THE TRAVELER'S KEY TO
NORTHERN INDIA

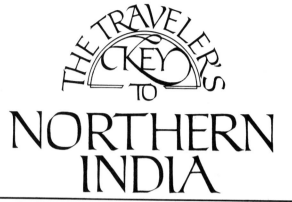

NORTHERN INDIA

A GUIDE TO THE SACRED PLACES
OF NORTHERN INDIA

ALISTAIR SHEARER

 Alfred A. Knopf   New York   1983

Note: The scales on illustrations are only approximate.

Cover photograph by Alistair Shearer
Cover design by Gun Larson

Library of Congress Cataloging in Publication Data
Shearer, Alistair.
The traveler's key to Northern India.
Bibliography: p.
Includes index.
1. Temples—India—Guide-books. 2. Shrines—India—
Guide-books. 3. India—Description and travels—
1981-   —Guide-books. I. Title.
BL2015.T4S53 1983   915.4′0452   83-47887
ISBN 0-394-51652-4

CONTENTS

PREFACE

Northern India has such a wealth of sacred sites that it has not been an easy task to choose which to include in this book. However, as this is the first volume of The Traveler's Key series, I have decided to select only the best known and most frequented sites out of literally dozens of possibilities and to concentrate on those places that are of outstanding architectural and artistic worth. Thus, some of the living pilgrimage centers, vibrant though they are, have not been included for lack of space.

So many people have helped in the creation of this book that it is impossible to name them all. At the top of the list, however, should be the Government of India Tourist Board, Air India, and Indian Airlines, without whose generosity in providing both international and domestic air travel the initial research would not have been possible. Mr. O. Terang and Mr. Kul Talwar, from the Government of India Tourist Office in London helped in planning itineraries and obtaining tickets. Once in India, I was assisted by many old friends, all of whom were unstinting in their generosity and help. Trade Wings Ltd., the travel agents, fixed all my arrangements; special thanks are due to Mr. M. P. Singh and Mr. S. J. S. Rikhy of the New Delhi office. Thanks are also due to Mr. Virendra Singh of Rājasthān Tours, Udaipur; Mr. Raghubir Singh Jhala of Peacock Travels, and Mr. Rām Gopāl Sharma of the Albert Hall Museum, Jaipur; Mr. M. N. Ganguli from the Government of India Tourist Office, and Mr. Hari K. Singh, in Banāras; Swāmi Sharānanda Bhāratī in Khajurāho; Mr. Bijay K. Rath from the State Museum, Mr. Ashokam in Bhubaneshwar, and Frederick and Katyāyanī Smith in Poona. I am grateful to Diana Eck for contributing two photographs of Banāras and to Air India for one other; also to Lauraine Schallop and Bury Peerless for photographs of Sarnath and Amritsar.

The actual production of the book has been something of a family affair. Ruth Trevenna was an invaluable help throughout. She not only accompanied me for six months research on the road in India but typed transcripts, took some of the photographs, and, most importantly, drew up roughs for all the illustrations. All the other photographs in the book are my own. Margaret and Jack Trevenna painstakingly read rough drafts of the manuscript and made many helpful suggestions, while Val Trevenna did a sterling job typing up the final version. Sue Conrad and Dennis Wesson of Ideas Design Ltd. (U.K.) produced the finalized illustrations. Many thanks also to Toinette Lippe of Alfred A. Knopf for her encouragement, her patience with my tardiness in delivering the manuscript, and her sensitive editing.

As regards inspiration, I have been greatly influenced by a loosely knit body of scholars and seers, among the most important of whom are Alice Boner, Ananda Coomaraswamy, Titus Burckhardt, Alain Daniélou, Carl Jung, Richard Lannoy, Stella Kramrisch, Benjamin Rowland, and Heinrich Zimmer. To anyone familiar with the work of these pioneers of human understanding, my debt will be obvious. This book is affectionately dedicated to all those who have responded to the magic of India, and all those yet to do so.

Sanskrit is a highly inflected language, but in this book I have tried wherever possible to simplify Sanskrit names and terminology so as to facilitate their pronunciation. The major change this has involved has been the rendering of both the retroflex sibilant *ṣ* and the palatal sibilant *ś* as *sh*, because this is how, to the untutored ear at least, they sound in practice. Thus *Viṣnu* is transliterated *Vishnu*, *Śiva* is *Shiva*, and so on. For the same reason, the Sanskrit *c* is rendered *ch* (thus *cakra* becomes *chakra*), *ch* becomes *chh* (*chattra* becomes *chhattra*), *ṛ* is *ri* (*ṛṣi* becomes *rishi*), and *jñ* is transliterated *gy* (*yajña* becomes *yagya*). In addition, the Sanskrit *v* is pronounced virtually the same as our *w*. Diacritical marks have been kept to a minimum throughout, with only the vowels being stressed when they are long, as this is vital to their correct pronunciation.

These guidelines for pronunciation also apply to the Persian and Arabic words in the text.

a	like the	u	in	*cup*
ā		a	in	*father*
e		ay	in	*say*
i		i	in	*bit*
ī		ee	in	*sweet*
o		o	in	*go*
u		oo	in	*foot*
ū		oo	in	*boot*
ai		i	in	*tight*
ph		ph	in	*cuphook*
th		th	in	*coathook*
dh		dh	in	*madhouse*
gh		gh	in	*doghouse*
bh		bh	in	*clubhouse*
kh		kh	in	*inkhorn*

NORTHERN INDIA

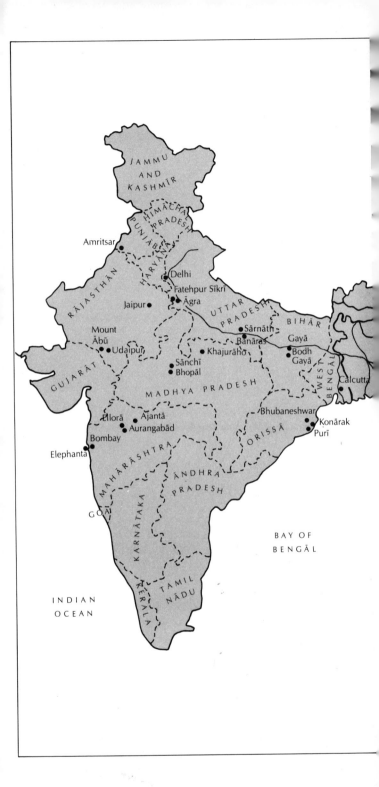

1
THE BACKGROUND

Pandit Nehru, the first prime minister of independent India, once called his country "a madhouse of religions." He had a point. No matter which way modern India may be aiming, her traditional culture is rooted in a world view with a spirituality so strong that it spread eastward to all the rest of Asia, shaping the civilizations from the Himālayas to Indonesia. Its echoes were heard in far-off China and Japan. To appreciate the importance of India's spirituality is to have an Ariadne's thread to guide one through the maze of her ancient culture. Secular India—her kings and their courts, the cities they built, their wily politicians—has largely disappeared. What we can still see are the remnants of sacred India: her temples and places of pilgrimage and worship. These are the remains of a culture that was once stable, powerful, and exceedingly subtle. It is to provide a key to understanding this culture that this book has been written.

The Religions Seven distinct religions have made significant contributions to Indian civilization. In order of importance these are Hinduism, Buddhism, Islām, Jainism; Sikhism, Christianity, and Zoroastrianism (the Parsees). The three major influences will be discussed in the following paragraphs. Of the four minor ones, Jainism and Sikhism will be dealt with in their context (Chapters 5 and 10, respectively). The Christian influence, where it occurs, is found in southern India and so falls outside the scope of this book; the Parsees forbid outsiders entrance to their places of worship.

Hinduism

Over 85 percent of Indians are Hindus. Strictly speaking, Hinduism is not a religion but a total way of life that governs the Hindu from the moment of conception to the grave. The word *Hinduism* is a foreign import, coined by Western observers to describe the wide variety of beliefs practiced in the subcontinent. The Indians themselves do not acknowledge it, referring to their faith as *sanātana dharma,* "the eternal Truth." As if to emphasize the all-inclusive quality of this faith, there is no separate word for "religion" in Indian languages. Hinduism has no historical founder, no central organization, and no head of the Church.

The best way to approach Hinduism is to look at its origins. When the Āryans entered northern India from the grasslands of Central Asia about 1800 B.C., they brought with them an extremely sophisticated religion known as Vedism (or Brahmanism). The principal scripture of this was the *Rig Veda,* a collection of some ten thousand hymns praising the creative spirit of the natural world in lines of great beauty with energetic and sensuous imagery. These hymns are addressed to sky gods that manifest themselves through the natural elements: Indra, the god of rain, the celestial storm warrior whose thunderbolt is the scourge of the unbeliever; Agni, god of fire and light; Rudra, "the howler," who destroys the unrighteous; Sūrya, the sun god; Varuna, prime mover of the universe; and Yama, god of death. Usha, the dawn goddess— one of the few female deities—is praised in terms of great tenderness. The *Rig Veda* was not at first committed to writing; the Vedic tradition was essentially an oral one. For the Āryans language had a mysterious power. If chants were correctly intoned, they could produce miraculous effects. Sanskrit, the language of the hymns and rituals associated with the sacrifices to the various gods, was considered a sacred trust. If it was written down, it lost its power. The sacrifices and their accompanying chants insured the continuing harmony of the different levels of the universe: divine, human, and infernal. If the chants were mispronounced or the rituals altered, their efficacy was diminished and the cosmic harmony disrupted. The inevitable result was suffering. The guardians of this vital ritual knowledge were the priests (*brāhmanas,* from which we get our word *brahmin*), and the whole body of priestly expertise was handed down from father to son in an unbroken oral tradition. In fact, the earliest written text we have of the *Rig Veda* dates from the fifteenth century, over three thousand years after it was first composed.

Even today this knowledge serves a purpose in Hindu society. Vedic rituals and hymns are still performed at every Hindu wedding. As recently as 1946, a Vedic sacrifice (*mahāyagya*) was performed at Banāras under the auspices of the Bengālī saint Ānandamayī Mā. It lasted continuously for three years (January 14, 1946, to January 14, 1949), took place on the banks of the Ganges, and included ten million offerings of oblation and ten million chantings of the *gāyatrī*, most sacred of the Vedic *mantras*. Its purpose was to promote the welfare of the entire world.

The Āryans left virtually no remains apart from their Vedic texts. Their principal cult object, the sacrificial altar, was set up in the open air, and what structures they did build—using brick, wood, hide, or bamboo—have long since perished. They left no artifacts, apart from evidence of pottery, from which we could build up a picture of their daily life, and the only architectural remains we have are a few burial mounds, for it seems they practiced both burial and cremation. Even at this early date, there was a thread of monotheism running through the highly esoteric teachings of these mysterious people, for, as the *Rig Veda* tells us: "Truth is one, though the sages call it by many different names." On their arrival in northern India, the nomadic Āryans met a culture that had already existed for perhaps fifteen hundred years, traded with the ancient Mesopotamian centers, and was a model of urban organization. This was the Indus Valley civilization, composed of more than a hundred sites along the river Indus. As the remains of the principal cities, Harappā and Mohenjodaro, show, the Indus Valley people built for permanence. Their cities were walled and laid out on a grid system; the water supply and drainage systems were extremely efficient. The civic sophistication of this culture puts it on a level with its contemporaries in ancient Sumer and the Middle Kingdom of Egypt. Much more would be revealed if the script found on numerous terracotta seals could be deciphered, but this task still defeats even the most modern computer. For our purposes, the most important aspect of the Indus Valley culture was the religion. As far as we can tell from the large number of clay figurines found, this was a fertility cult, centered on the Great Mother.

It was the mingling of the incoming Āryan stream with the indigenous peoples (the Indus Valley civilization, tribal societies, and the Dravidian cultures of the south) that gave birth to what we call Hinduism. The early history of this loose-knit body of beliefs and practices is by no means clear. If we date the Vedic period from ca. 1800 to 600 B.C., the next significant cultural era is the Buddhist period, lasting approximately from 550 to 150 B.C. This was in turn superseded by the Age of Invasions, lasting until the second century A.D., during which many different groups entered India from the northwest. Throughout this time, Hinduism was evolving alongside Buddhist and Jain cults, though details and dates, as with all early Indian history, are almost all speculative. It is Fa-hsien, a Chinese monk who came to India to obtain Buddhist scriptures during the reign of Chandragupta II (ca. A.D. 376–415) who gives us the first objective description of the emerging Hindu faith. He noted the peacefulness of India, the fact that it was possible to travel without danger or the need of passports, and that all respectable people were vegetarians, meat eating being confined to the lowest castes and untouchables. He also states that, although Buddhism was still flourishing, theistic Hinduism, particularly the worship of Shiva, was very widespread.

Hinduism combined the different characteristics of its two parents—on the one hand, the "paternal" Āryan strain of sky gods, esoteric ritual, magical Sanskrit chants, and abstract cognitions; on the other hand, the "maternal," indigenous strain of earth deities, fertility cults that worshipped the Great Mother (and her personifications in river and tree) and practiced animal sacrifice and animism. This combination resulted in a rich and diverse religion, that catered to the needs of the believer at a great variety of levels, from the heights of the most subtle and abstract philosophy to the most minute ritualistic ordering of day-to-day life.

The Hindus accept the Vedas as the ultimate scriptural authority, but they also have a number of other sacred texts that evolved at a later date. The *Upanishads* (from 800 B.C. onward) deal with the spiritual level of life that unifies the world of diversity, and the most important contain much material on yoga and meditation. The *Laws of Manu* and the *Dharmashāstra,* both finalized ca. A.D. 200, deal with the organization of society, the duties of its members, and the caste system. The *Rāmāyana* and *Mahābhārata* (400 B.C. to A.D. 400) are the great epics of India, which contain the legends of the gods and heroes. Much traditional education was based on these epics. The *Bhagavad Gītā* (200 B.C.) (the eighteenth chapter of the *Mahābhārata*) is the favorite scripture of the Hindus. The *Purānas,* which date from about the same period as the epics, are the historic-mythical accounts of the origins and adventures of the gods throughout endless cycles of time.

Contemporary with the Indus Valley civilization in other parts of India were various groups of indigenous peoples, all almost certainly worshipping the Great Mother as the source of life, in fertility cults such as are found all over the world.

These cults are the expressions of an animist view of life that sees the holy in everything. What we call Hinduism is a mixture of these archaic beliefs with the most sophisticated theological and philosophical doctrines. Traveling through India, one sees evidence of the ancient strata of folk belief everywhere. Trees, in particular, are sacred, and their roots can often be seen daubed with *sindūr* (powdered red lead, much used in folk rituals) or wrapped in silver foil. The most holy are fig trees, the *banyan* and the *pīpal* (the *bodhi* tree of the Buddhists) and the *bilva* (woodapple), which is sacred to Shiva. Many plants are sacred, as they have been since the days of the Āryans, when the divine *soma* plant, elixir of immortality, was hymned in the Vedas. Today the most revered plant is *tulasī* (basil), which is dedicated to Vishnu. It is considered an incarnation of Vishnu's consort, Lakshmī, goddess of fortune, and, as such, is married each year to an image of the Lord. More commonly, it is ritually married to the *shālagrāma,* a type of ammonite stone found on the bed of the Ghantakī River, and worshipped as a form of Vishnu. Among animals the most important is, of course, the cow. This preeminence is another legacy from the days of the pastoral Āryans. Not only is the cow considered the brahmin among animals, but its products—milk, curds, *ghī* (clarified butter), dung, and urine—are believed to be extremely purifying to both body and soul. Eating beef or handling leather is anathema to the strict Hindu. The cow is especially sacred to the Vaishnavas (worshippers of Vishnu) because of its association with the youth of Krishna, when he lived as a cowherd, but the Shaivas (worshippers of Shiva) also venerate it in the form of Nandin, Lord Shiva's bull. The feeding of cows brings religious merit; as the cows wander the streets, they are touched by the devout as a sign of respect. This reverence can be carried to an extreme: It is not uncommon for traffic to be slowed to a crawl as each vehicle carefully circumvents a cow that has decided to sit down in the middle of the road for a snooze!

After the cow the most revered creature is the snake. This cult is strongest in southern India, where the traces of the old faiths are most evident. In the north it is found in Mahārāshtra and, particularly, Bengāl, where there is a special snake deity, Manasa. The snake is the embodiment of the divine *nāgas* of Hindu lore, and in rural areas anthills are decorated and garlanded as the haunts of these deities. There is an annual snake festival, Nāga Panchamī, held in the Hindu month of Shrāvana (July–August). On this day snakes are fed milk and fruit and worshipped with great ceremony, and the pious farmer will not plow his field lest he inadvertently harm one. *Nāga* stones, carved with serpentine motifs, can often be seen piled up on the roots of a tree, where they are worshipped by devotees in a shrine combining three ancient focuses of devotion—tree, stone, and snake.

☐ THE MANY GODS, THE ONE SOURCE

Most Westerners' first reaction to Hinduism is confusion. Polytheism is unfashionable in our time; monotheism, the worship of "God," is considered a higher form of religion than the worship of "the gods." Perhaps this is why many people feel at a loss when they come across what appears to be the rampant polytheism of the Hindus: dozens of divinities of fantastic shape, color, and expression, all sprouting heads and limbs with a seemingly irreligious abandon. Leaving aside the esthetic differences between Western and Indian culture (which are considerable), much of this confusion can be dispelled by a brief examination of the Hindu view of life.

To the Hindu, the entire universe is alive, an ever-changing field of vibrating energy, permeated by the Supreme Consciousness. This is known as *brahman:* "the unbounded expanse." It is the source of all life, yet remains unaffected by its creations: "Weapons cannot cut Him, fire cannot burn Him, water cannot wet Him, nor wind dry Him away" (as the *Gītā* says). Totally free of the world of time and change, *brahman* is of the same status as the Allāh of the Muslims or the godhead of the Christian mystics: "Unborn, eternal, everlasting, ancient." This transcendental infinity of life is not directly accessible to worship. It is impersonal and cannot respond to human prayer or emotion. Nevertheless, it manifests as the endlessly diverse world, each particle of which contains a spark of the divine essence, and each part of which can thus legitimately be worshipped as the temporary seat of the divine. In this way the radiance of the Supreme is refracted through a series of ever denser levels; a continuum of vibration ranging from the transcendent, through the subtle, to the gross. As human beings we usually inhabit the grossest level, only dimly aware of the possibilities that lie beyond the range of our senses as they normally operate. But our capacity to experience can be enormously expanded, and to the Hindu such expansion is considered an intrinsic part of life. Mind, like matter, is merely a point of particular density in the continuum of life energy. One of the primary purposes of religious ritual is to refine and develop the mind's ability to perceive the depths of life, and ultimately the one spirit— *brahman*—within all things. In this sense, Hinduism is grounded in what the Indians call knowledge (*vidya*), which is what we in the West would call mystical experience.

The gross levels of life are based on the subtle; the subtle are based on the transcendent. The subtle levels—the invisible realms that form the unconscious springs of our thoughts and actions—are the abode of the gods. These hidden energies, which, although unseen, control and sustain our daily lives, are personified in the complicated Hindu pantheon. The Hindus acknowledge not only major and minor deities, all with their different forms and aspects, but numerous demigods, spirits, attendants, and a whole host of infernal and celestial creatures. Moreover, each member of this huge retinue interacts with each other member, just as in our microcosmic lives, events, thoughts, and feelings weave often unsuspected patterns. Thus demons win boons from the gods by prolonged worship and penance; humans can contact and utilize the strength of deities; celestial and infernal beings flit in and out of the human realm, taking any shape or form that suits their fancy. In the Hindu world *anything* is possible! Nor are the exploits of these subtle beings regarded as imaginary or, in our sense, "mythical," for the Hindu does not recognize the Western distinction between myth and history, legend and fact. To him, the outer world of "reality" and the inner world of "imagination" are constantly intermingling and influencing each other.

The complex web of relationships that is the universe operates through a network of correspondences that connect each part of the whole and link the subtle to the gross levels. The system operates as a vast hologram, any part of which not only contains the image of the whole but can be used to contact and utilize the energies of the whole. Thus each deity, itself mirroring the universal, is at the same time intimately associated with the world of particulars through its connection with a specific element (*bhūta*), sense (*indriya*), name (*nāma*), form (*rūpa*), sound (*mantra*), color (*rasa*), diagrammatic representation (*yantra*), set of symbols (*linga*), and so on. It is through these media that the deities, the causal energies of our world, manifest; they are the "body" of beings that are themselves immaterial. To ignore the realm of the deities is foolish in the extreme—to do so is to be like the gardener who tries to tend a plant while disregarding the roots on which its health depends. In any case, there is nothing we can think or do that does not depend on these elemental energies. The knowledge of how the deities manifest, what rituals they enjoy and which representation they favor, is the prerogative of the priest. He is the technician of the sacred. It is because he deals with the very roots of life that India has always considered sacred knowledge to be the greatest power. This accounts also for the respect traditionally paid by Indians to the priests even when their behavior, like that of all mortals, has not always warranted it.

Even for those of us not fortunate, or deserving, enough to have been born a male in the brahmin caste, the Hindu model of existence is an evolutionary one. Life is seen as a continuing process of spiritual alchemy whereby the individ-

ual being, through countless incarnations, is gradually purified in the fire of experience to the point at which it can
consciously reunite with the cosmic source, *brahman,* the
matrix of all life. The word used to describe the soul's journey
is *līlā,* which means "the divine play," both in the joyful and
the dramatic sense. The world is a stage, and each of us plays
our brief, allotted part to the best of our ability. According to
how well we learn the necessary lessons and pass the necessary tests of each incarnation, we proceed to the next life,
the next role in the cosmic drama that unfolds throughout all
eternity. And no matter how grim life may at times appear,
from the point of view of the divine, at least, it is blissful. The
Taittirīya Upanishad reminds us of this exalted perspective:
"From joy all beings are born, by joy all beings are sustained,
and into joy all beings again return." That this is the true
nature of things will not be clear to us until we accomplish
the purpose of our incarnation in a human body, which is to
realize our own inherent divinity.

The myriad gods are arranged in a strictly organized hierarchy. At the head of this chain of being sit three principal
deities: Brahmā, Vishnu, and Shiva. Each has at least one
consort, for the female energy (*shakti*) is indispensible to the
deity. Without it, the god's power remains latent—"Shiva
without *shakti* is a corpse (*shava*)." Each of the three is
identifiable by his form, attributes, accompanying vehicle
(*vāhana*), and consort, who also has a particular form and
attributes. These attributes express, in symbols, the qualities
and characteristics of the deity, and the area of life he or she
governs.

□ *BRAHMĀ: "THE UNBOUNDED"*
Brahmā is the embodiment, or personification, of creative
energy. As such he figures in many myths as the creator of
the world, and one reason given for the fact that he is little
worshipped nowadays is that, once a cycle of manifestation
has been set in motion, he becomes redundant. Largely
ignored by human beings, he is, however, worshipped by angels
and seers. Brahmā is usually shown with four heads and four
arms, symbolizing the four cardinal directions (space); the
four ages, or *yugas* (time); and the four Vedas, or sacred
books (causality). He holds attributes that refer to his role as
priest of the gods: a portion of the Vedas, a spoon for lustration, a vessel of holy water, and a rosary (*mālā*), signifying
meditation. His color is red or pink, and he is often shown as
bearded, to indicate his wisdom. His vehicle is the swan or
goose, symbol of the freedom gained through knowledge. He
is seated on the lotus of creativity.

Brahmā's consort is Sarasvatī: "the flowing one." She is the
goddess of speech, and represents the union of power and

intelligence from which organized creation arises. She plays the *vīnā*, from whose notes the sounds of the Sanskrit alphabet flow. As the patron deity of the "Word" or creative *logos*, she revealed language and writing to man. Sarasvatī is the patroness of learning, eloquence, music, the arts, and all forms of cultural refinement. She is the mother of poetry. She is depicted as white in color, seated on the swan, and with two or sometimes eight arms. She can be shown holding a variety of objects, including the *vīnā*, a book, a rosary, and an elephant hook, with which she catches and holds her devotees. As befits her role of patroness of refinement, Sarasvatī is always most graceful. She is the deity of students, artists, and intellectuals. On her annual festival none of her devotees is allowed to read books or play an instrument. These are cleaned, placed on the family altar, and worshipped as the abodes of the goddess.

□ VISHNU: "THE ALL-PERVADING"

Vishnu embodies the energy that sustains creation. He is the power of cohesion, the preserver of life. Whereas Brahmā represents the mind and knowledge, Vishnu represents the heart and devotion; he is the god of love.

Vishnu is usually shown with four arms, standing on the lotus. In his lower right hand he holds the conch, symbol of the five elements; in his upper right the discus, which, as a sun symbol, reminds us of his probable origin as a solar deity before the Hindu pantheon was finalized. In his upper left hand is a lotus, signifying fertility (or sometimes a bow he uses as defender of the righteous), and in his lower left is the mace, the emblem of both temporal and spiritual authority.

Vishnu is always dark blue or black—the color corresponding to infinity and the appropriate hue for the present age, the Age of Darkness (*Kali Yuga*).

His vehicle is the fabulous bird Garuda, "the Wings of Speech," who is half-vulture, half-man. Garuda is the personification of courage and immense strength and is the color of molten gold. His body is composed of the secret utterances of the Vedas, which transport one to the higher worlds, and in his red beak he crushes the serpent of Time. Lord Vishnu may be flanked by a royal parasol and standard, be garlanded, have a precious jewel on his chest, earrings shaped like the sea monsters that guard the treasures of the deep, a fly whisk, armlets adorning his arms, and a diadem on his head. All these adornments are attributes of royalty, for Vishnu is the member of the trinity who takes the most active interest in human affairs. In fact, whenever the forces of good are being overcome by the forces of evil, Vishnu incarnates onto the earth plane to redress the balance. In the *Bhagavad Gītā*, Krishna, who is the eighth incarnation (*avatāra*) of Vishnu,

explains his compassionate intervention into human affairs
to Arjuna, the archetype of the noble warrior:

> Whenever truth is in decay, and untruth flourishes, O noble
> one, then I create myself. To protect the righteous and destroy
> the wicked, to establish truth firmly, I take birth age after
> age.   (4.7–8)

To date, Vishnu has incarnated nine times. (As might be
expected, his tenth, and final, incarnation, which heralds the
end of this cycle of manifestation, is expected any day now.)
These incarnations trace the span of evolutionary growth,
from lowest to highest life forms. They are the Fish (*Matsya*);
the Tortoise (*Kūrma*); the Boar (*Varāha*); the Man-Lion
(*Narasingha*); the Dwarf (*Vāmana*); Rāma-with-the-axe
(*Parashu Rāma*); Rāma ("the Charming One"); Krishna ("the
Dark Lord"); Buddha ("the Enlightened One"); and Kalki
("the Destroyer").

The stories of these incarnations are to be found in the
Purānas, and also in the *Rāmāyana* and *Mahābhārata* epics.

Vishnu has two consorts: Lakshmī (also known as Shrī, or
Shrīdevī) and Bhūdevī. Lakshmī, "Good Fortune," embodies
beauty, success, and prosperity. She appears with Vishnu in
each of his incarnations—when he is Rāma, she is Sītā; when
he is Krishna, she is Rādhā. Lakshmī is usually represented
with two arms, occasionally with four, in eight principal forms.
One of the most popular of these is as Gaja Lakshmī—
"Lakshmī with the elephants"—often found over the doors of
temples. A good example of this can be seen at the Kailāsanātha Temple in Ellorā (see Chapter 3). Lakshmī stands on
a lotus and also holds the lotus, and though there are no
temples dedicated to her, she is worshipped in every home.
Her festival is the autumnal celebration of Divālī, "the darkest
night," when homes are freshly whitewashed after the
monsoon and all utensils are cleaned and new clothes bought.
Divālī is the festival of lights, when oil lamps are lit all around
the home to entice the goddess in to bless the household for
the coming year. Lakshmī is a favorite deity of merchants
and businessmen.

Lakshmī is also worshipped as "Destiny" (Mahālakshmī),
in which form she has eighteen arms, signifying the different
aspects of fate. Bhūdevī, goddess of the earth, like Lakshmī,
is shown as a beautiful young woman, a lotus sinuously twined
in her hand. When both consorts are shown with Vishnu,
Lakshmī appears on his right and Bhūdevī on his left.

□ *SHIVA: "THE AUSPICIOUS"*
The most fascinating of all the deities. You will often hear
that Shiva is the god of destruction, as opposed to Brahmā,
the creator, and Vishnu, the preserver. This is a misunder-

standing. The Hindus see three forces operating in the universe: creation, preservation, and dissolution. Shiva is the deity who presides over the process of change. Any creation involves destruction of a previous state: the bud is destroyed for the rose to be created. Shiva teaches that the universe is essentially dynamic, everything is constantly changing, evolving. Even the things we consider permanent—the mountains, the oceans, our own personalities—all are in reality transient: "All flesh is as grass." Shiva is the personification of the process of dissolution and re-creation that is constantly at work from moment to moment. He is life itself, which only exists by devouring life.

As befits the god of change, Shiva contains many seemingly contradictory elements. As Mahāyogi, "the Great Yogi," he is the supreme ascetic, living in seclusion, naked on a tiger skin, the crescent moon in his matted hair, and his body smeared with ashes. Yet he is also a Dionysian figure, seducer of the sages' wives, and orgiastic lover; as Natarāja, "Lord of the Dance," he creates the universe in a wild dance of frenzied joy, his hair streaming out behind him like the rays of the sun. As Maheshvara, "the Great Lord," he is worshipped as creator of the world and the giver of esoteric knowledge; while as Mahākāla, "Transcendent Time," he represents both the irresistible march of time and the eternal present that nullifies it. The *Mahābhārata* praises Shiva: "You are the origin of the worlds and you are Time, their destroyer." Shiva also has his fearsome aspect. He is the wrathful Bhairava, "the Terrible," garlanded with serpents and the skulls of his sacrificial victims, with glaring eyes and pointed fangs. Bhairava haunts the funeral pyres and cemeteries in search of devotees, to whom he teaches occult secrets of the left-hand path. Shiva is also Hara, "the Remover," who presides over sickness and death; and in his form as Bhūteshvara he is "Lord of the Ghosts," the wandering souls and creatures of the night.

Shiva, in fact, embodies the limitless possibilities of existence, reconciling life's complementary aspects into one dynamic whole. Pulsating with vitality, he is the personification of the unconscious mind, which is at once a Pandora's box and our greatest treasure. As the teacher of the ancient techniques of meditation, he shows us the way to uncover the wellsprings of our inner life.

Shiva is portrayed in many forms, depending on which aspect is being represented. Generally speaking, though, he will be shown with four arms, signifying universal power and the four directions of space. He holds his trident (*trishūla*), symbolizing past, present, and future; and his hourglass drum (*damaru*), the union of male and female principles, from whose intermingled rhythms all the vibrations of life spring forth. He has a noose to catch and hold his devotees and a number of weapons with which to fight the demons: a bow, a spear, an axe, and a club in which a skull is set. Shiva also wears a cobra around his neck. This represents the dormant energy, set free by yoga, known as *kundalinī*: "the Coiled Serpent." In its grosser form this power is sexual energy; in its subtle form it is the source of all spiritual growth. The most common image of Shiva, and the main image in Shiva temples, is the *linga* ("sign" or "emblem"). This phallic stone is the symbol of creative power, the power of the One to become many. Sometimes realistically carved as an erect penis, the *linga* obviously originated in the most ancient fertility cults. Scholars believe that Shiva originally belonged to the pre-Āryan stratum of Indian culture, and that what we see today as Shiva is a combination of the original deity and the Vedic god Rudra. On an abstract level, the *linga* symbolizes the male principle: light, spirit, and consciousness. For the myth of the origin of the *linga*, see page 103.

The potential creativity of the *linga* becomes actual with the addition of the female half. This is the *yoni* ("womb" or "vagina"), a stone base that encloses the shaft of the *linga*. The *yoni* can be a roughly hewn stone block, or it can be carved and shaped like the female reproductive organs. It signifies the feminine principle: darkness, matter, and primal existence. The union of male and female is the source of life, on a cosmic as well as an earthly level. This union is known as the *yoni-linga*, an image of the mystic *coincidentia oppositorum*.

Shiva's vehicle is the bull Nandin, "the Joyous," who embodies the qualities of the strong and the just.

As befits his polymorphous nature, Shiva has several consorts. His nature is expressed through three principal ones—Shakti, "Energy"; Pārvatī, "Daughter of the Mountain"; and Kālī, "the Power of Time."

Shakti is creative; she is the vibrant power of enjoyment, lust, and sensual pleasure. She is the giver of delight but also the giver of liberation, for it is by way of correct understanding of the senses that the wise arrive at dispassion. Shakti is also known as Devī, "the Shining One."

Pārvatī represents stability; she is gentle and peaceful. She is Shiva's official wife and the mother of his sons: Ganesha, the elephant-headed god, and Kārttikeya (known as Subrahmanya or Kumāra in southern India), the youthful god of war. Pārvatī shares Shiva's home on Mount Kailāsa ("the Abode of Pleasure"), and embodies the idealized qualities of woman: beauty, sympathy, and strength. Her vehicle is the lion.

Kālī is pure destruction. She is black, the supreme night that swallows all that exists, goddess of epidemics and cataclysms. The *Kālī Tantra* describes her:

Most fearsome, her laughter shows her dreadful teeth. She stands upon a corpse. She has four arms. Her hands hold a sword and a severed head, and show the gestures of banishing fear and granting boons. She is the auspicious divinity of sleep, the consort of Shiva. Naked, clad only in space, the goddess is magnificent. Her long tongue hangs out. She wears a garland of skulls. Such is the form to meditate on Kālī, she who dwells near the funeral pyres.

On the psychological level, Kālī has a dual meaning. As a positive force she represents the power of independence and the ability to cut through the bonds of reliance on parent or mate. But she is also the negative complement of the ideal wife Pārvatī, and as such can represent the negative aspect of woman: the suffocating mother and devouring lover.

Kālī is today worshipped principally in the northeast, especially Bengāl—those parts of India that have largely retained their tribal fertility cults based on blood sacrifice. The comparatively later overlay of the sophisticated religion that is Hinduism incorporated these existing beliefs and myths into its fold.

Kālī originally received human sacrifice. Indeed, even today there are many rumors of tribal children who disappear in the foothills and are never heard of again. But officially Kālī now makes do with cocks, water buffalo, and he-goats.

There are several sects of ascetics who worship the wrathful Shiva, or his consort Kālī, by identifying themselves with the demonic side of their deity's nature. One such sect are the Aghorīs. *Aghorī* means "fearless." These devotees are said to hold their rituals in cemeteries, eat human flesh (especially the brain), and do magic with the spirits of the dead. This is the darker face of Hinduism, turned to a world most of us never see.

But notice that Kālī makes the gesture of "Fear not!" with one hand and grants boons with another. She has a dual nature, not at first apparent. Although she destroys all that exists, she is the gateway to what lies beyond manifestation and attachment—the eternal peace of pure Being. If her devotee can accept her terrible form and surrender his attachment to fear, then the goddess reveals her true nature, which is infinite joy. Kālī is not for the weak. Hinduism celebrates what may at first seem unacceptable aspects of life. The Indian myth makers saw a great psychological wisdom in admitting the unpleasant and hostile forces of the mind, rather than repressing them or denying their existence. By acknowledging the destructive, they hoped to be able to transmute it, to exorcise its terrible power. The Hindu believes that destructive and malign forces are just as much a part of the divine play as the creative and benign ones; they are the left hand of God.

This ability to accept and cater to all aspects of the psyche, however unpleasant, distinguishes Hinduism and makes it the most human (which is not the same as humane or humanitarian) of the great religions.

□ WORSHIP

There are four main religious groups: (1) Shaivas, those who worship Shiva, (2) Vaishnavas, those who worship Vishnu, (3) Shāktas, those who worship the Mother Goddess, Shakti, and (4) Smartas, those who worship a consortium of five major deities—Shiva, Vishnu, Shakti, Ganesha, and Sūrya, the Vedic sun god.

Traditionally, the Hindu worships three types of deity: the local deity (*grāmadevatā*), the family deity (*kulādevatā*), and his or her personal, chosen deity (*ishtadevatā*). Thus it is quite possible for the local deity to be Shiva, the family deity to be some aspect of the Mother Goddess, and the personal deity to be Hanumān, an attendant of Vishnu. The Hindu sees nothing contradictory in such complete tolerance. Remember that each deity is just a facet of the One: the universal spirit that is beyond all form. Hinduism allows you to choose whichever deity suits you as the best way to approach this universal spirit. It is a fluid and open-ended system, catering to the different spiritual and psychological needs of each worshipper. To the Hindu there are as many ways to reach God as there are beings who want to reach Him (or Her!).

The local deity is worshipped in the local temple, and the pious Hindu goes to the temple each morning after his bath to offer prayers, fruit, or flowers. Once or twice a year there is a temple festival, with processions, music, and general celebration, in which all members of the community are expected to participate. The family deity is worshipped at home; those families who can afford it having a shrine set aside in their houses, to which a paid brahmin comes to perform the necessary rituals. Nowadays, especially among city dwellers, it is more common to find a *pūjā* table set up in one corner, often in or near the kitchen, where the family deity is worshipped each day. The chosen deity is worshipped in a private way. The devotee may perform *pūjā* to an image, wear a talisman of the god, or keep a picture of the god, which acts as a focus for worship. In addition to this, there are certain major festivals that all Hindus, no matter which sect they belong to, are expected to attend, such as the autumnal Durgā *pūjā*, when Durgā, a consort of Shiva, is worshipped; the spring festival of Shivarātri, when Shiva is worshipped with hymns and offerings throughout an entire night; Ganesha Chaturthī, which is sacred to Ganesha, and so on. All Hindu festivals are regulated according to the phases of the moon, in accordance with the lunar calendar. Full moon is especially auspicious. Astrology is of crucial importance in assessing the correct days and times of day on which to undertake certain actions, and the nine planets themselves are often portrayed in temple decoration and worshipped. So, too, are the "Guardians of the Eight Directions" (see page 467), who govern the cardinal points of space.

The Temple   The temple begins with the simple shrine. The shrine separates and protects what is holy ground: the place at which the gods were seen—either in a direct vision, or in a temporary form, or in the occurrence of some miraculous event. The shrine becomes the hub of the community. Healers, soothsayers, and dancers gather here to perform their arts. The shaman leaves his ritual masks here. These, as is still the case in such Hindu-influenced countries as Bali, are considered to possess magical power and are perhaps the first cult objects. It is significant that the most popular domestic gods in Hinduism are Ganesha, the elephant-headed son of Shiva, and Hanumān, the monkey general. The preeminence of these deities, together with the importance of Garuda (half-man, half-bird), attest to the remnants of a masked dance ritual at the very beginnings of Hinduism. Little by little the shrine grows and attracts the attention of the rich and powerful. A local chieftain prays for the continuance of his family or success in battle. Fortune smiles on him; he erects an altar in thanksgiving. In time other patrons come; leaf and branch are replaced by wood and stone. A permanent building rises up, perhaps long after the original reason for sanctity has been forgotten.

The temple never replaced the shrine. It was merely a more sophisticated and premeditated structure, which in time served ends other than the immediate apprehension of the mysterious deity. It could be argued that these little heaps and mounds that mark the devotion of the poor and uneducated are a truer witness to the religious feelings of the people than are the grandiose temples. As spontaneous and temporary dedications to visiting or seasonal gods, they have none of the permanence or sophistication with which the courtly temples strive for immortality. Certainly, many of India's greatest sites—Elephanta, Khajurāho, Konārak—were conceived and built as royal extravaganzas.

But this type of building was encouraged by the scriptures, which frequently mention the religious merit that accrues to the builder of the temple. The *Shilpaprakāsha*, an important text on temple building, reminds us that a religious patron "will always have peace, wealth, grain and sons" and adds that the builder's aspirations for permanence are quite legitimate because "everything vanishes in time, only a religious monument lasts forever." The glory of the royal patron is but a reflection of the greater glory of the gods. And, as if to verify the teaching of the *Shilpaprakāsha*, such places have indeed become centers of spiritual pilgrimage, and they have remained as such long after their patrons have gone. At the same time, it is significant that many of India's holiest temples, though dedicated to one of the sophisticated gods, such as Shiva, Vishnu, or Ganesha, have as their principal image an uncarved stone or simple wooden block that clearly betrays its origin in folk worship. The Vishvanātha temple in Banāras, the Kedāreshvara in Kedārnāth in the Himālayas, and the Jagannātha in Purī are among the most famous examples; there are literally hundreds of others throughout India.

The folk shrine belongs to an irrepressible level of religious vitality. It will often exist in the shadow of the most refined and articulate temple complex. The devout Hindu feels no conflict between the two. He may well visit both the temple and the shrine, perhaps worshipping the tree spirit of the shrine as an emanation of the power of the great god Shiva, or Vishnu, or whoever is commemorated in the temple proper. The temple is the place where mankind meets the gods. It is to the temple, in which its image stands, that the deity makes its temporary descent, and it is here that it may be worshipped. That the temple serves this function is evident from the variety of Sanskrit names for the building, such as *devagriha*, "house of god"; *devalāya*, "the god's residence"; and *mandira*, "reception hall." It is here that the deities—which, from the psychological view, are the personifications of the creative faculties waiting to unfold from the depths of the unconscious—appear to the devotee. Although the actual vehicle of the god's descent is the image (*mūrti*, which literally means "crystallization"), the whole temple is considered holy, itself a vehicle for divinity. Potent sites become the goal of pilgrims from all over the country. Places of pilgrimage provide the bridge to a higher mode of being; as such they are called *tīrtha*, "the place of crossing." As in medieval Europe, pilgrimage plays a vital part in the life of the Hindu, not only as a means of expressing devotion but as a source of travel, adventure, and celebration.

The building of a temple is an exact science, which aims to re-create, here on earth, the celestial abode of the gods. The texts on temple building, the *Vāstu shāstras*, stipulate the precise proportions, designs, and sculptural representation required to fashion a fitting place for the deities. These rules, rooted in sacred geometry and mathematics, must be followed exactly if the temple is to fulfill its role as mediator between heaven and earth. One of the most common names for the temple is *vimāna*, which means "the well proportioned."

Early Indian texts on architecture tend to deal with the

practical questions of sacred and secular architecture, whereas the later ones are more concerned with the theological meaning of temple structures. The earliest buildings would have been of wood and bamboo; we can see the legacy of this in many of the curved structures of existing temples, such as the horseshoe-arched windows, and ribbed barrel vaulting. What the original wooden temples looked like can be imagined from areas such as the Himālayan foothills and Kerala in the south, heavily wooded areas where the tradition of building in wood has continued up to recent times. But from the earliest days, stone was recommended as the best material. The texts say it is a hundred times more meritorious to build a temple in brick than in wood, but ten thousand times more meritorious to build it in stone.

Before any building could be started, the correct site had to be chosen. This must be favorable for the descent of the gods: peaceful, attractive, and near gardens, mountains, or rivers. The proximity of water not only purifies the atmosphere but serves as a means of ritual ablution for the worshippers. In the absence of natural water, sacred tanks were dug next to the temple.

Once the site has been chosen, it must be purified by certain rituals that drive off negative influences, personified as demons (*rākshasas*). This purification also takes place at certain critical points in the construction of the temple, such as the laying of the foundation stone or the installation of the image, and, once the temple is built, a large proportion of its external decoration, especially around the doors, will be devoted to images that ward off evil spirits. Thus the temple should remain a constant source of positivity in the community. Every stage in the construction of a temple must take place at an astrologically favorable time. Astronomy and astrology have always been two aspects of the one science in India, and many of the texts on temple building also contain a wealth of material on astrology.

When the site has been purified, the ground plan is drawn. This is an extremely complicated business, because its purpose is ritually to subdivide the cosmos into its component parts (the four cardinal directions) and to establish the temple as a microcosmic replica of the universe. The *Māvasāva shilpashāstra* stipulates that a pillar be erected and a circle drawn around it. The points where the shadow of this pillar cuts the circle at morning and evening are connected to form an east-west axis and are used as centers of two other circles, drawn with a cord as a compass, whose intersection provides a north-south axis. From this cross a plan is drawn out on the ground as a *mandala* in the form of a square subdivided by a grid into a number of smaller squares. One of the most popular ground plans in northern India was a matrix of sixty-four (eight by eight) squares, known as the *Vāstupurusha mandala.* The *Brihat Samhitā,* an important sixth-century text on temple building, confirms this by saying: "Let the area of the temple always be divided into sixty-four squares." But we know from other texts that there were no less than thirty-two permissible types of ground plan. Whatever type was used, the origin of these plans goes back centuries, to the construction of Vedic altars *(vedi).* Vedic cosmology symbolized the universe as being square, and the *vedi* signified the universe in miniature, with each brick representing a different part of it. Similarly, each of the squares in the microcosmic *mandala* corresponds to an area of the universe, and the main celestial bodies and presiding deities are marked in their respective places (Figure A). The temple is constructed

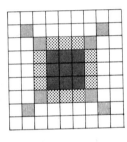

Divided into 81 squares (9x9), this plan is taken from the Brihat Samhitā, *a sixth-century Gupta text on architecture. The 9 central squares are assigned to Brahmā, the Creator, who is surrounded by assorted planetary deities. (After S. Kramrisch.)*

Figure A. Hindu temple ground plan mandala.

on this grid, each part related to the heavenly macrocosm. In the building of a temple, special care must be taken to protect the corners, for, being exposed, these are considered vulnerable to hostile forces. They are thus usually guarded by the "Lords of the Eight Directions" *(ashtadikpālas)* who preside over the cardinal points. The whole building is usually aligned along an east-west axis, to face the rising sun, although this is not always the case. Another type of ground plan recommended in the scriptures is the *Mahāpurusha mandala.* This incorporates a drawing of the body of the cosmic man *(mahāpurusha),* who, as personification of the eternal *brahman,* gives birth to the world by sacrificing himself. In this case, each part of the temple will be linked to a particular part of the body of the *mahāpurusha.*

Whatever the model, the center of the ground plan *mandala* is crucial. The plan, and thence the temple, radiates from its center, and it is here that the worshipper comes into most direct contact with the laws of nature governing the universe. Thus the center of the plan *(brahmāsthāna)* is assigned to Brahmā, the Creator, and corresponds to the holy of holies in the temple, the sanctum in which the image resides. This is known as the *garbha-griha* ("womb house"), which, as its name implies, brings about the spiritual rebirth of the worshipper. Indeed, the whole construction of the temple insures that the devotee moves from an area of profanity (the outside world) through successive stages of purity (the inner confines of the temple compound) until he comes face to face with the deity in the inner sanctum. That this journey is a return to the source is emphasized by the fact that the inner areas of the temple are invariably without natural light, and the sanctum itself is often approached through a passage that is dark, narrow, and constricting. As a result, the feeling is of entering the depths of some divine womb, from which one emerges again into the light of day, transformed.

The dark innerness of the temple mimics the cave. From earliest times ascetics and hermits have chosen the cave as their place of retreat, for the cave, representing the inner spiritual depths of man, is a physical analogue to the inner journey through prayer and meditation. This symbolic association explains, in part at least, why Indian builders showed a marked preference for cave sanctuaries up until a comparatively late date. Even in the eighth and ninth centuries, by which time many fine temples had been built, cave sanctuaries in the form of rock-cut temples were still being excavated, as we can see from Ajantā and Ellorā. And when, with reluctance, the builders turned to freestanding temples, the interior of these—massive, dark, and unadorned—were often fashioned after their natural prototype.

The cave is only one symbolic motif operating within the temple. Another is the holy mountain. To the Hindu, the mountains are the abode of the gods. Lord Shiva himself lives on Mount Kailāsa. Mount Meru, the "center of the universe," is situated in the high Himālayas, as are many of the most potent pilgrimage sites. The temple, as the cosmos in miniature, is also a representation of the holy mountain, a correspondence that can clearly be seen in the shape of many northern Indian temples as a series of levels ascending to a peak. This association is reinforced by the fact that many temples are actually named after mountains, such as Kailāsa and Meru; that the spire of the temple is known as the *shikhara,* which means "mountain peak"; and that the image inside is called the *achala* (literally "the unmoving"), a word also used to mean "mountain." The mountain motif is particularly well demonstrated in the temples of Khajurāho (see page 377).

The *shikhara* is aligned directly over the image in the holy of holies. This positioning establishes a third symbolic refrain: that of the sacred mountain acting as the center of the universe, or world axis *(axis mundi)*. The line of spiritual force that runs between the image and the finial serves as the connection between heaven and earth, linking the realm of the gods with the world of humanity. As such, the temple spire is the divine pillar, the stable axis around which the ever-changing universe revolves. In both its cosmic symbolism and its social role, the temple becomes what T. S. Eliot called "the still point of the turning world." So in its symbolic associations, the temple is not only a microcosm but embodies the three principal qualities of the divine: stability (axis), immanence (cave), and transcendence (mountain).

The Image   The image itself is not the deity; it is a temporary form into which the deity can descend. Rituals of worship are, in effect, an invitation to the deity to descend, and if they are correctly performed, he or she will be pleased to do so. Hence the importance of the priest. If the necessary rituals have not been performed, the deity is said to be "asleep" and does not inhabit the image. Nevertheless, in popular worship, the image is often treated as if it permanently housed the god. The fact that images are not considered sacred in themselves can be seen from the practice of annual festivals, when months may be spent making an image of the god from clay or wood. As soon as the climax of the festival is over, the image is taken to the sea or nearest river and ceremoniously thrown in. It has done its job in attracting the deity; when the same festival comes around the next year, a new image will be made. Similarly, if a stone image in a temple is damaged, there will be no attempt to restore it. A new image will be carved as a replacement.

In order to attract the divinity, an image must correspond exactly to the proportions laid down in the sacred texts dealing with iconography. Any deviation produces an unacceptable image, which becomes like a suit of clothes that is the wrong size and cannot be "worn" by the god. Adherence to the traditional form, and not esthetic considerations, is what governs the art of image making. An important iconographical text, the *Shukrānatisāra,* makes this distinction clear by stating that that image is "said to be lovely which is neither more nor less than the prescribed proportions." The proportions and procedures for image making are believed to have been received by sages *(rishis),* beings of higher consciousness who could communicate with the gods in states of deep meditation, and they are contained in a class of sacred texts collectively known as the *Shilpashāstras.* The science of image making has always been the prerogative of specific subcastes, and the skills have been handed down from father to son in a well-controlled guild system. The basic unit of measurement in any image is usually the length of face. As well as overall size, the facial expression, gestures, posture, attributes, costume, and color are all laid down. Once the image is completed and the temple has been purified with the required rites, the image is installed. A special ritual (*prāna-pratīshtha*) is performed to breathe life (*prāna*) into the image, and the eyes are symbolically pierced open. Now the *mūrti* is ready to be used as the earthly seat of the divine.

□ *RITUAL*

Despite the great variety of gods, rituals of worship are fairly standard, with only minor variations. When the Hindus worship an image, they are entertaining a royal guest. The deity is invited, received, and attended with procedures that go back to the very earliest times and that are stipulated in a vast body of canonical literature. It is true to say that, apart from an overall simplification, these rituals have altered very little since their inception.

Ordinary temple worship takes place four times a day: sunrise, noon, sunset, and midnight. Before he begins, the priest must purify himself by bathing and other acts of consecration. As he is the mediator with the divine and performs the rites on behalf of the community, there is no need for any of the congregation to be present at temple ceremonies. Nevertheless, devotees like to attend these occasions in order to have a glimpse (*darshana*) of the image and absorb some of the spiritual effulgence that results from the descent of the deity. The actual ceremonies begin with the opening of the doors of the sanctum in which the image is housed. This is done with great reverence. The divinity is alerted and evil spirits driven away by ringing the bell that hangs in front of the sanctum, and the priest addresses the god, asking permission to invoke it. Hymns are sung and *mantras* chanted, which purify the atmosphere and charm the unseen presence into the image. Now the priest can enter into communication with the deity and various *mantras* and formulas are recited and hand gestures (*mudrās*) performed that serve to concentrate the power of the god in its temporary abode. The visiting deity is made as comfortable as possible. The image is bathed and dressed in fine clothing, it is anointed with oils, camphor is burned to purify the atmosphere, and cooling sandalwood paste is applied to the body of the image. Various offerings are made: incense that sweetens the air and which the gods are said to enjoy, *sindūr* (vermilion powder), flowers, sweet fresh fruit, coconut, betel leaf, milk, ghee, honey, consecrated water, and so on. Cooked food is also offered, usually a number of rice dishes, as the main meal of the god. These offerings—especially in the big *pūjās* performed in the south of India, which has maintained temple traditions more than the north—can comprise dozens of dishes and can go on for hours. At an annual festival in the great temple of Tirupati in Tamil Nādu, thirty-two types of flowers, weighing a total of 5,400 pounds (2,450 kilograms) are offered. Light, in the form of burning camphor and ghee lamps, is waved in front of the image in a ritual known as *āratī*, and, where possible, circumambulation is performed several times. Finally, after more flowers have been offered, the doors of the sanctum are closed and the deity is considered to be asleep again until invoked by the next ceremony. Portions of the offered food are distributed among the congregation as consecrated gifts from the god *(prasāda)*.

The Hindu gods, like those of ancient Greece, are considered to have many of the characteristics of humans, only on a more rarified level. They have their likes, dislikes, jealousies, and so on. They are also susceptible to our more tedious weaknesses. At the famous Jagannātha Temple in Purī, for instance, the main image, a form of Vishnu, is considered to catch cold every time it is ceremoniously bathed in public, and spends a fortnight in a special sick bay after each bath.

As well as serving the needs of the divinity, temple ritual is designed to elevate the consciousness of the person who performs and witnesses it. Each offering has a symbolic meaning through which the senses and mind of the worshipper are offered up to the supreme spirit. Thus the ritual is in fact a series of techniques leading to self-transcendence. This reciprocal effect of the ritual is especially important, since the priest, in theory at least, should be the example and guiding light to his community. Moreover, to the devout Hindu all of life is a ritual. Every action has its importance and its consequences, and there are proper ways to perform each action. What we see in the temple is the external and public ritual, but all the events that constitute life have their own rituals as well. To the Hindu, the principal temple is the universe, and life itself is the service.

Between the four daily ceremonies, individuals can make offerings to the deity throughout the day, using the priest as an intermediary. Such offerings may be the mark of general devotion, or, more often, given in the hope of specific assistance in a time of trouble or illness or to secure success in some undertaking. They may also be in thanksgiving for a danger survived, an obstacle overcome, or a stroke of good fortune. There is a third level of offering, which does not involve the priest: just a simple gift of a flower or a few coins, left at the threshold of the holy of holies.

As well as ritual worship of the deity, the Hindu temple serves other, more congregational functions. The temple, like the cathedral in medieval Europe, has always been the center of learning and culture. This traditional role is still fulfilled today through temple performances of song and dance, which enact scenes from the *Rāmāyana* and *Mahābhārata*. These are staged primarily for the worship of the god but also serve a vital function as entertainment and instruction for the village or neighborhood. Stories from the epics and *Purānas* are recited by itinerant storytellers, who are masters of their craft and can hold a huge audience spellbound for hours into the night. Although each storyteller will spice his performance with little bits of local gossip and scandal gleaned on his arrival in the village, almost everyone in the audience will already know the tale by heart. It will be part of a body of legend that every Hindu child imbibes at his mother's knee. Novelty is not the point; what matters is repetition and reconfirmation of the time-honored stories. Sometimes learned *pandits* will chant and explicate the sacred texts, or a visiting holy man (*sannyāsin*) will give a discourse. Even today, such lectures are a very real means of education and therapy for the adults of the village. In a community hedged round with caste rules and stringent domestic etiquette, the *sannyāsin*, being a renunciate, acts as a neutral sounding board for social and marital grievances. All these activities take place in the hall, or confines of the temple, and are a very valuable social unifier.

Many of these public performances are staged as part of a particular festival that occurs at regular intervals, often connected with seed time or harvest. An intrinsic part of such festivals is the procession. This has special significance for the community because on these occasions the image or symbol is taken from the sanctum of the temple and paraded. This not only allows the devotee to present offerings directly to the image but in times past permitted those members of the community, who, for caste reasons, would normally have been forbidden entrance to the temple, to make their own devotions to the divinity. In practice, many temples have two sorts of image: the "fixed image" (*achala*), which remains in the temple, and its replica, or substitute, the "moving image" (*chala*), often made of bronze, which is processed at festivals. The image is transported in a chariot (*ratha*), which serves as a mobile temple for the duration of the festival. Such *rathas* are often works of art in themselves, huge wooden chariots covered with intricately carved panels of the gods and goddesses and surmounted by elaborate towered structures in bamboo, wood, and canvas. The superstructure is, of course, brilliantly decorated. The procession is accompanied by music, dance and general festivity, and that anarchic atmosphere of carnival, never far beneath the surface in Hinduism, is once again abroad.

Yoga

Running like a thread through the spiritual history of India is the discipline of yoga, which seems to go back even to the days of the Indus Valley civilization. The word *yoga* means "union." It refers to the ancient technique of quieting the restless mind and achieving union with the infinite within. The most authoritative text on yoga, the *Yogasūtras* of Patanjali (third century B.C.), opens with the succinct definition: "Yoga is the settling of the mind into silence." When the habitual chatter of the mind is totally calmed, we can experience the divine consciousness that shines within each one of us and illumines all creation. Yoga calls this consciousness the universal Self (*ātman*).

Union with the divine is called Enlightenment (*moksha*). Enlightenment is the goal of all spiritual life in India, and yoga and meditation are considered indispensable for true spiritual progress, no matter which deity is worshipped. All the great religious teachers, including the Buddha, used yogic techniques themselves and taught them to their disciples. Yoga is nondenominational, belonging to no particular cult or creed. Those who practice yoga are called *yogis*.

Yoga teaches that deep within the human nervous system are subtle channels (*nādīs*), which convey the life energy through the system. These channels converge periodically at plexuses (*chakras*), which lie along the spinal cord. The *chakras*, or energy centers, are represented iconographically by the lotus. There are seven major ones, each having a different color, number of "petals," and deity associated with it. Within the lowest *chakra* the psychic energy known as *kundalinī*, "the serpent power," lies dormant. When awakened through yoga, the *kundalinī* energy rises through each *chakra* in turn, purifying it. When all the *chakras* are purified, they open to the spirit as the lotus opens to the sunlight, and Enlightenment results.

Buddhism

Sometime around 590 B.C. a seeker after truth arrived at what is now the small town of Bodh Gayā in Bihār. He sat down to meditate under a *pīpal* tree and, after some time, achieved Enlightenment. His experience was to have a momentous effect not only on India, but on the whole of Southeast Asia, and in time its echoes were to be heard in most of the rest of the world. Who was this man, and what was his message?

The future Buddha was born Prince Gautama Siddhārtha, son of Shuddhodana, king of the Shākya people, in Lumbinī, on the India-Nepālese border. There is much controversy about his dates; the Mahābodhi Society of India believes he was born in 624 B.C., but many scholars prefer a later date, around 540 B.C. Whatever is the case, it is certain that Gautama was born a *kshatriya*—a member of the warrior caste. The legend is that King Shuddhodana was anxious to keep his son unharmed by the harsh realities of life and insured that he enjoyed an existence of princely ease and undisturbed comfort within the safety of the palace at Kapilavastu. In the course of time Gautama married and had a son.

But his life of luxurious ignorance was not to last. He was twenty-eight years old when, while out in his chariot one day, he happened to see in quick succession an old man, a sick man, a corpse being carried to cremation, and, finally, a wandering holy man. So great was the impression made by these intimations of mortality on the young Gautama that he decided there and then to renounce his life of pleasure and seek the Truth. He stole out of the palace in the middle of the night, accompanied only by a servant, and once he had crossed the river Anoma, he proceeded on his own. Gautama spent seven years studying under various spiritual teachers. He experimented with techniques of mind control and asceticism, and his fervor was so great that at one stage he nearly fasted to death in pursuit of his goal. Eventually he decided that such extreme practices were a waste of time, and coming to Bodh Gayā, he vowed not to leave the place until he had realized the Truth. After many hours of solitary meditation, he attained supreme Enlightenment (*nirvāna*). Gautama was thereafter known as the Buddha, "the Enlightened One." He is also referred to as Shākyamuni, "the sage of the Shākyas."

The Enlightened One called his teaching the *dharma* (Truth), which, he said, was "glorious in the beginning, glorious in the middle, and glorious in the end." The Buddha himself was not concerned with establishing a religion. He wished only to create a monastic order (*sangha*) of individuals who would be able to find out the Truth for themselves. His last words to his followers were "Be a lamp unto yourselves, be a refuge unto yourselves, seek no refuge outside of yourselves." He strongly discouraged any personal adulation, saying that all he had done was to discover a universal truth that was independent of any one person. It was only after his death that his followers began to organize what we call the Buddhist religion, which, as time progressed, became a less monastic and more popular worship, increasingly along the lines of the Hinduism the Master had originally rejected.

After the Enlightenment, the Buddha traveled to Sārnāth, near Banāras. Here he delivered his first discourse, in what the Buddhists call "the Setting in Motion of the Wheel of Truth." In this first discourse, often called the Deer Park Sermon, the Buddha delineated his message with a simplicity and clarity that were to become the hallmarks of his teaching. From its very beginning Buddhism had a fresh, translucent quality. It is straightforward and to the point, proceeding logically step by step through an analysis of the human predicament and culminating in the remedy. The *dharma* is like cool, clear water, which soothes, refreshes, and wakes us up. The Master often likened himself to a doctor who diagnoses the problem and presents the cure. As he himself said: "I show you suffering, and I show you the way out of suffering."

The first discourse presented "the Four Noble Truths." These are the basic tenets of Buddhism, as relevant to us today as they were when he expounded them, nearly twenty-six centuries ago.

☐ THE FOUR NOBLE TRUTHS

The Noble Truth of Dissatisfaction Human beings are basically dissatisfied. This dissatisfaction can express itself in any number of ways, ranging from a desire for fulfillment— whether material or spiritual—to a state of total depression, perhaps culminating in suicide. Most of us spend much of our lives somewhere between these two poles. Often our dissatisfaction is not recognized. It is disguised by our incessant mental or physical activity, which takes the form of ambition, pleasure seeking, the pursuit of success, and so on. But it is a common experience that no matter how much we have, we will always want more: more money, more prestige, more power, more security. There is no end to the desire for "more." It is very rare to find the person who is truly satisfied, who lives fully in the present, without hope, fear, or expectation.

The Sanskrit for "dissatisfaction" is *dukkha*, usually translated as "suffering." Such a translation is misleading, and the interpretation of the Buddha's teaching as "life is suffering" has led people to regard his doctrine as negative and pessimistic. Obviously there is much happiness in our lives. The Buddha's point was merely that this happiness, like everything else, is impermanent. It cannot last. And as such, it is basically unsatisfactory, because even in the very shadow of our happiness lurks the knowledge that one day circumstances will change and happiness will turn into its opposite. Youth turns to age, pleasure becomes stale, innocence hardens into experience. Even romantic love, the great human panacea, cannot be permanent. As a text puts it: "The meeting and parting of living things is as when clouds come together and part, or the parting of leaves from trees." So even happiness, if based on outer things or circumstances, is transitory, and thus comes under the category of "dissatisfaction."

The Noble Truth of the Cause of Dissatisfaction What is the cause of dissatisfaction? Unfulfilled desire. And desire springs from a feeling of lack. We do not have something; we want it. If we cannot get it—preferably immediately—we are dissatisfied, and from dissatisfaction is born suffering. Desire is deeply ingrained in us and has been operating for countless years. The Buddha traced it back not only to childhood and our mother's breast, but beyond, to previous lives stretching back interminably. There is always something more that we want, and there always has been. Our lives are a pattern of trying to fulfill this sense of wanting, whichever form it may take.

If dissatisfaction is the result of unfulfilled desire, then we must examine the root of desire. Buddha taught that this is the ego. It is the individual sense of "self"—"me" as opposed to "them"—which is always clamoring for fulfillment, because it is basically alone, fearful, and insecure. Because the ego is unsure of itself, it seeks to bolster its security by assuming the trappings of strength and identifying with something greater than itself. This something may be a football crowd, a political party, or the belief in a personal God who is going to save us at the last day. The ego tries to overcome its insecurity in many ways, and the attempt to conquer our sense of isolation is the basis of our relentless drive for achievement, success, and status. Conversely, it is the fear of losing what we have already gained that creates the violence and hostility that is unique to mankind.

Of course, most of us are unwilling to hear such home truths. This is partly because society unstintingly rewards those who ignore them the most. Human society is almost totally geared to the support and continuance of our vain attempts to amass security by dominating and exploiting each other and our surroundings. This is just as true of the communist as it is of the capitalist system; for men are equally blinded by the pursuit of territory, power, and status, no matter in which ideology they choose to clothe their ambitions. The Buddha's perception of the central conflict inherent in humanity cuts through mere social and political differences. He exposed dissatisfaction to be the very nature of the mind, as surely as a surgeon exposes the cancerous growth that is relentlessly destroying his patient.

The Noble Truth of the Ending of Dissatisfaction On their own, the sober facts uncovered by the first two Noble Truths might seem rather depressing. Fortunately, the Buddha's analysis of the human predicament included a solution! The only way to deal with the ego is to transcend it. Selfish fears and desires can never be repressed; they can only be replaced by something that is more satisfying to the mind, something beyond the individual sense of self, the isolated "I." In truth, the ego is falsely imagined. To get rid of this imagined isolation, we must become aware of a source of permanent fulfillment. Paradoxically, this fulfillment we crave can never be found outside ourselves. The answer lies within.

The Noble Truth of the Eightfold Path   The Eightfold Path is the practical side of the Buddha's message, the cure that follows his diagnosis of human ills. It consists of

Right insight Right aspiration	Wisdom
Right speech Right action Right livelihood	Morality
Right effort Right meditation Right ecstasy	Joy

The Path is a middle ground between the extremes of self-indulgence and self-mortification, both of which he had personally experienced. The crucial aspect of the Path is the practice of right meditation; this is the hub from which the other steps spread out like the spokes of a wheel, balancing and reinforcing one another. The mind is the root of all our problems, and it is the mind to which we must attend if they are to be solved. The *Dhammapada*, an important text from about the second century B.C. opens with the words:

> What we are today comes from our thoughts of yesterday, and our present thoughts build our life of tomorrow: our life is the creation of our mind. If a man speaks or acts with an impure mind, suffering follows him as the wheel of the cart follows the oxen . . . [but] if a man speaks or acts with a pure mind, joy follows him as his own shadow.

Self-knowledge is the key; anything else in the way of belief or theory, no matter how comforting, is an illusion, conjured up by a mind working in ignorance of itself. Such a mind is the victim of unconscious needs and fantasies; it can never find the Truth. Self-knowledge comes from meditation, which gradually reveals a level of being that is beyond the petty ego and opens up an inner peace that becomes the source of love, humor, and wisdom.

The goal of the Eight fold Path, and all Buddhist practice, is *nirvāna*. All sorts of nonsense has been written about *nirvāna*, even by the so-called experts. It has been variously described as a state of utter trance, a zombielike passivity, or even the extinction that comes with death. This confusion stems partly from the Buddha's unwillingness to pin the state down, for fear that his description would degenerate into yet another philosophical theory to divert people from seeking an end to their suffering. But he emphatically says that it is a state that is realized during life, and not some heavenly deliverance after death. A famous passage from the Hīnayāna scripture the *Udāna* tells us: "There is, O Monks, an unborn, unoriginated, uncreated, unconditioned state. If it were not for this state, O Monks, there would be no freedom possible here."

The word *nirvāna* literally means "blowing out" and refers to the extinction of the burning flame of selfish desire, fueled by egocentric ignorance. But *nirvāna* is not only a negative state. According to the Buddhist scriptures, the Master described it variously as "ultimate freedom," "the Highest," "the Imperishable," "total peace," and so on. It is the fulfillment, rather than the extinction, of the personality. Perhaps his most succinct definition was: "*Nirvāna* is the supreme bliss."

One of the attributes of this selfless beatitude is boundless compassion. The Enlightened One often taught his followers that, just as a mother would protect her only child at the risk of her life, so should one practice loving kindness toward all beings.

☐

The Buddha did not invent anything new in his realization of *nirvāna*. Rather he restated the fundamental insight of Indian religious experience that he had verified by his own experience: There is a state of beatitude that can be experienced only when the mind is completely silent and the agitation of desire has ceased. In this Buddhism is at one with Hinduism in its teaching of Enlightenment—which the Hindus call *moksha*. What the Buddha did criticize was the priestly mumbo-jumbo which he saw around him. He warned people not to depend on others nor to put their faith in unreasonable beliefs and superstition. Though he did not deny the existence of the gods, he asserted that they could never lead to ultimate truth. The Buddha was a man who discovered for himself the deathless state that is the essence of all religion.

The Buddha spent the rest of his life traveling around northeastern India in the kingdom of Magadha, teaching the *dharma* and establishing monastic communities for both men and women. He died at the age of eighty, in 544 B.C., at Kushinagara, the modern Kasia. His death is known as the *parinirvāna*, "the going beyond *nirvāna*."

The Buddha never wrote his teaching down; what records we have of it date from the early communities. That there was considerable disagreement among them on the finer points of the Master's message is clear from the fact that by 100 B.C. there were no less than eighteen separate sects, each with their own interpretation. This variety arose because the teaching was transmitted orally for its first five hundred years; it was only written down when the long passage of time threatened the accuracy of the monks' memories. Different groups had different versions of the teaching, hence the proliferation of schools. The most important of these sects was the Theravādin, "the school of the elders," probably formed around 200 B.C. Its teaching was somewhat austere and reclusive, the emphasis being placed on a solitary life of tranquillity and meditation. The goal of the Theravādins was the enlightenment of the individual monk. Their scriptures describe the enlightened monk (*arhat*) as being "in character as excellent as the gods, in meekness as the ascetic, and in wrath as the thunderbolt." At this time the Buddha was not worshipped or portrayed in images. Instead, he was represented by an empty throne, the Wheel of Truth (*dharmachakra*), the *bodhi* tree, or his footprints. Early shrines were simple and abstract, centered on the *stūpa*.

□ *THE STŪPA*

The *stūpa*, such as the Great Stūpa at Sānchī (Figure B), is basically a large hemispherical mound or dome (*anda*) that contains the relics of a Buddhist saint or teacher. This was in time surrounded by railings (*vedikā*), with gates (*toranas*) at

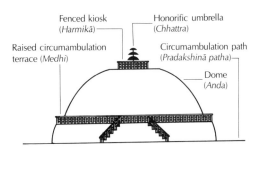

Fenced kiosk (*Harmikā*)   Honorific umbrella (*Chhattra*)

Raised circumambulation terrace (*Medhi*)   Circumambulation path (*Pradakshinā patha*)

Dome (*Anda*)

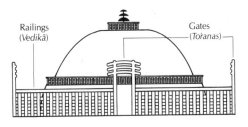

Railings (*Vedikā*)   Gates (*Toranas*)

Figure B. The Great Stūpa at Sānchī, ca. A.D. 100.

the four cardinal points. The top of the dome is truncated and surmounted by a railed enclosure (*harmikā*), beneath which the relic was buried in the body of the *stūpa*. The dome is crowned by an umbrella-shaped finial, the *chhattra*. In the earliest *stūpas* this *chhattra* had only one tier, but by the time the *stūpa* assumed its final form, there were three tiers, each one smaller than the one below. As well as having a paved path around their base to allow circumambulation (*pradakshinā*), the later *stūpas* also had a railed terrace (*medhi*) built onto the *anda*, to allow a second level of circumambulation.

Ancient monumental structures have always been built over a wide base, tapering to an apex of some sort. This is the best way to insure long life and structural stability for such essentially inflexible materials as brick and stone. Thus the weight of the mass is concentrated downward, and as long as the foundations are sufficiently strong, the building will endure. The pyramids of ancient Egypt, the zigurrats of Assyria, and the terraced Aztec temples in Mexico are all built on this principle. So, too, is the *stūpa*.

The historical model of the *anda* is the burial mound of ancient India. From Neolithic times on, it was the custom to bury the remains of kings or tribal chieftains in tumuli. These graves were always situated outside the village limits, just as death is outside the limits of life as it is normally understood.

The Buddhist architects adopted this circular model as the best expression of the perfection of the *dharma*. The hemisphere, as well as acting as a stabilizing and centralizing force, stands for the dark and motherly forces of the earth. It is a lunar symbol, referring to the unconscious in man and the transforming power of death and rebirth. This womblike hemisphere is called *anda*—"the egg." It alludes to the metamorphosis that awaits those who explore the depths of their mind. Not only did this shape remind the devotee of the "wheel of the law" and the recurring round of death and rebirth, which operates from moment to moment and from lifetime to lifetime, but in practical terms it allowed people to "make salutation" by the rite of circumambulation.

The umbrella rising from the plateau on top of the dome has several levels of meaning. As well as the cult of the dead centered around the tumulus, ancient man always had a cult of the living. This was situated in the heart of the village and was a shrine dedicated to the life-giving and preserving forces, those deities who bestowed good harvests, strong children, and long life. This shrine stood in the shade of, or actually was, the sacred tree of the village, protected by a fence of wood or bamboo. The *chhattra* harks back to this ancient idea by providing a vertical sign of the forces of light and life to balance the netherworld represented by the hemisphere.

Just as ancient Indians had placed offerings and cult images within the tree shrine, so the Buddhists placed the ashes of the Buddha and the saints in the *stūpa*, beneath the fenced enclosure around the *chhattra*.

The tribal king would sit under the shade of the main tree in the village, holding court and dispensing justice. When away from the village, his attendants would shelter him with a parasol that served the same purpose. In time the tree and parasol both became symbols of the royal authority. In recent times the *mahārājas* would give audience under sumptuously decorated parasols; revered holy men are also shaded in this way even today. It was natural for the Buddha, as world ruler, to have this ancient symbol associated with him.

Uniting both the sacred tree and the royal parasol theme is the Bodhi Tree, under which Gautama attained Enlightenment. The *chhattra* would serve as a reminder to the faithful of the historical fact of the Master's *nirvāna*. On a more abstract level, the *chhattra* represents the Cosmic Tree, which in Indian myths stands at the center of the universe, supporting on its branches all the multitudinous levels of creation. Both railings and gateways are based on their wooden prototypes that encircled the village in ancient India. They delineate the sacred enclosure and provide a protected pathway for circumambulation of the *stūpa*.

There have been various explanations for the rite of circumambulation, a rite common to many ancient cultures. Most of them link the practice to the course of the sun, by seeing it as a type of magical mimicry of the movement that sustains all life. This is a little too intellectual an explanation for what is a basic, instinctive response to an object or structure of veneration. It seems more likely to be an unconscious attempt to incorporate the object of worship, to make it your own by thoroughly imbibing its essence from all angles. There is no doubt that to walk around one of these ancient structures does provide a sense of completeness and reintegration.

Thus the *stūpa* is extraordinarily well suited to its role as the principal architectural structure of Buddhism. It unites several symbols and forms that are deeply embedded in the Indian psyche and is a physical expression of enduring psychological archetypes. It is also a succinct summary of the Master's teaching. Buddhism sees life and death as two sides of the same coin, not as antagonistic opposites. The goal of Buddhist practice is to die to the old behavior patterns and be reborn into a state of awareness that goes beyond birth and death, the state of *nirvāna*. This is why the early *stūpas* were erected in prominent places, gaily decorated and painted, and not set in seclusion, as earlier burial mounds had been. Buddism transforms the tumulus from a memorial to the dead to an inspiration to the living.

When the Buddha died, he was cremated with the honors befitting a king, and his ashes were distributed among the chief groups of his followers. These ashes were enshrined in the first eight *stūpas* of Buddhism. We are fortunate in having textual corroboration of the establishment of the *stūpa* as a cult symbol, for the important text known as the *Mahāpari-nirvāna Sūtra* is quite clear about the origin of the custom. Ānanda, the Buddha's favorite disciple, is asked by the people of Kushīnagara how the remains of a *buddha* should be disposed of. He replies that they should be treated like those of a king, explaining: "People, the body of a great king should be wrapped in muslin. Once it is wrapped in muslin, it should be wrapped in five hundred pairs of garments. Once it is wrapped in five hundred pairs of garments, it should be placed in an iron coffer. When this has been filled with vegetable oil, it should be closed with a double lid, made of iron. Then all kinds of scented woods should be heaped up and burned. The fire should be extinguished with milk, and the bones placed in a golden vase. Then one constructs a tumulus (*stūpa*) for the bones at a crossroads, and honors it with parasols, victory banners, flags, scents and garlands, incense, colored powder, and music. And one has a great festival, honoring, venerating and worshipping it."

In time there grew up three basic types of *stūpa*, which accorded with the classification generally applied to Indian sacred objects. These were the "physical *stūpa*" (*shārīraka-stūpa*), in which the relics of a holy person were enshrined; the "personal *stūpa*" (*paribhogika-stūpa*), which contained an object that had belonged to a holy person; and the "memo-rial *stūpa*" (*uddeshika-stūpa*), which commemorated a person or event.

□ *THE TWO SCHOOLS: HĪNAYĀNA AND MAHĀYĀNA*
Sometime around the beginning of the Christian era, a fundamental split occurred in the ranks of Buddhism. A new school emerged with a radical reinterpretation of the Buddha's message. It called itself the Mahāyāna ("the Great Vehicle") and dubbed the Theravādins the Hīnayāna ("the Little Vehi-cle"), the idea being that the Mahāyāna was by its nature able to lead many more people to the freedom of *nirvāna*. The new school saw *nirvāna* as being compatible with the mundane world and stressed that the attainment of *nirvāna* is possible for all.

With the development of the Mahāyāna, Buddhism became more of a popular religion, increasingly like the Hinduism the Master had originally rejected. The Buddha himself was viewed as more of a divine savior figure, who could be propi-tiated and adored, than as a historical mortal who was owed reverence because he had discovered the Truth. A celestial pantheon was adopted, and the original monastic teaching became increasingly overlaid with a subtle and colorful body of doctrine and philosophy. While meditation and insight still formed the core of the monk's life, a new dimension of popular devotion was added to embrace those who lived in the thick of life, beyond the monastery walls. From the Hīnayāna point of view, the new school was both a concession to the needs of the lay community, upon whom the monks depended for their existence, and an illustration of the general law that the more time that elapses from the founding of a religion, the more distorted that religion becomes. From the Mahāyāna point of view, however, their teaching was based on certain truths that the Master had only revealed to his closest disciples.

The philosophy of the Mahāyāna was based on a reinterpretation of the idea of *nirvāna*. Whereas the Hīnayāna had taught that *nirvāna* was a state of enlightened consciousness, attainable only by the reclusive monk, the Mahāyāna extended *nirvāna* into an absolute Reality that underlies and permeates all of life. It called this Reality the Void (*shūnyatā*), because it is devoid of qualities but holds all potential manifestation within it. The Void is not a state of nothingness but of pure potential, like the plenum-void described by Western mystics. Through meditation we can experience this Void as our own essential "buddha-nature"; Enlightenment is permanent experience of this "buddha-nature" that enlivens all creation. Immanent and yet transcendent, the Void is very like the *brahman* of Hinduism.

Overall, the doctrinal shift in the Mahāyāna was away from the historical Buddha, toward the buddha-nature inherent in all living beings.

The Void manifests through a series of stages, represented by a pantheon of celestial beings. The most important of these are the five *tathāgatas* ("enlightened ones"), or as they are popularly known, *dhyāni buddhas* ("buddhas of meditation"), which are assigned to the four cardinal points and the center. Each of these governs a particular part of the universe, and embodies a particular quality of the attributeless Void. The most popular of the *dhyāni buddhas* is Amitābha, who dwells in the Western Paradise and is the *buddha* of Boundless Light. The pantheon expanded into a number of celestial *buddhas* of the past, present, and future, each of which presides over a particular plane of existence (*loka*) and each of which can be worshipped individually. The historical Buddha, Gautama Siddhārtha, is thus just one of this pantheon, though as he is the *buddha* of our present age, he still retains great importance. Another important Mahāyāna deity is Maitreya, the coming *buddha*, who is yet to be incarnated on the earth plane.

A central figure in this elaborate cosmology was the

bodhisattva, "the pure-minded one." The *bodhisattva*, who is the spiritual son of the *dhyāni buddha*, acts as intermediary between the celestial and terrestrial realms, not unlike the saints in Catholic doctrine. These divine figures can also be worshipped, as they help mankind's spiritual endeavors from the heavenly realms, watching over humanity in a compassionate and concerned way.

In practical terms, the *bodhisattva* plays an important part in the spreading of the *dharma* on earth. Whereas the ideal of the Hīnayāna school was the lone *arhat* who strove for his own enlightenment, the heroic individual in the Mahāyāna is the person who has vowed not to become fully enlightened until all other sentient beings are also freed from ignorance. The *bodhisattva* dedicates his life to teaching others, spreading the message of the Buddha for the welfare of all, no longer concerned solely with his own spiritual progress. One aspect of the *bodhisattva*'s compassion is the practice of *parināma*, by which he turns over all his accumulated merit to the general mass of humanity.

As the Mahāyāna matured over the centuries, so its art became more ornate. In early Buddhism images of the Master were avoided—just as in early Christianity Christ was represented only by an empty space, the fish, or a plain cross. With the growth of the Mahāyāna, images of the Buddha proliferated. After the Buddha himself, the most common iconographic figures of the Mahāyāna are the divine *buddhas* and *bodhisattvas*. The principal *bodhisattvas* are Avalokiteshvara, "the Lord who looks down"—also known as Padmapāni, "the holder of the lotus"—and Vajrapāni, "the holder of the scepter." These deities symbolize, respectively, the Mahāyāna virtues of compassion and insight. The Mahāyāna figures, like their Hindu counterparts, are no mere creations of the artist's imagination, but divine archetypes that the artist has to cognize with an inner vision before he can faithfully represent them.

The *stūpa*, too, became more ornate, as can be seen from the various Mahāyāna caves at Ellorā and Ajantā. A particularly striking demonstration of the iconographic changes that expressed the doctrinal development can be seen by comparing the *chhattras* of *stūpas* from the various parts of the Buddhist world (Figure C). Broadly speaking, the Hīnayāna took a southern route, and flourished in those countries of Southeast Asia that received the early missionaries: Srī Lankā, Burma, Thailand, and Indochina. The Mahāyāna, on the other hand, took the northern route over the Himālayas to Tibet, Mongolia, China, and Japan. In practice, however, there is much intermingling, and even in those countries that are ostensibly Hīnayāna (that is, where there is no *bodhisattva* cult or extended pantheon) there is a form of popular worship

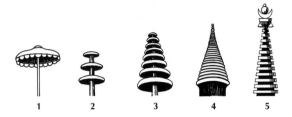

1 *Honorific parasol.* **2** *Indian* stūpa. **3** Chhattra *as tree of life.*
4 *Burmese/Thai/Srī Lankān* stūpa. **5** *Tibetan* chörten. *(After
Anagarika Govinda.)*

Figure C. Development of the chhattra.

directed toward the Buddha that the Master himself would
never have allowed. Thus in Srī Lankā and Thailand, for
example, Buddhism is a mixture of the original teaching,
fertility cults and local beliefs that predated its arrival, and
popular worship of the Buddha figure. Generally it is true to
say that the monks follow a purer form of the doctrine and
lead a life that the lay population hopes, in a future birth, to
aspire to. In India both schools flourished side by side—the
Hīnayāna with their scriptures in Pāli, the Mahāyāna with
theirs mainly in Sanskrit.

☐

Given its variety, why did Buddhism disappear so completely
from the land of its birth? One reason is historical. As time
progressed, the Buddhists faced challenges from both Hinduism and Islām. As what was virtually a reform movement
within Hinduism, Buddhism was continually at doctrinal
loggerheads with the Hindu orthodoxy. The Buddha had
rejected the authority of the Vedas, the scriptures that orthodox Hindus consider infallible. Socially the two religions were
incompatible because the Buddha also rejected the caste
system, which was the cement of Hindu society. Repeated
waves of Hindu revival, especially under the brilliant Shan-
kara in the ninth century, weakened the Buddhist strength.
Eventually Hinduism actually incorporated the teachings of
its wayward son, by making Buddha the ninth incarnation of
the compassionate god Vishnu, one of the Hindu trinity.

Yet, Hinduism and Buddhism existed side by side peacefully for many centuries, until the coming of Islām. When
the Islamic hordes poured into northern India from the eleventh century onwards, the pacifist Buddhists were no match
for the warlike invaders. Afghāns, Turks, Mughals—the cresent
of Islām swept through the Punjāb like a sickle through wheat,

took Delhi, and moved on eastward to the fertile Gangetic plain. Bihār, the birthplace of Buddhism, was right on their path. The great Buddhist seat of learning, Nālandā, which had been to the East what Alexandria had been to the West, was razed to the ground. In its heyday the university had had ten thousand monks of different orders, living peacefully side by side, debating, researching, teaching. It had been a center for learning, art, and culture; all of Asia was irradiated by its light.

Added to which, being primarily a monastic religion, Buddhism was dependent on the continued support of the community. In centers of population the proportion of Muslims steadily increased, but, due to its monastic celibacy, the Buddhist nucleus gradually declined. Thus Islām was bound to make increasing inroads into what had been Buddhist territory (exactly as is the case in present-day Ladākh).

What was left of Buddhism fled to countries already converted: either south to Srī Lankā, and thence to Southeast Asia, or north to the safety of the Himālayas. In later, more peaceful times, missionaries returned from these places to bring the *dharma* back to India, but even today, only three million of India's population follow the teachings of the Enlightened One. Many of these are low-caste converts from a Hindu order that has little to offer them.

Yet there is another reason, rooted as much in Indian psychology as in her history. The Indian psyche loves the lurid color and powerful emotions of Hinduism—its irrepressible fecundity that sprouts heads, arms, incarnations, and myths with the relentless energy of the life force itself. Though he never denied the existence of these forces, these benign gods and malign spirits that crowd the Indian imagination, the Buddha drew his teaching from an altogether more rarified world. His analysis of human ills was rational, his prescription based squarely on meditative discipline. The Indian psyche dwells in the realms of magical powers and the incomprehensible forces that govern life; the Enlightened One inhabited the transcendent. Like many great yogis before and after him, the Buddha lived beyond the astral worlds, in a kingdom too pure for the masses. His teaching was based on *nirvāna*, a state too abstract and distant for most of us, inextricably caught up in the petty dramas of our daily lives. If Buddhism was to survive, enlightenment had to give way to heaven. In those countries where the *dharma* flourished, it had to change its form, adopting the colorful garb of the local cults it met, and accommodating their beliefs in its metamorphosis into a popular religion.

Islām

Muhammad, "the Praised One," was born at Mecca, in what is now Saudi Arabia, on August 29, A.D. 570 His father, a merchant in the Quraish tribe, died before he was born; his mother, when he was five. He was brought up by an uncle. When he was twenty-five, Muhammad married a rich widow, by whom he had several sons, all of whom died in infancy, and four daughters. The youngest of these, Fātima, married Alī, and from them are descended the nobility of Islām: the Sayyids and the Sharīfs. When Muhammad was about forty, he began to have visions of the Angel Gabriel, who commanded him to preach the new religion of Islām—"unconditional surrender." The new prophet and his associates were persecuted by the Meccans; under threat of death Muhammad fled from Mecca in 622, for the safety of Medina some 270 miles (435 kilometers) to the north. Here he was publicly proclaimed the Prophet and established the first permanent community of true believers—the "Companions of the Prophet." In 630 Muhammad returned to Mecca at the head of an army of ten thousand. He conquered the city, destroyed the idols in the Temple of Abraham that stood on the site of the Kāʿba, the holy stone, and declared Mecca to be the religious capital of Islām. From then on, Mecca replaced Jerusalem as the focus of Muslim prayer. Two years later Muhammad returned to Medina. He died the same year and was buried there.

The religion of Islām rests on what are called the Five Pillars, the observances which every good Muslim follows. The most important of these is the Attestation of Faith (*shahāda*), which states: "There is no god but God, and Muhammad is His messenger." Islām is rigorously monotheistic, its central belief being the unity and inexpressible mystery of the One God (Allāh). Although the essential nature (*dhat*) of God far transcends our ability to comprehend it, we can get some idea of it by the Attributes, or Divine Names, which Allāh has condescended to reveal to His believers. There are said to be three thousand of these. One thousand are known only to the angels, another thousand known only to the prophets. Three hundred are in the Old Testament, three hundred in the Psalms of David. Another three hundred are in the New Testament, and ninety-nine are in the *Qurʾān*, the principal scripture of the Muslims, which was revealed to Muhammad by the Angel Gabriel. The final name is hidden, though it is believed that Allāh has revealed this to the purest of souls. In the *Qurʾān* Allāh is referred to by such names as "the Merciful" (*ar-Rahīm*), "the All-Knowing" (*al-Alīm*), and "the Eternal" (*as-Samad*). Muhammad is not the only prophet in Islām, for the Muslim accepts the authenticity of the tradition of Old Testament prophets beginning with Abraham and culminating in Jesus. But these are considered incomplete revelations; the perfect, and final, revelation was given to Muhammad, who is therefore known as the Prophet, or the Messenger, of God. Similarly, much of the Christian scriptures is accepted, though the complete and irrefutable scripture is the *Qur'ān*. Whereas the *shahāda* enunciates the unity of God, the other four Pillars express this unity in social terms. They are prayer (*salāt*), fasting (*siyām*), giving of alms (*zakāt*), and pilgrimage (*hajj*). Prayer should be performed five times a day: at dawn, noon, mid-afternoon, sunset, and nightfall. Daily prayers may be offered from a variety of places— an oratory, a prayer rug (which acts as a ritually pure portable oratory), or a mosque, and whatever the Muslim is doing at the time of prayer must be interrupted to attend to worship. Once a year, for a month, no food or drink is to be taken between sunrise and sunset. This month of abstinence is called Ramadan and includes prohibition of such activities as smoking and sex. When he instituted the practice, the Prophet said it would serve a dual function, to purify the believer and remind him of what it is like to go hungry. The giving of alms to the poor is a compulsory duty to the Muslim, and in general Muslim communities are scrupulous in looking after the welfare of their less fortunate members. The last Pillar, which is in many ways the climax of the believer's life, is the pilgrimage to Mecca.

□ *MECCA*
Mecca is the center of the Islamic universe, the birthplace of both the Prophet and the religion he founded.

At the heart of the city of Mecca stands the Kā'ba: a huge hollow stone cube, covered in a black cloth embroidered with gold. Muslims believe it is situated directly beneath the throne of God in Paradise. The site has been holy since time immemorial and goes back long before the time of Muhammad. Some say it was originally a shrine to the "great god of the ancient world," who, in comparatively recent times, split to become Dionysius in the West and Shiva in the East. The Kā'ba itself has been rebuilt many times. It is the *axis mundi* of Islām, the supreme symbol of a religion that sternly forbids naturalistic representation. The Kā'ba marks the place where the vertical axis of the divine and the horizontal axis of the realm of matter most perfectly intersect. Thus it serves the same function for the Muslim world as the Omphalos at Delphi did for the classical world or Mount Meru does for the Hindu: It is the navel of creation, the perfect, timeless origin of all.

Each Muslim is united to this magical center, and all the followers of the Prophet turn to face it when they conduct their five daily prayers. Whatever the place of prayer, it is united to the Kaʻba at Mecca by an invisible line of direction called the *qibla*. This acts as a divine axis that aligns the individual to the whole. In spiritual terms, it is an umbilical cord, connecting the worshipper with the source of his life.

□ THE MOSQUE

The word *mosque* is derived from the Arabic *masjid*, which means "place of prostration." The mosque is essentially the place from which prayers are offered. There are four types of mosque. The *masjid* itself is a local mosque that is used throughout the week for both private and communal prayers. There will be many *masjids* in a large Muslim community. The *jāmi* ("that which brings together") is the mosque for the entire community to assemble together in for the Friday service. This remains open throughout the week, but its importance lies in its Friday function. In India and Pakistan a *jāmi* is known as a *jāmi masjid* (or Friday mosque). The third type is the *madrasa*, or teaching mosque, which acts as the theological college, and the fourth type is the *khānaqāh*, or monastic mosque, in which the Sūfī brotherhoods—the mystics of Islām—live.

The life of any mosque—especially a Friday mosque—is its congregation; it is above all a social structure. In this way the mosque is very different from the Hindu temple. In a temple an individual encounters the divine, on his or her own. The temple, as the abode of the gods, is permanently and energetically charged with divine power. The Hindu believes that this *shakti* is present even if the temple has not been visited for some time; humans are, in a sense, irrelevant to it. Thus the temple is a building that receives and contains the immanence of divine *shakti*; its social function is secondary. The mosque, on the other hand, exists to unite the community of believers, and points beyond itself to the transcendent Allāh. Mosques, like Christian churches or Jewish synagogues, are always built with a sizable hall or outer courtyard to accommodate the congregation of the faithful.

But between the congregation and Allāh, so to speak, lies the Kaʻba. For this reason the heart, and raison d'être, of any mosque is its *mihrāb*, an arched niche, set into the mosque wall, that indicates the direction of Mecca. It is through the *mihrāb* that the *qibla* axis runs, connecting the worshipper with his distant focus of devotion. Thus in simplest terms, a mosque is no more than a building erected around the *qibla* axis, and the *mihrāb* delineates the direction of this sacred lifeline. The holiest part of a mosque is therefore the wall in which the *mihrāb* is set, for this is the wall nearest to Mecca.

The Kaʻba is, then, the infinite hub of an almost infinite

wheel. Around the many concentric circumferences of this wheel lie every Muslim shrine and mosque in the world, united to the hub by the spokes of the *qibla* running through their *mihrāb*. The Kā'ba plays the same centering role as does the temple for the Hindu: With its corners aligned to the cardinal points, it orients sacred space around a visible center from which the faithful may ascend to the realms of the invisible.

In this context it is worth adding that the Arabic word for the five fundamentals of Islām translated as "Pillar" means literally "corner," and the image here is of a square, centered on the first Pillar, the *shahāda*. The same universal symbolism of the infinite center expressed through the four cardinal points is once again in operation, though here on a social and doctrinal, rather than on an architectural, level.

The *mihrāb* serves an acoustic as well as a directional purpose. The prayer leader (*imām*) faces into the alcove when he leads the prayers, aligning the whole congregation to Mecca. (Even in small mosques there will be an *imām* leading the five daily prayers, though Muslims may and do pray individually at other times.) At the same time his voice is amplified by the concave vault, and bounced back to the worshippers assembled behind him.

The earliest mosques had no *mihrāb*. In the Prophet's own mosque at Medina, the *qibla* direction is indicated only by a simple stone set into the floor. But as the new faith spread rapidly along the trade routes of the known world, some way had to be found to keep the ever-increasing circle aligned to its hub at Mecca. The solution was brilliant and simple. An impromptu mosque wall, inside which the faithful could assemble, was traced out in the sand with a spear. The spear was then stuck, haft downwards, into the ground, its elliptical blade standing like a flame, illuminating the direction of the Holy City. For the first few years of the rise of Islām, while the armies of the Prophet were spreading far and wide to establish the new Empire of Righteousness, the spear served as *mihrāb*. Then, as permanent mosques and shrines began to be erected, the pointed niche took its place as *qibla* indicator. Coins have been found dating from the eighth century as evidence of this transition: They are engraved with a spear standing in the *mihrāb* niche.

But for the settled communities, who had permanent mosques from the start, the *mihrāb* arrived earlier. It is commonly held that the first one was built into a mosque wall by the Umayyad caliph al-Walīd, when he restored the mosque of the Prophet at Medina. He brought Coptic masons with him, who created the prayer niche, perhaps modeled on the apse in Coptic churches or (perhaps) on the liturgical niches in certain contemporary synagogues. But it is very likely that elsewhere in the Islamic world a simple marker, such as a false door, had already been used to indicate Mecca.

Whatever its historical origins, the *mihrāb* belongs to a worldwide symbolism. Its shape is the shape of the cave, and in all Eastern traditions, the cave is the place where the divine appears, whether externally in the world or internally in the heart. In this sense the *mihrāb* is an Islamic parallel to the *garbha-griha* of the Hindu temple: a physical focus that awakens the corresponding "place" in the consciousness of the devotee. The word *mihrāb* means "refuge," and in the *Qur'ān* this is used to refer specifically to a secret place in the Temple of Jerusalem (perhaps the holy of holies), where the Virgin Mary retreated to receive nourishment from the angels. This link enforces the feminine, receptive aspect of the *mihrāb* that its shape naturally suggests. It is in the heart that the worshipper receives the nourishment of grace, and it is only by emptying the mind and heart that such a transfusion can take place.

That this receptivity lies at the heart of Islām was made more explicit in many mosques in which the *mihrāb* niche was surmounted by a canopy in the form of a seashell. This is another universal feminine symbol, related to the ear and the vulva, which signifies both the hearing and the conception of the Divine Word. Again the connection with Mary, Mother of Jesus, is clear. But unlike the protuberant altar in a Christian church, the symbolism of the concave *mihrāb* demands that it remain empty and uncluttered at all times. The shape of this niche, whether in the *mihrāb* itself, the miniature *mihrāb* woven into the design of prayer rugs, or as a recurrent motif in architectural design, is the hallmark of Islām (Figure D).

In fact, simplicity is the essential tone of Islamic art. Islamic law forbids the making of naturalistic images, because this would be a blasphemous mimicry of the only true creator, Allāh. In the mosque simplicity is also functional. The mosque

The hallmark of Islamic art, originating as the shape of the mihrāb *indicating the direction of Mecca.*

Figure D. Arched niche.

is a ritually pure area, within which the impurities of the outside world are temporarily suspended. Walled off from polluting influences, the mosque serves to focus the believer's attention in prayer and contemplation. One way to encourage this quietening of the mind is to minimize its distractions; thus there is little in the decoration of a mosque that can divert the believer from his true reason for entering the place: worship. The early mosques were all extremely simple; it was only when rich and powerful dynasties, such as the Ottoman Turks, began to build mosques that they became extremely ornate. Generally speaking the purity of Islām, like its art, lies in omission.

□

Islām spread like a forest fire along the trade routes of the world. The Prophet died in 632; by 660 his religion stretched from Tunisia in the west to Afghānistān in the east. By 750 the empire of Islām ran uninterrupted from Spain to the borders of China, as far south as Yemen, and as far north as the Caspian Sea. It was the most spectacular spread of a religion the world has ever seen. Yet from its beginnings, Islām was marred by internal disharmony. Soon after the Prophet's death, a dispute arose among his followers as to the question of who should be the head of the faith. The Sunnis advocated the election of the leader and recognized a succession of four *kalifas* ("caliphs" or "vice-regents"): Abū Bakr, Omar, Othman, and the Prophet's son-in-law, Alī. The Shī'ites, however, believed in apostolic succession, decided by appointment, and regarded Alī as the first genuine caliph. Conflict between the warring factions was strong; Omar, Othman, Alī, and Alī's son Hussain were all murdered in the continuing struggle for power. This division between Shi'a and Sunni has lasted until today, and the world's four hundred million Muslims are principally divided between the two sects. A third sect, the Ishmailis, dates from the eighth century. Founded over a dispute concerning the rightful *imām* (spiritual head of the community), the sect has as its present head His Holiness Āga Khān IV, the forty-ninth hereditary leader. About 10 percent of Indians are followers of the Prophet, and most of these are Sunnis.

Islām reached India as early as the eighth century, but it did not become well established there until some four hundred years later, with the founding of the Slave dynasty by Qutbuddīn Aibak.

The impact of Islām on northern India was enormous. But it was rarely a peaceful interchange, for it would be hard to imagine two less compatible systems of belief than Hinduism and Islām. The Hindu lived in an ancient static society that was conservative yet tolerant of outsiders. This closed system accepted no converts, and was dominated by hierarchical caste rules and the dictates of the brahmin priests. The Hindu worshipped a thousand different forms of God, each one represented in the most fantastic and colorful way imaginable, and he held the cow sacred. The Muslim, on the other hand, belonged to a new, dynamic, and proselytizing faith that aimed to spread its message to all corners of the world, by force if necessary. Islām recognized no distinction of race, color, or class among its members. It had no priesthood but aimed to create an egalitarian society in which each member was individually responsible to the One God. This God was of such purity that any attempt to represent it, let alone identify it with a domestic animal, was blasphemy. The stage was set for a confrontation that has lasted, off and on, until modern times.

The situation was worsened by the fact that many of the new conquerors, though ostensibly Muslim, were little more than nomadic adventurers. Their conduct cannot be blamed on their adopted religion. In establishing Muslim dominance, they were often guilty of unpardonable behavior against the Hindu infidels. Thus, for example, if a Muslim judge found a Hindu defendant guilty, he had the right, in addition to sentencing him, to spit in his mouth. Quite apart from the unpleasantness of such an insult, to the caste Hindu it was doubly horrendous, as body secretions are considered the most ritually impure of all polluting substances. Fortunately, military conquest was not the only way that Islām entered India. From the early thirteenth century onward, many members of the mystical Sūfī brotherhoods escaped persecution by the Muslim orthodoxy in Persia by fleeing to India and established schools there. It was through these brotherhoods that the true spirit of Islām percolated into Indian culture, influencing music, architecture, poetry, and painting. The Sūfīs were given a warm reception from the Hindu devotional sects, especially the worshippers of Rāma (*Rāmabhaktis*). The most important of the Sūfī groups was the Chishtī order, based at Ajmer. It was one of its leaders, Sheikh Salīm Chishtī, who was spiritual adviser to the Emperor Akbar, and to him must go much of the credit for encouraging the Great Mughal's tolerant outlook.

And despite the bloodshed and vandalism that some of the Muslim conquerors brought with them, they also left India a legacy of unparalleled beauty and cultural accomplishment. Āgra, Delhi, Fatehpur Sīkrī, the courtly sophistications of Lucknow and Lahore—these are among the greatest wonders of India, renowned the world over as an integral part of her heritage. It is, however, a tragic and irrefutable fact that such achievements must be weighed against the wanton destruction of untold thousands of Hindu buildings, architectural wonders that had stood unharmed for hundreds of years before the green banner of the Prophet was first unfurled.

**The
Country**

India is a land of staggering variety. Physically, she ranges from the world's highest mountain chain— the Himālayas—to swamplands that lie below sea level. Her 125 million square miles (324 million square kilometers) make her as large as Europe, and within this land mass lies every sort of terrain imaginable. This variety is obvious in the north: The Punjāb boasts well-watered fields of wheat and paddy; Bihār struggles through flat and dusty plains that seem to go on forever; Orissā stretches from the inaccessible mountains of the Eastern Ghāts through lush foothills and steamy jungle, down to deserted palm-fringed beaches.

India is as varied climatically as she is geographically. Eight months of the year are comparatively dry, building up to a hiatus of oppressive, unrelieved heat in late April and May, when temperatures can rise to 120° Fahrenheit (50° Celsius). Then, about the beginning of June, the monsoon breaks. For the next four months, the land is intermittently drenched in torrential downpours. These bring life back to the parched earth but can also cause widespread flooding and horrendous damage. The oscillation between drought and flood is as regional as it is dramatic. Parts of Assam, in the northeast, have an average annual rainfall of sixty feet (yes, *feet!*), while areas of the desert state of Rājasthān, a thousand miles away to the west, have in recent history gone without rain for twelve years at a stretch. In India we are confronted with the almighty power of nature and her unpredictable extremes: What the Great Mother gives, She can just as easily sweep away. The resulting fragility of life is a fact that has been deeply etched into the Indian psyche throughout its long history.

**The
People**

India's peoples are as varied as her terrain. Her population is now nearing seven hundred million; it is increasing each year by thirteen million—about the total population of Australia. This vast mass is distributed over twenty-two federal states and several union territories—all of which owe allegiance to the central government in New Delhi. They speak between them 14 major languages (all of which can be seen on a one-rupee note), and linguists have identi- fied 220 minor languages and 845 dialects in the subcontinent. Each state has its own racial and cultural heritage, enjoying its own traditional type of dress, eating habits, religious customs, and festivals—in short, its own identity. Take women's dress as an example. The traditional attire of Indian women is the *sārī*—a length of material six yards long and a yard and a half wide (five and a half meters by one and an eighth meters) that is wound once around the hips, pleated six times at the front, then taken around the waist again and brought up across the chest to the left shoulder. In Gujarāt the women drape the loose end gracefully across their back and shoulders, whereas in Mahārāshtra and Tamil Nādu (in the south) they prefer a ten-yard (nine-meter) *sārī* that is worn loosely and tucked between the legs, so as to give greater freedom of movement and a more billowing effect. Each social occasion has its appropriate *sārī*, and each region its preferred material and weave. Thus in parts of Orissā the *sārīs* are woven with intricate *ikat* designs, in which both the warp and weft are dyed before weaving, whereas the Bengālī *sārī* is characteristically bordered with a plain band in a single color. But even the *sārī* is not universal! Punjābī ladies wear baggy trousers topped by a long, fitted shirt that reaches almost to the knee, with a long scarf that drifts off the shoulders. Muslim women wear a similar shirt and scarf over very narrow-legged trousers, often atop pointed shoes. And in the western states of Gujarāt and Rājasthān, the women wear voluminous skirts that are richly embroidered and often inset with mirrorwork. Their bodices are even more highly decorated and embellished, and they cover their heads with a half-length of *sārī* that is tucked into the waistband and sweeps up over the head. These basic differences are further complicated by variations in jewelry and adornment. Even the sign that a woman is married varies from region to region: a ring on the first toe of each foot; a vermilion line drawn in the central part of the hair; ivory bracelets stacked from wrist to elbow; a beaded necklace combining the symbols of the deities of her own and her husband's families—the list goes on and on. And what is more, any comprehensive survey of India's people would have to include the indigenous tribals, of whom there are an estimated forty million, each tribe with its own particular traditions and customs.

The History   Why such tremendous diversity? This question can partly be answered by looking at a map of Asia. Geographically, the Indian subcontinent is situated at the end of a corridor that runs unbroken from Turkey eastward. Through this corridor have flowed streams of invaders, traders, and travelers from time immemorial. But their journey east stopped at India, for India is a cul-de-sac, her north-eastern border closed by the impenetrable heights of the majestic Himālayas, which deflect all comers down into the funnel-shaped land mass to the south. This receptacle, stopped at the top by mountains and at the bottom by sea, has been a cultural melting pot, into which has been poured wave after wave of influence, each finding its own place in the richly varied mosaic it encountered.

The earliest of these waves that we know about was the Āryan invasion, which began about 1800 B.C. The Āryans (the word means "noble") were pastoral nomads from what is now southern Russia. They brought with them Sanskrit, the language of classical learning and priestcraft, and the Vedas, those scriptures which the orthodox Hindu of today still considers infallible. They also brought the art of sacrificial ritual and reverence for the cow and its products. The light-skinned, long-nosed Āryans were of a very different racial stock from the indigenous Indians they met; their sacred texts refer to the people they encountered by a variety of critical epithets: "cattle raiders," "the noseless," "the dark ones." The Āryans continued to enter northern India for the best part of a thousand years, establishing themselves as far as the Gangetic plain in the east. But, decisive though their influence was, the Āryans were only the first of many invaders. Next came the Persians under Cyrus and the famous Darius (521–485 B.C.), who conquered the Indus Valley and conscripted Punjābī troops to help him in his wars against the Greeks in 479 B.C. The Persians brought with them the solar cult and the use of pillars to commemorate victories and publicize laws and edicts. They also believed in the divinity of the monarch, an essential element of later Hindu society. Alexander the Great reached the Indus in 328 B.C., and left behind him craftsmen and sculptors who were to have a decisive influence on the artistic growth of India. Although Alexander himself died in 323 B.C., his successors in the province of Bactria—an independent Greek colony on the site of the modern Balkh in Afghānistān—were responsible for perpetuating Hellenistic artistic ideals in Asia. The direct result of this influence was the Greco-Buddhist school known as Gandhāra (after the ancient kingdom comprising what is now northern Pakistān and eastern Afghānistān), which produced some of the loveliest figures ever made in the subcontinent. While various native dynasties were rising and falling on the Indian stage, invaders continued to make inroads through the passes of the northwest frontier. After the Greeks came the Scythians (130 B.C.), then the Parthians from Persia, then the Kushānas from Central Asia. These last made their capital at Peshāwar and reached as far east as Banāras, establishing a dynasty that was to last until A.D. 200. They were followed by one of the greatest Hindu dynasties, the Guptas, who ushered in a golden age of Indian art and culture. But once again the open flank of the northwest was invaded, this time by the White Huns. In the fifth century these ferocious tribes from Central Asia streamed across Europe under their leader, Attila, to attack Italy; at the same time a wave of them flowed east, to overrun Persia and northern India. They are recorded as having reached as far south as Ujjain, in modern Madhya Pradesh.

But the most profound impact on the emerging Indian nation was to come from the Islamic invaders. The first Muslims to reach India were Arab traders, who landed on the west coast as early as the seventh century, not long after the Prophet's death. In 712 a seventeen-year-old youth called Muhammad bin Qasīm marched into Sind at the head of an army and won several battles before returning to his native Afghānistān. Yet it was another two hundred years before the first real Muslim invasion arrived. This was led by Mahmūd of Ghaznī, a ruthless Turco-Afghān freebooter who invaded India no less than seventeen times between A.D. 1000 and 1027. Mahmūd took all before him, devastating Hindu cities and temples from the Yamunā to the Ganges, destroying all in his path. Yet for all his savagery, Mahmūd found time to patronize Islamic art and literature. One of the greatest masters of Persian poetry, Firdausī, belonged to his court; so, too, did the great historian al-Birūni. Then, in 1192, came the consolidation of Islamic influence in India. An Afghan named Muhammad of Ghor took the Punjāb and then Delhi from the Rājput Hindus, and Islām had come to stay. Disunited among themselves, the Hindus were no match for the invaders. According to caste rules, only the warriors (*kshatriyas*) were allowed to fight; the rest of the population were reduced to mere spectators. Nor were the Hindus, who used elephants and foot soldiers armed with lances, able to withstand the assaults of the Muslim archers, many of whom were mounted. The Hindu ranks were slow and unwieldy by comparison, their elephants frequently turning on and trampling their own masters. Added to which, the Turk, Mongol, or Afghān was often bigger than his Hindu opponent. The advantage of size, together with crusader's zeal and plunderer's greed, made them unstoppable.

Once his rule was safely established over Delhi, Muhammad returned to Afghānistān, appointing his slave, Qutbuddīn Aibak, as his viceroy. Qutbuddīn in turn established the so-called Slave dynasty and inaugurated a Muslim ascendency that was to last, through a succession of sultanates, for over six hundred years. Turks, Afghāns, and Persians sat on the throne of Delhi; each dynasty contributing to the variegated mosaic of Indian culture. The most brilliant of these was undoubtedly the Mughal dynasty, founded by Bābur in 1526. Bābur's ancestors, like the Huns and Turks, came originally from Mongolia. Their name is derived from the Persian word *mughal*, meaning Mongol. The glory of the Mughals lasted until the death of the last Great Mughal, Aurangzeb, in 1707, but the dynasty actually continued until the British defeated the last Mughal emperor, Bahādur Shāh, in 1857.

The Great Mughals

Bābur	1526–1530
Humāyūn	1530–1556
Akbar	1556–1605
Jahāngīr	1605–1627
Shāh Jahān	1627–1658
Aurangzeb	1658–1707

The Mughal dynasty eventually gave way to the British. In fact, the Europeans had long been on the Indian scene, albeit in a limited way. The first to arrive were the Portuguese. Having explored the west coast of Africa and discovered the Cape of Good Hope and established settlements in East Africa, Portuguese navigators moved on to India. They came, as Vasco da Gama told a local chieftain, in search of spices and Christians, and by 1510 they had captured the port of Goa, just south of Bombay. The British came much later. On the last day of 1600 Queen Elizabeth I, contemporary of Akbar the Great, granted a group of London businessmen a charter to trade as the East India Company in competition with the Dutch, who at that time dominated the European spice trade. After establishing a base in Java, the company set up its first Indian base at Armagaum, on the Coromandel coast near Madras. Madras itself was leased to the company by the local *rāja* in 1639, and this, together with trading posts on the west coast, was the beginning of the British Empire in India. However, both the Dutch and the Portuguese were more favored at the Mughal court, and in 1674 the French, who were to present a serious challenge to the British ambitions a hundred years later, arrived at Pondicherry. By 1696 the British had set up a trading post at the mouth of the Hoogly River in Bengal, called Fort William. This was to grow into Calcutta, the city which, after the final defeat of the French in 1757, became the springboard of the East India Company's activities. It was to remain the capital of British India until 1911, when Delhi became the principal city.

The Power of Tradition

So to a land already populated by diverse ethnic groups were added successive waves of foreign influence, until India's diversity, like her size, was comparable to that of Europe. Her differences have been strengthened and maintained not only by the natural barriers of mountain, river, and desert, but by a unique type of social organization: the caste system. Āryan society was divided into three basic types (*varnas*): priests, warriors, and farmers. From this the caste system evolved. It became immensely complicated and has traditionally militated against change. The orthodox Hindu must marry within his caste or subcaste (*jati*), live in his native place, and follow his inherited occupation. Thus not only were the foreign elements in Indian society encouraged to find their own level and preserve their own identity, but even within the Hindu community itself, difference and separateness were valued and safeguarded.

To the new arrival in India this weight of tradition may well not be obvious. First impressions stick, and many incoming visitors judge the country by their first point of contact: the relatively cosmopolitan cities of Delhi, Calcutta, or Bombay. But these are misleading. Their Westernized inhabitants are, in some ways, as unlike the average Indian as is the traveler himself. For India is still predominantly a land of villages—some seven hundred thousand of them. In a world where education is synonymous with Westernization, 70 percent of these villagers are illiterate. Their lives are still ordered by those ancient patterns that no longer affect the modern urban dweller: the twin supports of agriculture and religion. The villager still inhabits a world where the cyclical rhythms of seed time and harvest are more important than the clock, and the time-honored symbols of priesthood and royalty carry more weight than the newfangled arguments put forward by the bureaucrats in far-away New Delhi.

Today the onslaught of the twentieth century is changing all this, and the latest wave of invaders, Western tourists, are agents in the inevitable process of change. But it would be a mistake to assume that the country will be transformed overnight. Tradition dies hard in India. Her society is still essentially tribal, composed of largely independent groups that function with little or no clear idea of national consciousness.

How, then, is the visitor to come to grips with the exotic panorama he sees spread out so colorfully and so invitingly before him? How can he begin to comprehend its almost overwhelming diversity? To many travelers, with limited time at their disposal, India seems just too vast and alien a civilization to handle. To understand her would take years—if not lifetimes! Ironically, the key to understanding this complex culture lies in an understanding of what at first may appear its most baffling aspect—the art and architecture.

The Nature of Indian Art   Virtually all the art in India, of whichever religion, can be classified as what Benjamin Rowland (see Appendix 2) has rightly called "traditional." Traditional art is an expression of devotion; it is the handmaiden of religion. Its purpose is the transmission of divine truths and the cultivation of religious feeling. As such, its character is universal; the nearest historical example for us being the art of medieval Europe. Traditional art is an integral part of the society's life. Its framework is the metaphysical order which governs that life, and its function is to mirror, explain, and perpetuate the harmonious functioning of that order. Thus traditional art is social, rather than individualistic, because it seeks to stabilize the community and remind its members that they are part of a greater, cosmic, whole—an order that is mirrored in the social order to which they belong. The premises upon which Indian art is founded stem from a world-view that would have been instinctively understood by Dante, Shakespeare, or Fra Angelico.

This traditional, or aristocratic, view of art sees it as a medium that is both educative and esoteric, using form, myth, and symbol to speak a language of hidden depths and multiple meanings. This language is both a teaching for the unlettered and a code for the initiate. Its primary purpose is instructive not esthetic, and its goal is integration and upliftment. In fact, considerations of esthetics, or even personal taste, are largely irrelevant, because the laws that are being followed are the realities of a plane of life that is prior to the human plane and unaffected by our likes or dislikes. Classical Western art was based on the norms of Greek and Roman culture. It endeavored to represent the "real world" in a naturalistic way, expressing clear and external fact with a fine perfection of form, of which the human body was the yardstick. Classical Indian art, on the other hand, belongs more to the world of dream than to the daylight world. It is oneiric rather than realistic, suggestive rather than definite. And it is preeminently symbolic, for its images are pointers to a higher and more abstract reality. It is this conformity to a hidden order in preference to a perceptible esthetic that has largely blinded Western eyes to the nature and appreciation of traditional Indian art.

It should be added that there is, in addition to iconographic regulation, a mature theory of esthetics in Indian thought. This theory is clearly defined in the *Nātyashāstra* (ca. A.D. 300), which speaks of the eight basic moods, or "flavors" (*rasas*), that can legitimately be expressed through the arts: the erotic, comic, pathetic, furious, heroic, terrible, odious, and marvelous. These *rasas* should elicit appropriate emotional responses (*sthāyibhāvas*) in the spectator: the feelings of love, mirth, sorrow, anger, energy, fear, disgust, and astonishment, respectively. We have here a parallel to Aristotle's dictum that the proper business of dramatic tragedy was to elicit the feelings of pity and terror in the audience. It was generally considered that drama was the most effective medium through which the *rasas* found expression, and a later text, the *Vishnudharmottara,* adds a ninth *rasa,* the peaceful, which elicits a feeling of tranquillity. On the part of the spectator, a receptivity very like what the poet Keats called "negative capability" is an essential prerequisite. The Indian authorities stress the need to approach a work of art with a quiet, open mind, so as to allow the dominant *rasa* gradually to impress itself on the consciousness and elicit the appropriate feeling-response. Nor should this feeling overwhelm the mind, but should be viewed dispassionately, so that its universal truth may be clearly understood. And even the *rasas* are referred back to their divine source, since they are believed to be displayed in their archetypal form by the god Shiva in his various exploits.

However, when he wished, the Indian artist was perfectly able to produce naturalistic art, full of loving and detailed observation, and sparkling with humor at the foibles of humanity. Such art is particularly to be found in the Buddhist sites (for example, Ajantā or Sānchī) because the Buddhists, in accord with the orientation of their faith, were generally more down to earth than their Hindu counterparts. Nevertheless, even in Buddhist art, there is an ever-increasing leaning toward the fantastic and the larger than life, which stamps it clearly as being in the Indian mold. This specifically Indian quality can be seen when we contrast similar Buddhist subjects treated in different civilizations, and compare the Buddhist art of India with, for example, its Chinese or Japanese counterparts.

Sacred art is essentially anonymous. In the West, at least since the European Renaissance, we have come to accept the idea that the artist is some especially gifted individual, with a unique and personal vision. This attitude reached its most exuberant expression with the Romantic movement and, although the greatest artists have always aspired to a universality that transcends the merely personal, still predominates. In traditional societies, on the other hand, the artist is seen above all as a channel that serves to transmit higher truths to the community. To such an artist, the limits set by sacred tradition are considered an indispensable anchor; they nourish and stabilize, rather than stultify, the individual creative talent. Another aspect of the functional nature of sacred art is that it sees no division between the artist and the craftsman; they are one and the same.

The religious responsibility of such an artisan necessitates a strictly defined set of guidelines, because if the purpose of art is to reveal the divine reality behind appearances, there is no room for error. As in all ritual, if the correct procedure is not followed, the ritual will not work. In India this procedure was laid down in the texts, explicated by the brahmin priests, and passed on through the master-disciple relationship within the framework of a guild organization regulated by the rules of family and caste. Artistic training was itself a spiritual affair, incorporating the twin disciplines of yoga and meditation to purify and refine the apprentice's perception to the point at which he could begin to transmit the divine forms.

The aim of Hindu art is twofold: to fashion an image into which the deity can descend and to re-create, generally in sculpture, the realms of the gods. Both these purposes necessitate iconographic accuracy as a necessary complement to the priestly science of invocation and worship.

Early Buddhist art arose from rather different needs. As we have seen, the Buddha rejected the rituals of the brahmin orthodoxy and taught instead a doctrine of meditation and insight. His early followers created structures and images designed to evoke specific feeling-responses in the worshippers, in an attempt to precipitate various emotional and spiritual states by reminding the devotee of the life, Enlightenment, teachings, and death of the Master. With the development of the Mahāyāna, however, came the need to create images, particularly of the celestial *buddhas* and *bodhisattvas,* that represented the celestial hierarchy; just as in Hinduism, the task of the sculptor or painter was to recreate heaven here on earth. The mechanics of this process are explained by the French scholar Foucher (quoted and condensed by Coomaraswamy—see Appendix 2) in a passage that could just as well refer to Hindu procedure:

> The artist . . . after ceremonial purification, is to proceed to a solitary place. There he is to perform the "Sevenfold Office," beginning with the invocation of the hosts of *buddhas* and *bodhisattvas,* and the offering to them of real or imaginary flowers. Then he must realise in thought the four infinite modes of friendliness, compassion, sympathy and impartiality. Then he must meditate upon the insubstantiality or impermanence of all things, for it is said "by the fire of the idea of the void, the five factors of ego-consciousness are destroyed beyond recovery." Then only should he invoke the desired divinity by the utterance of the appropriate *mantra,* and should identify himself completely with the divinity to be represented. Then finally, on pronouncing the *mantra* of meditation, in which the attributes are defined, the divinity

appears visibly, "like a reflection" or "as in a dream," and this brilliant image is the artist's model.

By the time of the later Mahāyāna schools (for example, in Tibet from the ninth century onward), Buddhist artists were creating an art every bit as fantastic and colorful as their Hindu counterparts.

Islām forbids images, condemning the image maker as a blasphemous imitator of the only true Creator. It is said in the *Qur'ān* that on the Day of Judgment God will mock the presumption of the image maker by setting him the impossible task of breathing life into his creation. Nevertheless, Islamic art seeks to effect the same spiritual alchemy as do its native Indian counterparts. It aims to provide the faithful with a constant reminder of the ordered beauty of the divine. The abstract perfection of Allāh is alluded to by the concrete forms of the artist. The most important of these are calligraphy and calligraphic embellishment on architecture, vocal chanting, and the general purity of design and decoration that characterizes Muslim holy buildings. All of these art forms operate on a variety of levels, from the decorous to the esoteric. Thus calligraphic inscriptions, for example, which express different levels of meaning to the believer, are analogous in their purpose to the figurative sculpture employed by non-Islamic iconography. By alluding to scriptural passages and historical events, the calligraphic word functions almost as an image. And in all Islamic art there is a conscious interplay between the literal and the allegorical. This tension reflects a fundamental insight of Islām, namely that all phenomena have two aspects: a revealed aspect (*zāhir*) and a hidden one (*bātin*). The task of the Muslim artist is to render the surface so perfectly that it reveals the underlying unity of its depths.

2

ELEPHANTA

THE CAVE
OF THE HEART

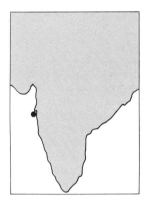

Elephanta Island lies in the harbor that separates the peninsula of Bombay from the mainland. Originally composed of seven islands separated at high tide by the sea, Bombay was once so notorious as a malarial swampland that, according to seventeenth-century travelers' lore, no European was likely to last there more than two monsoons. Despite her inhospitable reputation, Bombay has been visited by Western travelers and merchants from the earliest times. We know that the mighty empires of Assyria, Persia, and Rome traded with this part of the coast and that Ptolemy stopped at what is now Bombay in A.D. 150, calling it Heptanasia ("the seven islands"). It is also likely that there were considerable Arab connections from an early date. Precise Western association dates from 1498, when the intrepid Portuguese explorer Vasco da Gama landed at Calicut far to the south of Bombay. From this time, European influence began to exert itself in India in earnest. Bombay was ceded to the Portuguese by Sultan Bahādur Shāh of Gujarāt in 1534. It is said that the European name for the place derives from the delighted foreigners' description of it as Bom Bahia—"the beautiful bay." In 1661, Bombay passed into English hands as part of the dowry that Catharine of Braganza presented to King Charles II. He in turn leased it to the fledgling East India Company for the annual rent of ten pounds in gold, though it was not until 1783 that the area really became the springboard for the company's activities in the subcontinent.

Modern Bombay dates from the middle of the nineteenth century, for from this time onward a massive land-reclamation scheme, the building of the docks and cotton mills, and the erection of some of the finest Victorian architecture in India combined to change the face of the city. This urban progress continues apace today. Since being made the capital of the newly formed State of Mahārāshtra in 1961, Bombay has witnessed an astonishingly energetic building program, the biggest in the country.

To the provincial Indian, Bombay is a place of enormous energy and opportunity, a place where you can make those all-important connections, amass a quick pile of rupees, or taste unimaginably delightful pleasures. Part of the city's enduring glamour lies in the fact that it is the capital of the Indian film industry, the largest in the world, spawning a film a day, 365 days a year. To the foreigner at least, these films seem to follow a well-tried formula: stylized yet over-powering emotions, music, dance, the vicissitudes of romance, and the eternal conflict between good and evil—all enacted in the most fabulous of surroundings. And here, unexpect-edly, is a link with the ancient India. For the prototypes for the movie plots are those sacred myths that have for so many centuries fired her imagination, while the modern movie stars are to the mass of Indians almost superhuman beings who inhabit an inspiring, if unattainable, world.

One of the most perfect representations of these hallowed myths is the small cave-temple of Elephanta, a shrine carved out of the solid rock seven hundred years before Vasco da Gama set foot on Indian soil. The island is only about an hour's boat ride from the elegant Tāj Mahal Hotel, where the modern celluloid gods and goddesses love to meet, glitter, and hold their court.

The Elephanta cave-temple was excavated sometime in the eighth century A.D by the Rāshtrakūta dynasty, which ruled the Deccan from 757 to 973. It was probably intended as a private chapel for the royal family. Its exact date is unknown because when the shrine was desecrated by the Portuguese in the sixteenth century, they removed a stone panel containing a lengthy inscription, which presumably mentioned the date of the temple's dedication. One thing the Portuguese did leave was the name, Elephanta, derived from the colossal stone elephant that stood originally at the entrance to the site. (The remains of this can now be seen in the Prince of Wales Museum in the city.) Although the temple dates from after the Gupta period, the Golden Age of Indian art (A.D. 320 to 600), so assured and classical are the carvings here that, stylistically, they can be considered as the last noble testimony of the Gupta genius.

The Elephanta sanctuary was among the first sites to alert the West to the heritage of Indian art. The Portuguese botanist Garcia da Orta visited the island in 1534 as part of his survey of medicinal herbs in India, and he was so impressed by the monument that he included a short description of it in his otherwise purely scientific account:

> Another pagoda, the best of all, is on an island called Pori, which we call the Isle of the Elephant. . . . On the walls, all round, there are sculptured images of elephants, lions, tigers and many human images, some like Amazons, and in many other shapes well sculptured. Certainly it is a sight well worth seeing and it would appear that the devil had used all his powers and knowledge to deceive the gentiles into his worship. Some say it is the work of the Chinese when they navigated to the land. It might well be true seeing that it is so well worked.

To the early European travelers in India, Hindu art seemed to present a combination of the fantastic scenes from travelers' tales of antiquity—such as those Pliny collected—and the medieval visions of hell, squirming with many-headed monsters and fearsome hybrid creatures. Orta's mixture of admiration for the skill of the Hindu sculptors and confused suspicion about their purpose is an attitude that in varying degrees, has persisted in the Western mind until the present day.

While today's visitor to Elephanta cannot fail to be impressed by the power and beauty of the place, there is a symbolic level of meaning in its location that may not be immediately apparent to him. But to those whose consciousness is open to the mythic depths of life, Elephanta embodies two of mankind's oldest and most potent symbols: the sea and the island. The sea is both nourisher and destroyer and represents life in its raw, chaotic state, the ceaseless flux of becoming that is the world. As the matrix of all life, the sea is unlimited life energy (*prakriti*), containing all possible opposites, every variety of manifestation. On the human level, the sea is the mind, restless and creative, whose depths are the source of all thought and imagination, the womb of great beauty and unspeakable terrors.

The eternal movement of the sea is balanced by the stability of the island. The island is a place of solitude and refuge, which provides relief from the seas of chaos that threaten to overwhelm the traveler. To those in need the island is not only a physical haven; it also symbolizes a tranquil and undisturbed spiritual center (*purusha*) deep within the ever-restless mind. These images are universal. The myths of Mesopotamia tell us of the hero Gilgamesh, who has to dive to the bottom of the cosmic sea to find the elixir of life, the plant "Never-grow-old," which brings immortality and reprieves us from the clutches of time. In ancient Greece, Jason sets sail to find the Golden Fleece, and in Homer's *Odyssey,* the hero Odysseus sets out on the long and dangerous voyage to reclaim his island home, Ithaca, his real self.

In India the same images tell the same story. In Sanskrit—the language of the Hindu scriptures—the world of change is called *samsāra,* "the ocean of life." The saints of Jainism, a religion dating back at least to the sixth century B.C., are called *tīrthankaras,* "those who have crossed to the farther shore." The Buddha's last words to his disciples were: "Be an island unto yourselves, a refuge unto yourselves."

To a pilgrim brought up on these myths, the psychological impact of the sea voyage to Elephanta would have been enormous. Apart from anything else, it was a long and potentially dangerous journey; even today the voyage is impossible from June to October because of monsoon storms. The culmination of many years' planning and saving, the pilgrimage to the enchanted island would have been the perfect analog to the spiritual journey to find the light of eternity deep within the heart.

The shrine is dedicated to Shiva, the god who presides over the universal forces of change and re-creation. Shiva is probably the most ancient deity of the Hindu pantheon, and the most fascinating. The *Shvestāshvatāra Upanishad* (first century A.D.) tells us that: "beyond the cosmic darkness there is neither day nor night, but Shiva alone, the indestructible. Even the sun lies prostrate before him. From him springs forth the ageless wisdom."

The temple is not in regular worship, so shoes do not have to be removed except for the holy of holies.

The Entrance (Figure A)

As you enter the temple, you go through to your left to the original entrance (A.1). This was blocked by a rockfall some years ago, but it is only from here that you can clearly understand the cave as a whole. In fact, Elephanta is unusual in that there were originally three entrances, giving the temple a cruciform shape. Both east and west entrances had their subsidiary shrines as "side chapels" (A.2) and may well have been used for different rituals or festivals.

You are standing in the eastern entrance. The early morning sun filters through here and illuminates the path to the main shrine. Nearly all Hindu temples are built facing east

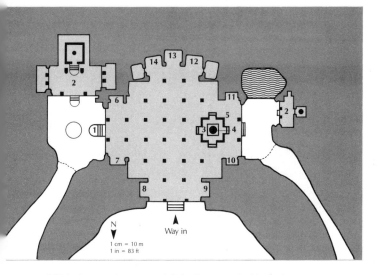

1 *Main (eastern) entrance.* 2 *Side shrines.* 3 Garbha-griha.
4 Yoni-linga. 5 *Door guardian.* 6 *Shiva and Pārvatī on Mount
Kailāsa.* 7 *Rāvana Shaking Mount Kailāsa.* 8 *Shiva as Lord
of Yoga (Yogīshvara).* 9 *Shiva as Lord of the Dance
(Naṭarāja).* 10 *Bhairava Killing the Demon Andhakāsura.*
11 *The Marriage of Shiva and Pārvatī.* 12 *The Descent of the
Ganges.* 13 *Shiva as the Great Lord (Maheshvara).* 14 *Shiva
as Androgyne (Ardhanārīshvara).*

Figure A. Elephanta Cave ground plan.

on this principle. The shrine (*garbha-griha*, A.3) at Elephanta
is also unusual because it is housed in a detached structure.
The sanctuary is normally attached to the back wall of the
temple, with a passage often being left for the devotees to
perform ritual circumambulation. The architects of Elephanta
introduced a striking innovation by detaching the shrine from
the rear wall and placing it in the middle of an aisle in the
main hall.

From here, on the steps, you can see the symbol of Shiva
that is the focus of attention in any Shiva temple: the *yoni-
linga* (A.4). *Linga* means "sign"; it is the phallic image signifying the elemental power of the deity. Framed dramatically
within its shrine doorway and against the uncut rock behind,
the *linga* confronts the pilgrim immediately with the imposing and mysterious power of Shiva. Moreover, you are inevitably led up to it by the avenue of pillars that flank the main
axis of the cave. Stepping into the temple proper now, you
can get a feeling of the place as a unity: pillars, panels, main
shrine, and the play of light and shadow continuously operating in the cave.

The garbha-griha *seen from the eastern entrance.*

The Pillars

Sanctuaries such as Elephanta are not, strictly speaking, caves (natural caverns in the rock) but temples that were painstakingly sculpted out of the rock face.

All the pillars you see here are purely ornamental, serving no functional purpose. The earliest rock-cut sanctuaries had no pillars. They became a regular feature only later, as a means of breaking up the inner space and adding subtlety and proportion to the different parts of the hall.

These pillars are essentially Dravidian (that is, southern Indian) in style. They have a high square base, tapering slightly up to a ribbed, rounded neck, on top of which sits a ribbed cushion capital. On each corner of the pillar, where the base gives way to the neck, there sits a dwarfish figure. This is the earth spirit (*gana*), who supports the nether regions of the world. Often one of the corners has Ganesha, the elephant-headed son of Shiva, whose name means "Lord of the *ganas*."

Notice how delightfully irregular these columns are. If you look closely, you will see that no two are exactly the same. Some are elegantly concave; some bulge as if squashed by the weight of the roof they appear to support. All are massive, yet each is unique—their organic mushroomlike form perfectly suited to the dark earthiness of this subterranean cavern. The lack of symmetry (originally much more pronounced than now, since they have been extensively restored) was in the first place due to the nearly impossible task of hewing each pillar out of the solid rock. But as well as adding charm and variety to the hall, this irregularity acts subtly to distort

Typical Elephanta pillar.

our whole sense of space, breaking down our habitual sense of solidity. Whereas perfectly regular aisles might have the effect of defining and hemming us in, these have the effect of expanding us into a detached and less limited perspective by counteracting the downward force of the rock itself.

The Shrine (Figure A.3)

In any sacred place the threshold is of crucial importance, because it is here that the sacred world of the inner shrine meets the profane, and potentially harmful, world outside. So the threshold must always be protected, both to guard the sanctuary from negative or evil influences and also to create the right feeling of awe and respect in all those who enter. The shrine has four doors, facing the cardinal points of north, south, east, and west, and radiating the spiritual influence of the shrine in all directions. Each door is flanked by massive door guardians (*dvārapālas*).

The best preserved of these door guardians is on the west face of the shrine (A.5), a graceful, elongated figure with a long, sweeping torso, full face, and royal headdress. In fact he has all the insignia of nobility: sacred thread over his left shoulder, belt, sash, and sword hanging by his side. He is like some royal attendant, guarding the king's private chamber. His left foot bears a patina from the touch of devotees.

The Yoni-Linga (Figure A.4)

This is the holy of holies. It should be circumambulated clockwise, following the movement of the sun. To go around the other way is to move in the direction of death and brings bad luck.

In the center of the unadorned sanctum stands the *yoni-linga:* the supreme symbol of the godhead for the worshippers of Shiva. Here the male and female energies that together create the universe are in a state of perfect equilibrium. The male *linga* is the image of Shiva: pure spirit waiting to create. The female *yoni* is the image of the creative energy of matter, without which the spirit could not take form. This energy (*shakti*) is essential to the play of life, and Hindus worship it in the form of many female and mother goddesses. There is a common saying among devotees of Shiva that "Shiva without *shakti* is a corpse." Here in Elephanta the *yoni* is a large and roughly hewn square block, representing the earth that "grounds" the *linga*. In other temples (for example, the Kailāsanātha in Ellorā) it is shaped like the female reproductive organs.

The inner sanctuary is plain and unadorned. We are beyond the realm of images here. Just the simple shape of the *yoni-linga*. The unity of these two—the squaring of the circle—is the sign of perfection.

The yoni-linga.

The Main Floor

Having circumambulated the *yoni-linga*, we retrace our steps to the main entrance to begin a circumambulation of the temple itself. Turn right to the panel marked 6 on the ground plan (Figure A).

□ *SHIVA AND PĀRVATĪ ON MOUNT KAILĀSA* (Figure A.6)
This is one of the most popular scenes in the mythology of
Shiva. Shiva is the faceless figure on the left of the panel as
we look at it. Sitting on his left is his wife Pārvatī ("the Lady
of the Mountain"), who is the aspect of *shakti* that embodies
the idealized attributes of womanhood: creativity, gentleness,
and maternal love. The figure between them is an attendant,
carrying a child to emphasize the domestic nature of the
scene. Shiva and Pārvatī live on Mount Kailāsa in the Himālayas. This celestial abode is believed to exist high up in the
mountain peaks, and is the center of the universe for the
worshippers of Shiva, as Jerusalem was for Christendom, or
Mecca still is for Islām. This spiritual axis around which the
world revolves is also the major center of pilgrimage, for all
pilgrimage serves to reestablish the order of the pilgrim's own
psyche and, by extension, his world.

Underneath Pārvatī we can see Nandin, the divine bull
that is the vehicle (*vāhana*) of Lord Shiva. The bull is the
earthly animal that most perfectly embodies Shiva's power,
signifying strength, creativity, and sublimated energy. The
headless figure by Shiva's right knee is Bhringi, one of Shiva's
most ardent devotees.

All the disfigurement of these figures was, sadly, the work
of the Portuguese. They were not as fanatical in their
destruction of Hindu temples as were the Muslims, and the
vandalism here was probably as much drunken target practice as religious zeal, but their desecration of Elephanta was
ruthless enough.

Above the main figures, in the top third of the panel, are
the celestial beings. We will see this division in most of the
panels here: celestial beings in the top third, principal deities
in the middle portion, and underneath them the terrestrial
worshippers, spirits, and attendants. Notice how the clouds
are represented as scalloped blocks, just as in some medieval
paintings in the West. Yet this is not just a stylistic convention; it gives great depth to the scene, especially when seen
as a contrast to the unworked rock face behind the principal
characters, Shiva and Pārvatī. The heavens really do seem to
extend upward infinitely, and, simultaneously, the whole thrust
of the clouds themselves is down, toward us. The celestial
beings are shown hovering, but very close to us, as if they
were ready to descend at any moment. There is a wonderful
feeling of imminent descent in them. They are definitely
inhabitants of some timeless world, far removed from our
mundane reality, yet they wait at the threshold of consciousness, as close to us as our dreams. Look immediately above
the central attendant with the child at the very fine ascetic
figure, holding his begging bowl. From the very earliest times,
asceticism has been considered a noble way of life by the

Indians. Devout ascetics are considered fit companions for the gods. The long-legged figures on either side of the ascetic, with their limbs streaming out behind them like tails, are the celestial dancers (*apsarases*). It is said that if they are pleased with you, they will teach you their arts. These figures are beautifully realized. Keep your eyes open for more friezes like this as we proceed. They are one of the highlights of Elephanta, though all too often overlooked.

The Hindu deities, like the gods of the ancient Greeks or the Nordic sagas, are often endearingly human. They have their moods, their love affairs, and their jealousies; they are forever plotting and scheming and exacting terrible revenge on those who dare to cross them. The story behind this panel is that Shiva and Pārvatī are playing a game of dice—one of the favorite pastimes of the ancient Indians. Pārvatī has lost, and is turning away from Shiva in a sulk. Shiva is telling her to stay and play.

Despite the quarrel Shiva and Pārvatī are here the ideal man and woman. Their mountain home is a haven of stability, on the earth but within reach of the heavens. An atmosphere of calmness pervades the whole scene; it is Adam and Eve before the Fall. Yet, as always in India, the domestic is balanced by the ascetic. We are reminded that spiritual advancement is never to be forgotten, and that the great sages dwell on the mountaintops, not in the valley.

Esoterically, this panel takes us a stage farther, in more concrete and pictorial terms, from the holy of holies. Spirit and matter have now been anthropomorphized into the figures of Shiva, the ideal male, and his wife Pārvatī, the ideal female. Pārvatī is turning away from her consort: Matter is beginning to be differentiated from pure spirit. As the creative *shakti* begins to take form, the process of creation is beginning, and the potential in the abstract *yoni-linga* is becoming actualized. This is why the actual center of the panel is not the divine couple but the attendant with the baby. This positioning emphasizes that the union of male and female energies is fruitful, whether on the human or cosmic level. The throwing of dice is a frequent image of the beginning of a cosmic cycle in Hindu texts. The divine drama is unfolding once again.

☐ *RĀVANA SHAKING MOUNT KAILĀSA* (Figure A.7)
The idyllic scene of the previous panel cannot last. With manifestation into duality comes the problem of good and evil.

In Hinduism evil is represented by any number of spirits and forces of darkness, who are constantly doing battle with the gods. The principal one is Rāvana, the demon king of Lankā. Fearsome tales are told of Rāvana's strength. In the

Rāmāyana, one of the great Indian epics, we are told that "where Rāvana remains, the sun loses his force, the winds cease to blow, the fires can no longer burn and the mighty ocean, on seeing him, stills its waves." The same text continues to describe this unnatural prince of darkness as being a giant with ten heads, twenty arms, eyes the color of burning copper, a huge chest, and teeth as white as the young moon.

Rāvana's mortal sin is pride. He is a great devotee of Shiva. (It is quite acceptable for a demon to worship a god if he thinks he can get some advantage out of it!) One day Rāvana decided that as he was so powerful he would travel to Kailāsa and bring the entire mountain back to his own kingdom of the island Lankā so that he could worship Shiva at home, without having to make the effort to travel all the way to the Himālayas whenever he wanted to make his devotions.

What happened when he got there is depicted in this panel. Rāvana is shown at the bottom, with back bent and shoulders bulging from the effort of trying to seize the mountain. There is wonderful movement here, as the demon king struggles to carry off his prize.

In the center of the panel sits Shiva, absolutely calm and undisturbed. Not only does he dominate the entire panel, but its physical center is actually his navel, so the entire sculpture seems to radiate out from him.

He is grasping two attendants to prevent them from falling off the mountain. Seated in the pleasing pose (*lalitāsana*), one leg tucked under him and the other extended, Shiva has only to stretch his toe down to secure Kailāsa. The great Lord's victory is languidly effortless, in marked contrast to the frenetic activity of his adversary. The Shiva figure is totally static: solid, broad-shouldered, and at rest. Emotionally he possesses a calm stability, like the adamantine rock behind him, partaking of its immovable strength.

The contrast between the two protagonists is heightened by the use of light. Blocked off from the top of the panel by the overhanging eaves of the cave, the light falls more on Rāvana. Shiva, cloaked in shadow, appears far more awesome and mysterious than his well-lit adversary below. This shadowing lends a majestic power to the central figure, which is heightened by the actual composition of the tableau.

The top frieze of celestials here conveys a tremendous feeling of transcendence. The figures seem to retreat into the rock, leading the eye upward, away from Shiva, so as to emphasize the majestic sweep of his head with its crown of matted locks. This is the exact opposite of the previous panel, where the heavens were brought within reach of us mortals and the angels were reaching down to us. Here the tension draws the entire composition upward, out of the grasping reach of Rāvana and into an invincible realm above.

The end of the story? Well, seeing the folly of his presumption, Rāvana finally repents and Shiva forgives him. But that is not quite the end: In a later age the god Vishnu in his form as Rāma has to deal with Rāvana, who has kidnapped his wife Sītā. The story of the kidnap, their battles, and the final victory of good over evil is told in the *Rāmāyana*.

☐ *SHIVA AS LORD OF YOGA* (Figure A.8)
This panel depicts Shiva as the Lord of Yoga (Yogīshvara).

Shiva is the Lord of Yoga and patron deity of yogis. He is believed to have given all the most important texts on yoga to mankind, and he himself is the archetype of the accomplished ascetic and yogi. There are many stories of his living in the forest, practicing meditation, and gaining the miraculous powers that it brings.

Yoga has basically two aspects: physical postures, which purify the body, and meditation, which purifies the mind. The postures prepare the nervous system for meditation. Shiva is shown sitting in "the lotus posture" (*padmāsana*), in which the legs are crossed and each foot rests on its opposite thigh. This self-contained position keeps the spiritual energy circulating through the body.

Shiva is also seated on a lotus, one of the most important of Indian symbols. It represents the watery, feminine, creative principle: the unconscious mind. The lotus also signifies enlightenment and the enlightened yogi himself. Just as the flower grows out of the mud at the bottom of the pond yet simultaneously rises above the water, white and pure, so the yogi lives in the world of *samsāra,* with all its mire, but is unattached and unsullied by it. He is in the world but not of it. Like the lotus, he emerges out of the darkness into the light.

Yoga teaches that deep within the human nervous system are subtle channels (*nādīs*), which convey the life energy (*prāna*) through the system. These channels converge periodically at plexuses (*chakras*), which lie along the spine. The *chakras,* or energy centers, are represented iconographically by the lotus. There are seven major ones, each having a different color, number of "petals," and deity associated with it. Enlightenment is said to be the result of all these *chakras* being purified. Then they open to the spirit as the lotus opens to the sunlight.

See how the god's hair falls in snaky coils on his shoulders. Long hair is a symbol of spiritual power to the Hindus, as it is in the Biblical story of Samson. When his ascetic side is being emphasized, Shiva is often portrayed with matted locks (*jatā*). Shaiva yogis grow their hair and often plaster it with cow dung and ashes.

The feeling of stillness in this sculpture is achieved partly by the uncarved rock behind the meditating figure. Yet this absolute stillness of the meditating yogi is really only half the picture because this panel forms a pair with the one opposite, just as the last two were a sequence. Shiva Yogīshvara both continues the story told by the two previous scenes (because yoga is the means to develop the strength and purity to overcome the evil symbolized by the demon Rāvana) and looks forward to the next scene: Shiva as Lord of the Dance.

☐ *SHIVA AS LORD OF THE DANCE* (Figure A.9)
This is Shiva as Lord of the Dance (Natarāja). We have seen the quiescent form of Shiva in the last panel. But to the Indian sages, life is composed of two equal halves: silence and activity. Underlying the ceaseless flux of life is an infinite calmness. This is the spirit, deep within matter. The yogi realizes this within his own mind; he develops an unshakable calm no matter what is happening outside him.

Shiva as Lord of the Dance (Natarāja).

In practical terms, the whole point of practicing yoga is to improve the quality of daily life. The way that the divine is brought into the human world is through a balance of rest (yoga) and activity. The mind is first quieted and rested through meditation, and then it is brought out to engage in activity. A calm mind is more powerful and effective than an excited one, and therefore the yogi accomplishes what he has to do with less effort and more joy. So yoga is a practical discipline that clarifies the mind, strengthens each thought, and improves activity. This is the practical teaching that this pair of sculptures conveys.

Shiva as Lord of the Dance is the natural complement to Shiva as the great yogi. The whole universe is danced by Shiva; he is the cosmic rhythm that creates form and life. His dance is the eternal round of life and death, creation and destruction. Physics tells us that all matter, even this solid and immovable rock we see all around us here, is nothing but a scintillating dance of energy. At the very heart of life, where the electrons whirl around the nucleus of the atom, we can see the great Lord's dance. Its rhythm is the pulse of time, its exhilaration the joy of living. Each of us has been assigned a part in this cosmic drama, yet no matter what the current situation may be, it will soon change, because this is the nature of life. Nothing is fixed or permanent; everything is part of the cosmic round of Shiva's dance.

Notice how each panel in Elephanta resembles a stage set, framed by the surrounding rock. Despite the heaviness of the rock, each scene has about it the delicacy of a dream. This atmosphere of an evanescent reality is entirely appropriate, for in Indian art, as in Indian philosophy, the world is seen as a divine yet ephemeral drama (*līlā*) set against the backdrop of eternity.

All the other gods are watching the dance of Shiva. Above his right shoulder is Brahmā, the four-headed god of creation, seated on a throne of swans. Below him, around a club, is the cobra, symbol of death and renewal, for Shiva's dance goes on forever. Next to Brahmā is a fine ascetic and his wife. He is shown with a long beard and hair coiled up in *jatā* on his head. The style has not changed since the days of the Gupta sculptors; such men can still be seen walking the length of the country from pilgrimage place to pilgrimage place, temple to temple. Below is Ganesha, the elephant-headed son of Shiva and Pārvatī. And see how the face of the attendant below Ganesha radiates bliss!

Opposite, on the right of the tableau, we can just make out Vishnu, god of preservation, on a line with Brahmā. Behind him is Indra, who rides an elephant, and underneath them, Pārvatī. These figures are too damaged to spend time on; we shall see them better in The Marriage of Shiva and Pārvatī (A.11).

The movement in this piece is tremendous. Shiva moves with an almost indolent heaviness. His face displays a languid self-assurance; he swings into his dance with a sensual swirl, hair streaming behind him. Yet his face is composed, self-absorbed. At the center of the dance is stillness.

Dancing was, from the earliest times, an integral part of worship in India. It was in the temples that classical dance originated and was perfected. The greatest authority on music and dance is Bharata. He is the composer of the *Nātyashās-tra* (ca. A.D. 300), the main text on both dancing and acting.

(In Sanskrit the same word—*nātya*—covers both.) He tells us that dancing brings "the reward of righteousness to those who abide by the moral law; pleasure to those who delight in lust; a restraint for those who are of an unruly nature; a discipline for the law-abiding; virility to the impotent; ardour to warriors and wisdom to the ignorant."

As we have seen, the celestial realms are full of angelic musicians (*gandhārvas*) and dancers (*apsarases*), who perform to delight the gods.

Even today, the student of classical dance must undergo a rigorous and lengthy period of training. This is, in effect, an apprenticeship to a *guru*. Mental equanimity is essential to the art. This is because nothing is left to chance or improvization. Each movement, each step, follows a carefully laid out pattern that must be learned so thoroughly that it becomes ingrained in the dancer's consciousness. In this sense the dance becomes impersonal, a ritual that must be performed correctly if it is to achieve its aim, which is to please God. Art is thus transformed into worship.

Bharata lists 140 basic poses (108 "easy," 32 "difficult"), which form the basis of the science. These cover movement of the limbs, face, eyes, hands, and feet. All these poses have to be well mastered before the dancer is considered competent.

☐ *BHAIRAVA KILLING THE DEMON ANDHAKĀSURA* (Figure A.10)

Many Westerners, influenced by centuries of Christianity, find the Indian view that life is essentially blissful hard to accept. Such an attitude seems frivolous and irresponsible.

Bhairava Killing the Demon Andhakāsura.

What about suffering and the problem of evil? The worshippers of Shiva reply that we suffer because we are ignorant of our own nature, which is eternal happiness. Hence the importance of yoga. Nevertheless, for those of us whose vision is still veiled by illusion, suffering and negativity are still very much realities. Just as Shiva can dance joy, so he can dance terror. The other side of the dream is always the nightmare. But remember that, ultimately, the negative is no less divine than the positive; it is merely another aspect of the great Lord's play, just as the Christian devil Lucifer was originally a fallen angel.

This fearsome aspect of Shiva is known as Bhairava, and he comes into being when there is evil to be destroyed and the blinding darkness of egocentric ignorance to be vanquished.

The word *andhaka* means "darkness." Andhakāsura is one of the chief demons, an ill-fated son of Shiva and Pārvatī, who was born both physically and spiritually blind. (The Sanskrit for demon is *asura*—which also means "darkness.") The story goes that if he was wounded, each drop of his blood, when it fell on the ground, would cause another demon to spring up (like the soldiers who sprang up from the teeth of the dragon guarding the Golden Fleece). So Shiva speared the demon on his trident and held the skull cup under the writhing body to catch the blood. Each time the cup was full, he would give it to his consort Shakti to drink. In this way the demon was finally defeated.

This is the most dramatic of all the subsidiary panels here. Just look at the massive figure of Bhairava, sword in hand, with two of his hands stretching the skin of a previous victim over his head. The mouth is open, his fangs showing, and his eyes bulging and staring into the middle distance—all traditional ways of portraying a deity that is expecting blood sacrifice. He seems to be leaning right out of the panel, but if you go to the side and look at the figure in profile, you can see that in fact it is hardly leaning at all. The effect of this movement is created largely by the foreshortening of the neck and the way the jaw is made to jut out, a visual trick that creates the impression that the enraged god is about to topple out of the wall and overwhelm you.

The best time to see this panel is in the early afternoon. From midday onward, as more and more light filters into the cave from the western entrance, the figure becomes progressively lit from beneath. This growing illumination increases the shadowed contrast within and around the main figure; the mouth seems to open in a wider snarl; the teeth protrude further; the skull in the crown becomes more hollowed and the whole face becomes more enraged and demonic. The entire figure struggles to emerge from the rock, encircled by a negative halo of shadow that pulsates, distorting the outlines of the body and adding to the terror it conveys. Spend some time sitting to absorb these sculptures. They all take time to come to you, so the longer you can observe and the more open your mind is, the more you will receive.

The historical origins of this myth are interesting. In all probability it dates from a time when the sophisticated pantheon of Hinduism was establishing itself as the dominant religious system. Many of the indigenous tribal cults were fertility cults, worshipping the Mother Goddess and involving blood sacrifice. The new religion had to incorporate these into its own teachings to keep the allegiance of the original tribal groups of the country. Generally speaking, these aboriginal traits are best preserved in the northeast of the country, and blood-sacrifice is still practiced widely in Bengāl, parts of Orissā, and the foothills of the Himālayas. In Nepāl, where blood sacrifice predominates, Bhairava—the wrathful Shiva—is the principal deity. Andhakāsura may originally have been a folk deity, this myth also illustrating his being overpowered and incorporated into the fold of mainstream Hinduism.

Iconographically there are definite similarities between this figure and the deities of the sacrificial cults of Nepāl and Tibet. Shiva's face is like a mask of a Tibetan wrathful deity, eyes protruding, mouth open in anticipation of offerings. He holds a sword in one right hand and a bell in the left, as do his Himālayan counterparts.

And yet, in the midst of all this gore, there are the sublime faces of the two worshipping sages on the right of the panel, behind the impaled demon. The back figure especially (right in the corner) shows the indrawn softness of worship. It is an exquisite cameo.

□ *THE MARRIAGE OF SHIVA AND PĀRVATĪ* (Figure A.11)
The terrible is balanced by the idyllic. What tenderness there is in this scene! Our attention is immediately drawn to the three main faces. Shiva stands with Pārvatī on his right. This shows us that the marriage has not yet taken place, as the customary position for the Hindu wife is always on her husband's left. Pārvatī looks down demurely at the floor, her head turned away from her future husband. Yet notice how her left hip is inclined toward him. Her whole body—her feelings—are irresistibly drawn to Shiva, desiring him, even while her rational mind, her head, makes her shy and hesitant. It is beautiful how these conflicting feelings are portrayed simultaneously in the one figure; the Gupta sculptors had an unerring ability to portray emotion through the position of the body rather than through facial expression—and an uncanny grasp of body language.

Behind Pārvatī stands her father, Himālaya, who is giving her away at the marriage ceremony.

The figure to the left of Pārvatī's father is Chandramas. He is the god of the moon—with the crescent moon behind his head. He is holding a pot of *soma,* the ambrosia of the gods that bestows immortality, which he has brought as a wedding gift to the divine couple.

Now look at the other side of the picture: The large figure to Shiva's left is Vishnu, the witness to the ceremony. Below him is Brahmā, who is acting as the officiating priest.

The Marriage of Shiva and Pārvatī.

Again, the celestial figures in the heavens convey an extraordinary effect of spiritual absorption. In fact a timeless quality pervades the whole scene. It radiates a delicate and sunny tranquility that completely contrasts with the panel opposite.

The story behind the happy event goes as follows: Shiva was sitting on Mount Kailāsa engaged, as was his wont, in deep meditation. He had lost all desire for women and was enjoying the solitary delights of asceticism. Pārvatī happened to see him one day and fell passionately in love with him. Realizing that her beauty, considerable though it was, could not tempt him, she decided to worship his image assiduously in the hope of gaining his attention. This, too, failed. She then became a yoginī (female yogi) and practiced the severest penances. One day an ugly brahmin appeared before her and asked her why she was torturing such a beautiful body. On hearing that she was in love with Shiva, the brahmin laughed and proceeded to denigrate the Lord as a dirty, unwashed, and bad-tempered oaf who haunted cemeteries and couldn't even earn a living. Eventually, Pārvatī's rage was such that she could no longer bear such insults. She burst out shouting at the brahmin and cried that even if what he said were true, she would never renounce her love for Shiva. At these words, lo and behold, the brahmin before her changed into Shiva himself. Pārvatī fell down at his feet in worship. She had passed the test; Shiva went to her father and they were married with the prescribed rites.

Of the twelve major ceremonies (*samskāras*) that the orthodox Hindu householder has to perform in his life, marriage is probably the most important and certainly the most expensive! The best time of year for the ceremony is the spring, and the exact hour must be fixed by the astrologers—just as the horoscopes of the couple must be exactly matched before any betrothal can take place. A sculpture such as this, showing the marriage of the gods, would act as a powerful reinforcement of the social necessity and obligations of marriage within Hindu society.

Before the ceremony is begun, Ganesha, the elephant-headed god who is the god of good beginnings, is invoked. This is why he is on the pillar to the left, facing the scene, ready to preside over the whole affair.

The longer you stay in Elephanta, the more the atmosphere of the place creeps up on you. The dappling of light and shade give the hall the quality of a vast underwater cavern. Perspective is destroyed as the light shifts from pockets of greenish brilliance to unexpected wells of darkness. The rock gathers an unearthly sheen, which has the effect of rendering the solid surfaces almost ephemeral. This is especially apparent as you approach the last three panels against the back wall of the cavern. The carvings are monolithic—especially the Mahesha—yet there is no sense of heaviness about them. On the contrary, they seem fashioned out of "such stuff as dreams are made on."

☐ *THE DESCENT OF THE GANGES* (Figure A.12)
All rivers are holy in monsoon-dominated India, and the holiest is the Ganges. In fact she is so holy, she is the goddess Gangā, worshipped by millions.

This is the story of the descent of the Ganges. Originally the river flowed only in heaven, because she was so pure her father had given her in marriage to the gods. She was brought to earth by King Bhagīratha, who is the figure kneeling at Shiva's right foot. Some of Bhagīratha's ancestors had had the temerity to disturb a sage who was meditating, and the sage, opening his eyes in fury, burned them to ashes with his gaze.

Since that time, all Bhagīratha's forebears had tried to have the curse revoked, but it was only the king's sincere efforts that at last won the promise that if the Ganges were to flow over their charred ashes, the wretched ancestors would be reborn in heaven.

Bhagīratha approached Shiva, and the god requested Gangā to flow down from heaven. Unwilling to leave her celestial abode, she refused and warned that her power was so great that the earth would be destroyed by the impact of her descent. At this Shiva commanded her, and the torrents were let loose, deluging the land, uprooting trees, and destroying mountains. But when Gangā came to Kailāsa, she was no match for Shiva. He broke her fall with his head, and ever since, the Ganges has flowed peacefully down from Shiva's matted locks.

So we have here a good example of how a natural occurrence is transformed into myth in the folk memory. Monsoon floods, which come down from the "heavens" of the Himālayas to water the parched Gangetic plain each year, are always potentially dangerous. Each time the disaster of flooding is avoided, the merciful intervention of Shiva is gratefully remembered.

Looking at the central figures, you can see three beings on Shiva's head. These are Gangā in the center with her two tributaries, Yamunā and Sarasvatī, on either side of her. Notice also how the sculptor has captured the look of blind adoration on the face of the curious little hump-backed attendant between Shiva and Pārvatī.

The figures of Shiva and Pārvatī are clear examples of the Indian ideal of beauty. The male should be like a warrior: tall, broad-shouldered, and narrow-waisted with a long torso and long limbs. The female should have narrow shoulders, large, full breasts, a wasplike waist, and ample hips—a veritable fertility symbol, the Mother Goddess. Pārvatī certainly fulfills these conditions here. She positively flows out from the waist down and she is full bodied, her right leg delicately turned to emphasize the breadth of her hips. Strictly speaking, the figure is out of proportion—the arms are rather heavy and the loins too massive—but the concern of the artist was not to produce a figure that was realistic by human standards but to create a representation of the feminine ideal. Imagine how differently the Greeks would have portrayed the same subject. Every muscle and bone would have been carved in the human style, rather than the long, tubular limbs these divine archetypes have.

Despite, or because of, the stylization, both figures are extremely graceful. They soar upward and are shown in the *tribhanga* ("triple-bend" pose: bent at the neck, shoulders, and hip)—a posture from classical dance that is frequently used in standing figures. There is as well an indrawn majesty in Shiva's countenance.

This panel is in good enough condition for us to examine the subsidiary figures. On Shiva's right is the four-headed Brahmā, the original god of creation. He is seated on a throne of swans. In the Vedas, Brahmā is described in glowing terms: "the first of the gods, framer of the universe, guardian of the world." Nowadays, however, his popularity has waned disastrously. There is only one temple in India—at Pushkar in Rājasthān—still dedicated to him. Presumably, now that this cycle of creation has begun, the Hindus consider him to be out of a job!

Brahmā is shown with four heads (the fourth is hidden from our view). These represent the four cardinal directions and the four Vedas. In fact, he originally had five heads. The story goes that he formed from his own immaculate substance a daughter. She was so beautiful that he became infatuated with her, and whenever she moved to hide herself from his unfatherly gaze, he sprouted another head to look at her. To avoid his attention, she sprang into the air—whereupon a fifth head appeared!

This fifth head was nipped off by Shiva, when it began to claim that Brahmā was superior to Shiva. Another legend says the great Lord cut it off because Brahmā finally managed to commit incest with his lovely offspring. Whichever version you prefer, we can see how sectarian rivalry works to shape religious myths. And, at the same time, the story contains profound psychological material.

You can see that Brahmā is holding a lotus, which is the symbol of his creative function. He was, in fact, born from a lotus, like his Egyptian counterpart, Horus.

Between Brahmā and Shiva sits the Vedic god Indra, on his mount the elephant. Like the lusty Brahmā, he is little worshipped nowadays.

On the opposite side of the panel, to the left of Pārvatī, sits Vishnu, the god of preservation. He is seated on Garuda, who is half vulture, half man. By now you may be baffled as to which god is which, and how to identify each one. Each god has his own mount and this, plus a quick look at what each is holding, is the way to recognize them.

So whereas Brahmā holds the lotus and rides on a swan, Vishnu rides on Garuda and holds a mace (in his right hand here) and a discus. These symbolize justice and authority.

☐ *SHIVA AS THE GREAT LORD* (Figure A.13)
As the Great Lord (Maheshvara or Mahesha), Shiva unites in himself the functions of creation, preservation, and destruction. The head on the right is Umā (Creation); the one on the

left Bhairava (Dissolution). The central head is Shiva Svarūpa—Shiva in his true form as the transcendent spirit that underlies and sustains all birth and death. This triune image is sometimes known as Sadāshiva—Shiva the Eternal One.

Let us look at this astonishing panel—the highlight of Elephanta—to understand its sublime message.

Umā: "Peace of the Night"   The feminine principle of creativity: graceful, delicate. See how her hair falls in ringlets and her royal headdress is scalloped to resemble a cornucopia—the unending source of life. Her nose is straight and well formed, her face smooth, her lips soft and very full. She is contemplating a lotus, fully opened. Springlike, she is the Indian Persephone, the gentle companion of Shiva's pleasures.

Shiva as the Great Lord (Maheshvara).

Bhairava: "The Wrathful"   The fearsome aspect: Shiva as destroyer of the old. His snake-coiled locks form a demonic crown composed of leaves, vines, and flowers—the organic and irrepressible growth, which springs relentlessly from decay and death itself. See the skull in his crown, with its pitted, staring eyes. This is Time, which is measured by change. Only Shiva, Lord of Time, is free from its ravages. Bhairava holds a cobra, the age-old symbol of death and resurrection, and even his hand is serpentine in its twists. His brow is puckered, his nose hooked and predatory, his nostrils flared, his cheeks bunched over lips bared in a snarl. A fearsome warrior, he sports a moustache. This is the demonic mask we saw in the killing of Andhakāsura. And yet, if you take a closer look, you will see he has the third eye in the middle of his forehead, the wisdom eye of enlightenment. It is only when we fully accept the inevitable processes of change that we understand its purpose and become free of its binding influence. The myth is that one day Pārvatī crept up behind Shiva and playfully covered his eyes. If the Lord's gaze fails, the universe will disappear, so, to prevent this, the third eye sprouted. The meaning of this story is that for the third eye of enlightenment to be developed, the normal eyes must be closed and the mind must go within. Detachment is wisdom.

Shiva Svarūpa: "Shiva in His True Nature"   Here we have the balance of the two complementary forces: creation-destruction; female-male. This is Shiva in his true form, totally impassive, serene, and undisturbed. He is the eternal quiescence that underlies and supports all creation and destruction: the unmoving Mover, the backcloth against which all our petty dramas are acted out, age after age. He is the silence at the heart of all activity.

His face radiates a silent, indrawn bliss. Like the Buddha he has the marks of wisdom: long earlobes, turning into earrings (the mark of an ascetic), and three wrinkles around the neck. Yet he is bejeweled like a king and wears the tall crown (*jatāmukuta*), which, like the Phrygian cap worn by Osiris, Zeus, and archbishops of Christendom, is the mark of freedom and nobility. His right hand is held up in the gesture that says, "Fear not!" (*abhaya mudrā*). In his left hand sits the unopened lotus bud. He holds all things in potential. He is "the auspicious one" (*shiva*).

It is amazing the way these sculptors managed to combine the spiritual and the sensual. All the figures have this deeply sensuous interiority. They are full-faced, their lips so heavy they are almost pouting, and yet the whole effect is ineffable. Notice how the eyes are closed, yet the lids are heavy and swollen; the whole face throbs with a latent energy, ready to burst forth at any second. It is the face of the sage in meditation, suffused with the glow of an inner fullness.

It is interesting that the Maheshvara, "the great lord," is aligned to a principle axis from the north entrance. It may well be that some rituals or festivals were performed to this image, using the north entrance; others to the *linga*, entering from the east or west. Whatever the original reason, this panel silently dominates the whole cavern. It is a remarkable achievement to render something so massive with such gentle delicacy. The figure is huge, yet there is no coarseness in it. It has more the quality of a miniature painting. Look at it also in profile. All these figures were created to be seen from many different angles. Explore!

☐ *SHIVA AS ANDROGYNE* (Figure A.14)

We finish our journey with an image of completeness: Shiva as Androgyne—half male, half female (Ardhanārīshvara).

A universal symbol of primordial perfection, the androgyne represents wholeness, paradise regained, the harmony of all opposites. In shamanistic or tribal societies the medicine man is often a transvestite. In Greek art Zeus is often shown wearing women's clothes, and Plato held that man was originally androgynous. The ancient Persian god of time, Zrvain, was portrayed as a hermaphrodite, and in alchemy the "Great Work" culminated in the creation of a being that was half man, half woman.

The mythological origin of this figure concerns the sage Bhringi ("the Wanderer"). He was a great seer, renowned for the severity of his penances. He worshipped only Shiva, however, and had no interest in Pārvatī. This preference excited Pārvatī's jealousy, and she vowed to remedy the situation. Bhringi used to worship his deity by circumambulation. Pārvatī decided to join herself to her Lord, so that when the sage walked around Shiva, he would also inadvertently worship her. As it happened, Bhringi was too clever to be caught by such a ruse. He transformed himself into a tiny insect, and so managed to do circumambulation of the half that belonged to Shiva only. As before, the central figure is surrounded by the other deities: Brahmā and Indra on the left and Vishnu, mounted on Garuda and holding the discus, on the right. Once again the celestial hosts are finely realized.

The balance of the whole sculpture is well maintained, despite its unconventional proportions. The female half of the figure slews the whole thing to the left at the hip, but this is balanced by the size of Shiva's bull Nandin, on which the Shiva half is resting. The bull is the sign of male energy; this has its corollary in the mirror that Pārvatī is holding. This is a traditional Indian pose of the woman beautifying herself, looking in the mirror, but it also signifies the self-knowledge that stems from a clear mind.

As far as the teaching of Elephanta is concerned, this figure is the logical fulfillment of the pilgrimage. We have seen that Shiva combines the forces of rest and activity: He is either dancing the universe as Natarāja or sitting in silent meditation as Yogīshvara.

To the Shaiva devotee, the ideal is to combine these two halves of life in one's own personality. Thus the enlightened being is resting and yet active simultaneously; he is dynamically peaceful. True wholeness is the unity of the male and female parts of the psyche. The rational, conscious mind is integrated with the intuitional unconscious. This harmony is the integration that existed before the Fall, which was brought about by the duality of the knowledge of good and evil, when

Adam and Eve became self-consciously aware of themselves as separate genders. To be excessively dominant or active, or excessively passive and submissive, is to be out of harmony with the flow of life. Spirit and matter need each other equally.

As regards yoga, which is the means India has employed to rediscover mental health, there is a physiological balancing that occurs. We know that the two hemispheres of the brain have complementary functions. The left hemisphere is "male," controlling the rational, temporal, and logical abilities, whereas

Shiva as Androgyne (Ardhanārīshvara).

its partner, the right hemisphere, is concerned with the "female" side of our personality: emotions, intuition, and spatial judgment. Experiments have shown that in meditation, the two hemispheres come into synchrony and physical coordination as they never otherwise do. The ancient seers intuited such truths, which they translated into art and symbol. Modern science is beginning to discover the same truths and to express them in its own vocabulary.

You have come to the end of your Elephanta pilgrimage. It began with the abstract totality of the *yoni-linga*, the supreme and most common image of Shiva. You traced the different myths that show the character of this deity and saw how his active side is always balanced by the peaceful, quiescent phase. The culmination of the journey is in the vision of Shiva as three-in-one, and the inner wholeness that results in the devotee from such a vision. The pilgrim is now reunited with the source. Fulfilled in himself, he is ready to leave the cave sanctuary and return to the outside world, across the seas of *samsāra*.

3

ELLORĀ

THE ART
OF THE ROCK CUTTER

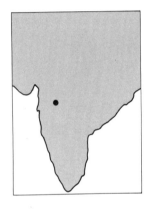

One of the most remarkable facts about Indian civilization is that almost all of its most important earliest monuments are caves. More than twelve hundred of these rock-cut sanctuaries (for they were man-made rather than natural) have been discovered, in all parts of the country. They were excavated over a period of a thousand years, between the third century B.C. and the tenth century A.D., by all the major religious groups—Hindu, Buddhist, and Jain. While the cave has always been a place of retreat for the hermit and ascetic, these sanctuaries served a communal as well as a monastic purpose; some of them are veritable cathedrals in rock. Originally created as more permanent alternatives to shrines built of wood and bamboo, they continued to be excavated long after the development of building techniques in durable materials made their original advantages obsolete. There are famous examples of rock-cut sanctuaries elsewhere in the world— Abu Simbel or Petra, for example—but nowhere else did cave architecture reach such heights of achievement or play such a central part in the development of civilization. It is as if the cave served a need that the Indian psyche felt with a peculiar intensity.

A particularly fine conglomeration of these sanctuaries is to be found at Ellorā, in Mahārāshtra State. The hills around Ellorā are honeycombed with over a hundred caves, of which there are thirty-four principal ones (Figure A). These divide into three groups:

Caves 1–12	Buddhist	A.D. 600–800
Caves 13–29	Hindu	A.D. 600–900
Caves 30–34	Jain	A.D. 800–1100

The Buddhist caves belong to the Vajrayāna sect (an esoteric sect of the Mahāyāna school); the Hindu caves are dedicated to Shiva, and the Jain caves belong to the Digambara sect of that religion. The fact that shrines of these three major faiths are found side by side testifies both to the religious tolerance of ancient India and to the archaic custom of establishing a religious monument in a place already sanctified and regarded as holy. Ellorā had probably been a pilgrimage spot long before the first caves were excavated here. Moreover, it lay near the junction of two major trade routes, which ran from the centers of Pathan to Broach, and Ajantā to Ujjain. Thus its position was ideally suited to the itinerant life of the monks who lived here and to the regular visits of pilgrims who made Ellorā one of their stopping places, especially at the time of seasonal festivals.

Two great dynasties were the patrons of the Ellorā excavations: the Chālukyas of the Deccan (A.D. 550–642) and their successors, the Rāshtrakūtas (A.D. 757–973), who also built the shrine of Elephanta. Unlike the famous caves at Ajantā, which lay deserted and forgotten for several centuries, Ellorā seems to have been well known as an active pilgrimage place for much of its history. There are references to the site in contemporary Rāshtrakūta inscriptions, and both Arab and European travelers refer to it in their journals.

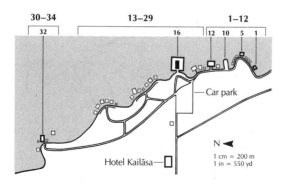

1–12 *Buddhist caves.* **13–29** *Hindu caves.* **30–34** *Jain caves.*
Figure A. Ellorā site plan.

General view of the Buddhist caves.

Of the thirty-four caves here, six give a good overall idea of the variety of the rock-cut sanctuary. Caves 1, 5, 10, and 12 show the development of the Mahāyāna sanctuary; Cave 16 provides the greatest achievement of monumental cave architecture in India; and Cave 32 gives us a glimpse of the florid sculptural art of the Jains.

Your car or bus will park opposite Cave 16 (the Kailāsanātha Temple). Do not enter here—we shall come back later—but take the path that goes to your right. Follow this to Cave 1 at the end. This way you will visit the caves in their correct sequence and be able to follow their development.

Cave 1

There are basically two types of Buddhist rock-cut sanctuary: the shrine, or chapel *(chaitya)*, and the monastery *(vihāra)*. Whereas the *chaitya* was built to house the earliest cult object, the *stūpa* or *dāgaba* (see under Cave 10, below), the *vihāra* was where the monks lived, ate, and studied. The word *vihāra* means "rainy season retreat." The original community of monks was itinerant, begging its food from place to place and teaching the doctrine of the Buddha as it went. It was because of the need for shelter from the ferocious monsoons (June through September) that the first *vihāras* were built. These were constructed out of wood, thatch, and brick. As time went on and the Buddhist communities became more established, largely due to the patronage of the kings and merchant classes, these temporary, free-standing structures gave way to the more permanent rock-cut sanctuaries.

This is the simplest type of *vihāra*—no pillars, no carving, just meditation cells around the walls.

Because of its extreme simplicity, it is often claimed that this cave was used as a storeroom or to house the workmen while they excavated the other caves. But it is more likely to have been used as a special retreat, somewhat isolated, where advanced meditation was practiced. Even today Buddhist monasteries have such buildings set aside for periodic intensive courses.

The whole place has a purity that is almost Islamic: totally unadorned except for an exquisite niche (probably for a lamp) set in the left-hand wall. Holes have been dug in the wall around the niche, from which objects can be hung. These may well have been made by local people who used the caves as a monsoon retreat after there no longer were permanent communities here. The cave's uncluttered style is the perfect analogue to the emptying of the mind that is the essence of Buddhist practice. There is something here that captures the very essence of the Master's teaching. Step into one of the cells—the silence is deafening.

Cave 5

This is a typical Mahāyāna *vihāra*, with its open frontage, flat ceiling, carved pillars, large central hall, and cells around the walls. By the time of the Mahāyāna (that is, after A.D. 100) *vihāras* were built with a shrine at the far end that contained a figure of the Buddha. Hīnayāna *vihāras*, of course, would not have had such an accommodation to the worship of the Buddha, since the earlier school was concerned with strictly following the Master's advice to "Be a lamp unto yourself" and did not put much faith in ritual, worship or supplication.

The two raised platforms that run the length of the hall would have served as tables—the monks sitting on the floor to eat or to read their scriptures. *Vihāras* have no kitchen quarters, since food was begged from the local community. In such Buddhist countries as Thailand and Burma you can still see the monks going out on their daily begging rounds before dawn. It is a rule in the Buddhist community (*sangha*) that a monk should not eat after noon; his only meal of the day is usually taken in the late morning. The Buddha taught that lust is a great eater and that too much food makes the mind dull and lazy, impairing the process of meditation. It is this injunction, rather than a desire to mortify the flesh, that lies behind the Buddhists' frugal eating habits. The ruling on vegetarianism varies from sect to sect, and within the hierarchy of any one sect. Thus novices may still eat meat, whereas senior members of the order generally do not. The Buddha taught that a monk should accept whatever food is placed in his begging bowl, meat or not.

The shrine at the back of the cave is guarded by the two principal *bodhisattvas* of the Vajrayāna. On the left is Padma-pāni: "He who holds the lotus in his hand." He holds this symbol of purity and enlightenment in his left hand, and is "born" out of the lotus on which he stands. His right hand holds a rosary of prayer beads (*akshamālā*) signifying contemplative discipline, and below his left arm is the head

Cave 5—interior.

of a deer. This deer represents meditation—a deerskin is the traditional seat for ascetics and the Buddha's first discourse was given in the Deer Park at Sārnāth. Padmapāni is flanked by two attendants and is shown with the traditional attributes of wisdom and beauty: long earlobes, elongated arms, and three folds of flesh (*trivali*) in the neck. His robe is finely traced, and his crown contains a miniature Buddha figure, symbolizing his divine status and the clarity of his compassionate wisdom.

The right-hand guardian is Vajrapāni, "He who holds the thunderbolt," the *vajra* symbol of esoteric knowledge. He is the principal deity of the Vajrayāna sect. Vajrayāna teaching emphasized the importance of meditation and esoteric ritual to gain enlightenment and was in some ways a reaction to the Mahāyāna reliance on the grace of the celestial *buddhas* and *bodhisattvas*. Great importance was given to the female energies personified as the consorts of the *buddhas* and known as *shaktis*. Also known as Tantric Buddhism (or Tantrayāna),

Vajrayāna was particularly popular in Tibet and the Himālayan kingdoms.

Padmapāni represents the compassion (*karunā*) and Vajrapāni the wisdom (*pragya*) of the Buddhist teaching. These two *bodhisattvas* are especially linked with the celestial *buddha* Vairochāna, who in turn represents that aspect of the Absolute that is the realm of space. In the Vajrayāna sect, the historical Buddha is often seen as a reflex, or manifestation, of Vairochāna, and thus the image here is, strictly speaking, of the Buddha as the historical manifestation of a celestial prototype.

Originally there would have been a wooden door to the shrine so that the image could be closed off when not being worshipped; the holes for the door posts are still visible. The image here is in an unusual position, sitting in the "European fashion" (*bhadrāsana*). This posture is only found comparatively late in Buddhist iconography; usually the Master is shown cross-legged or in the "lotus posture" (*padmāsana*). The Buddha is attended by two servants bearing ceremonial fly whisks (*chāmara*), one of the insignia of royalty. Behind him hover the guardians of the celestial realms, including some curious composite creatures (*vyālas*) that ward off evil influences. Thus, the Master is shown as having dominion over the heavens, the earth, and the nether regions; he is the lord of all sentient beings.

The face of the Buddha, as is usual for this period, is full and conveys a powerful feeling of compassion. He has the long earlobes, three folds in the neck, and the third eye, which are some of the thirty-two traditional marks (*lakshana*) of a *buddha*. Originally these *lakshana* were confined to Gautama, the historical Buddha, but with the growth of the Mahāyāna pantheon, they were applied to the celestial *buddhas* and, as we have seen, to the *bodhisattvas*. The squareness of the shoulders and the massive body is well offset by the delicately sculpted robe (*sanghāti*), which, as is the tradition, leaves the right shoulder bare. So finely is this etched that at first glance the figure appears naked. This is a characteristic of Gupta and post-Gupta images.

The position of the Buddha's hands is always significant, as it shows different aspects of his role as a teacher or refers to specific incidents in his life. These hand poses are known as *mudrās*, "signs," and, like the *hastas* of Hindu iconography, act as codes to the initiated (see Chapter 4, Figure E). Here the *mudrā* betokens the Buddha's first discourse in the Deer Park at Sārnāth, an event known as "Setting the Wheel of Truth in Motion" (see Chapter 17). The pose is technically called the *dharmachakra mudrā*, is also referred to as the "teaching *mudrā*," and was a very popular one with the Buddhist iconographers.

Emerging from the cave, one is struck by the sunlight rippling across the larval rock floor, which itself swirls like an eddying tide. There are some fine carvings on these Dravidian-style pillars with their cushion capitals: auspicious couples (*mithunas*), geometric friezes, here and there a protective monster. From its very beginnings Buddhist art incorporated the "old gods" of the new converts to the religion.

Cave 10

This is an interesting combination of *chaitya* and *vihāra*. The cave itself is the chapel for worship, but added to both the ground floor courtyard and the first (U.S. second) floor balcony are cells in which the monks lived.

The facade is particularly noteworthy. The original Buddhist *chaityas* were rectangular buildings housing a miniature *stūpa* at one end. The roof of these structures was barrel-vaulted in timber, covered in tile and supported by brick walls framed by timber pillars, thus the form was essentially similar to the Roman basilica. The open ends of the nave were horseshoe-shaped and covered with a screen of timber trelliswork that provided a door below and a vast sun-shaped window above, allowing light to filter into the hall. The window was the logical facade for such a building, and its shape was symbolically apt, since it mimicked the shape of the leaf of the *bodhi* tree under which the Master gained Enlightenment. As such,

Cave 10—exterior.

the trellised window of the *chaitya* provided an esthetic and symbolic function similar to that of the rose window of the Gothic cathedral.

When the monks began to excavate their sanctuaries out of the rock, they copied their freestanding structures exactly. The earliest rock-cut *chaityas* actually contained wooden beams and rafters and a wooden trellised facade. Though the practice of timbering died out by the first century B.C., the forms remained and were thereafter reproduced in stone.

By the time of this cave, the leaf-shaped motif has moved up to the first (U.S. second) floor, where it is not in fact a window but an entrance from the balcony to a gallery inside the hall. This doorway is flanked by *apsarases*—celestial nymphs—and surmounted by a fine frieze of auspicious couples (*mithunas*). Such couples are originally fertility symbols and act to inculcate the sense of completeness and harmony that a visit to the *chaitya* induces.

The stairs leading to the gallery, which is well worth visiting, are in the northwest corner of the courtyard—that is, immediately on the left as you walk in.

When you enter the *chaitya* itself, notice first the ceiling. Barrel-vaulted with rafters that are purely decorative, it is a replica of its wooden prototype. Similarly the pillars are decorative rather than functional and are reminiscent of an avenue of trees leading up to the *stūpa* at the end of the hall. The local name for this *chaitya* is "the carpenter's cave."

The mixture of wooden motifs and stone material is startling, almost creating an optical illusion that bends reality. Aside from the inherent and persistent conservatism of the Indian artist, why have these archaic wooden motifs been preserved so assiduously here, probably a thousand years after they actually existed?

They seem to show the Buddhist monks' unconscious nostalgia for the early days of their religion, the time when the Master was still alive and the community was itinerant and unfettered, listening to his teaching in idyllic forest groves, far from the pressure of worldly life. As time went on, and Indian society crystallized into an urban, work-oriented society, dominated by the mercantile classes, it became increasingly necessary to retain some psychic link with a freer, more natural life. This desire for a return to nature was only to be expected from a community that had originally come into being because of shared disillusionment with a life of mere worldliness and been united by the desire to find something more meaningful and permanent. It found its expression in the architecture, in a deliberate and stylized reproduction of forms that were organic, natural, and reminiscent of a time when the pressures of Hindu resurgence and the consequent dangers of loss of patronage were less.

The Stūpa

The focus of the chapel is the *stūpa*. The origin of the *stūpa* (which is sometimes in India, and always in Srī Lankā, known as a *dāgaba*) is linked with the earthen tumuli of pre-Buddhist funerary cults. The miniature structure also shared the larger *stūpa*'s symbolic function in representing the "death" of the Buddha and his rebirth into a higher state of being—the deathless wisdom of *nirvāna*. Like the large *stūpa* too, these monuments sometimes contained the ashes of a Buddhist saint. These literal and symbolic associations with death are implicit in the name *dāgaba,* which is a contraction of the words *dhātu* ("relic") and *garbha* ("womb," or "storehouse"). The early *stūpas* were unadorned and plain, representing the reclusive and austere doctrine of the Hīnayāna school. As the teaching became more of a popular religion, however, so the *stūpa* became more ornate. In this cave the *stūpa* itself represents the impersonal and eternal Truth that is the Buddhist teaching (*dharma*). The Buddha figure represents the movement of this teaching into time and history, into the figure of a particular human being who is a savior, showing the way to the Truth that he so perfectly embodies. The Buddha points behind him, as it were, to the *stūpa,* the supreme symbol of a teaching that transcends time and elevates humanity to divinity. It is noticeable that the Buddha here is almost life-size, someone to whom the worshipper can relate as a friend or helper.

The cylindrical pedestal of the *stūpa* is carved with repeated Buddha figures. Such repetition is a visual accompaniment to the repeated chanting of prayers and *mantras* by the circumambulating devotee. Such visual reinforcement would instill the image of the Buddha deep into the monk's consciousness, where it would lie as a seed, waiting to be enlivened through his meditation practice.

Cave 12   This monumental sanctuary has three stories and is an expanded type of *vihāra*. The first and second floors, which are relatively unadorned, have cells around the walls; the top floor, which served as a meeting hall, has no cells but some finely carved figures.

That it is later than its predecessors can be seen by the ornate development of the pillars on the ground floor. As well as incorporating the vase design (a northern Indian motif), which by now overflows with abundant foliage (in what is called the *pūrnaghata*), the capitals are embellished with auspicious couples (*mithunas*) and divine sea dragons (*makaras*). It is safe to assume that this splendid *vihāra*,

Vase-and-foliage (pūrnaghata) capital of column.

almost baroque in its effect, was built when the local *sangha* was being generously funded by the lay community.

The stairs to the first (U.S. second) floor are in the front right-hand corner (that is, southwest) of the ground floor hall, and at the top of the first flight there is a small chamber worth a visit. It contains a large Buddha in the "earth-touching pose" (*bhūmisparsha mudrā*). His right hand is extended to the ground in commemoration of his victory over the forces of evil. Just after the great Enlightenment, Māra (the Buddhist Satan) and his alluring daughters came to tempt the Master. When asked what proof he had of his exalted state, the Master replied, "The whole earth is my witness." Then he touched the ground with his hand.

Notice as well the sets of two parallel lines of small indented holes in the rock floor. We often see such depressions in these sanctuaries; they are probably the carved palettes of the artists who painted the frescoes that originally adorned all the caves.

The top floor is reached by the stairs in the northwest corner of the first (U.S. second) floor. This airy and expansive chamber was a hall for meetings and lectures; the head monks sat in front of the shrine facing the congregation, backed by the authority of the image behind them.

The shrine itself is flanked by two rows of seven seated Buddhas. The left-hand row shows the *mudrā* of meditation (*dhyāna mudrā*): both hands resting palms-up in the lap, right hand on top of left. The Buddha sits under a stylized frieze of the *bodhi* tree, emphasizing the indrawn, passive side of the *dharma*—the essential absorption of meditation. To balance this, the right hand row denotes the dynamic side of the doctrine—the activity of teaching all sentient beings.

Here the hands are in the teaching pose (*dharmachakra mudrā*). This transition from inner- to outer-directed activity is emphasized by the tree (representing the reclusive life of the forest) giving way to the royal parasol, which underlines the status of the Buddha as a teacher in society, a King among kings. Thus the whole thrust of Mahāyāna is embodied in these adamantine figures, steadfastly gazing out over the plains of the Ellorā Valley.

Between Caves 15 and 16 runs a path up the hillside. This is the old trading route. The view from the top is magnificent and provides a superb vantage point for photographs looking down into the Kailāsanātha Temple below. In fact the achievement of the Ellorā sculptors of Cave 16 can only fully be appreciated from this elevated angle. It is also a fine place from which to watch the sunset!

Cave 16
Kailāsanātha
Temple

This monolithic temple, cut from the living rock as a gigantic piece of sculpture, is dedicated to the Hindu god Shiva. It dates from A.D. 765 and was built by the Rāshtrakūta dynasty, under the patronage of King Krishna I. Although much of the carving inside was damaged by the Muslims at the end of the thirteenth century, the temple is both a masterpiece of the rock cutters' art and a storehouse of Hindu mythology. The temple is in the southern Indian (Dravidian) style, with some northern Indian (Indo-Āryan) elements.

Cave 16—exterior.

Kailāsa ("the abode of pleasure") is the mountain home of Shiva. Situated in the high Himālayas, it is the center of the universe, the axis of the world and the holy territory par excellence. Shiva is "Lord of Kailāsa" (*Kailāsanātha*).

The Entrance (Figure B)

As you look at the entrance, you can see the bells carved as a balustrade on top of the portal. These drive away evil spirits and provide celestial music for the gods. But the entrance to the celestial abode is also, in human terms, the entrance to the subconscious mind. So there are also serpent kings (*nāgas*) and queens (*nāginīs*), the guardians of the treasures of the underworld and esoteric knowledge. The threshold of any sacred place is always a delicate region that needs protection from the profane world outside. The doorway has two guardians on the doorjambs—the goddess Gangā (B.1) and her sister Yamunā (B.2). These goddesses take form as the sacred rivers of the same names, and, as do the water serpents, act to purify the pilgrim who passes between them. All these watery images also symbolize the creative depths of the mind, for to enter a temple is to penetrate to one's own core and emerge reborn. Originally, there was a tank outside the temple in which worshippers bathed before entering.

Just within the entrance are two seated sages. On the left is Vyāsa (B.3), the legendary author of the *Mahābhārata*. Opposite him sits Vālmīki (B.4), the poet of India's other great epic, the *Rāmāyana*. The pillars here (B.5) are a touch in northern Indian style, a further development of the vase-

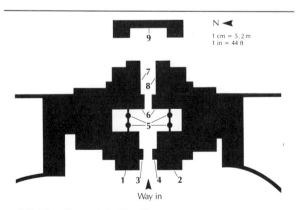

1 *Goddess Gangā.* **2** *Goddess Yamunā.* **3** *Vyāsa.* **4** *Vālmīki.*
5 *Pillars (northern style).* **6** *Kubera.* **7** *Ganesha.* **8** *Durgā.*
9 *Lakshmī.*

Figure B. Kailāsanātha Temple entrance.

and-foliage motif, a popular good omen indicating good harvest, fertility, and domestic happiness. On either side of the inner door we find forms of Kubera (B.6), the Hindu god of wealth. He is a jovial character, potbellied and grinning. (To this day a potbelly is esteemed in India and considered the mark of a handsome man!) The left-hand Kubera holds a conch, the right-hand one a lotus—both cornucopias, symbols of wealth and plenty. This is a common southern Indian motif. For the pilgrim who is a householder, there is no antagonism between material benefit and spirituality. They are the two sides of the coin of life, and worship of the gods brings material gain.

The last two figures to give you their blessing on the way in are Ganesha (B.7) and Durgā (B.8). Ganesha, the elephant-headed son of Shiva, is the most popular of the domestic deities, the god of good beginnings. He is worshipped at the start of any new venture or undertaking, and his image is always used to guard the threshold of a house or temple.

Opposite Ganesha is the panel of Durgā killing the buffalo demon Mahisha. Durgā is a wrathful form of Shiva's wife Pārvatī and in this aspect she is called *Mahishāsuramardinī* ("the Killer of the demon Mahisha"). According to the story in the *Mahābhārata*, Mahisha ("the Powerful") was a demon who conquered the heavens and drove out the gods. Durgā was created to destroy the interloper. Judging from this panel, she did a good job. The demon is shown coming out of the carcass and Durgā's vehicle, the lion, is polishing off one of the demonic attendants.

So before you have entered the temple proper, you have been sanctified by a number of beings who guard the threshold. The sacred rivers purify, the sages remind you that visiting the temple brings wisdom, Kubera assures material prosperity, Ganesha is propitiated, and the conquest of evil is assured by Durgā's presence. As this entrance is also the exit, the worshipper is again protected before he returns to the profane world outside.

Once safely through the initiatory portals, you are greeted by the figure of Lakshmī (B.9) flanked by two smiling attendants who welcome you to the temple proper. The consort of Vishnu, Lakshmī presides over wealth. She is the goddess of beauty, fortune, and prosperity. In the present decadent age she is worshipped only as the deity of money (you will see her picture in many shops and businesses), but originally she was the deity of both material and spiritual riches.

The main Lakshmī festival is the Hindu Financial New Year: Divālī, "the festival of lights," in October. At this time homes are freshly whitewashed and cleaned after the monsoon, new clothes and utensils are bought, gifts are exchanged, and the goddess is worshipped. It is believed that Lakshmī will make her abode in homes that are clean and

Gaja Lakshmī, Goddess of Wealth.

pure, and once she stays, good fortune will bless the place. According to the scriptures: "Lakshmī is all that is termed female." She is the Mother Earth, fertile and abundant with riches and water. This form of Lakshmī is called Gaja Lakshmī, because she is attended by elephants (*gaja*). As befits her feminine nature, she is usually shown sitting or standing on the opened lotus. A marvelous effect of rippling water is created here by the half-open lotuses that dance and bob like wavelets; tiny birds and frogs lurk among the flowers. Attended by celestial musicians and dancers, the goddess is shaded by a parasol, a regal symbol of wealth and power.

Lakshmī is being lustrated by a continuous stream of water, passed up by the smaller elephants to their larger companions. The effect of movement is given in the backward swing of the elephants' chain and bell. It is a delightful scene altogether, full of the little details that the Hindu sculptors loved to portray.

The Courtyard (Figure C)

Now turn left, down the steps into the courtyard.

On your immediate left are a number of panels. Of particular note is the third one from the end. This is Kāma, the god of desire (C.1). He is the Indian Cupid. He carries a bow of the sweetest sugarcane strung with humming bees, and he has five arrows, one for each of the senses. Their stinging points are tipped with flowers. So desire is a legitimate part of life, and the god of love has his place in the temple as one of the celestial host.

Continuing around the courtyard, you come to three figures

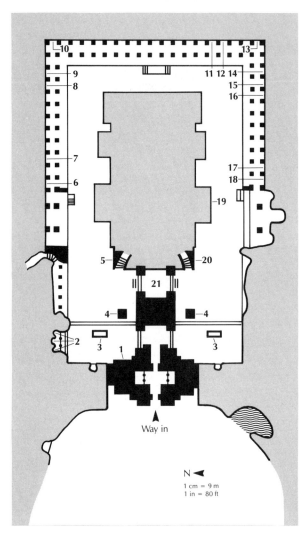

1 *Kāma* 2 *Goddesses Gangā, Yamunā, and Sarasvatī.*
3 *Elephant.* 4 *Pillar.* 5 Mahābhārata *panel.* 6 *Rāvana
Offering His Heads.* 7 *Shiva and Pārvatī.* 8 *Shiva Playing the*
Vīnā. 9 *The Dice Game.* 10 *The Marriage of Shiva and
Pārvatī.* 11 *The Origin of the* Linga. 12 *Dancing Shiva.*
13 *Shiva Tricking Pārvatī.* 14 *Krishna Stealing the
Buttermilk.* 15 *Narasingha.* 16 *Vishnu Reclining on the
Cosmic Serpent.* 17 *Vishnu, the Preserver.* 18 *Annapūrnā.*
19 *Rāvana Shaking Mount Kailāsa.* 20 *The* Rāmāyana
panels. 21 *Porch.*

Figure C. Kailāsanātha Temple, lower floor ground plan.

that immediately command your attention. These are the three sacred river goddesses (C.2): Gangā (in the center), Sarasvatī (on her right), and Yamunā (on her left). Gangā is mounted on a crocodile, Sarasvatī on a lotus, and Yamunā on a tortoise. Water is life-giving, so the rivers are female deities. Gangā, being the largest and most sacred, is the center, with her two tributaries leaning toward her. She is said to flow from Shiva's matted locks. Portrayed very gracefully in the *tribhanga* ("triply-bent") pose of classical dance, their bodies are bowed at the neck, shoulders, and waist. Their garments are skillfully rendered as transparent, clinging wetly to their bodies.

On the physical level, to bathe in the confluence of these three rivers at Allāhabād is one of the holiest acts for a Hindu. Many in India try to do this pilgrimage before they die, since it is believed to insure a good rebirth. So the rivers are portrayed here to give the worshipper in Ellorā the merit of the Allāhabād pilgrimage.

Symbolically, Gangā stands for purity, Sarasvatī wisdom, and Yamunā devotion.

Esoterically, these deities represent the three main nerves (*nādīs*) that convey the life energy through the body. These nerves are not physical but belong to the subtle nervous system. The principal nerve (*sushumna*) runs through the spinal column. It is the channel along which the *kundalinī* energy rises, and along which lie the subtle energy centers (*chakras*). When the life energy is drawn up this central nerve, enlightenment follows. The confluence of the three is the "third eye," in the middle of the forehead. The yogis who worship Shiva mostly practice *kundalinī* yoga.

This is a good example of how an image can convey several levels of meaning simultaneously, each one suited to a different type of worshipper.

The goddesses' shrine is fronted by Dravidian-style pillars. The huge elephant in the courtyard (C.3) is a symbol of majesty, dignity, and dependable strength. Kipling's "noble pachiderm" is probably the most loved and widely represented animal in Indian painting and sculpture. Shiva himself is said to "move with the pace of an elephant." Unfortunately, the iconoclastic zeal of the Muslims who defaced the Kailāsa statues didn't even spare this elephant's trunk, but he is still a handsome beast, and has long outlived his attackers.

Continuing around the courtyard, you see a massive pillar fifty feet high (C.4). Perfectly proportioned and balanced between plain and ornamented surfaces, this pillar (*stambha*) was probably erected as a symbol of King Krishna I, the patron of the temple. A stylized flagstaff, it is in the style of the classical Dravidian pillars we shall see in the main hall (*mandapa*). Since the time of the Buddhist emperor Ashoka (third century B.C.) it was the custom for Indian kings to

Shrine of the three river goddesses.

---

erect such pillars as testaments to their glory. (The Persian victory tower served the same purpose; see the Qutb Mīnār in Delhi, Chapter 7.)

This is a good vantage point from which to appreciate the achievement of this colossal temple. As you can see, it is not a structural edifice but a gigantic rock carving in architectural form. The whole place has been hewn out of the living rock. It was done by starting at the top and sinking three great trenches on the north, south, and east sides to create a quarry. Once these trenches were begun, wooden trunks were inserted into them, which were then soaked with water, the resulting expansion splitting the rock. In this way the builders slowly exposed the entire rock face. This left one huge block—over two hundred feet (sixty meters) long and one hundred feet (thirty meters) high—standing free. Starting from the top, this block was sculpted into everything you see: the temple with its crowning spire (*vimāna*), the subsidiary shrines, and the elephants. Workers laboriously cut and polished each section before moving on to the next, to avoid the use of cumbersome and dangerous scaffolding. All the carving was done with chisels, each about an inch (less than three centimeters) wide!

The external decorations of the temple—niches enclosing deities, colonnettes, engaged columns, and the heavy overhanging cornices, the "Bengālī roof" type—are all, like the main spire, typically Dravidian.

Over 200,000 tons (175,000 metric tons) of rock are estimated to have been removed, and the whole complex took over one hundred years to complete. No wonder the architect presiding at its completion is said to have exclaimed: "Oh

*General view
of Kailāsanātha
Temple.*

wonderful! Have I done this? How could I ever have accomplished such a thing?" To prevent the whole edifice being lost in the darkness of the pit, it was "raised" on a platform some twenty-five feet (seven and a half meters) high. Thus the structure is on two floors: the lower one a solid plinth, the upper containing the temple proper—Nandin shrine, hall, and holy of holies. Moreover, the building was originally covered in white stucco, which not only lightened the whole effect but served to mimic the snow-covered peaks of the gods' Himālayan home. Nevertheless, the overwhelming feeling here is one of massive solidity. Emotionally, this fulfills the purpose of the temple because it is through its special quality of stability that sacred architecture most faithfully represents the divine.

Before you leave the courtyard, there is a fine piece of carving on the north wall.

□ THE MAHĀBHĀRATA PANEL (Figure C.5)
Hindu temple art is a means of educating people in the eternal truths of their religion. Panels such as this act as a divine comic strip for the illiterate (who still make up 70 percent of India's population). The top five bands of the panel recount legends from the *Mahābhārata*, the bottom two from the life of Krishna. The *Mahābhārata* is one of the two great epics of India. (The other, the *Rāmāyana*, is on the south wall.) In its written form, over one hundred thousand verses, it was finalized about A.D. 300, but as an oral teaching it is far older.

The story starts in the top left-hand corner. Here we see Arjuna, the ideal man, who is the hero of the *Bhagavad Gītā* (the eighteenth chapter of the epic). He is doing yogic penance to win the boon of invincibility from Shiva in his battle with the forces of evil. Shiva and his wife have taken the form of a forest-dwelling couple. To test the hero's devotion, Shiva sends a boar across his path one day. Seizing his bow, the famous archer shoots the animal, but just as his shaft strikes it, another arrow appears and strikes the creature at the same time. A hunter appears from the trees, and a quarrel breaks out over who has the right to the unfortunate boar. They have an archery contest but even Arjuna, the greatest archer in the world, cannot beat the hunter. Then they wrestle, but again Arjuna loses. Then suddenly he realizes that only one being could be so accomplished: Shiva himself! He falls at the hunter's feet, and the figure immediately changes into the great Lord. Pleased by such devotion, Shiva grants the warrior the desired boon and sends him back to continue the battle.

Halfway along the same band, you see Yudhishthira, a king of ancient India, bowing down and honoring the god Krishna. Yudhishthira is chiefly renowned for his addiction to gambling, a favorite pastime of the Vedic Indians. The trouble was, he could never win. Villages, towns, palaces, whole kingdoms were lost at the throw of the dice. He even gambled away his entire family. He and his four brothers were exiled for thirteen years in the forest as a result. It is their battle to regain their kingdom that is the story of the *Bhagavad Gītā* ("the Song of God"), one of India's most popular scriptures.

The second panel shows the coronation of the hapless gambler, and the last three show various incidents from the war between Yudhishthira's family, the Pāndavas, who represent good, and their cousins, the Kauravas, who usurped their kingdom and represent evil.

☐ *THE KRISHNA PANEL*

These two bands read from the bottom right-hand corner. Krishna, the eighth and most popular incarnation of the god Vishnu, is India's most loved folk hero. He is in turn the ideal child, lover, warrior, ruler, and diplomat. In the battle of the *Mahābhārata,* he was Arjuna's charioteer, and it was he who gave the Song of God, the cream of Indian scriptures, to the world.

Vishnu incarnated as Krishna in order to rid the earth of a demon called Kamsa. Krishna was born to Kamsa's sister, and the panel begins with the divine baby being suckled by the wife of an agent of righteousness, Vasudeva. Vasudeva takes the infant from the household of his demon uncle and escapes to Gokula, an idyllic pastoral spot. In time, the wicked

Kamsa learns that Krishna has escaped and, like the Biblical Herod, orders a general massacre of all the children in Gokula. One of his demonesses, Pūtanā, has the nasty trick of poisoning all children who suck her milk. She offers Krishna her breast, but he sucks so hard she dies on the spot. (This is halfway along the band.) The rest of the lower band is taken up with scenes from daily life in Gokula.

On the upper band, you see Vasudeva's wife milking a cow. Krishna, the mischievous child, has been bothering her, so she has tied him to a grain thresher. But the baby pulls it over and crawls to the cream pot to steal the cream. Next we are shown Krishna killing demons in his childhood, twisting the neck of a demoness who has taken the form of a crow to attack him in his cot. Various other demons are dispatched as the band progresses, until ultimately we see Krishna fulfilling the purpose of his spell on earth by killing his demon uncle Kamsa. So we see how the hero myth is passed on to the succeeding generations through a combination of history and fairy story. It is significant that both Kamsa and Krishna are traditionally *kshatriyas,* members of the warrior, rather than the priestly, caste. They are both represented as dark in color. Thus they were most likely heroes of the ancient pre-Āryan mythology, incorporated into the mainstream Āryan fold at a comparatively late date.

☐

As you turn to the steps leading to the colonnaded passage, notice the fabulous creatures on the first register on top of the plinth. In most Hindu temples these magical animals (one here looks definitely sphinxlike) support the temple on their backs. They are called *yālis.*

The Shadowed Corridor

These cloisters are designed to instruct the pilgrim while providing a way to circumambulate the main shrine, keeping it, as is the custom, on the right. Although the quality of the carvings in this three-sided corridor are not of the highest order, the panels display some important myths of Shiva and, in the southern passage, Vishnu. We shall examine the most important.

☐ *FIRST NORTHERN PANEL:*
   RĀVANA OFFERING HIS HEADS (Figure C.6)
Rāvana, the demon king of Lankā who personifies evil in the *Rāmāyana* epic, was a great devotee of Shiva. One evening, just before the time for evening worship, the god decided to test this devotion by stealing the flowers Rāvana was going to offer him. It is the Indian custom not to pluck flowers for

the temple after sunset, because then they are asleep and unconscious of being offered to the gods. Faced with this dilemma, the pious Rāvana had no alternative but to offer his heads to Shiva in place of the flowers.

Here Rāvana has already offered nine of his ten heads. If a flower falls to the ground, it cannot be offered in *pūjā*, so the demon king is holding on to his last remaining head to make sure that it doesn't fall to the ground. Luckily, Shiva is pleased by such an extreme display of devotion and not only restores the king's heads but promises him that he will never be killed by the gods. In the *Rāmāyana,* when Rāvana is finally defeated, it is by Rāma, the archetypal human warrior.

The head symbolizes the ego, which has to be sacrificed if true spiritual progress is to be made.

☐ *THIRD NORTHERN PANEL:*
   SHIVA AND PĀRVATĪ (Figure C.7)
Shiva shown with his consort and his two most common symbols: the bull Nandin ("the joyous one"), and the phallic *linga*. Both represent the creative power of the Lord, potential that becomes actual through the energy of his consort *(shakti).*

☐ *NINTH NORTHERN PANEL:*
   SHIVA PLAYING THE VĪNĀ (Figure C.8)
Shiva as the origin of sound. According to Indian thought the universe comes into creation through sound. All matter is basically energy in motion, and all motion must produce sound. So as the Creator, Shiva is here shown playing the *vīnā* (a type of sitar), the notes of which create the universe. (There is a parallel here with the Greek figure of Orpheus, who made the sun rise with the notes from his lyre, and the creative power of the *logos* in Greek thought.) This sound manifests through rhythm, and thus Shiva is also the lord of dance (Natarāja), music, and grammar. The Sanskrit language is composed of the sounds that constitute the entire universe, and it is believed that any form can be created or destroyed by the correct intonation of its constituent sound.

Just as Shiva creates through sound, so the yogi returns to Shiva through meditating on sound *(mantra)* and transcends the world of name and form.

☐ *TENTH NORTHERN PANEL:*
   THE DICE GAME (Figure C.9)
As we have seen with the hapless Yudhishthira, dice was one of the favorite pastimes in ancient India. The gods were also addicted to gambling and were often very bad losers. Shiva is here being beaten by Pārvatī, who rises to go and so keep her winnings. Shiva, however, is holding her hand to restrain her, so that he can have a chance to recoup some of his losses.

The same theme is treated more fully in the Elephanta shrine (see Chapter 2).

Esoterically, this sculpture portrays the inseparable union of pure spirit (Shiva) and matter-energy (Pārvatī). Life is the divine play of these two forces; they are two sides of the same coin.

The lower half of the panel has a historical interest, since it demonstrates the remarkable continuity of images in Indian art. The hump-backed bull the children are playing with could have come straight off a seal from the Indus Valley civilization, over two thousand years older than this temple.

☐ *FIRST EASTERN PANEL:*
THE MARRIAGE OF SHIVA AND PĀRVATĪ (Figure C.10) One of the favorite themes of Hindu sculptors. Pārvatī is represented as the ideal Hindu bride: eyes shyly downcast, submissive to her husband. But in addition, she is obviously confused by the great event. See how she is playing with her feet, one crossed over the other, and how, in her haste to attend the ceremony, she has forgotten to put an anklet on her right foot. What is more, she is holding Shiva's hand, whereas traditionally the bride's hand should rest in the groom's palm.

The four-headed figure at the bottom is Brahmā, god of creation, who is the officiating priest at the wedding. In front of him is the sacred fire. The essence of the marriage ceremony is that it is witnessed by Agni, most truthful of the gods, in the form of fire. The sacred flames are kept burning in a pit in the center of the room, and at the climax of the ceremony the groom leads the bride around the fire. They take the seven sacred steps together. These steps are irrevocable. There is no divorce for the orthodox Hindu. All orthodox marriages are still arranged, the parents choosing a suitable spouse for their child.

☐ *FIFTEENTH EASTERN PANEL:*
THE ORIGIN OF THE LINGA (Figure C.11) The *linga* is the supreme symbol of Shiva. We shall see a fine example in the holy of holies upstairs. This is the story of its origin as told in the *Skanda Purāna:*

One day Brahmā (top right with four heads) and Vishnu (top left) were arguing as to which of them was the greater. As they squabbled, a fiery pillar appeared before them, without beginning or end. Astonished, the gods forgot their quarrel and resolved to find the origin of this immense pillar. Brahmā took the form of a swan and flew up into the heavens to find the top. Vishnu took the form of a boar (right) and burrowed into the earth to find the base. After eons of fruitless searching they returned. Vishnu admitted defeat, whereas

Brahmā claimed to have found the top. At this the flames parted, and the great Shiva emerged. The other two fell at his feet and acknowledged his supremacy. But Brahmā paid dearly for his lie: Shiva decreed that he would never be worshipped again, and to this day there is only one active Brahmā temple, at Pushkar in Rājasthān, though there are images of him in most temples and his name is invoked in rituals. The fiery pillar became the *linga*, the universal sign of the Lord Shiva.

☐

Look behind you. This spot gives a good view of the frieze of animals you saw earlier supporting the temple. There are some beautiful elephants here, their natural movements lovingly caught in the stone, with particular care paid to the rendering of their trunks, ears, and feet.

☐ SIXTEENTH EASTERN PANEL:
DANCING SHIVA (Figure C.12)

An unusual depiction of Shiva as Natarāja. The sculpture captures the taut energy about to erupt, coiled like a spring ready to unleash. Apparently this pose was the result of a dance contest between Shiva and Pārvatī. Modesty prevented her from dancing in such an uninhibited and revealing way, so Shiva won the contest! Shiva Natarāja is a subject often chosen by Indian bronze sculptors, especially of the Chola dynasty (A.D. ca. 900–1050).

☐ NINETEENTH EASTERN PANEL:
SHIVA TRICKING PĀRVATĪ (Figure C.13)

Shiva wishes to trap his future wife. He jumps into a lotus pond just as she comes out of her house, crying, "Save me! I am drowning! My foot is trapped!" (Actually, this is not a complete lie; we can see the little turtle nibbling his foot.) Pārvatī rushes to save him, innocently offering him her hand to pull him out. But the cunning Shiva extends *his* right hand—because this is extended to the bride in the marriage ceremony. Seeing his ploy, Pārvatī refuses to touch him, saying "Give me your other hand or drown!" He does so, she pulls him out, and he reveals himself to be her future husband, the great Mahādeva.

☐

As you turn into the southern corridor, you can see the way the rock overhangs the courtyard unsupported. The original engineers had an uncanny understanding of their material when they designed the temple: The perfectly balanced structure has stood for eleven hundred years.

□ *THIRD SOUTHERN PANEL:*

KRISHNA STEALING THE BUTTERMILK (Figure C.14)
Krishna, the eighth incarnation of Vishnu, has been taken
by all the Vaishnava sects of later times as having all the
attributes of absolute divinity. He is thus the only complete
incarnation (*pūrnāvatāra*). Although originally a non-Āryan
culture hero, Krishna ("the dark one") has become the most
popular deity for millions of the orthodox. As a boy he tended
the herds and played with the sons of the cowherds in the
paradisical pastures around Vrindavan. As a youth he graduated to the cowgirls (*gopīs*) and used to charm them by playing his flute. He is the great lover in Indian mythology and is
reputed to have had 16,108 lovers at once. His favorite was
Rādhā ("success"), the lovely daughter of his adoptive father
Nanda, and the love of these two is the subject of much
mysticoerotic verse and painting from the Middle Ages onward.
At the highest level, this love represents the insatiable yearning of the soul for God. In the Krishna legends, the principal
collection of which is the *Bhāgavata Purāna*, we can see a
glorification of the pastoral life of the early settlers in India,
before the advent of an urbanized society. These nomad Āryan
tribes lived off the cow and used its products for their religious rituals. Cow reverence, an essential part of Hinduism
and still practiced by the orthodox, dates from this time.

□ *FOURTH SOUTHERN PANEL:*

VISHNU AS NARASINGHA (Figure C.15)
Vishnu's fourth incarnation was as a creature who was half-
man (*nara*) and half-lion (*singha*). This was to enable him
to kill the demon Hiranyakashipu, an ogre who had worshipped
Brahmā so devotedly (Hindu demons are nothing if not
cunning) that the god had promised him that he could not
be killed by man, god, or beast. In addition, he could not die
by day or by night, neither within nor outside his own home.

Understandably, such divinely sanctioned immunity went
to Hiranyakashipu's head. Not only did he prohibit all worship
in his kingdom, but he persecuted his own son for worshipping Vishnu. The unfortunate youth was flogged, bitten by
poisonous serpents, trampled by elephants "as vast as mountains," thrown off cliffs, and submerged under water—all at
his father's command. Still he stubbornly worshipped Vishnu.
Eventually Vishnu took the form of Narasingha and, to honor
Brahmā's promise, attacked and killed Hiranyakashipu at dusk
(neither day nor night) on the threshold (neither inside or
outside) of his house.

☐ *FIFTH SOUTHERN PANEL:*
  VISHNU ON THE COSMIC SERPENT (Figure C.16)

An ancient text describes this creation myth: "Vishnu, Lord of the Universe, reposed for over a thousand years on the cosmic serpent, Ananta, 'the unending one.' He was quite alone, blissful, lying on the ocean of infinity. While the Lord was thus lying in self-communion, there issued forth from his navel a lotus with the shining brilliance of one thousand suns together. So large was the lotus that it could be the dwelling place of all the creatures. And from this lotus there sprang up Brahmā, the self-created. Being endowed with the power of the mighty Lord lying on the ocean of infinity, Brahmā created all beings and assigned to each of them its rightful name and form." This is one of the twenty-four iconographic forms of Vishnu and is known as Vishnu Nārāyana ("Vishnu the Universal Abode").

☐ *ELEVENTH SOUTHERN PANEL:*
  VISHNU, THE PRESERVER (Figure C.17)

A fine portrayal of Vishnu. His top left hand holds the discus (power), bottom left the conch (generosity). His bottom right hand is extended in the gesture of generosity, and the top right holds the mace (spiritual authority).

Vishnu is the most loving of the Hindu pantheon. He watches over his devotees with compassion and concern and is full of forgiveness. In many ways he is the nearest Hindu equivalent to the Christian concept of God. Usually colored black, he has a thousand names and ten major incarnations—each one of which can be worshipped as a separate deity (for example, Krishna, Rāma, etc.).

The worshippers of Vishnu are called Vaishnavas and are distinguished by perpendicular marks in ash, sandalwood paste, or red *kum-kum* paste on their foreheads.

☐ *TWELFTH SOUTHERN PANEL:*
  ANNAPŪRNĀ, GODDESS OF PLENTY (Figure C.18)

It is comparatively rare to see a representation of this goddess in a temple. Her name means full (*pūrna*) of food (*anna*); she is a form of Pārvatī. She holds a pot, a rosary, and some maize.

She was created because once the yogi Shiva was too incapacitated from smoking hashish to go out on his daily begging round. The long-suffering Pārvatī went out for him, and on her return, Shiva was so delighted with the abundant food she had begged, he embraced her, changing her into Annapūrnā. It should be added that many Shaiva yogis share their deity's love of intoxicants.

☐

Dravidian-style spire (vimāna).

On leaving Annapūrnā, do not go down the steps back into the courtyard but continue through the doorway ahead, which leads to an empty recessed chamber. The stairs up to the right lead to a fine view of the temple spire (*vimāna*). This is a classic example of the southern Indian style—basically a truncated pyramid surmounted by a domed finial known as the *stūpika* ("little *stūpa*"). The impression of soaring height is emphasized by the repetitions of this dome on the lower corners of the terraces of the pyramid, which act to balance the upward thrust of the intricately carved pilasters and niches. It is particularly dramatic against the backdrop of massive rock and open sky.

Now come down the stairs and continue into the courtyard, until you are face to face with the most assured panel of the temple.

The Courtyard Again

□ *RĀVANA SHAKING MOUNT KAILĀSA* (Figure C.19)
The ten-headed demon Rāvana was the king of Lankā and is the representation of evil in the *Rāmāyana* epic. At one point in his battles against the forces of good (led by Rāma), he decided that he had need of the spiritual power of Shiva's mountain home in order to continue the fight. So he went to

*Rāvana Shaking
Mount Kailāsa.*

Mount Kailāsa and, impudently disturbing Shiva and Pārvatī, who were making love at the time, tried to take the mountain back with him to his kingdom.

In this deeply shadowed stage set you see his attempt. The whole piece is beautifully balanced: the effortless way that Shiva, towering above the spectator, puts down his foot to steady the mountain, provides a dramatic contrast to the twisting demon, whose arms, like so many spokes of a wheel, are braced with the strain of seizing the mountain. The Lord is quite unconcerned—his left shoulder is lifted in what is almost a shrug of nonchalance—while Pārvatī clings to his arm and a terrified maidservant rushes in.

This is sculpture of the highest order. The stone has been carved to maximize the effect of light and shade in communicating dynamism and emotion. As at Elephanta, the feelings of the figures are conveyed through pose and gesture, rather than facial expression. The entire piece seems to recede into a space that is somehow limitless, while the figures themselves emerge from the depths of the rock, as the world emerges from the Infinite. We get the feeling that they could at any time sink back into it. We have here a visual representation of *māyā*—the divine illusion that is creation.

□ *THE RĀMĀYANA PANELS* (Figure C.20)
These eight panels depict stories from this epic. It is on the southern wall because the story takes place mainly in south-

ern India and Srī Lankā. Since Rāvana is the king of Lankā, the historical basis of the epic is probably the Indian attempts to conquer that island. You can see Hanumān, the monkey god, who is the general of Rāma's army, in many of these panels. Now continue around to the porch (Figure C.21).

The Porch

□ *SHIVA AS THE LORD OF KNOWLEDGE* (Figure D)
This inner porch contains two important sculptured panels. Taken together, they contain the entire teaching of Shaivism in symbolic form. On your right is a representation of Shiva as the Lord of Knowledge (Gyāna Dakshināmūrti). Here the great Lord assumes the form of a meditating yogi, seated in the "posture of the enlightened one" (*siddhāsana*). He sits on a lion throne, the emblem of both temporal and spiritual dominion. The three lions represent the three worlds—gross, subtle, and transcendent—and the three realms of time— past, present, and future. Shiva is Lord of all. His hair is piled into the ascetic's crown of matted locks (*jatā*), which merge into the tangled foliage of the sacred fig tree (*ashvattha*), which protects him. As well as conforming to the pan-Indian symbolism of the protective tree and royal umbrella, the fig tree here has an added dimension. What at first sight appear to be the branches are seen, on closer inspection, to be more like roots; they are tangled and knotted together, serpentine. This is probably an allusion to the passage in the *Brihadār-*

The Rāmāyana *panel (south wall).*

anyaka Upanishad (800 B.C.), which describes the universe as an everlasting fig tree having its roots in heaven and its branches spreading down into the manifest worlds. (In Islām, the Tree of Life that grows in paradise is similarly inverted.) Yoga teaches that this divine tree has its microcosmic counterpart in the human nervous system, which is nourished by the life energy (*prāna*) that flows down into the thousand-petaled lotus (*sahasrāra chakra*) above the head and sustains the whole organism. Shiva is here the archetypal yogi and teacher of supreme knowledge, unifying the realms of spirit and matter.

One unusual feature of the image is that it has eight arms; Shiva is more often depicted with four. Although several of these have been damaged, we can infer from iconographical rules which attributes they would have been displaying. The first right hand would have been in the attitude of explanation (*vitarka mudrā*), with thumb and forefinger touching, for it is knowledge that integrates all aspects of life. The second hand touches the knee, "grounding" this knowledge and bringing it down to earth. This hand would have held the pitcher of immortality, the same symbol that is placed as the *kalasha* finial on top of northern-style temples. The third hand holds a rosary (*akshamālā*), which signifies the repetition of sacred *mantras*. The fourth grasps the cobra—emblem of the esoteric knowledge that leads to psychic renewal through the awakening of *kundalinī*.

On Shiva's left side, the first hand is opened in the gesture of generosity (*dāna mudrā*), as he bestows the boon of liberation to his devotees. The second, now missing, would have held a book: the Shaivite scriptures (*āgamas*) that lay down the principles of worship. The third reaches out to support two sages (*rishis*) who teach Shiva's wisdom on earth, while the fourth holds a lotus that symbolizes enlightenment—the culmination of all wisdom.

The divine throne is surrounded by sages, celestial musicians, and the Guardians of the Eight Directions (*dikpālas*), who represent the whole universe, radiating out from the infinite Consciousness, which is personified as Shiva.

The panel is also interesting in the way it exemplifies some of the classical principles of Hindu sculptural composition. In much of what follows I am greatly indebted to the work of Alice Boner (see Appendix 2). It was her pioneering research that uncovered a wealth of hitherto hidden meaning in Indian art, which, although it had been suspected by a handful of sensitive art historians, had never previously been spelled out in terms of form and composition.

Boner has shown that in Indian iconography, sculptural panels (as opposed to freestanding sculptures) are an art form in their own right, with their own laws of composition.

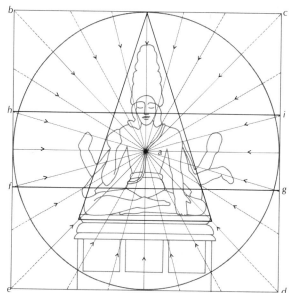

Figure D. Shiva as the Lord of Knowledge.
(After Alice Boner.)

The basic means of organizing space within the panel is the circle (*mandala*). To the ancient Indian artists, this shape was the most effective way of ordering and integrating the energies at play in the panel—giving coherence to the various structural elements, while at the same time being itself a satisfying abstract symbol of wholeness and perfection. Within the encompassing matrix of the circle the panel is organized from a point at its center, known as the "midpoint" (*madhya bindu*). In fact, the panel can be seen as "growing" organically out of this point, which is quite appropriate, since one of the most common meanings of the word *bindu* is "seed." The panel is then divided by two axes that pass through the midpoint: the horizontal axis (*madhya prastha*) and the vertical axis (*madhya sūtra*). Within the four areas thus created by the squaring of the circle, the panel is further subdivided into a network of intersecting energy lines that serve as a grid on which the composition of the tableau is constructed (Figure D). This composition, like the construction of a temple, thus becomes a *yantra*—that is, a formal and sacred organization of space into a whole in which the various component parts unite to express a particular aspect of the divine.

The *yantra* subdivisions *b-c-d-e* act to reinforce the message of the tableau. The image of Shiva is static and self-absorbed, as befits the state of meditation. The energy is centripetal:

drawn into the center from the peripheries of the panel, a movement emphasized by the contrast between the still central figure and the comparative activity of its arms and the attendant figures. The energy is drawn, as if by a magnet, to rest on the midpoint a, which falls exactly in the center of Shiva's chest. This corresponds not, as might be imagined, to the heart in the gross physical body, but to the *anāhata chakra* in the subtle body. This *chakra*, related to transcendence of the manifest world and entrance into the world of pure spirit, is used as a focus in certain meditation techniques. It is the gateway to the realm of pure Consciousness. The movement of the whole panel is thus inward and upward, which is itself the ascent of contemplation. The ascent from lower to higher is emphasized by the upward thrust of the triangular figure of Shiva. Firmly based on its throne, the great yogi's body broadens from waist to shoulder, rising like a fountain of life energy that fans out in the spread of his arms. Tne energy is not dissipated here but continues on to soar like a jet to the head and upward into the sacred tree and onward into the infinite expanse beyond. The triangle is a universal symbol of the ascent from matter to spirit; it also has a particular significance for Shaivas, who regard it as the supreme emblem of the male energy epitomized by their Lord. There is also here an allusion to the conservation of the sex energy, a technique practiced by the Shaiva yogi that leads to the state technically known as *ūrdhvaretas* ("with the energy flowing only upward").

The horizontal divisions of the tableau fall into three distinct strata. These correspond to the three realms of existence that Shiva rules. The lowest realm is earth (*bhū*). This stretches from the bottom of the panel to the mid-axis, which runs across the heads of the earth spirits that squat at the foot of Shiva's throne, and passes through his navel. The terrestrial nature of this realm d-e-f-g is emphasized by squared, subterranean cavities formed by the legs of the throne; the square being the symbol of earth and groundedness. In these caverns live the lions who guard the entrance to the depths of the unconscious mind. The middle stratum h-i-g-f signifies the subtle realms (*antariksha*): those levels of the mind that are accessible through meditation. This stratum finishes at the axis that runs across the tops of the sages' heads, for it is the sage who embodies the possibilities of this realm and who acts as a vehicle to transmit its energies down onto the earth plane. It is no accident that this axis runs through Shiva's nostrils. The lower two realms are said to be created by the Lord's life breath (*prāna*), and it is through regulation of his breath (*prānāyāma*) that the yogi releases his attention from the grip of sensory impressions to experience the subtle levels of his mind. The third stratum b-c-i-h represents the heavenly realm (*svarga*), which contains Shiva's head, the heavenly attendants, and the roots of the sacred tree ceaselessly drawing nourishment from the infinity beyond.

It is worth noting that the form of Shiva as the Lord of Knowledge is technically known as *Dakshināmūrti*: "He who faces south." The implication is that Shiva is here seated on Mount Meru, the center of the universe, high in the northern reaches of the Himālayas. From his mountain fastness, the abode of yogis and ascetics, Shiva looks down in compassion on the teeming worlds below and to the south. This is why his eyes are open.

□ *SHIVA SLAYING THE ELEPHANT DEMON* (Figure E)
Directly opposite the Lord of Knowledge is a panel that is its complement in every way. Whereas the former tableau depicts Shiva in his withdrawn state as master of meditation and esoteric knowledge, this panel celebrates the Lord's active role as the energetic destroyer of evil.

The technical name for this form of Shiva is Bhairava Gajāsura Samhāramūrti—the Wrathful Shiva Slaying the Elephant Demon. This refers to a legend (also represented in the cave temple of Elephanta; see Chapter 2) that comes from the *Purānas* (second century B.C.). The story tells how Shiva defeated the demon Andhakāsura ("Blinding Darkness"). Andhakāsura had been troubling the gods with his arrogance, and in exasperation they finally went to Shiva and beseeched his help. Meanwhile, Andhakāsura had himself gone to Shiva's home on Mount Kailāsa in order to abduct Shiva's beautiful wife Pārvatī, who was his own mother. In this unholy scheme he enlisted the help of his henchman Nīla ("the Dark Blue One"), who disguised himself as an elephant. Shiva fought and defeated Nīla and stripped off the elephant skin to use as a protective cloak. Then, taking his trident, he joined battle with Andhakāsura himself. But the demon had been granted a boon in reward for penances he had previously performed to the gods: If ever he was wounded, a replica of himself would spring up from every drop of his blood that hit the earth. Finding himself surrounded by hordes of replica demons, Shiva opened his mouth and breathed forth fire, out of which his consort (*shakti*) Yogeshvarī was born. She started to collect the drops of blood in a skullcup, before they hit the ground, and the gods sent the Seven Mother Goddesses to help her in her task. Thus Andhakāsura was unable to reproduce himself and fell victim to Shiva's mighty trident. Having slaughtered the demon, the Lord began a terrible dance of victory (*tandāva*) as a warning to all the worlds.

This is the moment depicted here. Shiva holds the elephant skin aloft in his upper four hands, its head hanging down to

Shiva as Bhairava, Slaying the Elephant Demon.

his right. The two front hands rest on his hips, as if ready to
spin his body round as it swings into the victory dance. He
holds a tusk ripped from the demon, and the two remaining
right hands hold his trident (*trishūla*) and the hourglass drum
(*damaru*)—two common Shaivite symbols. The upper left
hand holds the skullcup (*kapāla*), in which the demon's blood
was caught, and the lower one lovingly strokes Yogeshvarī.
Now that the battle is over, she is shown in her serene, peaceful aspect, sitting gracefully beside her Lord. Shiva wears the
jewelry that befits royalty, and a garland of skulls signifying
time lies across his chest. His head is flanked by celestial
companions, while below his upraised foot sit the Seven Mother
Goddesses (now headless) and between his feet his faithful
attendant, the emaciated yogi Bhringi, dances gleefully.
Historically, many of these details and indeed the legend itself
may relate to the process by which Hinduism incorporated
indigenous cults that practiced blood sacrifice and worshipped
the Mother Goddesses as fertility deities. Many of the myths
of mature Hinduism—which were not finalized until well
into the Christian era—contain elements that clearly belong
to the most ancient strata of folk religion.

The "midpoint" in this panel is the third energy center
(*manipura chakra*), which is situated between the navel and
lumbar regions. This *chakra* is associated with the element
fire, the movement of blood in the physical body, and the flow
of cosmic energy into the material world. The movement of
the panel is thus centrifugal, and the scene radiates out from
the *bindu* point *a* with explosive force.

Horizontally, the tableau is divided into the realms of heaven

Figure E. Shiva Slaying the Elephant Demon. (After Alice Boner.)

and earth by an axis *f-a-g* passing through the midpoint. The lower rectangle *f-g-d-e* shows the earth figures and is characterized by the vertical tension of these figures, Shiva's legs, the elephant head, and the sitting Yogeshvarī. The upper rectangle *b-c-g-f* contains the celestial attendants and is characterized by the movement outward into the radiating *mandala* of Shiva's arms and the fiery halo of his matted locks (*jatābhāra*). As in the previous panel there is an upward thrust of energy to be gathered into Shiva's chest, but here it explodes outward. Thus the predominant image is not one of an ascending jet of water (the lunar element of darkness and dissolution, allied to the unconscious depths of the mind) but of the rising sun (the solar element of light and creativity, allied to the conscious mind).

The upward triangle (male) has given way to the radiating star (female). This shift is emphasized by the presence of Shiva's female companions. In Hindu thought Shiva is only creative by virtue of the energy of his female consorts. While as Lord of Knowledge he was depicted in his spiritual and quiescent form as the solitary yogi, here, in his material and dynamic role as conqueror of evil, he is accompanied by both his *shakti* Yogeshvarī and the Seven Mother Goddesses.

☐

To judge from their stylistic similarity, these panels were carved by the same craftsmen. They act as a complementary pair, depicting both the active and passive aspects of the Great Lord who is himself the mysterious conjunction of all opposites.

The Upper Floor (Figure F)

Now continue through the porch and up the steps on the right, which lead to the upper floor. At the top of the stairs, turn right, and there is the Nandin pavilion (F.1). Nandin the bull is the vehicle of Shiva. His name means "giving joy." It is customary to have the vehicle of the god facing the main shrine, often housed in a separate pavilion or porch.

Now continue as far as you can and turn right. You will pass a little Ganesha on the left-hand wall—so much part of the stone that he seems to be growing out of it. Outside in

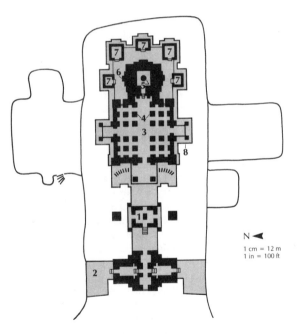

1 *Nandin pavilion.* 2 *Photo spot.* 3 Mandapa. 4 *Pillars (southern style).* 5 *Yoni-linga.* 6 *Offering bowl.* 7 *The five shrines.* 8 *Rāvana Abducting Sītā.*

Figure F. Kailāsanātha Temple, upper floor ground plan.

the fresh air, there is a balcony that provides a good spot for taking a photograph looking back into the temple itself (F.2).

Retrace your steps to the main hall (*mandapa*, F.3). On the ceiling just above the main door there is some of the original painted plaster, with charming details of elephants, reminiscent of the frescoes at Ajantā. The method used here was the same. The stone was covered with a base of straw, rice husks, and animal dung or clay, which, when hardened, provided a base for a coating of gypsum or fine white clay. This then served as the actual ground for the painting.

The *mandapa* is flat-roofed, seemingly supported on sixteen columns, arranged in groups of four. The hall extends in transepts, east-west, so the temple is roughly cruciform in plan. The pillars (F.4) are in the mature Dravidian style: with a square or polygon base supporting an octagonal shaft. Above the shaft is a fluted neck, leading to a similarly fluted bulbous cushion-capital.

You are now in what is the basic plan of any Hindu temple: a hall for the worshippers leading to an inner sanctuary. The feeling here is one of a subterranean and awesome darkness, as if you were entering the very bowels of the earth. This overwhelming atmosphere of compression drives the worshipper deep into his very self, down to the bedrock of the personality.

The shrine is again guarded by protective deities. Inside the plain, unadorned shrine is the *yoni-linga* (F.5), the symbol of Shiva's creative power. The phallic *linga* is surrounded by the *yoni*, female symbol, which holds the *linga* in its uterine grip. These make up a composite symbol known as the *yoni-linga*, which represents the totality of the male and female energies that together constitute the universe. Sometimes the top of the *linga* is carved to represent the glans of a penis or the shaft may be carved with faces of Shiva himself. The earliest artifacts from Indian civilization are seals depicting a deity with erect phallus sitting in yoga posture. This deity is the prototype of Shiva, who in some of his aspects plays the same role as the priapic Bacchus and Dionysius of the ancient classical world.

The *yoni-linga* is worshipped by lustration with holy water, milk, and clarified butter—a feminine ritual, stressing amniotic creativity and the liquid beginnings of life.

When a temple is under worship, the devotees bring their offerings—flowers, fruit, coconuts, *kum-kum* paste, sandalwood paste, money—and present them to the officiating priest, who is the only person allowed in the holy of holies. He offers them to the *linga*, chants the appropriate *mantras*, and performs libation. Some of the *kum-kum* is put on the worshipper's forehead as a sign that he or she has been blessed by the divinity. In addition, the mere sight (*darshana*) of the cult image is believed to convey great blessings. And there is no doubt that a place becomes holy partly by being considered so; worshippers bring a feeling of devotion to a shrine, and the feeling stays. After seeing the *linga*, you can proceed with the circumambulation.

The liquid used for lustration drains out of the sanctuary through the *yoni* and collects in the stone bowl outside (F. 6). The devotees can take it from here, drink it, or put it on their heads. So the symbolism of rebirth is here reenacted very graphically and would have great meaning to a mind uncluttered by the constant bombardment of impressions that swamp the intuitive sensitivity of modern man.

Around the back of the *garbha-griha* are five small shrines (*pancharatha;* F.7), each a replica of the main temple, elegantly reduced. Such subsidiary structures are often part of the later temple complexes. They serve to radiate the spiritual influence of the sanctum to all directions, as do the chapels that flank the apse of a Gothic cathedral. Their delicacy contrasts dramatically with the mass of unhewn rock behind.

There is some fine carving of blissful celestial figures on the back wall of the main shrine and the plaster is well preserved, giving us an idea of how the whole temple must have looked originally. No wonder the Muslims called it "the colored palace."

Continue around, back into the main hall, and walk through to the balcony opening off the southern transept (F.8). On your right, up on the wall beyond the door guardian, you will see what is one of the most exquisite cameos of this site: Rāvana Abducting Sītā.

This is the episode that sparked off the Trojan War of India, related in the *Rāmāyana*. The wily demon Rāvana plotted to kidnap Sītā, the beautiful young wife of his archenemy, Rāma, and add her to his *haram* in Lankā. So he asked his uncle, a magician, to assume the form of a golden deer and stroll past the forest hermitage where Rāma and Sītā were living in exile from the court of Ayudhyā. Sītā was so entranced by the deer that she begged her husband to go and fetch it for her. The ruse succeeded; while Rāma was away, Rāvana kidnapped his wife, taking her back in his flying chariot to his island kingdom of Lankā. Hearing Sītā's cries as they left the hermitage, the king of the birds flew to help her. He attacked Rāvana, but the demon showed no mercy and, as this panel with its sweeping movement shows, cut him down. Fortunately for the world, the bird king lived long enough to tell Rāma all that had happened, and after a long war, Sītā was eventually rescued.

□

Rāvana Abducting Sītā.

You can now return through the *mandapa*, down the stairs back to the courtyard. Our journey to the sacred mountain Kailāsa has been completed: You are ready to return transfigured, to the mundane world of mortals.

Cave 32

This cave is Jain, dedicated to Mahāvīra ("the Great Hero"), the last of the twenty-four saints (*tīrthankaras*) of Jainism. He was a contemporary of the Buddha in the sixth century B.C. and is actually believed to have studied under spiritual teachers with him. For a full description of Jainism, see Chapter 5. The most famous Rāshtrakūta king, Amoghavarsha (A.D. 815–877), adopted the Jain faith and was a generous patron of the Digambara ("the sky-clad") sect, who went naked and practiced austerities. This gave a tremendous impetus to the spread of Jainism in the western Deccan, which resulted in the decline of the power and influence of Buddhism.

Although the nucleus of the Jain religion is an extremely ascetic monastic order, their temples and sanctuaries are often profusely carved. This one is late (ca. 1100) and truly baroque, as we can see from what is the final phase of the vase-and-foliage pillar. The courtyard is especially interesting here; the combination of massive chunks of rock and ornately carved figures adding drama to the entrance. The carvings on the level of the first (U.S. second) floor balcony are very beautiful: animals, flying couples, and demigods. There is an exceptionally fine serpent king (*nāgarāja*) just below the balcony on the north wall, on the left as you enter.

Jainism shares many of the deities and symbols of Hinduism. As you come up the steps to the first floor, Matanga the god of wealth, a form of Shiva, is directly in front of you, seated on an elephant. He, through the "elephant power" (*mātangī*) establishes peace and prosperity on earth. Opposite him is a buxom fertility goddess, Sidhaika, surmounted by a tree laden with fruit. As with the Kailāsa temple, these figures promise material well-being to the devotee who enters the temple, and dissipate the worshipper's anxieties.

Inside the main hall there is a massive lotus on the ceiling, the ubiquitous image of enlightenment. The main shrine contains a well-proportioned image of Mahāvīra, with his emblem, the lion, underneath. Mahāvīra is flanked by door guardians of earlier *tīrthankaras*. On the left is Parshvanātha, the twenty-third *tīrthankara*; the snake's hood, representing the raised *kundalinī* and esoteric knowledge, serves the same protective and iconographic function as the *bodhi* tree or parasol of the Buddha. The right-hand guardian is an earlier saint, Gomeshvara, who is portrayed with a tree growing up around his legs. Again, as in Buddhism, the tree represents the cosmic knowledge and paradisical natural state of the enlightened being.

Cave 32—interior.

4

AJANTĀ

THE FLOWERING
OF BUDDHIST ART

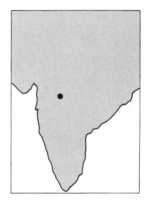

The town of Aurangābād sits right in the middle of Mahārāshtra State. It was once a provincial capital of the Mughals
and is named after the least loved of that dynasty, the fanatical Aurangzeb, who is buried here. Apart from his tomb, and
a couple of other Muslim monuments, present-day Aurangabād has little to commend it and hardly seems to warrant its
traditional importance as a revered place of Muslim pilgrimage and devotion. Nevertheless, almost everyone who comes
to India will pass through this dusty little town, for it is the
stepping stone to one of the country's most famous sites: the
caves of Ajantā.

As you leave Aurangābād and travel north, the country grows
progressively more deserted. Fertile fields of sugarcane, maize,
and cotton soon give way to scorched plain and dry scrub.
The few farmers you see seem to grow out of the very landscape, their sinewy limbs as gnarled and knotted as the twisted
stumps of dried-out trees that line the road. They are using
the most ancient methods to plow and water the parched
land. Bullock carts creak and sway along the road ahead.
Each ramshackle, mountainous load is topped by a figure
swathed in white cotton, crowned with an orange or cerise
turban of such brilliance that it almost hurts the eye. These
carts have all the patient unconcern of rural India, as they
lurch along with a rhythm that is somehow both graceful and

ungainly, their wooden wheels splayed out at fantastic angles. The road runs straight through a land that is flat, dusty, and unrelieved.

Little seems to have changed here since the Buddha walked the earth, five hundred years before Christ. Then, suddenly, after endless miles, a steep bluff rears up ahead. The heat is intense, and in the shimmering haze the bluff could well be a mirage, cruelly mocking the weary traveler with a promise of shelter. But no, it is real enough, as it curls around in on itself, protecting at its heart a steep, horseshoe-shaped ravine,

General view of the caves.

overlooking the Waghora River, which winds its way through the rocky gorge below. Cut into the side of this ravine are thirty caves. In their cool, silent shadows are hidden the most lovely and important Buddhist paintings in existence—the murals of Ajantā.

It is only comparatively recently that Ajantā has become a major tourist attraction. In the early years of the century only the most hardy and determined traveler managed to reach the place. In those days the journey involved twelve bone-shaking hours by bullock cart from the nearest railhead, followed by a four-hour scramble up to the caves themselves. The surrounding country was inhospitable and dangerous. The local tribe, the Bhīls, usually attacked strangers. Wild animals abounded—in fact the early expeditions tied white rags to bushes, as markers to warn where someone had recently been killed by a tiger. Worst of all, apparently, were the local bees. Ferocious colonies clustered in the ravine and often made it impossible to get to the caves. The first parties had to be accompanied by professional "bee exterminators," and there are stories of learned archeologists diving into the river to escape an enraged swarm.

Nowadays, of course, all this has changed. Daily buses ply in and out of the car park area beneath the caves. Crowds flock from Bombay or faraway Delhi. As always, it is the clusters of women who catch the eye: In their gorgeously colored *sārīs* they bustle and flutter like tropical birds. The weathered stone steps are thronged with chattering crocodiles of freshly scrubbed schoolchildren, wide-eyed with wonder, their thick black hair smoothed down with glistening coconut oil. Everywhere there is excitement and festivity: "At last! We've made it to Ajantā!"

Yet despite the twentieth century—the visitors, the hawkers, and the buses—Ajantā retains a powerful atmosphere, and when the people have gone and peace returns, its spirit emerges once more. Local legend says that the ravine has always been the abode of a particularly powerful *nāgarāja* god; at the twilight hours of dawn and dusk, you can believe it. Once you enter the caves, the outside world drops away; you are in another realm. The charm of this new world seeps into the mind surreptitiously and plants a strange seed, which, as it sprouts, will render ever more blurred the shifting boundary between illusion and reality.

Strictly speaking, the caves are not caves at all, but temples, hollowed out of the living rock. They were excavated by generations of Buddhist monks. Since 200 B.C. the Ajantā ravine had been a great monastic center. Initially it was used only as a shelter from the ravages of the monsoon, for the Buddha had instructed his disciples to lead an itinerant life, teaching the Truth (*dharma*) and living off charity. During the summer months they would set up a *vihāra*, which literally means "rainy season retreat." These shelters were made of bamboo, wood, and brick. They became the first permanent architectural structures of the new faith, fixed points on the pilgrimage paths along which the ocher-robed order traveled. The *vihāras* were usually situated on, or near, the trade routes, for the mendicant monks depended from the start on the goodwill of the community and the patronage of the merchant classes. Low down on the brahminical social scale, as fixed by the caste system, the merchants eagerly embraced the new religion, which taught that salvation comes from one's own efforts and understanding rather than one's birth or inherited status.

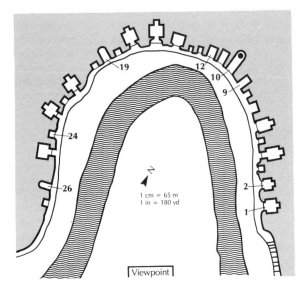

Figure A. Ajantā caves site plan.

In time the *vihāras* became well-established centers for the monastic community (*sangha*). Simultaneously another great Buddhist structure evolved, the chapel-shrine (*chaitya*). The *chaityas* were for worship, whereas the *vihāras* were principally for living. Both these types of architecture are well represented at Ajantā, and we can trace their development over several centuries.

Of the thirty caves here, five are *chaityas* (Caves 9, 10, 19, 26, and 29), and the other twenty-five are *vihāras*. They can also be divided chronologically into two groups. The earlier group (8, 9, 10, 12, 13, and 15A) belong to the Hīnayāna sect of Buddhism and are assigned to the second century B.C. The remainder belong to the Mahāyāna sect, and date from about A.D. 450 to 650.

Since the very earliest times, India has been honeycombed with natural and man-made caves. As in Egypt and Irān, they were used by anchorites for their solitary lives of contemplation. They were easy to maintain and relatively immune to the extremes of the Indian climate—cool in summer, warm in winter. Caves were permanent, or at least as permanent as anything can be in this ever-changing universe the Buddhists call *samsāra*. To the Buddhist as to the Hindu, the cave was an island of retreat and refuge from which to better understand the unstable and illusory world of flux. The monks dug, carved, and decorated with marvelous patience and skill here over a period of eight hundred years. Then, sometime in the seventh century, they abandoned the place. No one knows why.

By A.D. 650 Buddhism was already on the wane in India, deferring to a Hindu renaissance that flourished until the Islamic invasions that began in earnest in the eleventh century. Perhaps the patronage ran out; perhaps there was plague or persecution. Whatever the reason, Ajantā lay forgotten for twelve hundred years, lost to the world and hidden under creepers, shrubs, and jungle. Wild animals took over the caves, rain soaked and crumbled the walls, and most of the shrines were completely silted up.

Then, in 1819, it was rediscovered. A party of British army officers, attached to the Madras Army, were on exercises in the nearby Indhyahadri Hills. One free day, a group of them went hunting in the Ajantā area, famed for its wild animals. Following the riverbed in search of game, they met a local boy who insisted that the gorge below was full of tigers' lairs. He took them to the promontory that overlooks the curving ravine, now marked by the Viewpoint. Looking down into the ravine, a soldier suddenly noticed something peeping out above the tangled jungle below. It was the top of the facade of Cave 10.

It was some time before the importance of the find was fully appreciated. A dry paper read by a Mr. William Erskine to the Bombay Literary Society in 1822 described the caves as "having sitting figures with curled wigs. No traces of the Brahminical religion were discovered. The paintings were in a decent state of preservation."

A more enthusiastic visitor arrived in 1823. This was Lieutenant Alexander of the 16th Lancers. He had to run the gauntlet of the Bhīls: "They were a most savage-looking race," he tells us, "perfectly black, low in stature and almost naked. Our firearms prevented them from attacking us; and we were allowed to proceed unmolested." Alexander visited many of the caves and was delighted by "their marvellous freshness of colour." Other visitors came and went, many of them chipping off souvenirs from the frescoed walls. Gradually the caves attracted scholarly attention. In 1843 the famous architectural historian, James Fergusson, visited Ajantā and was worried by the combined attacks of the elements and the souvenir hunters. He begged the East India Company (which still had control of the area) to do something to preserve and protect the paintings "before decay and the recklessness of tourists has entirely obliterated them."

His plea resulted in the appointment of Captain Robert Gill, an artist attached to the Madras Army, whose brief was to copy all he could of the frescoes. Gill arrived in Ajantā in 1844 and spent the rest of his life there. He was utterly devoted to the place; the elemental hillside became his Walden.

Gill was indefatigable. He photographed the frescoes with a magnesium lamp; made painstaking tracings, copies, and colored drawings; painted by the flickering light of oil lamps.

For twenty-seven years he lived there. He spurned a comfortable bungalow in the Ajantā village, preferring to sleep in the caves themselves, or in a makeshift thatched hut he built himself on the hillside. He lived in constant danger from the Bhīls and the wild animals; in fact he is reputed to have shot 150 tigers with his own gun. Happily there was one relief from his dedicated life of austerity. He fell in love with, and married, a dark-eyed local beauty. In the evenings, after a day spent painting, he would watch her dance, as she moved with the same feline grace that animated his beloved frescoes.

They say there is a curse on Ajantā. Many years ago Indra, the King of Heaven, allowed the other gods and goddesses to descend to earth for one night's celebration, on the condition that they returned to heaven before the cock crowed the dawn. They came to Ajantā, and so great were their revels that they quite forgot the cock's warning crow. As a punishment they were frozen into the walls and statues of the caves, and there they will remain for all eternity. Yet despite their transgression, these foolish gods are still divine. Any mere mortal who tries to deface, or even reproduce, their fallen forms, will meet with untold misfortune.

Gill certainly had his share. He suffered intermittent illness, once nearly dying of dysentery. In 1857, during the Mutiny, he was forced to leave the caves. Shortly after his return he fell while climbing, broke his leg, and was out of action for many weeks. As he finished each batch of paintings, he had it shipped to London from Bombay. After twenty years' solitary work, he had virtually completed the mammoth task of copying all the most important paintings of Ajantā. All the facsimiles were gathered together in the Crystal Palace to be exhibited to the public. Then, in December 1866, the Palace was destroyed by fire. Three or four of Gill's paintings were saved, the rest went up in flames.

After the fire Gill struggled on for five years, but he was a broken man. In the end he sold off what was left of his drawings and equipment for a few pounds. Soon after he became ill and died. He is buried in the little cemetery of Bhusawal, just north of the caves he had loved so fruitlessly.

But at least the rest of the world was now aware of the immense importance of the site. In the 1870s the Bombay School of Arts sent out a team to the caves under its principal, John Griffiths. The team spent four seasons copying the paintings. As the facsimiles were finished, they were shipped back to London. Mindful of his predecessor's fate, Griffiths urged his London sponsors to photograph the paintings as they arrived. Unfortunately, the expense involved was considered too great. The paintings were stored in the annex of the Victoria and Albert Museum in Kensington. In 1885 fire broke out. Eighty-seven of the paintings—many of them canvases over thirty feet (nine meters) square—were destroyed. The extraordinary thing was, that though the fire raged for more than three hours throughout the large building, the only objects of value that were damaged were the Ajantā facsimiles.

In 1918 a team of Japanese Buddhist artists, under the leadership of Professor Sawamura, head of the Oriental Arts Department of Kyoto University, arrived at Ajantā. Their concern was primarily with the carvings. Their technique was to dampen rice paper and press it against the stone to obtain an exact impression from which reproduction molds could be made. Hundreds of these delicate casts were made and carefully shipped back to Japan. A few years later they were all destroyed by an earthquake.

Throughout the years the souvenir hunters continued to desecrate the frescoes, often cutting out whole slabs of painting. Some of these later found their way into the world's great collections. But things took a turn for the better in 1920. A lover of Indian culture, Lady Herringham, alerted the Nizām of Hyderabād, under whose jurisdiction Ajantā was, to the deterioration in the murals. On her advice he had two Italian restorers brought out: a Signor Cecconi and his assistant. They undertook work to fix the remaining paintings to the wall, principally by injecting casein into them. At the same time leaks in the caves were plugged, lights installed, and an effective guard system established. But the curse of Ajantā was operating, nonetheless. The Griffiths expedition had applied varnish to the paintings to render them more visible, and the two Italians now applied a coating of shellac and alcohol as a fixative. These varnishes gradually darkened with the years. In time they became increasingly opaque and then cracked, trapping dust between the layer of varnish and the actual surface of the paintings. Thus the paintings were again vulnerable to the damage by seepage, humidity, and bat urine that had plagued them since they were discovered.

Ajantā has been under the care of the Archeological Survey of India since 1951. Recent preservation work has been intensive. Flaked portions are shaved off, stains removed, and the paintings strengthened by a mixture of solvents to arrest further deterioration. Preservatives such as polyvinyl acetate are being applied. In the course of this work several new paintings have been uncovered, notably in Caves 6 and 17.

The original entrance to the caves was along the riverbed, each cave having a flight of stairs leading up to it. The first to be excavated was Cave 10. Then came the other Hīnayāna sanctuaries spreading out to either side of it. The Mahāyāna caves were added later on the ends of the existing crescent.

The caves have been numbered consecutively from the western entrance; their numbers bear no relationship to their dates. Although nearly all of them contain something of interest, on a short visit Caves 10, 9, 12, 19, 24 (unfinished), 26, 2, and 1 should be seen. If they are viewed in this order, the development of Buddhist rock-cut architecture becomes plain to see.

Cave 10 (Figure B)
Hīnayāna,
Second Century B.C.

The first cave to be excavated, Cave 10 is the archetypal Hīnayāna *chaitya*. The entrance is a massive arch, now covered by a screen of wood and

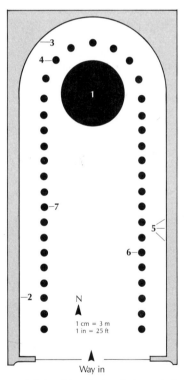

1 *The* stūpa. **2** *Painted inscription dating paintings.* **3** *The Rāja and His Retinue.* **4** *The Buddha with Two Attendants.* **5** *The* Chhaddanta jātaka. **6** *Buddha and the One-Eyed Monk.* **7** *Gautama the Buddha.*

Figure B. Cave 10—interior.

wire. This screen would originally have been made of plaited bamboo and thatch; it served to keep out the birds, bats, and animals. The first thing the architects would have done is to score out a rectangle on the rockface and then carve the arch within it, working from the top downward. The Hīnayāna shrines were generally plain and unadorned; the little Buddha figures to the right of the doorway are later Mahāyāna additions.

The Stūpa (Figure B.1)

As you walk into the huge chapel, your attention is caught by the cult object at the far end—the miniature *stūpa*. *Stūpas,* derived from pre-Buddhist funerary mounds, were focuses of pilgrimage for the early Buddhists (see Chapter 1). Often very large (for example, at Sānchī, Chapter 14), they contained the ashes of a Buddhist saint or revered teacher and were reproduced in miniature and enshrined in the *chaitya* as a symbol of the faith.

Here the *stūpa* is quite massive—a two-tiered drum that supports the spherical *anda* mound. On top of this dome rests the *harmikā,* modeled on the kiosk that contained the relic shrine in the larger *stūpas.* Around this shrine a wooden railing was erected in the original structures; here it has been reproduced in stone. Above the railings a "*chaitya* window" motif is carved. Originally inspired by the shape of the leaf of the *bodhi* tree, under which the Buddha attained *nirvāna,* this motif was to recur frequently in Buddhist art, especially as the principal design for cave facades. Surmounting the *anda* is the beginnings of the *chhattra,* the flattened honorific umbrella that was to assume a complex of symbolic meanings: the sign of royalty, the sacred tree under which the Buddha (like the village elders before him) sat, the dome of the heavens, and the thousand-petaled lotus that crowns the head of the enlightened being.

As well as its localized references to the burial mound and the funeral urn, the *stūpa* was the outcome of the Buddhist artists' struggle to represent something very abstract—the blissful state of *nirvāna.* Even if the Master had not been reluctant to describe the state, it would have been difficult to convey it in figurative art. Relying on unconscious intuition, the early architects evolved the *stūpa,* with its symbolic associations of the *anda,* the cosmic egg that is the universal symbol of spiritual death and resurrection. This regenerative motif was combined with images that were already pregnant with meaning for the Indian psyche: the sacred tree and its variants. Nevertheless, the whole effect of the *stūpa* is still one of abstract plenitude, a fullness of potential that is already mysteriously latent in us. This power is given awesome weight by the very size of the cave here; the merely human is dwarfed by the austerely plain hall, centered on the immense symbol of the eternal *dharma*.

The Ceiling

The cave itself, as well as the *stūpa*, shows some interesting archaic motifs. Most important of these is the ceiling. This was originally covered with a network of wooden beams and rafters, curved across the ceiling to form a wooden "backbone" to the cave. The slots that held the beams in place can be seen where the pillars join the ceiling, at the level of the cornice. This design was in conscious imitation of the earlier, freestanding shrines of wood and thatch. Already the Buddhist architects were showing the conservatism that characterizes all sacred, and especially Indian, art. In copying an earlier form, they were unconsciously harking back to the day when the Master was among them. This imitative style is also seen in the pillars that separate the nave from the aisles. They lean inward and resemble an avenue of trees, leading up to the *stūpa* at the end. After about the first century A.D. the caves no longer contained wooden beams, though they continued to be mimicked in stone as a decoration. We can see the beginnings of this transition in the vaulted roofs of the aisles here, which contain purely stone imitations of their wooden originals.

The Murals

Cave 10 also has some remains of murals. These can be classified into two groups. The early, Hīnayāna, work was done very shortly after the cave was completed. We know this from a painted record in the cave itself (left-hand wall, opposite the third pillar (Figure B.2). The later, Mahāyāna, painting, which often overlays the original, was added about six hundred years later, when the second phase of cave building was at its height. Many of the Hīnayāna caves were painted and decorated afresh at this time.

The main subjects of the Hīnayāna painting were the *jātaka* ("birth stories"), stories of the Buddha in his previous incarnations. The fabulous pantheon of the Mahāyāna, with its *bodhisattvas* and divine beings, had not yet been developed. These early paintings are also interesting for the details they reveal about the styles of dress and architecture of the period.

☐ *THE RĀJA AND HIS RETINUE* (Figure B.3)
On the rear wall of the left-hand aisle is a frieze entitled The Rāja and His Retinue. Here you see a king accompanied by ten ladies and a child, approaching the sacred *bodhi* tree to

pay it homage. This is a common theme in Buddhist art; no doubt each new patron identified with the original kings and merchants who supported the Master and his Order. The women are wearing jewelry, including bangles of ivory and conch shell, which cover almost the entire forearm. This style is still to be observed today all over the Deccan. Some of the ladies are wearing the bright *tikka* mark on their foreheads. The scarves and veils over the womens' heads are also noticeable. The Rāja is allied to the fabulous serpent king, by the way his jeweled headdress and topknot rise up over his head like the hood of the *nāga*.

On the other side of the *bodhi* tree are a lively group of musicians and dancers. They are elegant and carefree; their joy seems uninhibited. Their features are dark and rounded, identifying them as the indigenous tribal people of the northwest Deccan (in other words, around Ajantā). Altogether the energy of this soft-hued group is perfectly expressive of the unfettered tribal life of the times.

□ *THE BUDDHA WITH TWO ATTENDANTS* (Figure B.4)
The later phase of painting introduces a northern influence into the original Deccan style of representation. You can see this in a superb group of The Buddha with Two Attendants, on the eighteenth pillar of the left-hand aisle. Here the topmost attendant is pale in complexion and his robes are in the northern style, whereas the lower one is dark and holds the tribal necklace as an offering. All three figures display a languid grace that is a hallmark of the Ajantān style. They are shown on a forest floor, carpeted with flowers; the atmosphere is one of paradise, where all opposites are reconciled.

□ *THE CHHADDANTA JĀTAKA* (Figure B.5)
On the right-hand aisle wall, behind pillars 2 to 12, stretches a long frieze of the *Chhaddanta jātaka* (see page 350 for the story). Although the fable is not depicted chronologically, it is possible to make out its main details: Chhaddanta's life in the Himālayas, his favorite spot under the *banyan* tree, the hunting of the six-tusked elephant and the removal of the tusks, and, finally, the death of the vengeful queen. The frieze is full of the love of life and nature, depicted in beautifully observed detail. But it is the elephants that steal the show. As in the Sānchī sculptures, the artist here has managed to convey all the ponderous dignity of these noble creatures, as they graze, walk with their swinging gait, or apprehensively watch the movements of the hunters out of the corners of their gentle eyes. Although the composition is crowded, there is no feeling that the animals are restrained within the confines of the frieze. It is altogether a masterly achievement.

The Pillars

Lastly, the pillars themselves are worth studying, since they have some fine examples of the later phase of painting. The fifth, sixth, and seventh pillars in the right-hand aisle have some graceful figures of *bodhisattvas* in pink and white. Especially noteworthy is the exquisitely rendered Buddha and the One-Eyed Monk, on the sixth pillar (Figure B.6). The features and flowing robe of the Master show clear traces of the northern style of Gandhāra (Greco-Buddhist) art. This hybrid style lasted from the second to the sixth century A.D. and was the result of Greek influence in what is now Afghānistān and northern Pakistān over the three centuries before Christ. This Gandhāran style is even more obvious in the figure of the Monk, with the graceful folds of his toga and his fair features. The hands, feet, and faces of these two are lyrically depicted in the best traditions of classical Buddhist art.

The most impressive painting in the left-hand aisle is on the ninth pillar (B.7). This is a seated figure of Gautauma the Buddha, white-robed and simple. His gaze is serene and lucid, cutting through the world of illusion like a laser.

Cave 9—exterior.

Cave 9
Hīnayāna,
First Century B.C.

This *chaitya* shows certain stylistic developments over Cave 10, though its overall proportions are not as pleasing. The facade is particularly interesting, since it shows a clear example of the *chaitya* arch transposed to form the principal window of the sanctuary. The arch is ribbed and would originally have been screened with wooden latticework. You can get an idea of this from the five miniature *chaitya* window motifs above the cornice over the doorway and those above the window itself. This use of the *chaitya* window motif, or bull's-eye (*gavāksha*), in various sizes was to continue throughout the centuries, both as a structural and decorative theme. It was incorporated into much Hindu architecture as well.

The *stūpa* at the center of the apse has also developed. The *anda* has become globular, and the *harmikā* has been extended upward into the shape of an inverted pyramid. When the *chaitya* was in use, there were two wooden umbrellas (*chhattras*) surmounting the *harmikā*, as can be inferred from the sockets that held the shafts.

The vaulted ceiling of the nave and apse was originally crossed by wooden beams, as in Cave 10, though the aisle ceilings here are flat, not arched. The pillars are also similar to those of Cave 10: octagonal, slightly tapering, and inclined inward.

Cave 12
Hīnayāna,
Second Century B.C.

The earliest of the *vihāras*, this is a flat-ceilinged hall almost thirty-six feet (eleven meters) square. Whatever the front wall or facade was, it has entirely disappeared. The remaining three walls contain four cells each; each cell has two raised "beds" of stone, on which the monks slept and did private meditation. As the holes for hinges in the sills and lintels show, each cell would have had a wooden door. The four recesses around the walls would have been for utensils such as lamps or for manuscripts. The narrow doorways to the cells are topped by the *gavāksha* window motif, as are the ledges between the doors. Although these living quarters were once painted, their utter simplicity of design is a clear illustration of the life their inhabitants led.

Cave 12—entrance to monk's cell.

Cave 19

Mahāyāna,
Fifth Century A.D.

Cave 19 is a fully developed *chaitya*, belonging to the golden age of Buddhist art, the Gupta period (A.D. 320–650). You are immediately struck by the ornateness of the facade. The lotiform *chaitya* window is still in evidence as the principal source of light, though below it there is now a portico, supported on richly carved Dravidian pillars with squashed-cushion capitals. You will see more of these pillars inside. But the main development is in the profuse decoration of the wall surface. Every inch seems covered with carving. Niches are filled with standing or sitting *buddhas* and *bodhisattvas*, all carved in high relief. The arrangement of these figures is more or less symmetrical, and they represent the heavenly hosts of divine beings that make up the Mahāyāna pantheon. These beings, according to the Mahāyāna, intercede for mankind and generally look after his spiritual welfare. As such, they are a Buddhist equivalent of the ancient Indian hosts of gods and goddesses and are quite alien to the early Hīnayāna teaching, the simplicity and austerity of which is mirrored in its architecture. As with a Hindu temple, the architects' idea was to overwhelm the pilgrim with the majesty of the heavenly hosts, so that a visit to the shrine would be like a glimpse into the realms of the divine.

The assembled deities also serve to project a sort of positive force field around the temple, warding off any evil or negative influences. This protective role is clearly seen in the two guardian figures who flank the *chaitya* window. Their heavy, muscular bodies are intended to convey their spiritual strength. Here, as often in Indian art, esthetic considerations are not as important as functional ones. The figures are actually quite disproportionate: with bulging shoulders and trunklike legs. But this distortion is intentional, because their job is to display *power*, not beauty or grace. Nevertheless, their faces are suffused with a dreamy softness that is a hallmark of the Gupta style, and which you will be seeing more of later. The standing *bodhisattvas* are shown in *dāna mudrā*, the gesture of generosity: right arm hanging down with the palm extended outward. The seated *buddhas* are shown in the gesture of teaching, or Setting in Motion the Wheel of Truth (*dharma-chakra mudrā*). This style of covering the entire wall surface with *buddha* images was one aspect of Buddhist art to be copied extensively in the Chinese rock-cut sanctuaries, especially during the Tang dynasty (A.D. 620–910).

Another important detail on the facade is the miniature *chaitya* window as an ornamental cameo, eight to nine inches (twenty to twenty-three centimeters) high. A smaller version of the *gavāksha* you saw in Caves 9 and 10, this is known as the *kūdu*. *Kūdu* contain a face, animal, or loving couple

Cave 19—exterior.

Cave 19—detail of facade, showing guardian figure surmounted by kūdus *and* buddhas.

(*mithuna*). The Hindu temples of Bhubaneshwar (see Chapter 19) are covered with similar designs, adopted from Buddhist architecture in Orissā.

The Entrance Courtyard

Set into the left-hand wall of the small entrance courtyard is a panel of a serpent king (*nāgarāja*) and his queen, together with an attendant. All three figures have the supple grace of Gupta bodies. There is something utterly effortless about their stances, and the group is one of the masterpieces of Ajantā. Iconographically they are also significant, as they show the reemergence of archaic Indian symbols into the mainstream of Buddhist art. The serpent king may be a reference to Muchalinda, who sheltered the Buddha with his seven hoods at Bodh Gayā (see Chapter 18), or it may be a representation of the particularly powerful *nāga* spirit that was believed to rule the Ajantā ravine. Esoterically, the panel represents wholeness: the unity of the male and female aspects of the psyche.

The Interior

The initial impression of ornateness is confirmed by the baroque interior of the *chaitya*. The doorjambs are carved with a scroll, and the pillars of the aisles are decorated with bands of foliate ornament. Their shape has also changed: Now they have a square base leading to an octagonal section, which in turn leads to a round shaft. This shaft is "supported" by *ganas* (fertility spirits) and fluted either vertically or horizontally. At the top is a lotiform cushion neck that supports a bracket-shaped capital. The center piece of this capital is a seated *buddha*, and he is flanked by celestial musicians (*gandharvas*), nymphs (*apsarases*), and couples. These capitals are so close together as to form an almost continuous molded "frieze" around the nave. This frieze is topped by a triforium, with alternate seated and standing *buddha*s, separated by panels of scrollwork, interwoven with animal and human figures. Not only were all the surfaces intricately carved; it is clear from remaining traces that they were brightly painted too.

The ceiling is again ribbed with mock wooden beams in stone, the right-hand side showing traces of the original ceiling decoration.

The Stūpa

The *stūpa* continues its metamorphosis. The shape has changed from the grounded, circular drum of Cave 10 to a

Cave 19—interior, showing stūpa.

spirelike structure, full of vertical tension. It is now a richly carved monolith that reaches almost to the vaulted ceiling. The drum has been elongated, the *anda* shrunk, and the *harmikā* relic box stretched. Above this towers a three-tiered *chhattra* umbrella; each tier stands on its own drum and is supported by heavenly figures. The whole *stūpa* is crowned by the *kalasha* vase, filled with the nectar of immortality. The later the *stūpa*, the more important the *chhattra* portion becomes. Here it occupies half the height of the whole structure. This trend was continued in the Mahāyāna sects of the Himālayan countries. In Tibet and Nepāl, for example, the *chhattras* became very ornate and were often gold-plated or painted and hung with brightly colored cloth.

The development of the *stūpa* exactly parallels the development of the Mahāyāna teaching, with its celestial *buddhas* and its intricate pantheon. The multiple *buddha* images we see in this cave are illustrations of the myriad hosts known as the "Buddhas of All Directions," described in the Lotus of the Good Law (*Saddharma Pundarīka*), an influential Mahāyāna text of the third century. Moreover, the *sūtra* describes many fabulous structures that exist in the various heavenly realms. These were no doubt a divine model for the *stūpa*. In its towering ascendancy toward the heavens, the *stūpa* reflects the way the Mahāyāna moved toward a fantastic realm of magical belief. The Hīnayāna was uncompromisingly down to earth; it conducted the sober analysis of the here-and-now that the Master advocated. The later Mahāyāna, like the *stūpas* it inspired, ascended into the clouds.

Cave 24
Mahāyāna,
Sixth Century A.D.,
unfinished

This unfinished monastery would have been one of the largest and grandest at Ajantā had it been completed. As it is, the *vihāra* is worth study for one or two details of carving and, more importantly, for the light it sheds on the method of excavation employed by the monks here.

The verandah pillars have been largely restored, but there is some fine detailed carving on the original fragments that survive. Especially noteworthy is the right pilaster, the bracket capital of which is adorned with a vase-and-foliage motif (*pūrnaghata*) over which float a number of seemingly weightless couples (*mithunas*) representing the heavenly hosts. Neither of these themes is uncommon, but the delicacy and assurance with which they are depicted here are tantalizing evidence of the skill the Ajantān sculptors had developed by this time. The lintel of the door has a lovely frieze of flying figures, the two central ones holding a crown between them.

The interior of the *vihāra* shows how the caves were excavated. Once the facade had been incised and dug out, the work continued from the top downward, so that the ceiling was the first part of the sanctuary to be finished. The shrine was completed next, and at the appropriate places, columns of rough rock were left intact to be sculpted into pillars. The floor was the last part to be completed.

Quarrying, dressing, finishing, and painting went on simultaneously. Of the twenty pillars here, only one, to the right of the entrance, is almost finished. The carving on it, like the details of the facade, shows a high degree of skill and taste.

The cave shows a considerable advance on the early *vihāra* of Cave 12. It is much larger, the hall is pillared, and, most important, it contains a shrine at its far end. Here there is Buddha, seated in *bhadrāsana*, surrounded by attendants and flying figures. As the Mahāyāna developed, the *vihāras*, like the *chaityas*, became increasingly ornate. They also included carved figures of the Buddha and various deities for worship, as well as being profusely painted. We shall see the consummate examples of the extended *vihāra* in Caves 1 and 2.

The abandoned shrine is a subterranean graveyard, hewn out of prehistoric darkness. The uncarved stone lies in heaps around the floor like sleeping mammoths that will never waken. One thing that does emerge clearly from this cave is that the rock-cut shrine is an architecture of *mass*. As such it operates in quite a different way from the church or cathedral. These may induce an unconscious tension when you enter, as an instinctive response to the tensile stress of the building. The cave, on the other hand, induces, or rather forces, you to relax. It is as if the whole weight of the rock is bearing down, almost crushing the breath out of you. The total relaxation resulting from the body's natural response to the dynamics of the cave is, of course, exactly appropriate to its purpose, which is to foster a calmness conducive to meditation. Entering the bowels of the earth is a perfect physical preparation for delving into the depths of the mind. It is no coincidence that the yogis call the very deepest levels of meditative awareness "entering the cave of the heart."

Cave 26
Mahāyāna,
Sixth Century A.D.

A late *chaitya*. By now the ornamentation has become too florid and threatens to overwhelm the general symmetry of the cave. The *stūpa* has been virtually relegated to the background, and most emphasis is paid to the elongated drum on which it rests.

This huge drum is carved with a seated Buddha figure, in the European sitting position with legs down (*bhadrāsana*). The legs are somewhat out of proportion with the top half of the body; the whole is reminiscent of the Buddha of Cave 10 at Ellorā. The rest of the drum is profusely decorated with *bodhisattvas*, various attendants, and *ganas*.

Though the cave is perhaps too baroque, it contains two redeeming sculptured panels. These are both on the eastern wall.

□ *THE RECLINING BUDDHA*
Nearest the door is the celebrated figure of the Reclining Buddha. This is the *mahāparinirvāna*, or death, of the Master. *Nirvāna* itself is in no way to be confused with death, as far too many "scholars" continue to think. The Buddhist goal of *nirvāna* is enlightenment in life, whereas death is specifically known as "the great state beyond *nirvāna*" (*mahā·pari·nirvāna*).

The twenty-four-foot-long figure (seven meters) is angled to catch the sun as it filters into the cave. The shadow plays around the Master's mouth; the noble face is lit by a tranquil smile. There are some fine details, such as the little finger on his right hand, which is gently bent, the pliant bend of his left hand, and the softness of the cushion on which he rests his head. A late sculptural convention is that the robe is merely suggested. It has become so fine as to be transparent; we see only its border at his ankles and in his left hand. The figure radiates equanimity, balanced between the mourning humans below and the rejoicing gods above. This form of the Buddha is popular in both Srī Lankā and Thailand.

□ *THE TEMPTATION BY MĀRA*
The second panel is a lively representation of the Temptation by Māra. As the great Enlightenment was dawning, Māra, the Buddhist Satan, sent his seven beautiful daughters to seduce the future Buddha. They are shown at the bottom of the panel. To their left is Kāma, god of love, letting fly his flower-tipped arrows of lust. Māra is shown seated on an elephant, in the top left-hand corner. The Buddha is unperturbed; he sits in the "Earth Touching Gesture" (*bhūmisparsha mudrā*) to ground himself against the final psychic turmoil before Enlightenment. The scene here is the Buddhist equivalent to Christ's temptation in the wilderness, an ordeal shared in various forms by other Christian saints (for example, Saint Anthony).

□
Cave 26 has the largest Buddha at Ajantā. It also has the smallest. If you face the Buddha sitting on the *stūpa* and look

to his immediate right, you will see a standing *bodhisattva*, his face blackened by the touch of devotees. In the center of his crown sits a tiny *buddha*, waiting to be discovered.

Painting at Ajantā

It is as well to pause before tackling Caves 1 and 2, for they contain a wealth of material that should be approached with rested eyes. A word here on the technique of painting used at Ajantā. The rock surface was first prepared by being roughened with chisels so it would hold the plaster better. Then a layer of clay or cow dung, mixed with rice husks, straw, or hair, was applied. To this rough base a second layer of plaster was added and smoothed off. Lastly a coat of white plaster (gesso), the thickness of egg-shell, was laid down which provided the actual surface for the painting. On this surface the outlines were boldly sketched in cinnabar red; next came a flatwash, corresponding to the *terra verde* of medieval Italian painting. To this moist surface the mineral colors were applied: red and yellow from ocher, green from glauconite, white from lime, kaolin, and gypsum. Lamp-black was used for black; lapis lazuli, probably imported from Central Asia, provided the blue pigment. Gum was used as a binder (rather than the egg tempera of Italian frescoes), and once the outlines and tones had been strengthened, the whole mural was burnished to give it a glowing lustrous finish.

The murals in Caves 1 and 2 belong to the Gupta period (A.D. 320–650), the golden age of Buddhist art. These three centuries witnessed an unprecedented flowering of painting, poetry, drama, and architecture. Kālidāsa, the Indian Shakespeare, was writing; several of the Gupta kings were themselves accomplished dramatists or poets. All in all, Gupta art represents a high point that was never again achieved on such a wide scale. Despite their often poor condition, the Ajantā paintings still manage to convey a vision of a refined and aristocratic sensibility, expressed in luxuriant fullness.

Cave 2 (Figure C)
Mahāyāna,
Sixth Century A.D.

This cave is a full-size Mahāyāna *vihāra*, comprising a main hall surrounded by cells for monks, and a main shrine containing an image of the Buddha. The main shrine is flanked on either side by a subsidiary one. This *vihāra* is fronted by a narrow verandah (C.1), at either end of which is a small chapel with decorated facade (C.2). The *vihāra* would have been used both for daily living and worship.

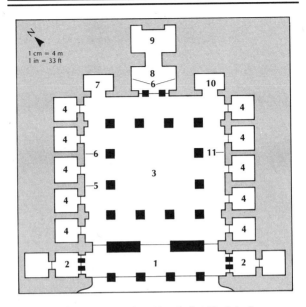

1 *Verandah.* 2 *Side chapels.* 3 *Main hall.* 4 *Monks' cells.*
5 *Birth of the Buddha.* 6 *The Thousand Buddhas.* 7 *The*
yakshā *shrine.* 8 *The antechamber.* 9 *The main shrine.*
10 *The Haritī shrine.* 11 *The story of Pandit Vidhura.*

Figure C. Cave 2—interior.

A richly carved doorway, with a window on either side,
leads into the main hall (C.3). This has twelve pillars, the
central ones of the front and back rows being carved in minutest detail. The left- and right-hand walls each contain five
cells. Although many are damaged, the murals here are
exquisite. They can best be seen by circumambulating the
gallery clockwise.

□ BIRTH OF THE BUDDHA (C.5)
This story stretches across the left-hand wall of the hall, from
the front pilaster to the door of the third cell. One night
Shuddhodana's chief queen, Māyā, dreamt that she was
carried away to the sacred lake Anavatapa in the high Himālayas and bathed by the heavenly Guardians of the Four
Directions. Then a white elephant, bearing a lotus flower in
his trunk, approached her and entered her side. The royal
bedchamber, where the dream took place, is shown in the
bottom-left panel, though it is much damaged. Above this we
see the royal couple—Queen Māyā telling her husband,
Shuddhodana, about the dream. The next top panel, above
the door of the second cell, shows the future Buddha, as a

bodhisattva in the Tushita Heaven ("the Heaven of Supreme Delights"), waiting to reincarnate on the earth plane. He is shown as a princely figure, seated in the teaching attitude, with an aura of spiritual radiance surrounding his head. To the right of this is a panel relating the interpretation of Queen Māyā's dream. Shuddhodana and his wife are squatting down in front of an astrologer, who sports a fine mustache. The *pandit* interpreted the dream to mean that the future child would be either a world ruler (*chakravartin*) or a Buddha. To the right of this again is a very significant portrayal of Queen Māyā. She stands between two pillars, absorbed in her own thoughts. She is shown with all the conventional emphasis on full breasts, rounded hips, and prominant vulva that characterizes fertility deities. Moreover, she rests her left foot against the pillar behind her. To this day a widespread fertility ritual centers round an unmarried virgin girl imparting her fecundity to a tree—and thence the village's crops— by kicking it with her heel. By showing the pregnant Māyā in this stance, the Ajantā artist was able to tell the story in terms his audience would understand. At the same time he showed the Master's mother to be the supreme embodiment of the universal force of creation—the Mother Goddess Shakti.

This connection is made even more explicit in the panel below, which shows the birth of Gautama, the future Buddha. He is held by one of three figures—possibly the Hindu deities Brahmā, Vishnu, and Shiva. Next to them stands Māyā, holding the branch of a tree. This refers to the story—again a variation of the tribal fertility theme just discussed—that she gave birth effortlessly, standing up while supporting herself on a *shāl* tree. In the bottom right of what remains of the panel we see Gautama taking his first seven steps immediately after being born. Where each step touched the ground, a lotus sprang up, as a sign that the seven *chakras* of his subtle body were to open in full Enlightenment. At this point he exclaimed: "This is my last life; I shall not need to take birth again."

☐ *THE THOUSAND BUDDHAS* (Figure C.6)
This theme is widespread in this particular *vihāra*. We also see it along the back wall of the main hall and in the ante-chamber to the main shrine. It refers to the story of the Miracle of Shrāvastī, when, to confound a heretic, Buddha took the form of a thousand celestial *buddhas*. The "blanket" technique of covering the wall surface with *buddha* figures is most effective and was much used by the iconographers of the Tibetan schools, both in their murals and their silked wall hangings (*thankas*). It is also reminiscent of the "Cave of the Thousand Buddhas" in Tun Huang, Central Asia.

☐ *THE YAKSHA SHRINE* (Figure C.7)

The *yakshas* are Dravidian nature spirits, associated with fertility. It is possible that these two figures are not *yakshas*, but forms of Kubera, god of wealth. In either case, they serve the same function of insuring the devotee material plenty. Their luxuriant tresses, falling to one side, show a type of hairstyle very common in the sculptures of Ajantā. No doubt it was in vogue at the time the cave was excavated.

The ceiling of this shrine is typical of the quality of the ceiling paintings in this cave, which have survived better than most. It is designed with a *mandala*, supported in two of the corners by a green dragonlike creature with vampire teeth. This was another motif that was to be developed in the Tibetan iconography. There it took the form of the "wheel of life" *mandala*, held in the grip of the fearsome deity Yama, Lord of Death. Especially fine here is an inner ring composed of twenty-three geese. They are all shown in different positions; each is naturalistic and gracefully buoyant.

☐ *THE ANTECHAMBER* (Figure C.8)

The walls of this little room leading to the main shrine are covered with seated *buddhas* in various postures. Although the detail of the individual expressions is not outstanding, the cumulative effect is very powerful. The murals elevate by their constant repetition; they act as a visual and hypnotic reinforcement of the repetitious chanting that would have been an important part of worship and initiation here. In fact, there is a painted inscription on the back wall of the antechamber, to the right of the shrine door, which records the donation of "a thousand *buddhas*" by a wealthy merchant.

The ceiling is in good condition and shows a *mandala* bordered by the Greek key design, probably a legacy of Greek influence on the Gandhāran art of the Kushāna territories. The *mandala* is surrounded by floral and geometric motifs, in the typical colors of Ajantan ceiling painting: black, white, and chocolate brown. It is significant that the Indian artists confined their ceilings to decoration and did not cover them with teaching or didactic scenes, as, for example, the early Christian churches have. Presumably the Ajantan artists considered ceiling panels too difficult to "read" with ease, especially in the flickering light of oil lamps. However, even the ceiling decoration had a purpose: Its swirling patterns were intended to create a dreamlike visionary effect on the worshipper below.

☐ *THE MAIN SHRINE* (Figure C.9)

The back wall of the shrine is carved with a seated Buddha, his hands in the teaching gesture (*dharmachakra mudrā*). He is flanked by the two protecting *bodhisattvas*: Padmapāni on the left and Vajrapāni on the right. Padmapāni signifies compassion, and Vajrapāni insight. Both figures hold the royal fly whisk (*chaurī*). There are also superb examples of these two important *bodhisattvas* in Cave 1.

Of the well-preserved wall paintings, those on the right-hand wall are particularly beautiful. On the top row are three exquisite *buddhas*, seated weightlessly on a carpet of flowers, reminiscent of Persian miniature decoration. The central *buddha*, with his head inclined at a gentle angle, radiates a compassionate delicacy. The attendants behind, with their dark, lotus-shaped eyes and supple gestures, exemplify the innocent spontaneity of Gupta art.

□ THE HARITĪ SHRINE (Figure C.10)

Haritī was an ogress, whose chief delight was eating other people's children. To cure her of this unsociable habit, the Buddha one day concealed her own favorite child. In a rage she attacked him but was converted by his calm wisdom. She agreed to stop eating children but bewailed the fact that now her own family would have to go hungry. The Buddha assured her that her family would always receive food at a Buddhist monastery. Thus she is often represented in *vihāra* sculpture.

Haritī is here shown with her favorite child on her knee. Beside her sits her consort. The attack on the Buddha and her subsequent conversion are shown in the top right- and left-hand corners of the panel. Below the couple is an interesting group of schoolchildren. From the right we see first three attentive pupils, scribbling away under the cudgel of the teacher; then two boys boxing; and lastly five boys goading a couple of rams to fight.

The wall paintings on both the left- and right-hand walls are entitled Votaries Bringing Offerings. They represent the classical style of Ajantā at its best and have been compared to Botticelli's *Primavera*. Dating from the fifth century, both panels are constructed around five main figures. These occupy a major portion of the wall. The subsidiary figures are only about half the size (as befits their lesser importance) and occupy the four corners. The scene of rocks and gardens breathes an atmosphere of carefree tranquility and is probably as near to a pure landscape as Indian artists ever came. The willowy women positively sway as they glide toward the shrine, displaying a restraint that is yet wholly sensuous. This feeling is echoed in the balanced use of colors, especially the opposition of the pale oyster-brown tinted with red for the women, and the greens for the banana leaves.

It is interesting to compare the achievement here with the murals in the *yaksha* shrine. Both tell the same story, but the Haritī shrine paintings are far more accomplished. They contain fewer figures, and convey an atmosphere of space and light. By comparison the *yaksha* shrine paintings seem crowded and uncomfortable. Presumably some considerable time separated the decoration of the two shrines.

☐ *THE STORY OF PANDIT VIDHURA* (Figure C.11).
This *jātaka* occupies a large part of the right-hand wall of the main hall. It tells the story of the *bodhisattva*'s life on earth as the pandit Vidhura, a minister in the court of the king of Kuru. Vidhura was so eloquent that a serpent king presented him with a necklace of priceless jewels. The serpent king's wife, however, was smitten with jealousy and said she would die if Vidhura's heart was not brought to her. The serpent king reluctantly persuaded his most beautiful daughter to seek a husband who would be brave enough to carry out her mother's wish. She did so and married a general called Pūrnaka. This Pūrnaka then lured the king of Kuru into a gambling match, offering him a fabulous jewel with magical qualities if he won. But the king lost, and Pūrnaka took the minister Vidhura as his winnings. He was unable to kill the pandit, however, and, after many attempts, presented him to the serpent king, saying, "This man must be divine." The serpent king recognized the *bodhisattva*'s true worth and, after much feasting and celebration, allowed him to return, unharmed, to the court of Kuru.

On the left you see Pūrnaka tempting the king of Kuru with the magical jewel. The animated discussion is well conveyed by the hands of the group, at the extreme right of which stoops Pūrnaka, holding the jewel. Behind him stands his horse. Moving to the right, you see the game of dice, with the king of Kuru seated in the middle of a group. The next scene to the right shows Vidhura instructing the repentant serpent king in the buddhist *dharma*. Behind him is Pūrnaka, seated on a cushion of intricate design. This panel is interesting not least for the evidence it provides of contemporary styles of textile design and architecture. The latter is shown by the steps and balustrades of the balconies. To the right of the game of dice there is a group of *nāga* chiefs. One of these, bearing a single serpent's hood on his head and shown squatting on the ground, is very fine. The drawing is vigorous and the dark olive of his face, jet-black hair, blue neck ribbon, and red-flowered background combine very successfully.

The innocent lyricism that inspires the paintings of Ajantā, and many of the *jātakas*, is well summed up by a description one version of this story gives of the serpent princess's wooing of Pūrnaka. We are told she "gathered all the flowers in the Himālayas that had color, scent, or taste, and having adorned the entire mountain like a precious jewel, she spread a couch of flowers upon it, and, after executing a pleasing dance, sang the sweetest of songs."

Cave 1 (Figure D)
Mahāyāna,
Sixth Century A.D.

The finest *vihāra* at Ajantā. It follows roughly the pattern of Cave 2, in containing a verandah, a main hall surrounded by aisles that lead to cells, and a main shrine preceded by an antechamber. But instead of side shrines, as in Cave 2, this cave has four cells on the end wall, two on each side of the main shrine. Every inch of the cave, including pillars and sculptures, was originally painted.

A feature of the late Ajantā architecture is the profuse ornamentation of the pillars. The verandah has six columns, each of which has a square base and an elaborately carved bracket capital. There is, however, considerable variety in the design of the shafts.

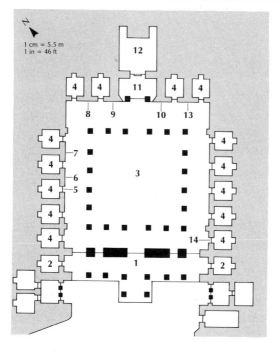

1 *Verandah.* 2 *Side chapels.* 3 *Main hall.* 4 *Monks' cells.*
5 *Dancing scene.* 6 *Mahājanaka on the Elephant.*
7 *Departure from the Palace.* 8 *Lustration and Renunciation.*
9 *The* Bodhisattva *Padmapāni.* 10 *The* Bodhisattva *Vajrapāni.*
11 *Antechamber.* 12 *Main shrine.* 13 *The* Champeya jātaka.
14 *The Palace Scene.*

Figure D. Cave 1—interior.

The Mahājanaka Panels

A clockwise circumambulation of the cave begins with the *Mahājanaka jātaka*, which covers much of the left-hand wall. This story deals with a favorite theme of the *jātakas*: renunciation—a theme that was to find supreme expression, of course, in the story of Gautama himself. In fact, many of the details of that story are mixed up with this *jātaka* tale.

In one of his previous lives, the Buddha took form as King Mahājanaka, an accomplished and revered ruler of Mithilā. He married the beautiful Princess Savilā and seemed set for a life of fame and fortune. Little by little, however, the king began to tire of wordly life, which he found less and less satisfying. Eventually he decided to renounce his kingdom and become an ascetic.

□ *DANCING SCENE*
   (Figure D.5; above the third cell door)
The panel begins with Mahājanaka and his wife sitting in the royal pavilion. The queen is seated leaning against him, her feet being pressed by a servant. Below the pavilion a lady is pounding *bhāng* (hashish) for a forthcoming celebration or perhaps preparing ointment to massage the king.

Appalled at her husband's decision, Savilā attempts to dissuade him by the allurement of beautiful dancing girls. The *jātaka* tells us:

> Queen Savilā sent for seven hundred concubines and said to them: "It is a long time, four full months, since we last beheld the King. We shall see him today; go and adorn yourselves and exhibit all your graces and persuasiveness, and try to entangle him in the snares of passion."

The dancers and musicians are shown to the right of the pavilion. Our attention is caught by the principal dancing girl. She is shown in a long jacket with full sleeves over a long striped skirt that allows her a swirling, sensual movement. The picture contains many fine details: the dancing girl's thumb ring with its tiny mirror, her intricately worked earrings, her headdress of stringed pearls. Her hair is plaited with flowers. She is surrounded by a group of five musicians, who play drums, cymbals, and guitar. Despite all the merriment Mahājanaka, to judge from his expression, is not impressed.

The hairstyles, clothes, and shape of the eyes here all exemplify the late Ajantā style.

□ *MAHĀJANAKA ON THE ELEPHANT*
   (Figure D.6; between the third and fourth cell doors)
Unaffected by the dancing girls, the king leaves the palace on an elephant (symbol of the *dharma*) to hear a Buddhist

monk preach in the forest. He looks most serene, his hand raised in a farewell gesture. The animal is well painted, too, with its leg raised to take a step, and its gentle eye twinkling with happiness at its mission.

The scene continues above: Mahājanaka in the forest with the white-robed monk. There are two deer here, symbolizing the Buddha's first discourse in the Deer Park at Sārnāth. The monk holds a rosary, and the king listens with folded hands, in rapt attention.

☐ *DEPARTURE FROM THE PALACE*
(Figure D.7; between the fourth and fifth cell doors)
An especially beautiful part of the panel, which well conveys the poignancy of the king's departure. He breaks the news to his wife, surrounded by attendants. The variety and feeling in their expressions is masterly; there is an air of solemnity about the whole scene. The group of five ladies between Mahājanaka and the white gate of the palace is particularly beautiful. They are portrayed with a great economy of line yet intense feeling, communicated through their posture and the contours of their lovely faces, with slanting eyes and raised eyebrows.

The story continues as the king leaves the palace on a white horse, the traditional symbol of renunciation to Buddhist and Hindu alike. Again, the detail is finely observed, in, for example, the horse's solemn expression or the man blowing a conch to announce the royal departure—his eyes bulging and cheeks puffed out with the effort.

☐ *LUSTRATION AND RENUNCIATION* (Figure D.8)
Another episode from the *Mahājanaka jātaka* is shown on the end wall of the left-hand aisle, between the two cell doors.

On the extreme left of the panel sits a monk in ocher robes, holding a begging bowl. Four ladies are paying homage to him: The heads of all the figures are gracefully inclined, and the monk smiles serenely. To the right of this are water bearers carrying water into the hall where King Mahājanaka is being bathed. They are realistically portrayed with shoulders straining under the weight of the pots. The king is also distributing alms prior to his departure to the forest, so there are assorted mendicants around the doorway: ascetics with matted hair piled up, beggars, and a Buddhist monk carrying an umbrella.

The right end of the panel shows the king sitting cross-legged on a throne while two servants are pouring water over him from above. We are told that once the king had decided to leave for the ascetic's life, "he bathed himself with sixteen pitchers of perfumed water and adorned himself in all his magnificence." The king is surrounded by delightful young

Cave 1—Mahājanaka jātaka, *lustration scene.*

ladies, three on the left and two on the right. All exhibit elegance and charm reminiscent of the votaries bearing offerings in the Haritī shrine of Cave 2. The two women are dressed in garments that are almost transparent, revealing their firm breasts and hips. The balance of color tones is most successful, the various skin colors and the red of the pillars contrast well with the dull olive green of the palm leaves overhead. Throughout the panel, oranges, reds, and ochers predominate, and the wall radiates a burnished glow, as if illuminated from within. All the figures display a rhythm that is almost ritualistic, and there is a subtle contrast between the restrained presentation of the future Buddha and the lyrical grace of the women. The spiritual and the sensual go hand in hand.

The Antechamber Entrance

☐ *THE BODHISATTVA PADMAPĀNI* (Figure D.9)
The masterpiece of Ajantā. Padmapāni ("He who holds the Lotus")—also known as Avalokiteshvara ("The Lord who looks down")—is the embodiment of compassion, the supreme Buddhist virtue. According to the scriptures, Padmapāni has been performing the duty of the Buddha since he died and will continue to watch over humanity until the Buddha returns in his form of Maitreya, the coming world savior. This superb figure is worth detailed analysis.

Size The first thing that strikes us about the *bodhisattva* is his size. He is very much larger than the attendant figures and dominates the entire panel. This scale is an hieratic device: It shows that the deity is immeasurably more important than the rest of the figures in the panel; physical stature and spiritual stature are here equated. But the *bodhisattva* is also relatively large for compositional reasons. One of the conventions of Indian art is the technique known as *charana* ("pillar") composition, by which the principal figure serves as a dominant vertical axis around which the rest of the tableau revolves. Thus the *bodhisattva* acts to stabilize the swirling world of figures, animals, and plant forms that teem around him. As the divine manifesting himself to his devotees, he is the "still point of the turning world." It is this function, rather than any laws of spatial composition, that is considered important by the Indian artist. Common-sense considerations of so-called reality have little to do with it. What is important is to convey a feeling mood to the observer, by which he can actively participate in the revelation that the panel depicts.

Tone   Another important Ajantan technique is the use of tones. It will be noticed that the tone of one color in this panel is very close to the tone of another; there is a remarkable lack of contrast between the figures. This sameness is not a result of the artists' inability to differentiate various areas of the painting, but is a deliberate technique. The idea is to suppress the apparent depth of the painting in order to

Cave 1—the bodhisattva *Padmapāni.*

allow the figures to emerge very gradually into vision. Initially, your eye is held by the "pillar" of the *bodhisattva*, but the longer you look at the mural, the more you see. Little by little, figures emerge from the shadows, surreptitiously advancing toward the eye. Not only is each figure inseparable from its surrounding environment, but each one reveals another in turn. Every body has a counter-body to balance it; the outline of one figure is the inline of another, and the figures fit together like pieces of a jigsaw. The effect of this technique is to enwrap the observer ever more completely in a visual blanket that surrounds him. He is progressively immersed in the scene, until he almost becomes part of it himself. The separate sense of self begins to dissolve into the scenes that float buoyantly across the walls in rhythmical undulation. This deliberate use of tonal equality is not unique to Ajantā. In Western art certain painters—Bonnard and Matisse, for example—employ it to create visionary effects. What is unique to these caves is the consistent and deliberate use of the technique. The Buddhist cave art is dedicated to altering consciousness and to re-creating in the observer that expanded sense of being that is the goal of Buddhist practice. Thus these murals are one enormous *mandala*, the object of which is to slow the mind down so that the chattering of thought and sense perception can subside into silent awareness. You will notice that any attempt to "read" the paintings quickly, or to focus on, and hold, a particular detail, is frustrated. You cannot view them from a fixed reference point, because another detail is always quietly coming into view to alter your stance. This effect of "all-around vision" is heightened by the fact that a figure's limbs are often painted from slightly different angles. This creates the sensation that you are viewing the figure from two, or more, vantage points simultaneously. Nor is there any "vanishing point" of Renaissance perspective, around which the eye can orient itself. The art was designed to be seen with an open, unfocused mind—the attitude that Keats called "negative capability." This choiceless awareness is in fact the state of meditation—calm, attentive, and receptive. The murals, especially when combined with the rhythmical chanting that would have echoed and reechoed around the walls, were designed to lead the mind beyond the boundaries of thought and ego-centered perception. Ajantān art is mystical. In the true sense of a much-debased word, it is "psychedelic."

The tonal sameness does not create a feeling of lifelessness. On the contrary, these panels glow with an inner luminescence, especially when seen (as they were intended) by the flickering of oil lamps. The figures emerge, floating toward us like characters in a dream. Again, this effect is calculated. The Buddhists hold that all creation is impermanent—illusory, lacking real substance. A common Mahāyāna simile is that the world of phenomena is like a rainbow, and the art here is a perfect expression of this *māyā*. All the figures are in perpetual flux, and this moving caravan of life emerges from a background that is limitless and intangible. There is no solidity behind the figures, just limitless space. The Mahāyāna seers described the universe as emanating from an infinitely creative void they called *shūnyatā* (literally: "emptiness"). The actual experience of this infinite source is possible when the mind is silent. Ajantan art seeks both to illustrate and to induce such an experience.

The parallels between the painter's skill and the true perception of reality are made clear in the *Lankāvatāra Sūtra*, an important Mahāyāna text of the second century A.D.

> As a picture shows height and depth, while there is really nothing of the sort in it . . . so the Void is like the painter's canvas, on which there is no depression or elevation as imagined by the ignorant.

The Figure Itself   The figure of the *bodhisattva* is a stunning achievement. Delicately balanced between rest and movement, he sways gracefully, with head and hand tilted, as if he were about to come to life. In accordance with the canons of Indian art, his body is drawn with reference to the universal forms of the animal and vegetal worlds—both considered more enduring, and thus more real, than the human realm. His face has the perfect oval of the egg, the eyebrow follows the curve of a drawn bow, the heavily lidded eyes mimic the lotus. The massive shoulders are modeled on the elephant, the adamantine body on the lion. The beautiful hand, holding the blue opened lotus, itself has the pliant springiness of a sap-filled plant. In fact the whole figure undulates like a heavy-headed flower, both graceful and tender.

The *bodhisattva*'s face is filled with compassion. The skin is smooth, the expression abstracted and dreamy, as in all mature Gupta art. Padmapāni is hardly of this world; his beauty comes from a purity that is more divine than human. Yet there is a strongly sensual element to his spirituality. Like some of Michelangelo's demigods, Padmapāni combines two worlds that we normally assume to be irreconcilable. This sensuality is partly conveyed through the judicious use of toning on the flesh, which seems to be modeled in light and shade. Areas of shadow—for example, on either side of his nose—are accentuated to increase the sense of form and solidity. Thus this *sfumato* technique is used to convey mass, rather than light. It was used, for example, by Giotto and his school in Western art, nearly seven hundred years later.

□

The spiritualized sensuality of Gupta art expresses perfectly the philosophy that underlies it. The Mahāyāna teaches that all life should be glorified. The senses should not be repressed, but cultured and gradually refined, until they can lead the mind to what lies beyond them. But most of us are too engrossed in the petty concerns of daily life even to set out on this journey to Truth—hence the poignancy of the *bodhisattva*'s compassion.

□ *THE BODHISATTVA VAJRAPĀNI* (Figure D.10)
Complementing Padmapāni, on the other side of the entrance to the antechamber of the main shrine, is the *bodhisattva* Vajrapāni: "He who holds the Thunderbolt of Knowledge." Compassion and knowledge are the twin pillars on which the whole magnificent edifice of the Mahāyāna rests. These two *bodhisattva*s represent the full development of the qualities of heart and mind, feeling and insight, in the fully developed human being.

Vajrapāni is a stylistic, as well as a doctrinal, complement to Padmapāni. Whereas the latter is a good example of the northern style of representation—with his Āryan features, fair skin, and courtly demeanor—Vajrapāni represents the indigenous tribal races of the Deccan. He is dark-skinned, round-faced, full-lipped. He wears the heavy jewelry typical of the southern region, and his native vitality is emphasized by the fact that, against the background of green, his dark figure stands out with greater relief than that of his counterpart. These two figures must be seen as a pair; only then will their balance of Apollonian restraint and Dionysian vitality be fully appreciated. The tension between these two aspects of human nature has always been present in Indian life and art. It has generally been externalized in the conflict between the indigenous tribal societies and the more sophisticated invading ones. It is partly because Ajantā manages to reconcile these aspects so clearly and so consciously that her art is so psychologically satisfying to us today.

Vajrapāni holds the thunderbolt (*vajra*), the symbol of esoteric knowledge. This emblem was to play a central part in the Mahāyāna sects of the Himālayan kingdoms, especially Tibet. The thunderbolt is a masculine (phallic) symbol, complementing the feminine (vulva) symbol of the lotus of creativity. It corresponds to the staff of Hermes, or the trident of Neptune, in Western mythology.

Vajrapāni leans on an attendant, who, like his master, is profusely bejeweled. Below the *bodhisattva*'s right arm are two other interesting figures: one with a shaven head and, next to him, a girl. She is known as the "Dark Princess" and is finely modeled and embellished, her expression of tranquil thoughtfulness emphasized by the contrast of the dark complexion against the lighter background. Her eyes, above all, captivate the onlooker. They radiate a warm friendliness that is highlighted by the soft hazel pupils and the red spots in the corners of the eyes. Although a late painting, the Dark Princess avoids the exaggerated stylization from which many of its contemporaries were already beginning to suffer.

The Main Shrine (Figure D.12)

□ *THE BUDDHA*
Seated majestically within the main shrine is the third member of this Buddhist trinity, the Master himself. He represents the Absolute: calm, unshakable. This Absolute manifests through the activities of the two *bodhisattvas*: Pure knowledge expresses itself through the functions of compassion and insight. Thus the Buddha bears a similar relationship to the *bodhisattvas* here as God does to the angels in Christian theology. The Buddha is aligned to the Infinite Void; the *bodhisattvas* are his agents who operate throughout the celestial realms to influence the gross world of human life.

This hierarchy is emphasized by the contrast of the media employed. When the Indian artist wanted to represent permanence, he always used stone. However much the paintings of the *bodhisattvas* may decay, we feel the figure of the Buddha is here to stay.

The Master sits in the teaching attitude (*dharmachakra mudrā*). He is flanked, again, by Padmapāni and Vajrapāni, in stone this time, and two celestial attendants (*gandharvas*) hover above. The face is full, soft, and noble. The earlobes are long, there are three slight folds of flesh in the neck, and the snail curls of the hair rise to form the *ushnīsha* protuberance on top of the head that signifies the thousand-petaled lotus of enlightenment. All these are traditional signs (*lakshana*) of the Buddha. The whole figure is simple, massive, unadorned, and immensely powerful. The Buddha's teaching role is emphasized by the Wheel of Truth, the symbol of the eternal *dharma*, which protrudes from under the Master's throne. It is flanked by two deer; they symbolize the Deer Park at Sārnāth, in which the first discourse was delivered (see Chapter 17). On the left of the wheel are the first five disciples of the Buddha, on the right some noble visitors to the Master.

There is an ingenious trick with the lighting in the shrine. When the statue is lit from the left of the chamber, the face of the Master appears somber. He is contemplating the impermanence of all phenomena. When the figure is lit from the right, the shadows play around the mouth, causing the face to smile in serene joy. When the light is placed by the

Wheel of Truth, right underneath the Buddha, his face expresses utter tranquility. It is calm, undisturbed, beyond all opposites of pleasure or pain. The Ajantan sculptors have achieved here effects by light that their Hindu counterparts in Elephanta rendered in stone in the magnificent Shiva Maheshvara panel (see page 77).

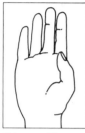

Abhaya mudrā
(Fear not)

Vitarka mudrā
(Explanation)

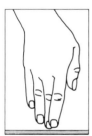

Bhūmisparsha mudrā
(Earth touching)

Dāna mudrā
(Generosity)

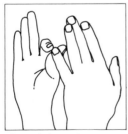

Dharmachakra mudrā
(Teaching—Turning the
Wheel of Truth)

Figure E. Mudrās

Dhyāna mudrā (Meditation)

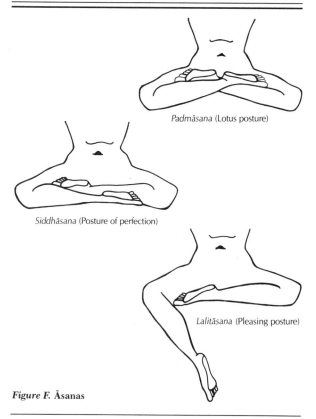

Padmāsana (Lotus posture)

Siddhāsana (Posture of perfection)

Lalitāsana (Pleasing posture)

Figure F. Āsanas

As with all sacred art, these images operate on a variety of levels. To the simple worshipper, the Buddha and the *bodhisattvas* are external figures, who can intercede for helpless humanity and who listen to our prayers. On a more sophisticated level they represent the faculties that can be awakened in the human mind. If insight and compassion are cultivated through meditation, they will eventually reveal themselves to be the workings of the infinite consciousness in all minds, the eternal buddha-nature within.

Continuation of the Circumambulation

□ *THE CHAMPEYA JĀTAKA* (Figure D.13)
This *jātaka* panel is composed of two tiers. On the top level we see the king of Banāras, Uggasene, holding court in his royal palace. He is the figure on the left, sitting on his throne, framed by the pillars.

The bottom tier is a wealth of finely observed detail. It shows the Buddha in a former incarnation, delivering a lecture to a group of people. His message is evidently being received in a variety of ways. The woman seated under his right elbow is entranced by what she hears. But behind him another woman looks skeptical, while another listener, directly above the Master, looks frankly disbelieving. The variety of expression in the faces of the audience is remarkable: each one unique. To the right-hand side of the scene, next to the pillar, there is an example of the comic relief that abounds in these frescoes. A woman devotee stands in rapt attention, holding a tray of fruit she intends to offer the Buddha. Behind her, a pale-faced character wearing a cap is more intent on the fruit than the sermon. He is actually stealing some of it from the tray. But he hasn't gone unnoticed. Two women next to him, along the back row, have spotted his game. One of them is actually pointing out the theft to the woman holding the tray. Altogether the scene is beautifully observed, with an affection for human foibles that is almost Chaucerian. It is a mark of the maturity of the Ajantan outlook that the artists can move from spiritual to mundane subjects with such consummate ease. The slightly stylized presentation of the characters in this drama remind us that in Indian painting states of mind, or moods, are always represented by pose, gesture, and glance. In this treatment of the emotions, painting follows dance and drama. All three art forms use a formalized vocabulary to communicate certain things to their audience. The wonder is that, in using these conventions, a lively and natural quality is never absent.

☐ *THE PALACE SCENE* (Figure D.14)
The right-hand wall of Cave 1 is badly damaged. However, there are some fine fragments. One of the best of these is the Palace Scene, above the last door before the exit. The principal figure, the queen, is shown squatting in front of a *rāja*, surrounded by a number of other women. Many of these are in the characteristically relaxed pose we have come to associate with Ajantā: Full-breasted, with stomachs out and hips thrown forward, they twist and turn like sensuous creepers. The predominant colors are a rich orange and burnished ocher. The panel is late, and some indication of this can be seen in the heavy heads, large mouths, and elongated eyes. But it would be wrong to attribute the apparent distortion of limbs to a mere carelessness of an art in decline. The crouching queen, in particular, shows us the Ajantan painters' technique of presenting a figure from different angles simultaneously. The queen supports herself by placing the full weight of her body on one arm, her hand at the level of the viewer's eye. But her navel is viewed from about ten inches higher, her breasts from the side, and her foot from above. Moreover the hand which supports her entire body does not even touch

the ground, but floats almost twelve inches (thirty centimeters) above it. The net result is that the queen floats weightlessly in front of us, almost in 3-D. Her lightness is accentuated by the fact that the ground on which she sits has no solidity either, but dissolves into flower-sprinkled space. Such a posture, if posture it can be called, is fairly common in these paintings. It illustrates perfectly the shifting play of *māyā*, the dreamlike world of flux that we all mistake for solid "reality." It is also possible that such figures were inspired by the actual practices of the monks here. It is well known that the cave sanctuaries were used for perfection of supernormal powers (*siddhis*), which are the outcome of intensive meditation. Significantly, several of these *siddhis* are concerned with "levitation," "moving through the air at will," and "walking on water." It is only natural that the cave art should be influenced by the experience of such yogic phenomena.

The Ceiling

Before we leave Cave 1, notice the ceiling. This has a flatter, more decorative style than the walls. The surface is divided into a number of square or rectangular panels, many of which are filled with flower and vegetal motifs. The flowers in Ajantan painting deserve a study on their own. There is no doubt that the Ajantā area was the source of an enormous number of plants and flowers that found their way to the countries of Southeast Asia, China, Japan, and Korea, via the traveling monks. The flowers, fruits, animals, and birds all constitute an aspect of Ajantan art that is more decorative than didactic. The flower and leaf forms, in particular, show the Indian artists' ability to extract the essentials of natural form and convey the feeling of abundant growth and fecundity in a restrained, almost abstract style. The result is that the ceiling appears to be covered by some vast and intricate paneled textile, woven in muted colors.

As you leave the enchanted ravine, becalmed once more in the evening stillness, the words of Shakespeare's great magician Prospero accompany you:

> Our revels now are ended. These our actors,
> As I foretold you, were all spirits, and
> Are melted into air, into thin air:
> And, like the baseless fabric of this vision,
> The cloud-capp'd towers, the gorgeous palaces,
> The solemn temples, the great globe itself,
> Yea, all which it inherit, shall dissolve,
> And, like this insubstantial pageant faded,
> Leave not a rack behind. We are such stuff
> As dreams are made on, and our little life
> Is rounded with a sleep.

The monks of Ajantā would have loved these lines.

5

MOUNT ĀBŪ

THE HOLY MOUNTAIN
OF THE JAINS

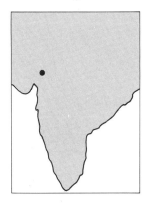

Mount Ābū lies in the southwest corner of Rājasthān, right on the border of Gujarāt. It forms the southern tip of the Arāvalli Mountains, which stretch diagonally down from Delhi, cutting Rājasthān into two unequal parts. The road to the hill station climbs eighteen miles (twenty-nine kilometers) up from Ābū Road, twisting and turning all the way up to a plateau that varies from thirty-five hundred to fifty-six hundred feet (one thousand to seventeen hundred meters) above sea level. It is the highest peak between the Himālayas and the Nīlgiri Hills, in the far south. The landscape has a Mediterranean atmosphere. White buildings nestle among foliage that is thick and luxuriant. Ābū is famed for its bird life. The brilliant Indian roller can be seen, flashing iridescent turquoise through the trees; so can the turtledove, with its velveteen gray and brown plumage. Black-faced langur monkeys swing and chatter through the forests that border the road, and farther into the hinterland bear and panther roam freely. The mountain is also famous for its flowers, especially orchids, and for its varieties of mushrooms. After the monsoon the whole place is dotted with delicate pink and yellow lantana flowers. It is a veritable oasis after the roads from Jaipur or Udaipur, which seem to stretch for mile after unending mile of semidesert country.

Mount Ābū is a pleasure resort for the hot months, providing a welcome respite from the scorching heat of the plains below. The social hub of the town is Nakki Lake. Here the scene is incongruously Edwardian. On the lake rowing boats bob up and down, their fringed canopies shading groups of Indian tourists, who sing college songs with self-conscious gusto. Married couples promenade demurely along the shore, taking the air. The lawns are covered with picnickers. Each group centers on an enormous matron, swathed in voluminous *sārī*, around whom sit circles of children, ranged in diminishing size, like the foothills around maternal Annapūrnā, the Himālayan mountain named after the Hindu goddess of food.

Eager photographers take holiday snaps of painfully formal family groups. They will live forever, staring stiffly down from the mantelpieces of faraway Baroda or Madras. Ice cream vendors stroll around or pursue the smartly dressed parties of giggling college girls. Here and there a doe-eyed beauty glides past. Tightly chaperoned by mama, perhaps she dreams of being discovered by a movie director, on holiday from Bombay. At any moment the strains of Gilbert and Sullivan should break out from the faded bandstand.

In ancient times Mount Ābū was the home of the great sage Vasishtha, guru to Rāma. He lived here with the wish-fulfilling cow Nandinī, who was able to grant mortals any boon they asked. The place was known as Nandivardhan—the "place that increases joy." One day Vasishtha was grazing Nandinī by a great lake when she fell in. Fearing for her life, the sage flew to the Himālayas to ask the gods to save her. They replied by sending Arbuda, the cosmic cobra, carrying an enormous rock on its hood. Arbuda dropped this rock—the present Mount Ābū—into the lake. The water was displaced, Nandinī saved. Thereafter the spot became known as Arbudāchala: the hill of Arbuda, from which its present name derives.

Vasishtha is also celebrated as the father of the most powerful Rājput tribes. The story goes that Vishnu, in his incarnation as Parashu Rāma, totally destroyed the *kshatriya* caste to avenge his father, a pious brahmin who was murdered by a group of *kshatriya* princes. Alarmed at the resulting imbalance in society, the gods came here to Mount Ābū to implore Vasishtha to do something about it. He performed an ancient ritual fire sacrifice at his hermitage, and, out of the flames, he created the four "fire-born" Rājput clans. Ever since, these clans have been the most powerful defenders of *kshatriya dharma*. They include the royal families of Jaipur and Udaipur.

The legend of Parashu Rāma points to an ancient conflict between brahmin and *kshatriya*, a feud between "church and state," which the former won. It is also probably an allegorical account of how invading tribes of Central Asian Huns were initiated into the Hindu fold by sacred fire rites and thus became the "fire-born" Rājput dynasties.

The sacrificial firepit and Vasishtha's hermitage can still be seen at Gaumukh, a charming little temple complex about six miles (ten kilometers) from the town. Here religious novitiates (*brahmachārins*) study under their guru in an idyllic clearing surrounded by mango forests. The pattern of life here has not altered for centuries.

Although most sects have had temples and ashrams on Mount Ābū, it has been specially sacred to the Jains since the eleventh century.

Jainism

It is often thought that Jainism was founded by Mahāvīra, a contemporary of the Buddha, who died in 526 B.C. But the Jains hold that Mahāvīra, "the Great Hero," was only the most recent in a line of twenty-four teachers that stretches back into remotest history. The word *Jain* comes from *jina*—"the Conqueror"—and the Jains are the "followers of the Conqueror," the first great teacher Ādinātha. The twenty-four teachers are known as the *tīrthankaras*, which means "those who have crossed the ocean of becoming." They are the models, teachers, and inspiration of Jainism, who have reached the farther shore of enlightenment. Each Jain temple is dedicated to one of these *tīrthankaras* and has his image in its central shrine. Jainism belongs to the oldest cultural stratum of India; it is a religion whose roots go back to the earliest philosophies on earth. Before the Āryan invasions of the third millennium B.C., the ancient Middle Eastern world was united by a loosely knit body of belief. This took the form of strictly dualistic mythologies that recounted the eternal battle between the forces of light and the forces of darkness. Our Judeo-Christian tradition developed one aspect of this conflict between good and evil. Zoroastrianism, the religion of ancient Persia, developed another. In India the conflict is most clearly expressed in Jainism and yoga, both of which express the eternal conflict as the antagonism of spirit and matter. There are clear connections between Jain myths and those of the ancient Middle East. The stories of Pārshvanātha, Mahāvīra's immediate predecessor, are in several cases the Indian version of the myths of Cain and Abel, or Jacob and Esau in the Old Testament. These in turn are linked to the "Tale of the Two Brothers" of ancient Egypt.

Each *tīrthankara* is associated with an animal or object that best represents his qualities. These symbols are really the only way of identifying the different *tīrthankaras*. The heroic Mahāvīra is represented by a lion; Ādinātha, the first

Image of a tīrthankara
seated in meditation.

teacher, by a bull. This association may well link Jain cosmology with the bull cults of the ancient Mediterranean and
Middle East. Furthermore, Ādinātha's son is called Bhārat-
varsha, from which the Indian continent Bhārata gets its
name. The religion of Ādinātha may thus be connected to, or
even contemporary with, the first emergence of India as a
distinct country, independent of the land mass to her west.

Jainism teaches that within each individual lies an immor-
tal and totally detached spirit (*jīva*). The goal of life is to
become aware of this eternal spirit by transcending the
coverings of matter and *karma* that normally obscure it. To
experience the spirit is to be free, enlightened.

In one of the oldest Jaina texts we read that the seventh
and most important principle of the religion is: "Freedom.
Spirit [*jīva*] and nonspirit [*ajīva*] together constitute the
universe. All that is necessary is to discriminate between
them."

The Jains do not deny the gods, but they do not believe in
any one personal creator of the universe. In this they agree
with the Buddhists. The world functions solely by the universal law of *karma*, the invariable law of cause and effect. All
our actions have an effect on the universe for good or evil,
and these effects eventually return to the doer. "As ye sow, so
shall ye reap." Negative thought or action will return to the
doer as bad luck, ill health, and so on. This will in turn have
the effect of increasing ignorance and obscuring the *jīva*

with ever denser coverings of ignorance. Conversely, positivity will bring positive benefits, which are conducive to greater purity, detachment, and freedom. There is no doctrine of grace in Jainism, whereby the effects of one's actions can be short-cut. The only thing to do is to lead a life of scrupulous morality and perform acts of merit, such as building temples, to accumulate the good *karma* necessary to win eventual enlightenment.

The cardinal virtue for a Jain is nonviolence (*ahimsā*). He considers the whole cosmos to be alive, and thus worthy of respect. All orthodox Jains are strict vegetarians. Not only are the gross occupations of butcher, hunter, or soldier taboo, but even farming is prohibited, lest one unwittingly kill insects or small animals. This concern for even the humblest levels of the animal kingdom reaches astonishing lengths. In a Jain community, ants, snakes, and even rats are fed as a religious duty. In places with a large Jain population, such as Bombay, you may see a man being carried around on a bed. He makes his living by being paid to provide nourishment for bedbugs! As a result of their exaggerated concern for life, Jains have always specialized in business. Traditionally they have been moneylenders, jewelers, merchants. Today the banking and cotton businesses are largely in Jain hands, and wherever Indians have settled, many of the greatest industrial houses are watched over by the serene image of one of the *tīrthankaras*.

The Jain community is pious as well as rich. The householder must observe certain stringent vows: He must not lie, he must not use another's property without permission, he must be chaste and limit his possessions, he must avoid excess or inauspicious travel, and he must eschew useless or sinful talk, thought, or action. In addition he must worship regularly at morning, noon, and evening. He must pay great heed to eating only pure food, and he must fast on frequent occasions. Mahāvīra, like all the great gurus, taught that one's state of consciousness, and thus the quality of mind and behavior, was directly influenced by the type of food eaten. Lastly the Jain must give daily charity, in the form of knowledge or money.

The Jains do not subscribe to the authority of the Vedas, nor do they believe in the caste system. In this sense they are a reform movement within Hinduism, like the contemporary teachings of the Buddha. Nevertheless, in their popular domestic rituals, the Jains worship such Hindu gods as Ganesha and Lakshmī for the boons of health, wealth, and happiness. But the supreme object of Jain worship is the *tīrthankara*. He is at the summit of the celestial hierarchy. Because he is enlightened, he is superior to the gods. But he is not worshipped as a savior figure; the *tīrthankara* cannot intercede on behalf of the devotee. The enlightened ones are to be viewed as examples, inspiring all of us on our long and arduous ascent to spiritual freedom. As such, it is a sober and stoic religion. It bridges the gap between the full-blown theism of Hindu devotion and the ascetic schools of Hīnayāna Buddhism.

There are many parallels between Buddhism and Jainism. The Mahāvīra myth resembles the story of the Buddha. Both have similar legends about their miraculous birth, and sooth-sayers prophesied that each would be a "World Redeemer." Both were the sons of princes who grew up to despise wealth and privilege, which they renounced in order to seek enlight-enment. Both practiced austerities, and some accounts say they studied together under the same teachers. On the verge of *nirvāna*—the word is common to both traditions—each was tempted by the personification of evil: Mahāvīra by Samvara and the Buddha by Māra. Both founded orders and taught in northeastern India; both saw meditation rather than ritual as the key to spiritual life. But Jainism is more ascetic. Only a monk can reach enlightenment, according to the Jains. In this they differ from the later Buddhists, who hold that *nirvāna* is open to all. The hub of the Jain lay community is thus the monastery.

The monk lives under strict vows of avoiding violence, stealing, lying, sexual activity, and possession of property. The ideal of nonviolence goes to extreme lengths. He should wear a veil over his mouth to avoid inadvertently swallowing any flying insects; and he should carry a soft white broom to sweep the ground before him or the seat where he is about to sit, in order to avoid crushing any unsuspecting creature. Even if thrown off a ferryboat, perhaps by some wicked passengers incensed at his unworldliness, he should not make too violent efforts to swim ashore, lest he harm the atoms in the water! Such an outlook makes it not unsurprising that there are only a few Jain monks in India today. Few can fulfill such demands.

In addition, the Jains are famous for being one of the most severely ascetic monastic orders. Their practices used to include meditating in the full sunlight of the Indian summer and maintaining difficult postures for hours on end. Some have even starved themselves to death in an attempt to divorce the spirit from the physical body that obscures it.

The Two Sects

The earliest Jain monks went about naked to show their complete freedom from the shackles of caste, society, and worldly life. Their detachment from identification with the mortal body was complete. They were called "the sky-clad"

(*Digambaras*) and predominated in the south, in modern Mysore. After the time of Mahāvīra, whose teaching was less ascetic, there arose the second sect, "the white-clad" (*Shvet-āmbaras*), so called from the simple white cotton garment they wore. They were strongest in western India. Mahāvīra also gave women the right to enlightenment by allowing an order of nuns to be formed.

At the time of Alexander the Great's raid across the Indus in 326 B.C., the "sky-clad" were still numerous enough to attract the attention of the Greeks, who called them gymno-sophists: "the naked philosophers." In fact they existed in large numbers until the eleventh century, when the Muslims forced them to wear clothes. But it is still quite possible to come across members of this group in rural Gujarāt and Mahārāshtra. In fact, naked ascetics are still to be seen in all parts of India except the capital.

In the Middle Ages western India flourished under the stable rule of the Solānkī dynasty. The western seaboard abounded in natural harbors, and through these flowed trade from the West, which enabled the country to become rich and powerful. With their increasing domination of trade and banking, the Jains were able to finance both temples and monasteries in abundance. Religious patronage was not left solely to private enterprise. There was also a tax levied each market day from the local merchants. Each shopkeeper gave a spoonful of every grain he sold, or as much cloth as could be held in the hand. These tributes went directly to the religious foundations, or were sold off to provide them with money.

The Jains created a number of temple complexes. These were not cities as such but sacred citadels, conglomerations of temples that, within their walled precincts, were self-contained communities.

The first extensions to the temples themselves were monasteries and sleeping quarters for monks and lay pilgrims. From these in turn sprang libraries, schools, hospitals, and orphanages. These complexes were the energy centers of a virile and prosperous community. Today there are about one and a half million Jains in India, but they exercise a power out of all proportion to their numbers. The most renowned of their citadels is Dilwara, one and a half miles (two and a half kilometers) from Mount Ābū.

Dilwara Temple Complex (Figure A)

Strategically surrounded by hills, the citadel looks like an encamped army. Domed temple roofs are protected by high walls, which in turn are ringed by palm trees, mute sentinels on guard. Flags flutter over the buildings—the only splash of color against the austere whitewashed brickwork. On the left as you approach, the rest house for pilgrims rears up. Its massive walls are pierced by tiny windows, regularly spaced. The whole place has the air of some fortified retreat, prepared to offer vigilant resistance to the evils of the outside world that besiege it. A few village huts cluster around the walls, as if hoping for eventual admittance to the reclusive sanctuary within. This is unlikely. The temple authorities have long been wanting to buy the buildings and lay large gardens in their place. But the proffered sum is not large enough, so there is stalemate.

Although Jain architecture is a hybrid of Buddhist and Hindu styles, its military and rather forbidding exteriors are unique. They are also misleading. For within these unadorned buildings lies some of the finest sculpted architecture in the world, hidden like the translucent pearl encased in the rough shell of the oyster.

Having shed all your leather at the entrance, you enter the complex proper. On your left stands the Chaumukha Temple, locally known as the Stonecutters' Temple (A.1). It is said to have been built by the masons in their spare time, free of

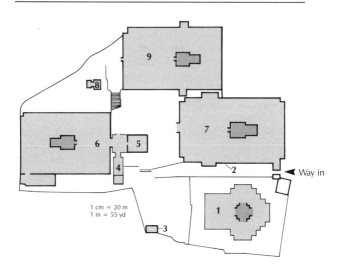

1 *The Chaumukha Temple.* **2** *Ganesha.* **3** *Temple offices.* **4** *The Vimala Shāh Temple entrance shrine.* **5** *The Hall of Vimala Shāh.* **6** *The Vimala Shāh Temple.* **7** *The Unfinished Temple.* **8** *The Digambara Temple.* **9** *The Tejapala Temple.*

Figure A. The Dilwara temple complex

charge. A mixture of thirteenth- and fifteenth-century styles, this building is inferior to the two main temples. It has three stories, the upper ones open only to men. The ground floor contains a cella opening onto a colonnaded hall. Inside the shrine is a remarkable image of the twenty-third *tīrthankara,* Pārshvanātha. This is four-faced, symbolizing the mission of the enlightened ones to spread the teaching to the four directions. This is a Jain version of a pan-Indian iconographic convention. In Buddhism one form it takes is the arrangement of the *toranas* of a *stūpa;* in Hinduism the placing of the subsidiary shrines in a *pancharatha* temple plan, or a Shiva *linga* carved with four faces (*chaturmukhalinga*).

When a *tīrthankara* reaches enlightenment, the gods create a sumptuous hall where the teacher sits to preach the doctrine to all corners of the universe. The Stonecutters' Temple signifies such a hall. Some of the door guardians to the shrine are interesting, but the carving here is somewhat distorted and overstylized.

There is a fine little standing Ganesha (A.2), set into the southern wall of the unfinished temple, on the right of the entrance path. Ganesha always sanctifies the entrance to a home or temple. As the god of domestic success and business, he is especially popular in the mercantile communities that make up a large part of Gujarāt and Mahārāshtra. Each September his festival, Ganesha Chathurthī, is celebrated with great enthusiasm in these states. This figure looks very pleased with himself. He has a fine rollicking gait as he carries a dish of sweets (*modakas*), with his potbelly stuck out like some successful Gujarātī trader. His eyes are elongated into the lotus shape, a convention in all forms of Jain art.

A courtyard on the left leads to the temple administration office (A.3). The blue-doored quarters are for visiting monks. In any city the temple quarter served as a nucleus of the Jain community. Much local government policy was decided within its walls, and family trees and records were kept there. A temple council is in charge of the day-to-day running of the Jain temples. Daily and annual rituals are, as is often the case, performed by brahmin priests. This ability to coexist with the brahmin hierarchy, as well as to incorporate Hindu deities, helped save Jainism from sharing the fate of its sister reform movement, Buddhism.

This entrance to the Vimala Shāh Temple is shaded by a champak tree, its yellow flowers exuding a heavy musk perfume. The champak is one of the favorite flowers of Kāma, god of lust, who tips his arrows with it. Champak trees are often grown in temple compounds, so that the flowers, as a symbol of sensual desire, can be offered and surrendered to the divinity.

Vimala Shāh Temple Entrance Shrine (Figure A.4)

This contains an image of Mahāvīra, the last of the twenty-four *tīrthankaras* of the present age. The figure is naked and unadorned, apart from its silvered eyes, which catch the light. Various subtle energy centers are picked out on the body. The chief of these is the heart *chakra,* which is shown on all images of *tīrthankaras* in a diamond shape known as the *shrīvasta.* This *chakra* is connected with experience of transcendence and thus is the most important, as far as the Jains are concerned, because it "connects" man with the Absolute. The Jain artist was concerned to show the saints as barely human personifications of this Absolute. *Tīrthankaras* are the most spiritualized beings of all, superior to the gods, who, hovering around them, have yet to achieve enlightenment.

If the images are to represent the absolute side of life, personality has no part to play. That belongs to the changing, mortal man. Here personality is not the enduring individuality it is in the Western traditions, but a temporary covering of the soul. This covering changes from day to day and incarnation to incarnation. We are told in the *Bhagavad Gītā* that the spirit in man adopts and discards bodies and personalities as we change our clothes. Thus the Jain images are impersonal, austere, and stark. Theirs is a purity that is divine, far beyond mere corporality. According to Jain teaching, "The body of a *tīrthankara* is of a wondrous beauty and a miraculously pure fragrance. It is not subject to disease, and it is devoid of perspiration as well as all the uncleanness that originates from the processes of digestion."

The Jains are great system makers. They have analyzed and catagorized ad infinitum the various levels of existence and types of soul. Their temples are encoded with the details of their exhaustive cosmology. On the left of the main shrine is a marble tablet that shows Mahāvīra surrounded by the various other sacred persons of the Jain system. Altogether there are twenty-four *tīrthankaras* of the present age, twenty-four of the coming age, and another group of lesser divine beings numbering a hundred and six. A detailed list of all these great souls, preeminently holy as they are, is likely to bore anyone who is not himself a Jain ascetic.

The door to the sanctuary is barred by a silver chest. It is for the offerings of the devout and reminds us that the Jain community has always specialized in business. Beside the shrine stands a camphor holder. The camphor is lit and waved in front of the image as *āratī,* part of the Jain *pūjā* honoring images of teachers. The light represents pure spirit.

The ceilings of the shrine are covered in mural friezes of typical Rājasthānī and Gujarātī design. They combine sacred and secular motifs. These scenes of worshippers, musicians, armies, animals, and so on are common in western India as decorations on house walls, paintings in miniature, or wood-block prints for fabrics.

The Hall of Vimala Shāh (Figure A.5)

This contains a figure of the patron of the temple, Mahāsethjī Vimala Shāh. The "great merchant" is seated on a horse. He was the chief minister of the Solānkī King Bhīm Deva of Gujarāt and commissioned the temple in 1031, at the estimated cost of over 180 million rupees. It is not uncommon in the north for the patron to be immortalized facing his temple. At the back of the hall is a small figure of Ambikā, a form of the great goddess Durgā, who was the family deity of the Shāh family.

Immediately behind Vimala Shāh is an interesting model of the universe in miniature. This is in the form of the holy mountain of Shatrunajaya, in Saurāshtra. Shatrunajaya is the holiest of the four Jain mountains—the others being Girnar in Saurāshtra, Sametshikhara in eastern Bihār, and Ābū here in Rājasthān. There is a fifth, transcendental mountain that, like the Hindu Mount Meru, is not in this world. This is called Astapada and represents the infinite center, with the other peaks representing the four cardinal points. Shatrunajaya is the navel of the Jain universe and the scene of a massive pilgrimage on the full moon of each Kārttika (October–November). Groups of pilgrims from all over the country flock there, and part of the rite consists of processions carrying huge pictures of the mountain through the streets that lead to the sacred site. Many Jain temples contain pictures, or images, of the mountain, to align them to the sacred cosmos. Sometimes an entire temple is identified with Shatrunajaya. Then it is worshipped as the holy mountain, circumambulated, and praised with hymns.

The model here is carved with channels for the libations to run down. The water that flows down the slopes of the sacred mountains is as holy as the elixir of life. It runs into the rivers, which are themselves focuses of pilgrimage.

The Jains often use milk for libation. This is because milk symbolizes nourishment and divine childhood and is precious, since it comes from the cow. There is also an esoteric reason. Milk signifies the spirit, and milk mixed with water is a common symbol of the spirit mixed with matter. It is said that the sage has such fine discrimination that he can discern the absolute spirit at the heart of the relative world. For this reason he is like the swan (*paramahansa*), the only bird whose discrimination is fine enough to sift the precious milk from the water with his beak.

The mountain is protected on each side by the standing *tīrthankaras* who delineate the four directions that arise from the sacred center. Thus the cult of the mountain is in essence another version of the archaic and universal orientation rite, by which the cosmos is ordered and the relationship between heaven and earth, gods and men, is established.

The room is full of elephants, familiar symbols of stability and royal power. These magnificent beasts lugged the stone for these temples all the way from the mines of Makarāna, nearly three hundred miles (five hundred kilometers) away. The effort and expense necessary to realize this astonishing feat of engineering are staggering. But effort and expense were no object. As they increased, so did the glory of the patron, and his spiritual merit. Like the Mughals after them, when the Solānkīs wanted the best, they chose white marble. Its uniform purity was especially appropriate to the Jain architects, whose main concern was to re-create on earth the abstract and unsullied world of pure spirit.

The Vimala Shāh Temple (Figure B)

The entrance to the temple proper (Figure A. 6) is guarded by *makaras*, sea monsters who protect the treasures of the deep. Below them is another watery images, a pair of conches. The conch is a symbol of the origin of existence. It has the form of a single point spiraling into ever-increasing spheres. When blown in temple ritual, it produces a sound that resembles the primeval sound (*OM*) from which creation evolves. In the microcosm, the conch represents the human ear, through which the pilgrim hears the truth that sets him free.

Vimala Shāh Temple—pillared mandapa.

Entering the temple is like stepping under water, into a pure and crystalline world, dappled by sunlight. Every inch of the cool white marble is intricately carved into layer within layer of detail. Pillars, linked to one another with elaborately scalloped arches, positively writhe with tendril forms. Above them the ceiling rises and disappears in a gradated series of ever more deeply undercut figures of animals, deities, and cusped lotuses. Yet there is no busy-ness, nor does the tracery degenerate into some birthday-cake extravagance. The place has an order and restraint that is more classical than baroque. Despite the fantastic elaboration of the carving, the effect is somehow simple.

In many a Hindu temple similarly exuberant carving evokes

Vimala Shāh Temple—cusped arches and ornate capitals.

the jungle, with its sinuous and irrepressible organic energy. Here the effect is more crystalline. We are inside a faceted jewel, a snowflake, or a cavern of salt-bleached coral. This astonishing effect is the result of several factors. The restrained quality of the white marble adds lightness to intricacy and prevents the carving from becoming too fussy. The walls of the temple are open to the sun and air. This creates a feeling of lightness and expansion and counteracts any tendency of the carving to be too cluttered or oppressive. Organic forms are judiciously tempered by geometric motifs; male and female energies are balanced. The alternation of areas of light and shade creates a restful atmosphere that is very powerful. This tranquility is enhanced by a silence that is audible, increased, rather than diminished, by the fluttering of birds that pains-takingly build their nests in the fretted recesses.

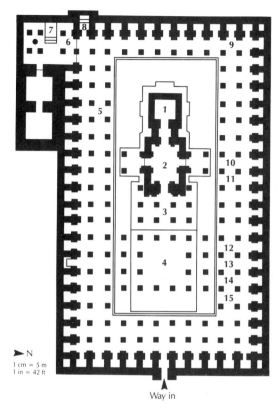

►N
1 cm = 5 m
1 in = 42 ft

▲
Way in

1 *Sanctum.* 2 *Vestibule.* 3 *Portico.* 4 *Hall* (mandapa).
5 *Chakrasurī.* 6 *Corner shrine.* 7 *Ādinātha.* 8 *Ambikā.*
9 *Krishna and the Serpent.* 10 *Krishna and the Gopīs.*
11 *The Goddesses of the Four Directions.* 12 *Shītalā.*
13 *Sarasvatī.* 14 *Padmavatī.* 15 *Narasingha.*

Figure B. The Vimala Shāh Temple ground plan.

The Jains usually adopted or adapted existing regional styles.
Thus the layout here is similar to the Hindu temples of Gujarāt.
The main building stands on a single axis, focused on the
sanctum (B.1), which contains the image of the first *tīrthankara*, Ādinātha. This is preceded by a larger vestibule (B.2),
whose side entrances give the plan a cruciform shape. The
sanctum is emphasized externally by a compact pyramidal
roof. The main shrine and vestibule are linked to a portico
(B.3), which is in turn united with a platform (B.4), that is a
few steps lower. Such open hexagonal *mandapas* are a
speciality of Gujarātī temples. The sunken platform is used
for ritual dances and congregational purposes. It is surmounted

by a shallow dome, perhaps twenty feet (six meters) wide, supported on eight finely carved dwarf columns. These columns are joined by scalloped arches to form an octagon. Running around the edges of the temple is a double colonnade of intricately carved pillars. Lining the walls of the courtyard are fifty-two side shrines, each containing a *tīrthankara* seated in meditation. Reminiscent of the cells around a Buddhist *vihāra*, where the monks slept and meditated, these shrines represent the fifty-two temples that adorn the central mountain of the mythical continent Nandīshvar-advīpa, "the abode of the Lords of Joy." In this Jain paradise the *tīrthankaras* are incessantly adored by the gods.

In a Jain temple no deity is worshipped as a dispenser of salvation. The enlightened Masters act as ideal prototypes, spurring men on to ever greater heights by their calm and unshakable presence.

The repetition of these figures serves to instill in the pilgrim's mind the form of the perfected ones. They act as an example, for although a *tīrthankara* cannot intercede, his life and history are a constant encouragement to the Jain to seek his own *nirvāna*. The mere repetition of the forms here soothes the mind, like a chant or *mantra*. The place of images in Jainism is explained in an old story. A king entered a Jain temple. Approaching one of the many wall shrines, he paused, thinking to himself: "Why should I bow down before this lifeless image? What good will it do me?" As fate would have it, the Jain saint Vipulamati was in the temple at the time. He answered the king with these words:

> An image affects the mind. If a red flower is held up before a glass, the reflection will be red; if a dark blue flower is held up, the reflection will be dark blue. Just so the mind is modified by an image. The mind that contemplates the image of a passionless *tīrthankara* in a Jain temple will automatically be filled with the feeling of renunciation—just as it will become restless at the sight of a courtesan. No one can regard the peaceful form of the Lord without imbibing some of His qualities; and this influence becomes stronger the more one worships. The mind immediately becomes purified. Given purity of mind, one is on the road to absolute bliss.

The ceiling of the colonnade has some lovely panels. Many of them contain images of deities. The most important panels are discussed below.

□ *CHAKRASURĪ* (Figure B.5)

Chakrasurī, "Disk of Brilliance," was the personal deity of Ādinātha, the first *tīrthankara*. She is attractively carved and surrounded by a frieze of musicians, which is picked out in fine detail in the delicate orange grain of the marble. The details of her legs, waistband, and heavy ornamental jewelry

have been lovingly depicted. Chakrasurī has six arms. They
hold two discuses, a bow and arrow, a thunderbolt, a noose,
and an elephant goad. The bow and discus, together with the
fact that Chakrasurī is mounted on the mythical bird Garuda,
identify her as an esoteric consort of Vishnu. Garuda, "Wings
of Speech," is half-vulture, half-man. He represents the power
of mystic utterance and *mantra*. He devours the serpent,
symbol of time. The discus, a sun symbol, stands for creativity and the mind. It also refers to the *chakras* of the subtle
body, themselves depicted as lotuses. The bow symbolizes
the ego. The arrows are the senses, by which we are trapped
in the illusion of the world. The noose is used by Chakrasurī
to capture the restless minds of her devotees. Her goad is a
type of mace, representing the power of knowledge. The
thunderbolt (*vajra*) is also a common tantric symbol of spiritual power—in particular the power that comes from sublimated sexuality. Chakrasurī is flanked by attendants, who
fan her with yak-hair flywhisks (*chaurīs*), signifying the eternal law (*dharma*), which winnows the unrighteous from the
righteous. So this little figure contains a concentrated teaching. Chakrasurī catches the mind of the devotee who meditates on her, destroys his ignorance, and leads him to
enlightenment.

□ *CORNER SHRINE* (Figure B.6)
The southwest corner of the courtyard has been renovated.
The shrine here houses a massive *mūrti* of Ādinātha (B.7),
which sits over eight feet (two and a half meters) high. This
vast figure not only emphasizes the spiritual stature of the
tīrthankara but refers to the fact that in previous ages, when
humanity was purer and happier, we were a race of giants.
Men born in the Golden Age were two miles (three kilometers) high and had 256 ribs! All mothers gave birth to twins,
a boy and a girl, and the population of the sexes always
remained equal. There was no need for work, cooking, or
religion, and a long and healthy life was assured. These idyllic conditions gradually deteriorated until the present age,
which is the most miserable and debased of all. After mankind
has reached its lowest point, we slowly work our way back to
a Golden Age. In time, this again begins to degenerate, and
so the cycle rolls on, through all eternity.

Ādinātha was reputed to have been five hundred bow shots
high, and to have lived for eons. The story goes that the land
at Dilwara originally belonged to the brahmins. When Vimala
Shāh wanted to build here, they replied that he could only
have the land if he proved that it originally belonged to the
Jain community. He prayed to the goddess Ambikā, who told
him in a dream that he was to dig under the *champak* tree
that was on this spot. He did so and found this huge *mūrti*

of Ādinātha. The brahmins accepted the miraculous sign and granted him the land. Opposite the seated sage are several figures representing Vimala Shāh and his wife. At the southern end of the shrine stands another representation of Mount Shatrunajaya. The little shrine next door (B.8) has a fine figure of Ambikā, the Mother Goddess, draped in bright *sārī* material. *Pūjās* are performed here every morning and evening to commemorate the miracle of the building of the temple.

□ *KRISHNA AND THE SERPENT* (Figure B.9)
One of the many legends of Krishna's childhood tells how he overcame the cosmic serpent Ananta, "the Unending." Krishna was playing with his golden ball one day when it fell into the River Yamunā and was captured by Ananta, who was lurking under the water. Unafraid, Krishna dived in to retrieve it. The serpent, out of respect, put up its hands in salutation. The young god effortlessly held the serpent at bay with his hand and retrieved the ball without coming to any harm. This simple story has deeper meanings. On the level of folk myth, it celebrates the god's miraculous ability to "retrieve" the sun from the clutches of night. Each morning the "young" deity reappears with the life-giving light. Esoterically, Ananta is the serpent-power *kundalinī*, which awakens higher levels of consciousness and psychic powers in man. The water is the mind. If one "dives" innocently into the mind and faces its unconscious levels without fear, the power of *kundalinī* is waiting there to be utilized. As a sun symbol, the golden ball represents the true self.

□ *KRISHNA AND THE GOPĪS* (Figure B.10)
A well-known myth of the young god. The dance of delight (*rāsalīlā*) is the basis of many folk dances in western India. It later became a common motif of Rājasthānī and Gujarātī painting. Krishna's favorite cowgirl was Rādhā ("Success"), and their love has throughout the ages been the supreme Hindu symbol of the individual soul's yearning for God. The story has given rise to some of India's most beautiful poetry, on a level with the Song of Songs and the devotional verses of the Sūfis. Jayadeva, the medieval author of the *Gītā Govinda*, describes Krishna:

> His azure breast glittered with pearls of unblemished lustre, like the full bed of the brilliant blue Jamunā, interspersed with curls of white foam. From his graceful waist flowed a pale yellow robe, which resembled the golden dust of the water lily, scattered over its blue petals. His lips glistened with the liquid radiance of smiles, and his locks were interwoven with blossoms, like a cloud variegated with moonbeams. On his forehead shone a circle of odorous oils, extracted from the sandalwood, which glowed like the moon just appearing on the dusky horizon.

Vimala Shāh Temple—Sarasvatī and attendant.

Krishna was born to establish the religion of love at the beginning of the *Kali Yuga*, the present age of universal strife.

□ *THE GODDESSES OF THE FOUR DIRECTIONS*
(Figure B.11)
Aligned to the cardinal points, these four goddesses orient the temple in space. They were originally worshipped in a daily ritual, as manifestations of space (*akāsha*), the substratum of the cosmos and the source of all forms.

□ *SHĪTALĀ* (Figure B.12)
The goddess of smallpox. Especially popular in Bengāl, she still commands widespread worship.

□ *SARASVATĪ* (Figure B.13)
Sarasvatī, "the Flowing One," is the goddess of eloquence, of wisdom, and of learning as well as the patroness of arts and music. She is the consort of Brahmā, the creator, and represents intelligence. One of the names of this Indian Minerva is Vāch: "The Word." She revealed language and writing to man. She is the mother of poetry.

As a personal rather than a popular deity, she is worshipped quietly at home, in keeping with her refined nature. Her festival falls on Vasanta Panchamī, the fifth day of the spring month of Māgha (January–February). On her festival none may read books or play musical instruments. These are cleaned, placed on an altar, and worshipped as the abodes of the goddess.

Sarasvatī sits on a swan or peacock, and always holds the *vīnā*, a type of *sitar*. The *vīnā* is the indigenous classical stringed instrument of India, and is particularly popular in southern Indian, or Karnātaka, music.

□ *PADMAVATĪ* (Figure B.14)

A tantric deity. She carries the *trishūla* and the snake, both emblems of Shiva that signify yogic skill. The sword is for cutting asunder the knots of attachment that bind us to the world. The double *vajra* is the symbol of male energy; the bell of female energy. United, these two energies create a balanced harmony. Her vehicle is the three-headed *nāga*, symbolizing the *kundalinī* energy and the three principal arteries of the subtle body. She is crowned by the seven-headed serpent king Muchalinda, who represents the full unfolding of wisdom. Padmavatī is the ruler of the lower hemisphere, which in the microcosm is the unconscious mind.

□ *NARASINGHA* (Figure B.15)

Vishnu in his fourth incarnation. He disembowels the evil demon Hiranyakashipu, the personification of arrogance and cruelty. The cult of the man-lion is an ancient one. Like Ganesha, the elephant-headed god, or Hanumān the monkey god, Narasingha is one of the earliest Indian deities. These cults probably originated in the masked dances of tribal ritual. In the man-lion, bravery is worshipped as an aspect of divinity. Narasingha was especially popular with the kings and warriors who converted to Jainism.

□ *THE MANDAPA CEILING* (Figure B.4)

This intricate marble *mandala* is the highlight of the temple. The domed ceiling rises in a series of eleven concentric circles, each more minutely carved than the last. The *mandala* culminates in a pendant, which hangs down like some exqui-

Vimala Shāh Temple—ceiling mandala.

site stalactite over the head of the worshipper. All the architectural energies of the hall seem concentrated here. To stand
underneath is like being in the center of some pearly flower
that is huge yet weightless.

The ceiling is at once the dome of the firmament and the
inner flower of enlightenment; both images are contained in
the lotus motif. On the macrocosmic level, the lotus refers to
the creation of the universe. While the Supreme Lord Vishnu
was lying on the cosmic ocean, he put forth a lotus from his
navel. This was the goddess Earth, born of the unending
Waters. Out of this Earth the holy mountains rise up. All
these peaks are the abodes of the gods and perfected souls.
These mountains are the filaments of the lotus, filled with
precious gems. The outer petals are the distant lands of
foreigners. The undersides of the petals are the realms of
demons and serpents. In the center of the pericarp is the
mythical Nandīshvaradvīpa.

On the microcosmic level this flower is the thousand-petaled
lotus of enlightenment, radiant as the sun. Whenever a yogi,
purified by incessant austerities and perfected through initiation, achieves full realization, he crosses the ocean of change.
He becomes a *tīrthankara* and assumes his rightful place in
the unchanging halls of the blessed, safe on the farthest
shore.

All these messages are subliminally coded into the architectural forms of the temple. It acts as a repository of all the
Jain wisdom and accumulated lore. Images and stories that
have been imbibed since childhood are hidden here, waiting
to be intuited and experienced afresh.

Vimala Shāh Temple—ceiling mandala *(detail).*

The lower rings of the dome are straddled by brackets in the form of goddesses whose gaze is distant yet benign. These personifications of wisdom offer a protective warmth of feeling that is a welcome contrast to the overall masculinity that characterizes the temple. So fine is the carving that the very texture of the stone seems destroyed, and the deeply undercut figures appear quite fragile. Vimala Shāh had a novel way of insuring that his masons produced the finest work possible. Once the figures were carved, the masons set to with their files. The dust produced by each man in refining his carving was collected and weighed, and he was paid accordingly. Indeed, we have here a jeweler's art transferred to marble.

□ *THE SANCTUM* (Figure B.1)
The image of Ādinātha is secluded in the holy of holies. Only the priests are allowed past the red and gold threshold. The image, like the image in a Hindu temple, is treated as a monarch. It is bedecked with a headdress and fanned by attendants with the silver flywhisks (*chaurīs*) that are hanging on the right of the door. But in Jainism, temples have a particular purpose: to destroy the power of time. They were built where a *tīrthankara* was born, or initiated, received enlightenment, taught, or dropped the body. Similarly, the holy mountains commemorate significant events. Neminātha, the twenty-second *tīrthankara*, became enlightened at Girnar, and Pārshvanātha, Mahāvīra's predecessor, did so at Sametshikhara.

Thus pilgrimages in Jainism are not a matter of worshipping a god but of repeating and reenacting such holy events. In this way sacred time, which is imbued with eternity, is reestablished over profane time, which merely marks the inevitable progress of decay from birth to death. By regularly reenacting the events of a life that transcended mortality, the Jains seek to overcome the passage of time for themselves. This purpose also applies to daily temple ritual. The cult image is bathed in milk to symbolize the birth of the *tīrthankara*. Outside the shrine door stands an embossed silver pagoda of several tiers. This commemorates the heavenly pavilion (*samāvasavāna*), from which the *tīrthankara* first preached. At certain festivals a small image of the *tīrthankara* is placed in this pavilion and moved across in front of the door. Then he sits under the protective *pandal*, the embroidered cloth, which has the same symbolic function as the buddhist *chhattra*. On these occasions devotees sit in the *mandapa* and sing hymns (*bhajans*) of praise to the image. Scriptures are read as if the *tīrthankara* were actually alive and preaching to the devotees.

The Jains, like all Indian sects, believe that reality is that which never changes. To the *tīrthankara*—as to the Buddha and to the Hindu yogis—the world of change is *māyā*, a cosmic illusion. But whereas the Hindu temple is the abode of the gods and the Buddhist *stūpa* is a reminder of the eternal *dharma*, the Jain temple is paradise on earth. It represents the hall in which the enlightened sit and preach. By visiting the temple, a Jain is reminded of a level of reality that is always here but is usually obscured by our mundane concerns. This is the world of the spirit, as pure and as simple as the naked figure of the *tīrthankara*.

This sense of static perfection is reinforced by architecture. Repetition of design, images, and motifs combines with the white marble to create an effect of unchanging uniformity. When successful, this technique makes the temple seem somehow frozen in time.

The Unfinished Temple (Figure A.7)

This was begun in the late thirteenth century by Brahmā Shāh, chief minister of the Mahārāna of Udaipur. It was never completed because the Mahārāna was at that time engaged in a war with neighboring princes in Gujarāt. Faced with the choice of finishing his temple or financing the war, the loyal Brahmā Shāh chose the latter.

The temple is dedicated to Ādinātha. It was originally intended to outshine all the other temples here. As it is, all that remains of note is the image itself. Made of *pancha-dhātu*—an amalgam of gold, silver, copper, brass, and zinc—it is reputed to weigh 108 *maunds* (4.76 tons, or 4.32 metric tons). With its fine luster and third eye glowing in the half light, the figure is reminiscent of a Himālayan icon. Tantric influence can also be seen in the roof animals. Together with the style of some of the panels in the colonnade of the Vimala Shāh Temple, this suggests that the Ābū builders employed craftsmen from the northeast—the original home of Jainism and the home of Tantra. They would have brought their traditions of iconography with them.

The temple platform overlooks the rather futuristic domed roofs of the temples to the south. These are basically a combination of Buddhist and Hindu styles. The flattish dome of the *stūpa* is surmounted by a typically Hindu finial—the *āmalaka* fruit supporting the pitcher of ambrosia. The view from here is particularly lovely at sunset.

The Digambara Temple (Figure A.8)

This is the only shrine at Ābū belonging to the "sky-clad" sect. Its image is even more austere and unadorned than usual, reflecting the extreme asceticism of the sect. The only embellishment on the body is the *shrīvasta*. The altar is hung with Jain flags, on which the *svastika* is a prominent motif. This goes back to the earliest days of Indian civilizations. Bricks at the city of Mohenjodaro (2000 B.C.) have been found stamped with the sign. It derives from the cross. Here the four cardinal directions spring from the unmanifested central space. This is the development of the multiple world from the basic unity of spirit. But the arms of the *svastika* are bent away from the center. As regards the macrocosm, this implies the continual and cyclical movement of time. As regards the microcosm, it teaches that we cannot regain the basic unity through the gross forms of the universe. The spirit is hidden. The *svastika* can face either way (see Figure C). Similarly there are two ways to the spirit: the "right-hand path" of ritual and worship or the "left-hand path" of esoteric techniques. Since the state of enlightenment conquers time, it is represented diagramatically as the opened lotus surmounting the cycle of history and rebirth, just as it surmounts the head.

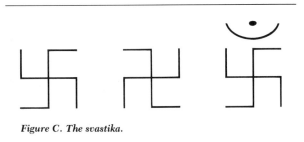

Figure C. The svastika.

Tejapala Temple (Figure A.9)

This was built in 1230, by two brothers, Tejapala and Vāstupala. These wealthy merchants also built the triple temple on Mount Girnar. The temple here is dedicated to Neminātha, the twenty-second *tīrthankara*.

The Tejapala follows the same design as the Vimala Shāh, having a holy of holies, a vestibule, a portico, and, at a lower level, an open hall. But its atmosphere is quite different. Whereas the earlier temple created an effect of lightness and expansion in the visitor, here the effect is more one of concentration. As soon as you enter, your attention is held by the heavily fronded arches that ring the hall. These serpentine scrolls lead the eye to the shrine doorway, where the figure of the *tīrthankara* is just visible as a faint glimmer in the inner darkness. Approaching the image is like penetrating to the very heart of matter. The doorway is surrounded not by figures but by geometrical shapes that resemble rock strata. Again, the domed ceiling of the *mandapa* is superb.

Mathematical patterning is the dominant theme of the carving here. The ceiling panels of the colonnade contain deeply cut motifs that are like Islamic designs executed in high relief; the effect is of a crystalline regularity and order.

These incised panels are bordered by carved frames that act as low lintels spanning the cloistered walkway. These repetitive overhead beams, and the images sitting silently in their niches one after the other, combine to produce an almost hypnotic effect on the circumambulating pilgrim. Often the panel is divided into a number of small designs that seem in their regularity to mimic molecular structure. It is as if the masons had managed by their yoga to experience, and then reproduce, the very structure of matter. The creamy stonework of the northeast corner of the colonnade has some particularly fine examples of this visionary art.

At the back of the courtyard stands a hall for the figures of the patrons of the temple. It runs the width of the compound.

Tejapala Temple—lattice screen (jālī) in courtyard.

Here the two brothers, their wives, elephants, and various *tīrthankaras* are immortalized in stone.

Many of them stand stiffly upright, like soldiers of the spirit, impervious to the ravages of time. The theme of the standing *tīrthankara* has both historical and mythical importance. A common representation of the universe in Jain cosmology is the giant in human form, the Cosmic Man. The lower part of its body is the underworld, the dwelling place of the demons. From the waist to the head are the heavens, where the gods live. The crown of the head is the place of the *tīrthankara*.

The theme of the Cosmic Man is enacted at the holy mountain of Shravana Belagolā, the principal pilgrimage center in the south. Here there stands a sixty-foot (eighteen-meter) statue of Bahūbali, eldest son of Ādinātha. Every twelve or fourteen years there is a festival of libation. It is attended by hundreds of thousands. Priests build scaffolding over the statue to a height of seventy feet (thirty-six meters). At the climax of the ceremony, 1,008 copper pots of sacred water are poured over Lord Bahūbali's unflinching head. Then he is anointed with the sixteen sacred substances. These include milk, ghee, curds, silver, gold, jewels, flowers, vermilion, saffron, and sandalwood.

Tejapala Temple is perhaps too stylized to be considered in the same class as its predecessor; it presents too rigid an image of cosmic order. This inflexible regularity exemplifies the mechanical formality that characterizes too much of later Jain art. Nevertheless, it has a great deal of charm when seen as a complement to the Vimala Shāh. Taken together they constitute what must be reckoned one of the architectural wonders of the world.

6

JAIPUR

A MAHĀRĀJĀ'S LEGACY

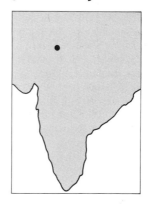

The *mahārājas* ("great rulers") were the governing princes of India. Until Independence and Partition in 1947, they reigned as absolute and hereditary sovereigns over a third of the Indian subcontinent and a quarter of her population. After independence the princely states were merged into the Indian Union, but the *mahārājas* kept their private lands and possessions and were awarded privy purses from the government. As the years went by, these stipends were slowly whittled down, until they were finally abolished by Mrs. Indira Gandhi in 1973.

Since the gradual onset of British rule in India, the *mahārājas* had constituted what was virtually a second tier to Her Majesty's government. They had been allowed to keep their independence and administer their own territories. In fact this arrangement suited the British well, since it removed much of the burden of attempting to govern an enormous and diversified land that in the past had absorbed all the foreign rulers who had tried to impose their will on it. This policy of autonomy had paradoxically been strengthened after the Indian Mutiny—or, depending on your viewpoint, the first Indian War of Independence—in 1857. The Mutiny had brought home sharply to the *Rāj* the difficulty and possible danger of attempting to rule India. Henceforward the government was happy to let the Indian princes keep their autonomy as long as they acknowledged the ultimate authority of the Queen Empress in England and her representative, the viceroy, in Delhi. The *mahārājas* could thus act as bulwarks between the British and their subjects.

The Indian princes' loyalty also took more tangible forms, especially in the military sphere. The *mahārājas* themselves sometimes fought for Britain and distinguished themselves on the field of battle. The Mahārāja of Jaipur was one of the leaders of the assault on Monte Cassino in Italy in 1943, and Bundi Mahārāja won the Military Cross for his part in the Burma campaign of the same war. Moreover, many of the princes kept private armies. These were raised, equipped, and maintained entirely at their own expense and were often loaned to the British in time of need. The camel corps of the Rājasthānī Mahārāja of Bikanīr fought for Britain in two world wars and saw active service in France, Palestine, Egypt, Burma, and even China. Gwālior sent infantry and hospital ships to help the British in World War I, and it was the Mahārāja of Jodhpur's cavalry that led the charge that took Haifa from the Turks in General Allenby's Palestine campaign in 1917.

Jodhpur himself is perhaps more famous for inventing the riding breeches named after him. On the way to Queen Victoria's Diamond Jubilee celebration in London, His Highness's luggage was lost at sea. The prince was reluctantly forced to reveal the secret of how his favorite trousers were made to a London tailor, and the Western world added another garment to its wardrobe.

There were 565 members of the Chamber of Indian Princes, and it must have been the strangest and most eccentric governing body ever to meet under one roof. Some rulers, such as the Mahārāja of Kashmīr or the Muslim Nizām of Hyderabād, had kingdoms as large and as populous as European countries. Others, such as Kāthiāwār, ruled territories not much larger than Disneyland. In fact, over four hundred of the princes had domains that were less than twenty square miles (fifty-two square kilometers). Their characters were as varied as their kingdoms. Some were truly remarkable men, intelligent administrators genuinely concerned with the progress and advancement of their people. In this century the princes of Baroda, Bikanīr, and Mysore were notably enlightened rulers. They worked to abolish such customs as caste untouchability, polygamy, and the educational inequality that they felt hindered their country's entrance into the modern world. Others were great patrons of traditional Hindu *dharma* in its religious and artistic expression, seeking to preserve all that is best in Indian life. The present Mahārāja of Banāras, Vibhūti Nārāin Singh, is an outstanding example of this type of leader.

But it is for their extravagant eccentricities that the *mahārājas* are mainly remembered. They were perhaps the last frivolous flourishing of the truly exotic in a world that has grown increasingly gray and apprehensive in the years since they departed from the scene. Even in the period between the two world wars, some of the *mahārājas* managed to indulge themselves in memorable follies. Gwālior Mahārāja had an obsession with toy trains. He had over 250 feet (75 meters) of solid silver rails running from the kitchens to the royal dining room, and the food was brought along the tables in exquisitely decorated carriages pulled by model trains. Unfortunately, during one particular banquet, there was an electrical fault and the trains went beserk, spilling food all over the guest of honor, the viceroy. The Mahārāja of Junagadh's obsession was not trains, but dogs. His favorite was a bitch called Roshanā. When the time came for her to be mated, she was married in the style of a royal princess, by brahmin priests and according to ancient Vedic rites. The radiant bride was adorned with necklaces of pearls, rubies, and gold, and her husband, Bobby, was proudly arrayed in a cloth of the finest Mysore silk, his neck and ankles hung with chains of solid gold. The ceremony was witnessed by over seven hundred guests from all over India; the viceroy was one of the few to decline the invitation, declaring the whole affair to be "a piece of unprecedented silliness." Silliness or not, a great time was had by all, and the celebrations were sumptuous. The Mahārāja was so pleased with the marriage that the royal kennels were increased to a thousand dogs, and Roshanā spent the rest of her days on velvet cushions in an air-conditioned apartment, fed on the finest food.

Bhūpinder Singh, the seventh Mahārāja of Patiāla in the Punjāb, devoted himself to a life of the pleasures of the flesh. He had a *haram* of over 350 women, and he even had a resident team of plastic surgeons on hand to alter the shape of any woman he felt could do with a little improvement. He was also fond of food. The current favorites of the *haram* were served a dinner of a hundred dishes on golden platters. The less favored had to make do with only fifty dishes on plates of solid silver, whereas those who were out of favor had only twenty dishes, served on brass plates. Bhūpinder Singh himself was always fed off gold plates studded with precious stones, and the number of dishes served to him was never less than 150. The Nawāb of Jeora was regularly advised by a panel of six councilors drawn from the ranks of the local lunatic asylum, whereas the Nizām of Hyderabād, who was the richest man in the world, had the reputation of behaving as if he were the poorest. His palace was huge, as befitted the seat of government of a kingdom that, with a total area of over eighty thousand square miles (two hundred thousand square kilometers), was larger than that of England and Scotland combined. Every corner of the run-down building was stuffed with money or jewels. Bundles of bank notes wrapped in old paper bags or newspaper were squashed into cupboards, gold coins flowed out of ancient teapots and dusty jars in every room. In the ramshackle grounds there was a fleet of dozens of trucks, stranded and abandoned, sunk in the mud with the weight of their cargo of thousands of gold ingots.

From childhood on, the Nizām's chief delight had been in rummaging through the stacks of wealth he had inherited from his forefathers. The palace cellars were full to overflowing with gold, silver, and jewels. Throughout his life he never allowed anyone but himself to carry the keys of these vaults. He slept with them in his hand, and he had a list of his personal jewelry, which never left his pocket, day or night. So vast was this bulk of wealth that when it was transferred from the palace at the time of Independence in 1947, the vaults of the Imperial Bank of India in Bombay filled to overflowing. The residue was taken to the Mercantile Bank of India, which in turn had to improvise special cellars to contain it all, once their own considerable safe deposits were full. In addition to all this, the Nizām had property and lands worth millions.

The Nizām's wealth was matched only by the meanness of his character. At the time he acceded to the throne, he threw several members of the family out of the palace; some of these became street beggars and died penniless. A chain smoker, he smoked the cheapest brand, and he even smoked the butts that his visitors left in his ashtrays. If any visitor offered him a superior make, he would take the cigarette and hoard it for days. If anyone went to have tea with the Nizām, they were served one cookie, no more no less. To save money the electric current in the palace was kept at such a low level that no machine could run properly! The Nizām's bedroom was like a rubbish heap: furnished with an old bed, a battered table, and three kitchen chairs, all covered in cigarette ash. It was cleaned only once a year, on the great man's birthday. His dress was simple to the point of being slovenly: an old shirt, pajama trousers, battered slippers, and a fez reputed to be thirty-five years old!

But although it is men like Bhūpinder Singh and the Nizām of Hyderabād who capture the headlines of the world's imagination, probably the most remarkable of all the *mahārājas* lived in Rājasthān in the eighteenth century. His name was Sawai Jai Singh II, and his enduring monument is the beautiful city of Jaipur.

From an early age Jai Singh exhibited a tremendous interest in all branches of learning and showed a mature self-assurance that was to stand him in good stead throughout his life. When he was only seven, he met the last of the great Mughals, Aurangzeb. The emperor, fanatical in his hatred of the Hindus, rose to meet the young lad.

"Your ancestors gave me much trouble," he thundered. "I trust you will not be the same!" So saying, he grabbed the boy's arms, sneering. "And what use are these little arms now?" Unperturbed, Jai Singh coolly replied: "Your Highness, when a bridegroom takes his bride's hand in marriage, he is duty bound to protect her for life. If the Emperor of all India has taken both of my hands in his, what have I to fear? I need no arms other than thine."

Aurangzeb was so impressed that he predicted that the young Jai Singh would be one and a quarter (*sawai*) times as great as his illustrious ancestor and namesake, Mīrzā Jai Singh. "So let Sawai be the title of you and your successors," concluded the delighted Mughal. The name stuck, and the founder of Jaipur and his descendants adopted the sobriquet.

Sawai Jai Singh ascended the throne of Amber at the age of thirteen, in 1700. His kingdom was then a comparatively small state in Rājasthān, the home of the martial and chivalrous Rājputs. The Rājputs are to India what the conquistadors and troubadours were to Europe: civilized knights who lived under their own codes of chivalry, dedicated to the twin deities of love and war. They claimed to be the original *kshatriyas*—warriors—of the ancient Hindu social system, born out of the fire offering of the gods on Mount Ābū. These hardy and romantic people were probably descended from tribes of Scythians and Huns who had come into India from the northwest at an early date, going south to the flat lands of Rājasthān rather than east to the Gangetic plain. The Rājputs modeled themselves on Rāma, the god-hero of the *Rāmāyana* epic, and they saw themselves as protectors of the Hindu *dharma* against foes and invaders. Their offerings to Durgā, the goddess of war, were blood and wine, and they rode into battle drugged on opium and painted with saffron. In peacetime their relentless energy was poured into hunting and the pursuit and conquest of beautiful women.

Sawai Jai Singh was more a diplomat than a man of the sword. He distinguished himself early by his grasp of the intricacies of politics, and the first twenty years of his reign were largely devoted to establishing good relations with his powerful Mughal neighbors to the north. It was a time of crisis and uncertainty for the young ruler. Relations between the Rājputs and their Muslim overlords were at their worst. Under Aurangzeb the wise policy of religious tolerance adopted by Akbar had been bloodily reversed; persecution and bigotry were rife. The situation was complicated by the fact that there was also a threat to Jai Singh's southern flank from the Marāthā armies in Gujarāt and Mahārāshtra. It was the young king's victories over these claimants to power that won him back the favor of the aging Aurangzeb and allowed him enough political stability to develop his considerable contribution to the history and culture of India.

During these uncertain years, Jai Singh had not neglected his intellectual pursuits. In fact, his mathematical nickname Sawai proved to be prophetic, for the young king was especially interested in mathematical and scientific knowledge. He avidly studied the ancient texts on astronomy under his guru Jagannātha Samrāt, who was a master of Sanskrit and Persian. He had Samrāt translate works of Ptolemy and Euclid into Sanskrit, and he sent an ambassador to Central Asia to find out about the astronomical researches of Mīrzā Beg, the grandson of Tīmūr the Lame (Tamburlaine), who had built himself an observatory at Samarkand in 1425. He sent another emissary to study the observatory of the famous Persian astronomer Tusi, and had his tables brought back to Amber for scrutiny.

It is not unusual to find a Hindu king who was patron of the ancient learning of his own country. What was remarkable about Jai Singh was that he was also very much a man of his time, devoted to the study of contemporary sciences with the open-minded enthusiasm of his counterparts in Europe. The seventeenth century saw an unprecedented zeal for exploring the physical universe, and here in the wilds of Rājasthān, the young prince was a conscious part of this enlightenment, a citizen of the world of Copernicus, Galileo, and Newton.

The fruits of these years of study ripened in the years after 1720, when the throne was secure. Jai Singh decided to build his own observatories at Delhi, Banāras, Ujjain, and Mathurā. He discarded the brass instruments he had had brought from Europe, saying that they were too small; he built masonry ones instead. For seven years he studied the stars, cross-checked existing tables and compiled new ones, and ironed out problems in the construction and maintenance of his instruments. Then, satisfied with his experiments, he moved on to construct the most ambitious of all his observatories, the Jantar Mantar, which lies at the heart of the city of Jaipur.

Jaipur: The New Capital

The foundations of the new capital were laid in 1727. It was to be called Jaipur, "City of Victory," and was to be an impregnable center of civilization, less vulnerable than the old capital of Amber. The chief architect was another exceptional young man, the brahmin scholar Vidyadhār Bhattachārya, from Bengāl. Vidyadhār worked in close collaboration with Jai Singh to realize the king's dream. It took about four years to complete the main palaces and central square, and from this the axial roads were extended in a grid pattern and the buildings bordering them laid out. Six years after the founding of the city, Jai Singh rode round it on a tour of celebration. He was in a ceremonial chariot pulled by four magnificently caparisoned elephants. Typically enough, the chariot was of his own design.

The Nine Squares

Although there existed classical Indian works on architecture and town planning dating from the Gupta period (sixth century), the design of Jaipur was an original and brilliant conception. Vidyadhār's plans were based on the mathematical grid of nine squares (see Figure A). It was a satisfyingly symmetrical and stable design, with the palaces and administration blocks at the center, surrounded by the populace. The north was protected by a lake and gardens, and only the royal priests and scholars were allowed to live on this flank. This area is still known as Brahmāpurī, "City of God." The design was not only practical, with the heart of the city, the palace, being well protected, but it was also satisfying symbolically. The nine-square grid was an ancient Indian map of the universe, with Mount Meru, the home of Shiva, occupying the central and northern portions. In the case of Jaipur the most northwest square of the design was displaced to the southeast corner, allowing the hill fort of Nahargarh—

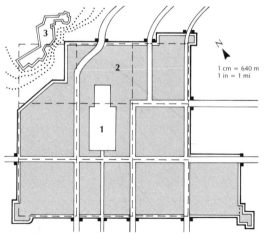

1 *The Royal Palace area.* 2 *Brahmāpurī.* 3 *Tiger Fort.*

Figure A. The Pink City mandala.

"Tiger Fort"—to occupy this corner, and protectively overlook the capital. This fort still provides a superb vantage point over the entire city, from which the grid structure of its design is clearly revealed. Any visit to Jaipur should include a trip up to the fort; it is well worth the climb.

There are interesting similarities between the layout of Jaipur and the design of some of the great Chinese imperial cities of the sixth and seventh centuries, such as Changan, but as far as we know, Jai Singh had no access to such plans. The isolation provided by the surrounding hills allowed the new capital to be a place of safe withdrawal from the surrounding political uncertainty and nurtured the flowering of a fine example of introverted medieval architecture.

□ THE PALACE
The heart of the central square was the seven-storied Moon Palace—Chandra Mahal—which was surrounded by various other public buildings and spacious squares. The ground floor was incorporated into a formal garden laid out in Mughal style and was called "the Abode of the Beloved." The first (U.S. second) floor was highly decorated with Persian floral motifs and called "the Abode of Comfort," whereas the second (U.S. third) floor was inlaid with exquisite mirrorwork—a feature of most Rājasthānī palaces—and known as "the House of Pleasure." The next floor was "the House of Decoration" and contained most of the royal artistic treasures, and the top floor was an open pavilion commanding a magnificent view over the whole city. It was called "the Crowning Glory." Most of the palace is still the private residence of the *mahārāja*, and not open to the public, except for the area known today as "the City Palace," which we shall come to later.

□ THE DESIGN OF THE CITY
At the southeast and southwest corners of the royal square were impressive public squares, called *chaupars*, each of which had a central pavilion and ornamental fountains, as a gathering place for social use. The water for these fountains came from an underground aqueduct, which also supplied water at street level at regular intervals throughout the city. The first thing that strikes the visitor to Jaipur even today is the width and spaciousness of the streets. These were graded according to their use. The principal streets are 108 feet wide (108 being the most sacred number to the Hindu). The smaller streets and lanes were scaled down in proportion—small streets 54 feet wide, lanes 27 feet, and alleys 13.5 feet. Thus the whole city was in perfect relation as far as its arterial system was concerned. Similarly, the shops lining the streets were of a standard size, and there were 165 shops on each side of the main streets between the two *chaupars*. Another feature of

Jaipur streets was their unusually wide sidewalks. These were designed to encourage and accommodate pedestrian traffic, and each sidewalk was also a colorful bazaar which extended out from the shopfronts themselves. When the city was laid out, great respect was paid to the existing villages in the valley, and any temples were carefully left *in situ*, undisturbed. This is why you still see many little temples dotted around the city, often in the middle of the road.

The houses were carefully related to the streets they overlooked. The general pattern was to have the buildings about 54 feet high—that is, half the width of the street. The first (U.S. second) floor was staggered inward several feet, so that the building rose gracefully by stages from the street below, and there was absolutely no chance of the sidewalks becoming overshadowed or oppressed.

Generally speaking, the function of the first (U.S. second) floor space was to act as a gallery overlooking the precinct below. There were both arcades and temples at this level, looking out through the numerous carved and fretted balconies that adorn the main facades of the city. Thus the whole place was designed to facilitate the viewing and enjoyment of parades, processions, and religious festivals. To maximize the uncluttered vista, no trees were originally planted in the main streets, but there were parks and gardens placed at regular intervals around the city.

The building from the second (U.S. third) floor upward would project forward again, over the public space of the second floor, which enjoyed a fluid continuity with the sidewalk area below. This upper part was devoted to private residences.

One of Vidyadhār's problems in designing Jaipur was to deal with the sun, which beats down mercilessly for most of the year. He solved it by designing the shopfronts to minimize the effect of direct sunlight, keeping the interiors cool and shaded and the air circulating. One way he achieved this was by incorporating horizontal stone slabs into the walls, which, supported by sturdy yet delicate brackets, kept large areas of the wall sheltered from the sun. These masonry sun shades (*chhajjas*) present a visual sweep to the wall surface that is balanced by the vertical thrust of the numerous verandahs and window projections that cover the walls of the buildings. These projections, like charming little dovecotes, are often connected by balconies domed by the Rājasthānī-style cupola (*chhatrī*). They are like jewels worked in stone, studding the surface of a building that is perfectly suited to its environment in combining the elegance of a palace with the safety of a fort. The shopfronts were protected by deep awnings, which served to shade the sidewalk and, no doubt, increase business.

The basic social unit of Jai Singh's India was the same as it is today: the joint family. The normal family building was the *haveli*, a residential block, usually three to five stories high, built around a shaded communal courtyard. This courtyard was the public space for the several families who shared the *haveli* and worked as a social and often economic unit. It contained the well, washing facilities, and so on, and it acted as a safety valve for the high-density accommodation, being both a play space for the children and a forum for the elders. Well shaded, the courtyard was kept cool by the rising of the air when it heated up, being displaced by the cooler air that filtered in through the trellised stone screens fronting the lower stories. Each *haveli* was protected from the street by a sturdy gate that delineated the boundary between public and private space. This introverted architecture, insuring the maximum of domestic privacy with consideration for water and shade, is strongly reminiscent of housing throughout the Islamic world. Indeed, the word *haveli* was originally Persian, meaning "an enclosed space."

The city was constructed from the basic building block of the *haveli*. So many *havelis* comprised a district (*mohalla*), and about four hundred districts formed a section (*chokri*). Each district or group of districts housed a particular trade, another feature of medieval cities that reflected the clear-cut divisions then prevailing in society. These social divisions were of course strengthened in India by the caste system, which demanded that certain occupations be kept separate from others for reasons of ritual purity. Not only did each district thus have its peculiar codes of conduct enjoined by caste rules and the dictates of its trade guides (*baradāris*), but it would also have its own temple, whose deity was most appropriate to the type of occupations carried on by the people who lived in that particular district.

This systematic patchwork can still be seen in the city today. The jewel cutters live in Johari Bazaar, the marble workers in Chandpole Bazaar. These trades, like carpet weaving and fabric dying, belong traditionally to the Muslims, who form about 10 percent of Jaipur's population of just over a million. The Hindu cloth merchants, on the other hand, are concentrated in the aptly named Nehru Bazaar.

☐

Tradition dies hard in Rājasthān. One of the most revealing exhibits in the excellent Albert Hall Museum is a tableau of models on the top floor. This shows the dress, facial characteristics, and occupations of the various tribes and castes to be found in the state. One feels that the social organization of this part of India has changed little over the centuries, dictates from the government in New Delhi notwithstanding.

Today Jaipur is a thriving commercial center, known for its banking, jewel merchants, and goldsmiths, as well as its traditional cloth trade. Yet the minute you step off the plane you are in a different world. The overwhelming impression is of being in some ancient Middle Eastern country—a land of camels, hookah pipes, and forbidding walled cities.

The Rājasthānīs are a handsome and noble people. The men are high cheekboned, with strong straight noses and long drooping moustaches. They carry wickedly curved knives or ancient muskets, and they wear embroidered shoes with curling toes, straight out of the Arabian Nights. Their women are extraordinarily beautiful, tall and straight with none of that dissatisfaction one senses in many Indian women. They walk like warriors, as is fitting, for the Rājput women used to fight alongside their men in battle. Here the *sārī* is superseded by a three-piece outfit. A three-yard length of cloth acts as a head covering (*odhnī*) flowing down gracefully over a short half-sleeved bodice (*kanchlī*) that leaves the midriff bare. The skirt (*ghagra*) is heavy, full, and ankle length, and it swirls in a rollicking way when the women move, giving them an extraordinary air of virile femininity. The *ghagra* may take as much as five yards of cloth to make. The color of these garments is breathtaking. Every piece is a deep well of pure color, often inset with sparkling mirrorwork and bordered with heavy bands of intricately embroidered finery. These gorgeously appareled ladies have the knack of combining blocks of brilliant color that should clash but never do—sunflower yellow on vermilion, saffron with deep lime green, turquoise next to ruby red, royal blue and carmine. The dressmakers' skill is highly prized and a valuable dowry asset, and what little spare time there is is largely spent making, mending, and stitching clothes.

Each woman is a walking treasury of jewelry, displaying her family's wealth from head to foot. This is a custom throughout India, partly as a safety precaution to keep the wealth mobile in case of invasion and attack. Rājasthānī women wear heavy nose rings and earrings of solid silver; the earrings (*jhumkas*) are in the traditional pattern of a bell. The hair at the forehead is often decorated by a heavy round boss (*borla*), whereas the neck is hung with closely worked gold and silver necklaces (*hanslī*) that must weigh pounds. Their firm arms are strung with ivory bangles that are the sign of marriage (sometimes tinted red), which can stretch up to the armpit, as well as jangling bracelets that sparkle in the bright sun. Finally there are heavy silver anklets and delicate toe rings that jingle as the women pad barefoot about their business. Far from being encumbered by their finery, these women (like women everywhere in India) are ceaselessly active: not only cooking, cleaning, looking after the children and animals, but also working in the fields and on the roads, where they lift great blocks of stone and carry sand and cement in curved dishes on their heads. Whether standing, squatting, or gliding along, they seem always to exhibit a mixture of self-possession and unconscious sexuality.

The men are usually dressed in white: long shirt or full-sleeved close-fitting vest over the *dhotī*, an untailored piece of cloth (about five by two yards) that is worn tucked up like loose trousers. This plainness is offset by a turban of brilliant orange, yellow, or cerise. The well-to-do Rājasthānī wears the traditional Rājput outfit of close-fitting trousers (*churidār*), a shirt of fine muslin under a long coat with high collar (*achkān*), and a full turban. This is a strip of cloth eighteen yards (yes, *yards*!) long and a mere nine inches wide (sixteen meters by twenty centimeters), embroidered at each end and wound around the head in various ways. Each area in Rājasthān has its style of tying the turban; those who know can tell a man's native place at a glance.

These people radiate a quality the West has all but lost: dignity. A mosaic of tribal and racial types, Jaipur is like some vast caravanserai for nomadic wanderers, temporarily resting before they move on again. The Rājasthānīs themselves exude the nomad's air of proud independence. They squat smoking their hookahs, leaning against well-laden camels. Like their animals, they watch the encroaching modern world with a heavy-lidded gaze of distant disdain.

The weight of tradition is almost tangible here. This is especially noticeable if one has come north from the glitter of Bombay, or south from the offices of Delhi. Neither of these places is really India; Jaipur has far more the flavor of the real country, and, despite its modern facade, is ancient, impassive, and—not far beneath the surface—quite wild.

Bordering the long, straight road that runs from the airport to the center of the city are the camps of an itinerant tribe of metalworkers. These are the Luhars, a people who once inhabited the fortress of Chittor in central Rājasthān. They left when it was taken by the Muslim Alāuddīn Khaljī at the beginning of the fourteenth century, and they vowed never to return while a foreigner was on the throne of Delhi. They have been traveling the country in their ornately carved carts ever since. The Luhars are gypsy astrologers, and their carts have the signs of the zodiac emblazoned on the spokes of their wheels. In 1947 Pandit Nehru, the first prime minister of free India, offered the Luhars their ancestral home again. They refused, saying they would prefer to remain nomadic and free rather than be brought into a union of states they despised. And it comes as no surprise to learn that it is in Rājasthān that there has been the most widespread return to *satī*: the ancient custom of a widow burning herself to death on her husband's funeral pyre. The state has always been a stronghold of the cult, and scores of queens have died here along with the royal concubines on their husbands' pyres. Ten wives and three hundred of the *haram* died with Rāja Suchet Singh, and when Rāja Ajit Singh of Jodhpur died in 1780, sixty-four wives went with him. There have been several cases in the last few years, and the rite seems set for a revival. A recent case was in the spring of 1980, when a sixty-five-year-old woman committed *satī*. She had announced her determination to perform the rite several years before, and so when her husband died, the family locked her in the house on the day of the funeral to prevent her gruesome prediction coming true. It was to no avail. Somehow the woman escaped from her captivity, reached the cremation grounds, and, wearing her wedding dress as the custom demands, eluded the grasp of the horrified onlookers and threw herself on the blazing funeral pyre. She died in flames without a murmur. While the media expressed shock and horror (*satī* has officially been illegal since 1829), the local people also expressed their feelings. The next day the streets of the capital were thronged with thousands of women who had marched in from the surrounding villages. They had not come to protest. On the contrary, they were demonstrating to show their respect and support for the *satī* wife who had died the day before.

Jantar Mantar—the Observatory (Figure B)

Jantar Mantar means "instruments for measuring the harmony of the heavens" and is the name given to Jai Singh's obser-

General view of the Jantar Mantar.

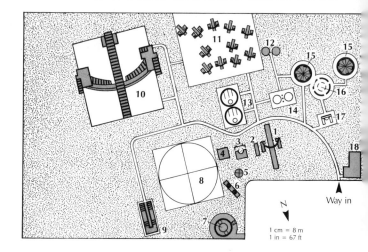

1 *Small* samrāt yantra. 2 Dhruva yantra. 3 Narivalya yantra.
4 *Observer's seat.* 5 *Small* krānti yantra. 6 Rāj yantra.
7 Unnathāmsa yantra. 8 Disha yantra. 9 Dakshina yantra.
10 *Large* samrāt yantra. 11 Rāshivalayas yantra. 12 *Small*
rām yantra. 13 Jai prakāsh yantra. 14 Chakra yantra.
15 *Large* rām yantra. 16 Diganta yantra. 17 *Large* krānti
yantra. 18 *Office.*

Figure B. The Jantar Mantar Observatory ground plan.

vatory. Construction began in 1728 and was completed in
1734. The young king wanted to build an observatory that
would dwarf all the others of his time, and he chose stone as
the material for instruments of unparalleled grandeur. From
a practical point of view, stone lasts longer than brass and
wears better. Where clearly visible surfaces were needed for
complete accuracy, he used marble. The observatory is still
in use today, both for teaching and calculation purposes, and
retains extraordinary accuracy.

These futuristic instruments have a surreal, abstract beauty.
Walking into the observatory is like stepping into some lunar
landscape; the visitor is surrounded by elegant yet alien
structures whose purpose remains a mystery. But there is
nothing abstract about the workings of these massive geometric
instruments. Each serves a particular function in charting
and mapping the movements of the brilliant endless sky that
stretches above.

□ *SMALL SAMRĀT YANTRA* (Figure B.1)
This is a sundial. It consists of a right-angled triangle, the
hypotenuse of which is parallel to the earth's axis and which
casts a shadow on one of the two quadrants below it. Each

Small samrāt yantra.

edge of the quadrants is marked in hours, minutes, and degrees. It gives the time to an accuracy of twenty seconds. To read the time, stand facing the steps that form the hypotenuse. The arc on your left will show the time from sunset to midday; the one on your right tells the afternoon time. To get an accurate reading, read the dial at the point where the shadow is sharpest. All the sundials here are constructed at the latitude of 27 degrees north—Jaipur's latitude—and the time is local Jaipur (that is, solar) time. To correct this with the Indian Standard Time, anything from 1¼ to 32 minutes must be added, according to the time of year and the sun's position. There is always a board by the instrument showing how much must be added.

□ *DHRUVA YANTRA* (Figure B.2)
A brass instrument for finding the position of the Pole Star at night. It also serves to show the position of the twelve zodiac signs, each comprising 30 degrees of the celestial circle, and measures the declination of the sun (that is, how many degrees north or south of the equator it is).

The instrument is graduated and inscribed in Hindi characters, showing both time and position. While nowadays the Hindus reckon angles in degrees and minutes, as does the West, their traditional method of calculating time is based on a different system. The basic unit of this system is the human breath, reckoned to be equivalent to a length of 6 seconds.

$$4 \text{ breaths} = 1 \textit{ pala} \text{ (24 sec.)}$$
$$60 \textit{ palas} = 1 \textit{ gati} \text{ (24 min.)}$$
$$60 \textit{ gatis} = 1 \text{ day (24 hrs.)}$$

☐ *NARIVALYA YANTRA* (Figure B.3)

A sundial with two masonry dials, one facing south and the other north. The former is used when the sun is in the Southern Hemisphere, from September 21 to March 21, and the latter when the sun is in the Northern Hemisphere, from March 21 to September 21. The central iron pin points to the pole. At noon the sun falls on the north–south line; before noon the shadow will lie to the west, and after noon to the east. The time is read in the normal way.

☐ *OBSERVER'S SEAT* (Figure B.4)

Jai Singh's private little building from which he supervised the observations that were carried out.

☐ *SMALL KRĀNTI YANTRA* (Figure B.5)

An astrolabe made of masonry and brass. One of the circles rotates in the plane of the equator, the other in the plane of ecliptic (the circle of the sun's path). It is used for the direct measurement of the longitude and latitude of the celestial bodies, and it can be used day or night.

☐ *RĀJ YANTRA* (Figure B.6)

"The king of instruments." This astrolabe is a map of the visible portions of the celestial sphere, which can be used to calculate a vast amount of astronomical data. A telescope is fixed to a rod that passes through the central hole. The back of the *yantra* is fitted with a bar used for sighting. The plain disk to the left is intended for use as a blackboard, to record observations and calculations as they are made.

The *rāj yantra* is still used once a year (in August) to calculate the Hindu calendar. All the details and festivals of this calendar are based on the Jaipur Standard, as they have been for the last 250 years.

There are twelve divisions or months in the traditional Hindu calendar, spread over the six seasons of spring (March–May), hot season (May–July), monsoon (July–September), autumn (September–November), winter (November–January), and cold season (January–March). In practice, though, the Western calendar is in use throughout India, but there are also two indigenous calendar systems which are sometimes referred to in inscriptions and datings. In the north there is the *Vikrama* era, which dates from 57 B.C., and in the south there is the *Shaka* era, which began in A.D. 78. Thus 1983 is 2040 in the *Vikrama* era, and 1905 in the *Shaka* era.

☐ *UNNATHĀMSA YANTRA* (Figure B.7)

A huge graduated brass circle used for finding the altitudes of celestial bodies. Notice the brass pointer attached to the center of the circle and fitted with sights for observation. The circle can be revolved so that observations can be made at any time, day or night, and the sunken steps allow any part of the circle to be read.

☐ *DISHA YANTRA* (Figure B.8)
Points to the north.

☐ *DAKSHINA YANTRA* (Figure B.9)
A wall built aligned along the north–south meridian. The inscribed arcs on either face of the wall are made of marble and marked in degrees and minutes. It was used for observing the position and movement of heavenly bodies when passing over the meridian (an imaginary circle linking the poles that the sun crosses at midday).

☐ *LARGE SAMRĀT YANTRA* (Figure B.10)
An enormous sundial that towers majestically over the observatory. It operates on the same principles as its smaller counterpart, but it is ten times bigger and thus accurate to two, rather than twenty, seconds. The scale is measured in divisions of one minute, six seconds, and two seconds.

The complete stability of the instrument is assured by the arches cut in the gnomon wall, which allow the wind to pass through them. The gnomon is ninety feet high and is used for finding the time and declination. Its edges are graduated, as are the arcs, and the observer climbs the steps to read them.

Every year on *guru pūrnimā*, an especially holy full-moon day in the Hindu month of Shrāvana (July–August), on which the guru is worshipped, Jaipur astrologers climb the central stairs and fly a white flag from the top of the gnomon. On the basis of the direction the flag takes the texts are consulted, and the length, heaviness, and outcome of the monsoon are predicted for the surrounding area. Like weathermen the world over, the astrologers claim great accuracy!

On either side of the *samrāt yantra* are a remarkable pair of sextants. These are high, narrow chambers set within the walls of the *yantra*. Each chamber has two small square openings high up in the south wall, the only place that light can enter. Each day, at noon, the sun shines through these apertures for about a minute, and the light falls on a graduated arc, made of plaster. From reading the position of the dot of light, the altitude, declination, zenith, and distance of the sun can be seen. The variation in the sun's diameter can also be accurately measured, and even sun spots could easily be observed.

☐ *RĀSHIVALAYAS YANTRA* (Figure B.11)
Twelve sundials, one for each sign of the zodiac. You can easily find your own sign. Each instrument works in exactly

Rāshivalayas yantra.

the same way as the *samrāt yantras*. The instruments have been so constructed that one is available at the instant each zodiacal sign crosses the meridian; hence they enable observations to be made approximately every two hours. Each constellation has its own position, and this can be read off the appropriate instrument.

Astrology and astronomy were two parts of the one science, as far as the Indians were concerned; astronomy was the pure science, and astrology the applied. Because all human and earthly activity was considered to be inescapably bound up with the movement of the heavens, astrology had tremendous importance in determining which days were auspicious, who had what sort of character, what the future held, and so on. This importance has hardly diminished. Even today, eminent politicians, businessmen, and scientists consult their astrologers regularly and plan their lives accordingly. The matching of horoscopes is still the crucial criterion for arranging a marriage.

☐ *SMALL RĀM YANTRA* (Figure B.12)
This is essentially a working model of the large *rām yantra,* for measuring the altitude and azimuth of the sun. In case of damage, all the large instruments have exact scale models for reference.

☐ *JAI PRAKĀSH YANTRA* (Figure B.13)
This elegant instrument is the *pièce de résistance* of the Jaipur Observatory. It acts as a double check on all the other instruments and is unique to the Jantar Mantar.

The *jai prakāsh* measures the "rotation" of the sun. It consists of two hemispherical cavities set in the ground. They are complementary; if put together they would form one complete hemisphere, which would be a map of the heavens.

Crosswires are strung north to south and east to west. Where these join is a small circular iron plate with a hole in the center. The shadow cast by this ring falls on the marble hemisphere below, indicating the sun's longitude and latitude and the sign of the zodiac through which it is passing.

If the shadow falls on an empty space in one hemisphere, it will fall on a solid, uncut portion in the other. The bowls have been segmented and separated so as to allow accurate reading. The observer only has to descend the stairs to get a close view of exactly where the shadow is lying. If the hemisphere had been undivided, such an accurate reading would not have been possible. Moreover, other heavenly bodies can be directly observed from the well of the instrument. This is done by looking upward from the appropriate point on the graduated inscription and observing the passage of the body across the intersection of the wires. There is an underground passage connecting the two bowls.

This is a fine example of Jai Singh's love of things that were both practical and esthetically pleasing. One of the most charming and ingenious of his instruments, it is ideal for demonstrating the apparent motion of the sun and is much used to this day in introducing novitiate astronomers to the science.

☐ *CHAKRA YANTRA* (Figure B.14)
A graduated brass circle that can be revolved about a diameter parallel to the earth's axis, this gives the ascension and declination—that is, angle of an object from the equator. It is an exact counterpart to the modern instrument known as an equatorial.

On either side of the *chakra yantra* lies another instrument called the *kapali*. It is a miniature version of the *jai prakāsh* we have just seen, though here there are no pathways cut in the bowls.

☐ *LARGE RĀM YANTRA* (Figure B.15)
This, and its smaller version (B.12) have the same function. What the *jai prakāsh* does with a sunken hemisphere, the *rām yantra* does with an upright building. These two structures fit together to make one whole instrument. A sector in one building corresponds to a space in the other. There are twelve sectors in one building and eighteen in the other, and the walls have notches for placing sighting bars. The *yantra* is used to find the altitude and the azimuth of the sun.

☐ *DIGANTA YANTRA* (Figure B.16)

A simple and useful instrument, for measuring the azimuth—that is, the angle of any celestial body with the horizon. The central pin and inner wall are the same height; the outer wall is twice as high. The inner wall can be walked along to read the graduations of the outer.

☐ *LARGE KRĀNTI YANTRA* (Figure B.17)

The same as the small *krānti yantra* (B.5).

The City Palace, 1728–1732 (Figure C)

Just around the corner from the Jantar Mantar, shaded by an enormous *pīpal* tree, is the entrance to the City Palace.

☐ *OUTER COURTYARD* (Figure C.2)

The building in the center of the courtyard was the Guest Pavilion (C.3). In Jai Singh's palace the ladies of the *haram* wandered quite freely, so this pavilion was to keep the guests'

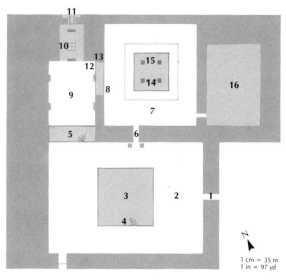

1 cm = 35 m
1 in = 97 yd

1 *Entrance gate.* **2** *Outer courtyard.* **3** *Guest Pavilion.*
4 *Textile and Costume Museum.* **5** *Arms and Armour
Museum.* **6** *Gate to inner courtyard.* **7** *Inner courtyard.*
8 *Entrance to the* zanāna. **9** *Zanāna courtyard.* **10** *Chamber
of Privy Council.* **11** *Ornamental fountains (leading to
gardens).* **12** *Krishna door.* **13** *Portrait of Madhu Singh II.*
14 *Silver urns.* **15** *Hall of Private Audience.* **16** *Art Gallery.*

Figure C. City Palace site plan.

living quarters separate from those of the *mahārāja*. The building is a gem of Indo-Islamic architecture, with its lace-like carved porticos of white marble, whose delicately fringed arches offer tempting pools of shade. The marble is from Makarāna, and the brown sandstone that forms the impressive tympanum over some of the doors is also from near Jodhpur. You can see an ancient form of cooling still being employed; reed matting hung over the doorways, which would originally have been soaked in perfumed water to create a fragrant breeze.

The ground floor of the Guest Pavilion now houses administrative offices of the City Palace Museum. All the material in the Textile and Costume Museum (on the first floor, U.S. second), the Arms and Armour Museum, and the Art Gallery are now no longer the private property of the present *mahārāja* but belong to the Museum Trust.

□ *TEXTILE AND COSTUME MUSEUM* (Figure C.4)
When Jai Singh moved his court from Amber to Jaipur in 1734, four out of the thirty-six imperial departments were devoted to costumes and textiles. This keen interest was continued by his descendants, and the museum collection reflects this artistic patronage with a wide range of exhibits. There are examples of handcrafts that are still practiced today; particularly tie-dye work from Jaipur, and hand-block prints from the little village of Sanganer, twelve miles from the city, which has been famous for its cloth for two hundred and fifty years. Dazzling brocades from Banāras lie next to Gujarātī embroidery, Kashmīrī shawls of the finest workmanship—the original paisley patterns—jostle with decorated silk from Aurangabād or Mysore, and curtains and coverlets from Mughal times. There are several complete costumes and *sārīs*, with excellent embroidery in gold or silver thread (called *zārī*) as well as carpets in wool, cotton, and silk, some of them dating from the seventeenth century. Ornately decorated musical instruments and toys from the royal nursery are also on display.

□ *ARMS AND ARMOUR MUSEUM* (Figure C.5)
In the northwest corner of the courtyard lies the Arms and Armour Museum. Even warfare was conducted as some sort of a divine pageant; the weapons here are embellished with a refined esthetic taste. The chain mail of Rāja Mān Singh, the famous Rājput commander-in-chief of Akbar the Great's army, is here, and next to it his two-handed sword, weighing eleven pounds and curved like a scimitar. In fact the swords here are especially fine. One of them is engraved with the Persian royal insignia, and two of them belonged to Shāh Jahān, whose name is elegantly inscribed in Persian callig-

raphy. There are many knives and daggers that would have been used in hand-to-hand fighting. Their handles are carved from jade, crystal, agate, or ivory, or they are fashioned from gold and silver. The collection of early guns is renowned and includes pistols, flintlocks, blunderbusses, and enormous guns that were mounted on camel saddles to form the first tanks! Especially notable is the huge collection of powder horns, made out of carved wood, mother-of-pearl, horn, shell, or ivory and decorated with delicate embroidery in gold and silver thread or tiny pearls.

Originally the common room of the *haram*, the gallery is very ornate, repainted in the traditional style by local craftsmen in 1924.

Entrance gate to inner courtyard.

☐ *THE INNER COURTYARD* (Figure C.7)
The main gate of the inner courtyard is flanked by two elephants, each carved out of a single piece of marble and bearing the Jaipur royal sun crest emblazoned on their wise old foreheads. The alcove behind these beasts has some excellent inlay work *à la* Tāj, with semiprecious stones set in the marble. There is the running *svastika* border too, an ancient Hindu good-luck motif transformed into an Islamic arabesque.

A magnificent pair of brass doors protect the inner court. Rājasthān is particularly rich in copper and zinc, so brass abounds in the royal palaces. We shall see many fine doors here. Each year, for Divālī, the autumn "Festival of Lights," these doors are painstakingly scrubbed with a mixture of freshly cut lemons and very soft sand, too fine to scratch the shiny brass. The patterning on these doors again reminds one of Islām; they could be from the Alhambra Palace in Moorish Spain.

You emerge into the full sunlight of the second courtyard, a blaze of deep, browny coral light. Each part of the palace is a mellow well of honeyed color—pink, gold, yellow, coral—highlighted by the brilliant red turbans of the white-clad bodyguard of the *mahārāja* who patrol the precincts. In the center of the courtyard sits the Hall of Private Audience (C.15), while on the left rises the grilled wall of the *zanāna*, or *haram* quarters, from which the royal ladies would avidly have watched the goings-on in the courtyard below.

Zanāna *courtyard.*

Within the gateway of the *zanāna* hangs a large picture. This is of the late *mahārāja* in the procession to celebrate his second marriage. He was Sawai Mān Singh II, the world's greatest polo player, who died after a fall from his pony at Cowdrey Park in England. The *mahārāja* is on top of the elephant, as the traditional Hindu bridegroom going to meet his bride, and the little man with the cloth cap is Mahātma Gandhi.

Each day at noon, ceremonial music is played in honor of the *mahārāja*, from a gallery over this gateway. It is a strange sound, reminiscent of Sūfī dervish music or the martial tunes of the esoteric Turkish cavalry, the janissaries.

The main attraction of the *zanāna* courtyard (C.9) is its doors, Indo-Islamic again, with their vivid swirls and zigzags of peacock blue, turquoise, amber, and aquamarine. Each doorway is surmounted by a tiny marble figure of a Hindu god guarding the threshold. To the north of the courtyard looms the Moon Palace, proudly flying the five-colored flag of Jaipur when the current *mahārāja* is in residence. He is Lieutenant Colonel Sawai Bhawāni Singh, known to his friends as "Bubbles," and a good example of how the *mahārājas* have adjusted to their new, diminished status in independent India. Equally at home in his Rājasthānī palace or on the Riviera, "Bubbles" resisted the temptation to emulate some of his fellow princes and blow the remains of his fortune on fast women and slow horses. Instead he kept up the family's military tradition by serving in the Indian army, and then he turned to business.

☐ *THE CHAMBER OF PRIVY COUNCIL* (Figure C.10)
This is where the *mahārāja* would hold private consultations with his ministers. He would sit on the couch, propped up by sumptuous cushions with his hookah pipe beside him. The silver table in front would have a silver tray laden with betel leaves ready for chewing, and, as these were mixed with very fine tobacco, there is a large silver spittoon beside the couch. The chandeliers here are of Bohemian glass; the paintings around the walls are illustrations from the works of the Indian Shakespeare, Kālidāsa, done about fifty years ago by a Jaipurī artist.

Ornamental fountain.

Following the steps around, you come to a *mandala* made of rifles, around a central spear, in the shape of the sun—the royal crest of the Jaipur family. The ceiling in this hall is very fine goldwork done by local artists in the late eighteenth century. The attendant will switch on the lights so the gold-work can be seen properly. Walking out toward the garden, you pass covered palanquins in which the royal ladies traveled, carried by eunuchs. The fountains (C.11) are beautiful examples of Mughal ornamental work, and, together with those in the garden, are still turned on for special festivals when the palace is closed to the public and the *mahārāja* entertains. The walls and ceilings of this corridor were painted in the Versailles style by an Italian prisoner during World War II. There is a delightful portrait of Sawai Jai Singh near the eastern end of the corridor, and there are pure ivory doors under protective glass.

The garden was laid out in the Mughal *chahār bāgh* style, and the vista extends over the private temple of the *mahārāja* (dedicated to Krishna), at the end of the lawns, to the Tiger Fort, up on the steeply escarped hills overlooking the city.

Retracing your steps, you pass the famous brass Krishna door (C.12), embossed with scenes from the god's life. Particularly charming is the panel with the handle, showing the young god perched in a tree, having stolen the *sārīs* of the bathing cowgirls, much to their delighted embarrassment.

The door is sealed in the traditional way, with a rope secured by sealing wax over the lock. Keys can be duplicated, but a seal cannot be broken. This method is still used to lock up the palace at the end of the day. Each afternoon, just before

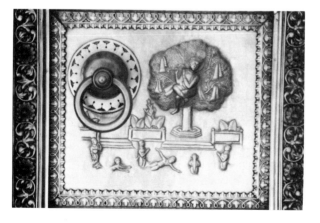

Krishna Stealing the Sārīs, *brass Krishna door (detail).*

five o'clock, one of the palace attendants lights a fire in the courtyard by the Guest Pavilion and heats up the wax to seal the locks.

At the end of the corridor you come to the portrait of the present *mahārāja*'s grandfather, Sawai Madhu Singh II (C.13). He was quite a character. A devout Hindu, he was loath to soil his hands with the touch of a non-Hindu (who, to the strictly orthodox, used to be considered as bad as an outcast). So whenever his duties required him to meet a representative of the British government, including the viceroy, he would wear white gloves to protect his royal skin from the pollution of a European handshake. But that was not all. After the meeting was over, he would immediately undress, bathe himself completely in purifying Ganges water, and give his clothes away to the sweeper.

When he went to England for the celebration of Queen Victoria's Diamond Jubilee, he went suitably equipped. He bought a P&O liner and had the entire ship refitted. Part of it was turned into a temple of Lord Krishna. The crew were to be strictly vegetarian, as he was, and a sacred cow accompanied them. The *mahārāja* always used Ganges water, and so two great urns (C.14) of solid silver, weighing 680 pounds (309 kilograms) each, were filled with the ambrosia and taken on board. It is said that when the *mahārāja* presented himself to Victoria, he took off his gloves, shook hands, and replaced them so quickly that only those right next to him could see that he had at last broken his own taboo.

The gigantic silver urns are still on display in the Hall of Private Audience (C.15), the interior of which is painted in the pale coral shade that originally tinted the whole city.

□ *ART GALLERY AND MUSEUM* (Figure C.16)
This was the Hall of Public Audience. The magnificent ceiling was painted in 1886 and cleaned before the visit of the Queen of England in 1961. The museum is really a tribute to the power of patronage and is especially famous for its collection of miniature paintings.

From the sixteenth century on, there had always been a lively tradition of miniature painting in India, stemming originally from the illuminated manuscripts of the Jains (especially in Gujarāt), which had existed since the twelfth century. This tradition was further vitalized by the influence of the Mughal schools of painting, through direct contact with the emperor's court and the establishment of provincial schools throughout northern India. As with so many things, it is Akbar we have to thank for this cultural cooperation; much of it was due to the fact that he had Hindu and Muslim artists working alongside each other in his atelier.

The Rājput princes had always been great patrons of this

art, and we can see the full flowering of the Indian artistic genius in the Rājput schools such as Bundi (ca. 1590–1800), Kotah (ca. 1630–1850), Mewar (ca. 1600–1900), Jaipur (ca. 1640–1850), Basoli (ca. 1660–1850), and Kāngrā (ca. 1760–1850). The Rājput courts maintained varying degrees of independence from the central court of the Mughal emperor, and the degree of independence can be seen in the amount by which the painting style is influenced by Mughal norms.

Generally speaking, Rājasthānī painting can be divided into three overlapping styles. The early work was predominantly devotional and illustrated religious texts and themes. Particularly popular were the stories of the much loved god Krishna, whose *bhakti* cult was very widespread during this time and coincided with a literary revival in Hindu India. The stories of the god's romantic dalliances were no doubt seen as the prototype of the chivalric and romantic codes of conduct practiced at the Rājput courts. Illustrations of the *Gītā Govinda* (the story of Krishna as told by Jayadeva, a twelfth-century Bengālī poet), the *Shrīmad Bhagavatam* (the life of Krishna), and the *Bhagavad Gītā* were especially popular with patrons.

A second theme was the pictorial presentation of musical modes in a genre known as *rāgamālā*. The theory behind these paintings was that any emotion or feeling can be expressed in form and sound. Thus each of the thirty-six musical modes (*rāgas*) has its corresponding pictorial form, was linked to a particular time and season, and evoked its particular emotion. This type of work, based on the ancient Sanskrit treatises on sound and vibration, is peculiar to Rājasthān and was especially explored by the Bundi artists.

A third theme was the secular representation of courtly life, depicting scenes from the hunt and battle. After about 1760 this genre was influenced strongly by Mughal schools. The Jaipur school produced some very fine paintings in this style, many of which tend to be flat in perspective, with black detailing.

Rājput painting has probably never been more succinctly described than in the words of Ānanda Coomaraswamy as quoted by Benjamin Rowland (see Appendix 2):

> Sensitive, reticent and tender, it perfectly reflects the self-control and sweet serenity of Indian life, and the definitely theocratic and aristocratic organization of Indian society. It lends itself to the utterance of serene passion and the expression of unmixed emotions.

Both religious and secular subjects are well represented in this excellent gallery. In all the paintings the brilliant color of Rājasthān is in evidence. The paints were made of such minerals as cinnabar, vermilion, and lime, and ground precious and semiprecious stones that the state has in abundance. The portrayal of women is always in the Indian convention:

long narrow eyes, firm breasts, slim waists, and flowing dress. What is here is only a fraction of the royal collection (the *mahārāja* still has twenty thousand paintings in his own possession), but even these are stunning and well worth a prolonged visit. In addition to the miniatures there are fine carpets displayed. Particularly worthy of note are the Herat and Lahore specimens, originally used in the Amber Palace, which date from 1630. On the central dais are some aged *howdahs* and palanquins, including one of solid silver.

Fortunately the traditional arts of Rājasthān are still very much alive in Jaipur. There are several ateliers in the city that can be visited (see Appendix 4).

7

DELHI'S QUTB MĪNĀR

THE COMING OF ISLAM

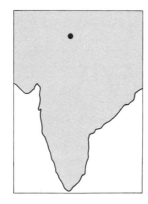

And so to Delhi, the capital of modern India. Your first impression of the place will depend on how you arrive. If you fly in, your drive from the airport to your hotel will be through New Delhi, along wide, well laid out boulevards flanked by large houses with elegantly ramshackle gardens strewn with languid bougainvillea and jasmine. These boulevards are the legacy of the British. They are the arteries of an administrative capital built only fifty years ago to house the government and those who governed. Today the streets of New Delhi are often eerily empty; traffic is light and pedestrians few. Time seems to stand still over their shaded sidewalks; somehow it is always the middle of a hot afternoon, and all activity hangs suspended. Much of New Delhi, the city that was intended to be the greatest creation of its British architects Edwin Lutyens and Herbert Baker, now stands like some imperial ghost town, occupied only by the silent echoes of its former glory.

If you come in by train, the scene is very different. You arrive right in the middle of Old Delhi. Even before the magnificent steam engine has pulled to a halt, passengers are scrambling on and off, clambering over each other to find or vacate a place—for it seems no one in India has yet discovered that it is more efficient to let disembarking passengers off first! Cases and trunks are heaved through open windows and doors; stalwart porters in red jackets stride along, massive tin trunks and khaki bed rolls balanced on their red-turbaned heads. Portly gentlemen, immaculate in freshly pressed white *kurtā* and *dhotī*, amble down the platform; tiny old ladies with faces of angels and elbows of steel barge their way past you, wielding furled umbrellas with deadly accuracy. The station vendors have long since descended upon the train like a swarm of locusts, all uttering their piercing cries: *"Garam chāy!"* (hot tea); *"Pān, achchha pān!"* (good-quality *pān*—a betel-leaf concoction); *"Bīdis!"* (aromatic but lethal cigarettes); "Thumbs up!" (Indian Coca-Cola). Food sellers, shoe shiners, money changers, fortune-tellers—they're all there; fixers of every sort hurry along the platform, sharp eyes looking for business. Somewhere above the din you catch the haunting sound of a blind beggar singing praises to the boy-god Krishna. Everywhere there is baggage, hooting, shouting, and the hiss of steam. You are submerged in the unforgettable pandemonium of an Indian station.

Outside the station the heat, sights, sounds, and smells are even more intense. People are everywhere. The sidewalks spawn a seemingly endless variety of wayside stalls, selling everything under the sun—fruit, swathes of eye-dazzling cloth, shoes, pots and pans, sizzling hot *samoosas* and curry served on leaf plates, engine parts, tea and crushed sugarcane juice, fragrant bundles of incense and Technicolor pictures of the gods (with maybe a movie star or two thrown in for good measure), toothbrushes, vegetables, and *sārīs*. You name it, you can buy it on the streets of Old Delhi.

On the main road auto-rickshaws (scooter taxis) nip through the crowds, buzzing like angry hornets. Cars and bicycles vie with humans and animals. Donkeys, horses, water buffalo, even the odd camel or elephant wander about, and here and there a crowd gathers around a troupe of performing monkeys. Cows, surprisingly, are rare, for during the Emergency in 1975 Mrs. Gandhi banned the ancient symbol of India from the streets of her modern capital. The air is rent with bells and horns, for it is *de rigueur* on Indian roads to blow your horn as often and as loudly as possible. You can hardly hear yourself think. Pity the innocent traveler who arrives unprepared in the middle of this perpetual carnival!

And yet, the scene is not so chaotic as it may first appear. On closer study, you can see there is a dreamlike logic to it all. The cars always seem to brake or swerve just in time, an Indian version of the Keystone Cops, managing to avoid the most horrendous pileups. The cycles manage to miss the animals or pedestrians who step blithely out in front of them without a moment's notice. And if two cars do happen to touch each other, there are usually no grim-faced melodramas about insurance claims and lawsuits, just a reproving grin and wagging finger. Somehow the whole thing works with an astonishing amount of good humor, and every piece of the jigsaw fits unerringly, if unexpectedly, together. The people of Old Delhi live right in the middle of the rummage sale we call the world, and they play their parts faithfully. Perhaps it was in the midst of just such bazaar life that the tenacious desire for renunciation was first born in the Indian psyche.

One thing is certain about urban India: the lack of violence. Considering the press of people and the stress of living in a place like Old Delhi (or Calcutta or Bombay), Indian cities are remarkably peaceful. Compared with the major cities of the West—especially those of America—they are still a relative haven, where even women can walk at night without undue fear of being raped, mugged, or murdered. This is all the more remarkable when one remembers that three or four nights in a five-star tourist hotel in Delhi costs more than the average Indian earns in a year.

The two worlds of Old and New Delhi meet, rather to their mutual surprise, in Connaught Circus. This is the hub of Delhi, a wheel-shaped complex whose spokes radiate out as the main roads of the city. It is the main tourist area for shopping, eating, and generally getting things done. The inner circle of Connaught Circus is called Connaught Place. It surrounds a public park that offers a welcome respite from the hectic traffic.

Delhi's history goes back to earliest times. The historical epic the *Mahābhārata*, compiled between 400 B.C. and A.D. 400, mentions it as Indraprastha. Just northwest of modern Delhi lies Kurukshetra, the site of the cosmic battle between good and evil that took place over three thousand years ago, which is described in the eighteenth chapter of the *Mahābhārata*, known as the *Bhagavad Gītā*, "The Song of God." One of the most popular of the Indian scriptures, the *Gītā* has done more than any other text to acquaint the West with the main teachings of Hinduism.

In more recent times Delhi has borne the brunt of every foreign army that has streamed into the country from the northwest. Because of her strategic position at the entrance to the fertile Gangetic basin, the city has stood guarding the land to the east, like a rock which each fresh wave of invaders has had to submerge or against which it has shattered. Each would-be conqueror has learned the truth of the old saying "He who holds Delhi holds India."

As a result, the city is an archeological palimpsest, with layer upon layer of succeeding civilizations etched into her dusty soil. Fortunately, though, each new layer has not entirely erased its predecessors. So great was the conqueror's need to establish his identity on the flat and seemingly endless expanse of land that is northern India that almost every newly victorious general chose to build a new city to commemorate his arrival. This desire for immortality has left us with the remains of seven distinct phases in the turbulent history of northern India—the so-called Seven Cities of Delhi.

The Seven Cities   The story of the Seven Cities begins at the end of the twelfth century, with the Muslim conquests. At that time Delhi was ruled by the Tomar Rājputs, one of the fierce military clans from Rājasthān. They had selected the hostile and barren Arāvalli Hills south of Delhi as their royal seat, comparatively safe from the attacks of other warring Rājput tribes. But in 1192, an Afghān freebooter named Muhammad of Ghor led his troops into India. He defeated and killed the Tomar King Prithvīrāja Chāhamāna at the Battle of Tavāin. Muhammad then returned to Afghānistān, leaving his slave, Qutbuddīn Aibak, as his viceroy in India. Qutbuddīn captured Delhi the next year. He celebrated his victory by raising the first Muslim city of Delhi, Qila Rai Pithora (Figure A.1—now known as the Qutb Mīnār complex) in the ruins of Lāl Kot, a fort that had been established in the tenth century by the Tomar Rājputs. In 1206, on the death of Muhammad of Ghor, Qutbuddīn had himself crowned sultan of Delhi. In so doing, he inaugurated the first of the five Delhi sultanates that were to rule over most of northern India until the coming of the Mughals, over three centuries later.

The second city, Sīrī (A.2), was built by Alāuddīn Khaljī, early in the fourteenth century. Alāuddīn rose to power by murdering his uncle, who had established the second of the Delhi sultanates, the Khaljī dynasty (1290–1321).

The third city, Tughluqābād (A.3), was created by Ghiyāthuddīn Tughluq. A man of humble origin, Tughluq had risen to power under Alāuddīn Khaljī, whose forces he led in twenty-nine victorious campaigns against would-be Mongol invaders. Tughluq was rewarded for his persistent gallantry by being made governor of the Punjāb. After a brief power struggle on Alāuddīn's death, Tughluq established his dynasty, which lasted from 1321 until 1414. The walls of his giant citadel still stand, as does his tomb, with its massively thick walls and white marble dome.

Tughluq's son and successor, Muhammad bin Tughluq, built his own capital, which he called Jahānpanāh, "The Refuge of the World" (A.4). Muhammad is remembered as "the mad Tughluq." He had plans to outdo even Genghis Khan and conquer the whole of the civilized world. But before

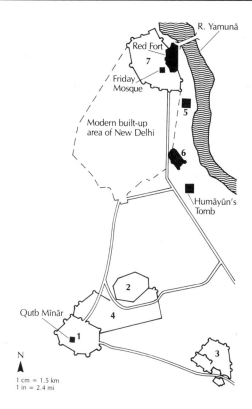

1 *The Qutb Mīnār complex; first city (end of twelfth century).* **2** *Sīrī; second city (ca. A.D. 1300).* **3** *Tughluqābād; third city (early fourteenth century).* **4** *Jahānpanāh; fourth city (mid-fourteenth century).* **5** *Fīrūzābād; fifth city (late fourteenth century).* **6** *Shergarh (Purāna Qila); sixth city (mid-sixteenth century).* **7** *Shāhjahānābād ("Old Delhi"); seventh city (mid-seventeenth century).*

Figure A. The Seven Cities of Delhi.

he could embark on such a grandiose scheme, the southern flank of his empire had to be protected against the warlike Hindu tribes —Rājputs and Marāthās—of the Deccan. More-over, Muhammad believed that a rich harvest of money and materials awaited him in the south. Thus in 1330, "the shadow of God," as Muhammad called himself, decreed that the entire population of Jahānpanāh should shift eight hundred miles (thirteen hundred kilometers) south, to Daulātābād, not far from the caves of Ellorā. The move was a disaster. Thousands died on the enforced march, and the conditions at Daulātā-bād proved to be far from satisfactory. After a mere seventeen years, water ran out there, and the whole population, or what was left of it, straggled back to the old capital. Muhammad's dream had turned into a nightmare.

With the death of "the shadow of God" in 1351, the council of nobles were left in a quandary. There was no heir. They decided to petition Muhammad's cousin, Fīrūz Tughluq, to ascend the throne of Delhi. Reluctantly, he agreed. The new sultan built Fīrūzābād, the fifth city (A.5), along the banks of the Yamunā. Contemporary accounts speak of the city thriving: "The people's homes were replete with grain, property, horses and furniture; everyone had plenty of gold and silver; no woman was without her ornaments, and no house without good beds and *dīwāns*; wealth abounded and comforts were general." Even allowing for the obligatory amount of flattery, by all accounts Fīrūz Shāh was an enlightened ruler, and his reign one of peace, plenty, and accomplishment.

But such settled times were not to last, and northern India soon reverted to her pattern of conflict between warring factions. Various members of Fīrūz Tughluq's family usurped the throne in turn, and Delhi became increasingly unstable. Worse still, in 1398 the Mongol chief Tīmūr the Lame (also known as Tamburlaine) invaded India and plundered the capital mercilessly. Although Tīmūr left the next year, it took the country a long time to recover from the effects of his devastating raids. Political instability continued through the next two dynasties—the Sayyids (1414–1444) and the Lodīs (1451–1526). As a result, comparatively little was accomplished during this time in terms of architecture as town planning. The Afghān Lodīs did leave some mosques and a number of splendid tombs—often embellished with double domes and Persian tiling—but they never established a city as such.

Then, in 1526, a new era began in Indian history. The sultan, Ibrāhīm Lodī, was a treacherous and unpopular ruler. One of his chief nobles sent an invitation to Bābur, king of Kābul, to invade India and take over the throne of Delhi. Bābur was descended on his father's side from Tīmūr the Lame and on his mother's from Genghis Khān. True to his heritage, Bābur accepted the invitation, duly marched into India, defeated and killed Ibrāhīm Lodī at the historic Battle of Panipat, and established the Mughal dynasty. Bābur and his descendants were to govern northern India for the next three hundred years and to bequeath to the country some of its finest treasures, including the Tāj Mahal. The arrival of the Mughals ushered in a renaissance of Indian art and architecture.

The new dynasty got off to an unpromising start. Bābur's son Humāyūn, a dreamy character with a penchant for opium and astrology, was driven out of India in 1543 by Sher Shāh

Sūrī, an Afghān prince who had settled in Bihār and who had designs on the throne. Humāyūn fled to Persia and Sher Shāh built the sixth city of Delhi, Shergarh (A.6), just south of Fīrūzābād, on the very site where Humāyūn had hoped to establish his own capital. When Humāyūn eventually returned to India, in 1555, he had only one year left to live. But he brought with him artists and architects from Persia, and their skills were to have an enormous effect on subsequent Indian culture. Thus Humāyūn, who in many ways seems the least successful, though not the least endearing, of the great Mughals, was indirectly responsible for the consolidation, and above all the refinement, of the Indo-Islamic style that had its beginnings when the first Muslim armies marched into India in the twelfth century. And, in addition, Humāyūn bequeathed the country a son who was to be one of the most remarkable rulers of all time, Akbar the Great.

It was Akbar's grandson, Shāh Jahān, the builder of the Tāj, who established the seventh city of Delhi. Akbar had moved the capital south to Āgra, and then, for a time, to Fatehpur Sīkrī. In 1638 Shāh Jahān moved it back to Delhi. As a testament to the glory of God and the emperor, he created the magnificent Shāhjahānābād (A.7), which covered the area we now know as Old Delhi.

The architecture in and around Delhi can conveniently be classified into four groups, according to date and style:

Early Indo-Islamic (1193–1320)
including the Qutb Mīnār complex, and the Jamaāt Khāna Mosque at Nizām-ud-dīn.
This group develops from an initial adaption of Hindu materials and style to Saracenic requirements, into a genre characterized by elaborate and beautiful decoration in buildings with "true" arches and domes.

Middle Indo-Islamic (1320–1414)
including Tughluqābād and Tughluq's tomb, Kalān Masjid; Mosque of Fīrūzābād; Hauz Khās tomb, and the mosques of Nizām-ud-dīn, Khirkī, and Begampur.
This group develops from buildings in local stone or red sandstone with sparing use of marble, to buildings with sloping walls of stone and mortar plastered all over and domes supported on columns of stone pillars.

Late Indo-Islamic (1414–1556)
including the tombs of the Sayyid and Lodī kings; the Old Fort (Purāna Qila) and mosque; Jamālī Mosque; Īsā Khān's tomb and mosque.
This group is distinguished by elegant domes and the attention paid to ornate decoration with marble, colored tiles, and plasterwork.

Mughal (1556–1660)
including Humāyūn's tomb; Āzam Khān's tomb; the Red Fort; Jāmi Masjid; Fatehpurī Masjid; Motī Masjid (at Mehrauli): tomb of Safdar Jang.

The earlier buildings in this group are usually of red sandstone with restrained use of marble. The use of white marble gradually increases and the decoration becomes more free, the domes become increasingly bulbous, and the minarets loftier. The late Mughal buildings tend to become overelaborate and baroque in their decoration.

To get an idea of the development of Delhi's rich heritage, you should at least visit the Qutb Mīnār complex, which contains some of the earliest and most impressive ruins in the city, and the two principal monuments of Shāhjahānā- bād, the Red Fort, and the Friday Mosque (*Jāmi Masjid*).

Qutb Mīnār
Complex

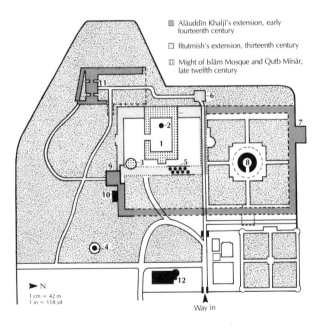

1 *The Might of Islām Mosque.* 2 *The Iron pillar.* 3 *The Qutb Mīnār.* 4 *Major Smith's cupola.* 5 *Iltutmish's extension.* 6 *Iltutmish's tomb.* 7 *Alāuddīn Khaljī's extension.* 8 *The Alāī Mīnār.* 9 *The Alāī Darwāza.* 10 *The Tomb of Imām Zāmin.* 11 *Alāuddīn Khaljī's tomb and* madrasa. 12 *ITDC restaurant.*

Figure B. The Qutb Mīnār complex site plan.

The Might of Islām Mosque (Figure B.1)

The Might of Islām Mosque (Quwwatul Islām Masjid) is the earliest extant mosque in India. It was begun by Qutbuddīn Aibak in 1192, immediately after his conquest of Delhi, and was completed by 1198. The mosque was built from the remains of no less than twenty-seven Hindu and Jain temples that stood within the walls of the city of Rai Pithora.

The Muslim chronicler of that time, Hassān Nizāmī, records his master's energetic building program:

> The conqueror extended the city; and its vicinity was freed from idols and idol worship, and in the sanctuaries of the images of the gods, mosques were raised by the worshippers of the One God.

The most important of these new mosques, which came to be known as the Might of Islām, stood on the site of what must have been the most glorious of the temples of the "idol worshippers": Prithvīrāja's personal Hindu temple, the foundations of which now lie five feet under ground level. It was common practice for conquering Muslim armies to erect mosques on the sites of idolators' temples. The old buildings were destroyed, then elephants were used to flatten what remained and the new structure erected on the level ground.

The architectural heritage that the Muslims brought with them when they entered India was very different from what they encounterd when they arrived. Spreading from its birthplace in the deserts of central Arabia, Islām moved rapidly through Irān, Central Asia, and Afghānistān, establishing itself in India five hundred years after the Prophet's death in A.D. 632. As it spread, the new religion incorporated those existing styles of building practiced in the countries through which it passed, adapting them to build its mosques, tombs, and caravanserais. These styles were variations on a single theme of building in brick—both mud and fired—and embellishing with glazed tile decoration. To this tradition the Muslim builders added an already mature system of architectural mechanics inherited originally from Roman, Byzantine, and Sassanian sources, which made use of the pointed arch, the squinch, and the true dome. A squinch is an arch set diagonally across each of the four corners of a square chamber, thus converting the square into an octagon (Figure C). This can again be changed into a sixteen-sided shape by the addition of a further set of squinches. These arches then act as a platform on which a dome or an octagon can be raised. The squinch is thus a pendentive device, that effects the transition from the square of the chamber to the circle of the drum or dome that surmounts it. And Muslim buildings were, of course, enlivened by what has come to be regarded as the hallmark of the Islamic esthetic—a passion for decorative

Figure C. The squinch.

finery that expressed itself in ornamental calligraphy and in arabesque and geometric patterning.

The indigenous Indian styles of architecture sprang from a different root. All of them—Hindu, Buddhist, and Jain—relied on the post-and-beam (trabeated) system of construction in which spaces were spanned by an elaborate system of corbels. Indian builders used mainly stone, which, since earliest times, had been intricately carved with representations of the divine beings that people the Indian imagination.

What generally happened in the genesis of Indo-Islamic architecture is that the Muslim architects designed buildings that conformed to their own architectural principles but which utilized local Indian materials and were built by local craftsmen. These craftsmen embellished their work with carving that employed traditional Indian motifs and was executed with traditional Indian skill. A good example of the hybrid style that resulted from the meeting of these two strands can be seen in Akbar's ghost citadel, Fatehpur Sīkrī. But it seems

Courtyard of the Might of Islām Mosque.

that Qutbuddīn Aibak was in too much of a hurry to wait for the quarrying of local stone for his victory mosque. Instead, he made use of the remains of the idolators' temples he had flattened. Broken pillars, walls, and roofs were reassembled in a new order, and the stone that had writhed with all the fantastic beings of the Indian universe reformed itself to become a sober Islamic building that proclaimed the glory of the One God. What passed through the minds of the Hindu craftsmen as they built the new master's victory mosque out of blocks of stone they had patiently and lovingly carved for their own gods can only be imagined. They must have viewed him as as much of a barbarian as he viewed them, not only because he was an iconoclast of the first order, but because he chose to erect his building in complete ignorance of the fundamental laws that they considered to govern all sacred architecture. The building that resulted from Qutbuddīn's impatience must, to modern eyes at least, have been an incongruous patchwork affair. But to Ibn Batuta, the Muslim chronicler who saw it in the 1340s, it appeared to have no equal in beauty or grace. We can get some idea of how it looked from what remains of its cloisters, three aisles deep, in which pillars from the Hindu temples are rather indiscriminately piled on top of one another to achieve an equal height all around the central courtyard. The Hindu character of many of the pillars is obvious.

Detail of pillar, showing Hindu vase-and-foliage motif.

☐ *THE ARCHED SCREEN*
One feature of the Might of Islām Mosque must, without doubt, have been staggeringly impressive. This is the arched screen that runs along the western end of the courtyard-*cum*-prayer-hall. This was added a couple of years after the main mosque was finished, perhaps to elevate what had proved to be an esthetically unsatisfactory experiment. In building this screen, Qutbuddīn may have recalled what his envoys had told him of the architectural triumphs achieved by the Seljuk Turks in the holy cities of Damascus or Baghdad, or he may have mimicked the Caliph Osman, who, in the seventh century, built a brick screen to separate the sanctuary from the courtyard in no less a building than the Prophet's own mosque in Medina. Whatever the influence, the result was a masterpiece. Qutbuddīn's screen formed the facade of the mosque. Facing Mecca, it united the community of believers socially, as an impressive focal point, and also liturgically, as the focus of daily prayers. The screen consisted of a central arch, fifty-two feet (sixteen meters) high, flanked by two similar, but smaller arches, on either side. These side arches had four much smaller openings above them so that the whole screen appeared pierced by a series of elegant doorways that led invitingly over the horizon to Mecca. The arches were all ogee-shaped (that is, they had a double curve that formed a flattened S shape). They were a fusion of Hindu and Islamic styles, being corbeled in the Hindu trabeated style of post-and-beam construction but having a few stones laid as radiating voussoirs at the apex, in the manner of the "true" arch favored by the Islamic architects (see Figure D). The sandstone screen is carved in Indo-Islamic style. The geometric and arabesque motifs of Islām intermingle with lotuses, spiraled borders, and serpentine tendrils that clearly betray the painstaking hand of the indigenous craftsman. Running like a unifying thread through the decoration is qur'anic calligraphy, which serves not only to beautify the mosque but

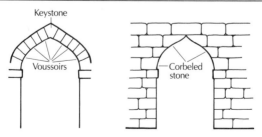

Figure D. The Islamic "true" arch (left) and Indian trabeated arch (right).

Qutbuddīn's screen.

to insulate it from harmful forces. The verses of the *Qur'ān* are the Muslim's direct link with Allāh; in the absence of representative images, it is the written word that most accurately and powerfully conveys the nature of the divine to the worshippers. This mediating role of the Word was emphasized by the physical grandeur of the screen. As Nizāmī records:

> Upon the surface of the stones were engraved verses of the *Qur'ān*, in such a manner as could not be done in wax, ascending so high that you would think the *Qur'ān* was going up to Heaven, and descending in another line so low that you would think it was coming down from Heaven.

□ THE IRON PILLAR (Figure B.2)

An interesting feature of the mosque is the iron pillar that stands in its courtyard. This dates from the fourth century A.D. and bears a Sanskrit inscription in the contemporary Gupta script. The inscription tells us that the pillar was erected as a flagstaff (*dhvaja*) in honor of Vishnu, in memory of the Gupta king Chandragupta II (375–413). Originally the pillar was topped by an image of Garuda, the sacred bird who is Lord Vishnu's vehicle, and it probably stood facing a Vishnu temple. Why and when it was moved to its present position is not known, though tradition says that it was brought here by Anang Pāl, the Tomar king who built Lāl Kot, the nucleus of the first city of Delhi, in the tenth century.

What is of interest is the composition of the pillar. It is wrought iron, 98 percent pure, and the fact that it contains no manganese suggests that it was probably charcoal fired. That the pillar has withstood its sixteen hundred years of life

*The Qutb Mīnār with
the Alāī Darwāza
below it and Imām
Zāmin's tomb in the
foreground.*

without rusting or decomposing is a tribute to the metallur-
gical skill of the ancient Indians. In fact, the only damage it
seems to have suffered was at the hands of man: About four
feet (a little over a meter) above the inscription is a dent
caused by a cannonball of some invading army. A local tradition regards the pillar as having magical qualities. If you can
stand with your back to it and join your hands around the
pillar, all manner of good fortune is said to await you!

The Qutb Mīnār (Figure B.3)

The Might of Islām Mosque was not the only reminder of his
glory that the turbulent Qutbuddīn Aibak left behind him. In
1199 he began work on what was intended to be the most
glorious tower of victory in the world. Probably influenced by
the brick victory pillars he had seen in Ghāznī in Afghānistān, Qutbuddīn built the Qutb Mīnār not only as a victory
tower but to serve as the *mīnār* attached to the Might of
Islām Mosque. From here the *muezzin* could call the faithful
to prayer. This positioning of the *mīnār* at a little distance
from the mosque itself was a practice that had already found
favor in some ninth-century mosques in Samarra, Syria, and
Egypt. Qutbuddīn erected what was to be the prototype of all
the *mīnārs* in India; later every mosque would incorporate
its minarets, smaller versions of this awe-inspiring structure.

Symbolically, the *mīnār* united heaven and earth. It thus served the same spiritual purpose as the Vedic sacrificial post (*yūpa*) and the ancient pan-Indian symbols of the royal parasol, the tree of life, and the sacred mountain. As a constant reminder of the glory of the sovereign as God's representative on earth, the *mīnār* built by Qutbuddīn stood as a stable axis around which the community and, by extension, the world at large revolved. It stood as a pivot of Truth (*qutb*), Justice, and Righteousness. The inscriptions carved in *kūfī* script around the tower tell us that the building was erected "to cast the shadow of God over both East and West." This divine sundial measured the eastern limit of the world of Islām for Qutbuddīn and his contemporaries. It had its counterpart in the equally impressive tower of Yusuf I, built in Seville in Spain, which marked the western limit of the empire of the One God. The immense variety of the lands that lie between these two geographical limits bears eloquent testimony to the flexibility of the message of the Prophet, and its relevance to those who heard it.

The Qutb Mīnār is 238 feet (73 meters) high and rises in five stories. The three original stories are heavily indented with different styles of fluting: alternately round and angular on the bottom story, round on the second, and angular on the third. To judge from inscriptions carved on the tower, Qutbuddīn's successor, Iltutmish, embellished the original structure and added the fourth story. Other inscriptions, in both Persian and northern Indian (*nāgarī*) script, tell us that the *mīnār* was damaged twice by lightning—in 1326 and in 1368. While repairing the second of these disasters, Fīrūz Tughluq, builder of the fifth city of Delhi, partly rebuilt the fourth story and added the top one. He used marble to face the red and buff sandstone, but he left the lower portion of the fourth story in its original condition. This was the first time that contrasting colors of stone were made a deliberate feature of Indian architecture. It was a technique that was to be utilized to full effect by the Mughals. Fīrūz's addition was topped by a graceful cupola, but this fell down during an earthquake in 1803. A new cupola was added in 1829 by a Major Smith, but it looked so out of place on the *mīnār* that it was removed in 1848. Major Smith's cupola now stands in the gardens, to the southeast of the tower (B.4).

The imposing *mīnār* is saved from being too stark both by the warmth of its red sandstone, which glows in the sunlight, and the beauty of its decoration. Originally it was girded by stepped balconies (a fragment of one remains over the doorway), but these had disintegrated by the time of the earthquake and had to be replaced. Nevertheless, the honeycomb work beneath the first (U.S. second) floor balconies is exquisite and reminds one of the stalactite work at that other

Detail of the Qutb Mīnār, showing balcony and carving.

extreme of the Islamic world, the Alhambra Palace in Moorish Spain. The calligraphic bands of qur'ānic verses are florid in the extreme, but never overdone. Altogether the decoration manages to preserve a fine balance between voluptuousness and restraint.

Iltutmish's Extension (Figure B.5)

The Might of Islām Mosque was enlarged twice. In 1230 Qutbuddīn's son-in-law and successor, Shamsuddīn Iltutmish, doubled the original size of the mosque by extending its colonnades and prayer hall. This extension was to accommodate a larger congregation of the faithful, for in the comparative stability of Iltutmish's reign the religion of Islām had gained further ground among the local population. Iltutmish also extended the arched screen at the western end of the enclosure. Though the new arches were still principally corbeled, without voussoirs, they can be seen as a stylistic advance on those built by his predecessor. They may at first appear to be mere duplicates, on a larger scale, they are in fact less ogee-shaped and more pointed. In this they are nearer the shape of the "true" arch and are similar to the Gothic pointed, or "equilateral," arch that appeared in England at about this time. Iltutmish's arches are thus cleaner in their lines than the original ones built by Qutbuddīn. There is also a change in decoration. The extended facade is very richly embellished with carving, but on close inspection the new decoration will be seen to be somewhat more rigid than what went before. The style now is Saracenic; it is as if the native exuberance of the Hindu stone carvers has been tempered and restrained by the demands of a more sober, and more truly Islamic, sensibility. This development of Indo-Islamic decoration is a marked feature of Iltutmish's architecture. We can see the same process of stylization in his completion of another mosque begun by Qutbuddīn, the Arhāidinkā Jhonpra at Ajmer, in central Rājasthān.

Iltutmish's Tomb (Figure B.6)

Iltutmish left the Qutb Mīnār complex with one of its most impressive buildings: his own tomb. It was common practice for the sovereign to build his own mausoleum, and tomb building had from earliest times been an important feature of Islamic sacred architecture. This, of course, was quite foreign to the Hindus, who, at least since the Purānic period (ca. 400 B.C.) had practiced cremation. Iltutmish had had experience in such building when he erected a mausoleum for his son, Sultan Ghārī, in 1231. But his own resting place is a marked advance on this rather austere prototype, which stands not far from the Qutb Mīnār complex.

The tomb lies northwest of the Might of Islām Mosque, and it was completed in 1235. The outside is relatively plain, with three doorways framed by pointed arches, which are in turn fringed by delicate calligraphic patterns. There are also false windows, similarly decorated.

The interior of the shrine is a dance of intricate ornamentation; to step inside is like entering a tent hung with Persian rugs and tribal wall hangings. As so often in early Indo-Islamic architecture, you are reminded of the nomadic origin of the first Muslim lords of Delhi. The sandstone walls of the thirty-foot- (nine-meter-) square hall are closely carved in low-relief patterns, which include verses from the *Qur'ān* in a variety of scripts: *kūfī* in square blocks, *naskh* in ornamental flourishes. The calligraphy is pointed here and there with white marble, providing both textural and tonal relief from the reddish stone. Altogether the chamber, protecting its subterranean crypt, is a most harmonious blend of Hindu and Muslim styles: the familiar Indian motifs of the wheel, bell and chain, lotus, and diamond providing a balance to the sober geometrical and arabesque patterning of the Saracenic designs.

The western wall is inset with three *mihrābs*, the arched alcoves that indicate the direction of Mecca in any Muslim shrine, (see Chapter 1). Iltutmish's tomb was originally roofed by a shallow dome supported on squinches. This marked an important new departure in Indo-Islamic architecture. The technique used to construct the dome was, however, the indigenous Indian method of corbeling, as we can tell from the huge slabs of stone that lie scattered around the tomb. These are the remains of Iltutmish's dome; corbeling proved too unstable a technique to support such a dome against the ravages of time and the Indian climate. There is still a long way to go before we reach the domed perfections that the Mughals erected in the seventeenth century. Nevertheless, Iltutmish's prototype was an imaginative and important new step in the emerging style.

*Interior of
Iltutmish's tomb,
showing squinches.*

In better shape than the dome itself are the squinches on which it rested. The squinch appears in India for the first time in this building. The squinch was a device inherited by Islām from Roman and early Byzantine buildings, though here in Iltutmish's tomb they are corbeled, as was the dome, in the native Indian fashion. Another indigenous building technique was the method of fixing the stones to each other. This again was typically Indian, iron dowels being used to clamp the blocks of masonry together. They can be seen in the eastern wall of the chamber. In later Indo-Islamic buildings the Islamic technique of bonding by lime plaster was used.

Alāuddīn Khaljī's Extension (Figure B.7)

Almost a hundred years after Iltutmish's death, the Might of Islām Mosque was again enlarged; this time the builder was Alāuddīn Khaljī, creator of Sīrī, the second city of Delhi. Khaljī waded through much blood in his conquest of Delhi, and he was a man who had few doubts about his own divine right to govern the peoples of India. He formally had himself proclaimed "God's representative on Earth" and told the dismayed elders (*ulamā*) of the Muslim congregation: "I do not know whether this is lawful or unlawful, but whatever I feel to be for the good of the state or suitable to the circumstances, that I decree. As to what may happen to me on the day of judgment, that I do not know."

Alāuddīn is chiefly celebrated by contemporary historians for his tireless and bloodthirsty military campaigns, but he also had considerable architectural ambitions. One of his first projects was to double the size of the Might of Islām Mosque. Sadly his death in 1316 curtailed the scheme, and all we have of the mosque itself are its foundation courses. But before he died, Alāuddīn did extend the site to the north and east, so as to include those buildings that had already been erected by his predecessors Qutbuddīn Aibak and Iltutmish.

The Alāī Mīnār (Figure B.8)

To complement this new mosque, Alāuddīn conceived of a new victory tower, which was to be twice the height of the famous Qutb Mīnār, and make the latter pale into insignificance. But his grandiose plan was not to materialize, for he died when the tower was only one story high. His supreme monument, the Alāī Mīnār as it was to be called, now stands to the north of the compound, a massive heap of rubble, testifying to the unending ambition of man.

The Alāī Darwāza (Figure B.9)

But Alāuddīn did have time to complete what is the finest building here: the southern gateway to his new extension, known as the Alāī Darwāza. No less than three inscriptions woven into the ornamentation of its surface tell us that the gateway was constructed in the Muslim year 710 A.H. (that is, A.D. 1311). The architectural success of the Alāī Darwāza was partly the result of the vicissitudes of history. Since the beginning of the thirteenth century, regular waves of Mongol invaders had been sweeping down from Central Asia, spreading east and west. By the time of Alāuddīn, these invasions had effectively destroyed the mighty civilization of the Seljuk Turks in Western Asia. As a result refugee poets, artists,

The Alāī Darwāza.

architects, and craftsmen fled eastward into India. Alāuddīn (whose own dynasty was Afghān and had come to power by usurping the ruthless Turkish Sultan Balban) received them gratefully. For the Seljuks brought with them several distinctive features of an extremely refined architectural tradition that harked back to the glories of Byzantium. Many of these features came to be incorporated into Indo-Islamic architecture and are well demonstrated in the Alāī Darwāza.

The gatehouse is a massive yet airy sandstone cube, fifty-five feet (seventeen meters) on each side, and over sixty feet (eighteen meters) high. Its facades are divided into rectangular panels, into which are set miniature cusped arches or horseshoe arches inset with carved screens. The panels are framed by alternating bands of inscriptions in *naskh* characters and geometric and floral designs. Altogether the profuse ornamentation, set in red sandstone and white marble, conveys the warm shimmering of some fantastic Central Asian tapestry and has the effect of softening the stonework, even in the harsh glare of the Indian sun.

□ *THE INNER CHAMBER*
The inner chamber is thirty-six feet (eleven meters) square, with a doorway in each of its four sides. Three of these are pointed horseshoe arches and high and narrow built on the principle of the "true arch," with radiating voussoirs. This is the first appearance of the Islamic arch in India, and thus Alāuddīn's gatehouse marks a watershed in the development of all subsequent Indo-Islamic architecture.

Above each of these doorways is an Arabic inscription, with Alāuddīn's name and one of his favorite, though more modest, titles; "the Second Alexander."

The northern doorway is the most elaborately carved of the four. Whereas the others are pointed horseshoe arches, fringed with prominent "lotus-bud" embellishment, the northern door is semicircular but gently scalloped into three sections. As the actual entrance to the mosque enclosure, this would have been the most important door, and would probably have led onto a pillared portico. The shape and ornamentation of all these arches is a particularly delicate example of the new maturity of architectural style.

Significant too is the dome, for this is a "true" dome, raised on squinched arches and stable enough to have remained standing for nearly seven hundred years. The dome is wide and shallow, topped by a buttonlike finial. It rises on an octagonal base created by concentric circles of arches to form the squinch.

All in all, the Alāī Darwāza displays an assurance and accomplishment of technique that has not been seen before in Indian building of this sort. Certain elements are directly traceable to Seljuk influence: the arches with their "lotus-bud" fringes, the flattish dome and rounded finial, the alternating courses of wide and narrow embellishment, and the general treatment of the facade. These now came to be the hallmarks of mature Khaljī architecture. They were to determine the stylistic development of the Indo-Islamic genre, until the traditions of the Delhi sultanate buildings were superseded by the Persian-derived innovations of the Mughals in the middle of the sixteenth century. It was not until the construction of Humāyūn's tomb in 1565 that the principles established by the Alāī Darwāza were to give way to an even greater architectural achievement.

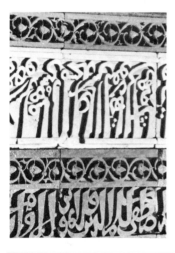

Detail of the Alāī Darwāza, showing calligraphic ornamentation.

Imām Zāmin's Tomb (Figure B.10)

Immediately to the east of the Alāī Darwāza stands the tomb of Imām Zāmin, a sūfī saint from Turkestān who came to India at the very beginning of the sixteenth century. The tomb, with its octagonal drum surmounted by a plastered sandstone dome, has finely worked *jālī* screens, characteristic of the Lodī style of embellishment.

Alāuddīn Khaljī's Tomb (Figure B.11)

Alāuddīn Khaljī was buried to the southwest of his uncompleted mosque. An *L*-shaped group of ruins marks the site of his tomb. He was buried within the confines of the teaching college (*madrasa*) that he had established to propagate Islamic doctrine. This is the first time in India that a tomb and *madrasa* are combined—another custom inherited from the Seljuks. There are some examples of these tomb-colleges still extant today, particularly in Anatolia, where the *baraka* of a Sūfī saint continues to inspire the students who come to imbibe the teachings of the Prophet.

Detail of the Alāī Darwāza, showing northern doorway.

8

DELHI'S RED FORT

THE MIGHT OF THE MUGHALS

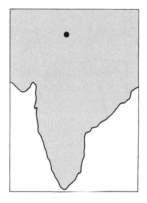

By the reign of Shāh Jahān (1627–1658), the Mughal dynasty had reached its zenith. Consolidated by the wise and tolerant policies of Akbar and firmly grounded on the administrative and revenue system established by the Hindu Rāja Toda Mal, the empire had proved strong enough to survive even the twenty years of self-indulgence that marked the rule of Shāh Jahān's father, Jahāngīr. A man of refined sensibility, Jahāngīr was a ruler whose patronage stimulated great esthetic achievements in the world of the arts, but his love of beauty could hardly justify the excesses that enervated his life. As his reign advanced, Jahāngīr became increasingly plagued by ill health and his addiction to alcohol and opium. It was only the considerable strength and skill of his wife Nūr Jahān, who was always the power behind the throne, that kept the empire sufficiently intact to hand it on, undamaged, to his son.

The young Shāh Jahān soon showed himself to have the energy and application of a true emperor. He was a tireless soldier and spent many of his early years campaigning against dissidents in the Deccan, particularly the rebel kingdoms of Ahmnedagar and Bījapur. To begin with, he was very much under the influence of the orthodox Muslim hierarchy at the court—the *ulamā*. These divines had been so scandalized by the religious tolerance shown by both Akbar and Jahāngīr that, with the new emperor, they saw their chance to redress the religious balance. Thus the early part of Shāh Jahān's reign was marred by outbreaks of persecution against both the Hindu and Christian communities, and the country had a grim foretaste of what was to happen under Shāh Jahān's own son, Aurangzeb. However, the emperor seems to have mellowed as he grew older, and today he is remembered chiefly as a ruler whose influence raised the esthetic and architectural standards of his time to new heights.

The backbone of the empire was the road that ran, straight and tree-lined, 400 miles (650 kilometers) from Lahore in the west to Āgra in the east. This road, along which the imperial armies and messengers fanned out north and south, ran through Delhi. Shāh Jahān, who since his childhood had shown a genius for architecture, was determined to beautify these three principal cities of his kingdom. He built himself a splendid marble palace in each of them. This entailed reconstructing many of Akbar's sandstone buildings in Lahore and Āgra. Indeed, if there is one feature that characterizes the architectural taste of Shāh Jahān's reign, it is the transition to an enthusiastic but judicious use of the soft, gray-white marble from the mines of Makarāna, near Jodhpur in Rājasthān. This milky stone was costly, but it was the perfect material for a man who frequently said that he "loved beauty more than life itself." Aurangzeb was to accuse his father of emptying the royal coffers to finance fruitless building schemes, but the judgment of history has smiled more favorably on Shāh Jahān's passion for building than on his son's passion for righteousness. It was in Delhi that Shāh Jahān's passion was given unfettered scope, for here he created Shāhjahānābād, the so-called seventh city of Delhi. He officially transferred his capital here from Āgra in 1638. The city was laid out in blocks, with wide roads, residential quarters, bazaars, and mosques. Its principal street was Chandni Chowk, which had a tree-lined canal flowing down its center and which rapidly became one of the most celebrated markets of the East. Even today, Chandni Chowk retains some of its legendary magic. A long, straight road lined with a jumble of shops, temples, hotels, mosques, and billboards, it is a bargain hunter's paradise. Running off the main street are dozens of twisting little alleys where the craftsmen of the city have their workshops. Here you can find goldsmiths, silversmiths, jewelers, ivoryworkers, silk merchants, and embroiderers. Lose yourself in the alleys off Chandni Chowk and you step back in history.

The city of Shāhjahānābād was protected by rubble-built

walls, some of which still survive. The walls were strengthened by bastions and pierced by fourteen main gates. The most important ones still in existence are Ajmerī Gate, Turkmān Gate, Kashmīrī Gate, and Delhi Gate.

Between his new city and the River Yamunā, Shāh Jahān built himself a fort, encircled by a forbidding red sandstone wall, modeled on his grandfather's citadel at Āgra. The Red Fort (Lāl Qila) was begun in 1639 and completed after nine years, in the spring of 1648. It is said to have cost a crore (ten million) of rupees, half of which was spent on the marble palaces within.

The Red Fort Complex (Figure A)

The Red Fort is built as a huge, irregular octagon, measuring about 3,000 feet by 1,800 feet (900 meters by 550 meters), with two longer sides on the east and west (see Figure A). It was surrounded by a moat that was fed from the river on the east. The northern end is joined by bridges to Salīmgarh and overlooks the site where Yudhish-

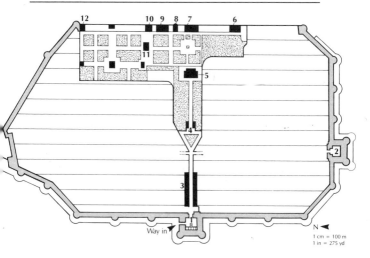

1 *The Lahore Gate—main entrance.* **2** *The Delhi Gate.* **3** *The arcade—Chhatta Chowk.* **4** *The Drum House—Naubat Khāna.* **5** *The Hall of Public Audience—Dīwān-i-Ām.* **6** *The Palace of Jewels—Mumtāz Mahal.* **7** *The Palace of Colours— Rang Mahal.* **8** *The Private Palace—Khās Mahal.* **9** *The Hall of Private Audience—Dīwān-i-Khās.* **10** *The Royal Baths— Hammām.* **11** *The Pearl Mosque—Motī Masjid.* **12** *The Water Tower—Shāh Burj.*

Figure A. The Red Fort site plan.

thira is said to have performed the Royal Horse Sacrifice to celebrate the victory of the Pāndavas over the Kauravas in the battle described in the *Bhagavad Gītā*. There were originally five gates; now the main entrance is through the Lahore Gate on the west of the fort (A.1). The defensive barbican that fronts the gate was built by Aurangzeb, much to the disgust of his father, who commented sadly: "You have made a bride of the palace and thrown a veil over her face."

Once through the Lahore Gate, you enter an arcade called Chhatta Chowk (A.3). This originally housed the courtiers and members of Shāh Jahān's retinue; now it contains some of the best antique shops in Delhi.

The Drum House (Figure A.4)

Continuing through Chhatta Chowk and into the fort, you next reach the Drum House, or Naubat Khāna. This marked the entrance to the inner apartments of the fort, and here all except princes of the royal family had to dismount and leave their horses. It was also known as Hāthīpol—that is, the gate where visitors leave their elephants (*hāthī*).

As well as being a gatehouse, the Drum House was a music gallery. Five times a day ceremonial music was played to the glory of the emperor.

The three-story (U.S. four-story) building is particularly remarkable for its carvings. The red sandstone is pointed with flower designs typical of late Mughal art. These display a combination of stylization and naturalism that is in part traceable to European herbals copied by the artists of Jahān-

The Drum House, from the first court.

The Drum House, showing detail of flower motif.

gīr's court after the emperor's trip to Kashmīr in 1620. By the time of Shāh Jahān, these flower patterns had become a dominant motif in architecture and were to become very common in carpet and textile design. Panels such as these on the Drum House were originally painted in gold and other colors, traces of which are still visible on the interior of the gateway.

In Shāh Jahān's day, the Drum House gave onto an inner courtyard, 540 feet (165 meters) wide and 420 feet (128 meters) long, around which ran galleries. Here the palace guards were stationed. But the internal structure of the fort has undergone many changes since then, especially during the British period, when it became the headquarters of the army. It suffered considerable damage during the Indian Mutiny (1857). The courtyard is now a lawn, flanked by shrubbery where the galleries once stood.

The Hall of Public Audience (Figure A.5)

Between the first inner court of the fort and its heart, the royal palaces, stood the Hall of Public Audience (Dīwān-i-Ām). This was the farthest the normal visitor would be allowed into the royal residence. The Hall of Public Audience was designed to be a functional building, in which much of the administrative work of the empire could be conducted, but also to act as a showpiece, overwhelming the visitor with its splendor and hinting at the unimaginable sumptuousness contained in the palace quarters it protected. The hall is beautifully proportioned, presenting a facade of nine openings made by double-cusped arches, standing three bays deep.

The emperor's throne in the Hall of Public Audience.

To get an idea of how the place would have looked, it is essential now to use the imagination. The red sandstone interior was covered by a shell plaster of ivory polished *chunam*—a speciality of the craftsmen from Rājasthān. This was then painted—not inlaid—with floral motifs in many colors, especially gilt. The hall was hung with thick curtains and spread with rugs and tapestries from the western reaches of the empire—Afghānistān, Pakistān, and Balūchistān.

□ *THE DAIS*
At the back of the hall stands a platform, on which the throne of the emperor was placed. Persian influence is discernible in the inlaid floral decoration. The dais is surmounted by a marble canopy in the form of a Bengāl roof—modeled on the roofs of eastern India. These were originally made of spliced bamboo, their sloping eaves well suited to draining off the monsoon rains, particularly heavy in that part of the country overlooked by the Himālayan foothills. Bengālī influences were introduced into Mughal architecture via the Bengāl sultanate; an Indian motif has here been perfectly married to a Mughal idiom. What is perhaps more remarkable is that in this seventeenth-century setting, amid all the splendors of a court that was in touch with post-Renaissance Europe, we see again the archaic Indian convention of the sacred tree-umbrella, which has been protecting sovereigns and teachers since at least the time of the Buddha, over two thousand

years before. Behind the marble canopy are twelve marble panels inlaid with *pietra dura*. These are the work of one Austin of Bordeaux, a French jeweler, who probably worked on the inlay designs of the Tāj Mahal. As well as the floral and bird motifs, we can see evidence of classical influence in the figure of the Greek god Orpheus with his lute, who was perhaps a favorite of the music-loving Shāh Jahān.

☐
Below the dais stands an inlaid marble platform. This was for the prime minister (*wazīr*) to stand on and conduct the business at hand.

The whole hall was restored by Lord Curzon in 1903, and the *pietra dura* restored a few years later by a Florentine named Menegatti.

We are fortunate to have quite detailed accounts of daily life in the court of the later Mughals. Shāh Jahān rose at dawn and, after ablutions and morning prayers, would begin the day's business by showing himself to the people in the daily sunrise ritual known as the "Audience from the Balcony" (*jharoka-i-darshana*). This took place from a tower adjoining the sleeping quarters in the Private Palace (Khās Mahal). Once this ritual was over, the emperor proceeded to the Hall of Public Audience, where all those who had business in the court that day had long since been standing in strict order of rank, awaiting the arrival of their sovereign. According to Bernier, the seventeenth-century French traveler, the respectful subjects waited with "their eyes bent downward and their hands crossed." It was now eight o'clock. The emperor entered the hall to the accompaniment of trumpets and drums, and, mounting a flight of movable marble steps, he took his seat. Security was of course extremely tight. We know that Jahāngīr's throne was protected by no less than forty of his hangmen, including the chief executioner, all of whom carried whips and hatchets to deal with any trouble. The actual steps up to the throne were forbidden to all but the most trusted officials. In 1654 an assassin tried to rush up them; he was cut down before he had climbed the first step. And, at the top of the steps, Bernier continues, "glittered the dazzling figure of the Grand Mughal, a figure to strike terror, for a frown meant death."

The business conducted in this public audience seems to have been a mixture of official and domestic administration. As well as dealing with reports from the outlying provinces of the empire, tax and revenue matters, and official appointments, Shāh Jahān liked to busy himself with more personal affairs. Dreams, illnesses,and anecdotes of the sovereign and his ministers were often announced and recorded in these sessions, and sometimes elephants and horses from the royal stables were paraded in the courtyard for inspection or approval. Wednesdays were devoted to justice. Sentences were often brutal and always rapid; sometimes the punishment of beating, dismemberment, or death was carried out on the spot. Nevertheless, despite, or perhaps because of, its severity, Shāh Jahān's justice was respected throughout the empire, and it was claimed that his judicial system was of an exceptionally high standard. The public audience usually lasted about two hours (except on Fridays, the Muslim holy day, when there was no official business). Then sometime after ten, the emperor withdrew to the Hall of Private Audience for more detailed and intensive consideration of important matters of state.

Behind his Hall of Public Audience, Shāh Jahān set six miniature palaces along the eastern wall of the fort, overlooking the Yamunā. These formed the most intimate areas of the royal household, including the *haram* quarters, and were connected by a channel of scented water that flowed through them, called the Stream of Paradise (Nahr-i-Bihisht). All but one of these palaces survive.

The Palace of Jewels (Figure A.6)

The southernmost of the six is the Palace of Jewels (Mumtāz Mahal). This was one of the buildings devoted to the *haram*.

View from the Palace of Colours, looking south.

*Lotus fountain,
the Palace of Colours.*

The lower half of its walls and pillars are of marble, and it contains six apartments. It is now the site of a small but excellent collection of the Delhi Archeological Museum, consisting mainly of paintings, materials, letters, and *objets d'art* from the Mughal era. It should not be missed.

Moving northward, the next palace was called the Little Sitting Room (Chhotī Baithak), but it has now disappeared.

The Palace of Colours (Figure A.7)

Next comes the Palace of Colours (Rang Mahal). This was the residence of the chief *sultāna*, and as such, the principal part of the *haram*. It is divided into six apartments recessed into sixteen bays by cusped arches set on piers. Privacy was insured by marble *jālī* screens. The northern and southern apartments were both known as the Palace of Mirrors (Shīsh Mahal), since their walls and ceilings were set with tiny pieces of mirror to catch and reflect the light. This type of decoration was a favorite in India before the Mughals; many of the Rājput palaces in Rājasthān have Shīsh Mahal apartments. Through the center of the Palace of Colours flows the Stream of Paradise channel, and in its center is a marble basin in the form of a huge lotus in which was set an ivory fountain. The whole building, as indeed the fort complex itself, was designed to maximize light and air. As its name implies, the palace was lavishly painted, and the sinuous scrolls and foliage motifs were inset with colored semiprecious stones. The whole effect must have been of tremendous luxury. In fact a contemporary chronicler tells us that "in luster and color the Palace is far superior to the palaces of the promised Paradise." In a strict Muslim society, this was praise indeed!

The Private Palace (Figure A.8)

North of the Palace of Colours stands the Private Palace (Khās Mahal). This consists of three parts. The north end, facing the Hall of Private Audience, is the Chamber for the Telling of Rosaries (Tasbīh Khāna). Here Shāh Jahān would worship privately, using his rosary of ninety-nine beads, one for each of the mystical names of Allāh. Behind this are three rooms known as the Royal Sleeping Quarters (Khwābgāh). Attached to the east of these chambers, overlooking the river, is the octagonal tower from which the emperor showed himself to the population each morning, in the ceremonial *darshana*. This ceremony, a vital part of temple worship with the figure of the god, would have been instinctively understood by the Hindus in the crowd. A balcony was added to the tower in 1809, and from this balcony George V and Queen Mary appeared in the coronation *darbār* of 1911, which celebrated their coronation and coincided with the moving of the capital from Calcutta to Delhi. This great *darbār* marked the height of British power in India.

To the south of the Royal Sleeping Quarters is a long hall with painted walls and ceiling: the Robe Chamber (Tosh Khāna). At the northern end of this room is a very fine alabaster panel over a lacelike screen of pierced marble that bridged the Stream of Paradise channel. The panel is carved with the scales of justice surrounded by the heavens—crescent moon, stars, and clouds. The detail and workmanship deserve careful study and show how far the native Indian craftsmen had developed in their depiction of Indo-Islamic motifs.

All these rooms overlooked the area that lies between the walls of the fort and the Yamunā. This stretch of ground was an arena, in which animal fights (for example, between lions and elephants), tournaments, and other such diversions were performed for the delight of the emperor and his court, who watched from above.

The Hall of Private Audience (Figure A.9)

The fifth palace along the wall was the hub of the court: the Hall of Private Audience (Dīwān-i-Khās). It is a one-story building, topped by four Hindu-style cupolas (*chhatrīs*), built

Pierced marble screen, Robe Chamber.

wholly of white marble. A rectangular central chamber is surrounded by aisles of cusped arches. The dado of the interior walls and the lower parts of the pillars were exquisitely inlaid with precious and semiprecious stones. The ceiling was originally of silver, but this was removed by raiding Marāthā tribes in 1760. The present painted wooden ceiling was restored in 1911. The hall used to be fronted by a marble pavement and surrounded by an arcaded court; these sadly are now gone. In the center of the hall stands a marble pedestal on which the fabulous Peacock Throne stood. Shāh Jahān outdid even his father, Jahāngīr, in his love of jewels and was quite a connoisseur of them, sometimes able to give a more accurate assessment of their value than a professional jeweler. A contemporary witness tells us that the emperor even preferred examining his jewels to sampling the delights of his dancing girls, despite their "lascivious and suggestive dress, and immodest behavior and posturing." It was reckoned it would take an expert fourteen years to catalogue and value his private collection, and the ostentatious display of precious stones coupled with the use of white marble were to become the hallmarks of the splendor of Shāh Jahān's reign.

On his accession, the new sovereign commissioned the Peacock Throne, to be a fitting symbol of his glory. The throne was six feet (two meters) long and four feet (one and a half meters) wide and was made of solid gold. It had six massive

The Hall of Private Audience.

feet; and the whole thing was studded with sapphires, rubies, emeralds, pearls, and diamonds. It was surmounted by a canopy, supported on twelve emerald pillars, which was fringed with pearls. On top of the throne stood two peacocks, their tails unfurled, on either side of a tree that was inset with all kinds of precious stones. Sitting in the tree was a parrot carved out of a single emerald.

But even the Peacock Throne was not immune from the vagaries of history. In 1739 the notorious Nādir Shāh, a Turk who had overthrown the Safavid dynasty in Persia two years before, invaded Delhi. The first couple of days of his occupation were quiet enough, but then a riot took place in which some nine hundred Persian soldiers were killed. To avenge this uprising Nādir Shāh ordered the entire population of Delhi to be massacred. For a whole day the carnage continued, and by evening thirty thousand corpses littered the streets of the city. Nādir Shāh's army stayed only long enough to collect its reward. So great was the haul of booty that the Shāh was able to suspend taxes in Persia for the next three years. Among the treasures he took back with him, together with a thousand heavily laden elephants, two hundred carpenters, and a hundred masons, was the Peacock Throne. But he was not destined to sit on it for long. In 1747 he was murdered, and the throne was broken up by his assassins.

Nādir Shāh's brutal invasion marked the complete decline of the Mughal dynasty. The irony is that it almost exactly paralleled the invasion and sack of Delhi by Tīmūr, which, over three hundred years earlier, had acted as the prologue to his descendant Bābur's inaugurating the Mughal line in India.

The Hall of Private Audience was the center of Shāh Jahān's

empire. Here he would debate important matters of state, argue and formulate policies, and receive foreign ambassadors and important visitors. It was also the final court of appeal for high officials to defend themselves against charges. And here the emperor would inspect paintings and architectural plans submitted for his approval. The parade of animals—always an important part of a Mughal ruler's daily routine—also continued here, but only such refined beasts as cheetahs and falcons were presented in such elegant surroundings.

Two hours, from ten to noon, were spent on business in the Hall of Private Audience each morning; then the emperor would retire for an even more select conference that only the princes attended. This took place in the octagonal tower. Then, after a meal, siesta, and afternoon prayers, he returned to the hall for more work, which lasted until six or seven in the evening. After this, he retired for dinner and music with his women in the *haram*, and by ten o'clock he was in bed. As he lay in bed, he was read to by court readers with especially pleasing voices. His favorite subjects were travelogues, lives of saints, or history. He was particularly fond of hearing passages from the *Bābur-nāma*, the memoirs of his great-great-grandfather, Bābur.

The Hall of Private Audience, together with its sister building in Āgra, is the most elegant of Shāh Jahān's administrative buildings. It stands as a reminder of a dignified and luxurious civilization at the peak of its power, for after Shāh Jahān the decline began in earnest. The splendor of the inner court was legendary even in its own time. Above the corner arches of the northern and southern walls of the hall are inscribed the famous words of the fourteenth-century poet Amīr Khusrau:

> If on earth there be a Paradise of bliss,
> Oh! It is this, it is this, it is this!

The Royal Baths (Figure A.10)

North of the Hall of Private Audience lie the Royal Baths (Hammām). These are three apartments, separated by corridors. Their floors and dados are of marble, inlaid with semiprecious stones in floral patterns. The two rooms flanking the entrance were used by the royal children. The eastern apartment has three fountain basins, which emitted rose water. The western apartment was used as a steam bath.

The Pearl Mosque (Figure A.11)

West of the Royal Baths is the Pearl Mosque (Motī Masjid), built by Aurangzeb, for his personal use, in 1662. This small building, almost hidden behind a high wall of red sandstone, exudes an air of privacy. It is of polished marble, and its architectural features incorporate all the elements that are typical of later Mughal style: cusped arches, sinuous decorative designs, curved "Bengālī" cornices, and bulbous domes. In fact the domes, originally copper-plated, are perhaps too bulbous here, since they appear to be rather constricted at the drum. With their exaggerated lotus moldings and elongated finials, they give the mosque a fairy-tale quality. All the surfaces of the Pearl Mosque are highly decorated, in both inlay and low relief, to the extent that the separate elements of the building tend to lose their distinctiveness—a trait shared by the contemporary rococo architecture in Europe. Here, this blurring of distinction is emphasized by the gray veining in the marble. One unusual feature of the mosque is that its prayer hall is on a raised platform, above the entrance courtyard. This hall is inlaid with the outlines of individual prayer mats (*musallās*) in black marble. In order for the mosque to be correctly aligned to Mecca, some architectural juggling was necessary. The outer walls of the mosque were aligned to the cardinal points, for this was the alignment of all the other buildings in the Red Fort. The inner walls, however, were twisted several degrees to the south so that the building was ritually correct in its orientation.

□

The gardens to the north of the Pearl Mosque were called the "Life Bestowing Gardens" (Hayāt-Bakhsh-Bāgh), and, like all Islamic formal gardens, were intended to replicate the heav-

The Pearl Mosque.

enly gardens of paradise. Though their present layout is new,
they were originally landscaped in the Persian *chahār bāgh*
style, with pavilions, fountains, and water courses dividing
the garden regularly between beds planted with ornamental
shrubs and flowers. The water for the gardens and the Stream
of Paradise was drawn up from the river to a tower in the
southeast corner of the fort (the Shāh Burj, A.12) and from
there fed into the various channels. Contemporary accounts
tell us that special pavilions were erected for the Hindu festival of Teej, which marks the onset of the monsoons. The royal
ladies would sit in silver swings suspended by silken cords
and watch the rains as they poured unremittingly down.

9

DELHI'S FRIDAY MOSQUE

IN THE NAME OF ALLĀH

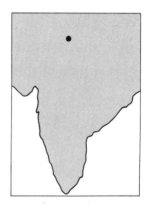

About a thousand yards (nine hundred meters) west of his Red Fort, Shāh Jahān built a royal mosque whose aristocratic splendor was intended to dwarf all that had gone before it. Each Friday the emperor and his retinue would travel in state from the fort, along the Khās Bazaar—which ran across what is now Edward Park—to the Friday Mosque (Jāmi Masjid), where they would take part in the midday prayers—the principal service of the Muslim week.

The fort and the mosque dominate Old Delhi. Their vast structures tower above the antlike scurry of the crowded streets below like the twin peaks of some massive chain of red sandstone mountains, haughtily proclaiming the joint power of Church and State. They stand as enduring monuments to the mighty aspirations of monarchy, and the vast gap that separated the world of the monarch from the world of the subjects that supported him. All the ancient monuments of Delhi share this larger-than-life quality. It was a quality that Lutyens and Baker inherited, and perpetuated, when they designed what was to be the nerve-center of the government of India, the huge parliamentary and secretarial complex on

Raisina Hill at the heart of New Delhi. Working in the 1920s, these British architects unconsciously imitated what every invading ruler had done since Qutbuddīn Aibak had first arrived at the end of the twelfth century: They built on a vast scale, in a brave attempt to pit their strength against the apparently endless sky and plains of northern India. To the modern traveler, these mammoth buildings are impressive still, but they are also somehow poignant—eminently suited to a country where man has always been acutely aware of his smallness in the face of almighty Nature.

The Friday Mosque is the largest mosque in India. It was begun in 1650 and finished six years later, at a cost of ten *lakhs* (that is, one hundred thousand) of rupees. Five thousand workmen are said to have labored on it day and night. The mosque rises on an elevated plinth from the bazaars clustered below, whose fish and poultry markets come as a rude shock after the vegetarian markets of Hindu India. Three pyramidal flights of steps—on the east, north, and south— lead up to the main courtyard.

The Gates

The largest and most impressive gateway is on the east (Figure A.1); its doors are inlaid with brass arabesques half an inch (over a centimeter) thick. In Mughal times this entrance was reserved for the royal family, who gathered in a private gallery in its upper story. Today the general public is admitted through the northern gate (A.2), while the faithful enter through the eastern gate on Fridays and on the occasion of the two annual Īd festivals: Īd al-Fitr (Feast of the Breaking of the Fast), which celebrates the end of Ramadan, and Īd al-Adhā (Feast

The Friday Mosque, looking over Edward Park.

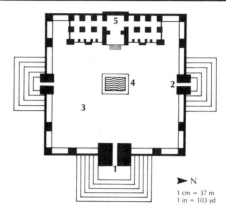

1 *Eastern gate.* 2 *Northern gate (main entrance).* 3 *Main courtyard.* 4 *Ablution tank.* 5 *The* Mihrāb.

Figure A. Friday Mosque site plan.

of Abraham's Sacrifice), which commemorates Abraham's sacrificial offering of his son Ishmael.

The purpose of these fine gateways is symbolic as well as practical, for they divide the area within the mosque from the profane area outside. In any sacred architecture, the threshold is a place of vital importance that must be clearly demarcated, for it is the place of transition from a lower to a higher order of reality, and such transitions require certain rites of passage. Thus, at the entrance to a mosque shoes must always be removed (as at the entrance to a Hindu temple). This is both to prevent any ritually impure substances being inadvertently brought into the mosque and to instill a feeling of respect in the visitor. Similarly, the worshipper should cover his head, out of respect for the divinity he is approaching. The convention of the skullcap arose in Islām, since, being brimless, it is the most practical head covering to wear for prostration of prayer. These observances, together with the elevated and fortified position of the mosque, create the feeling that you are leaving the humdrum world of everyday reality behind, and entering into some rarified citadel of the spirit.

The Courtyard (Figure A.3)

The courtyard (*sahn*) of the mosque, which acts as an extended prayer hall, is over a hundred yards (ninety meters) square and can accommodate more than twenty thousand worshippers. It is enclosed by pillared cloisters (*riwāqs*) with finely sculptured arches, which are linked by gateways and domed pavilions. To appreciate fully the proportions of the building itself, it is best to view it from the eastern gate, and see it as Shāh Jahān himself would have seen it as he arrived each Friday.

□ *THE ĪWĀN*

The initial impression is one of restraint. The facade of the mosque is dominated by the two four-stage minarets, one at each side of the building, and the central arched opening (*īwān*). The *īwān* is flanked by five smaller arches on each side, leading rhythmically into the interior prayer hall (*liwān*). Behind and above the *īwān* sit three bulbous domes, the larger central one flanked by two smaller ones, raised on their drums and set well back from the facade of the building. Shāh Jahān had learned to avoid the imbalance, often seen in Persian and early Indian mosques, caused by the domes looming too close to the raised *īwān*. Moreover the retiring position of the domes, together with the repetitive chorus of small arches echoing the sweep of the central *īwān*, has the effect of drawing the spectator's attention into the interior of the building. The deep shadowy recesses beckon you into the cool inside; the mosque is a spiritual oasis, offering relief from the heat of the exposed courtyard. This is not only esthetically pleasing, it is also liturgically correct. For, no matter how beautiful a mosque may be, its primary purpose is always functional rather than esthetic. A mosque exists to unite the congregation in prayer and to orientate it toward Mecca. This purpose is made quite clear architecturally by the way in which the concave *īwān* entrance echoes the shape of the *mihrāb* and beckons the believer within.

□

The Friday Mosque, from southeast of the courtyard.

Shāh Jahān's Friday Mosque is noticeably simpler in its ornamentation than his secular buildings. The white marble domes are judiciously striped with red sandstone, the sandstone minarets are set with marble stripes, and the cusped arches are decorated with marble frames and surmounted by inscriptional panels picked out in black and white marble. The decoration is used to emphasize the architectural features, rather than for its own sake. Similarly the internal embellishment is kept to a minimum: Simple niches and arabesques, the basic motifs of all Islamic art, act to relieve the expanse of red sandstone wall. The total effect of such combinations of marble and sandstone is almost austere. You are a long way here from the silks, satins, and gilts that adorned the royal apartments in the fort.

The function of the mosque, together with its simplicity, can combine to mislead the casual visitor. Although the courtyard here is dotted with people—sleeping, gossiping, conducting their individual prayers—the sheer enormity of the place overwhelms them. It is as if the mosque itself were only half-alive; it hangs in suspended animation. And this in a sense is true, for, as the Friday Mosque, it only really comes alive each Friday at noon, when the community assembles for communal prayer (*madhana*).

□ *THE ABLUTION TANK* (Figure A.4)
In the center of the courtyard stands a tank for ablution. Water plays an almost sacramental role in Islām as a means of initiation. If the historical reason for this can be traced to the importance of water for the desert-dwelling Arabs, its universal justification is that water is the vehicle for purification. Nor is this purification merely physical; for to bring the body into contact with water is to restore a state of undifferentiated being, to start afresh. Such symbolic baptism is found throughout the world, not least in Christianity. Thus in a mosque the ablution tank (*hauz*) is placed between the inner and outer parts of the building, as in Christian churches the font is placed just inside the west door, to remind the worshipper that it is through the ritual of baptism that one first enters the community of believers. The degree of ablution needed to sanctify the worshipper for prayer depends on the degree of ritual pollution that precedes it, a matter that is exactly determined by Islamic law.

□ *THE DIKKA.*
In front of the ablution tank stands a raised platform about ten feet (three meters) high, called the *dikka*. Muslim congregations grew so rapidly that by the eighth century it was already necessary to introduce a second prayer leader (*muballigh*) into the communal services, whose job was to

Arched cloisters
and domed chhatrī
pavilion.

copy the postures and chants of the *imām* within the actual
building, and thus relay them to that part of the congregation
for whom the *imām* was neither visible nor audible. Thus the
respondent acted as a human amplifier of the prayers and
coordinated the responses of the vast crowd assembled behind
him. In the largest mosques, such as this one, there are more
than one *dikka*, the second one here being located at the
entrance to the *īwān*. With the advent of the loudspeaker,
dikkas became largely obsolete. Practical though this
modernization may seem, in fact it heralded the decadence
of Islamic liturgy. For the human voice, as used in recitation
of the *Qur'ān* and qur'anic prayers, is one of the most cultivated arts of Islām, being second only to the art of calligraphy.
As with Christian plainsong, the purpose of Muslim cantilla-
tion is to transport the mind to silence, an effect that is almost
impossible to achieve over a public address system.

☐ *THE KAWTHAR INSCRIPTION*
Nevertheless, we have in the Jāmi Masjid evidence of a sacred
building's power to encourage mystical experience. At the
northwest corner of the white marble tank is an inscription
surrounded by a low railing. Set up in 1766, this commemorates the spot where a worshipper had a vision of the Prophet
standing beside the Kawthar, or celestial "Tank of Abundance" in paradise. According to Muslim belief, it is here that
the Prophet will stand on the Day of Judgment to intercede
with God for the faithful. The inscription reads in part:

Kawthar of Muhammad, the Messenger of God. Saints and the people of God have seen the Prophet here; it is right that this stone also should become a place of pilgrimage.

The Mosque Itself

□ *THE INSCRIBED PANELS ON THE FACADE*
One particularly interesting feature of all Shāh Jahān's buildings is the use of calligraphic inscription. Islamic buildings are usually inscribed with passages from either the *Qur'ān* or the *Hadīth* ("Sayings of the Prophet") in Arabic script. Shāh Jahān, however, preferred Persian inscriptions that were eulogies praising both the building and the builder, the great emperor himself. These eulogies were composed in the elaborate and verbose style that was then fashionable at court and much used to flatter royal patrons.

The ten inscribed panels on the facade of the Jāmi Masjid record (from right to left, of course!) the details of the date, cost, and history of the building of the mosque. The calligrapher has also signed his name at the very end of the inscription, telling us he was Nūr Allāh Ahmed, probably the son of the man who did most of the work on the Tāj Mahal. The inscription proudly proclaims that even those who have traveled throughout the world have not seen "an adorned building of such loftiness and strength." Such inscriptions were calculated to impress visiting ambassadors and subjects with the devotion and accomplishment of the emperor.

Yet there is more to these panels than Shāh Jahān's well-attested vanity. Hints are given in them that the Jāmi Masjid is to be taken as the earthly counterpart of the Bait al-Mamūr, "The Frequented House," which, situated in the highest heaven, is believed to be the celestial prototype of all mosques. It was here that Muhammad had his meeting with God after ascending to Paradise from the Dome of the Rock in Jerusalem. And the four or five short qur'anic phrases that are included in these inscriptions allude to the subtle connections that exist between Paradise and sacred buildings set up on earth.

□ *THE MIHRĀB* (Figure A.5)
The most important of these qur'anic passages are located around the *mihrāb*. Above the niche, within the rectangular cartouche, is a passage that refers to the compassionate nature of God—"He who forgives all sins." This formula was especially popular with the faithful, who used it as a ritual invocation of divine mercy, and is to be found on many mosques and tombs. Flanking the cartouche on either side is a passage

that refers more directly to the mosque as an earthly micro-cosm of Paradise:

> There is a mosque whose foundations were laid from the very beginning on piety. It is best that thou stand therein to pray. Within it are men who strive to be purified—for God loves best those who make themselves pure.

Two identical circular medallions are inscribed in the span-drels of the *mihrāb* arch. These read *Yā Ghaffār*: "O Forgiver," and are to be taken in conjunction with the similar medal-lions on the main arch of the facade, which read *Yā Hādī*: "O Guide"—both well known among the ninety-nine names of Allāh.

So here, in the heart of the mosque, are inscriptions that go some way to offset the imperial boasts of the facade inscriptions, reminding us that Shāh Jahān, in part at least, built his mosque upon piety, rather than pride.

In front of the prayer niche hangs a lamp. This is common in mosque architecture and reminds the Muslim of the famous "verse of light" in the *Qur'ān* in which the Divine Presence in both man and the world is compared to a lamp in a niche:

> God is the light of the Heavens and of the earth. The symbol of his light is a niche wherein is a lamp; the lamp is in a glass, and this glass shines as a radiant star. The light is nourished by a blessed olive tree, whose oil glows though fire touches it not. Light upon light. God guideth to his light whom He will, and God fashions symbols for mankind, and God knoweth all things.

□ *THE MINBAR*

To the right of the *mihrāb* is a flight of steps. This is a pulpit (*minbar*) from which the *imām* addresses the congregation, and it is only found in a Friday mosque, because it is only the Friday service that includes a sermon. The Friday service is compulsory for all male members of a Muslim community, but it is voluntary for women.

The *minbar*, with its steps and domed top, looks like a cross between a bishop's chair and a king's throne. In fact in a sense it is just this, as Islām has never really divorced religious from political power.

In the beginning, Muhammad was both the spiritual and temporal leader of the Muslim community. Having delivered the sermon, he would descend from the *minbar* to lead the prayers. In the early days of Islām, sermons were more polit-ical than dogmatic. The institution of the caliph combined both religious and secular power, and later it was often the ruler of a province who acted as *imām* and also delivered the Friday sermon. By Mughal times the *imām* had become a separate religious office, but whenever a Mughal king ascended the throne, or conquered new territory, the Friday sermon (*khutba*) was read in his name in the appropriate *jāmi masjid*.

The prototype *minbar* was a three-stepped wooden stool on which the Prophet sat to address the Companions. Whereas Muhammad sat on the top step, resting his feet on the middle one, his successor, the first caliph Abū Bakr, sat on the middle step, with his feet on the bottom one. This hierarchical sense of levels has been maintained ever since, and to this day the top step is always left vacant for the Prophet to return. As time went by, the *minbar* became an architectural feature in its own right, and grew ever more elaborate. Wood inlaid with ivory or mother of pearl, marble, and limestone became popular materials; the most magnificent *minbars* being those of Ottoman Turkey (1281–1924), which, to match the splendor and size of the Ottoman mosques, often rose as high as thirty feet (nine meters) and were beautifully embellished. *Minbars* are frequently flanked by flags. This not only emphasizes the connection between spiritual and political power in Islām—which the form of Indo-Islamic architecture also states strongly—but bears witness to the continuity of tradition in the religion, for it harks back to the fact that Muhammad would approach the *minbar* flanked by standard bearers. In many later *minbars* (since the time of the Seljuk Turks, ca. 1070–1380) folding doors were added at the bottom of the stairs and a domed canopy at the top.

And though it came to be a symbol of authority, the *minbar* never lost the esoteric significance of the different levels of being—gross, subtle, and transcendent—that was implicit in Muhammad's initial choice of a three-tiered stool. The topmost level, an empty canopied throne, comes then to represent the Prophet, his teaching, and the level of enlightenment he attained, just as in early Buddhist art the vacant throne under the *bodhi* tree represents the Buddha, the *dharma*, and *nirvāna*. We have here yet another example of the universal character of symbols operating within the apparently diverse forms of different religions.

10

AMRITSAR

THE GOLDEN TEMPLE OF THE SIKHS

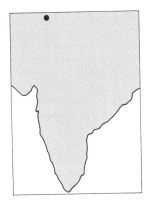

Amritsar is a wild frontier town, only fifteen miles from the Pakistānī border. It is a traditional junction of the trade routes that wind their laborious way across the roof of the world. Though modern politics has disrupted ancient mobility, Amritsar is still a melting pot. The town is a tribal rug of a place, its rough variegated texture woven from all the nomadic strands of Central Asia. Every race from Kābul to Katmandu seems represented here. Sturdy traders from Bokhāra and Balūchistān rub shoulders with Yarkāndīs, Turcomāns, and long-faced Kashmīris; laughing Tibetans and sure-footed little Nepālese jostle with surly Irānians. The mud streets of the bazaar are lined with wooden booths selling ivory and copper goods, silk, gold-and-silver threaded embroideries, and, above all, wool. Amritsar is famous for *pashmīna*—that down-soft fleece of the Himālayan goat. It is woven into shawls, scarves, and blankets, either in its natural shade of dark mushroom or embroidered with colored silks. The traders who come down from the mountains bring their own goods too—rugs, turquoise, and blankets made of yak's wool.

Amritsar is hardly India; it has more the atmosphere of a northwest frontier post. The streets resound with the rough clamor of the warlike tribesmen who have ruled the mountainous borders of Afghānistān and Pakistān for so long. The men are bigger here than they are further south. Their faces are faces of warriors: bearded, swarthy, and aloof. A tangible aura of independence surrounds them, as they herd their dusty pack animals through the narrow twisting alleys. Many carry rifles and wear leather bandoliers slung across their chests. You are on the edge of one of the great smuggling routes of the world here, and smugglers along this border deal in anything: whiskey, guns, hashish. They are regularly shot by police patrols.

Western influence is on the retreat in Amritsar. Urban India's ugly infatuation with polyester has given way to traditional native dress. Long, baggy shirts and trousers are topped by short vests and turbans. Pointed sandals kick up the dust, their embroidered leather as dry and as cracked as the mountain passes they have crossed to get here. Horse-drawn carts jingle by. We are in the land of Alī Bābā and the forty thieves.

But Amritsar's bustle is not chaotic. The town exudes an atmosphere of energetic industry. Its population of half a million seems well organized and prosperous. This is just as it should be, for Amritsar is the capital of India's most vigorous and united community: the Sikhs.

The Sikh brotherhood was founded by Guru Nānak in 1497. Nānak was born in 1469 in the village of Talwandi near Lahore. At that time northern India was ruled by the Afghān dynasty of Lodī sultans from Delhi. It was a period of turmoil and disintegration. Most of the political institutions derived their character from Muslim law, and a corrupt and decadent Hinduism was on the defensive. Nānak was born into an orthodox Hindu family, but he soon showed signs of the individualism that was to characterize his life. Since earliest childhood he had preferred the company of holy men and religious teachers. When he was nine, he refused to undergo the sacred thread ceremony by which every male member of the three highest castes officially becomes one of the "twice-born." He argued that there was no sanctity in a mere cotton thread and that real purity was an inner thing. He continued to quarrel with his family about religious and caste matters and left Talwandi for good in 1484. He married and had two sons, but his heart was never wholly in the householder's life. He spent more and more time in solitary meditation, and he eventually renounced the world in 1497. He spent the rest of his life traveling and teaching all over northern India.

Nānak was a social and religious revolutionary. He campaigned against superstition, idolatry, and priestly exploitation. He denounced all forms of inequality, including the caste system, and proclaimed the brotherhood of all men and women, irrespective of race, caste, or creed.

Nānak was greatly influenced by the mystic Kabīr, a weaver from Banāras who was one of India's most loved saints, and whose simple teachings, ready wit, and dedicated life had a profound effect on medieval northern India. Kabīr strove to unite Hindu and Muslim. It is said that when he died in 1519, there was a dispute between his Muslim and Hindu disciples as to whether the body should be buried or cremated. The elders of both communities decided that some fresh flowers be placed by the corpse, one bunch for the Hindus, one for the Muslims. Whichever flowers faded first, that community would yield. In the morning, not only were all the flowers as fresh as they had been when picked, but the body had disappeared. It was agreed that the shroud be divided in two equal parts. The Muslims buried their half, the Hindus cremated theirs.

Nānak continued Kabīr's tolerant teachings. One of his favorite sayings was "There is no Hindu, no Muslim." Many stories are told of his conflicts with orthodoxy. Once he visited Hardvār, the great Hindu pilgrimage center on the Ganges. Here he saw the faithful performing their early morning ritual of offering the holy water to the sun. Nānak joined them but turned around and started throwing water in the opposite direction, toward the west. When asked what he was doing, he replied, "I'm watering my fields." The crowds started laughing, and jeered, "How can the water reach your fields?" To which Nānak replied: "If your water can reach your fore-

Guru Nānak.

fathers who died so long ago, surely my water can reach my village, a mere three hundred miles away?"

On another occasion he performed the pilgrimage to Mecca like a good Muslim. But here as well, his refusal to compromise with dogma got him into trouble. He fell asleep in the holy city with his feet pointing toward the sacred stone of the Ka'ba. He was taken before the authorities for such blasphemy. In his defence Nanak protested that since the Ka'ba, as the infinite center of the Muslim world, represented Allāh, it was everywhere. He challenged his interrogators to take his feet to a place where the omnipresent Ka'ba was not.

Nānak taught that God is One and accessible to all. He drew disciples from all sects and all walks of life. A prolific poet, he taught by hymns and songs, which he composed spontaneously. The followers of his egalitarian creed were called Sikhs (from the Sanskrit *shishya*, meaning "disciple"), and before his death he chose one of these disciples to be his successor. In so doing he founded the line of ten Sikh *gurus* that was to stretch unbroken until 1708. Nānak died at Kartapur in 1539. Both his Hindu and his Muslim followers built their own mausoleums to the *guru*, separated by a common wall.

The Sikh *Gurus*

Guru Nānak	1469–1539
Guru Angad	1539–1552
Guru Amar Dās	1552–1574
Guru Rām Dās	1574–1581
Guru Arjun	1581–1606
Guru Hargobind	1606–1645
Guru Har Rai	1645–1661
Guru Har Krishan	1661–1664
Guru Tegh Bahādur	1664–1675
Guru Gobind Singh	1675–1708

Under the first four *gurus* Sikhism remained a peaceful religion, pervaded by the spirit of Kabīr and Nanak. But the brotherhood was to face severe challenges. The popularity of the fifth *guru*, Arjun, among both Hindus and Muslims aroused the suspicion of the Emperor Jahāngīr. He wrote in his autobiography *Tuzki Jahāngīrī* that Arjun

> had captivated the hearts of many simple-minded Hindus and foolish and stupid Muslims by his ways and means. They called him *guru*, and from all directions fools and fool-worshippers were attracted to him and expressed full faith in him. For three or four generations they have kept this shop warm. For years the thought had been occurring to me that I should either put an end to this false traffic or that he should be brought into the fold of Islām.

When the emperor heard that Arjun had blessed the cause of his rebellious son Prince Khusrai, it was the last straw. As

soon as the revolt was suppressed, Jahāngīr imposed an enormous fine on the whole Sikh community. Arjun refused to
pay. His days were numbered. Jahāngīr wrote: "I fully knew
his heresies. I ordered that he should be brought into my
presence, and having handed over his houses, mansions, and
children to Murtāza Khān [the prime minister] and having
confiscated his property, I ordered that he should be put to
death with tortures."

The emperor's orders were carried out. Arjun was tortured
to death in 1606. His successor, Guru Hargobind, sanctioned
the wearing of swords by the Sikh community as a defensive
measure. He himself wore two swords at his installation ceremony. They are the emblems of temporal and spiritual authority
and are shown crossed in the Sikh crest. This was the first
step toward the transformation of Sikhism into a militant
church.

The ninth *guru*, Tegh Bahādur, was persecuted by Aurangzeb. He was accused of proselytizing, and associating with
both Kashmīrī Hindus and Sūfī saints, neither of which
Aurangzeb approved of. The Mughal summoned him to Delhi.
When Tegh Bahādur refused to embrace Islām, he was
tortured. He still refused. Then, as a final humiliation, the
Sikh leader was accused of "presuming to gaze from the roof
of his abode upon the apartments of the ladies of the royal
haram." He was publicly beheaded in Chandni Chowk, the
main street of Old Delhi. His body was cut into four pieces
and hung at the four gates of the city.

Before his departure to Delhi, the *guru* had wisely
bequeathed his sword to his son Gobind. The boy swore
undying vengeance. It was he, as the tenth *guru*, Guru Gobind
Singh, who organized the Sikhs as we see them today. From
his accession at the age of nine, he began to develop the
brotherhood into a fighting force. He called the Sikhs the
"Pure Ones" (*khalsa*).

The new *khalsa* brotherhood was established at Ānandpur,
on March 30, 1699, when Gobind Singh was thirty-three.
Here the *guru* set up a tent. He assembled the community
and, holding up a sword, announced: "I want a head. Let any
one of my true Sikhs come forward and give me his head."
He had to repeat the request three times. Eventually a man
stood up and offered his head. He went with the *guru* into
the tent. A few moments later, the *guru* emerged, his sword
dripping with blood. Again he demanded another head. Again
a man volunteered. The assembled crowd was struck dumb.
Five times this happened. Then the *guru* drew aside the tent
flap. All five inside were alive. But they had died to their past
and were reborn as true Sikhs. Then the *guru* produced an
iron pot, mixed fresh river water and sugar in it, and, stirring
it with his sword, made the "nectar of baptism." Each of the

"five beloveds" took five handfuls of the nectar, and were baptized as the first members of the *khalsa*.

Under Aurangzeb's orders there was a price on any Sikh head. To insure that none of its members would disown the sect, Gobind Singh laid down the "Rule of the Five K's" (*kakaras*). This established the signs by which all true Sikhs can be recognized. The first K is *kesha*—hair. No Sikh should cut his hair. Hair conducts spiritual and physical energy and should not be wasted. The second is *kangha*—the comb around which the uncut hair is rolled. This is a symbol of order and discipline, as well as a practical way of keeping long hair in order. The third K is *kaccha*—a pair of shorts. The *guru* established these as the most efficient clothes for a warrior. They are also a reminder of the strict marital fidelity that is enjoined on all Sikhs. The sword—*kirpan*—was the fourth K and the chosen weapon of the *khalsa*. The word comes from *kirpa* (blessing) and *anif* (honor). This power of the sword was considered both a necessary means of protecting honor and a blessing from God. The last mark of identification was the bangle—*khurra*—worn on the right hand. Gobind Singh said the Sikhs were sparrows who had been given the power to kill hawks. In order that they should not abuse this divine trust, they should wear the single bracelet as a symbolic handcuff to remind them never to do anything unworthy of the brotherhood.

Every Sikh was henceforth to be known as "Lion" (Singh). This was already a common name among such martial communities as the Rājputs and Mahrāthās. So all Sikhs are Singh, but not all Singhs are Sikhs! Added to which, the Sikh should take the name Sardār, which means "Chieftain." Even if they were being abused, their nobility would remain. (Today Sikhs are colloquially known as *sadārjīs*.) Gobind Singh also encouraged those who wished to worship Durgā, the Hindu goddess of war.

The custom of baptism is still performed. At the Ceremony of the Sword the initiate drinks water stirred by a double-edged dagger and eats cakes made of consecrated flour. If a Sikh does not undergo the ceremony (*amrutchāgana*), he technically reverts to being a Hindu. In practice he is known as one of the "easy-going" (*sahidhāris*) who do not wear the distinguishing marks.

By organizing the Sikh community into a militant and self-aware brotherhood, Gobind Singh alienated not only the Mughals but also the neighboring *rājas*, in particular the Nawāb of Sirhind. After a lifetime of fighting, Gobind Singh was summoned by the dying Aurangzeb to try to negotiate a peaceful solution to the problem of the Punjāb. After the emperor's death, Gobind Singh helped the rightful heir to the throne, Bahādur Shāh, to overcome his usurping younger brother at the battle of Jajau. The prince was so grateful that he presented an address of honor to the *guru* at Āgra in 1707 and it finally looked as if Mughals and Sikhs could be peacefully reconciled. But this happy state of affairs was not to last. Bahādur Shāh had to travel south to continue defending his throne, this time against his younger brother. Gobind Singh accompanied him as far as the Deccan. Here, before any settlement could be reached regarding the Punjāb, the Sikh leader was assassinated by an agent of his old enemy, the Nawāb of Sirhind. He died at Nandeo in the autumn of 1708.

A hundred years later the Sikhs were the last of the Indian peoples to acknowledge the British domination of the subcontinent. In the hour of need another brilliant soldier emerged as their leader. This was Ranjīt Singh, the "Lion of the Punjāb." Contemporary reports paint an unflattering picture of a man who was "short, deformed, blind in one eye, and illiterate." Despite these handicaps, Ranjīt Singh was a born leader of men. He rallied the Sikhs in continued defiance of the British Rāj. After several battles a treaty was signed in 1809 that recognized the River Sutlej as the boundary between British and Sikh territory. Ranjīt Singh died thirty years later. At about the same time, the British were ignominiously defeated by the Afghāns at Kābul. In 1845 the Sikhs seized what they saw as their chance to win back land they had ceded to the British, and crossed the Sutlej to attack Delhi. After a series of bloody battles they were badly defeated. Three years later they took the unprecedented step of joining forces with their traditional enemies, the Afghāns, and launched the Second Sikh War. At Chilianwāla they routed the British cavalry. The victory is especially remembered for the way the British horsemen executed a "backward charge" through their own infantry and artillery, scattering even the wagon lines at the back. But in February 1849 the British scored an overwhelming victory at Gujarāt, and the Sikh nation surrendered.

The defeat of Gujarāt fulfilled the prophecy Ranjīt Singh had made almost half a century before. On being shown a map of India he had screwed up his face in disgust saying: "Soon it will all be red!" In the Mutiny of 1857 the Sikhs sided with their new conquerors against both Hindus and Muslims.

Relations between the British and the Sikhs were not to remain cordial for long. In 1919 there was the infamous massacre of the Jallianwāla Bāgh Gardens in Amritsar, when British soldiers, under the orders of Major Dwyer, opened fire on a crowd of demonstrators, many of whom were killed. Thereafter the Sikhs played an active though nonviolent part in the Independence Movement. One of the most famous freedom fighters was Bāba Karak Singh, the president of the Punjāb Provincial Congress Party, the local branch of Gandhi's

Congress Party. Imprisoned for sedition in 1922, he refused to wear clothes as a protest against the government's ban on prisoners being allowed to wear the black turban of militant Sikhism. Although the ban was later withdrawn, Karak Singh remained naked until his release in 1927, four and a half years later.

The last and most bloody chapter in the annals of Sikh military history had yet to be written, as the world learned to its horror in 1947. This was Partition. When the new Muslim state of Pakistān was born, it was the Punjāb, the homeland of the Sikhs, which was ripped apart. The new boundary left over five million Sikhs and Hindus in Muslim Pakistān, and as many Muslims in Hindu India. Both sides, terrified by the prospect of losing everything they had worked all their lives to achieve, turned on each other with unparalleled ferocity. The result was a staggering and convulsive collapse of all civilized values. India has always been a land of extremes; the wholesale carnage of Partition was no exception. All across the state villages and bazaars were reduced to smoldering rubble. The gutters, irrigation canals, and wells of the Punjāb ran red with blood. The hacked and the mutilated were left to the ravages of heat, flies, and vultures. No one was spared. Men, women, and children were indiscriminately beheaded and disemboweled, as centuries of accumulated antagonism between Hindu and Muslim was unleashed in one terrible orgy of slaughter.

Amritsar witnessed some of the worst scenes of this utter and inhuman devastation. The Sikh capital was, as it still is, the principal town on the railway line between Delhi and Lahore, the capital of the new state of Pakistān. Every train crammed with Muslim refugees on their way to their new homeland had to stop here. The militant Sikhs were waiting for them. One after another that summer, trains pulled out of Amritsar station, their carriages running with blood and piled high with dismembered bodies. When word got through to Delhi about what was happening, the trains tried to go straight through the town. It was to no avail; they were ambushed farther down the line. Similar scenes took place in Lahore, the old capital of the Punjāb, which had been famous as a stately pleasure dome since the time of the Mughals, and was known as the Paris of the East. Now the streets of the old city reeked with piles of Hindus, slaughtered as they tried to make their way into India. Neighbor attacked neighbor; old friends turned on each other with a maddened fury. Frenzied mobs roamed the city looting, murdering, raping, pillaging.

All that terrible summer the roads of the Punjāb were filled with streams of refugees going one way or another. Decimated by malnutrition and disease, especially cholera, they straggled along, clutching their pathetic little bundles of belongings. To cap it all, when the long overdue monsoon finally arrived, the Punjāb was devastated by floods. Thousands of refugees were drowned in their improvised camps. Homes that had somehow escaped the mobs were washed away like matchwood. It was as if the gods were trying to wash away all trace of what had been the most appalling outbreak of civil strife in history. Their attempt was in vain. In six blood-soaked weeks, from August to mid-September 1947, half as many Indians died as did American soldiers in World War II. These are the official figures. No one knows the real number of victims. Three quarters of a million is a conservative estimate. The number of surviving refugees is known, however: eleven and a half million.

No one is exclusively to blame for the horrors of Partition. Both the Hindu Congress Party, under Nehru, and the Muslim League, under Muhammad Alī Jinnāh, were intransigent at various times. Had they been able to compromise, the tragedy might well have been averted. Gandhi was against Partition from the start, foreseeing the violence it would unleash. But he paid for his pacifist views with his life. The Mahātma was assassinated by a Hindu fanatic's bullet in Delhi, in 1948, as he began his customary evening prayer meeting. Some have blamed the British for the atrocities of Partition. But they were under pressure from all sides to resolve an impossible situation with impossible speed. In a sense, disaster had been inevitable since 1909, when separate electorates were established for Hindus and Muslims. This meant that in the future any one corner of the Hindu-Muslim-Rāj triangle would be in a position to neutralize the other two. In effect, this is just what happened. Jinnāh outmaneuvered both Congress and the British, so that the state of Pakistān became inevitable. The speed with which the Partition was effected has also been criticized. But when the British lawyer Cyril Radcliffe was given the thankless task of drawing up the world's most complicated frontier, time was already running out. During the summer of 1946, communal riots in Calcutta had already left five thousand dead. Most of them were Hindus. To avenge what they saw as Muslim aggression, the Hindus retaliated with equal ferocity in Bihār. By 1947, as the last viceroy, Admiral Lord Mountbatten, later commented, "India was a ship on fire in mid-ocean with ammunition in the hold." Sooner or later it was bound to explode. In essence, the conflict that erupted in 1947 went back before the days of the British, before even Guru Gobind Singh. It went back a thousand years, to the day the first army marched through the Khyber Pass bearing the green flag of Islām.

Today, the Punjāb seems a land of peace and plenty. By Indian standards, it has been blessed by nature. The soil is rich and well watered. The word *punjāb* means "the land of the five rivers"—the Sutlej, Beās, Rāvī, Chenāb, and Jhelum. These vital arteries flow down from the western end of the Himālayas and cross the plains of the Punjāb to unite in the mighty Indus, which empties into the Arabian Sea. But it is not only nature that has made the Punjāb the granary of India. The industry and organization of the Sikhs is also responsible. As a community they have the gift of resilience. They survived not only Partition, but also the Pakistānī wars of 1965. As the chief component of the Indian army, the Sikhs were again prominent in these clashes. Yet they can survive in peacetime, too. In the Punjāb they have made a mighty contribution to India's Green Revolution. To them must go much of the credit for the golden fields of wheat and mustard, the glittering rice paddies, the white cotton fields, and the leafy green sugarcane plantations. It was the Sikhs who, before the crippling droughts of the mid-1970s and the world oil crisis, had brought India to the verge of being able to produce enough food grains for her 650 million people.

When you drive through the Punjāb today, you feel an atmosphere of optimism. Even the poorest villages are paved and drained. The villagers not only look after their fields, but they weave assiduously as well. Almost every home has a loom and turns out woolen goods, often on a subcontract basis for a local manufacturer. Coops of healthy-looking chickens abound, and plump pigs trot along the roadside. Much of the cooking is done on gas, rather than those twig and dung fires you see further south. There seem to be more tractors here than in all the rest of India put together. Moreover, the nine million Sikhs have a strong sense of identity. They still retain the pride that knit them together as a nation under their first *guru* five hundred years ago.

They are great eaters—fish, chicken, liver, rice—and the Punjāb boasts the largest brewery in Asia. Their appetite befits a martial people. The Norsemen ate and drank like this; so did the Saxons. So too did the Āryan invaders, who swept through the Punjāb on their way to the plains of India four thousand years ago. In this land of hunters the presence of these Āryan ancestors can perhaps be felt more clearly than anywhere else in India. Even the British Rāj, many of whose early members were at a loss to understand the "effeminate Hindu," could grudgingly appreciate the virile qualities of the Punjābī.

Endowed with an almost mystical affinity with machines, the Sikhs are the drivers of India. Wherever there is a bus, lorry, taxi, or scooter, there you will find a Sikh. They were the drivers in the Indian army, and they have kept this monopoly ever since. It seems to be due to a combination of their innate mechanical skill and other peoples' reluctance to risk driving on the same road with them.

The Sikhs are equally at home with India's steam trains, those gleaming dinosaurs that huff and puff their way all over the country. Amritsar is the destination of some of the finest, that rejoice in names like the 42 (up), A. C. Express (Deluxe), or the Frontier Mail. Nowadays these much loved and carefully tended giants provide shocks less terrible than they did in 1947. There is the story of the innocent traveler at Amritsar station. The train from Delhi was late. After some minutes he sought out the station master, immaculate in suit, beard, and turban.

"Excuse me, is the train from Delhi late?"

"Yes, *sahib.*"

"Is it very late?"

"Yes, *sahib.*"

"Any idea how late?"

The station master extracted a silver pocket watch from his waistcoat. Flicking it open, he studied the dial gravely for some moments.

"Three days, six hours, and forty-two minutes, *sahib.*"

The Golden Temple (Figure A)

The heart of Amritsar is the Golden Temple. Set in a tank of water surrounded by a walkway of Jaipur marble, the temple is the Mecca of India's five million Sikhs. Every pious member of the brotherhood hopes to make at least one visit here and bathe in the holy water.

The following rules for visitors must be obeyed:

1. Tobacco, narcotics, and intoxicants in any shape or form are not to be carried into the temple precincts.
2. Shoes, used socks, sticks, and umbrellas are to be left outside at the cloakroom area (Figure A.2). They are looked after free of charge.
3. Visitors without socks should wash their feet outside the entrance of the temple.
4. All visitors should keep their heads covered while in the temple precincts.

The site dates from the times of the fourth *guru*, Rām Dās (1574–1581). In 1577, while living at nearby Gurukatchak, Rām Dās heard that a cripple had been miraculously cured by bathing in a pool here. He had the pool enlarged, and named the tank *amrit sovar*: "the Pool of the Nectar of Immortality." The land around the tank was formally ceded to the Sikhs by Emperor Akbar, but Rām Dās insisted on paying its value to the local Jhāts who owned it. Rām Dās

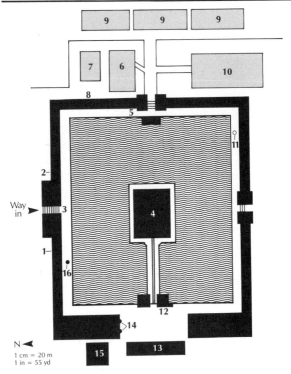

1 *Temple office.* 2 *Cloakrooms.* 3 *The Clock Tower and main entrance.* 4 *The Golden Temple.* 5 *The Sixty-eight Holy Places.* 6 *The dining hall.* 7 *The kitchen.* 8 *Residence of Bāba Karak Singh.* 9 *The temple guest houses.* 10 *The Assembly Hall.* 11 *The Shrine of Bāba Deep Singh.* 12 *Arjun Dev's tree and the* Guru Granth Sahib. 13 *The Akhāl Takhat.* 14 *The flagstaffs.* 15 *The Shrine of Guru Gobind Singh.* 16 *The tree shrine.*

Figure A. The Golden Temple site plan.

then invited Sikh merchants to come and live in the vicinity and allocated each his special place in the bazaar. The town became the religious capital Amritsar.

Rām Dās's son and successor, Arjun, enlarged the tank and built the original temple in its center. The temple was begun in 1589 and was completed in 1601. In keeping with the tolerant attitude of the new faith, the foundation stone was laid by a local Muslim saint.

The temple's history is as turbulent as that of the *khalsa* itself. It suffered most at the hands of Ahmad Shāh Durāni, an Afghān freebooter who invaded India in 1747. He occupied the temple in 1757 and desecrated the shrines. The Sikhs united and drove him out. Four years later he returned

The Golden Temple.

by a different route and defeated the Sikh armies at Ghallu-
ghara. On his way back to Kābul he sacked Amritsar and
blew up the temple. After Durāni's departure, the Sikhs
reconquered the Punjab, the temple was rebuilt, and the tank
reset. Both have remained in their possession ever since. It
was Ranjīt Singh, the Lion of the Punjāb, who gave the temple
its present form. In 1830 he donated 220 pounds (100 kilograms) of gold to the temple trust. This was applied as gold
leaf on copper sheets to the outside and inside of the building.
Each square foot (929 square centimeters) of the upper part
has between a third and a half of an ounce (ten and fifteen
grams) of gold. The lower part of the walls is white marble.

In its prodigious use of gold, the Golden Temple exemplifies the universal symbolism of gold representing the celestial
levels of creation. It has always been used as the highest
earthly representation of heavenly luminescence (this quite
apart from its commercial value), and the craft of the goldsmith has correspondingly been considered the highest of
the crafts.

The Clock Tower (Figure A.3)

You enter the temple by the north gateway, the Clock Tower.
As the early morning mist lifts off the water, the temple
emerges, glowing dully in the early light. The air is filled with
singing and the poignant sound of the harmonium. This
singing is the central point of Sikh worship. After he had
built the temple, Arjun compiled a collection of the hymns of
the great medieval saints: Kabīr, Rāmānanda, Nāmdev, Nānak,
and others. This became the Sikh scripture, the *Ādi Granth*
(the "Original Holy Book"). It was installed in the temple as

The Clock Tower and main entrance to the Golden Temple.

the focus of devotion and the practical teaching of the brotherhood. From then on the temple was the "House of the Lord" (*harmandir*). The *Ādi Granth* was revised by Gobind Singh, the tenth and last in the line of Sikh *gurus*. He refused to name a successor, saying that from then on the Sikh *guru* would be the Holy Book itself. From his time onward the *Ādi Granth* was known as *Guru the Granth Sahib* (the "Holy Book as Guru").

☐
Around the tank are a number of places of special sanctity, milestones marking significant events in Sikh history.

The Sixty-eight Holy Places (Figure A.5)

This is the name given to a stretch of the eastern side of the tank.

☐ THE SHRINE

First there is a shrine, built around a *jūbi* tree. This tree is believed to be the place where the cripple took his healing bath. It is now used as a special bathing place for the sick, who hope to repeat his miraculous cure. There is a covered area for ladies to change in. Next to this is a shrine containing a copy of the *Guru Granth Sahib*. Here, and at other kiosks in the compound, the Holy Book is read for devotees.

Sikhs register their names with the temple authorities to have the scripture read on their behalf in exchange for a donation to the temple. The reader (*granthi*) is an employee of the temple trust. Each *granthi* reads for three hours. One complete reading takes forty-eight hours.

The name of the area comes from the sixty-eight spots of Hindu pilgrimage. When the tank was built, Arjun Dev told his followers that rather than waste time and money being cheated by the brahmin priests at all the orthodox pilgrimage places, they should just bathe here. The benefit they acquired would be many times greater.

☐

Beyond the east gateway lies an important part of the temple precinct. It includes dining hall, kitchen, administrative offices, and guest houses.

☐ THE DINING HALL AND KITCHEN
  (Figures A.6 and A.7)

The dining hall is a modern red brick building with white domed roof. It holds over three thousand at a sitting. Lunch is from eleven until three, and dinner from seven onward. There is no charge. The food is vegetarian, though many Sikhs eat meat. This custom of the community kitchen (*langar*) dates from the time of the third *guru*, Amar Dās (1552–1574). He noticed that the disciples who came to see him would sit and eat separately, as dictated by caste rules. He abolished the custom, saying that if his followers sat together to listen to him, they should eat together as well. Since that time, each Sikh temple runs a kitchen that serves food to whoever wants to eat. The food is paid for out of temple funds. All sit together on the floor to eat, men and women, rich and poor, Hindu and Muslim. This egalitarianism runs right through Sikh history. The mighty Akbar once visited Amar Dās to seek his blessing. The *guru* consented to see him provided the emperor first sat on the floor and ate with the common people. Akbar did so. The kitchen is run by volunteers, and voluntary service (*seva*) to the temple and its associated institutions is an important part of Sikh practice. Ultimately, *seva* is directed to God, and the ideal of Sikhism is that one's whole life should become *seva*. The kitchen here feeds ten thousand people a day.

☐

Between the kitchen dining area and the tank is the residence of Bāba Karak Singh (A.8), who is hailed by the Sikhs as a saint. His followers are distinguished by orange turbans. Temple employees and members of the Akāli sect, one of the most militant in the brotherhood, wear blue or black turbans. The Akālis are currently lobbying for an autonomous Sikh state to be established in the Punjāb. The whole area around the dining hall is in the process of being extended and renovated. Opposite the dining hall is the impressive Assembly Hall (A.10). It is the largest of its kind in Asia.

☐ *THE TEMPLE GUEST HOUSES* (Figure A.9).
Outside the compound proper lie the guest houses (*dharamsālas*, or *bunghas*). These are available for pilgrims and visitors, who can stay for three days and nights free of charge. The largest one (Rām Dās *dharamsāla*) has three hundred rooms, all clean and well kept.

☐

The administrative offices of the temple trust are also in this area. Originally, the temple was managed by a committee under the local *mahārāja*. During the British period, a manager was appointed by the deputy commissioner of Amritsar. The affairs of the temple were mismanaged. The desire of the Sikhs to manage their own administration dovetailed with the general Indian desire for Home Rule. In 1925 the Gurudvāra Act transferred the running of all Sikh affairs to a trust committee elected by the Sikh community itself. The trust is staffed by 140 unpaid members. Elections are held every five years. At present the trust holds about fifty million rupees and runs schools, colleges, and hospitals as well as temples all over India.

Continuing the Circumambulation of the Tank

☐ *SHRINE OF BĀBA DEEP SINGH* (Figure A.11)
In the southeast corner of the compound is an area reserved for ladies to bathe in, screened off from public view. Between this and the south gateway is the shrine of the warrior Bāba Deep Singh. In 1758 Ahmad Shāh Durāni attacked the town. Deep Singh was engaged in copying out the *Granth Sahib* when he heard the news. He vowed to defend the temple to his death and led his followers out to fight the invaders. About four miles (six kilometers) from the town Deep Singh was mortally wounded and his head was hacked from his shoulders. But so great was his determination to die within the hallowed walls of the temple that he managed to fight on, holding onto his head with one hand. He fought his way back to the temple and collapsed and died on this spot. The shrine is held very sacred.

☐ *THE SOUTHERN SIDE*
To the south of the temple precincts lie the Temple Gardens. They cover thirty acres (twelve hectares) and contain pome-

granate, orange, and other fruit trees, and some pavilions. At the southern end is the Bāba Atal Tower, another grim reminder of the violent history of the *khalsa*. The tower is named after Atal Rai, who was the youngest son of the sixth *guru*, Hargobind. When he was nine, the boy used his psychic powers to cure a child of snakebite. His father reproved him, saying that supernatural powers should be displayed in purity of life and not in flashy miracles. To which his son replied that if he had withheld a life that was required by God, he would donate his own. So saying, he lay down and died.

There is some fine carving along this side of the tank. Donors to the temple also have their names carved into the marble floor, and you can often see the scribes at work.

□ THE WESTERN SIDE

The western end of the compound is undergoing extensive renovation. A marble causeway, 204 feet long, lined with nine gilded lamps on either side, leads to the temple proper in the middle of the tank. At the entrance is a tree shrine (A.12), next to which stands a booth where the *Guru Granth* is read. The tree was a favorite spot of Arjun Dev, who would sit here and meditate.

The square in front of the entrance is a great gathering place for visitors. Conspicuous among them are groups of fierce-looking warriors dressed in blue. Those are the Nihāng Sikhs, a sort of Knights Templar group within the brotherhood. The word *nihāng* means "crocodile," and alludes to their fierceness. They consider themselves the truest followers of the militant Gobind Singh and are always heavily armed. They carry swords, lances, or curved daggers and have razor-sharp steel quoits in their turbans. They often travel on horseback. Officially there are so *sādhus* (ascetics) in Sikhism. Nānak decreed that all Sikhs should marry and be householders, and he denounced asceticism, saying, "A hungry man is in no mood to worship the Almighty." But wandering asceticism is in the Indian blood, and the Nihāngs are to all intents and purposes Sikh *sādhus*. They live off the land. Some of them take *bhāng*; many of them are fine musicians.

The Temple Itself (Figure A.4)

The siting of the temple serves several symbolic purposes. It represents the island, a haven of calm amid the ever-changing flux of life. With its four doors open to the four directions, it is the central point of the Sikh universe. It is accessible to all, in time as well as in space, for none of the gateways have doors, and they are always open. The temple is thus a permanent refuge. Like the Hindu temple or the square Muslim Kā'ba, it signifies the primordial division of the cosmos into

Interior of the Golden Temple—the reading of the Guru Granth Sahib.

four, a division that orders the manifesting universe as it emerges from the womb of the Absolute, the cosmic waters.

When it was built, Arjun Dev likened the temple to a ship that crosses the ocean of ignorance. As such it is a physical analogue of the Name of God, on which the Sikhs meditate. The "Name" is an inner sound, which serves as a *mantra* to take the attention from the gross surface level of the mind to its inner depths. The *Granth Sahib* calls this name "a ship by which the devout cross the miseries of the world." All Sikh temples are known as *gurudvāras* ("the doors to the *guru*").

□ THE GROUND FLOOR
The temple has three floors. The ground floor, entered by fine silver doors, is the shrine containing the Holy Book. It sits on a sumptuous platform under a canopy studded with jewels. Professional singers (*rāgis*) take turns singing the verses from the book, accompanied by musicians. The *rāgis* are employees of the temple and enjoy a position of tremendous honor. The singing is continuous from 4 A.M. to 11 P.M. in the summer, and from 5 A.M. to 10 P.M. in the winter. Each evening the Holy Book is taken in a golden palanquin, with a sumptuous procession, accompanied by music, to the Akhāl Takhat (A.13), where it stays overnight. Each morning it is brought back again into the temple for the next day's chanting. The equipment used in the procession can be seen in the treasury, on the first (U.S. second) floor of the entrance to the temple, opposite the Akhāl Takhat. It includes a golden canopy set with rubies, emeralds, and diamonds, silver poles,

a diadem with strings of pearls. Before the chanting begins, the book is opened at random and a quotation selected. This is then posted on a board outside as a text for the day. The *Granth* is in old Punjābī, written in the *gurumukha* ("Guru's Mouth") script. It contains nearly thirty-five hundred hymns.

Throughout the day pilgrims place their offerings of flowers or money on the sheet spread on the floor and then take their place around the book to join in the singing. Entrance is absolutely unrestricted. There is no other formal or ritualistic worship, and the lack of compulsion to donate money is a welcome change from some of the Hindu temples. The place is saturated with an intense atmosphere of devotion.

The ground floor shrine is surrounded by a path for circumambulation. Its marble walls are decorated with plaster and mirrorwork, gold leaf, and beautiful designs of animals, birds, and flowers in semiprecious stones. This inlay is as fine as any Mughal craftsmanship.

☐
The rest of the temple is virtually all covered in copper gilt, inscribed with quotations from the *Granth*. The whole effect is sumptuous yet tasteful.

Throughout the day pilgrims are provided with *prasāda*, holy food consecrated by its presence to the *Granth*. This is bulgar (cracked wheat) liberally sweetened and fried in ghee. Its smell pervades the entire compound!

☐ *THE FIRST (U.S. SECOND) FLOOR*
On the first (U.S. second) floor there is a balcony overlooking the holy of holies downstairs. Here three venerable Sikhs perform the *akhand path*, "the unbroken reading." This is a version of the same idea as the perpetual adoration in Christianity: In order to preserve the purity of the cosmic order, there must always be someone focusing on the prime object of devotion.

☐ *THE TOP FLOOR*
On the top floor there is a small Hall of Mirrors (Shīsh Mahal), where the *gurus* used to sit. It has a curved roof in Chinese style. Here another reader performs *akhand path*. This little pavilion is as richly decorated as downstairs. Hymns are inscribed on the walls in letters of gold, and the place is swept with brushes made of peacocks' feathers.

The Akhal Takhat (Figure A.13)

This domed temple stands opposite the entrance to the causeway. It is the seat of the supreme religious council. It was originally built in 1609 by Guru Hargobind, when he began organizing the brotherhood into a political order. All decisions affecting the community are made here. The ground floor of the present building dates from 1874; the upper stories were added by Ranjit Singh. A number of weapons, including Guru Gobind's sword, are kept here. There is also an ark made of gold, in which are stored the vessels used for initiating new members into the brotherhood of the pure.

To the north of the Akhāl Takhat is a side shrine (A.15), dedicated to the tenth *guru*, Gobind Singh.

Continuing Around the Tank

☐ *FLAGSTAFFS* (Figure A.14)
These symbolize the two pillars of religion and politics. They are joined in the middle by the emblem of the Sikh nation: the two swords of Guru Hargobind, representing both temporal and spiritual authority. The circle is inscribed with the principal Sikh *mantra: Ek omkara* ("God is One").

☐ *THE TREE SHRINE* (Figure A.16)
The gnarled tree is four hundred and fifty years old. It was the favorite resting place of the first chief priest of the temple, Bāba Gujhajī. He would sit here and supervise the construction of the temple. Although he was chief priest, he would, in accordance with the doctrine of *seva*, do his share of the building work, and was particularly fond of grinding the lime for cement and mortar. Nowadays it is not the memory of the old priest that draws the attention of the pilgrims to the tree. Guru Nānak's teaching against superstition notwithstanding, thousands of women flock here to beseech the tree for a son. They tie strings to its withered branches, as Indian women have always done, hoping to be blessed by the primeval fertility spirits that choose such places as their abode. It is also a favorite spot to arrange and sanctify marriages, despite the protests of the temple authorities. It is as if an irrepressible nature worship creeps back into all Indian religion. Even here in the midst of modern Sikhism are the sacred trees and the reverence for water that have always been found in India. Nevertheless, in their social awareness, energetic organization, and strength of devotion, the followers of Guru Nānak are sincere and impressive examples of the four great principles of their faith: equality, industry, generosity, and optimism.

11

ĀGRA'S TĀJ MAHAL

THE PEARL IN THE MUGHAL CROWN

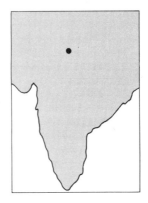

The Tāj Mahal has some indefinable quality, something you cannot put your finger on. Whole forests have been pulped and gallons of ink spilt to produce the hundreds of books, articles, and letters singing its praises, yet the place remains an enigma, beautiful and inscrutable. This Mughal tomb is one of the great visual clichés of our time; it is the supreme symbol of India. We have all seen countless photographs of it: postcards, book jackets, travel posters, holiday snaps. Yet despite this familiarity, the Tāj always surprises those who visit it for the first time. For some it is more breathtakingly beautiful than they ever imagined. Others are initially disappointed. But, as with most sites in India, the place grows on you, slowly but surely. Even for those who are initially skeptical, a second, third, or even fourth visit confirms its charm—and they are captivated forever. What is this elusive quality that makes the Tāj the most magical building in the world?

To begin with the facts: The Tāj Mahal was built by the fifth Mughal emperor Shāh Jahān (1627–1658) as the tomb for his favorite wife, Mumtāz Mahal, "the Jewel of the Palace."

She died while giving birth to their fourteenth child, and the emperor never really recovered from his loss. It is said that he observed mourning for two years, eating only the plainest of food and living a life of complete simplicity. Whereas previously he had been a man of action who loved the challenges of running his empire, he now became progressively reclusive and devoted his attention to what, apart from Mumtāz, had always been his passion: architecture. He resolved to build his wife the most magnificent memorial on earth. Saddened also by the treacherous revolts and rivalries of his sons, one of whom was the eminently unlikable Aurangzeb, Shāh Jahān enshrined his memories of happier times in a marble-faced tomb he had built across the River Yamunā from his own residence in Āgra fort. This palace was known as "the Crown of the Locality" (tāj-i-mahal). In later life, the emperor would sit at his windows in the fort gazing out at the mausoleum of his beloved wife. He intended to build his own tomb in black marble on the opposite bank to the Tāj and link the two by a bridge that would symbolize a love that transcended the flow of time itself. This dream never materialized; but even on its own the tomb of Mumtāz Mahal stands as the masterpiece of Mughal art.

The Tāj was begun in January 1632 and finished in February 1643, its completion coinciding with the twelfth anniversary of Mumtāz's death. Its cost in those days was well over five million rupees and, by today's standards, incalculable. No one knows who drew up the plans. Architects, designers, and craftsmen were summoned from all over the known world. Among the team assembled were Shāh Jahān's chief architect, Ustad Ahmad Lahwārī, a Persian architect named Mulla Murshīd from Shiraz, and a Turkish designer, Muhammad Afandi. There were also European master craftsmen involved: a French goldsmith, Austin of Bordeaux, and a jeweler from Venice called Veroneo. Wooden models were submitted to the emperor, who no doubt contributed himself to the project; at the least, he deserves credit for selecting the final plan.

An English traveler, Peter Mundy, witnessed the start of the mighty project in 1632 and tells us: "The building is begun and goes on with excessive labour and cost, prosecuted with extraordinary diligence; Gold and silver are esteemed common metal, and Marble but as ordinary stone." Indeed, the mausoleum was constructed by a veritable army of labor. Twenty thousand artisans worked on it, including five hundred carpenters and three hundred blacksmiths. Elephants, bullocks, camels, and mules were used to ferry materials and work the construction pulleys. The marble came from Makarāna in Rājasthān. For this journey alone, over a thousand elephants were used, each one able to carry a block of up to two and a half tons (two and a quarter metric tons).

R. Yamunā

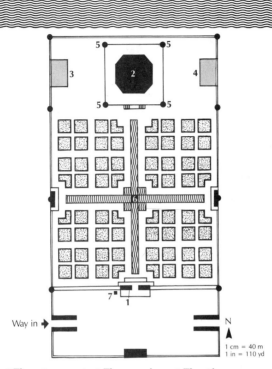

1 *The entrance gate.* 2 *The mausoleum.* 3 *The side mosque.*
4 *"The Answer."* 5 *The minarets.* 6 *The central tank.* 7 *Ticket office.*

Figure A. The Tāj Mahal site plan.

The precious stones for the inlay also came from far and wide: carnelian from Baghdad, turquoise from Tibet and Persia, malachite from Russia, diamonds and onyx from central India. It is as if all the skill, expertise, and resources accumulated by the eclectic, adventurous Mughal dynasty came together at one point in time and space to create what has become the most enduring romantic symbol of human love.

The Entrance Gate (Figure A.1)

You approach the Tāj through a wooded park that was originally an extension of the grounds of the tomb. Already the white top of the dome peeps tantalizingly over its red sandstone surroundings. A small entrance gate, flanked by the Tomb of the Royal Serving Ladies (on the left) and the Stonecutters' Mosque (on the right), leads to a long arcade. This

The entrance gate.

was the main bazaar of Mumtāzābād, the city that sprang up around the construction of the shrine. The arcade still houses shops, selling everything from marble replicas of the Tāj to hair oil and, of course, those ubiquitous Kashmīrī handicrafts. This avenue opens out into a large, shaded court now used as a meeting point and carpark. You are in the front courtyard of the Tāj compound—the sacred space walled off from the hustle and bustle of the marketplace and originally free from the hawkers who now throng it. It is here that you get your first glimpse of the massive entrance gate, an integral feature of the tomb too often ignored. It is worth spending a couple of minutes appreciating this gate.

In sacred architecture the entrance is that delicate yet absolute demarcation line between the sacred and the profane. Here, it is intentionally massive and awesome, as it had a practical as well as symbolic function: It protected the enormous wealth of gold and jewels originally within the actual building inside.

This monolithic sentinel stands one hundred feet (thirty meters) high and is in effect an enormous triumphal archway, attesting to the glory of its royal builder as well as the glory of God. The domed pavilions (*chhatrīs*), Hindu in style, that sit on top of the gate enhance the military effect; they resemble the tents and banners of some vast encamped army, at rest but vigilant.

To the Muslim such a gateway has a specific spiritual purpose. It symbolizes the transition from the realm of the senses to the realm of the spirit and is thus the entrance to paradise, the door to the womb of spiritual rebirth. This purpose is made explicit by the verses from the eighty-ninth chapter of the *Qur'ān*, which frame the central portals. In an assured and graceful Arabic script they remind you that the tomb garden is a replica of paradise. They end: "O soul that art at rest, return to the Lord, at peace with Him and He at peace with you. So enter as one of His servants; and enter into His garden." Notice how the lettering appears to be the same size from top to bottom. In fact, this is a skillful trick of Shāh Jahān's engravers. The letters are gradually lengthened as their distance from the eye increases so as to preserve the illusion of consistency.

The massive brass door is recent, a substitute for the original, which was solid silver and decorated with eleven hundred silver nails, whose heads were contemporary silver coins. They, along with other treasures, were removed from the mausoleum by the Jhāts, a local Hindu tribe who plundered much of the Mughal Empire after its collapse.

The transition from the profane to the sacred is carefully and deliberately orchestrated and can only be appreciated by walking very slowly. As you mount the steps into the entrance hall, you get your first glimpse of the tomb (A.2), which is revealed gradually through the darkened frame of the doorway of the entrance hall. The arch of this frame is echoed on the tomb ahead: first by the shape of the large arched alcove of the main face (*īwān*), then by the smaller, latticed arch that actually surrounds the dark doorway itself. Step by step your view expands to include the other faces of the building, and by the time you are standing on the threshold of the hall, the whole dome is in sight, its elegant finial just falling within your line of vision. As you walk through the entrance chamber, the vista expands to include not only the tomb but the backdrop of limitless sky behind. It is as if you had gone very deep into the heart of some tiny jewel and there discovered infinity. Many people's first reaction is: "Oh but how *small* it looks!" for we have all been brought up on photographs of a building taken out of its context. In fact, this apparent lack of size is another optical illusion. The dome is actually over 230 feet (70 meters) from the ground and is made to look small by the skillful use of proportion, as you can see if you compare the size of the people on the marble platform halfway down the garden against the building itself. They are dwarfed by it.

A couple of points about the entrance gate before you descend into the gardens: Do try and get up to the balcony on the first (U.S. second) floor because only from here can you see and photograph the Tāj in true relation to its auxiliary buildings. These are an integral part of the overall design. Sometimes the balcony is open to the public, sometimes the officials need a little gentle persuasion to let you up, but the view from there is magnificent. The gate also provides the

Initial view of the Tāj Mahal.

best vantage point for viewing the Tāj by moonlight. In addition there is an interesting collection of old photos of the Tāj in the last century, displayed in the office in the southwest corner of the entrance hall. Few people seem to know about this; a polite and friendly approach to the supervising officer will get you in.

If you move to the left of the gateway, you will be in the best spot to analyze the composition of the Tāj and begin to discover its secret. Beauty resides in proportion; if you examine the two interlocking parts of the complex—building and garden—you see that the whole achieves its effect by being a finely balanced synthesis of a number of deliberate contrasts.

Viewing the Outside of the Building

☐ *THE MAUSOLEUM* (Figure A.2)
The principal contrast is between the bulbous, full-blown dome, and the flat planes of the building on which it rests. If you look at a plan of the Tāj (see Figure B), you see it is basically a square with its corners cut off to form an irregular octagon. The octagon breaks down into four smaller octagons, all the same size and linked around a central, fifth one. This *mandala* is unified by the dome—a circle whose center is the center of the middle octagon and whose circumference links the centers of the other four. The truncated outside corners of the building have the effect of leading the eye around its edges and inviting us to explore what lies beyond, thus giving a dynamic tension to what would otherwise have been too flat, too like a house of playing cards.

The central dome rises high over the main *īwān*; in fact it appears to be a continuation of it, so gracefully do the lines move upward. Actually, the dome is set on a high drum some way behind the *īwān*, thus avoiding any sense of crowding as there had been in the earlier domes of Iran and India. This main dome is echoed by four balancing cupolas, which, being slightly flatter in outline, serve to contain its swell by exerting a stabilizing pull downward. This restraining tension is extended out to the corner towers, each of which is topped by a similarly flattish cupola.

The convex swell of the dome is also balanced by the concave recessed niches that cover the facade. Whereas the dome draws light to it, and radiates it out like some giant lustrous pearl, the *īwān* niches provide deep and cool caverns of shadow. Nor is this shadow at all heavy; the faceted surfaces of the inside of the niches break it up into its own variety. This device is most effective when it is most necessary: in the glaring light of the middle of the day. It saves the tomb from becoming too massive, preventing its monumental strength from degenerating into mere heaviness, and it saves the facade from being too one-dimensional.

The resemblance of this dome to a huge pearl is not accidental. There is a well-loved saying of the Prophet that describes paradise as containing the throne of God, surmounted by a gigantic dome made of white pearl, supported by four corner pillars. On each pillar is written a letter (*R, H, M, N*). Together these spell the word *ar-Rahmān* ("the All-Merciful"), one of the ninety-nine names of Allāh. From each of the four letters there flows a river of grace.

Moreover, in Islamic symbolism the pearl represents the eternal nature from which manifest creation arises at the will of Allāh. Thus, the pearl is the prototype of all that is female

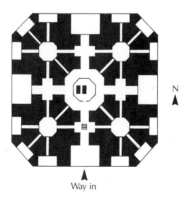

Figure B. Octagonal plan of the Tāj mausoleum.

and peculiarly suited to represent the emperor's beloved Mumtāz.

The cosmological purpose of the domed building (*hujra*) is to unite heaven and earth. The squared, grounded shape of the building represents the material universe, whereas the circular dome is the vault of heaven. The transition between the two is effected by the octagon. This symbolism is repeated in the shape of the finial, which has three spheres, representing the worlds of animals, men, and angels, and which, crowned by the crescent moon of Islām, points to Infinity.

□ *THE SIDE MOSQUE AND THE ANSWER*
(Figures A.3 and A.4)

On the left of the mausoleum is the tomb mosque in red sandstone. It is common in Islām to build a mosque next to a tomb: It sanctifies the place and provides somewhere for the family and mourners to offer up prayers (smaller tombs have a *mihrāb* set into the *qibla* wall). The tomb replica opposite, on the east of the platform, is known as "the Answer." It cannot be used for prayer, since it faces away from Mecca; it was added purely to preserve the symmetry of the complex.

□ *THE MINARETS* (Figure A.5)

The Tāj is surrounded by its four corner towers, standing like silent sentinels guarding the tomb within and lending it balance, space, and elevation. Look at them closely: Yes, they *are* slanting! Each was constructed off plumb—intentionally, unlike Pisa—the one on the southwest corner by eight inches (twenty centimeters), the others by two inches (five centimeters). This was so that if there was ever an earthquake, they would fall away from the tomb itself, not onto it.

The Garden

In all Islamic art, the garden symbolizes paradise, or the primordial unity of being we enjoyed before the Fall. The message inscribed over the entrance portal to the Tāj is an echo of an earlier saying at the gate to Akbar's tomb in Sikandra: "These are the gardens of Eden: Enter them to dwell therein eternally." In fact, the words for "garden" and "paradise" are the same in the Persian language as they are in Hebrew.

It is easy to see how important an image the garden was for a desert people. Its shaded, watered greenness provided a restful and sustaining oasis in the midst of an inhospitable environment. The Mughals, originally from the plains of Central Asia, shared their nomadic ancestors' love of gardens. In fact, their main complaint against India was its lack of verdant and well-watered places. The founder of the dynasty,

Bābur ("the Tiger") designed his own gardens in Kābul and actually helped in laying them out. He passed on to his descendants his love for Kashmīr, with its forests, lakes, and waterfalls, and also for the fertile valleys of Afghānistān, laden with fruit-bearing trees.

The guiding principle of the Islamic garden is one of a contrived and tranquil symmetry. It is a man-made replica of the perfection of Allāh. The rectangular plan of the Tāj complex measures 1,900 by 1,000 feet (580 by 300 meters) in a north-south axis (see Figure A). Of this, the garden occupies a central square, whose sides are one thousand feet (three hundred meters) long. The remaining rectangles comprise the tomb, with its balancing buildings in the north, and the entrance area, including what is now the carpark, in the south. This central garden is essentially Persian and follows the traditional *chahār bāgh* design: based on the number four, which signifies completeness and is sacred in Islām. The garden is divided first into four squares by the intersection of two marble water courses. These meet at a square tank in the middle of the lawns (A.6), on each side of which are identical benches and stairways.

Water is cooling, purifying, and symbolic of initiation, and the Tāj, like a Hindu temple, is situated on the banks of a river. Because it lies between these two stretches of water, the cenotaph is reflected on both sides. This reflection has a dogmatic, as well as an esthetic, purpose. The Muslim paradise is the opposite, or mirror image, of this world. Thus Muslim art makes great use of the principle of reversibility. The *Qur'ān* is thought to be the mirror image of a tablet in heaven; the Tree of Life grows upside down in the paradisical garden. This is the esoteric meaning behind both the use of reflection in water here and the inverted Hindu lotus motif that crowns the dome.

The four lawns are in turn subdivided into four, to produce a total of sixteen flowerbeds. Each bed was originally planted with four hundred flowers. The canals were lined with trees: cypress symbolizing death, fruit trees symbolizing life. In its heyday, the garden must have been breathtaking. The waters were filled with fish and the gardens with nightingales, peacocks, and rare birds of beautiful plumage. The lawns were patrolled by guards in white robes, whose duty was to scare off birds of prey. Their weapons were peashooters! Quite the antithesis of the dreary funerary gardens of Christianity, these Islamic grounds were visited by the nobility for picnics and celebration, and Shāh Jahān held *darbārs* here. This is why there are stables and outhouses around the southern walls.

With the decline of the Mughal dynasty, the gardens also waned, becoming overgrown and weed-ridden. By the nineteenth century the Tāj and its surroundings were a favorite spot for courting couples, and open-air balls were held under the brilliant white dome. It was also a haunt of British soldiers, who held drinking parties there. Indeed, the Tāj was the setting for what must have been the most damning story of the Rāj in India. The villain of the piece was Lord William Bentinck, who was governor-general of all India from 1828 to 1835. Bentinck is chiefly remembered for his abolition of *satī*, his campaign against the robber gangs called the Thugs (who worshipped Kālī and ritually strangled their victims with a yellow scarf weighted with a silver coin), and his educational policy of replacing Persian with English as the official language of India. Bentinck decided that the Tāj could be a good source of a little rapid money. Shāh Jahān's mausoleum was to be demolished, shipped back piece by piece to England, and auctioned off to the wealthy, who, in the Victorian manner, could sprinkle their gardens with these quaint imperial souvenirs. Believe it or not, the scheme actually reached the stage when there were cranes erected in the Tāj gardens, poised to begin demolition. The only reason that this never happened was that a pilot auction held in England, with marble shipped back from the Āgra fort a few miles downriver, failed to arouse the anticipated interest and cash. The reason we can stand and marvel at the Tāj today is solely that Bentinck's scheme was not, in our ugly modern phrase, "financially viable."

Fortunately for the British record, the balance of Bentinck was redressed by the work of Lord Curzon, a man who loved the country and did much to awaken India to its own cultural

The Tāj Mahal from the gardens.

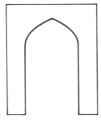

Figure C. The keel arch.

heritage. He renovated much of the damage done by the Jhāts, reset the marble platform around the Tāj, and cleaned up the gardens, restoring them to something of their former glory.

The Tomb

Now proceed to the tomb itself. As you will notice, most tourists troop dutifully down the central aisle, look at the monument and return. While this is one way to approach the building, do not forget that there are side paths and that the compound is meant to be explored from every angle. Not only are these side aisles quiet, even when the place is crawling with visitors, they also offer the best and most shady vantage points for unusual shots of the tomb, framing it with deep green foliage or setting it against a host of brilliant scarlet and yellow canna lilies. The side gardens are themselves worth a look, providing a dappled contrast to the play of light on the bright marble. Approached obliquely, the Tāj reveals its facets one by one, decorously.

As you approach you can also observe how the overall unity of the building comes partly from the simple uniformity of its basic decorative motif. This is the keel arch set within a rectangle—the archetypal shape of Islām (Figure C). This shape is repeated on different scales throughout the complex; in both the entrance gateway and the main *īwān*, the smaller recessed niches and the trellised doors and windows they contain, the podium on which the building stands, the ornamentation on the drum of the dome, the eight-cusped arches of the roof cupolas, and the turrets that surmount the four towers. Everywhere one looks, this refrain is repeated in different keys, each reinforcing and echoing the others. The upward thrust of these arches adds a sense of elevation to the central dome, which seems to have burst out of its rectangular frame and to be soaring heavenward.

Whichever angle you approach from, the initial illusion of the smallness of the building gives way to another one. With

The Tāj Mahal—detail of facade showing latticed window in the shape of the keel arch, with calligraphic and floral decoration.

each step we take, the dome appears to grow larger, swelling ripely as if being gradually inflated. Once you arrive under the looming dome and look up, the backdrop is just the blue expanse of sky, unending and unrestricted. Against this the marble bud seems to be floating in space, like the birds that wheel around it. It is monumental, yet somehow insubstantial, massive yet simultaneously filled with an airy lightness.

□ THE DOORWAYS

This synthesis is partly achieved by the balance of plain surfaces and intricate ornamentation. The entire text of Chapter 36 of the *Qur'ān* is inscribed over the four main doorways of the mausoleum, beginning with the front door and moving around clockwise to finish at the eastern one. This text, which reads from right to left, is recited to the Muslim on his deathbed and ends with the words: "Therefore, glory be to Him in whose hands is the glory of all things, and to Him you shall be brought back." The same trick of lengthening the Arabic letters is employed here as on the front gate.

The inner niches around the doors are also inscribed with qur'anic texts. It is sometimes forgotten that calligraphy is the most important of the arts in Islām. The *Qur'ān* was dictated to Muhammad by the angel Gabriel, and therefore the spoken and written word is the nearest we can come to expressing the inexpressible Allāh. There are seven major types of Islamic calligraphy, from the original geometric and simple *kūfī* script to the script of the intrigue-ridden court of the Ottoman Turks, which was so ornate that it became a cipher for sending coded messages. The script used on the Táj is *naskh*. The outside is also decorated with lovely floral arabesque motifs. The calligraphic inscriptions here give us a further indication that the Táj was constructed as a replica of paradise. It is unique among Islamic funerary monuments in the number and length of the qur'anic passages it bears—twenty-five altogether, totaling no less than 241 verses. This is especially remarkable when contrasted with the other buildings of Shāh Jahān, which, although mosques, contain but a few qur'anic passages amid the Persian inscriptions, most of which are concerned primarily with praising the building or its builder.

□

The Táj has often been called a sentimental building, but surely this is only true of the legends that surround it. Architecturally, the cenotaph has a purity which is almost classical. This sense of intellectual restraint extends to the decoration. For all its famed embellishment, there is something unshakably austere about Mumtáz's shrine.

□ *THE CENTRAL CHAMBER*

Inside the darkened central chamber lie the cenotaphs (*zarīhs*) of the emperor and his beloved queen. The actual bodies are buried in a crypt (*maqbara*) below (see Figure D); it was the custom to have both a public tomb and a private one (*qabr*) reserved for the members of the family. They were originally surrounded by a screen of silver, encrusted with precious stones, but this was removed by Aurangzeb in 1672, as he feared it might be stolen. The latticed marble substitute, again octagonal, is a beautiful piece of work, however: finely carved and with some exquisite inlay work. Mumtáz rests directly beneath the center of the dome, her gravestone marked by the female slate; Shāh Jahān's is to her left, marked by the male pen-box. It was squashed in as something of an afterthought, by Aurangzeb, who was too mean to make the dream of the Black Táj a reality.

Perhaps the imbalance here at the heart of the Táj reflects a fatal flaw in the dynasty itself—like some worm in the Mughal bud. It is a fitting, and ironical comment on a family that was such an extraordinary mixture of barbaric cruelty and esthetic refinement.

The beauty of the inlay work on these tombs is legendary: thirty-five types of precious stones are used, and one flower, only an inch (a couple of centimeters) square, can contain up to sixty pieces of stone. Take your flashlight and examine the work; it is breathtaking. By holding the flashlight flat against the marble you can see the translucence of the stones.

Above the tombs hangs a lamp that never goes out. The original was stolen by the Jhāts; this replacement was added by Lord Curzon, who had it made in Egypt.

Around the octagonal chamber are the four other octagonal rooms, originally meant to house the graves of other members of Shāh Jahān's family. But again, Aurangzeb failed to honor his father's wishes.

Figure D. Cross-section of the Tāj elevation.

The acoustics, especially in the central chamber, are marvelous. The domed ceiling was designed to act as an echo chamber for the chanting of the *Qur'ān* and the melodies of the court musicians. The slightest noise is picked up and reverberated around the vault, trailing off after many seconds into silence. If you want an idea of how the dome was designed to be used, listen to the records of the Canadian flautist Paul Horn, recorded inside the chamber.

And here is the final illusion presented by the Tāj. The domed ceiling you are looking at is not the actual dome. The building was constructed with a double dome (see Figure D), which is how it rises to such a height and yet remains stable. This device of a double dome was Central Asian in origin. With the Tāj, Shāh Jahān's architects brought to fruition an experiment first tried in Humāyūn's tomb in Delhi, some ninety years earlier.

□ *THE FACADE*

After the cenotaph, walk around the building a couple of times, to get an idea of the surface inlay. Because the faces of the building are flat, the angularity forces you to readjust your perspective continually, and to look at the building afresh at each moment. A circular structure, like a *stūpa* for example, has a greater monotony, which suits its spiritual purpose of creating a certain state of mind. But the effect of the Tāj is created by the contrast of planes, the play between the different facets of its surface, and the three distinct levels of the garden, the parapet, and the building itself.

□ THE MINARETS

From here outside the tomb we can get a close-up view of the four minarets. Aldous Huxley, who was not overimpressed by the Tāj, called these towers "the ugliest structures ever erected by human hands." There is indeed something ungainly about them—out of keeping with the whole. In comparison with the almost contemporary stone needles that grace the mosques of Ottoman Turkey and pierce the skyline of Istanbul, these towers are hardly minarets at all. Nevertheless, despite their rather lavatorial tiling with its heavy black pointing, they reinforce the purpose of the mausoleum to remind us of the power of death and the littleness of human destiny in comparison.

□

Everyone has a favorite time of day to see the Tāj. Just make sure you avoid the middle of the day, for to paraphrase Noel Coward: "Mad dogs and tourists go out in the midday sun." Between ten and three, not only is the heat oppressive for much of the year, but the full light of day does not show off the Tāj at its best. It sits like some enormous beached whale, patiently enduring the tourists who scurry like ants all over it. But in the early morning or evening—which are the traditional times of worship in India—its dignity returns. In the softer light the marble can glow pink, bluish, or a delicate lilac. Just after sunrise the place is especially lovely. The early sun picks out scintillating clusters of tiny lights in the marble, and the sandstone has a honeyed mellowness it does not regain till the golden light of the early evening strikes it. The place is quite still, only the birds are on the move: Flocks of brilliant parakeets flash against the white marble, and the first of the somber black kites start their wheeling homage.

If you go to the back of the terrace and look down over the river, you will see a small white Hindu temple to your right. Here are people doing their ritual washing and praying as they have done for countless years. The river is still and flat, dung cakes spread out to dry on the bank. This is the time to sit quietly, watching the play of light and shade all around you, and wait for the day to begin. There is nothing quite like it. Except perhaps the Tāj by moonlight . . .

12

ĀGRA'S TOMB OF ITIMĀD-UD-DAULA

AN EMPRESS'S JEWEL CASKET

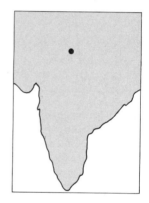

The story behind this small exquisite building has all the romance and intrigue one could hope for from the highly colored pages of Mughal history.

Sometime at the end of the sixteenth century, a Persian noble called Ghiyās Beg fell out with the Safavid king Abbās of Persia and fled with his wife and young daughter to India. His wife was pregnant, and at one time on the journey their money and morale were so low that they decided to abandon their baby daughter to speed the journey, and perhaps return for her when their circumstances were better. As fate would have it, a caravan traveling behind the wretched couple found the baby and returned her to her parents, who took the miracle as a sign from Allāh that the little girl was especially blessed. Penniless, Ghiyās Beg made his way to the court of the Mughal emperor Akbar the Great to try his luck at fame and fortune in the imperial service. Things went well for him. His natural abilities were rewarded, he rose in the ranks, and when Akbar's son Prince Salīm ascended to the throne as

Jahāngīr ("the Seizer of the World") in 1605, Ghiyās Beg was made prime minister. He was also given the title Itimād-ud-Daula ("the Pillar of the State").

Ghiyās Beg's rescued daughter, Mehrunissa, had grown into a young woman of great talent and, to judge from contemporary reports and portraits, great beauty. She was married to another Persian, Sher Afkun, a general in the army whom Jahāngīr posted to the far reaches of the empire in Bengāl. On her husband's sudden death in 1607, Mehrunissa, who was only thirty, returned to the court at Āgra to serve as a lady-in-waiting to one of Akbar's widows.

Since the days of Jahāngīr's grandfather Humāyūn, it had been a Mughal tradition that once a year the royal ladies would set up stalls in the Meena Bazaar and play at being shopkeepers, the emperor and his nobles moving freely among them and sampling their wares. This custom no doubt acted as a safety valve in a life dominated by court protocol, and it also allowed both sides a degree of lighthearted and open flirtation unheard of in the tightly controlled *haram* society. It was in this carnival atmosphere that the young Jahāngīr met Mehrunissa in the spring of 1611. Two months later they were married. Jahāngīr had coins struck in the new queen's name and bestowed on her first the title of Nūr Mahal, "Light of the Palace," and later Nūr Jahān, "Light of the World."

There is another version of the story that claims Jahāngīr fell in love with Mehrunissa long before and had her husband murdered in Bengāl, and that Mehrunissa resisted his advances for six years, unable to forgive him for his murder of her husband. Despite its persistence, this story has never been proved.

Whatever the truth, Nūr Jahān was a remarkable woman. Besides her legendary beauty she was an accomplished poet and artist, designing fabrics, jewelry, clothes, and even carpets in styles that were to enliven the fashion-conscious court for years. She was also fond of hunting and was an excellent markswoman; demurely enclosed in a veiled *howdah*, she would shoot tiger from the back of an elephant. As the years went by, she was also to prove herself an exceptionally able administrator and stateswoman who took over the government of the empire from her increasingly dissolute husband. That Nūr Jahān was the power behind the throne was obvious even to visitors. Sir Thomas Rowe, the English ambassador to the Mughal court from 1615 to 1619, wrote home to the governor of the East India Company that "all justice or care of anything or publique affayrs either sleepes or depends on her, who is more unaccessable than any goddesse." His view of Jahāngīr's daily life was equally unflattering. "I sawe what was to be seene," he tells us disapprovingly, "presents, elephants, horses and many whoores."

The Mausoleum as seen from the entrance gate.

As time went by, Nūr Jahān's family became steadily more powerful at court, until eventually they were virtually an extension of the royal family itself. Itimād-ud-Daula was afforded the extraordinary privilege of being the only man, apart from the emperor, who was allowed to enter the *haram* and see the royal concubines unveiled. Nūr Jahān's neice married Shāh Jahān, Jahāngīr's son by the Rājput princess Jagat Gosayinī, and was to achieve immortality as Mumtāz Mahal, the Lady of the Tāj. This was only one of a number of tactical marriages, and within seventy years of Itimād-ud-Daula's arrival from Persia, his family could boast two successive favorite wives and three successive prime ministers. It was this Persian influence that largely accounts for the great artistic developments of Jahāngīr's reign. Always a man of esthetic sensibility, Jahāngīr was an untiring patron of the arts. He was particularly keen on miniature paintings, especially those portraying wildlife, which he loved, being himself a talented and energetic naturalist with a rare gift of loving observation. Some of the finest miniatures come from his school. It was his reign, too, that saw the transition from sandstone to marble as the preferred building material of the dynasty. He added the white marble superstructure of Akbar's sandstone mausoleum in Sikandra and, much more successfully, rebuilt the tomb of his godfather, the Sūfī saint Salīm Chishtī, in Fatehpur Sīkrī. These buildings sowed the seed that was to blossom into the marble masterpieces of Shāh Jahān in Āgra, Delhi, and Lahore.

But hand in hand with Jahāngīr's love of fine things went an addiction to luxury. Never a strong-willed person, he became increasingly befuddled by wine and opium, and the reins of government passed ever more firmly into the capable and determined hands of his wife. A contemporary historian, Mutamid Khān, records that "her authority reached such a peak that the king was such in name only." With the decline and death of Jahāngīr in 1627, the bitter family feuds that had temporarily abated under the wise rule of Akbar began to reemerge in earnest.

The Tomb of Itimād-ud-Daula

Itimād-ud-Daula built himself, in the style of the day, a splendid pleasure garden on the banks of the River Yamunā. When he died in 1622, Nūr Jahān built his tomb in the center of the garden. It is said that her original plan was for the mausoleum to be of solid silver, but because of the risk of vandalism she agreed to settle for white marble inlaid with semiprecious stones. The tomb took six years to complete and was finished in 1628.

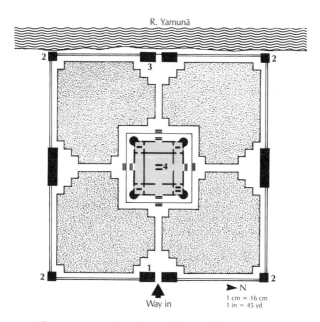

1 *Eastern gate, main entrance.* 2 *The watchtowers.*
3 *Riverside gate.* 4 *The mausoleum of Itimād-ud-Daula.*

Figure A. Itimād-ud-Daula site plan.

Stylized flowers and wine flasks, details from the entrance gate.

□ *THE ENTRANCE* (Figure A.1)
You enter the tomb of Itimād-ud-Daula by the eastern entrance, a splendid Mughal gateway of red sandstone inlaid with white marble. The main motifs of the inlay are stylized flowers, Persian wine bottles, which make their appearance into Indo-Islamic design at this time, and a combination of geometric and floral patterning that you will see to perfection on the building within.

The Tomb Itself (Figure A.4)

The first thing that strikes the visitor about the tomb itself is its smallness. Only 70 feet (21 meters) in diameter, it sits on a square base in what is a comparatively spacious garden whose walls are 540 feet (165 meters) long. Each wall is broken by a gate in the middle and has a watchtower at either end (A.2). The riverside gateway (A.3) was used for the royal family to visit by boat. This symmetrical framing emphasizes the building's compactness—an impression heightened by the intricacy of the surface design, which focuses your attention down onto the delineation of the structure, rather than acting to expand its boundaries.

□ *THE EXTERIOR*
The four identical sides of the tomb are squarely circum-scribed by heavy, shadowed eaves (*chhajjas*) and the broad,

almost squat, corner minarets, which are really little more than truncated towers topped by Indian cupolas. Yet any heaviness in the design is counterbalanced by both the vitality of the surface inlay and its fretted counterpart in the arched openings on each side. The upper story has a miniature pavilion that contains replicas (*zarīhs*) of the two tombs of Nūr Jahān's parents on the lower floor. This pavilion sits neatly on its base, like the snugly fitting lid of some sparkling jewel casket.

Indeed, it is the jeweler's art that is best exemplified here, for it is in its ornamentation, rather than its outline, that the genius of Itimād's tomb lies. It not only develops what had gone before in Indian decorative work, but it was in fact the model on which many of the techniques used in the Tāj were tried out and perfected. And, in its own way, Nūr Jahān's little masterpiece is not inferior to its more famous successor.

Whereas the earlier Mughal ornamentation consisted of carved stones being laid together on a flat ground, here the stones are actually inlaid into cavities cut in the marble, as you can see from where so many of them have, unfortunately, been removed by greedy souvenir hunters. Considering the hardness of the material, and the flowing arabesque shapes of many of the inlays, this is an astounding achievement. The European version of this technique is known as *pietra dura*, and it is often assumed that the skill passed from Italy to India via European craftsmen. But the designs of *pietra dura*

Floral and geometric inlay, detail from exterior of the Mausoleum.

are nearly always naturalistic and virtual imitations of painting, whereas these figurative and ornamental motifs stem directly from the earlier Mughal tradition of mosaic inlay, such as we find on the gates that Jahāngīr added to his father's tomb at Sikandra in 1611. The technique here has progressed to what is more the Persian cloisonné, in which the ground material is so minutely embellished that it becomes a mere frame for the stones it contains.

The ancestry of such surface inlay is ancient. Polychrome panels had been a feature of Greek, Roman, and Byzantine buildings, principally in floors and lower wall surfaces. This type of decoration was transposed to the earliest Islamic shrines, such as the Dome of the Rock in Jerusalem and the Great Mosque at Damascus. It spread with Islām along the Arab trade routes of the ancient world, becoming more intricate and curvilinear as time progressed, for the nomadic consciousness is dominated by rhythm and movement. From Persia it came to India, and here at Itimād's tomb, the patterning reaches such a delicate height of intricacy that the very surface of the marble stone is dissolved, and the whole becomes a whirling yet perfectly ordered dance of energy. It is as if the Muslim craftsman, prohibited by his religion from making images, turned his attention to delving deep into the very structure of matter itself, and thereby exposed, rather than created, a patterning that is remarkably close to what the modern electron microscope reveals. This effect of atomic crystallization not only ennobles the material world but leads beyond it, for it corroborates exactly the saying of the Prophet that "God is beautiful and He loves beauty." The graceful symmetry of organic creation indicates the perfection of the Creator.

The exterior designs of the shrine alternate between geometric and floral motifs. To the Muslim the regular and stable quality of the divine intelligence that orders creation is best displayed in mathematical and geometric harmony: the faultless interrelation of parts within a whole. This masculine, static consciousness is balanced by its vegetative and dynamic complement: the fecund, creative energy traditionally ascribed to the female and best represented by organic plant and flower forms. These two—male spirit and female matter—together create a unity that transcends both.

□ *THE INTERIOR*
On the ground floor the main inlay is in white, black, and yellow marble, with mottled jasper for the flowers. In the alcoves and the small towers around the upper story, semiprecious stones such as lapis, jasper, onyx, topaz, and carnelian are used to weave delicate arabesque.

Nor were these stones chosen only for their mellow color-

Minaret, looking toward the river.

ing of yellows, oranges, grays, browns, and blacks. Each piece was picked for its texture, for being a textile designer, Nūr Jahān was well aware of the importance of the feel of any material. When designing her father's mausoleum, she no doubt chose the stones that afforded the greatest tactile pleasure. Close your eyes and run your hand over these surfaces; Jahāngīr's queen has created an architecture of braille.

A third motif is discernible in the decoration: the wine glass or wine bottle, often in proximity to the cypress tree. These Persian designs, like the florid ornamentation of the brackets supporting the balcony over the principal doorway, are on one level indicative of the effect of Jahāngīr's love of luxury and fine living. Under his patronage the art of the Mughals became increasingly sumptuous. On another level the cypress tree symbolizes eternity (*khuld*), and the wine vessels divine intoxication (*fanā*). Both are enjoyed by the Sūfī.

Once inside the mausoleum, we can see that it is designed after the model of a Persian house: a square court surrounded by octagonal chambers. These hold the tombs of seven members of Nūr Jahān's family; their tombstones (*maqabriyya*)are of a striking yellow-orange marble. The floor, ceiling, and even the squinches of the central chamber are decorated with marble inlay. Her father and mother rest in the central chamber, all the male tombs are marked by the raised pen-box (*qalamdān*) on the top of the gravestones, representing active authority, the female by the flat slate (*tāwīdh*) signifying receptive and gestative nature. These traditional roles are still integral to the Islamic world today.

□ THE UPPER STORY

Access to the upper story is by a small circular staircase in each of the four minarets. There is a fine view from the top, and the deep marble awnings with their heavy Indo-Islamic struts are especially noteworthy.

Though the lower floor is remarkable chiefly for its ornamentation, it is the carved screens surrounding the false white marble tombs of Nūr Jahān's parents that most impress upstairs. There is, of course, also beautiful inlay up here, and the swirling marble and jasper floor of the pavilion is especially fine: a Persian carpet of inlaid stone. But to step inside the softly dappled chamber is to enter another world. The "walls" of the kiosk are reduced to the merest spiderwebs of latticed stone, which ventilate the chamber and filter underwater light in shifting shafts of brightness. This light is not random but patterned with geometric regularity into crystalline and snowflake forms, which play on and around you. The effect is to dissolve your usual sense of bodily solidity and break down your accustomed barrier with your environment. As with the inlay downstairs, all sense of individual form is smoothly eliminated, and the personality dissolves into an impersonal unity. These screens, each faultlessly carved from a single piece of marble, without a joint, accomplish visually what repetition of chants or prayers does audibly. Both allow the mind to detach itself from solid thoughts or images and ascend in contemplation. Here art is in the service of transcendence. As such it facilitates movement into a higher and more universal state of being by transporting our perception from the gross to the celestial. As the poet Hopkins said: "Glory be to God for dappled things."

13

FATEHPUR SĪKRĪ

AKBAR THE GREAT'S DESERTED CITADEL

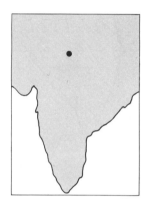

About twenty-three miles (thirty-seven kilometers) due west of Āgra, a rocky outcrop of the Vindhya Hills rises steeply up from the flatness of the surrounding plains. On the top of this sudden bluff, overlooking the dry countryside of Uttar Pradesh, rests a silent and petrified sandstone city, where time has stood still for the last four hundred years.

This time capsule is called Fatehpur Sīkrī, and it is the creation of the greatest of the Mughals, the emperor Akbar. It was Akbar's grandfather, Bābur, who founded the Mughal dynasty in 1526 when he defeated the Rājput king of Delhi at the Battle of Panipat.

Bābur, "The Tiger," came from a line of great warriors; he was descended on his mother's side from Genghis Khān and on his father's from Tīmūr the Lame (also known as Tamburlaine), who had ravaged Delhi in 1398. It was also Bābur who sowed the seeds for his grandson's interest in this altogether inhospitable part of the country. In following up his victory at Panipat, Bābur defeated a local Hindu prince here in 1527. He named the village where the battle took place Sīkrī, from the Arabic *shukria*: "Thanks be to God." As a youth, Akbar had hunted near Sīkrī, and in 1564, eight years after he ascended to the throne, he built a pleasure resort not far from the village. In the following year Akbar began the construction of the imperial fort at Āgra, the capital of the empire. The stone used for the fort was sandstone, quarried from the Sīkrī area, and it was the stonecutters, camped here on the ridge, who first spread the word about the miraculous powers of a local saint, Sheikh Salīm of the Chishtī order of Sūfīs. It was the fateful meeting between the holy man and the emperor that resulted in the majestic citadel of Fatehpur Sīkrī.

Despite all his achievements, Akbar had failed in the first duty of a Mughal—producing a son and heir. In 1568 he visited the now renowned saint in his hermitage and begged the sheikh to add his powerful prayers for the birth of a son. Salīm Chishtī smilingly replied that the emperor would father not one, but three sons, and the line would be secured.

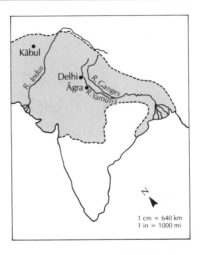

Figure A. The Mughal Empire at Akbar's death in 1605.

Sure enough, the next year, Jodh Bāi, one of Akbar's Rājput wives and the daughter of the Mahārāja of Amber, gave birth to a son. He was named Salīm, in honor of the holy man, and was the future emperor Jahāngīr. (The other two sons followed in due course.) Akbar was so overjoyed that, while he was staying at Sīkrī on his way back from a pilgrimage to the seat of the Chishtī Sūfīs at Ajmer, he announced his intention to move the royal capital from Āgra to Sīkrī so as to be as close as possible to the saint. The emperor himself selected the site on the ridge and had it leveled for the building of the citadel. Work began immediately. The best architects, masons, stonecutters, and sculptors from all parts of the empire arrived to help build what was intended to be the most sublime of all capitals. Akbar himself even took a hand in quarrying stone and, according to his biographer Abul Fazl, "sometimes put his hands to other menial tasks." The pillars, columns, capitals, and brackets were chiseled, carved, and polished at the quarry and then brought to the site for assembly.

The new capital came to be known as Fatehpur, "City of Victory," after Akbar's victory over Gujarāt in 1573. The development and beautification of the city continued for about fifteen years. In his memoirs, Akbar's son Jahāngīr records: "In the course of fourteen or fifteen years that hill, full of wild beasts, became a city containing all kinds of gardens and buildings, and lofty elegant edifices and pleasant places attractive to the heart." Then, in 1584, the place was abandoned; no one knows why. The reason usually given is lack of water, though we have no contemporary records of unusually severe droughts at that time. Perhaps the emperor tired of his achievements here; perhaps he felt Fatehpur Sīkrī was too isolated to remain the capital of his empire. Jahāngīr stayed here for three months in 1619 to escape an epidemic of the plague in Āgra, and his son, Shāh Jahān, the builder of the Tāj, visited the city on a couple of occasions to pay homage to Salīm Chishtī's tomb. But to all intents and purposes, Fatehpur Sīkrī was abandoned after only eighteen years. Since then it has stood deserted, a silent and empty stage on which once performed one of the most sumptuous courts of all time, the court of Akbar the Great.

Fatehpur Sīkrī is one of the boldest achievements in the history of world architecture. Akbar could have had a few examples on which to model his capital. He would have been impressed by the grandeur of Amber, the Rājasthānī capital of Rāja Bihārimāl, the father of his chief queen, Jodh Bāi. And another Rājput stronghold, the fortress at Mandu, would have inspired him, with its fifteenth-century buildings, the legacy of the Khaljī sultans of Delhi, who brought Central Asian building styles with them from Afghānistān. But the enormity of conception and the unity of design that had to combine to form such an imperial citadel were Akbar's alone. To found his capital here, in the middle of nowhere, in an age when communications were difficult, materials hard to come by, and all work had to be done by hand, was a decision that illustrates both the emperor's self-confidence and his idiosyncratic nature. Even by the heroic and eccentric standards of the Mughals, Akbar's decision to build his dream city at Sīkrī must have seemed a glorious, if foolhardy, undertaking.

Architecturally, Fatehpur Sīkrī belongs to the Indo-Islamic genre: a fusion of native Indian and imported Islamic styles. These Islamic influences had been seeping into India with each wave of Muslim invaders, from the end of the twelfth century onward and even by the first decades of the Delhi Sultanate (1206–1526) a virile and esthetically convincing style of architecture had evolved. But the finest development of Indo-Islamic architecture came with the great Mughals (1526–1707) and is largely attributable to Akbar's father, Humāyūn. Defeated by Sher Shāh in 1544, the hapless Humāyūn fled to Persia. When he returned from this exile, he brought with him Persian artists, architects, and craftsmen. It was the combination of these influences with the native Hindu architectural, and especially sculptural, skills that created the distinctive Mughal style that was to revolutionize building in northern India during the sixteenth and seventeenth centuries. What we see at Fatehpur Sīkrī is the emergence of the style as Indian materials and techniques struggle to adapt themselves to Persian forms and ideas.

The Royal Citadel (Figure B)

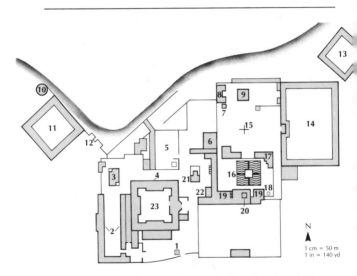

1 *Ticket office.* 2 *Royal stables.* 3 *Rāja Bīrbal's palace.* 4 *The Palace of Winds.* 5 *The* zanāna *garden.* 6 *The Fire-Storied Palace.* 7 *The Astrologer's Seat.* 8 *the treasury.* 9 *The Hall of Private Audience.* 10 *The Elephant Tower.* 11 *Caravanserai.* 12 *The Elephant Gate.* 13 *Imperial workshops.* 14 *The Hall of Public Audience.* 15 *The Pachīsī board.* 16 *Musician's Tank.* 17 *The palace of the Turkish wife.* 18 *Rosewater fountain.* 19 *The emperor's private quarters.* 20 *The House of Dreams.* 21 *The palace of the Christian wife.* 22 *The royal kitchens.* 23 *Jodh Bāi's palace.*

Figure B. *Site plan of the Royal Citadel, Fatehpur Sīkrī.*

The Royal Stables (Figure B.2)

Akbar's bravery and skill in the hunt was legendary. One of his favorite routines was to have an area of about fifty miles (eighty kilometers) enclosed by a ring of hunters, which would gradually tighten, trapping the animals in the middle. When the enclosed area was about three miles (five kilometers) in diameter, the emperor would ride into the middle and spend an entire day hunting the trapped beasts. Only when he had had his fill could the others be allowed to join the kill.

Altogether Akbar maintained enormous numbers of animals: twelve hundred horses, four thousand camels, and two thousand elephants. These royal stables were for the sixty camels and one hundred ten horses he kept for his private use. The niches in the walls are for fodder and the rings below for securing the animals.

The large courtyard is pleasingly simple and spacious. It is bordered by a vigorous corridor, whose carved brackets and corbeled eaves *(chhajjas)* supporting a heavy roof are typically Hindu.

Rāja Bīrbal's Palace (Figure B.3)

This building is popularly designated as the palace of Rāja Bīrbal, Akbar's prime minister, though some authorities claim that it was an extension to the *haram* quarters, being reserved for Akbar's two senior queens. Whatever the truth, the building has always been associated with Rāja Bīrbal.

Bīrbal was a brahmin, famed for his wit and sharp tongue, and he was perhaps the most brilliant of the "Nine Jewels of Akbar's Court," the most dazzling minds of the day. Many of his verses composed in Hindī are still recited and sung throughout northern India today. Akbar pursued a conscious policy of integration with the Hindu population and married into Hindu royal families as well as drawing many of his ministers and advisers from Hindu ranks. In this respect he was the most tolerant and far-sighted of the Mughal emperors.

Bīrbal's palace was built in 1572. It has two stories: the lower with four rooms, the upper with two entrance porches and two domed pavilions. Now open on all sides, it was originally enclosed by stone trellised screens. The building is exquisitely carved, both inside and out. The heavily corbeled eaves and arches of the main door, decorated with the lotus motif, are typically Hindu. So too are the pilasters, worked in low relief, with their bases carved with a deep double semicircle ringed with a fanlike halo. Between each pilaster is a recessed arch, entirely enclosed by an ornate band of carving. The arches rest on a heavily indented sill, again typically Hindu. But the cusped arches (see Figure C) are derived

Rāja Bīrbal's palace, seen from the royal stables.

from Jain architecture, and the mixture of floral and geometric patterning displays Islamic influence. So do the small stone screens above the upper doors. Nevertheless, the overall impression of the building is unmistakably Indian.

The central principle in the construction of this palace was to maximize the coolness of the interior. Thus the cupolas over the top rooms and the pyramidal roofs over the porches are built as double domes, with a hollow space between their inner and outer shells. In this way the heat is deflected to the greatest degree possible. It is a Persian technique.

The ceilings of the ground floor have some finely carved lotus motifs, though we can see from their ornateness they are not truly Islamic. Here again, the desert purity of Islām has been tempered by the jungle fecundity of India: The result is a decoration that is practically *art nouveau*. Red sandstone, especially on unlit interior surfaces, is always in danger of seeming dull and lifeless. Here the molding is done with such intricacy that it maximizes the effects of light and shade and relieves the flatness of the surface.

Figure C. Cusped arch (left) and Indo-Islamic chhatrī (right).

As you leave Bīrbal's palace, notice the wall ahead, surmounted by cupolas. These cupolas are the Indo-Islamic *chhatrī* (see Figure C)—trabeated kiosks topped by rounded domes, surmounted by a finial of inverted lotus shape. The *chhatrī* is especially common in the palaces of Rājasthān and western India. On your right is the wall of the royal ladies' summer palace, which comprises the north wing of the principal *haram* building, popularly known as Jodh Bāi's palace (B.23).

☐ *THE PALACE OF WINDS* (Figure B.4)
Attached to this wing is the Palace of Winds (Hawā Mahal). This type of building was often incorporated into northern Indian houses. The first (U.S. second) story is open; the second (U.S. third) is screened by beautiful *jālī* work. The idea comes from Persia, where towers were built that deflected the prevailing wind down into a lower chamber. Akbar's Rājput princesses lived in the Hawā Mahal, and here they would sit in the cool evenings and entertain their emperor, or watch pageants performed below. It also seems likely, from Abul Fazl's description, that Akbar often slept in this cool palace, which he also used to perform the Hindu domestic ceremonies, such as the fire sacrifice (*homa*) that his Muslim *mullās* so abhorred.

☐ *THE ZANĀNA GARDEN* (Figure B.5)
On your left is the garden of the *haram* (or *zanāna*). Originally it was entirely enclosed by walls and quite private. The garden was set out in the Persian style with *ashoka* trees for shade, pavilions, and a pigeon house for the birds of Akbar's mother, Maryam Makani. (Her name means "equal in rank to Mary, mother of Jesus," and she was always treated with reverence by her son and his court.) At the far end of the wall lies the ladies' mosque (*nagīna masjid*). This was exclusively for the ladies of the *haram,* of whom there were over five hundred and is a common feature of Mughal palaces.

☐
Next to the garden is a water tank that supplied the citadel. You can still see the guttering channel around the outside. Walk around the tank, down the steps and between the pillars on the left, and around to your right, to an arched colonnade that leads to one of the most impressive buildings of the site.

The Five-Storied Palace, Panch Mahal (Figure B.6)

This elegant pavilion was a pleasure palace for the enjoyment of the emperor and his ladies. It was used mainly in the summer. One problem faced by Akbar's architects was the Indian heat. To counteract this, all the buildings were designed with massive, overhanging eaves, so that the amount of shadow was maximized and the contrast between light and shade accentuated. Wherever possible, shaded arcades were adjoined to the exterior of the buildings—a feature that was to be incorporated into all later domestic Indian architecture. Another method of cooling a building that came to be very popular was to install an empty basement chamber (*tahkhāna*), which allows cool air to circulate at the bottom of the house. This Persian device would have been enormously difficult and expensive to install on top of the stone ridge at Fatehpūr, so the builders employed another imported method of insuring coolness—the Persian "wind tower" (*bādgīr*). In the Panch Mahal, Akbar's architects adapted the *bādgīr* to its new Indian setting and created a unique structure. Whereas a *bādgīr* is a tower, and has only three stories including the ground floor, the Panch Mahal has five open stories, each of the top four floors rising in diminishing stages above the lower one. Thus in style it is reminiscent of a common type of Buddhist *vihāra*.

In the hot weather screens made of a fragrant grass (*khass*) were hung from the eaves, and the screens were dampened with water so as to produce a fragrant coolness. This method of using scented grass curtains (*khass tattīs*) is still widely used all over India.

Supported on the columns of the ground floor, the building contains a total of 176 carved pillars: 84 on the ground floor, 56 on the first (U.S. second), 20 on the second (U.S. third), 12 on the third (U.S. fourth), and 4 on the top story. The building rests on 84 pillars, a highly auspicious number to the Hindus as it is the result of multiplying the seven planets by the twelve signs of the zodiac. Akbar would sit in the top kiosk in the cool of the evening, looking out over his capital.

The pillars on the first (U.S. second) floor are well worth a visit. Each is of a different design: Some have the Hindu vase-and-foliage motif—an ancient design symbolizing good harvest and material well-being—others show the temple bell hung on a long chain. Hindu motifs are freely mixed with Muslim ones. There is *muqarna*—the Islamic stalactite design—and a particularly remarkable group, on the north edge of the platform, could almost come from a Gothic cathedral, with their deep fluting and *fleur-de-lis* patterns. The railings (*katahra*) around the edge of each story are also charmingly varied, the ground and top stories having fine *jālī* work.

On the way to the top floor we get a good view of the massive stone slabs that form the overhanging eaves of the top floors, clearly echoing their wooden prototypes. In fact the style of Fatehpur Sīkrī is reminiscent of the contemporary Tudor architecture in England, though the Indian craftsman

Ground floor of the Five-Storied Palace.

was working in sandstone rather than oaken beams. History does not relate how many unfortunate revelers met a drunkenend by toppling off these steep and unprotected steps—but even in the soberest of moods, they are quite a difficult climb. We can get an even better view from the comparative safety of the roof of the Hall of Private Audience.

The Astrologer's Seat (Figure B.7)

Although Akbar was not as addicted to astrology as was his father Humāyūn, who would not move without consulting the auguries and ran his entire empire according to astrological portents, the astrologer played an important role in the day-to-day running of court affairs. Akbar kept both Hindu astrologers (*jyotishīs*) and Muslim astrologers (*nunajjims*).

This pavilion is remarkable chiefly for the ornamental *torana* arches, whose foliated cusping comes from the Jain architecture of the eleventh and twelfth centuries—for example, the temples of Mount Ābū (see Chapter 5).

Because of its proximity to the treasury, it is possible that this kiosk was also used by the court treasurer, the eunuch Phūl Mālik. It may even have served as the emperor's seat when he wished to witness the payment of his courtiers and subjects. On these occasions the courtyard was heaped with piles of copper coins, which were distributed to the deserving.

The Treasury (Figure B.8)

This three-roomed building was the imperial treasury for gold and silver. It is often claimed that this was where Akbar

Exterior of the Hall of Private Audience.

played "hide and seek" with the royal ladies, but since he had the entire citadel to devote to his romantic ploys, this seems highly unlikely. Added to which, he was a hardworking and conscientious ruler, in fact a paragon of sobriety compared with some of his descendants.

There are two notable features here: First, the struts that project from the walls, supported on corbels. The struts emerge from the jaws of the mythical sea dragons (*makaras*) of Hindu mythology, who are the guardians of the treasures of the deep. These serpentine scrolls again derive from the Jain architecture of western India. Second, the arrangements of the inner rooms. There are three chambers, each protected by a narrow corridor around it. These walkways were for sentries to patrol and, combined with a system of double doors, insured that each chamber was safely guarded. The deep holes in the wall alcoves were probably for storing jewels.

The Hall of Private Audience, Dīwān-i-Khās
(Figure B.9)

This is the gem of Fatehpur Sīkrī. Raised on a square plan, with a door on each of its four sides, it appears to be a two-storied building, but as you walk in, you will see that it in fact consists of a single vaulted chamber, open from floor to ceiling. The whole building revolves around the massive central pillar dominating the hall.

□ *THE LOTUS THRONE PILLAR*
As Akbar grew older, he became increasingly interested in developing a religion that would embrace all the great faiths. Always tolerant and eclectic in his tastes, whether in favorite wives or architectural styles, he strove to formulate what he

called "the Ultimate Faith" (*Dīn-i-Illāhi*). Many of his religious debates took place in this building. The central pillar, which actually supported Akbar's throne, has an interesting variety of design, which illustrates the universal outlook of the new religion. The bottom tier is carved in Muslim designs, the second Hindu, the third Christian, and the fourth Buddhist. In itself, the octagonal column is an extraordinarily profuse image, incorporating all the most ancient and important of Indian archetypes. It is simultaneously the tree of life (of which the *bodhi* tree of the Buddhists is a version), the lotus flower stretching to the heavens, the royal umbrella that protects the king and shelters his subjects, and the nail of Indra, which, in the earliest Hindu myths was the axis of the world, keeping the heavens and earth apart and in proper relationship to each other. From ground level the double row of thirty-six uniform brackets, repeating themselves around the pillar, could be lotus petals or the serpentine hoods of the sacred cobra (*nāga*). Not only is the pillar the center of the hall; everything seems to be hanging off it as finely balanced branches from a central trunk. The corners of the chamber are also embellished with decorative brackets, which writhe and twist like baroque serpents.

□ THE THRONE PLATFORM
If you climb to the balcony by the stairs set into the walls of the hall, you can see the central platform on which the

Interior of the Hall of Private Audience, showing Lotus Throne Pillar.

emperor's throne was placed. Akbar reached the throne by marble steps that were slid under the platform. Here he would sit in solitary splendor, lord of all he surveyed. The design of the Hall of Private Audience follows the archaic universal pattern of establishing a hallowed spot as the center of the universe, from which spiritual influence is radiated to the four directions, bringing order to the surrounding world. Here Akbar was literally the center of attention: The whole of the imperial capital revolved around his every command. Courtiers, visitors, even Jesuit missionaries hoping for a conversion they never got, would sit around the edges of the gallery, engaged in debate, flattery, or gossip, depending on the great man's mood. There is some good *jālī* work on the balustrades of the platform and the passages that bridged the world of Akbar, resplendently seated like some Hindu deity on a lotus, and the world of lesser mortals.

☐

If you climb the stairs again, you reach the roof. From here the entire site spreads out beneath you. Facing north, you can see the remains of some of the buildings below the citadel.

☐ *THE ELEPHANT TOWER* (Figure B.10)
On the far left is the Elephant Tower. This is the tomb of Akbar's favorite elephant, Hiran, "the Golden One." This tower is octagonal at the base, circular in the middle, and tapers to a Hindu-style cupola. Its walls are studded with a thousand masonry "tusks," sticking out like spikes. Hiran's particular task was to crush convicted criminals under his not inconsiderable feet. However, if he refused to squash the wretch three times in a row, the emperor wisely abided by the animal's decision and the happy criminal was pardoned and set free.

☐ *THE CARAVANSERAI AND THE ELEPHANT GATE*
  (Figures B.11 and B.12)
East of this tower lie the remains of a caravanserai where traders and visitors would stay, and next to this the well and water channels that supplied the citadel. The system involved five tiers of wells and aqueducts, and on each tier the buckets were lifted by windlasses turned by men, not animals. From here you can also see the Elephant Gate, one of the nine gates that pierced the massive city walls. The story goes that Akbar intended to construct a fortress next to the gate to protect the city, but he abandoned the idea on hearing of Salīm Chishtī's prophecy that if such a fortification were ever built, the emperor's power would immediately decline.

☐ *THE IMPERIAL WORKSHOPS* (Figure B.13)
On the right-hand side of the precinct you can see an arched colonnade with black domed roofs surrounding a large courtyard. This probably housed the imperial workshops (*kārk-*

hānas), including the royal mint (*taksāl*), which manufac-
tured articles needed in the palace. These would have been
sold and distributed in the nearby market. Opposite the workshops was the imperial treasury (*khazāna*), so this was the
financial area of the capital.

☐

This northern side of the ridge was the original Sīkrī village.
Turning round and facing south, you overlook what was the
town of Fatehpur, which grew up to serve the royal citadel. It
was protected on three sides by a massive rubble-built wall
and on the west by an artificial lake. You can still see the
remains of the wall, which stretched for seven miles (eleven
kilometers). The strategic advantage of Fatehpur Sīkrī is
obvious; any approaching army could be seen from miles off,
and the citadel itself must have been virtually unassailable.

Coming out of the south door of the Hall of Private Audience, cross the courtyard, up to the second level. You are
retracing Akbar's steps; when he had decided some policy, he
would walk this way to announce it to the waiting crowds.

The Hall of Public Audience, Diwān-i-Ām
(Figure B.14)

This building is basically an extensive courtyard enclosed by
cloisters on three sides and the royal balcony on the west. If
you walk through the hallway, you emerge onto this balcony.
The emperor would sit in the middle and give audience, with
the royal ladies on either side of him behind the beautiful *jālī*
screens (the lower halves of which were restored by Lord
Curzon). The nobility would watch the proceedings from the
cloistered verandah along the western wall.

Akbar would also dispense justice and hear litigation from
this place. He was the ultimate legal authority and would
make judgment sternly but, his biography assures us, "without harshness or ill will." Nevertheless, the method of
punishment could be harsh enough: The half-buried circular
stone in the middle of the lawn is where Hiran trampled his
hapless victims to death!

On the way out notice the doors. They are new but show
the original system of having two sets of doors, with room for
an armed guard to stand watch between them.

☐

After a strenuous session dispensing justice or reviewing the
royal animals, the emperor would no doubt have been in the
mood for some relaxation. Crossing through the gardens, which
would have been watered by gently tinkling fountains, he

would have arrived at the famous *pachīsī* board (B.15). Here Akbar and the favorite of the moment would sit on the royal bench and play *pachīsī* (a type of ludo) with his courtiers. The cross-shaped board is carved out on the stone, and each player's pieces were slave girls, attired in brilliant dresses of different colors.

Akbar's relaxation was happily not limited to *pachīsī*. He was a great patron of all the arts, and it was during his long reign that the artistic achievements for which the Mughals are renowned were firmly established. Although illiterate himself, Akbar loved to have books read to him and was a patron of poetry and scholarship. A part of his private residence was devoted to a library where extensive translation was undertaken, mainly of old Sanskrit texts into Persian. Even when traveling on battle campaigns at the far ends of the empire, he would take with him the famous Mughal library of over fifty thousand manuscripts, most of them gorgeously illuminated by Persian artists and calligraphers.

The Musician's Tank (Figure B.16)

Music was also a great love of the emperor's. His favorite musician was Tansen, a Hindu who was one of "the Nine Jewels." Tansen was probably the greatest singer India has produced, and much of Hindustānī (northern Indian) music bears his imprint. He was a master of sound—a *nāda* yogi—and it is said that by singing the appropriate *rāga* he could cause rain to fall or fire to break out.

Tansen would perform from the platform in the middle of the Musician's Tank, outside the emperor's private quarters, and the tank would be filled with scented water, on which hundreds of flowers were floated. When Akbar was in a particularly good humor, he would have the tank drained and filled with gold and silver coins. Then, with great ceremony, in the words of a local guidebook: "numberless arms were distributed to the poor."

The Palace of the Turkish Wife (Figure B.17)

Despite her inability to provide him with a son, Sultāna Ruqāyya Begum, who came from Istanbul, was Akbar's favorite wife. In building her this elegant little pavilion, surrounded by a verandah resting on columns, the emperor created a masterpiece of carved ornamentation. The detail is so intricate here that one forgets it is stone, where not one mistake can be made. It has more the appearance of richly worked wood, and to go inside is like entering some Chinese lacquered box and closing the lid. We have here the native Indian craftsmen's genius for stone carving producing motifs that, farther west in the world of Islām, would have been rendered in tile and stucco. Indeed, the ceiling and walls would have originally been set with glass and precious stones to create a *shīsh mahal*, "palace of mirrors," which, when illuminated by flickering lamps and candles, would have twinkled like the stars on a clear night. You can see where some of the flowers and animals were studded with jewels. Notice also the panels at knee height. These show strong Chinese influence in their exotic landscapes. Akbar's eclectic tastes are shown further in the pillars outside: Some have vine motifs that are quite European. In creating this masterpiece for what must have been a remarkable woman, the emperor drew on all the craftsmen at his command.

The workmanship in this building anticipates the intricacy of decoration that was to characterize the art of Shāh Jahān's reign.

☐

Leaving the Turkish queen's palace, go to the end of the courtyard. The large circular bowl (B.18) was a fountain that was filled with rose water. Turn right, keeping the square tank on your right, and then turn left into the building.

The Emperor's Private Quarters (Figure B.19)

This area was originally screened off from the courtyard. It was officially known as "The Abode of Good Fortune" (*Daulat Khāna*), and when entering it, whether the emperor was present or not, all had to kiss the threshold. It comprises two main rooms on the ground floor; the eastern one still preserves traces of the rich painting that once adorned it. The recesses in the walls would have contained personal possessions, such as albums of paintings and the manuscripts Akbar loved to have read to him. This was probably used as a dining room. Behind the first chamber is a larger room with a platform, supported on square columns, against the southern wall. This would be covered with rugs and cushions, with silk canopies and tapestries draped overhead, and here the emperor would sit and hold court. The platform was reached by marble steps that were slid underneath, as in the Hall of Private Audience. It was from a window in the southern wall that Akbar would show himself each morning to the waiting population below, and it is said that the most devoted subjects would not eat until they had glimpsed their king. We also know from historical records that a brahmin *pandit* named Devī would be hoisted up on a string bed (*charpoi*) to this window and instruct Akbar in the finer points of Hindu thought, especially the *Mahābhārata* which the emperor particularly enjoyed.

☐ *THE HOUSE OF DREAMS* (Figure B.20)

On the first (U.S. second) floor, above this room, is Akbar's private bedchamber (*khwābgāh*), the House of Dreams. He would retire here for privacy; it also provided easy access to the *haram* quarters. This intimate chamber was probably the most informal room in the whole of Fatehpur Sīkrī, for here Akbar could relax, have his favorites around him, and engage in impromptu philosophical or religious discussions till all hours of the night. He often took an afternoon nap here, too. The room was originally richly embellished with Persian frescoes and inscriptions painted in gold and ultramarine and floral motifs, some of which are still just visible. There are also traces of a mural depicting an angel with a child in its arms, probably representing the birth of Salīm, the future Emperor Jahāngīr. There was some restoration in 1905, thanks to Lord Curzon, and some of the Persian inscriptions are legible. They liken the beauty of the palace to heaven and claim that the angels visit it because of its beauty. The script is *nastalīq*.

The Palace of the Christian Wife (Figure B.21)

From here proceed to the palace of the Christian wife, either by continuing along this first (U.S. second) floor and through the doorway in the wall, or by descending to the ground floor again and crossing the courtyard.

Akbar's Christian wife was called Maryam and came from Goa. The building was originally painted in gold and known as the Golden Palace. It has four rooms and a flat roof, with an open pavilion supported on eight square pillars. This was used for sleeping in the summer. There are some unusual sculpted brackets here: some carved with lion heads, others with elephants and geese, all in the Hindu style. The Persian inscriptions on the beams of the verandah are verses by Faizī, Akbar's poet laureate, another of "the Nine Jewels." Some scholars claim that this palace belonged to Akbar's mother, also called Maryam.

☐

As you come out of the palace, notice the highly carved building on your left. These were the royal kitchens (B.22), which may originally have been attached to the *haram* quarters by cloisters that have not survived. The intricacy of detail is astonishing. The outer walls are carved with a mixture of floral and geometric patterns, including bands carved with the so-called ear-ornament motif.

Abul Fazl tells us that the emperor's food was mixed with Ganges water, holy to the Hindus. It must have worked; we have no records of a hospital in Fatehpur Sīkrī!

Jodh Bāi's Palace (Figure B.23)

Named after Jodh Bāi, the daughter of the Mahārāja of Amber and the mother of Akbar's son Jahāngīr, this is the principal building of the *haram* quarters. It served as the palace of the emperor's Hindu wives, of which there were many. Akbar was especially partial to the proud and beautiful Rājput princesses. Jahāngīr's younger brother, Danial, was the son of the daughter of the Mahārāja of Bikanīr, and there were several other Rājasthānī women in the royal *haram*. Such alliances were shrewd investments. The Rājputs were the only force in India that could offer a serious threat to the stability of the Mughal Empire. Fiercely independent, they had from earliest times enjoyed a reputation for fanatical bravery on the battlefield. Moreover, Rājasthān was on the western flank of the Mughal Empire, in inhospitable desert country that mocked any would-be invader. By accepting many of the Rājputs into his service as regional governors and generals in his armies, Akbar managed to keep the allegiance of what would have been a potential enemy. Only the Mahārāna of Mewar (Udaipur) steadfastly refused to compromise with the Mughal powers. With fathers in the royal army and daughters in the royal bed, the Rājput threat was considerably diminished. It was the fanatical Aurangzeb who finally reversed many of his great-grandfather's tolerant policies and sowed the seeds for continued hostility between Hindu and Muslim in India.

□ THE ENTRANCE GATE

Jodh Bāi's palace is assured privacy by its heavy, plain thirty-foot (nine-meter) wall. The front gate, which was always guarded by eunuchs, looks like the entrance to a fort: forbidding and well protected. This is just what one would expect of the *haram* quarters, for our word *harem* derives from the Arabic *haram*, meaning "forbidden by religious law." The parts of a house or palace reserved for the women were always carefully separated from the rest of the building by Islamic custom. In India, the *haram* quarters, and the institution itself, were usually known as the *zanāna*.

This gate is, again, a blend of Hindu and Muslim styles. Basically it is the Islamic keel arch (see page 289) enclosed within a rectangle, a design repeated, in niches of different sizes, all over the facade of the building. But, as in all the important buildings at Fatehpur Sīkrī, this arch is fringed with the Hindu pot and bell design. And the doorway itself is classically Indian: a square lintel with heavy brackets. The preference of the Indian architect was always for a pillar and beam doorway, with brackets or corbeling to span the open space. The "true" arch was an Islamic import.

The designs in the spandrels of the rectangle are also interesting (see Figure D). These six-pointed stars (*satkona*), enclosing a lotus, are tantric motifs, signifying the union of male and female. They are also to be found on Rāja Bīrbal's palace, Salīm Chishtī's tomb, and above the *mihrāb* in the Jāmi Masjid.

Once you enter the massive gateway, staggered to prevent anyone seeing in, you are in a dark chamber, whose overbearing heaviness is reminiscent of a Hindu temple. The niches here would have contained statues of deities and, in their serpentine pot designs, are influenced by Jain architecture.

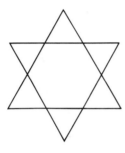

Figure D. Satkona—six pointed star.

☐ THE QUADRANGLE

You emerge into the large quadrangle, simply and integrally arranged. The symmetrical buildings around the square were the living quarters of the royal ladies: single-storied blocks with double stories in the center and corners of each side. The lower chambers were heated in winter, and the open rooms above were airy and cool in summer. The central block on the eastern side forms a vestibule to the main gate we have just passed through. There is a Turkish bath (*hammām*) for the ladies attached to the south wall of the palace.

The northern and southern wings—to your right and left, respectively—were known as the Summer and Winter Palaces. They are roofed in azure tiles from Multān and provide a welcome relief from the sea of flat, and often dull, sandstone. They give you a hint of what the place must have been like when it was hung with brilliant tapestries and awnings, and the floors were covered with rugs and carpets from Central Asia, Turkestān, and Kashmīr. The whole courtyard is nicely balanced and gives the impression of freedom from within. In fact it reminds one, as does the whole of Fatehpur Sīkrī, of a tented city, frozen in stone. You can see the influence of the Mughals' ancestry in the nomadic tribes of Central Asia.

Opposite the main gate, in the western cloisters, is the Hindu temple, and in the center of the courtyard there is a square brick structure which contains the *tulasī* plant (basil), sacred to Vishnu. It is a common custom in India to put this plant in the courtyard, or near the front door of a house, as a protective measure. Akbar performed Hindu ceremonies in this temple. He would spend much of his time in the Palace of Winds, which we have already seen from the other side. According to his biography—*Āin-i-Akbarī (The Institutes of Akbar)*, he would spend most of his nights here, and when he wanted solitude, would retire to the House of Dreams.

☐

There is much variety in the treatment of the pillars throughout Jodh Bāi's palace. The bases, columns, and capitals are carved in Hindu style with lozenges, lotuses, bell-and-chain ornaments, and so on. The columns are sometimes square or octagonal, sixteen-sided or circular.

As we leave this part of Fatehpur Sīkrī, it must be admitted that the unrelieved terracotta sandstone can sometimes appear flat and dull. Only in the early morning and evening does it radiate the mellow warmth of its yellow counterpart (for example, at Khajurāho); in the full light of day there is a certain heaviness to the place. This heaviness is partly due to the very Indian-ness of the architectural style. Despite the intricate ornamentation there is something a little too solid about the surfaces. We are witnessing the struggle of the Mughal style to find its feet, and develop its own rhythm and expression—each successive building will show an advance and maturity over the one before. To realize just how Indian this new style was, it is worth remembering that Akbar's capital is roughly contemporary with the Safavid city of Isfahān in Iran, in which architecture and embellishment were married with all the delicacy of a Persian illuminated manuscript.

The Friday Mosque   The second half of the site comprises the Friday Mosque and the tomb of Sheikh Salīm Chishtī. The Friday Mosque (*Jāmi Masjid*) is always the principal mosque in any Muslim community. Friday is the holy day of Islām, when all the male members of the community gather together to offer prayers. Here in Akbar's capital, the sacred is intentionally kept separate from the secular, so as to increase its sanctity. Built on the highest point of the ridge, the holy enclosure dominates the whole surrounding area.

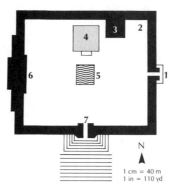

1 cm = 40 m
1 in = 110 yd

1 *The King's Gate.* **2** Jamāat khāna *hall.* **3** *The Tomb of the Ladies.* **4** *The mausoleum of Sheikh Salīm Chishtī.* **5** *The sacred tank.* **6** *The* mihrāb *shrine.* **7** *The Victory Gate.*

Figure E. The Friday Mosque ground plan.

The King's Gate (Figure E.1)

The first thing that you see is the majestic King's Gate, so called because Akbar would pass through this on his way to the mosque. Here the red of the city is relieved by honey-colored sandstone, and the two-toned stonework is inlaid with some fine marble in Islamic geometrical design, principally star and octagon motifs. The arch itself is cusped with the Hindu lotus.

There is certainly no lack of money changers in this particular temple; every corner of the entrance vestibule is crammed with souvenir sellers. The best policy is to ignore them totally; the quality is low and the prices are high.

The Congregational Courtyard

Once you are past the vendors, a vast courtyard *(sahn)* opens up in front of you, stretching 361 feet (110 meters) from north to south and 438 feet (134 meters) from east to west. This enormous open area is actually the congregational hall of the mosque, the *mihrāb* shrine of which is opposite you, on the western wall, crowned by three elegant domes. The mosque (comprising the shrine, the courtyard framed by cloisters, and the two massive gates on the south and east sides) was modeled on the Bībī Khānam in Samarkand and was built by Akbar in 1571–72 at the cost of seven hundred thousand rupees. The balance of the cloisters *(riwāq),* each portion of the colonnade framed by a delicate keel arch and surmounted by a *chhatrī* dome, is very satisfying. As with much Indo-Islamic architecture, there is a definitely military feel here, which adds to the ordered and sober atmosphere of the whole.

The north side of the courtyard is sprinkled with Muslim graves, many of them finely inscribed with verses from the *Qur'ān*. These are the tombs of the descendants of Salīm Chishtī, whose fourteenth-generation descendants still live in Fatehpur village. His favorite disciple, Hājjī Husain, is buried in the building against the northern wall popularly known as the Tomb of the Ladies (E.3), as it also contains the graves of the women of the saint's family. During the last years of his life, Salīm spent much of his time in a room here, where he gave audience to his disciples and listened to Sūfī devotional music (*samā*). (The Chishtī order makes particular use of music to promote mystical ecstasy.) This type of congregational hall is known in Sūfī terminology as a *jamāat khāna*, or *khānqāh* (E.2), and developed on the pattern of Buddhist *vihāras* and the monasteries of the Syrian Christians. It is not uncommon in Islām for the graves of both princes and commoners to be grouped around the tomb of a saint. Occasionally these come to form regular cities of the dead, like the Mamlūk tombs of Cairo.

The Mausoleum of Sheikh Salīm Chishtī (Figure E.4)

This pristine structure dominates the courtyard: an island of white marble in a sea of red sandstone. The holy man died in 1571, but the tomb was completed some ten years later on the orders of Akbar. It was built on the site of the *sheikh*'s

Cloisters of the Friday Mosque, topped by chhatrīs.

The mausoleum of Sheikh Salīm Chishtī.

private meditation cell (*zāwiya*). The tomb was originally designed to harmonize with the surrounding courtyard: the verandah and dome being of red sandstone, the rest of the tomb faced with marble. Jahāngīr's foster brother added the outer marble screens in about 1606 and paved the ambulatory with marble at the same time. The dome was covered with a marble veneer in 1866, by order of the district magistrate of Āgra. The shrine is maintained by the government and managed by a board consisting of descendants of the saint.

There is a great variety of surface texture here; what is a heavy and potentially unrelieved top half of the building is skillfully offset by the pierced marble screens that are the lacelike "walls" of the shrine, and the *pointilliste* marble and jasper inlay of the podium and floors. The dome and eaves thus seem to float on thin air.

☐ *THE ENTRANCE*

Notice, as you go in, the unusual bracketing that supports the heavy eaves (*chhajjas*). Here is a Hindu serpentine design, surrounded by delicate *jālī* work. These outside pillars are actually hollow and act as gutters, draining out through the spouts at their base.

The entrance doorway is framed by qur'anic texts of particular significance to the Sūfī.

Around the arched entrance to the shrine itself the names of God, the Prophet, and the four caliphs of Islām are inscribed, flanked by floral motifs. The original ebony doors to the sanctuary are very fine, and the canopy frame is of ebony, held together by brass nails and studded with mother-of-pearl.

This was renovated in 1905, but you can get an idea of the original magnificence of the shrine, the interior of which would have been profusely decorated and inscribed. The cenotaph (*zarīh*) itself is covered by a green cloth; green being the holy color of Islām. As with many Muslim mausoleums, the actual grave (*qabr*) is kept sacrosanct and inaccessible to the general public, in a vault (*maqbara*) immediately below. What we see here is a replica, for devotional purposes.

□

It is a widespread practice in Islām to bury saints or holy men near the spot where they lived and taught. Whereas the mausoleums of princes were constructed by those who expected to be buried in them, those of the saints (in Arabic: *wali-Allāh*, "friend of God") were donated by disciples. To the Muslim the tomb of a saint is far more than just a reminder of the great man. It is believed that, even after death, such a person radiates a spiritual influence (*baraka*), which can be absorbed by those visiting his grave. In fact, the *Qur'ān* states that those who have dedicated their lives to God are, in some subtle way, still alive after the physical body has died: "Say not of them that were killed in the way of God that they are dead; in truth they are alive but you perceive them not."

Detail of mausoleum, showing serpentine gutter bracket, with the King's Gate in the background.

Every saint's tomb is also a reflection of the tomb of the Prophet, which, after the Kā'ba at Mecca, is the most sacred place of pilgrimage to the Muslim. This is why you will see devout disciples praying at such tombs and even listening to the "replies" that the departed spirit gives. Here at Salīm Chishtī's grave it is also the practice to tie little pieces of red cotton on the fretted screens that surround the tomb. Each of these signifies a wish or something prayed for. When the prayer is fulfilled, the person returns and removes the cotton, leaving instead some flowers and money as a token of thanks. This custom is especially followed by women who, like Akbar over four hundred years ago, are hoping for a son.

□ *THE MARBLE SCREENS*
Coming out of the darkened sanctuary, walk around the shrine to appreciate the quality of the carved marble screens. Each one is different; each is carved out of a single block of stone. The workmanship is superb, the crystalline geometric patterns give you the effect of being surrounded by a spider's web, dappled with light so that your normal perception of space is broken up into a flickering play of light and shade. The sober and orderly perfection of these patterns was intended to convey the perfection of the Creator, as demonstrated by the lives of his saints on earth. These motifs are truly Islamic—they could come from north Africa or Spain—and are a type of decoration that demonstrates the unity of all those who put their trust in Allāh. The most impressive of these screens is in the southeast corner, facing the Gate of Victory.

The Mihrāb Shrine (Figure E.6)

The *mihrāb* shrine lies on the western wall, facing Mecca, the sacred center of the Islamic universe. The whole wall has an imposing grandeur, with its central chamber flanked by halls with Hindu-style pillars and then colonnades of richly ornamented arches. These pillars are especially significant. Their shafts are composed of sections that are square, then octagonal, then sixteen-sided, and culminate in a second octagonal section. This was the first time for over three hundred years that the Muslim architects had incorporated such a purely Hindu style into a mosque. They were probably inspired in this design by the temple buildings of Gujarāt in western India, which had recently come under Mughal rule.

The dome of the central chamber is painted in Persian style, and near the central *mihrāb* (the niche that actually orients the whole building, and thence the worshippers, to Mecca) is the pulpit *(minbar)* a simple marble structure of three steps. The Friday sermon *(khutba)* is given from here, and whenever a Mughal emperor took over a new territory, it was the custom to have the Friday sermon read in his name. Prayers for the welfare of the sovereign were also offered up from this point. There is some interesting decorative work in both the *mihrābs* and the north and south aisles leading off them: the red sandstone being inlaid with glazed tiles in green, blue, turquoise, black, and white, getting increasingly plain the farther one moves from the main *mihrāb*. Notice also the Hindu *satkona* design.

The Victory Gate (Figure E.7)

This triumphal gateway was erected in 1573, and completed a couple of years later, to commemorate Akbar's victory over the rebellious Ahmedabād, in Gujarāt. It is the most monumental structure of his reign, and it set the style for all the other imposing gateways built by Akbar himself, as well as his descendants Jahāngīr and Shāh Jahān. It was also mimicked in a more humble way in palaces, caravanserais, and domestic buildings. The gate is approached by a flight of steps 42 feet (13 meters) high and rises up 134 feet (41 meters) over the top step. One can see how it would dominate the surrounding countryside, being visible for miles, silently proclaiming the glory of the emperor and his religion. This gate both protects the sacred citadel within and offers a challenge to all outside. With the cupolas and crenelated walls, the feeling is of a fortress, buttressed against the world. In practical terms, the steep steps and elaborate chambers of the vestibule would have made any unwelcomed entry into the compound virtually impossible.

The military character of the gate is emphasized by its comparative plainness, the inlaid marble rosettes and cusping of the arch providing a restrained contrast to the unadorned spandrels. The lower part of the gates are covered by horseshoes and bits of metal. Like the cotton strips on the saint's tomb, they were fixed here by his devotees to secure his blessings.

Standing in the central hall and looking back into the mosque courtyard, you can see a famous verse from the *Qur'ān* inscribed in *naskh* script on the right of the main arch. It reads:

> Said Jesus, on whom be peace: The world is but a bridge; pass over but build no houses on it. He who hopes for an hour, hopes for Eternity, for the world is but an hour. Spend it in devotion, for the rest is unseen.

This somber thought is perhaps a fitting farewell to Fatehpur Sīkrī. There is something slightly unsettling about the place. Perhaps this is because of its construction: No symmetrical axes are used, there is no center, no monumental approaches or even regular streets around which the visitor can orient himself. The result is a feeling of suspension. And there is also a tangible feeling of emptiness here—*"Deus abest."* The place cries out that it has never really been lived in. Despite its brief hour of glory the imperial citadel is like some enormous new mansion that, after four hundred years, is still a little forlornly awaiting its new occupants.

14

SĀNCHĪ

IN MEMORY
OF THE BUDDHA

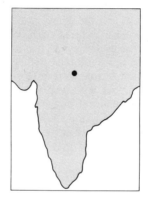

Sānchī is one of the most beautiful and important Buddhist sites in the world. Well off the usual tourist track, the place is visited mainly by pilgrims and is suffused with an atmosphere of sunny tranquillity. As you come out of the rural train station, a wooded hill rises up gently ahead of you. On top of this hill, its rounded shape peeping up over the surrounding trees, sits the Great Stūpa, the best preserved and most important of all Indian *stūpa*s. It is Sānchī, together with the slightly later ruined *stūpa* at Amarāvatī in southern India, that has provided archeologists with their most complete data on the development of this principal monument of Buddhism. Indeed, the Great Stūpa is the prototype of all Buddhist memorial structures: the *dāgaba* of Srī Lankā, the elongated *stūpa* of Burma, the *chedi* of Thailand, the high-spired *chörten* of Tibet, and the *pagodas* of the Far East.

With its commanding and majestic position overlooking the plains below, the Great Stūpa is an eloquent testimony to the Master's teaching on the building and function of sacred monuments. In the collection of Pāli texts known as the *Dīgha Nikāya*, the Buddha tells Ānanda, his favorite disciple:

> As they treat the remains of kings, so Ānanda, should they treat the remains of an Enlightened One (*tathāgata*). At the four crossroads a cairn should be erected to an Enlightened

One. And whosoever shall there place garlands, perfumes, or paints, or make salutations there, or become in its presence calm in heart, that shall long be to them a profit and a joy.

The foundation stone of the Great Stūpa was laid by the Mauryan emperor Ashoka ("the Sorrowless"), sometime in the middle of the third century B.C. The pious Ashoka is said to have erected hundreds of *stūpas* throughout his empire in his zeal to spread the teaching of Buddhism, and we know for certain that he laid the foundations both for the Sārnāth *stūpa* (commemorating the Buddha's first discourse in the Deer Park) and the temple at Bodh Gayā, where the Great Enlightenment occurred. Apparently Ashoka's wife, Devī, was no less devout; she founded a monastery at Sānchī even before the *stūpa* was constructed. Sānchī rapidly became a spiritual center. It was from here that Ashoka's nephew Mahendra (Pāli: Milinda) journeyed to Srī Lankā in about 240 B.C., taking with him the sacred relic of the Buddha's collarbone. This he placed in the *stūpa* he erected at Anurādhapura to commemorate his bringing of the *dharma* to the island.

After the death of Ashoka in 232 B.C., the Mauryan empire and dynasty crumbled and was replaced by the Shunga dynasty under their first king, Pushyamitra. This heralded a return to Hindu ascendancy and the consequent retreat of the Buddhist orders from the centers of urban influence. Nevertheless, Buddhist monasteries were still well supported throughout the Shunga period by the mercantile and trading classes, and despite the lack of direct royal patronage, funds

The Great Stūpa.

poured in to establish new monasteries and *stūpa*s or enlarge existing ones. The most important structure to benefit from this wave of practical piety was Ashoka's *stūpa* at Sānchī, which had been badly damaged sometime before the middle of the second century B.C. About 150 B.C., the emperor's semicircular mound, built of burned brick and mud mortar, was virtually doubled in size, its height being increased from 30 to 54 feet (9 to 16 meters) and its diameter from 70 to 120 feet (21 to 37 meters). The whole dome was given a casing of ashlar masonry, and a circumambulation terrace 16 feet (5 meters) from the ground, with a double flight of steps, was added. Both the dome and the terrace were thickly coated in mortar, and then covered with a fine layer of plaster. Other important changes were made. The top of the dome was flattened off, and the crowning member of a three-tiered umbrella, enclosed by a railing, was added. Inside this railing a heavy stone relic coffer was placed. A circumambulatory path was placed around the *stūpa* and paved in mortar. Lastly, sandstone balustrades were added on the stairs and ground level, many of them carved with floral and animal motifs. These were constructed in the technique used for wood: octagonal uprights with cross-bars mortised into them and crowned by massive copings that are rounded at the top. Many devotees contributed to these balustrades and pavements, as we know from the fact that their names are inscribed on them.

The next additions came about seventy-five years later (ca. 75 B.C.) during the reign of the Sātavāhanas, probably at the behest of King Shātakarni. These were the four elaborately carved gateways (*toranas*), which are the highlights of Sānchī. They will be discussed in detail later.

The last embellishment to Ashoka's monument came nearly five centuries later. During the Gupta period (probably ca. A.D. 450) four images of the Buddha seated in meditation under a canopy were installed facing each of the four gateways, their backs against the *stūpa*. Of these, the one facing the eastern entrance is the best preserved. You will notice that these four entrances are staggered. This is an ancient custom to keep out evil spirits, who are often believed to be only capable of proceeding in a straight line. This idea is found all over Southeast Asia, as for example in Hindu-influenced Bali, where a wall is built within the entrance gate of the temple for the same purpose.

After the demise of Buddhism in India in the twelfth century, Sānchī lay half buried and deserted for six hundred years, until it was rediscovered by a General Taylor in 1818, a year before the Ajantā caves were unearthed. What followed is a familiar story in Indian archeology: Amateur investigators and treasure hunters caused considerable damage to the site before an expert belatedly stepped in to preserve and restore

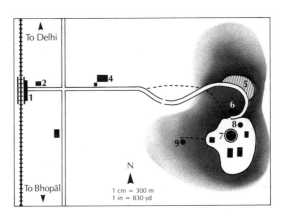

1 *Railway station.* 2 *Buddhist rest house.* 3 *Ashok Travellers' Lodge (ITDC).* 4 *Museum and ticket office for site.* 5 *Sānchī village.* 6 *Mahābodhi Temple.* 7 *The Great Stūpa.* 8 Stūpa *number 3.* 9 Stūpa *number 2.*

Figure A. Sānchī site plan.

the monument. In this case it was Sir John Marshall, the director general of archeology in India who, from 1912 to 1919, worked to restore the site to its present condition. The encroaching jungle was cleared, the Great Stūpa was partly dismantled and rebuilt, and the subsidiary *stūpas* were restored.

You approach the Great Stūpa by the northern gate. The original entrance was from the southern gate, but this one is in much better repair and is the logical place from which to begin your tour. Nevertheless, the south side of the complex provides the best overall view of the *stūpa* and its constituent parts, so you should make two circumambulations: First go around the four gateways, pausing at the southern one to view the *stūpa* from a distance, and then around the inner circumambulatory path so as to see the rear of the gates. Notice that the *stūpa* is ringed by a magic circle of stones. This protective ring was often used by the earliest cults and persists today in various forms in many Buddhist countries— for example, the eight boundary stones (*sīmā*) that delimit the consecrated ground on which Thai Buddhist assembly halls (*bot*) are built, with the ninth stone being embedded in the monument itself.

A gateway leading into a *stūpa* is called a *torana*; it is a stone version of the wood and bamboo gates that protected the village in ancient India. The basic model is two pillars, joined by three architraves. These architraves were built as if they actually passed through the upright posts, again in imitation of their wooden prototypes. The capitals of the gate pillars are carved with protective emblems. On the northern gate they are in the shape of four royal elephants, back to back. The elephant is a common symbol of strength and justice that is also frequently found "supporting" parts of the Hindu temple. As you will see, the elephant plays an important part in the mythology of Buddhism. Originally these fine beasts would have had ivory tusks set into the now empty cavities.

The highlight of Sānchī is its carving; the four *toranas* are consummate examples of the stone carving that most aptly expresses the Indian artistic genius. The earliest decorative carving in India was done by wood or ivory workers who transferred their skills to the more permanent medium of stone. Here at Sānchī, with its light-yellowed sandstone, the link is especially clear, and there is an inscription on the west pillar of the southern gate recording that its decoration is the work of the ivory carvers of the nearby town of Vidishā. What is so remarkable is that none of the minute detail and precision has been lost in the transition to stone. The figures and details in each panel are deeply cut into the background and are thus framed in dark shadow. This technique maximizes the play of light and shade and renders the scenes visible even in the strong glare of the Indian sun. Visibility was important not only for esthetic reasons but because these carvings were primarily intended as illustrated manuscripts to convey the teachings of Buddhism to an illiterate following. The method of telling the various stories was one of continuous narration, in which any normal unity of time is subservient to the unity of the story being told. Thus events that took place many years apart may be portrayed next to each other, or those that occurred in close temporal proximity be spatially separated, according to the particular points the artist wished to emphasize. This technique of continuous narration (which is also to be seen in the Ajantā murals or the scroll paintings of the Far East) is allowed particular scope at Sānchī because of the rectangular elongation of the architraves, each one terminating in a spiraled volute end, like a rolled manuscript.

These exquisitely carved panels are typically Indian in the way that every inch of the surface is covered with detail. Each outline is also an inline, and altogether the scenes appear to be emerging from the unifying matrix of stone with an organic and irrepressible energy. Yet notice how formalized the settings are throughout. You have already seen some of the conventional representations employed in later Indian sculpture (for example, at Elephanta), where cubes symbolize rocks and, on a larger scale, mountains and where trees are represented by leaves stuck onto stylized trunks. Here at

Sānchī, the carvers display great skill in conveying the lush-ness of vegetation—it is one of the most persistent themes—but this abundant vegetation is not portrayed for its own sake nor in any attempt to inaugurate a school of landscape repre-sentation. As with Giotto and his followers in European paint-ing, what was important to the Sānchī artist was to convey the essence of the scene as rapidly and directly as possible. One *banyan* tree represents a forest, wavy lines represent water or a river, a village hut or town palace conveys a community. Only as much as is necessary for the communi-cation of the important information is included. The message must be transmitted in its most readily apprehensible form, for its job is to *instruct* by reminding the viewer of specific, well-known scenes and stories. To this didactic end, conven-tional rules of proportion are irrelevant. Thus a particular species of tree may be represented by leaves that are enor-mously enlarged relative to their surroundings, or the parallel wavy lines indicating a river may flow over the head of a figure farther on in the narrative sequence. The method of presentation is above all conceptual rather than "realistic" (as in a child's painting), and its aim is to present each element in its most typical, and thus most recognizable form. This is not to say that realism is missing from these reliefs—as you will see, there is much charming and realistic portrayal—but, as with all native Indian art, naturalism is a secondary bonus rather than a primary concern.

The principal subjects covered in the Sānchī carvings fall into three categories:

1. Scenes from the life of the Buddha
2. Events in the subsequent history of Buddhism
3. Stories from the *Jātaka Tales* (legends concerning the Buddha's previous lives before he incarnated as Gautama Siddhārtha). The *Jātakas* are the main source of popu-lar Buddhist mythology and draw heavily on Dravidian folk myths that were part of the Indian heritage prior to the life of the Master. In turn, they influenced many European folk tales, including the collection known as Aesop's fables. Their didactic purpose is to teach such virtues as compassion, selflessness, and honesty.

Northern Gate—Front

☐ *THE GREAT RENUNCIATION* (Figure B.1)
The Buddha was born as Prince Gautama of the Shākya clan in Lumbinī, in southern Nepāl. He led a protected life within the precincts of his father's palace at Kapilavastu. One day, however, on a journey outside the safety of the palace walls, he happened to see in quick succession an old man, a sick

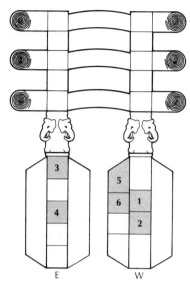

1 *The Great Renunciation.* **2** *Buddha Preaching to the Shākyas.* **3** *The Miracle of the Mango Tree.* **4** *The Miracle of Walking in the Air.* **5** *Foreigners Worshipping at the* Stūpa. **6** *The Monkey Offering Honey.*

Figure B. Northern gate (front view).

man, a corpse, and a wandering ascetic. These sights had such a profound impact on the young Gautama that he resolved to renounce his life of ease and seek the Truth. The right-hand side of the panel shows these fateful journeys.

The bottom left corner shows the final departure from the palace. The future Buddha, symbolized by the riderless horse, is watched over by celestial hosts, who are all rejoicing in the momentous decision he has made.

□ THE BUDDHA PREACHING TO THE SHĀKYAS (Figure B.2)

The Buddha is also known as Shākyamuni: "the sage of the Shākyas." *Muni* ("sage") means literally "the one with the silent mind." Seven years after the Enlightenment, Gautama returned to the family palace at Kapilavastu to preach to his family. Several of them, including his father, Shuddhodana, and his wife, Yashodharā, became his disciples, and the Buddha and his followers took up residence in a *banyan* park donated by the king. While speaking to the Shākya clan, the Buddha astounded them by levitating. The psychological teaching in this story is that reconciliation with the parents is an important marker on the journey to true individuation.

□ *THE MIRACLE OF THE MANGO TREE* (Figure B.3)
A wealthy merchant of Shrāvastī, near Kapilavastu, became a convert to Buddhism and donated some land for the *sangha* to build a monastery. He bought his land from its owner, Prince Jeta, by paying as many gold coins as were needed to cover the ground. The Buddha gave a discourse here to a huge crowd, including the local king, Prasenajīt, who, according to contemporary records, squandered much of his wealth on spiritual charlatans.

Among the audience at Shrāvastī were six teachers of heretical doctrines. To convince such disseminators of false-hood of the superiority of his teaching, the Master performed several miracles. One of these was to cause a mango tree to sprout, fully laden with fruit, out of midair. The Buddha then sat underneath it and preached the *dharma*. This story illustrates a universal connection in folklore between the spiritual health of a community and natural fertility of the region. If the people are acting in harmony with the laws of nature, then good harvests and general well-being will result. Spiritual ill health is frequently symbolized by drought, famine, and natural calamities—as in the Arthurian legend of the Fisher King. Many of the Buddhist myths show evidence of this connection.

□ *THE MIRACLE OF WALKING IN THE AIR* (Figure B.4)
It was on this occasion, according to Buddhist tradition, that the Buddha performed the miracle of walking in the air. This was done to curb the pride of the heretical teachers and demonstrate the superiority of the *dharma*. When they had this visible proof of the Master's spiritual status, the people, including the king, prostrated before him.

Now you can move under the arch of the *torana* and look at the carvings on the inside face of the pillar.

□ *FOREIGNERS WORSHIPPING AT THE STŪPA*
(Figure B.5)
A fitting way to start your tour. Buddhism was from its earliest days a proselytizing faith. Monks went to all parts of Asia and also Western countries to spread the teachings of the *dharma*. Added to which, the Buddhist monastic centers built near to *stūpas* became great cultural and religious magnets, drawing the educated and artistic leaders of society, as well as the common pilgrim. The veneration paid by the visitors is watched approvingly by the divine beings at the top of the panel. From its earliest days, Buddhist art, like its Hindu counterpart, overflows with these celestial beings drawn from folk mythology. There is genuine love of life in the depiction of detail here, emanating a feeling that is quite contrary to the pessimistic image of Buddhism as it is popularly misun-

Miracle of the Monkey Offering Honey, detail from the northern gate.

derstood in the West. Look at the merriment on the faces of these musicians, exhorting us all to join the general celebration. The Master's teaching is one of joy.

☐ *THE MONKEY OFFERING HONEY* (Figure B.6)
The animal kingdom was no less devoted to the Buddha than the human one. This depicts one of the eight most important events of the Master's life when a monkey spontaneously offered him some honey at a town called Vaishālī. Symbolically, the restless mind is always represented in Indian iconography by the monkey, which leaps from branch to branch and is never still. Just as the monkey can only be tamed by the lure of a pot of honey, so the mind can only be calmed by the nectar of enlightenment.

Notice that at this early stage in Buddhist art, the Master was not represented, but his presence merely indicated by the empty throne.

Eastern Gate—Front

☐ *YAKSHĪ* (Figure C.1)
Among the folk motifs Buddhist art assimilated were fertility figures, the local deities that had from time immemorial been the auspicious bringers of good harvests and material wellbeing. There is a particularly fine example of such a figure

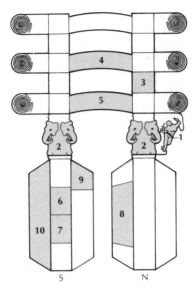

1 Yakshī. 2 *Elephants.* 3 *The Lustration of Queen Māyā.* 4
The Great Departure. 5 *Emperor Ashoka Visiting the* Bodhi
Tree. 6 *The* Bodhi *Tree Shrine.* 7 *The Buddha Walking on the
Water.* 8 *Queen Māyā's Dream.* 9 *Life in Uruvelā.* 10 *The*
Makara.

Figure C. Eastern gate (front view).

here: the female divinity (*yakshī*) that is a bracket on the
right-hand pillar. *Yakshīs* are tree spirits, fertility symbols
(originally Dravidian) that hark back to the earliest Indian
mythology. A recurrent theme is the ability of maidens or
yakshīs to cause a tree to burst into blossom by their mere
embrace, and an annual festival, still performed in rural India,
consists of the youths of a village gathering the flowers of the
shāl tree to insure the coming year's harvest. The *yakshī* is
the bride of the tree, a crystallization of its life sap, and as
such performs the same protective function as the amorous
couples (*mithuna*) on the outside of a Hindu temple. Indeed,
the *yakshī* actually personifies the tree, as the Dravidian artists
chose to represent every aspect of nature, whether hostile or
benign, anthropomorphically, in the form of a spirit-*cum*-deity,
just as the Greek artist represented the wooded grove in the
form of the dryad.

This figure, with her large breasts, ample hips, and
pronounced *yoni*, is delightfully portrayed. The heavy ripe-
ness of her body is emphasized by the constriction of her
belt, beaded with amulets, her necklace, and her bangles—
all of which provide a firmness that serves to accentuate the

areas of soft flesh they adorn. The aura of moist fecundity she exudes is echoed in the sappy fruit and leaves—themselves *yoni*-shaped—that hang from the mango tree she leans against, her right arm curled like some sinuous creeper around its branch. The mango (like the peach in Chinese art) is a symbol of the life force expressed as sexuality.

The distribution of the nymph's weight is beautifully conveyed. She leans easily out into space, her weight thrown onto the sumptuously curved left hip, her left leg straightened to take the strain. Notice the fine depiction of detail—the folds of flesh around her navel and waist and under her right breast. As both a protectress from evil and an invitation to a fullness of life that culminates in religious devotion, this figure is a perfect illustration of that intermingling of the spiritual and the sensual that is found in the best of Indian art, in no matter what period or medium.

□ *THE ELEPHANTS* (Figure C.2)
The Sānchī sculptors were as talented in their portrayal of the animal kingdom. Next to the *yakshī* are the moving elephants. The one next to the nymph looks slightly bemused by the whole affair. Again, the moment of balance is caught exactly: his leg raised and with his trunk acting as a fifth leg to support the ponderous weight. And the craftsman has again depicted the folds of skin—between the two front legs, on the nose, and even the wrinkles around the eyes. The *mahouts* carry a banner as a royal canopy, one of the symbols of the

Yakshī, *bracket from the eastern gate.*

Buddha, the spiritual ruler of mankind. The sense of movement of these four elephants is conveyed by the swinging
bend of their legs and trunks, giving a horizontal balance to
the upright tension of the pillar and at the same time transforming the functional into the decorative.

In fact, you could call this the Elephant Gate. The elephant
is India's most beloved animal. Quite apart from its practical
value, Kipling's "noble pachyderm" represented stability,
strength, and majesty. In ancient India the white elephant
was worshipped as a fertility god, and it plays this role in the
legend of the Buddha's conception (see Figure C.8). Today
many temples keep them for their processions, and you can
often see itinerant holy men traveling the country, their meager
belongings piled on an elephant, which to the ascetic symbolizes the regal state of renunciation.

□ *THE LUSTRATION OF QUEEN MĀYĀ* (Figure C.3)
If you look up above the four elephants, past a panel of fabulous birds that look like gryphons, you will see a woman being
lustrated by elephants. This is probably the Hindu deity
Lakshmī, goddess of wealth, transposed to represent the
mother of Buddha being anointed before the birth of the great
teacher. Such iconographic overlapping is not uncommon.

□ *THE GREAT DEPARTURE* (Figure C.4)
The middle architrave shows the Great Departure in more
detail than on the northern gate panel. Gautama left his wife
and child secretly in the middle of the night, accompanied
only by his charioteer, Channa. After crossing the Anomā
River, he sent Channa back with his horse. Here the four
riderless horse figures illustrate the progression of the journey, and on the extreme right Channa is shown taking leave
of the prince by bowing down to his footprints. Below this is
his sad and solitary return to the palace.

The tree enclosed by a railing in the center of the panel is
a *jambū* tree, reminding us that the Buddha's first meditation
as the child Gautama took place under one of these trees. It
was at a plowing festival, and when the celebrants returned
in the evening, they noticed that the boy's body threw no
shadow on the ground—a sure sign of his divine status.

□ *EMPEROR ASHOKA VISITING THE BODHI TREE,*
   AT BODH GAYĀ (Figure C.5)
We know from his own inscriptions that this visit actually
took place. Ashoka is first shown getting down from the
elephant, and again approaching the tree with hands folded
in respectful greeting.

Ashoka is closely connected not only with the spread of

Buddhism but the popularizing of the *stūpa* as a cult object. When the Buddha died at Kushinagara, the capital of the Malla clan, his body was cremated. The bone relics were divided among the Mallas and seven other groups, each of which erected a *stūpa* to enshrine them. It is said that sometime in the third century B.C. Ashoka opened up seven of these in order to redistribute the relics in *stūpas* erected by himself.

□ *THE BODHI TREE SHRINE* (Figure C.6)
Here we see a chapel has been constructed around the *bodhi* tree. The tree was the first cult object of the new faith, and its cuttings were planted wherever the *dharma* was established for the first time. Relatives of the *bodhi* tree continued to supply these cuttings, such as the one that Milinda took to Srī Lankā when he founded Buddhism there in 240 B.C. A common practice was to lustrate the tree with holy water, Ashoka himself is reputed to have emptied 1,008 vases over the roots of the Bodh Gayā tree. In time, a protective railing was erected around the holy trees, and a paved walkway laid to enable ritual circumambulation and afford protection from the muddy ground. Slowly the superstructures grew and the trees became increasingly enclosed. When the *stūpa* became more widespread, its symbolic role as the successor to the *bodhi* tree was made clear by the addition of the *chhattra* (which represented the sacred tree) to the dome of the *stūpa* tumulus. What had previously been a funerary mound was now transformed into a living symbol of the Buddha, the *dharma,* and the *sangha*—the "Three Gems" (*triratna*) of Buddhism. This *triratna* is represented not only in the three tiers of the *chhattra* but in a triune emblem, visible on top of the right-hand end of the topmost architrave here. There is another one clearly visible on top of the northern gate; both are best seen from the second level of circumambulation— the raised terrace around the *stūpa* itself. A miniature replica of the *stūpa* in turn becomes the devotional focus of the Buddhist chapel (*chaitya*), as can be seen at Ellorā and Ajantā. Thus this panel, as well as being a decorative masterpiece, provides important links in our understanding of the development of Buddhist iconography.

□ *THE BUDDHA WALKING ON THE WATER* (Figure C.7)
The ability to walk on water is one of the well-known supernormal powers (*siddhis*) gained through yoga. The Master is reported to have walked over the river Nairanjā, near Uruvelā, when it was in flood. This feat symbolizes mastery over nature and control of the restless mind. The sages with beards and long hair bundled up into topknots echo this idea. Saints in India are often depicted with long hair which signifies control

over the senses and spiritual strength (compare the Biblical story of Samson).

☐ *QUEEN MĀYĀ'S DREAM* (Figure C.8)
Perhaps the finest panel on the gateway is on the inside of the right-hand pillar. At the top left of the panel we see Queen Māyā, the mother of the Buddha, lying asleep. Just above her feet there is an elephant. This refers to the dream she had one night that she was transported to the divine lake Anavātapa in the Himālayas. There she was bathed by the heavenly guardians of the four quarters of the universe, after which a white elephant, bearing a lotus in his trunk, approached her and entered her side. The next morning the astrologers of the court interpreted this dream to mean that she had conceived a divine being as a son, who would turn out to be either a world ruler or an enlightened spiritual teacher. In due course Gautama was born in a grove of *shāl* trees near Lumbinī, his mother standing upright holding onto a tree during the birth. The infant stood up immediately and took seven steps, declaring that this was his last incarnation on the earth plane.

The heaviness of sleep is well conveyed in the figure of the queen, and the scene is enlivened with some lovely cameos— such as the little faces peeping out at the top right-hand corner of the panel. We can also gain some idea of contemporary architecture from the buildings shown here.

Just below the sleeping queen is the return of the Buddha to his family home at Kapilavastu; the Master is shown by the empty canopy atop the royal elephant. The animals in the procession are especially well rendered. Notice the horse's head at the rear of the column. In the extreme bottom left is a *banyan* tree, symbolizing the Master's residence in the *banyan* grove outside Kapilavastu.

☐ *LIFE IN URUVELĀ* (Figure C.9)
Uruvelā was the scene of some of the Buddha's most spectacular miracles. This is a charming domestic scene, illustrating the unity of all life, which lies at the heart of the Buddhist philosophy. Here we see daily life in the village—a routine that has hardly changed since these panels were carved. Women sit outside their huts, pounding grain and kneading dough for *chapattis*. They are surrounded by goats, cows, Brahmā bulls, grouped around the village pond with its lotuses. There's a tremendous feeling of domestic harmony in this idyllic scene, which is suffused with the same gentle atmosphere as some of the Kāngrā miniature paintings (ca. 1780–1850).

☐ *THE MAKARA* (Figure C.10)
This theme of the unity of all life is picked up in a more

abstract fashion on the outside of the column. Here organic life spills from the mouth of the mythical sea dragon (*makara*) at the bottom of the panel. Indian art is full of aquatic images—serpents, lotuses, plants—that convey the irrepressible fecundity of life. This is particularly understandable if we remember that at the time sites such as Sānchī were created, much of northern India was still fertile with forest and jungle and that even today the onset of the monsoon brings a dramatic resurgence of vegetation to the parched landscape.

☐

Now follow the path to the south side of the complex. From here we can get the best overall view of the *stūpa* and its component parts. The best vantage point is the rather Greek-looking temple with tall columns.

The Structure of the Stūpa (Figure D)

From here you can clearly see the different parts of the mature *stūpa*. The hemispherical dome (*anda*) rises like a nourishing breast and is flattened at the top to allow a railed enclosure (*harmikā*) around the three-tiered finial (*chhattra*). This sits above where the relic casket would have been buried in the dome. The dome is surrounded by a railing (*vedikā*), which has four ornamental gateways (*torana*) and which encloses a circumambulatory path (*pradakshinā patha*). An inner terrace (*medhi*) is built onto the side of the *anda* to allow a second, more intimate, circumambulation.

We have already discussed (in Chapter 1) the complex layers of symbolism that accrued to the *stūpa* and made it a supreme expression of the Master's teaching. From here another level reveals itself. The *stūpa*, like the Hindu temple, has the symbolic function of reenacting the primordial act of creation that established the emergence of the manifest world from the divine womb of pure, undifferentiated Being. This reenactment transports the worshipper to that same level of purity by a process of spiritual osmosis. He or she is unconsciously affected by the architecture and its meaning and experiences this as a transformation of consciousness (*metanoia*), which has a healing effect of positive regeneration. It is the creation of this effect that stipulates the rules governing sacred architecture, whether that architecture be the American Indian shrine or the medieval Gothic cathedral. The most widespread creation myth in India is that of the Golden Egg (*hiranyagarbha*) that emerged from the primordial waters and then divided itself into two halves, thus creating the world of spirit and matter, day and night, male and female. When mankind consciously reenacts this event in

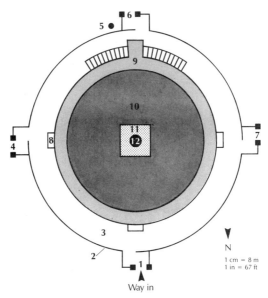

1 *Northern gate* (torana). 2 *Railing* (vedikā). 3 *Circumambulation path* (pradakshinā patha). 4 *Eastern gate* (torana).
5 *Ashokan pillar.* 6 *Southern gate* (torana).
7 *Western gate* (torana). 8 *Seated Buddah.* 9 *Raised terrace for circumambulation* (medhi). 10 *Dome* (anda). 11 *Fenced kiosk* (harmikā). 12 *Honorific umbrella* (chhattra).

Figure D. The Great Stūpa ground plan.

establishing a temple or shrine, the Indian pattern is first to erect a pillar that separates earth from the heavens, and to use this pillar as the module of the structure. In Vedic times this pillar was the *yūpa* or sacrificial post to which the animal was tied. In subsequent Hindu texts it is referred to as Indra's Nail (*indrakīla*), by which the various levels of the cosmos are separated and kept in their proper order, and erecting this pillar was the first step in the construction of a Hindu temple (see page 19). Once this axial pillar has been erected, it becomes the center from which the four cardinal points emerge, and with the fixing of these, the basic rite of creating order out of pure potential has been accomplished. This orientation rite is like a divine seed, which contains all its subsequent manifestations in spatial and architectural form. If it is not performed, all that follows is meaningless.

The *stūpa* incorporates this process very clearly. The dome is the *hiranyagarbha* (*anda*: "egg"), the cosmic seed. The fact that the *anda* contained relics is quite apt, since the processes of life and death are indivisible to the mythical mind. We have already seen how aquatic imagery is widespread on the *toranas* and *vedikā*, and there is evidence that some of the early *stūpas* had their *pradakshinā patha* paved with blue glazed tiles, surely an allusion to the cosmic waters from which the Golden Egg emerges. The central pillar is here the *yashti,* which, with the addition of the umbrella members, becomes the *chhattra*. As well as fulfilling the function of separating heaven and earth, it recalls the *bodhi* tree and the sacred umbrella of royalty. It is interesting to note that all early *stūpas* had a wooden pillar running down from the base of the *chhattra* to the bottom of the *anda,* where it terminated just above ground level. This pillar served no functional purpose whatsoever, and can only be explained as a symbolic version of the archetypal axial pillar around which the cosmos revolves. The themes of Golden Egg and axial pillar also intermingle in the ritual of lustrating the *bodhi* tree and the subsequent erection of an enclosing, domelike structure around it that is illustrated in the panel on the eastern gate. The final stage of this archaic orientation procedure, the establishment of the cardinal points, is enacted with the erection of the four *toranas*. That these gates in the case of Sānchī were erected some time after the original mound in no way destroys the mythic unity of the rite. The present gates and railings merely replaced wooden originals that were contemporary with Ashoka's *stūpa,* for the demarking of the threshold is an indispensable part of the erection of a religious structure. And again, the archaic pattern is well suited to the Buddhist need (or perhaps we should say that Buddhism is a particularly pure expression of a mythic archetype), since the *toranas,* open to the four quarters of the universe, proclaim "Come and see for yourself!" (Pāli: *epihasso*). This is precisely the word the Master used to describe the *dharma*—a teaching that was open to all and a matter of direct experience rather than abstract philosophy.

The Ashokan Column (Figure D.5)

Just to the right of the gateway is the stump of the pillar erected by Ashoka, who spread the teachings of Buddhism through edicts carved on stone columns throughout his extensive empire. The inscription on this one warned the nuns and monks of the order that they faced expulsion if they tried to create heretical schisms. The column was vandalized by a local *zamindar* (landlord) who reputedly used pieces as a sugarcane press. The capital, with the four lion heads, is now in the museum. Like its counterpart at Sārnāth, the column is made of a highly polished sandstone. The supporting capital is carved in the form of lions—a pan-Indian symbol of royalty. The Buddha's throne was also supported by lions.

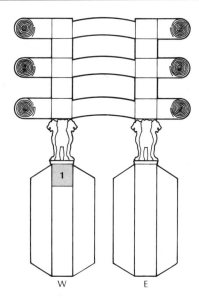

1 *The Wheel of Truth.*
Figure E. Southern gate (front view).

Southern Gate—Front

This gate is unfortunately badly damaged. Most of the missing panels are preserved in the museum.

□ *THE WHEEL OF TRUTH* (Figure E.1)
This very popular emblem represents the first sermon of the Buddha at the Deer Park in Sārnāth. The sermon is called "the Setting in Motion of the Wheel of Truth," and the *dharma-chakra* is here shown mounted on a pillar, like a spiritual lighthouse radiating the Master's teaching to all corners of the world. The deer at the bottom of the panel allude to the Deer Park at Sārnāth. The wheel is a widespread Indian symbol. Originally signifying the sun, it came to represent the ever-turning wheel of life, death, and rebirth, and thence the law of *karma*, which states that the effects of any action return to the doer, either in this life or a future one. A form of this wheel is to be seen on the Indian flag.

Western Gate—Front

□ *OUTSIDE FACE* (Figure F.1)
A fine panel of floral and animal decoration. The intertwined design here is like some medieval manuscript or a meander

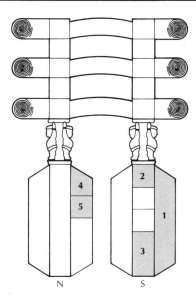

1 *Outside face.* 2 *The* Mahākapi jātaka. 3 *Heraldic lions.*
4 *The* Sāma jātaka. 5 *Muchalinda the Serpent King.*

Figure F. Western gate (front view).

of Celtic art. It does remind us how lucky we are to have this carving in such good condition after two thousand years; it is a miracle worthy of the Buddha himself! Notice as well the variety in the expressions of the potbellied dwarves (*ganas*) who form the capital supporting the architraves. These, like all the figures of the Sānchī capitals, are set back to back in the manner of the art of Persepolis. One is positively groaning under the weight, another looks rather bored, a third is really enjoying his task and grins from ear to ear.

□ *THE MAHĀKAPI JĀTAKA* (Figure F.2)
In one of his previous births, the Buddha was the leader of a band of eighty thousand monkeys and lived with them in a mango grove on the banks of the Ganges. The entire band lived off one miraculous tree. One day the king of Banāras came to pluck for himself the fruits of this fabulous tree which could support so many creatures. He arrived with a mighty retinue (bottom of panel) and was about to kill the monkeys to get at the fruit. The future Buddha leaped to the far bank of the river, and, tying a length of bamboo to his leg, made a bridge of his own body so his followers could escape across the river (top of panel). One of his rivals, the wicked Devadatta, took the opportunity to jump so hard on the Buddha

that he died. But before his death, the Buddha managed to preach the *dharma* to the king (top left). So contrite was the sovereign that he had the saintly monkey buried with full royal honors.

This homily is delightfully illustrated, with the stylized river and its fish depicted in a childlike way, reminiscent of early Abyssinian bas-reliefs.

□ *HERALDIC LIONS* (Figure F.3)
A fine set of lions, again similar to medieval heraldic motifs. Notice the script above the lions' heads. This records the patrons who financed the building of the gates and railings. Such inscriptions, the only way that we can date early Indian material, are comparatively rare.

□ *THE SĀMA JĀTAKA* (Figure F.4)
This *jātaka* teaches the value of filial love. In former times the Buddha was born as Sāma, the son of two pious recluses who dwelt in the forests (top right). His parents had both lost their sight through being bitten by a poisonous snake, and Sāma had dedicated his life to looking after them. One day Sāma went to the river with his pitcher to get water (bottom right). The king of Banāras (who is the villain in many *jātakas*), was out hunting and accidentally shot the boy with an arrow (bottom left). The king was so distressed by his mistake that he offered to serve the blind couple in place of their dead son. The parents' grief was so great, however, that a sympathetic goddess was moved to restore the boy to life, and the family was happily reunited (top left).

The Sāma jātaka—*detail of panel from the western gate.*

Again, the sculptors have caught the domestic tranquility of rural life very well here: the gentle cows around the huts of the recluses, the mischievous monkeys squatting on the thatched roofs. And look at the water buffalo swimming in the river (bottom right). The way the creature lazily floats his jaw on the water has been captured exactly; he is really enjoying a luxurious bask in the sun. You can see just the same scene in the tank on the way up the hill today, twenty-five hundred years after this was carved. And, as if to emphasize the importance of all forms of life in India, if you look between the cracks in the pillars here you will see the local wildlife—lizards sunning themselves, bats snoozing in the heat of the day.

☐ *MUCHALINDA THE SERPENT KING* (Figure F.5)
After the great Enlightenment at Bodh Gayā, the Buddha spent seven weeks in the vicinity of the *bodhi* tree, enjoying the bliss of freedom and considering whether he should teach the truth of *nirvāna* to the rest of the world. The fifth week was spent under a goatherd's tree, and during this time a tremendous storm blew up as a sign of the cosmic purification that the Master's Enlightenment had caused. Muchalinda, a serpent king (*nāgarāja*) who lived nearby, spontaneously came and protected the Buddha by raising his hood over the Master's head like a royal umbrella. Here the sacred tree-parasol theme is extended to incorporate the esoteric teaching of *kundalinī*, the "serpent power" that lies dormant, coiled at the base of the spine, until it is awakened by yoga exercises. When the nervous system is pure enough, this life energy rises up the spine to the thousand-petaled lotus (*sahasrāra chakra*) above the head, and there is no obstruction to the free flow of cosmic energy through the gross and subtle bodies. As a result the individual can consciously experience enlightenment.

Muchalinda, the king of the unconscious depths, is shown below the Buddha's seat under the tree. He and his retinue are in the service of all those who have learned to control their mind.

☐
Now you can leave the western gate and continue around the *stūpa*, keeping it on your right as is the custom, and begin the second circumambulation. Proceed to the eastern gate, where you will see the best-preserved of the four Buddha figures (D.8).

Despite being damaged, the seated figure has the unmistakable stamp of Gupta genius. The oval face, soft yet firm, with full, sensuous lips and heavy-lidded eyes, positively throbs with indrawn life energy (*prāna*). The very stone seems to glow with the joy of meditation. The Buddha is attended by two divine beings, backed by a finely carved halo (*prabhā-mandala*) and has the conventional *lakshana* of snail-shell curls of hair, wisdom bump (*ushnīsha*) on top of the head, elongated earlobes, and three folds of skin (*trivali*) around the neck.

If you now continue around to the back of the southern gate, you will come to the stairway leading up to the *medhi* terrace, from where you will be able to see the carving on the backs of the architraves more easily.

Southern Gate Architrave—Rear

□ *THE CHHADDANTA JĀTAKA* (Figure G.1)
In a former life the Buddha was born as Chhaddanta ("Six teeth"), the six-tusked elephant. He lived in the Himālayas with his two wives. One of these became insanely jealous of the other and prayed to the gods that she might die and be reborn in another body to take revenge on Chhaddanta for not showing her enough attention. Her wish was granted, and she died and was reborn as the wife of the king of Banāras. In this form she persuaded her new husband to have the elephant killed and his tusks brought to her. Besotted by his wife, he agreed. The noble beast was so full of compassion for his slayers, however, that he even helped the hunters to saw off his own tusks. But justice was done. The queen was so overcome by remorse when she saw the severed tusks that she died of shame.

We can see the elephant four times here: twice near the *banyan* tree in the center of the architrave, once in the far-left corner playing amid the lotuses, and once in the right,

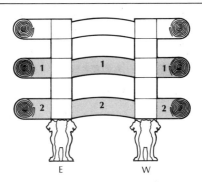

1 *The* Chhaddanta jātaka. 2 *The Siege of Kushinagara.*

Figure G. Southern gate (rear view).

facing the hunter's deadly arrow. There are also some fine figures seated on water buffalo at the right-hand end of the panel.

☐ *THE SIEGE OF KUSHINAGARA* (Figure G.2)
The Enlightened One died at Kushinagara in about 540 B.C. Seven kings claimed his remains after the cremation, and there was a dispute during which the city was besieged. Eventually King Drona persuaded the Mallas, who had the bones in their possession, to divide them into eight portions and give one portion to each of the claimants. These relics were taken to various parts of India, and the first eight *stūpas* erected over them. This siege is also depicted on the rear of the western gate, in the top two architraves.

Western Gate Architrave—Rear

☐ *THE SIEGE OF KUSHINAGARA* (Figure H.1)
A repetition of the scene you have just seen on the southern gate; it was a favorite subject for the Buddhist craftsmen, perhaps because it incorporated military subjects, which attracted the interest of royal patrons.

☐ *THE TRANSPORTATION OF THE RELICS* (Figure H.2)
Once the relics were divided up among the eight claimants, they were taken to different parts of the country and the first eight Buddhist *stūpas* erected over them. Unfortunately, we have no reliable evidence of these *stūpas* still existing, though many places claim to have some of these original relics (*bija*, literally "seeds") in their possession.

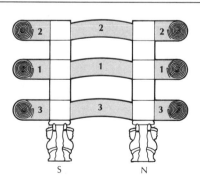

1 *The Siege of Kushinagara.* **2** *The Transportation of the Relics.* **3** *The Enlightenment and the Defeat of Māra.*

Figure H. Western gate (rear view).

Some especially fine figures are at the left-hand end of this panel, particularly three relaxed figures in a boat.

☐ *THE ENLIGHTENMENT AND THE DEFEAT OF MĀRA*
(Figure H.3)

Another favorite subject in early Buddhist art. While the Buddha was meditating under the *bodhi* tree, he was visited by Māra, the Buddhist Satan. The Evil One tried everything in his power to distract the future Buddha from his meditation, including offering him his enchanting daughters. But Gautama remained unmoved. At last Māra accosted him and asked him what right he had to be here under the tree seeking Enlightenment. To this the Buddha replied, "This earth is witness to my right" and so saying "grounded" himself by touching the earth with his hand. As he did so, the earth thundered "I am the witness." At this the Evil One fled, and the Buddha was encircled by celestial beings, all rejoicing in his victory.

Here we see the *bodhi* tree in the center of the panel, and to its right are the defeated hosts of Māra, scrambling to get away in their panic-stricken confusion. On the left of the band are the calm and majestic celestial beings, a model of tranquil order compared with the energetic disarray of the demons.

This event is signified by the earth-touching posture (*bhūmisparsha mudrā*) in Buddhist iconography.

Northern Gate Architrave—Rear

☐ *SUJĀTĀ'S OFFERING* (Figure I.1)

At dawn on the day of the great Enlightenment Sujātā, the daughter of the king of Uruvelā, offered Gautama a dish of milk rice (*pāyasa*). The future Buddha broke his fast and accepted; this was the last meal that he took before entering *nirvāna*. At the extreme left of the panel you can see Sujātā, holding the tray of food in her left hand and a pitcher of water in her right, approaching the *bodhi* tree. On the right-hand side of the scene is another depiction of the hosts of Māra, who are portrayed with a Bosch-like intensity. As in the story of the temptation of the Christian Saint Anthony, these demons personify fears and negativity that have to be faced in the dark corners of the mind on the journey to self-knowledge.

☐ *THE VESSANTARA JĀTAKA* (Figure I.2)

A tale illustrating the virtue of generosity. In a previous life as Prince Vessantara, the Buddha was banished by his father from the court of Sibi because he had given away a magical elephant with the power to bring rain to some brahmins from the drought-stricken kingdom of Kalinga. He went to live in a forest hermitage with his wife, Maddi, and their two children. Sometime later the future Buddha was approached by some begging brahmins and gave away not only his children but also his wife! The gods were so pleased with his unstinting generosity that they intervened in the dispute between the prince and his father. As a result the future Buddha was reunited with his family and his kingdom.

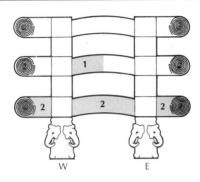

1 *Sujātā's Offering.* 2 *The* Vessantara jātaka.

Figure 1. Northern gate (rear view).

The panel is to be read from the right. At the end you can see the family arriving in the forest to begin their exile: a domestic scene with people weighing up fruit, sitting outside their huts. In the middle is the hermitage life; next the prince giving away his children; then giving away his wife; and finally, the reunion of the family and the journey back to the court. The detail on this gate is particularly fine. Indeed, the forest hermitage scenes are depicted especially well at Sānchī and in general elicit a very high standard in all periods of Indian art. At the time these gates were carved, the tribal life of northern India was giving way to a more urbanized and caste-ridden grouping; and organized work was replacing a more relaxed type of rural living. Much Buddhist art displays a nostalgia for a way of life that was fast disappearing, a stability that had existed since the time of the *Upanishads* and later, when Buddhism was well patronized and there were many communities of tranquil forest dwellers, Buddhist and otherwise, throughout northern India. This nostalgia was also evinced by the conscious imitation of earlier wooden architecture in the Buddhist rock-cut sanctuaries, such as Cave 10 at Ajantā (see Chapter 4).

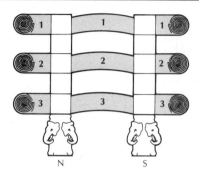

1 *The Mānushi* buddhas. **2** *The Buddha Worshipped by Animals.* **3** *The* Stūpa *of Rāmagrāma.*

Figure J. Eastern gate (rear view).

Eastern Gate Architrave—Rear

☐ *THE MĀNUSHI* BUDDHAS (Figure J.1)
The Mānushi *buddhas* (that is, the six *bodhisattvas* who were the immediate predecessors of Gautama) are a popular subject for the Sānchī artists; there are representations of them on each gateway, often covering a considerable portion of the architrave. We have seen that in Buddhist art the personal image is predated by the symbol. It can also be said that the symbol transcends the image metaphysically, because, being less personalized, it is less limited and is thus more readily identifiable with an archaic substratum of myth that has been operating in the folk consciousness since time immemorial. In accordance with this preference, the Mānushi *buddhas* are represented at Sānchī either by trees or by *stūpas*. As may be imagined, identification is not easy, though each of the *buddhas* has a particular tree for his symbol. The group is sometimes depicted by alternating trees and *stūpas* placed side by side; here on the top architrave they are shown by a row of trees alone. Notice that they are garlanded, just as trees, dignitaries, and holy men still are today.

☐ *THE BUDDHA WORSHIPPED BY ANIMALS* (Figure J.2)
One of the most endearing aspects of the *dharma* is its non-violence (*ahimsā*) and love of all life. Here the Master is being worshipped by the animal kingdom—parrots, cattle, water buffalo, camels, lions, dogs, deer, serpents, even the fabulous gryphons—another example of the minute and sympathetic observation that the Indian sculptor brought to

bear on his subject, in this case the animals he lived among and loved.

☐ *THE* STŪPA *OF RĀMAGRĀMA* (Figure J.3)

Our tour of Sānchī began with Ashoka; it also ends with him. One of the eight original *stūpas* was situated at Rāmagrāma, the royal seat of the Koliya clan. Ashoka is said to have opened up seven of these *stūpas* in order to redistribute their relics in *stūpas* he himself erected. But when he arrived at Rāma-grāma, he found that the mound was guarded by a fierce family of *nāgas*, who refused to let him desecrate the *stūpa*. The emperor and his retinue are shown to the right of the *stūpa*, the celestial serpents to its left. Together they repre-sent both the historical and the eternal guardians of the Master's teachings.

15
KHAJURĀHO
A HYMN
TO THE GODDESS

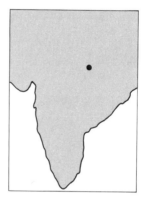

Khajurāho lies about 200 miles (320 kilometers) southeast of Delhi. Now it is a sleepy little town disturbed only by the daily planeload of tourists, but it was once the religious capital of the Chandella Rājputs, a tribal dynasty who ruled this part of India from the tenth to the twelfth centuries. At that time there were over eighty temples here, and the whole area was enclosed by a wall with eight gates, each flanked by two golden palm trees. It is possibly from the preponderance of these trees in the area that Khajurāho—"the road of the date palms"—got its name. Twenty-two of the temples remain, in various states of repair, scattered over an area of about eight square miles (twenty-one square kilometers).

Forgotten and unvisited until the mid-1960s, the place is now, after the Tāj, India's biggest single tourist attraction. It is also one of her greatest embarrassments, for Khajurāho has what is probably the world's greatest display of erotic sculpture.

These ancient temples are the source of one of the more delightful cultural ironies that abound in the meeting of East and West. The initial Occidental reaction to a place like Khajurāho is surprise. We are taken aback that a place of religious worship can be covered with a myriad of explicit carvings showing men and women making love, fondling each other and themselves, indulging in oral sex and even bestiality. This surprise is generally followed by a feeling of relief and then admiration that a religion can incorporate such all too human and enduring facts of life into its world picture. To Hinduism, everything is grist to the mill, and it goes up in our estimation because of its broadmindedness. "Aha!" says the Western intellectual. "Those wise old Hindus knew a thing or two. This art is the result of a mature attitude to life; it shows a lack of inhibition that we had arrogantly thought was the prerogative of our own, post-Freudian 'liberation.' Mmm, maybe I'll buy a copy of the *Kāma Sūtra* after all."

The educated Indian, however, tends to see things the other way around. He finds himself confused. On the one hand, he is heir to a tradition that took an unashamed delight in sexuality. Kāma (the Indian Eros) is a god and so is due worship as much as any other god. Khajurāho, the dozens of other erotic temples, the Hindu myths, and the profuse tradition of courtly miniature paintings all show us that sexuality has been a central and continuing concern of the culture. And this is right and proper, for to the Indian psyche, the very nature of existence is sexual—life is a ceaseless and creative exchange of energies, in which differences combine and mingle to produce ever new forms of the One. Nor is there any clear-cut distinction between the sexual and the sacred, because to the Hindu gods—like their ancient Greek counterparts—life is a celebration that Dionysius himself would have been proud of. Even in yoga and the philosophies of renunciation, the amoral yet potentially divine power of sexuality plays a central, if sublimated, role. Shiva, for example, is both the god of yoga and the wielder of the *linga* and its creative power.

So far so good. But on the other hand, the modern Indian finds his naturally fastidious temperament rebelling. This temperament has been sapped partly by traditional taboos of purity imposed by caste and partly by a Westernized and Victorian educational legacy. The result is that he is largely out of sympathy with the earthy energy of his ancestors, and all too often he affects a disdain for his own cultural heritage that he mistakenly assumes all Westerners share. This sense of discomfort is especially strong today, when the moral decadence of the West, with its groping permissiveness and soaring divorce rate, is the one thing the materially less developed East can feel superior about. It was only a couple of years ago that a kiss could be shown for the first time in an Indian film. This prohibition is all the more remarkable when you realize that Bombay is the world's biggest film capital, producing a film a day every day of the year! The sexual dalliances of the comely figures that cluster lithely around the walls of the temples of Khajurāho rather give the lie to the often voiced

Maithuna *couple, Lakshmana Temple.*

and quite erroneous cliché that the West has been concerned
with the material, while the East has been concerned with
the spiritual. The prevailing view among modern Hindus is
that the spiritual life entails austerity, celibacy, and renunciation. The Khajurāho couples, by contrast, celebrate the
wondrous pleasure of the material world and the joys of
sexuality.

As a confused reaction to these carvings, a prurience often
latent in the intellectual Hindu may raise its ugly head. Such
puritanism is nothing new. Some years ago, a former colleague
of Mahatma Gandhi stood up in Parliament and solemnly
suggested that the outsides of these temples be concreted
over, or at least walled round, so that their sculptures would
be hidden from view. That they were not was largely due to
the efforts of the Nobel Prize–winning poet Rabindranāth
Tagore. Although such singular philistinism is luckily the
exception rather than the rule, this unease about Khajurāho
still persists. Because it is explicit about sex, Khajurāho is
often seen as the all-too-fleshy skeleton in the country's
cultural closet. Officials in high places feel worried that the
foreigners might take too close an interest in these carvings
and conclude that India is not a land of moral purity and
conjugal fidelity. It is for this reason that a permit to photograph certain temples is limited to "general views only."

A similar fear haunts the man in the street. A typical
conversation at an airport or in a train, once it has been
established where one is from and how long one has been in
India, goes like this:

"And do you like India?"

"Oh yes!"

"Have you seen the Tāj Mahal?"

"Yes, I've been there."

"And, er, Khajurāho?"

The attempted nonchalance of the question is transparent. Since virtually every tourist answers yes, perhaps the Indians think that we Westerners are solely concerned in exploiting the East with our decadent and all-consuming desire for sexual titillation. Is the visitor to Khajurāho merely a slightly more highbrow version of the German factory workers who are flown into Bangkok by the regimented hundred each week to enjoy the delights of "Thai massage"? And is Khajurāho really no more than a medieval peep show for modern decadents and an unending source of revenue for dirty postcard sellers?

To begin with, it is worth remembering what is often forgotten: that the erotic scenes are only one of a number of subjects treated in the carvings. In fact, there are more elephants than lovers on the temple walls, and almost as many deities. Nevertheless, the whole question of the loving couples as a recurring theme in Indian art is an interesting one and worth looking at. From their beginnings, Hindu, Buddhist, and Jain shrines often featured auspicious couples (*mithunas*) among their carvings, especially near the entrances. These harked back to archaic fertility deities, and protected the temple from evil spirits by a type of sympathetic magic that evoked the abundance of nature. But what is the role of the erotic carvings (*shringāras*), in particular those loving couples locked together in sexual union (*maithuna*)?

Many explanations have been given for such figures. One book coyly suggests that the goddess of lightning was an innocent virgin, and the carvings acted as a sort of lightning repellent that worked by scaring her away with their explicitness. Another authority states that the languid ladies and copulating couples were a test of the monks' celibacy. Some say that the figures were a graphic reminder to the worshipper that he must leave all such earthly thoughts behind before he entered the temple's hallowed precincts. The most absurd explanation was one put forward by an all-too-serious European scholar. He claimed that the temples were built at a time when the population was in a serious decline, and the carvings were a sort of celestial sex education to show the people what they should do about their waning numbers! Surely a two-minute walk along any Indian street and a quick glance at the statistics—one baby born every thirty seconds nowadays—would convince even the most bookish of us that this is one area in which the Indians have always excelled!

Intellectual explanations such as these miss the point. Indian erotic art is dedicated to the senses, not the mind. It utilizes sensation as a way of teasing the mind out of thought and taking it to the bliss that lies beyond. This inner bliss is called *rasa*, which means "sap" or "essence," and is the legitimate goal of all artistic or spiritual endeavor according to the ancient treatises on esthetics. The senses must be so refined as to lead the mind to a state of pure feeling, which is beyond the individual ego and the constrictions of time. Erotic art uses the sensual as a path to the spiritual. Sex is a divine ritual to this end. As the expression of some of our most intense physical and emotional feelings, sexual love is an obvious path to divine awareness. Such an attitude is not exclusively Indian, of course. The Christian marriage service is talking about the same thing when the groom says to the bride: "With my body I thee worship."

But organized religion has a habit of stifling the joy it originally promoted. Khajurāho is the litany of an ancient faith that existed before the days of priests and prohibition. It is a hymn to those capricious gods that preside over beauty and pleasure, a celebration of the mysterious power the Indians call *shakti*.

Shakti is the life energy. Everything in the universe is the creation of *shakti*. All forms; everything in the past, present, and future is *shakti*'s play: created, maintained, and dissolved by *shakti*'s power.

Shakti creates through desire. The One desired to be many, and the whole creation arose out of this spark of desire. An ancient text from 600 B.C. tells how this act of creation took place:

> Pure Being, thinking to itself "May I become many, may I take form," created light. Light, thinking to itself "May I

Deity flanked by nymphs, symbolizing shakti, *Kandāriyā Mahādeva Temple.*

become many, may I take form," created the waters. And the waters, thinking to themselves "May I become many, may I take form," created the earth.

Chāndogya Upanishad

Shakti is female. She is Shiva's consort, the creative energy of the unmanifest Lord, personified as the deity of the same name. Shiva without Shakti is a corpse. Shakti is the goddess, Mother Nature, the feminine principle. India has always worshipped Shakti in her many forms: as Mā, the mother of all; as Pārvatī, the ideal wife; as Kālī, the destroyer; and Durgā, the terrible; or as Shrī, bringer of wealth and prosperity.

Shakti is incarnate in woman. It is woman who carries potential life within her, nurtures this new life when it is quickened, gives birth and sustains it, so perpetuating the family and tribe. The goddess Shakti is especially popular in the lush northeast of India, the part of the country which has most retained its aboriginal fertility cults. Even today India's

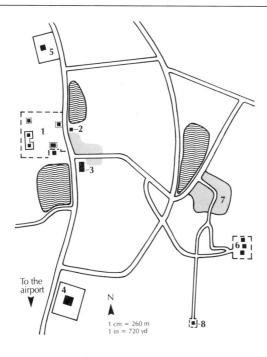

1 *Western group of temples (Hindu).* **2** *ITDC information office.* **3** *Archeological Survey Museum.* **4** *Hotel Chandella.* **5** *Ashok Travellers' Lodge (ITDC).* **6** *Eastern group of temples (Jain).* **7** *Khajurāho village.* **8** *Dūlādeo Temple.*

Figure A. Khajurāho.

tribal societies lead an uninhibited and natural sex life, in marked contrast to the taboos and prohibitions that enclose the behavior of a caste Hindu. It is significant that the Chandellas were a tribal dynasty, and thus comparatively unfettered in their enjoyment of the pleasures of life.

The goddess is worshipped in many ways, and her temples are as numerous as they are varied. Some are small wayside shrines, improvised under a holy tree or on top of a sacred rock daubed with vermilion and laid with incense and flowers. Some are magnificent buildings that have stood for years, protected by the maternal Nature whose glories they proclaim. And some are whole cities of such temples, each of which is dedicated to one aspect of the universal and infinitely varied Mother. It is this abundant female energy, stylized and refined into the courtly accomplishments of beauty, love, and creative arts that Khajurāho celebrates.

The temples of Khajurāho (see Figure A) can be conveniently divided into three groups: the western, eastern, and southern. We shall concentrate on the most important, the western group.

The Western Temples (Figure B) Ancient historical records tell us that the whole area now covered by the western group was originally a sacred lake, with the temples rising like the islands of the blessed above its waters. The lake has gone now, and the complex is green and lush, its buildings set in well-cared-for gardens, dotted here and there with brilliant bougainvillea. But the temples still stand on high plinths, restored versions of their original bases, and in the early morning it is not hard to imagine the time they were surrounded by water. As the sun rises, they loom out of the mist like fantastic galleons— unearthly godships laden with divine beings, their hulls encrusted with a vibrant honey-colored coral of strange deities and fabulous beasts.

We also know that Khajurāho was a center for Tantra, the ancient and esoteric religion that worships the goddess Shakti. The great tantric *guru* Gorakhnātha is said to have lived and taught here, and the fourteenth-century traveler Ibn Battūta writes of coming across tantric initiates:

> In the centre of that pond there are three cupolas of red sandstone each of three stories; and at the four corners of the pond are cupolas in which live a body of yogis who have clotted their hair and let it grow so that it becomes as long as their bodies; and on account of their practising asceticism their colour had become extremely yellow. Many Muslims follow them in order to take lessons from them.

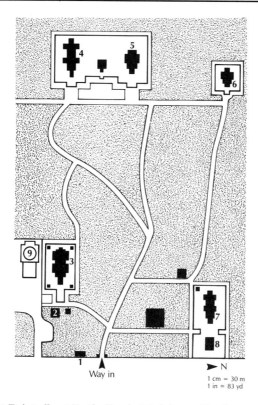

1 *Ticket office.* 2 *Varāha Temple.* 3 *Lakshmana Temple.*
4 *Kandāriyā Mahādeva Temple.* 5 *Jagadambī Temple.*
6 *Chitragupta Temple.* 7 *Vishvanātha Temple.* 8 *Nandin Pavilion.* 9 *Mātangeshvara Temple.*

Figure B. Western group of temples, site plan.

The jaundiced yogis may have gone, but their temples remain as one of the architectural wonders of the world, created with a loving virtuosity that will never again be seen on earth.

Varāha Temple, ca. A.D. 900 (Figure B.2)

This charming temple is dedicated to Vishnu, in his form of Varāha, the boar. Vishnu has ten major incarnations (*avatāras*), and whenever the world is in danger of being overrun by evil, he takes form to redress the balance and restore righteousness. Varāha was his third incarnation.

The story is that a demon, Hiranyāksha ("the Golden-eyed"), stole the earth and dragged it down to his lair in the underworld beneath the sea. The gods in heaven, alarmed that no one was left to offer them their customary worship, went to Vishnu and implored him to do something about it. Vishnu, renowned for his soft heart, agreed. He took the form of a boar. In this guise he was able to dive down through the oceans and reach the demon's kingdom. But the demon was cunning, and hid himself at the very depths of the nether-world. Varāha, however, using his tusks, was able to dig his way down. When he finally arrived, he found that the demon had created a thousand identical replicas of himself, each one goading Varāha to chase him. Once again the god's boar nature came to the rescue. Using his powerful sense of smell, he was able to sniff out the real Hiranyāksha and destroy him.

The same text describes Varāha: "His shoulders were round, fat and large; he strode along like a powerful lion; his haunches were fat, his loins slender and his body was smooth and beautiful."

Whoever sculpted the figure of Varāha that fills this shrine managed to capture this mixture of strength and grace. The figure is carved out of a highly polished sandstone. The earli-est temple on the site (the Temple of the Sixty-four Goddesses) was made of the local granite. This proved too hard for the fineness of carving the builders wanted, so soft sandstone from Panna—about fifty miles (eighty kilometers) away—was used. Figures such as this were probably carved at the quar-ries and then carefully transported to the site.

The boar's massiveness is relieved by the hundreds of tiny gods and goddesses that cover it. Here Varāha is a version of an archaic and universal symbolic convention of portraying creation as the multiple offspring of a single animal or cosmic being. Figures such as this can be found in the art of civili-zations as far distant as Celtic Europe and the Polynesian islands.

As a form of the all-pervading Vishnu, Varāha is Lord of the Three Worlds—the realms of water, earth, and heaven. By his feet are the watery beings, such as the crocodile, next come humans, and finally the gods and goddesses. On his jaws sit the nine planets (five on one side, four on the other), and on his snout is Sarasvatī, patron goddess of artistic creativity, who is the Indian equivalent of Minerva in Western mythology. Between the boar's legs lies the cosmic serpent Shesha, on whose head the world rests. The broken feet belong to a sadly missing figure of the earth goddess, Prithivī, grate-fully worshipping her savior. Above Varāha there is an exqui-sitely carved lotus ceiling.

All these figures—boar, serpent, earth goddess, lotus—are, of course, symbols of the elemental energy and creative drive of subconscious depths of the mind. As such, they represent the power of *shakti*, in both her human and cosmic phases.

The Varāha tableau is both an astonishingly satisfying symbol and a beautifully realized piece of monolithic sculptural art.

☐

Although each temple here is dedicated to a different deity, such as Vishnu or Shiva, each of these deities expresses its own particular nature through the creative energy of *shakti*. This expression takes the form of the deity's consort. Generally speaking, the deity is male and passive, while the consort, as the embodiment of *shakti*, is female and active. Thus Vishnu's creative nature is expressed through his consort Lakshmī, Shiva's through Pārvatī or Kālī, and so on. And, as we have just seen, Vishnu also manifests through his ten incarnations. If you are having difficulty following this complicated mythology, just remember that all these characters are different aspects of the one godhead. Each mythological figure represents one facet of the divine *shakti*.

Often the only way of identifying the deity to which a temple is dedicated is by looking at the cult image in the sanctum. Architecturally, the temples here are very similar, all conforming to a pattern that is the classical model of the medieval temple in northern India, in what is known as the *nagara* or Indo-Āryan style.

☐ THE FORM OF THE TEMPLE

The lofty yet compact buildings are raised on an elevated plinth that forms an ambulatory terrace around the temple. They are all aligned on an east-west axis and so designed to admit the early morning light into the sanctuary. The basic interior design is also uniform and its essential elements (see Figure C) are present in all the temples. These consist of entrance porch (*ardha mandapa*), hall (*mandapa*), vestibule (*antarāla*), and sanctum (*garbha-griha*). Though the smaller temples have just this, the larger ones have additional transepts, terminating in balconied windows. These

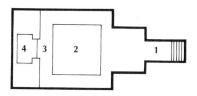

1 *Entrance porch* (ardha mandapa). **2** *Hall* (mandapa).
3 *Vestibule* (antarāla). **4** *Sanctum* (garbha-griha).
Figure C. Ground plan of typical Khajurāho temple.

transepts were sometimes added as later enlargements of an existing temple. They extend the basic hall into a "great hall" (*mahāmandapa*). Larger temples also have an ambulatory passage around the main shrine, which necessitates another transept with windows for ventilation and light.

Thus the full temple forms a Latin cross in plan. A further embellishment in the later temples is the addition of a subsidiary shrine at each corner of the platform. This creates what is called the "five-shrine complex" (*pancharatha*), of which a good example is the Lakshmana Temple (see Figure D).

The four subsidiary shrines were built to house different forms (or consorts) of the principal deity and to govern the four directions and the four elements—earth, water, fire, and air. They thus reenact the archaic rite of orientation that divides the cosmos into its center (the main temple) and the four quarters.

□ THE CARVINGS

Cult Images These occupy the sanctum and are carved in the round, according to iconographical conventions.

Deities These are to be found in the niches around the temple walls, and include the "Guardians of the Eight Directions" (i.e. the four quarters and their midpoints), which are set at the appropriate corners of the building. These *dikpālas* are often shown with animal heads, spectacular headdresses, and carrying their attributes, usually in two hands. They may be accompanied by their vehicles—for example, Shiva holds a trident and a drum and is accompanied by his bull, Nandin.

Heavenly Nymphs These delightful creatures are the most numerous of the figures at Khajurāho and can be found on outer or inner walls, pillars, and ceilings. They are known as *alasa kanyās*, —"languid maidens," or *apsarases*, "heavenly nymphs." They are shown in a variety of postures: dancing, at their toilet, bathing, and so on. They represent all the varieties of traditionally feminine activity and feeling in a graceful and elegant manner, and are the celestial attendants at the courts of the gods.

Secular Figures These include couples standing together (*mithuna*), couples amorously entwined (*maithuna*), as well as scenes of dancers, military life, teachers and disciples, musicians, and so on. The secular figures are found widely distributed.

Vyālas These are fabulous beasts of heraldic and symbolic importance. One of the most common is a leogryph (*shār-*

dūla), or rampant horned lion, bearing an armed warrior and often shown in combat.

Abstract and Geometrical Motifs These are found all over the site. Often overlooked, they provide a fine contrast to the wealth of naturalistic sculpture.

Subsidiary figures are often enclosed in an ornate niche called a *mundi* (see page 373).

Lakshmana Temple, ca. A.D. 950 (Figure D)

This is the earliest and best preserved of the large temples, and the only one with all its subsidiary shrines intact.

□ *INTERIOR*

The entrance is flanked by an arch composed of mythical sea dragons (*makara torana*), similar in design to the Jain marble architecture of western India—for example, at Mount Ābū. These creatures are the guardians of the treasures of the deep. The ceiling of the entrance porch is deeply worked with intricate cusping in the shape of an opened lotus blossom (D.2). These ornate carvings in the entrance portion give way to a darkened inner chamber, which at first seems plain and angular by contrast. But as we grow accustomed to the light, the wonders of the place reveal themselves, emerging like hesitant creatures out of the shadows.

The raised platform in the middle of the hall would have been used for dancing and tantric sexual rituals in praise of the deity. Such rituals were not orgies but the culmination of many years' discipline in esoteric practices, under the supervision of a *guru*. Until the early years of this century many temples kept *devadāsīs* ("slaves of God"), women whose role it was to be the female partner in such rituals. However, it must be admitted that the more the genuine tantric practices declined, the more the *devadāsī* became a very unspiritual source of revenue for lazy priests and crumbling temples.

At each corner of the platform are pillars with excellently carved brackets around their capitals. Celestial musicians and *apsarases* beam down joyfully on the worshippers below. Some of them have holes clearly visible in the chest or stomach, which reveal the original technique of construction. At one time there were other figures, attached to them by iron rods that fitted in the holes. In fact the basic Hindu method of joining socketed blocks of stone with interlocking iron dowels was the only one employed at Khajurāho. No mortar, cement, or plaster was used in India until the coming of the Muslims in the twelfth century. There are eight figures on each column, representing the eight sects of Tantra, and the doorway to the holy of holies (D.4) is framed by 108 figures, symbolic of

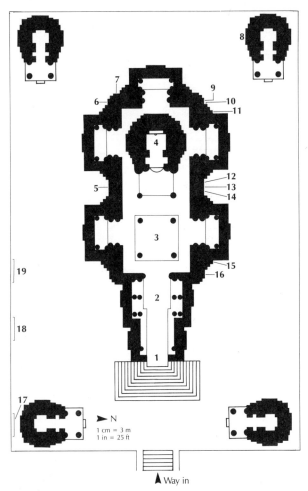

Interior. 1 *Entrance arch.* **2** *Entrance porch ceiling.*
3 *Columns and platform.* **4** *Sanctum.*

Exterior. 5 Maithuna *couple (lower register); attendants
(upper register).* **6** *Lady applying* tikka *(lower register); lady
with a ball (upper register).* **7** Nāgarāja *(lower register).*
8 *Ganesha (lower register); yogi (upper register).* **9** *Lady
removing thorn (lower register).* **10** *Lady drying herself
(lower register).* **11** *Lady painting (lower register).*
12 *Couple and monkey (upper register).* **13** Maithuna *couple
(upper register); Lady applying* tikka *(lower register).*
14 *Drunken couple (upper register).* **15** *Lady writing letter
(lower register).* **16** *Lady playing flute (lower register).*

Plinth. 17 *Orgy scene.* **18** *Man and horse.* **19** *The* guru *and
his disciples.*

Figure D. Lakshmana Temple ground plan.

the 108 techniques of stilling the mind taught by Shiva to his consort Pārvatī in the ninth-century tantric text the *Shiva Sūtra*. Thus the devotee was always reminded that the movement from the outside to the sanctum of the temple was an analogue of the descent into the depths of his own being. The image at the heart of the temple is a three-headed and four-armed Vishnu, with a human central head and the side heads of a boar and a lion. While such images would be the focus of common worship, like all Hindu art they served different purposes at different levels. Thus the initiates would contemplate this Vishnu to awaken its archetype in their own psyche. Such visions were considered milestones on the path to enlightenment.

□ EXTERIOR

The outsides of the temple are covered with hundreds of carvings—humans, divines, animals, abstract geometric and floral motifs. These designs follow an ascending sequence: the bottom layer of carving is a lotus-leaf design; then come floral motifs; then sea creatures (the guardians of the deep); then elephants (the symbols of stability and royalty often found "supporting" temple walls); and finally the human-divine figures who form two registers of frieze around the bulding. So the whole of creation is represented here: the vegetable, aquatic, animal, human, and divine realms. The elephant frieze, at shoulder height, is particularly worth study; each noble animal is different, and carved with loving attention to detail.

□ SOUTH FACE

Lower Register (Figure D.5)   The central panel presents a typical Khajurāho theme: a loving couple (*maithuna*) surrounded by celestial nymphs. These languid beauties are the most numerous sculptures here. They are shown either as attendants of the gods, bearing offerings to their masters, or as idealizations of femininity, enacting all a woman's daily rituals: washing, brushing their hair, beautifying themselves, making love, playing music, and so on. In both roles they are the personifications of *shakti*, the eternal creative energy that manifests through the female principle. These figures display an innocent grace and charm, and their movements and emotions have been unerringly captured by the sculptors' skill.

Although blackened by rain mold, these figures are worth close study. The central panel shows a couple entwined in close embrace. Oblivious to all but each other, they radiate an intense absorption, and seem to be melting into one another. This absorption is a characteristic of the Khajurāho couples, who illustrate the description of the spiritual state found in the *Brihadāranyaka Upanishad* (800 B.C.): "As a man in the embrace of his beloved wife is distracted by nothing, either without or within, so one in the embrace of the Universal Self is distracted by nothing, either without or within."

And notice how the woman is stretching up on tiptoe to reach her lover—a beautiful detail. They are flanked on the right by an attendant who, absent-mindedly fingering herself, seems to be joining in the fun, and on the left by another damsel, enviously casting a glance over her shoulder at the couple.

Following this frieze around to the left, you come to a woman gracefully combing out her hair with a flowing elegance. At the extreme left is another woman, her supple body bent backward in what could be a posture of yoga or dance training. This fluid movement of the body is a hallmark of Chandella sculpture, and something you will see much more of.

Upper Register (Figure D.5)   The central panel is also flanked by two figures. On the left, immediately above the lady combing her hair on the lower band, is a woman at her toilet, scrubbing her long leg with a bathbrush. Her opposite number is combing her hair in a natural and graceful manner.

All these figures radiate an elastic vitality; they are flowing with the sap of life. The whole lower part of the temple seems positively to writhe with lively movement, as each of the myriad figures sinuously twists and turns in a different and complementary direction to its neighbor.

One important feature of these temples is that sculpture and architecture blend into each other. The dividing line between them is totally blurred; one cannot say where one ends and the other begins. In fact, this fusion has been traditonally criticized by Western art critics, who claim that Indian buildings are too concerned with decoration and ignore the architectural considerations of light, space, proportion, and so on. But Indian architecture is above all sacred architecture, and thus always has a purpose that is more important than mere esthetic considerations. The Indian temple is not primarily concerned with form, or even functional convenience. Its principal aim is to create the cosmos in miniature by following the rules of sacred geometry, and thence to create a particular emotional effect on the beholder, thereby transforming the consciousness of all who see or enter it. Often the intended effect is to communicate a realization of the overwhelming power and diversity of the divine, the irrepressible creative *shakti* with which the One creates the many. This diversity includes not only the gross world of matter perceptible to our senses, but the subtle realms as well. To give us a vision of this diversity the Indian artist or sculptor will relentlessly pile image upon image, figure upon figure, in order to be true to the reality he is trying to express. It is the *feeling* of this reality, as much as a naturalistic representation of it, that Indian art tries to convey. So one of the aims of temples like these at Khajurāho is to give us a glimpse into the celestial abodes of what the Bible calls "the angels, archangels and all the company of heaven." In realizing this aim, the form and function of the Khajurāho temples unite triumphantly.

Lower Register (Figure D.6)   Two beautiful figures flank the deity on the end of this wall. One is a woman looking into a mirror and applying a *tikka*—the colored dot—to the middle of her forehead. Her whole body is bent back and her arm stretches over the top of her head with a serpentine grace. This supple posture allows us to see her face and the rest of her body, which would have been shielded from view if she had appeared in conventional position. As it is, the sculptural necessity has created a lithe and sensuous figure. The flesh too is molded carefully here and has a soft tactile quality as it folds gently around her navel.

On the other side of the standing deity is a woman whose face radiates bliss. Eyes closed, lips parted, she is the embodiment of *ānanda*—that feeling of sheer joy, which to the Indian is the true end of all sensual or spiritual endeavor.

To the right of this woman is a loving couple. Again, the taut and elastic tension of flesh is well caught in the figure of the woman, whose back is arched backward over the man's waist, her face twisted round to meet his. And again, there is a delicate little crease of skin under her breasts as she twists round. The firm fullness of the lovers' limbs is also very graceful and conforms to the Indian ideal of beauty.

Like the lady with the *tikka*, the figure has been carved to expose the maximum amount of body surface, and create a posture which, at the same time, conveys the greatest intensity of feeling. These creations show an uncanny marriage of form and content.

Can such charming figures really be called pornographic? Pornography seeks to stimulate the observer and is a manipulative art, devoid of innocence and emotionally flat. These figures are absorbed in pleasure yet they retain an innocence. They seem to belong to a blissful and timeless world, a sensuous eternity; their passion is without tension or compulsion; it is totally unneurotic. No matter how absorbed the bodies may be, the faces are serene and detached in their expression. It is worth mentioning that the men are very rarely shown with full erections in an attempt to arouse or shock the spectator, but are usually depicted in a state of semi-arousal that is languid and quite free of urgency.

Pornography leers knowingly at the camera, but these relaxed and natural lovers are quite unaware of us. We are like visitors from another, more inhibited planet, eavesdropping on their daily rituals of beautification and pleasure. Their sightless eyes look right through us, for we are invisible to their refined and sensuous world. The hosts of Khajurāho are the embodiments of the divine force of desire (*rati*), the courtly entourage of Kāma, god of love. As such they dwell at a higher level than us, inhabiting those celestial realms that are bathed in the limpid light of pure feeling.

Upper Register (Figure D.6)   Immediately above the lady with the *tikka* is the figure of a woman playing with a ball. Like her companion below, this nymph's body is a supple bend, displaying the soft fleshy molding of her back. The back is arched, the buttocks thrust out. This impishly charming posture has a structural as well as decorative purpose. It continues the line of the *tikka* lady below, serving to lead the eye around the corner of the building, drawing you round the temple. Again, the form is the function.

Lower Register (Figure D.7)   Here there is a fine, unbroken serpent king (*nāgarāja*), with five snake heads coiling above him. A symbol of the power of *shakti* energy, which at one level is expressed as sexuality and at a higher level as spiritual experience. The philosophy of Tantra is to use the former to achieve the latter. A tantric maxim goes: "Use the senses to go beyond the senses."

☐ *NORTHWEST SHRINE—SOUTH FACE* (Figure D.8)
On the first register here there is a lovely Ganesha panel. Ganesha is the elephant-headed son of Shiva, a much loved domestic deity. Temples will always have a few Ganeshas dotted round. Usually he is shown seated; this panel has him standing in a portly way, perhaps about to break into a dignified dance. He holds cornucopias in each hand, which, like his potbelly, signify material well-being and comfort. There is a fine realistic detail here too; Ganesha's weight is thrown onto his right leg, which is taut with the strain, his little fingernails are delicately etched into the stone, and his trunk is rakishly curled.

Above Ganesha is an extraordinary panel. Only about eight inches (twenty centimeters) square, this eloquent cameo depicts a yogi surrounded by attendants. To judge from the *rudrāksha* beads around his neck, he is a devotee of Shiva. This sage has an expression of utterly peaceful detachment. He looks past us with an unbroken serenity, free from the bonds of pleasure, dispassionate. He has reached the goal of Tantra and lives in enlightenment.

Mundi *niche, Khajurāho style.*

The honey-colored stone of the side temple is well preserved. Among its carvings are some good standing figures interspersed with dragons, and also a frieze of jovial musicians. Above the sage we can see clearly a type of abstract design that is common at Khajurāho but often too high up to be seen easily. It is the *gavāksha* or *kūdu* design and derives from the *chaitya* windows on the facades of Buddhist rock-cut temples.

☐ *NORTH FACE*
This side of the temple repeats many of the themes we have already seen. The following details are especially remarkable.

Lower Register (Figure D.9)   Here a woman is having a thorn taken out of her foot. It seems to be a recurring problem with the Khajurāho nymphs!

Lower Register (Figure D.10)   In the corner stands an *apsaras* drying herself after her bath. Despite being damaged, this is an exceptionally fine piece. There is once more liveliness in the way her rippling back arches. Her *sārī,* tucked well up above her knees, emphasizes this effect, stretched taut and clinging over her wet buttocks. The contours of the cloth are finely etched as lines running across her body, similar to the Gandhāran Buddhist sculptures a thousand years earlier. And once more you have the timeless aspect of India: You can see women in just this pose and dress every day at any tank or by any lake in the country.

Apsaras *drying herself, Lakshmana Temple.*

Upper Register (Figure D.12)   Here in the corner, an amorous couple is disturbed by a monkey. As well as being a humorous incident, the sculpture has an esoteric meaning. In Indian thought and art, the monkey often symbolizes the mind, which is ever restless—jumping from one thing to another as the monkey leaps from branch to branch. Here the teaching is that the mind must be transcended, otherwise it will "interfere" with the ecstasy of sensual love, the object of which is to reach a state of bliss beyond the limited individual ego.

Upper Register (Figure D.13)   The middle panel shows a beautiful *maithuna* couple. One of the partners is poised with the right hand elegantly shaped in an esoteric gesture (*mudrā*), another allusion to tantric ritual.

Lower Register (Figure D.13)   Below the couple is another lady applying her *tikka*. This mark is still worn today as a beauty spot, often matching the color of the *sārī*. Originally, so the story goes, a Rājput chief going to battle would cut his thumb and mark all his women on the forehead with his blood, so he could recognize them when he returned. It is not, as sometimes thought, a caste mark, but esoterically, as when given by the priest at a temple, it signifies the third eye of wisdom. It is popularly regarded as a protection from the evil eye.

Upper Register (Figure D.14)   In the left-hand corner is a carousing couple. Perhaps they are tantric initiates who have overdone the ritual intoxicant *soma*. Their staggering gait is a lovely piece of satire.

Lower Register (Figure D.15)   At the end of the frieze is a woman writing a love letter. Her expression has been caught as she smiles pensively while composing some alluring invitation to her lover.

Further along this lower register stands a flute player (D.16), her back turned toward us. Here, the detail is superb. Even her fingers are shown, curling around the holes of the flute, and we can make out the ornaments on her hand.

Next to the musician stands Shiva, and on his other side another *apsaras*, painting with a small brush on a canvas. These ladies are the members of a celestial court, where the accomplishments of music, art, and lovemaking play as important a part as they did in its earthly counterpart.

□ *PLINTH*

If a temple was built to the glory of the gods, it was also intended to commemorate their glorious representative on earth, the king. The daily life of the monarch and his armies forms an important subject of the temple carvings. We have an exceptionally well-preserved example of this type of narrative in the frieze around the plinth of the Lakshmana.

Circumambulating the temple base clockwise, we come to the royal insignia of the Chandella dynasty, a magnificent dragon-lion, often shown fighting a man. The frieze at head height depicts the social history of the time in a lively manner. It includes erotic scenes—the participants displaying more energy than subtlety; sages with hair coiled up on their heads; camels, elephants, and horses and all the paraphernalia of an army on the march; and musicians with flutes, drums, and dancers. Particularly remarkable in this Rabelaisian tableau are an orgy scene (D.17) and the man with the horse (D.18). Whether this sculpture was a warning of what happens to soldiers in a campaign who go too long without rest and recreation, or whether such horsing around was an accepted part of Chandella sexual life, we don't know. But at least the figure covering his eyes does not approve of what is going on! Interestingly, there are no depictions of homosexuality in these carvings.

Farther along is a superb group, the *guru* and his disciples (Figure D.19). The potbellied teacher sits surrounded by his attendants: one fanning him, one with refreshments, another carrying a notebook. In front of him sit the disciples, with long hair and beards to show their status. They are also wearing meditation belts that go around the knees as a support, a common iconographic feature in early sculpture.

The guru *and his disciples, plinth of Lakshmana Temple.*

As always in such detailed carving, the Indian sculptor showed his love of animals. Some of these, particularly the young elephants on the west face of the plinth, are rendered with a loving observation that reminds us of the achievement of such places as Sānchī. It is an ivory carver's skill transposed to stone.

Vishvanātha Temple (Figure B.7)

☐ *ARCHITECTURE*

The next stage in the development of the Khajurāho temples can best be seen in the Vishvanātha Temple. This was completed in A.D. 1002 and thus comes between the Lakshmana and the later Kandāriyā Mahādeva in both time and architectural style. As such, it is an interesting anticipation of the greatest of the Khajurāho temples, the Kandāriyā.

Approaching the Vishvanātha you can get a clear idea of the exterior lines of the Chandella temple. As well as being mounted on a lofty terrace, the building has an unusually high basement story. This is finely molded and provides a dramatic relief surface for the play of light and shade. It allows a striated effect that prevents the stone from appearing too monumental and unattractively heavy.

The stable base gives way to the walls of the temple. They form the central "body" of the building. The surface is fluted horizontally by bands of carving, and broken by the balcony porches. The carved bands, as well as containing the beautiful figures we have just seen, make full use of alternating projections and recesses, which give the surface a vitality and lightness.

Above the walls rises the fourth portion of the temple, the roof. This consists of a series of graded peaks that rise rhythmically to their summit like a range of mountains stretching to a peak. In fact, in the texts on architecture, the Hindu temple is often likened to a mountain because the mountains are the abode of the gods. The mountain is sacred in all religious traditions, as a place of spiritual power and pilgrimage, and to the Hindu, Mount Meru is the center of the universe and the home of Lord Shiva. The devotee, in going to the temple, undertakes a pilgrimage in lieu of actually visiting the Himālayan shrines.

☐

Each portion of the Khajurāho temple—entrance porch, hall, vestibule, and sanctuary—has its separate roof. These rise from the lowest over the entrance to the highest over the sanctum. Whereas the roofs of the first three parts are pyramid-shaped, composed of a series of tiers ascending to a peak, the roof over the sanctum is a taller spire (*shikhara*), curvilinear in shape. This rises elegantly upward, its ascending motion emphasized by the fact that whereas the other parts of the roof are layered with horizontal tiers, the *shikhara* has vertical bands that carry the eye upward. Each roof culminates in a *kalasha*, a pot-shaped finial, which as an ancient symbol of fertility signifies both material and spiritual well-being. The finial of the *shikhara* spire is supported

Vishvanātha Temple.

on a fine ribbed "cushion" (*amlā*), whose multiple segments contrast pleasingly with the plainer surfaces of the spire below (see Figure F). The *kalasha* and *amlā* have esoteric significance. The *kalasha* is said to contain *soma*, the nectar of immortality, and is situated in the human nervous system at the crown of the head. It is intimately connected with the "thousand-petaled lotus," the highest *chakra*, here symbolized by the lotiform *amlā* member. This derives its name from the *āmalaka* fruit not only because of the physical resemblance between the two but because the *āmalaka* fruit is used extensively in yogic diet to stimulate the nervous system into the subtle glandular and chemical activity associated with the production of *soma*. The flow of *soma* through the nervous system brings longevity, joy, and unassailable calm. When we remember that the temple is a microcosmic replica of the Cosmic Man (*mahāpurusha*) who creates the universe by self-sacrifice, and who is, in the human realm, especially represented by the yogi, the complex interlocking layers of symbolism operating in the form of the temple are exposed. It should perhaps be added that this yogic symbolism acts as a counterpoint to the basic symbolic themes of mountain, cave, and cosmic axis discussed in Chapter 1.

Originally a five-shrine temple, the Vishvanātha now has only two of its subsidiary shrines standing. The temple is dedicated to Shiva (*Vishvanātha* means "Lord of All") and enshrines a *linga*. According to the inscription built into the wall of the *mandapa*, two *linga* were dedicated when the temple was completed: one of stone and one of pure emerald. Perhaps not surprisingly, only the stone one remains.

The ceilings of the entrance porch are especially fine here, crystalline *mandalas* rendered in stone tracery. The sculptures on and inside the temple are up to the high standard set by the Lakshmana. Particularly impressive are the divine couples and a flute player inside the *mandapa*, and an *apsaras* plucking a thorn from her foot on the outer southern facade.

Nandin Pavilion (Figure B.8)

This stands opposite the entrance to the Vishvanātha. Nandin, "the Joyous," is Shiva's vehicle and worshipped along with his master. The worship of the bull goes back to the very beginnings of Indian history. Seals with a sacred bull have been found among the ruins of the Indus Valley civilization which dates from 2500 B.C. Like his counterpart Apis in ancient Egypt, Nandin has always been an important deity, particularly for the followers of Shiva. Like Varāha, he represents the procreative energy of *shakti* and the fertile power of the subconscious mind. Nandin is the embodiment of what the Indians call *prakriti*, or nature, the material counterpart to the pure spirit, or *purusha*.

Nandin is said to be as white as snow, with broad shoulders, sleek haunches, and a black tail. His horns are hard as diamonds, and he is decorated with a golden girth. Nandin represents instincts, especially sex. But Shiva rides on the bull and is the master of lust.

Tantra teaches that the yogi must emulate Shiva by sublimating (not repressing) sex energy and harnessing its power to attain spiritual ends.

There is tremendous latent energy in this highly polished sandstone figure. With his flared nostrils, eyes gazing up at the peak of the *shikhara*, and heavy, solid flanks, he is massive and awesome. Yet there are touches of delicacy about him, too, in the garlands draped around his neck and back, his gently curving tail and little hooves, and the embellishment over his ears. The decorative scrolls and meanders on his harnessing could come from Celtic art. The bells on his brow and the dragon-head motifs around his body also signify the power of the subconscious impulses, and his protruding testicles are obvious fertility symbols. Devotees, especially women wanting children, still touch these respectfully today; in some temples they are painted red and garlanded and receive impromptu offerings.

Kandāriyā Mahādeva Temple (Figure E)

Completed in about 1030, this is the most fully developed and impressive of the temples. It is also the largest. Dedicated to Shiva, the Kandāriyā continues the development started by the Vishvanātha, but on a grander scale. The basement is loftier and more molded, the roof rises in greater scale and ornamentation, and it has three full bands of carved sculpture running around the walls, producing the largest number of recesses and projections of any of the temples. The Kandāriyā is one of the most sublime achievements of Indian architecture.

As you approach the temple, you can see quite clearly how it mimics the mountain range, as the molded horizontal layers (*bhūmis*) ascend in stages to the peak. The stratified layers give the stone the effect of shimmering; the whole temple seems to be composed of pure, vibrating energy. The doorway is a dark cave, which, fringed by its deeply cusped arch, is like some cosmic *yoni* that promises death and rebirth. The building is designed to draw the worshipper like an irresistible magnet, its every line leading us inward and upward.

At the bottom of the stairs are bushes of *datura* plant, a powerful hallucinogenic drug used in tantric rituals. Its flowers, moist with sap, are offered to Shiva.

*Kandāriyā
Mahādeva Temple.*

You pass into the temple under minutely worked arches and ceilings. The inner ceilings were carved as echo chambers to reverberate the sacred chants, and send intoned *mantras* humming around the hall, but this effect was lost when the building was enlarged and the balconies added.

As you step onto the platform within, the main shrine is framed before you as a tall rectangle of darkened space. The line of the pillars, the door frame, the steps up from the vestibule, all lead the attention to converge on the upright *linga* gleaming in the darkness. The clean lines create a disciplined, purifying effect, which cuts out inessentials, spatially and psychologically. The supreme and abstract symbol, the *linga,* points beyond itself, to that which transcends all form. Its role as a mediator to the divine reality is very clearly stated in tantric texts, as in the following passage from Karapātrī's *Lingopāsanā-rahasya:*

> Those who do not recognise the divine nature of the phallus, who do not measure the importance of the sex ritual, who consider the act of love as low or contemptible or a mere physical function, are bound to fail in their attempts at physical as well as spiritual achievement. To ignore the sacredness of the *linga* is dangerous, whereas through its worship the joy of life and the joy of liberation are both obtained.

The passage around the sanctum is marbled by shifting light and shadows reflected from deeply indented walls. The

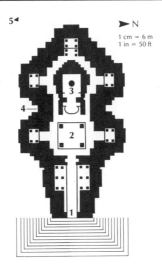

1 *Entrance doorway.* 2 *Dance platform.* 3 Linga. 4 Vajroli
scene (lower register). 5 *Viewpoint for* shikhara.

Figure E. Kandāriyā Mahādeva Temple ground plan.

place is bathed in the luminescence of the forest, where all
such shrines originated long ago. The real merges into the
dream; the mind begins to float.

You return from the darkness along the tunneled entrance,
to be reborn into the light of day. Emerging barefoot, you
walk again on holy ground.

☐ *EXTERIOR*

The figures on the Kandāriyā are more elongated than those
on the other temples; the emphasis here is on sinuously
tapering limbs and slender bodies. Each decorative band is
crammed with figures, stretching and unfurling themselves
like the petals of a flower teased into life by the warm rays of
the sun.

Yet despite the exuberant profusion of its detail, the wall as
a whole has a unified cohesion of design, akin to that of the
great Gothic cathedrals in Europe. This cohesion is an integral part of the architect's skill. It is partly achieved by the
fact that the figures all move in complementary directions. If
one bends to the left, her neighbor inclines to the right; if
one stoops, another stretches, and so on. The overall structure of the sculpted surfaces is as carefully orchestrated as
its details. Thus the movement of the figures is always
contained and ordered within a framework of balanced horizontal and vertical tensions. Whereas the standing figures of

Vajroli *scene, Kandāriyā Mahādeva Temple.*

the carved friezes carry the eye soaring upward, their vertical thrust is always balanced by the horizontal movement of the bands of decorative carving that run in layers around the building. The resolution of these two complementary tensions is masterly. Naturalistic figures are interspersed with abstract decorative designs, many of them reminiscent of Mayan or Celtic art. Moreover, the almost incessant movement of the wall surfaces is broken periodically by the open porches of the balconies with their overhanging eaves. These act to provide a temporary resting place for the attention. As a result, the effect is never one of overcrowding or busy-ness.

What is usually not understood is that many of these sculptures are an esoteric code, full of meaning to the initiated. Let us look at one such panel on the south face of the temple.

□ *THE VAJROLI SCENE* (Figure E.4)
At first glance, this extraordinary *maithuna* sculpture on the bottom register looks like a remarkable piece of sexual gymnastics. The woman, supported by her attendants, straddles her partner who is standing on his head. Not only does he seem to be thoroughly enjoying this (literally) mind-blowing experience, but he is so at ease that he is casually fondling the *yonis* of his lover's attendants at the same time! The panel is intricately composed. Despite the fact that it is damaged and the attendants' legs are missing, there is balance and feeling here. The way the woman carefully arches her back, and the way she is just lightly resting her arms on her attendants' shoulders while carefully lowering her full weight onto her partner's upturned body is conveyed with extraordinary skill.

But there is another level of meaning to this accomplished "sexercise." Tantra teaches that within the human body there is a finer, subtle body, made of an extremely refined type of matter, imperceptible to the gross senses. This body is the seat of thought and emotions, and conveys the life energy to the gross body. Life energy (*prāna*) is conducted along thousands of very subtle nerves (*nādīs*). There are three principal *nādīs*: called *idā*, *pingalā*, and *sushumnā*, of which the most important is the *sushumnā*. In the *vajroli* technique, the male partner controls the movement of his semen, which is the most concentrated form of the life energy in the gross body. Instead of ejaculating as in normal orgasm, he draws the subtle *shakti* energy that would normally manifest as semen up through his subtle body, along the *sushumnā nādī*, which runs along the inside of the spinal column. When this energy reaches the top of the head, it connects with the highest subtle energy center (*chakra*), the "thousand-petaled lotus." All thought, desire, and individuality are transcended; there is only the bliss of inner union.

In order to convey this abstract teaching, the sculptors of Khajurāho, acting on instructions from the tantric teachers, put it into pictorial form. The three female figures represent the three *nādīs*; the attendants are the *idā* and *pingalā*, while the lady in the middle is the *sushumnā*. In order to show that in *vajroli* the normal downward direction of the life energy leaving the body during orgasm is reversed, the male figure has been inverted. The *vajroli* scene is an extraordinary example of the esoteric and artistic sophistication of ancient Indian culture.

□ *THE SHIKHARA* (Figure E.5)
From the corner of the plinth you can get a clear idea of the development of the *shikhara*. Whereas the simple *shikhara*

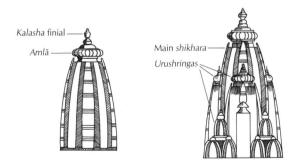

Figure F. Development of the shikhara.

was a tall, comparatively unadorned spire topped by the *kalasha* finial, by the time of the Kandāriyā, the architects had sufficient skill and self-confidence to develop what they had already achieved in earlier buildings. They sought to cover the spire with miniature replicas of itself. These replicas (*urushringas*) cluster round the seven segments of the cubical block on which the main *shikhara* rests (see Figure F). As they rise, they become more elongated to accentuate the upward thrust of the spire. The result is a surging and rhythmical movement, which culminates triumphantly in the finial that crowns the temple. You have already seen how the *kalasha* and *amlā* members allude to the yogic teaching on the subtle body, and how the temple as a whole both mimics and links the Cosmic Man and the human being. Firmly grounded in the world of vegetal and animal life, mankind is potentially divine. Like the temple, he has within him the potential to rise stage by stage in an ever more glorious ascent to his goal, the transcendent. This ascent is attained not through renunciation or life denial but through the spiritualizing of sensual life.

16

BANĀRAS

SHIVA'S EARTHLY ABODE

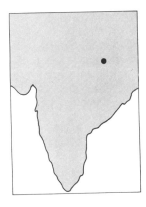

No matter what you call it—Kāshī, Banāras, or Vārānasī—it is probably the oldest and most exciting city in the world. Legend says that Kāshī, "the City of Light," was the first of all cities, built by the first king, in a forest carpeted with sacred *kusha* grass. Before the days of Babylon, Solomon's Temple, or the glories of Nebuchadnezzar, Kāshī was already a thriving religious and commercial center. Long before Christ it was mentioned in the Buddhist *jātakas* as a center of civilization. The *Mahābhārata* traces the name Vārānasī to the fact that the city lies on the banks of the Ganges between the rivulets Varanā in the north and Asi in the south. It was the Muslims who coined the name Banāras, and the British adopted it when they came.

Nowadays one and a quarter million people throng these narrow streets. At times of major pilgrimage, this population increases fivefold. All the color, sights, tastes, and smells of India are concentrated here—and all her seeming contradictions. Banāras is the quintessence of Hinduism. The place is quite a test for the Westerner, because it picks him up by the scruff of the cultural neck and shakes him hard. All expectations and priorities are challenged; nowhere else is India so radically different from what he is used to. For those visitors for whom plenty is assured, death disguised, and religion little more than a comfortable justification of corporate business life, Banāras may be too powerful. It is not for the faint-hearted. Getting nudged out of the way by a sacred cow may be just tolerable, but seeing a corpse crackle as it is devoured by the hungry flames can be too much reality to take. The impact of the place is overwhelming. Whether you love or loathe the city, you cannot remain indifferent. Once you have been to Banāras, your life will never be the same again.

Kāshī is the holiest place on earth for the Hindu: his principal goal of pilgrimage and where he hopes to die. Lord Shiva himself is believed to live here, and the entire city, with its two thousand temples, is dedicated to him. Kāshī is the city of knowledge. In the microcosm Kāshī is the summit of the head, where knowledge resides and the thousand-petaled lotus of enlightenment flowers. Kāshī is the navel of the world.

Kāshī is what it is because of where it is: on the banks of the great goddess Gangā. This flat, calm stretch of water that seems to go on forever is the artery through which the life blood of Hinduism flows. Starting as a crystal-clear rivulet at the "Cow's Mouth" of Gangotrī among the Himālayan peaks, she widens and lengthens, twisting her 1,250 miles (2,000 kilometers) through the parched plains of Uttar Pradesh, on through arid Bihār, then the lush green backwaters of Bengāl, finally to explode in the profusion of rivulets that empty joyously into the Bay of Bengāl. As she winds, she sanctifies site after site: Rishikesh, Allāhabād, Hardvār. Gangā Mātā—"Mother Ganges"—is the Hindu's link to the Himālayan vastness, where only the saints and the gods can dwell. She is the bringer of life and the comforter of ills. The Hindu gods migrated to her banks because they were already holy, and to the Indian her journey is the symbol of man's own winding way through life. But the goddess is fickle. Every so often, displeased with the persistent folly of men, she bursts her banks and wreaks havoc on great and small alike. The ancient part of Kāshī has been engulfed many times by her great waters. Yet the Ganges gives Kāshī a sign that the city is especially favored, for here the mighty river turns north and flows back toward her Himālayan home. What clearer indication could there be that Kāshī is unique? Once in the city all human limits are left behind. The place is paradise on earth. The moment you arrive, your past sins are absolved. To die here is to be assured of not just a place in heaven, nor even a favorable rebirth, but total liberation from the eternal round of birth and death (*samsāra*). Such is the power of Kāshī for those who believe.

This divine preeminence has not spared Banāras a turbulent history. The city remained under Hindu rule until the twelfth century, when, as the religious capital of the north, it suffered badly at the hands of Islām. First the Pathān kings

The riverfront at Banāras, looking south from above Panchagangā Ghāt, with the Alamgir Mosque on the skyline.

came across from their capital at Delhi to loot and plunder. Qutbuddīn Aibak's forces were said to have destroyed a thousand temples here in 1194. Then the Mughals arrived. Shāh Jahān, builder of the Tāj, had seventy-six temples destroyed, and his son Aurangzeb continued the reign of persecution and bigotry. He reimposed the *jazia*, a special tax levied on non-Muslims by their Mughal overlords, destroyed temples, and did what he could to abolish or impoverish Hindu cultural institutions. He even forbade music at his court because it was idolatrous and seduced the people from their true end of contemplating Allāh. In 1659 the holy temple Krittivāsa was pulled down on the emperor's orders. The year 1669 was even blacker for Banāras: Two of its most sacred shrines, the Vishnu Temple of Bindu Mādhava and the Shiva Vishvanātha Temple were destroyed, and mosques were built in their place. The Alamgir Mosque, which dominates the northern skyline of the waterfront, stands on the site of the Temple of Bindu Mādhava. Aurangzeb even changed the name of the city to Muhammadabād and set up the royal mint there to issue coins bearing the new name. Banāras has more reasons than most places to remember the fanatical Mughal.

Brought to its knees many times, Banāras continued to rise again. With characteristically Indian patience, the city incorporated each new element thrust upon it by the latest invaders. And her misfortunes increased her sanctity; for nothing drives man into the arms of God as swiftly as suffering. There is something here so essential to India that it could never be destroyed, no matter how often the temples were sacked. Whatever may change on the surface, Banāras goes on. All human life is here, and as long as one Hindu remains alive, Banāras will continue to exist.

Banāras has always been the center of Sanskrit learning in northern India. The oldest of the Indo-European languages, Sanskrit was originally spoken by the Āryan invaders of Vedic times. It is the classical language of India. Like Latin in medieval Europe, it is a language of learning and religious ritual. All the most important texts of Indian lore remain in Sanskrit, so a knowledge of the language is important for a deeper understanding of the culture. Banāras, being the religious capital of the north, maintained a healthy tradition of Sanskrit learning long after understanding had degenerated elsewhere. Since the twelfth century this knowledge has been increasingly the preserve of the priests, a small but powerful elite. In recent times the vitality of the tradition has been helped by migrations of brahmin sanskritists from the Hindu strongholds in Mahārāshtra and the south. So even today there are about forty Sanskrit schools and colleges in Banāras with over two thousand sanskritists. The best known of these is Banāras Sanskrit University where there is a remarkable collection of 150,000 rare manuscripts.

The traditional means of teaching this knowledge is the institution of the *pandit*. He is the ultimate authority on textual and ritual matters; any dispute will be settled by his verdict. These *pandits* teach in the time-honored *guru*-disciple relationship. There are perhaps fifteen hundred of them, each having a maximum of twelve disciples. For the most part the *pandits* live and breathe in an atmosphere of the Middle Ages. They speak Sanskrit, some even scorning its derivatives such as modern Hindī. They often delight in being out of step with the changes taking place around them. Nowadays only astrology and *ayurveda*—the indigenous Indian system of medicine—can provide a *pandit* with a comfortable living. However, *pandits* are devoted to maintaining even the most obscure branches of Sanskrit learning, despite a growing lack of interest in these traditional customs and values among the young. As custodians of a heritage they feel is the only bulwark against the complete collapse of society, they are keen to preserve the brahmin conservatism for which Banāras is famous.

The old city stretches from the area around the main square—the Chowk—down to the river. It is a labyrinth of unmarked lanes and alleys, wide enough only for pedestrians and animals. You cannot even navigate by the sun; the walls are too high. The winding alleys (*galī*) twist and turn into ever more mysterious darkness. There is a bustling activity; the place reeks of intrigue as cows and goats jostle with pilgrims, merchants, and wild-eyed ascetics. The temples themselves are often dark and forbidding; many of them officially closed to non-Hindus, who would pollute the place with their mere presence. But temple doorkeepers are human, and who can blame them for supplementing their income by turning the occasional blind eye? And, providing the price is right, perhaps the priest inside will perform the rituals for you. For Kāshī is preeminently a priestly city, with all the strengths and weaknesses that implies.

Vishvanātha Temple (Figure A.1)

The holiest temple is the Vishvanātha, in the heart of the old city, surrounded by little shops that are fascinating to browse in. The temple is open from four in the morning till eleven at night, and twenty liters (over five gallons) of milk are used daily to bathe its *linga,* which is set in solid silver. Though the temple dates only from the late eighteenth century, it is hallowed by the faithful, and there are five principal *āratīs* performed to the *linga* each day. Added to which the surrounding courtyards are full of shrines, many of which are believed to have special sanctity. The Vishvanātha Temple is closed to non-Hindus, but an open area around the "Well of Wisdom" (Gyāna Vāpī), which lies between the back of the walled temple compound and the Gyāna Vāpī Mosque, gives some view of it. The temple has a domed roof and two spires (*shikhara*). One of these rises over the *linga* and was plated with gold in 1839 by Ranjīt Singh, the "Lion of the Punjāb"—hence the Vishvanātha is commonly known among tourists as the Golden Temple.

The Golden Temple is the sacred center of Kāshī. As such, it is protected by seven concentric circles, each composed of eight Ganesha images, which spread out through the holy city. These Ganesha *mūrtis,* one for each of the points of the compass, combine to form the "fifty-six Vināyakas" (Vināyaka, "the Great Leader," being one of Ganesha's titles), and the pious pilgrim will endeavor to visit them all in turn. Many temples in Banāras are considered so sacred that access is restricted even for the faithful. In Varāhi Devī Temple the stone image of the goddess is kept in an underground sanctum, and the devotees are allowed to peep at it only through a window from the floor above. In the Kāshī Karavat shrine near the Golden Temple, the image is kept in a dry well with a sword next to it. In their zeal to please the god, it is said, worshippers used the sword to sacrifice themselves. No one is now allowed to descend into the well, but you can view the image from above by dropping little chunks of lighted camphor into the darkness. There is no doubt, too, that parts of this ancient city are touched with blackness. Some of the twisting alleys have that almost tangible atmosphere of blood sacrifice performed to the implacable Kālī.

Down the centuries nearly every important saint, philosopher, or religious teacher has had some connection with Banāras. Despite, or perhaps because of this, the city has also always been renowned for the lighter side of life. Classical music, ivory and brasswork, weaving, silkwork, perfume making, and fine food are among its specialties.

In the seventeenth century the French traveler Bernier wrote:

> Large halls are seen in many places called *kārkhānas*, that are workshops for the artisans. In one hall embroiderers are busily employed, superintended by a master. In another you see goldsmiths; in a third, painters; in a fourth, varnishers of lacquer work; in a fifth, joiners, turners, tailors, shoemakers; in a sixth manufacturers of silk, brocades and those fine muslins of which are made turbans, girdles with golden flowers and drawers worn by females that are so delicately fine as frequently to wear out in one night.

Such *kārkhānas*, though on a more modest scale, still exist today, especially in the silk, brocade, copper, and brass industries. Banāras silk, of course, has always been famous throughout the world. Much of the raw material is now imported, but the weaving, largely in the hands of the Muslim community, continues as fine as ever. Although they make the silk, traditional Muslims prefer, for reasons of religious purity, to wear good cotton.

A Hindu regards silk as the material most suitable for religious purity because it insulates him from psychic influences, but if possible, he will wear raw silk made from the cocoons left empty by moths so as to avoid causing any death. This raw silk is a specialty of Banāras and is suitable for furnishings as well as clothes.

Fine silk is still embroidered with the silver and gold threadwork known as *zārī*. These materials have been prized for centuries, and the historian Macaulay records that in the eighteenth century "all along the shores of the venerable Ganges lay great fleets of vessels laden with rich merchandise. From the looms of Benares went forth the delicate silks that adorned the balls of St. James and Versailles."

In fact Banāras was once the pleasure capital of Hindu India, as was Lucknow to the Muslims, though her sumptuous brothels are no more and the dancing girls no longer live in the elegant surroundings they did. These girls were generally the unmarried daughters of the professional musician caste. They were not attached to any particular temple, nor "married to the god," but were engaged to sing at festivals and celebrations: chanting the praises of Rāma, performing the classic poems of Tulsīdās, or telling the stories of the amorous Krishna. They also had an extensive repertoire of secular songs for parties. They were famous for their generosity; in old age, when virtue became a necessity if not a pleasure, they gave freely to the many charities in the city.

Another specialty here is *bhāng*, a decoction of hashish. The *galīs* are full of little booths selling this in various forms. You can drink *bhāng lassi*, a yoghurt drink laced with the stuff; eat *bhāng kulfi*, cones of ice cream; or wade your way through various doctored pastries and sweetmeats. The availability of *bhāng* perhaps partly accounts for Banāras's popularity among young travelers; it may also help explain the Banāras character. For natives of the city are known throughout Asia as a law unto themselves—volatile, carefree, perhaps a little crazy, and always on the lookout to make a quick rupee with the least possible effort. Their sense of humor is also renowned as ribald and uninhibited. The Banārsī exhibits a love of good living and culture that is positively infectious; the city throbs with what the locals call *mastī*—an exuberant *joie de vivre*.

The Banāras cycle-rickshaw drivers exemplify the city's character. There are over forty thousand of these, each with his own line, his own stories, his own vendettas. They know the city backwards and will be good guides for a day's sightseeing, as long as the price is fixed beforehand. Their motto is: "You want? I have." They are an untiring source of information and adventure.

The Ghāts
(Figure A)

The old part of the city leads down to the river and the *ghāts*, which are the terraced steps that front the Ganges. The word *ghāt* means "sloping place" and can equally well be applied to a range of hills—for example, the "Western Ghāts" in Mahārāshtra. The *ghāts* are the roots of Banāras; exposed in drought, submerged in flood, but always drawing nourishment from the mighty river. When you are in Banāras, you must visit the *ghāts*, and you must see the sun rise over the Ganges. If you do nothing else, do this. It is an unforgettable experience, and if you shirk it because you can't be bothered to get up that early, you deserve to be reincarnated as a slug.

The main *ghāt* from which to start your journey is the Dashāshvamedha Ghāt (A.2). Here you can hire a boat (your driver will no doubt have a friend up his sleeve) and spend an hour or two on the river, watching one of the most breathtaking sights on earth.

When you leave your hotel bleary-eyed but fortified by aromatic southern Indian coffee, the sky is still dark and the air surprisingly cold. But the moon is giving way to a faint light in the eastern sky, and already there is a subtle feeling

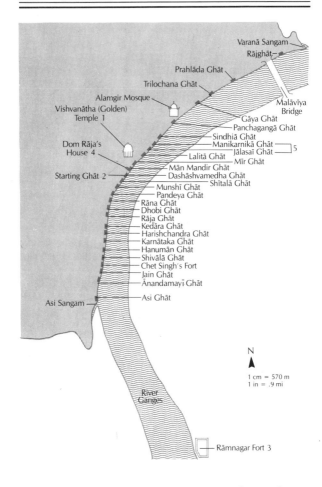

Varanā Sangam
Rājghāt
Prahlāda Ghāt
Trilochana Ghāt
Alamgir Mosque
Vishvanātha (Golden)
Temple 1
Malāvīya Bridge
Gāya Ghāt
Panchagangā Ghāt
Sindhiā Ghāt
Manikarnikā Ghāt
Jālasaī Ghāt
Dom Rāja's House 4
Lalitā Ghāt
Mīr Ghāt
Māna Mandir Ghāt
Starting Ghāt 2
Dashāshvamedha Ghāt
Shītalā Ghāt
Munshī Ghāt
Pandeya Ghāt
Rāna Ghāt
Dhobi Ghāt
Rāja Ghāt
Kedāra Ghāt
Harishchandra Ghāt
Karnātaka Ghāt
Hanumān Ghāt
Shivālā Ghāt
Chet Singh's Fort
Jain Ghāt
Ānandamayī Ghāt
Asi Sangam
Asi Ghāt

N

1 cm = 570 m
1 in = .9 mi

River Ganges

Rāmnagar Fort 3

Figure A. The Ganges riverfront at Banāras, showing the ghāts.

of expectation abroad. As your rickshaw bumps and jingles toward the city center, the sidewalks and doorways are still full of huddled bundles that proclaim the Indian's ability to sleep where he drops. There are more animals around than humans—water buffaloes, cows, goats, and pigs—for the street sweepers do not start work till ten o'clock, and there are four hours' good scavenging till then.

Gradually figures wrapped in blankets and shawls begin to wander through the streets, emerging like shadows from hidden lanes and alleys. Yawning cycle-rickshaw *wallahs* wipe the dew off their machines, flexing their bony shoulders for another day's work, scarves wrapped around their heads as if to hold their jaws on. You may drive through a Muslim quarter, where heavily veiled women are already up and about, as their men, in black vests and astrakhan hats, begin to make their way to the mosque.

Dark doorways splutter into life with the sudden glare of kerosene lamps and paraffin stoves; everywhere figures crouch preparing food. Mats are brushed, bedrolls shaken out, front steps swept, as sleepy-eyed children wander out into the new day. Gradually the air is filled with the familiar sounds of life: birdsong, human voices, bicycle bells. The great ritual of morning ablutions is beginning. People stand around street pumps or communal wells gargling, spitting, cleaning teeth, and finishing up with that horrendous retching that sounds like the peculiarly drawn-out death rattle of some unfortunate barnyard creature, but is actually only India clearing her early-morning throat.

The tea stalls are opening up now. Early customers cluster around the first kettle of the day, as it bubbles and hisses with that sweet, thick *chaī* that has a kick like a mule. Smoke begins to rise from a hundred hidden fires, casting a thin pall over the dilapidated streets with their crumbling plaster and faded paint. All around you the decayed grandeur of Banāras is emerging, a motley tattiness that nevertheless manages to be more sacred than sordid.

As the light grows in the eastern sky, the streets become more crowded, mainly with pilgrims returning from their early morning bathe in the river. Most of these are women, dripping hair pulled tightly back and *sārīs* clinging wetly to their bodies. They carry flowers on leaf platters, handfuls of rice sprinkled with vermilion, and their foreheads are daubed with *kum-kum* and sandalwood paste. All have little brass pots that glow dully, full of holy Ganges water taken from the great goddess herself to be offered in the temple of their choice or on the family altar at home. The trickle increases to a stream, threading its way through the flocks of black-headed crows that strut around, imperiously pecking at whatever they can find.

You may run into a temple procession bearing a flower-decked image on a brass throne and accompanied by one of those anarchic bands that sounds as if everyone in it were playing a different tune. Or you may come across the remnants of an all-night music contest: a platform set up in the middle of the road, garlanded with fairy lights that shine red, green, blue, and yellow with a garish hungover brightness in the early morning light.

As you approach the *ghāt*, the excitement becomes palpable. The crowd is swelled by people who appear from every nook and cranny. Blind street singers, their empty eyes turned toward heaven, children scuttling here and there with steam-

ing brass pots and kettles, pilgrims swathed in faded orange
and yellow—all are irresistibly drawn by the magnet of the
river. Just before the *ghāt*, the road opens into a large square.
Dozens of rickshaw *wallahs* stand around waiting to take
bathers back home. Their battered machines are brightly
decorated with pictures of the gods, garlands of marigolds,
Shiva's trident, or plastic flowers. Vegetable stalls spread out
their wares, and already the housewives, as tough as they are
tiny, are getting down to the serious business of the day's first
haggle. Wooden-flute sellers stroll nonchalantly around,
enormous stacks of instruments balanced like shiny Christ-
mas trees on their shoulders. Pavement stalls sell heaps of
flowers, rice, and leaves for offering to the river, or perhaps
bundles of *neem* twig toothbrushes or bolts of softest cotton.

Suddenly, in the midst of this holy fairground, you catch
your first glimpse of the river. It lies silver gray in the steely
light, unreal, the far bank shrouded in ghostly mist. And
between you and the river sit the beggars. The holier the
place, the more beggars congregate there. Some, whose faces
have melted away from leprosy, or those whose bodies end at
the waist and turn into trolleys on wheels, are enough to
shock even the most hardened traveler. But the strange thing
is that pity is quite out of place here, for these sufferers suffer
so little. On the contrary, many of them have that stoic dignity
that comes from acceptance. Their robust fortitude shames
our complaints against ills that are infinitely less exacting.
Whatever happens, they will cope, just as they have always
coped, and they are included as part of a scene that rejects
nothing, no matter how strange. India accepts things the
West has long since left behind or shut away, and she bears
her afflictions with a patience and good humor that seem
inexhaustible. What happens is God's will, and there is always
another life. The same thing applies to those frail bundles of
hope who have come to breathe their last on these steps.
They face their imminent end with a happy tranquility, for
they have fulfilled their life's ambition to die here by the
Ganges. Death holds no fears for them, and to that extent
they are better off than most of us.

It is worth remembering that the beggar occupies a legitimate place in Indian society. A pious Hindu gains religious
merit by giving alms, so to the traditional, a beggar is not an
object of scorn or contempt. As far as he can, the householder
will support an ever-widening circle of dependents. The joint
family extends from relatives to friends, servants, employees,
and the sick. At the outer edge of this circle sit the wanderers, the crazies, and the beggars.

Public welfare is a burden to be borne by individual charity,
not the state. Indians are used to emergencies—drought,
famine, flood—and used to sharing what they have, in the

faith that when they themselves are in need, someone else will be equally generous with them. Even those who are desperately poor set aside money for charity. To see the generosity of those who have so little can be truly humbling.

Nor need a beggar who looks destitute necessarily be so. Those who station themselves at temples or holy sites can earn good money. A journalist recently posed as a beggar at one of the big temples in the south. In one day he took ninety-five rupees, a princely sum by Indian standards.

This is not to romanticize or condone begging but merely to point out that this is one of the many aspects of India that a Western visitor going on his instinctive reactions is likely to misjudge. Begging is a way, perhaps not the best way, but still a way, for the disabled and deficient legitimately to fit into Indian society and play their part. In seeking to include every aspect of life into its fold, Hinduism tries to provide what every Hindu wants—a clearly defined place in the total scheme of things. Be it ever so low, this place is self-evident and guaranteed, and that is what matters, for a traditional Hindu derives his identity from what he *is*, rather than from what he does. And, contrary to popular belief, Hinduism is essentially optimistic, for it believes that we are all slowly progressing up the ladder of being, however disadvantaged we may now appear to be.

☐ *DASHĀSHVAMEDHA GHĀT* (Figure A.2)
Dashāshvamedha Ghāt gets its name from one of the most ancient legends of Kāshī. Long ago, the world was suffering from a terrible drought that threatened to destroy the very planet. Brahmā, the god of creation, realized that there was only one being on earth who had the ability to restore order to the world, a wise king called Divodāsa, who had renounced his throne to spend his days in meditation on the banks of the Ganges at Kāshī. Divodāsa agreed to accept the kingship of the earth only on the condition that all the gods retired from Kāshī so he could go about his task unhindered by their interference. Even the great Lord Shiva, who loved the city as his life, was forced to leave. Shiva brooded on his exile. He eventually realized that if Divodāsa could be proved to be lacking in kingly or ritual expertise, then the gods would have the right to return to Kāshī and Shiva would once again rule the city. So he sent Brahmā, in the form of a brahmin priest, to Divodāsa's court and had him request the king to be the patron of an extremely powerful and complicated Vedic ritual consisting of ten (*dashan,* simultaneous horse sacrifices (*ashvamedha*). The wily Shiva was confident that the king would make some mistake in such an enormous undertaking, for it is the patron's job to provide all the ingredients and see that all the arrangements are perfect. But Divodāsa played

his part flawlessly, and Shiva's plan was thwarted. The sacrifice was performed, with Brahmā as chief priest, on what is now known as Dashāshvamedha Ghāt—"The place of the Ten Horse Sacrifices." Since then it has become one of the most sacred *tīrthas*, and it is believed that bathing here gains almost as much religious merit as performing the sacrifice itself.

☐

Here on the *ghāt* all India is present in microcosm. The steps are already alive with *sārīs*—red, orange, green, blue—brilliant in the soft, clear light. The place bustles with activity—cows, people, flowers, goats, pigeons, incense, crows. The air is filled with the sound of bells, prayers, and sonorous chanting. All mingle together in a gently undulating tableau that has been reenacted every morning since the beginning of time.

Down in the water crowds jostle as they perform the ritual bath and offer their worship to the rising sun. Now it is a huge red ball just peeping over the horizon and casting its golden glint upon the water. Some are standing with hands folded in supplication; others hold brass pots aloft, offering Ganges water to the sun; others sit in rapt contemplation, red and orange prayer shawls around their shoulders. All are absorbed in their own, intensely personal worship, yet the whole tableau has a sense of unity. Each separate individual knows his place and what he is doing here. The movement is orderly, unhurried, and, above all, purposeful. India loves ritual and repetition; nowhere is this love more clearly demonstrated.

The never-ending flow of life is what the Indians call *karma*. *Karma* means "action; activity." Everything in this universe partakes of the movement of *karma*, even solid matter, which is in truth nothing but dancing energy. On the human level *karma* is that web we weave around ourselves by all our social and emotional interactions.

Most of us are content to spend our brief days immersed in what the world has to offer and asking the gods' help in daily life. But India has always glorified another way: the way of renunciation. To the itinerant holy man (*sādhu*), the web of life is a trap. Entanglement in the mundane snares the spirit. The fetters of *karma* must be burst asunder if true freedom is to be found. Renunciation and austerities are the arduous means by which life can be forced to reveal its secrets, or so the conventional wisdom goes. But can one really renounce all activity? The heart must beat, the blood must flow around the body. Yet here on the *ghāts* is a man who tries to deny even this much involvement with life. He lies inert as a log. His emaciated body is smeared with ash from the funeral pyre, flecked with vermilion, and heaped with rosaries of *rudrāksha* beads, sacred to Shiva, Lord of Death.

The *sādhu's* eyes are unblinking, like those of some reptile caught out of its rightful element. In the West this character would be certified and bundled into some institution. But here no one minds. Mortification is a valid path to God, even if it reaches these extremes, and anyway, he's not doing anybody any harm as he lies here, observing his silent covenant with whatever god he worships. Even this petrified life form will later slowly stir to lift the meager handful of featherlight coins which approving pilgrims have dropped onto his dusty blanket.

What on earth motivates this *sādhu?* What motivates those who give him alms? "Unfathomable are the ways of *karma*," answers the *Gītā.* Yet he is part of Kāshī, for Kāshī contains all life, all possibilities. Even in his renunciation the *sādhu* participates in the human comedy. He has his role on the stage of life, however much he may scorn the rest of the cast.

Each and every piece of the variegated jigsaw somehow fits unerringly together. We outsiders can only watch and marvel, for the total pattern is incomprehensible to the non-Hindu. Perhaps it is so even to the Indian, who unconsciously takes his or her place without pausing to think about it. Such a pause would interrupt the flow, and Kāshī flows as smoothly as the mighty river on which it is built.

Is all this magic, superstition, or sublime faith? Perhaps a bit of each. But the sheer number of people here, moving as one heartfelt body, is enough to forestall any cynicism. The scene is awesome in its emotional intensity. The sun expresses the nature of divinity more directly and appropriately than any other symbol and to this the Hindu instinctively reacts.

Are the Hindus right? The question is out of place. They are undoubtedly right for themselves, and that is all that can be said about it. Who can deny the worth of such a pilgrimage, even if it only provides the strength to continue with the more enduring pilgrimage of daily life? Every morning the scene here is the same; every morning it is totally different. No matter how often you see it, it never fails to be profoundly moving.

Upriver

Once out on the river you can see the whole panorama of the *ghāts,* diffused with an atmosphere of devotion that spreads like rays of the rising sun. Prominent on the steps are the bamboo umbrellas, like so many magic mushrooms. Under each sits a brahmin priest, an enigmatic oracle: perhaps India's version of the hookah-smoking caterpillar in *Alice in Wonderland,* who promised so much but spoke in riddles. These are the *ghātiās.* Their job is to look after the pilgrim's clothes

Early morning ritual bath.

and belongings while he bathes and worships the sun and to mark him with the sacred *tilaka* afterward. *Ghātiās* also perform rituals for the pilgrim, especially those to do with the *pinda dāna* rites, in which sons and grandsons offer balls of rice or other grains (*pindas*) to the souls of their departed forefathers to bring them peace and satisfaction wherever they may be in the universe. The *ghātiās* may own or lease the part of the step they occupy. Few of them know Sanskrit, and their rituals are performed in the vernacular and often perfunctorily. Some of these *ghātiās* have a calf tethered beside them. This alludes to the ancient custom of presenting a ritual gift of a cow (*godāna*) to a priest in exchange for his services. Nowadays the *ghātiā* keeps the animal as a symbol, and receives his fee in more useful commodities. However, this custom of receiving ritual payment for services rendered on the actual *ghāts* breaks a brahmin taboo. As a result *ghātiās* are looked down upon by the higher echelons of the priestly caste, and the orthodox brahmin will not marry into a *ghātiā* family. *Ghātiās* either marry lower subcastes (*jatis*) of brahmins than themselves, or they take concubines from lower castes altogether.

Another level in the brahmin hierarchy is the *pandā*. He is attached to a temple and meets pilgrims at the bus or railway station. He escorts them to a lodging house, temple, or particular *ghāt* and guides them round the city. Often a *pandā* will become "assigned" to several families, which will send all their pilgrims to his care. The father of the family will write and inform the *pandā* which relatives are coming to Banāras and when; and the *pandā* will be there to meet them. In this way the *pandā* builds up a regular clientele, and the pilgrims deal with someone they know and trust. There are also free-lance *pandās*, who, like most people in Banāras, work on a percentage basis!

Neither of these two types of brahmin officiates in temples. That is the job of yet another category, the *pūjārī*. *Pūjārīs* may own the temple they work in, lease it from a trust or another individual, or be employed in it. If the priests own the temple, the revenue goes to them. As you might imagine, some of the temple owners are immensely wealthy. Curiously, *pūjārīs* are not always brahmins. There is a Durgā temple here, for example, where the *pūjārī* is a *kunbi* (a member of the vegetable-growing *jati*).

You leave Dashāshvamedha Ghāt with the sound of the harmonium from the Gangā Mātā Temple humming in your ears. As your boat goes south, the people on the *ghāts* thin out a little. Dashāshvamedha is one of the holiest *ghāts* and so most crowded. On the last day of Kālī *pūjā*, in the month of Kārttika (October–November) there is a particularly impressive ceremony here when the images of the goddess are ceremoniously cast into the river. Made of clay, they are destroyed each year and new ones prepared for the next festival.

□ SHĪTALĀ GHĀT

Immediately to the south of Dashāshvamedha Ghāt is Shītalā Ghāt, so called from a temple dedicated to the goddess of smallpox. The temple is a small boxlike structure with bars; nothing much to look at but much visited by worshippers, who sprinkle the image with Ganges water. The *ghāt* is especially popular with women bathers. Everywhere there seems to be cloth flapping—scarves being unraveled, shawls hung out to dry, *sārīs* being changed or folded away. Some people are swimming out toward the rising sun, which is turning the sky pink, and troops of monkeys run along the buildings, chattering with excitement. Many of these buildings that rise up behind the *ghāts* were built by *mahārājas* as riverside palaces. Now they are rest houses for pilgrims or those who come to spend their last years here in meditation. Some of these hostels are free; others charge a nominal rent.

□ MUNSHĪ GHĀT

Next comes Munshī Ghāt, used by the Muslims, who form about 25 percent of Banāras's population and are particularly active in the cloth and mechanical trades. They come here for an early morning bath, and they treat the Ganges as they would any other river.

□ PANDEYA GHĀT AND RĀNA GHĀT

Then comes Pandeya Ghāt, distinguished by the incongruous graffiti of Japanese writing, the legacy of a Japanese artist

who lived here. The *ghāt* was donated by a chief minister of
Bengal. Farther along is Rāna Ghāt, built by the Mahārāna
of Udaipur.

☐ THE FOUR STAGES OF LIFE

By now the *ghāts* are almost empty. A sense of uncluttered
quietness returns, a silence intensified by the gentle and
regular slapping of the oars in the water. Smoke spirals up
from the roofs, odd faces appear at little windows overlooking
balconies draped with washing. Hawks circle overhead,
expectantly. Here and there sits an ascetic, doing his morning meditation. Although these holy men have renounced the
world, they are still very much part of Hindu society. Indeed,
some would argue that they are its very backbone. Manu, the
ancient Hindu lawgiver, laid down an ideal pattern of life,
which was composed of four stages. The first stage was *brahmachārya*. This was a period of celibate studentship, when
one lived with one's teacher and learned the wisdom of the
scriptures from him. The second stage, *grihastha*, was the
stage of householder, devoted to marriage, raising a family,
and securing the material benefits of a career. The third
stage, *vānaprastha*, represented a partial withdrawal from
active life. Once their children were well established as independent, the parents withdrew to the forest for a life of
contemplation and religious study in a hermitage. This period
would also be celibate. The final, optional stage was *sann-*

Meditating sādhu, *a
devotee of Shiva.*

yāsa, complete renunciation of society. Then the *sannyāsin* took a formal vow, threw away his clothes, and put on the ocher robe. He broke his sacred thread, the symbol of belonging to one of the three top castes—for he was beyond social divisions now—shaved his head, and was released from the performance of rites and ceremonies. His life was dedicated to wandering the country, learning, teaching, and debating. Life became a perpetual pilgrimage, for the laws of *sannyāsa* forbid staying more than three days in any one place. This fourth stage was open to anyone at any time; thus many of the great spiritual teachers became *sannyāsins* while still in their teens and dedicated their entire lives to the state. Those who do not take the formal vows of *sannyāsa* but nevertheless renounce and wander around the country as ascetics living on alms are called *sādhus* ("good men").

Though these four stages represent an ideal that is hardly practicable today, there are still many who try to follow a modified form of the old pattern, adapted to modern conditions. And there are still many who live the itinerant life; at the last census (1971) there were an estimated ten million *sādhus* or *sannyāsins*. Many of them spend time in Banāras, especially for the major festivals.

☐ *DHOBI GHĀT*

Past Rāna Ghāt is the Dhobi Ghāt where much of the city's washing is done. The *dhobi wallahs* are professional washermen, washing the clothes of all but the strict brahmins, who always do their laundry at home to avoid caste pollution. The *dhobi wallahs* soak the clothes in a special mud, not detergent, and leave them in the sun before washing the mud off. Amazingly it seems to work, though their energetic beating of the clothes tends to effectively demolish all buttons. Mark Twain had a point when he defined a Hindu as: "one of a large number of people who think they can smash up rocks with wet laundry." Most of the *dhobi wallahs* are illiterate, but they mark the clothes with special insignia, and in a village they would know by sight which article belonged to which household. The washing is transported by donkeys, who stand patiently high up on the *ghāt*, watching the incessant activity with resignation.

By now the sun is a brilliant ball of flaming red, too bright to look at. High over the horizon, it has risen with great speed, flooding the water with silken light and turning the soft pink of the sky to blue.

☐ *RĀJA GHĀT*

Beyond Dhobi Ghāt lies Rāja Ghāt, named after a *rāja* of Poona. Here the high-water levels are recorded on the walls of the buildings. Each year in the rainy season the lower parts of the *ghāts* are submerged and the bathing and worship take place higher up the steps, sometimes within the temples and houses at the very back of the *ghāt*. Each autumn the silt is dug out from the lower temples and shrines. But every so often the river floods disastrously, and the highest levels are marked in yellow as a grim reminder of the goddess's power.

The *ghāts* are being swept now. An old woman, bent double, lays out pats of cow dung to dry in the sun. A housewife scrubs her pots and pans with sand from the river bank. Her neighbor soaps and washes, without a trace of embarrassment, while talking to a priest with a belly as big as Ganesha's. All around are dilapidated houseboats that in their better days were used by the nobility for festivals and outings on the river. Now the party is very much over, and they are reduced to housing black-headed crows and the odd hippie, who rents them for next to nothing. Fish, and sometimes dolphins, leap and play in the warming water, and birds perch on a bamboo pole anchored to the riverbed by some pious Jain. A grinning fisherman rows by, his baskets squirming with gigantic catfish, their whiskers twitching sporadically.

□ *KEDĀRA GHĀT*
Farther south is Kedāra Ghāt, dominated by a Shiva temple painted in faded candy stripes of terracotta and white. Here is also the palace of the southern Indian Mahārāja of Vijanagar. The *ghāt* takes its name from the famous pilgrimage spot Kedārnāth, high in the Himālayas. It is especially popular with the Bengālī and southern Indian communities that inhabit this part of the city. The women have characteristic Bengālī *sārīs*, colored plain with a very wide decorated border. Halfway down the steps is a tank, called "the Well of Gaurī" ("the White One," another name for Pārvatī), which is thought to have healing properties. The steps are covered with picturesque stone *lingas*. Mondays—sacred to Shiva—are always busy here, especially in the holy monsoon month of Shrāvana (July–August).

□ *HARISHCHANDRA GHĀT*
Past an orange Hanumān and Ganesha at the water's edge, you come to Harishchandra Ghāt, one of the most holy. Harishchandra was a king famous for never telling a lie and never refusing a guest. He worshipped Brahmā. One day Indra, in one of his interminable arguments with the creator god, taunted him that Harishchandra's devotion was only skin deep. Brahmā protested and, to prove the king's unshakable loyalty, resolved to test him. He disguised himself as a wandering brahmin priest and approached the king asking for alms. He asked for Harishchandra's entire kingdom. The king gave it. Then, in order to pay the customary fee

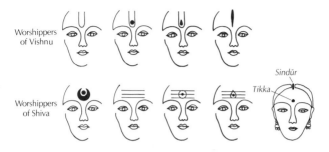

Worshippers of Vishnu

Worshippers of Shiva

Sindūr

Tikka

Figure B. Sectarian marks.

(*dakshinā*) to the priest for performing certain rituals, Harishchandra was forced to become a servant to the chief of the Banāras crematorium. His wife was sold to a flower seller. Then their son died of snakebite. The grieving woman took him to the burning *ghāt*, where her husband was employed. Having no money to pay the cremation fee, she ripped her *sārī* in half and gave half to the undertakers. Even Indra was impressed by such unflinching acts of devotion, and he ruefully admitted that he had lost his wager. Whereupon Brahmā immediately restored the child to life and declared that not only would the king have his kingdom back, but the *ghāt* would become especially sacred and be named after him. The *ghāt* is often considered the most sacred for cremation, but the other cremation *ghāt*, Manikarnikā, which is north of Dashāshvamedha, is in fact more popular. Here at Harishchandra you can see the wood piled up for the pyres in front of a green-and-black-striped Shiva temple. Towering behind is the blue and green top of the high gateway (*gopuram*) of a southern Indian temple, quite different in style from the ones in the north. This area caters to pilgrims from the south.

□ KARNĀTAKA GHĀT
Next is Karnātaka Ghāt, a southern Indian *ghāt*. Each different state has virtually its own *ghāt*, with priests and *pandās* who speak the appropriate language and know the eating customs and the regional festivals of the pilgrims who come. Thus the waterfront is a microcosm of the whole country— infinitely varied yet managing to stay united. The temple and palace here were built by the Mahārāja of Mysore.

□ HANUMĀN GHĀT
After Karnātaka comes Hanumān Ghāt, famous as the birth-place of Vallabha, a devotee of Krishna who lived at the end of the fifteenth and beginning of the sixteenth century. He inaugurated a revival of the Krishna *bhakti* cult. Here wres-

tlers and bodybuilders toil in open-air gymnasia on the steps, for Hanumān, the monkey god, was the devoted warrior of Lord Rāma, and epitomizes the virtues of manly strength and physical fitness.

□ SHIVĀLĀ GHĀT AND CHET SINGH'S FORT

Then comes Shivālā Ghāt and Chet Singh's Fort. The fort was the old palace of the Mahārājas of Kāshī. It fell to the Muslims in the seventeenth century, but was recaptured by the royal family, and occupied by Mahārāja Chet Singh at the time of Warren Hastings. In 1781 the Mahārāja was imprisoned in his own fort by the British authorities for refusing to agree to their tax demands, but he made a spectacular descent from the balcony into the river which, being in flood, accepted him gracefully. He then swam six miles upriver to escape, and rallied an army that sent the British packing.

□ JAIN GHĀT

Beyond the little red and white shrines that look more like Edwardian bathing huts than the abodes of the gods lies Jain Ghāt. This area is reserved for the Jains. The yellow spire of a monastery rises up behind the steps, its almost military architecture reflecting the austerity of the faith. Jains are strictly nonviolent; even fishing is prohibited in this stretch of the river. The monastic order is well supported, as lay Jains give generously and are mostly successful business families.

□ ĀNANDAMAYĪ GHĀT

Ānandamayī Ghāt follows, named after the famous Bengālī saint Ānandamayī Mā ("The Mother who is made of bliss"), who died in 1982 and whose disciples maintain her *āshram* here. Mā was the uneducated daughter of a poor Bengālī family who since her childhood had lived in the presence of God. She spent the whole of her long life since her spontaneous enlightenment at the age of seventeen traveling around the country, teaching and establishing charitable missions and *āshrams*. She never presented a formal dogma but guided her devotees through intense devotion and personal contact. One of her most remarkable characteristics was to awaken a keen desire for the spiritual life in all who were fortunate enough to see her. Here on the *ghāt* there is the *āshram*, a school, and an orphanage for girls, and Mā stayed here whenever she was in the city. The *āshram* is very well worth a visit. It is saturated with an atmosphere of peaceful joy (*shānti*). Mā was unquestionably a genuine saint. She was rightly revered as someone who had known God all her life and could awaken in others the same realization.

Ghāt *steps, with* ghātiā *under his parasol (left) and high-water marker and dung cakes drying (right).*

□ *ASI GHĀT*
The turning point in your trip is Asi Ghāt. Beyond this stands a tall water tower, and then trees give way to flat banks stretching into the distance. Asi is the southernmost *ghāt* in the sacred city, and is very popular with early morning bathers. Asi is interesting because, with its clay banks, it shows how the *ghāts* originally were before they were covered with stone and concrete steps—most of which were built by Marāthā kings in the eighteenth and nineteenth centuries. The center of worship here is a large *linga* set beneath a *pīpal* tree on the muddy bank. As you look back downriver from here, the city is unreal, lost in a soft haze that shimmers like *māyā*—the divine illusion.

□ *RĀMNAGAR FORT* (Figure A.3)
On the opposite bank, a little farther upstream, stands Rāmnagar Fort, the residence of the present Mahārāja of Banāras, Vibhūti Nārāin Singh. A devout and diffident man, the Mahārāja exemplifies all that was good about the old system of princely patronage. He is a sincere supporter of many projects to further religion and Sanskrit scholarship in his former kingdom. He has established and funded the Kāshī Trust, an organization dedicated to the preservation and publishing of Sanskrit texts, and is totally traditional in his

observance of Hindu *dharma*. As a result, he lives modestly and is rarely seen outside the fort.

One exception to this seclusion is the annual festival of Rām Līlā. Every autumn India celebrates the victory of Prince Rāma, the hero of the *Rāmāyana*, over Rāvana—the personification of evil. The Banāras Rām Līlā is a little special, since it is taken from the poem *Rāmacharitmānas*, the popular Hindī version of the *Rāmāyana* by the seventeenth-century poet-saint Tulsīdās, who lived here. Though Rām Līlā is celebrated in each district of the city, the one at Rāmnagar is the most lavish, and is financed by the Mahārāja. The "stage" covers an area of four and a half square miles (twelve square kilometers), and the performance begins as the sun is setting. The highlight is the brief episode when Rāma returns, after fourteen years exile, to the royal court, and the climax is played out with tremendous noise and gaiety under dazzling fireworks. The Mahārāja always arrives on a golden *howdah* atop an elephant.

Downriver

From Asi Ghāt you can drift back downriver. The *ghāts* were laid out by Mahārāja Balwant Singh in the seventeenth century, in such a way as to insure that the river did not deposit sand on the left bank, which is the built-up one. The current flows downstream, hits Rāmnagar Fort, is diverted to the opposite bank at Shivālā Ghāt, then on to Dashāshvamedha Ghāt and down to Rājghāt. This way, the river flows in a straight course, and does not silt up the *ghāts* themselves, whereas elsewhere it leaves heavy deposits of sand on both its banks.

☐ *MĀN MANDIR GHĀT*
Back below Dashāshvamedha Ghāt is Mān Mandir Ghāt, built by Mahārāja Mān Singh of Amber in about 1600. The palace here is one of the oldest buildings in Banāras and was a fine specimen of the architecture of that period, though now it is much restored with brick and plaster. But there is still the beautiful stone balcony to be seen high up on the northeast corner of the building. This is one of the architectural gems of Banāras. In 1710 Jai Singh, the great Hindu astronomer and builder of Jaipur, converted the palace into an observatory. The instruments are still within, but they are not in working order and the observatory is not as impressive as its Jaipur counterpart. Near the entrance to the observatory is a little Shiva temple known as Dalbhyeshvara. Here the shrine is a *linga* submerged in a cistern. At times of drought water is poured in and the temple filled to overflowing as a charm to bring rain.

Dom Rāja's House.

□ *DOM RĀJA'S HOUSE* (Figure A.4)

Next downstream is the House of Dom Rāja, the chief cremator of Banāras and one of its most respected citizens. The
doms are the untouchables who are responsible for crema-
tions. They manage the burning *ghāts*, look after the cleaning and upkeep of the pyre beds, accept the fees for cremation, and supply the flame on a staff from a nearby temple,
where it burns day and night. All dead matter is ritually impure
to the Hindu, corpses especially so. Thus the *doms* are
untouchables—on a level with scavengers—yet their presence is absolutely essential in the Hindu system. A cremation
is considered correct and according to scriptural procedures
only if it is performed by a *dom*. Cremation at Manikarnikā
Ghāt is thought to insure instant salvation, but only if the fire
is provided by a *dom*.

The leader of the *dom* community is the Dom Rāja, and he
is immensely wealthy. His house is easily identifiable: white,
with tigers on the balcony and a figure of Shiva as Mahāyogi
sitting on the roof. There is always a flag of India flying above
the house. The Dom Rāja claims descent from the cremator
who employed King Harishchandra as a servant, his elevated
status being a gift from the gods for his part in that famous
episode. His wealth comes from the cremation fees, which
range from a minimum of 11 rupees ($1.50) to a maximum
of 501 rupees. His income is estimated at over 1,000 rupees
a day, and he lives in great style. The position is hereditary
but does not pass automatically to the eldest son. The retiring Dom Rāja chooses whichever son he deems fittest for
the job. For the past three generations the youngest son has

succeeded his father. The Dom Rājas have also had a reputation as wrestlers, which continues to the present day.

□

North of the Dom Rāja's house is Mīr Ghāt, built by a Muslim *fakīr*. Here there is an *āshram* for white-robed widows, from which the plaintive sound of a harmonium, cymbals, and chanting drifts out over the river. Then comes Lalitā Ghāt, famous for its Nepālī temple. Half hidden by magnificent tamarind and *pīpal* trees, the temple is built of wood and brick in pure Himālayan style, with a sloping two-storied roof and great eaves supported by brackets elaborately carved with erotic sculptures.

□ *JALASAĪ AND MANIKARNIKĀ GHĀTS* (Figure A.5)
You are now approaching the holiest spot on the waterfront: the burning grounds of the Jalasaī and Manikarnikā Ghāts. PHOTOGRAPHY IS FORBIDDEN HERE. Manikarnikā is popularly considered the holiest of all the *ghāts*. Every pilgrim will try to include this and the Dashāshvamedha Ghāt in his daily round of the city's shrines. Legend has it that the Lord Shiva passed here in a frenzy, because of the death of his wife Satī, who had committed suicide because her father had insulted Shiva. She was slung over his shoulder. As he passed Banāras, Satī's earring fell off and landed in the well above the *ghāt*. The brahmins managed to salvage the jewel (*manikarnikā*) from the earring, and returned it to Shiva, who was so delighted that he blessed the place to be especially sacred ever after. The tank remains a great pilgrimage spot; offerings of *bilva* flowers (sacred to Shiva), milk, sandalwood, and sweetmeats are thrown into it. Between the well and the *ghāt* is a stone pedestal, on the marble top of which are two imprints, believed to be the footprints of Lord Vishnu. To be cremated here is the special privilege of only a few families.

□ *SAMSKĀRAS*
Cremation is only the last of a number of ritually prescribed ceremonies that govern the life of an orthodox Hindu. These are called *samskāras*. There are forty major *samskāras* and they guide the life of the pious from the moment he is conceived to the moment his ashes are scattered here in the Ganges.

One of the cardinal duties of a householder is to honor his ancestors by offering them food and performing certain rituals to them. Only a son can do this, hence the importance of the male child. Largely because of this necessity to perform rites, procreation is a duty enjoined on the householder. Thus the first *samskāra* is the conception ceremony, when the priest prays for the couple: "May you beget shining, wealthy children. May they donate liberally to the needy and attain enlightenment. May God make you fit for conception."

In the second month of pregnancy another ritual is performed "to quicken the male child in the woman." A few drops of the juice of a *banyan* stem are poured into the right nostril of the woman, with a prayer for the birth of a worthy child, preferably male. A sanctified thread is tied to her left wrist to ward off the evil eye. "May the immortals live in this house. May Indra bless me with sons. May I have handsome children."

At about the seventh month of pregnancy the hair of the woman is parted at the center, "to remove undesirable shocks" and to insure that she stays cheerful and positive before the birth. In this ceremony a porcupine quill is used, to bring the child an intellect that is sharp and penetrating, and the deity of the full moon is invoked, so that the child may be as beautiful as the moon itself. Music is played, in particular *vīnā* music, which increases the suckling power of the mother-to-be. She is given glass bangles that she wears until they break. At the close of the ceremony the woman touches a male calf, symbolic of her future child.

A month before the expected date of delivery, a special maternity room in the southwest of the house is selected on an auspicious day. A couple of days before the birth, the woman worships the family elders and family deities, and, accompanied by ringing bells and music, along with experienced and friendly mothers of the neighborhood, she enters the room. They supervise her special diet, massage her with oils, and prepare her for the birth. The room is kept dark, so as not to shock the baby. At the onset of labor *mantras* are chanted to ward off evil spirits. An elderly woman in the house unties several knots of rope to symbolize the loosening of muscles for the birth. The woman is surrounded by healing leaves. If delivery is difficult, special verses from the scriptures are chanted. When the baby is born, it is bathed in warm water and a small fire is lit for purification of the room and the child and its mother. Special seeds and grains are thrown into the fire.

There are a number of rituals the father also has to perform at this time, the principal one being to bathe in cold water with his clothes on. Ideally he should jump into a river or a lake, and make such a big splash that the water rises as high as a palm tree!

The father then touches the tip of the baby's tongue with honey touched by a gold ring, to endow it with intelligence. A secret name is given to him, his private identity free from harmful influences. Brahmins are summoned to bless the child by breathing on it. The father prays for the child: "Be a stone, be an axe unto your enemies; endure like the imperishable gold."

Early morning devotion.

There is a name-giving ceremony on the tenth or twelfth day after birth. Boys are called after the gods, and their names should have two syllables (for example, Hari, Shiva, Gopāl, and so on). Girls are generally named after goddesses or flowers. Their names should have three syllables and should end in "ī" or "ā." Sometimes possible names are written on pieces of paper and a little lamp set by each. The lamp that is the last to go out indicates the name to be chosen. Brahmins and elders are asked in, to call the new baby by its name and stabilize the personality it is acquiring.

The next major ceremony is the feeding of cooked rice. This is performed when the child is about six months old. The father feeds the child a little sweet rice anointed with gold, to ensure that its senses will be gratified and it will lead a long and happy life.

When the child is three, there is the tonsure ceremony. On a suitably auspicious day the hair is cut and thrown to the four directions. A knotted tuft of hair is left on, and this is meant to be kept for the rest of the child's life to insure the favor of the gods. This tuft is called the *shikha*.

One of the most important *samskāras* is the ceremony of the sacred thread. This ceremony is for males only. A brahmin takes the thread when he is eight, a *kshatriya* when he is eleven, and a *vaishya* when he is twelve. All dates are carefully calculated from the time of conception, which, to the Hindus, is when life begins. This is the child's second birth, when he was traditionally given over to his teacher to begin the *brahmachārya* stage of life. The *guru* becomes his father, and the *gāyatrī mantra* his mother. Those who have taken the sacred thread (i.e., members of the top three castes) are called "the twice-born." The ceremony makes the child fit to study the scriptures and begin a conscious, spiritual life.

The sacred thread is composed of three strands, which symbolize, among other things, the three chief deities: Brahmā, Vishnu, and Shiva. Different materials are used, depending on caste: silk for brahmins, cotton for the other two castes. The thread is worn over the left shoulder, across the chest, and should never be removed. Before the sacred thread ceremony an orthodox brahmin will never eat with his son, because the boy is not yet purified as one of the twice-born.

The most important of all the *samskāras*, from a social point of view, is marriage. It is certainly the most expensive. All marriages are arranged by the parents. Child marriage is now officially illegal, though it still takes place in remote parts of the country. The marriage proposal always comes from the girl's family; the father of a boy knows his son will be married and should not have to suffer the indignity of bargaining. Nor should the girl's father go directly to the prospective groom's family. The family priest (*purohita*) or, initially, the matchmaker is used as an intermediary. Matchmakers, along with money lenders, are well known as rogues; they are necessary evils in society. They are notorious for their greed and the unscrupulous flattery they will heap on the head of a youth they hope to get married, and from whose grateful parents they expect their fee. If the couple seem a possible match, the astrologer is then consulted, to insure that their astrological charts are compatible. Next the family pedigrees are mutually checked. If there is no genealogical objection, and the all-important question of the dowry is amicably settled, then the date is fixed for the engagement ceremony. This is really little more than a public declaration of the forthcoming marriage. A few close friends, the couple, the family priests, and, of course, the astrologer assemble together to bear witness to the betrothal.

The marriage season is in the spring. Not only the lucky day but the lucky hour and minute must be fixed by the astrologer for the wedding. The ceremony itself is a long drawn-out affair. The couple sit beside a sacred fire and repeat Vedic texts and verses uttered by the priest. He ties a sacred length of cloth to their clothes, binding them symbolically together. Toward the end of the ceremony, the couple take the "Seven Steps" around the sacred fire. This seals the marriage contract; it has now become a sacrament. Great feasting follows. The wealthy sometimes prolong the affair for ten days, and, of course, the brahmins are on hand for all the supplementary ceremonies that should be performed after the main one.

The final *samskāra* is cremation. Tradition has it that the *samskāras* performed while you are alive help you to conquer earth, while those performed at death help you to conquer heaven. To the Hindu life and death constitute a continuous process. At the time of death one merely drops the body, and the mind or "subtle body" withdraws to a subtler level. Here it joins the ancestors and may remain for some time before reincarnating onto the earth plane in another body. In any event, death is not something to be avoided or lamented. In fact any display of grief actually delays or prevents the departing person from entering whichever heaven he or she is destined for. Special texts are read at this time to divert the minds of the relatives and friends whose sad feelings might otherwise act as impediments to the departing soul. The *Gītā* sums up the Hindu attitude when it says that the soul takes on a new body just as the living change their clothes. It is unattached.

Because death is a sacrifice, fire must be used to burn the body. Only children under five, *sannyāsins*, and those who died from snakebites and smallpox are buried, preferably in the Ganges itself. Each pyre uses about 650 pounds (300 kilograms) of sandalwood, which is on sale at shops behind the *ghāt*. Clarified butter (*ghī*) is used as the fuel. It is the duty of the eldest son to light the pyre—another reason for the need to have a son. He undergoes various ritual purifications, including shaving and bathing, and is not allowed to eat food prepared by anyone else for thirty days after the funeral. When the body is burned, he throws a potful of the sacred Ganges water over his shoulder onto the smoking pyre, and walks away without looking back.

☐

Manikarnikā Ghāt is overlooked by the five-spired Temple of Durgā, goddess of destruction. Its walls are blackened by the smoke of pyres that never go out. Corpses are laid on the *ghāt* ready for the flames: men and widows wrapped in white cloth, women who died before their husbands in red. The *doms* carry huge baskets of smoking ashes down to the water's edge. Even if he is not fortunate enough to die in Banāras, a good Hindu will urge his relatives to bring his ashes here and scatter them in the river so as to speed the process of rebirth. There is no attempt to prolong the existence of what is only a physical shell; the impermanent is purified by fire, and the soul is set free. Everything is very matter-of-fact; there is no fuss. *Doms*, dogs, and mourners all mix together, as the inevitable round of life and death goes on. Strange ascetics are seen here—the Aghorīs. They use cremation grounds as their places of meditation and are reputed to indulge in fearful rituals with corpses and the spirits of the deceased. Even these wild-looking magicians are part of the scene with their matted hair piled up and their bodies smeared with ashes.

Figure C. Shiva's trident, the trishūla.

As a tribute to Shiva, Lord of Death, the *ghāts* seem to be crumbling before your very eyes. Temples lie half-submerged in the river; the steps are covered by little shrines and stones that mark the places of *satī*, where a pious wife immolated herself on her husband's pyre in emulation of Satī's suicide. The whole place breathes impermanence. Yet despite the drifting smoke, the wheeling kites, and the logs piled up like stacks of grotesquely contorted limbs, there is nothing morbid here. Just a sobering sense of inevitability and the fact that life goes on, no matter how many individuals die.

☐

If proximity to the Ganges guarantees holiness, then the priests sitting on their platforms only inches above the water have achieved perfection! Everywhere is now gleaming golden in the light of the sun, as the daily routine gets into full swing. The warm Chunār stone of the steps is splashed with the color of *sārīs*, as the women pick their way along the *ghāts* like the figures on a painted frieze from Pompeii. Sindhiā Ghāt, a favorite haunt of wandering *sādhus* of various orders, was named after a *mahārāja* of Gwālior, whose widow, Baīja Baī, started to build a palace and bathing *ghāt* here. But the tremendous weight of the masonry caused a landslide, and the buildings toppled into the river and had to be reconstructed.

☐ *PANCHAGANGĀ GHĀT*

The next large *ghāt* is Panchagangā Ghāt, beneath which the five holy rivers—Ganges, Sarasvatī, Yamunā, Kiranā, and Dhūtapāpā—are said to meet. This confluence gives the *ghāt* a special sanctity, and it is one of the five main places of pilgrimage in Banāras. It is certainly one of the most impressive. Five colossal flights of steps lead up to the main city.

Below them are clustered dozens of little cubicles, some containing images and some empty for meditation, which for much of the year are submerged under the river. Above them towers the Alamgir Mosque, which despite its curiously truncated towers, is still a commanding building in a fine position. It was built by Aurangzeb, on the site of the Bindu Mādhava Vishnu Temple, which, according to all reports, was one of the most impressive of all Indian temples. The French jewel dealer and traveler Tavernier, who was here in the mid-seventeenth century, describes it at some length in his journals—indeed the "great pagoda," as he called it, was the only temple in Kāshī he wrote much about. He was especially impressed with its six-foot (two-meter) image of Lord Vishnu, covered with gold, pearls, rubies, and emeralds in the Hindu style.

Here on the steps you might see a group of women clustered around a professional storyteller (*vyāsa*) who recites episodes from the *Rāmāyana* or *Mahābhārata*. He holds his audience spellbound. The confluence of the five rivers refers in esoteric symbolism to the flow of *soma*, the elixir of immortality, that the yogi experiences in the subtle nervous system. Much of the Vedic literature is concerned with this nectar and how to make it flow. Shiva is a god of the moon, and *soma* is lunar ambrosia. On the full moon of Kārttika (October–November) women come here, bathe, and then place food—often sweet rice dishes—in the moonlight to catch the *soma* as it falls from heaven. In the same month, as part of a Bengālī custom for the Divālī festival, the bamboo poles that

Riverside scene, Panchagangā Ghāt.

cover the *ghāts* are set up. Each has a lamp attached to it. These lights are to guide the ancestors (*pitris*) down to earth, so that when the moon is on the wane, they won't lose their way in the dark. It is worth climbing to the Alamgir Mosque for the view it affords over the river. From the top of its minarets you can see the *stūpa* at Sārnāth, and the Mīrzapur Hills stretching to the west.

□

Past Gāya Ghāt, where an enormous figure of a sacred cow stands on the steps and where the goddess Shītalā is especially worshipped in her form as the snake goddess (Nāgeshvarī Devī), lies Trilochana Ghāt, with two turrets half-submerged in the river. There is a temple here to Shiva in his form as the "Three-Eyed" (*trilochana*), from which the place gets its name. Although they are now somewhat subsidiary in their importance, until about the twelfth century, Gāya and Trilochana marked the southern end of the sacred city of Kāshī. All the *ghāts* you have so far seen were at that time in the rural outskirts of the city, known as the Forest of Bliss, and this area was the most frequented part of the city. Many of the holiest temples that were here were damaged when the original city was razed by the Muslim armies of Qutbuddīn Aibak at the end of the twelfth century; they were then moved farther south to where the present Kāshī stands. This part of the city is still largely Muslim, and thus there are no temples that would draw Hindu patronage and invest the area with vitality. The only exception to this is Prahlāda Ghāt, which has traditional sanctity for devotees of Vishnu.

The last *ghāt* on your journey is Rājghāt, the northern limit of the pilgrim's route. Excavations carried out just farther north on the Rājghāt plateau have revealed remains of the old city wall that date back to the ninth century B.C. The plateau, now a grassy knoll, was originally the very heart of the sacred city. In ancient times the river was most easily forded here, and it was no doubt here that the Buddha took the ferry across the Ganges on his way from Bodh Gayā to deliver his first discourse in the Deer Park at Sārnāth.

□ *ĀDI KESHAVA VISHNU TEMPLE*
On the far end of the Rājghāt plateau is where the river Varanā meets the Ganges. At their confluence stands the Ādi Keshava Vishnu Temple. This is one of the five places in the Panchatīrtha pilgrimage route which, ideally, all pilgrims should follow, bathing at each of the *ghāts*: Asi, Dashāshvamedha, and Ādi Keshava, then back to Panchagangā and finishing off with Manikarnikā. In following this route they have covered the entire city, in a ritual circumambulation, while offering their devotions at its holiest points.

☐

To the first-time visitor, Banāras, like Hinduism itself, may seem too overwhelming a mixture of new sights, sounds, and sensations. But the longer you stay in this ancient city, the more the hallowed atmosphere of the place creeps into you and the more its peculiar charm is revealed. For Banāras is the living proof that when a place is held to be holy for sufficiently long, the divine takes up its residence there.

17

SĀRNĀTH

IN THE FOOTSTEPS OF THE BUDDHA

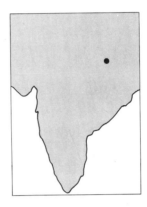

Buddhism was born in Sārnāth. Here in the Deer Park, only five miles (eight kilometers) from Banāras, the bastion of Hindu orthodoxy, the Enlightened One gave his first discourse sometime around 590 B.C. This event is known as "the Setting in Motion of the Wheel of Truth" and is one of the four most significant events in the story of the Buddha, along with his birth, Enlightenment, and death. The first discourse, popularly known as the Deer Park Sermon, was delivered with the clarity and incisiveness that were to become the hallmarks of the teaching (see page 27). From it came the creation of the *sangha*, the monastic order that was to spread the message of the Master throughout the world.

The Buddha's audience was composed of the five ascetics who had abandoned him when he decided to pursue his quest alone. Won over by the man they had earlier scorned, they became his first disciples.

Within a short time of "the Setting in Motion the Wheel of Truth," the Buddha had sixty disciples, the most prominent being Yasha, a wealthy householder from nearby Banāras. Buddhism rejected the caste system and from the beginning was associated with the merchant class. These disciples became the first monastic community. Based at Sārnāth, they

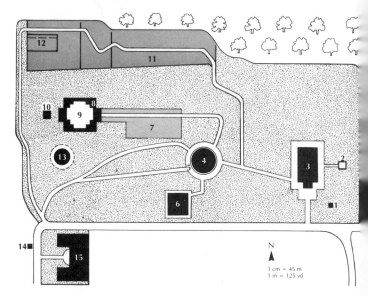

1 *Statue of Anagarika Damapala.* 2 Bodhi *tree.* 3 *Mūla Gandhakutī Vihāra.* 4 *Dharmekha Stūpa.* 5 *Gupta carving.* 6 *Jain temple.* 7 *Courtyard and walkway.* 8 *The Main Shrine.* 9 *Railings.* 10 *Ashokan column.* 11 *Monasteries.* 12 *Underground passage.* 13 *Dharmarājikā Stūpa.* 14 *Museum ticket office.* 15 *Museum.*

Figure A. Sārnāth site plan.

traveled throughout northern India, obeying the Master's instruction:

> Go forth, O Monks, and wander forth for the gain of the many; for the welfare of the many; in compassion for the world; for the good, the advantage and well-being of gods and men. Proclaim, O Monks, the glorious doctrine; preach a life of holiness, perfect and pure.

The park at Sārnāth is well laid out, with orderly green lawns and pink graveled paths bordered by beds of vivid red canna lilies. The place has a settled atmosphere, perhaps emphasized by the low contours of the remains, most of which are at little more than knee height. The tranquility is increased, rather than diminished, by the flood of pilgrims who ebb and flow around the monuments in a cadence of devotion. Many of these pilgrims are monks, their brilliant robes dotting the park with solid blocks of pure color—saffron, burgundy, deep amber, or black.

But the peace here is not inviolate; every so often it can be shattered by a group of visitors. Most incongruous of these are the cadres of Japanese monks, frenetically clicking away at everything with their duty-free cameras, while their leader bellows out the story of the Lord of Silence through a megaphone made of luminous orange plastic.

As so often at these Buddhist shrines, it is the Tibetans who are particularly impressive. Unfailingly cheerful and friendly, they seem little dispirited by the atrocities and exile they have suffered at the hands of the Chinese communists in the name of freedom and international brotherhood. Since the Cultural Revolution invaded Tibet in 1959, the three thousand temples, shrines, and monasteries there have been systematically destroyed; now thirteen remain. But Tibetan eyes twinkle humorously with the knowledge of human folly, and their leathery faces, lined by the joys and sorrows of life, are as creased and shiny as an old pair of well-loved shoes.

The women, girded round with striped aprons that are the sign of marriage, wear their jet-black hair in long plaits, sometimes coiled up around their heads. Their men sport huge earrings—lumps of coral and turquoise as big as pigeons' eggs—and each group of adults has its quota of mischievous russet-cheeked children, bottoms cut out of their baggy trousers to sidestep the problem of diapers. Tibetan hands never seem to be idle. Either they are spinning or knitting long strands of wispy yak or goat wool, or they are engaged in devotion: telling a rosary of dark wooden beads or spinning its automatic equivalent, the prayer wheel. Whether fixed in walls or small and portable, each prayer wheel contains a prayer, block-printed on rice paper, which ascends to the heavens as it whirls around. And wherever they go, these hardy people exude an unmistakable and pungent Tibetan odor—the result of incense, wood smoke, butter tea, and a congenital reluctance to wash.

India does not really want them—she has enough refugees of her own—so they live in their own villages and monastic communities scattered around the country. Luckily, Tibetans have a razor-sharp business sense, for they have always been traders. Although their handicrafts are often exorbitantly priced by Indian standards, a stubborn refusal to bargain, coupled with their plight as displaced persons, usually defeats the tourist. And even if they do overcharge, who cares? They do it with such charm that you don't mind joining in the game.

The spiritual head of the international Tibetan community is the Dalai Lama. This gentle man, whose name means "Lake of Great Peace," lives at Dharamshāla, in the Himālayan foothills. So far he has wisely resisted the attempts of the Chinese to lure him back to his old capital, Lhasa. He has said he will return to Tibet only when he can be sure that his people are genuinely happy under Chinese occupation. No such proof has yet been forthcoming.

The Deer Park
(Figure A)

You enter the park by the eastern gate, which faces the Mūla Gandhakutī Temple. On your right is a statue of Anagarika Damapala, the founder of the Mahābodhi Society (A.1). The Society pioneered a revival of Buddhism in India at the end of the last century. Today it is responsible for the upkeep of the Mahābodhi Temple at Bodh Gayā, which marks the site of the Buddha's Enlightenment, and looks after the Mūla Gandakutī temple here at Sārnāth. It also runs several missions throughout the world.

To the right of the temple is a *bodhi* tree (the *pīpal* or *ficus religiosa*, A.2). In 240 B.C. a cutting from the original tree at Bodh Gayā was taken to Srī Lankā by Mahendra, the nephew of the Buddhist emperor Ashoka. In 1931 a sapling from the descendant of that tree was planted here by Damapala to commemorate the resurgence of the *dharma* in its native country.

Mūla Gandhakutī Vihāra (Figure A.3)

This modern temple was built in 1929–31 and is modeled after the Mahābodhi Temple at Bodh Gayā. Apart from a good collection of Buddhist literature on sale inside, the chief interest of the temple lies in its frescoes. These were executed by a Japanese artist, Kosetsu Nosu, and depict scenes from the Buddha's life. Some of the incidents come from the *jātaka* tales and show a blending of known historical fact with ancient and universal myth. They are a good example of modern Buddhist art and avoid the technicolor excesses of their Hindu counterparts.

We shall begin with the south wall—that is, the one containing the main entrance, opposite the shrine.

The South Wall

☐ *THE DEVAS REQUEST THE BODHISATTVA* (Figure B.1)
The *devas* (celestial beings) ask the future Buddha to take birth on the earth plane. By the merit accumulated in previous births, the future Buddha had acquired the status of *bodhisattva* (pure-minded one). Now he is asked to incarnate on earth as Prince Siddhārtha Gautama of the Shākya clan, in order to teach the *dharma* for the welfare of all mankind.

☐ *QUEEN MĀYĀ'S DREAM* (Figure B.2)
The future Buddha's mother, Queen Māyā, dreamt that a white elephant entered her womb from the right side. This is

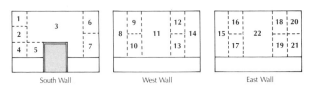

South Wall   West Wall   East Wall

1 *The* Devas *Request the* Bodhisattva. **2** *Queen Māyā's Dream.* **3** *Birth of the Buddha.* **4** *Distribution of Alms.* **5** *Asita Visits the Child.* **6** *Siddhārtha's First Meditation.* **7** *Siddhārtha Leaves His Family.* **8** *Siddhārtha Leaves the Palace.* **9** *Siddhārtha Meets a Philosopher.* **10** *The Offering of the Milk Rice.* **11** *The Great Enlightenment.* **12** *The Buddha Meets His Former Companions.* **13** *The Buddha Preaches to King Bimbisāra.* **14** *The Gift of a Monastery.* **15** *The Buddha Ministers to the Sick.* **16** *The Buddha Reconciles Two Warring Armies.* **17** *The Buddha Meets His Father.* **18** *The Buddha with Celestial Attendants.* **19** *The Buddha Converts a Murderer.* **20** *The Plot Against the Buddha.* **21** *Ānanda Accepts Water from an Untouchable.* **22** *Death of the Buddha.*

Figure B. Walls of Mūla Gandhakutī Vihāra.

the sign that a divine being will be born from her. Later the Buddha, describing the birth of a *bodhisattva* on earth, said that the mother is always pure, virtuous, honest, and averse to taking life or alcohol. She perceives the *bodhisattva* within her as a perfect and flawless being, and seven days after the birth, she dies and goes to the highest heaven.

☐ *BIRTH OF THE BUDDHA* (Figure B.3)
The future Buddha was born effortlessly and without pain in the Lumbinī Gardens, on the borders of modern Nepāl. He was born under the holy *shāla* tree, on which Queen Māyā leaned like the *yakshī* tree spirits of Indian lore. As soon as he was born, he stood up and took seven steps in the four directions, thus proclaiming himself spiritual ruler of the world. Lotuses sprang up where his feet touched the ground, and the surrounding trees burst joyfully into blossom.

☐ *DISTRIBUTION OF ALMS* (Figure B.4)
The Buddha's father, King Shuddhodana, celebrated the birth of his son by distributing alms to the poor and sick. Temples were decorated, there was great rejoicing, and the boy was given the name Siddhārtha: "the fulfillment of all desires."

☐ *ASITA VISITS THE CHILD* (Figure B.5)
An aged sage called Asita, respected by all for his wisdom and piety, dreamed that a divine child would be born in the royal palace of Kapilavastu. He visited the infant Siddhārtha, prophesied he would be a spiritual leader, and died shortly

afterward (an interesting forerunner to the Biblical story of Simeon).

☐ *PRINCE SIDDHĀRTHA'S FIRST MEDITATION* (Figure B.6)

During the annual plowing festival, the young prince sits under a *jambu* tree and meditates. It was noticed that he cast no shadow, and, when he put his hand to the plow, it turned to gold—sure signs of his divine status.

☐ *SIDDHĀRTHA LEAVES HIS FAMILY* (Figure B.7)

Siddhārtha lived a life of luxury and ease, married, and had a son. One day he traveled out of the palace and saw, in quick succession, an old man, a sick man, a corpse being taken to cremation, and an ascetic. These meetings so stirred him that he resolved to leave Kapilavastu and seek Truth. That night he left his sleeping wife, Yashodharā, and son, Rāhula, and stole out of the palace.

The West Wall

☐ *SIDDHĀRTHA LEAVES THE PALACE* (Figure B.8)

With his faithful charioteer Channa, the prince leaves the palace of Kapilavastu, mounted on his horse Kanthaka. (A white horse is a traditional sign of renunciation in India.) At dawn he sent the servant and horse back to the palace and continued alone to begin his quest.

☐ *SIDDHĀRTHA MEETS A PHILOSOPHER* (Figure B.9)

Now wearing the orange robe of an ascetic and carrying a begging bowl for food, Siddhārtha goes to visit a famous philosopher, Ālāra Kālāma, in his forest hermitage. He became his pupil but found no satisfaction. He studied with several other teachers, but in the end he, together with five brahmin ascetics, decided to undergo severe austerities in order to find Truth.

☐ *THE OFFERING OF THE MILK RICE* (Figure B.10)

Siddhārtha decided to abandon austerities, and his ascetic companions deserted him in disgust. He continued alone and, after several years of wandering, came, when he was thirty-five, to what is now Bodh Gayā in Bihār. One day, while meditating, he was approached by a young woman called Sujātā. She was bringing a golden dish of milk rice as an offering to the spirit of the tree under which Siddhārtha was sitting, in thanks for her newly born child. Seeing the nobility of the man, she bowed down before him and offered him the rice instead. Siddhārtha accepted and broke his fast.

☐ THE GREAT ENLIGHTENMENT (Figure B.11)

Shortly after this incident, Siddhārtha took up his seat under the *bodhi* tree, and, after prolonged meditation, on the evening of the spring full moon, entered *nirvāna*. From that time he was known as Buddha, "the Enlightened One." The mural shows him surrounded by the forces of Māra, "the Evil One," under whose power the world is kept in illusion. These figures represent the negative aspects of the subconscious that have to be faced and resolved on the journey to complete integration. The Buddha is touching the earth, which bore witness to his Enlightenment, thus "grounding" himself to ward off the psychic barrage let loose on him by Māra.

☐ THE BUDDHA MEETS HIS FORMER COMPANIONS (Figure B.12)

After the Enlightenment, the Buddha decided to teach the Truth to the world. His first thought was to find his old teachers and expound the insights of *nirvāna* to them, but Ālāra Kālāma had died seven days earlier and the others were not to be found. So the Buddha traveled to the Deer Park at Sārnāth, and there met the five ascetics, his former companions. At first they did not wish to have anything to do with him, but they were eventually unable to resist his spiritual power. One took his bowl, another prepared his seat, while a third brought water and a towel. When the Buddha had washed his feet, he explained to them the Four Noble Truths and thus took place "the Setting in Motion of the Wheel of Truth."

☐ THE BUDDHA PREACHES TO KING BIMBISĀRA (Figure B.13)

Bimbisāra reigned over Magadha, an important kingdom of northern India in which the Buddha did much of his teaching. Here the king is shown seated on his throne respectfully listening to the Master.

☐ THE GIFT OF A MONASTERY (Figure B.14)

A wealthy merchant who had heard the Buddha speak approaches the crown prince of Kosala, Prince Jeta, to see if he might buy some of the prince's land and donate it to the newly founded order (top). At first the prince was hesitant, but, on hearing of the Enlightened One's teaching, he sold the land to the merchant at half price.

The East Wall

☐ THE BUDDHA MINISTERS TO THE SICK (Figure B.15)

One day the Enlightened One and his closest disciple, Ānanda, came across a monk who was lying seriously ill. The

Master washed and cared for him and rebuked the other monks who had selfishly left their brother to die because they thought there was no hope for him to recover.

□ *THE BUDDHA RECONCILES TWO WARRING ARMIES*
    (Figure B.16)
When he returned to his home at Kapilavastu after seven years of Enlightenment, the first thing the Master found was that his family was about to go to war with their neighboring clan, the Koliyas, over water rights. Here he reconciles the enemies.

□ *THE BUDDHA MEETS HIS FATHER* (Figure B.17)
At first unwilling to receive his son in the robes of a simple ascetic, King Shuddhodana soon accepted his greatness. That night both the king and the Buddha's wife, Yashodharā, entered the Buddhist order.

□ *THE BUDDHA WITH CELESTIAL ATTENDANTS*
    (Figure B.18)
Here the Buddha stands surrounded by attendants after his return from the highest heaven where he had been preaching the *dharma* to his mother, Queen Māyā. Buddhism does not believe in an individual soul that goes to heaven after death but teaches that the "subtle" (that is, mental) body leaves the physical body at death and travels to one of a number of celestial or infernal realms. It remains there until the time comes for it to reincarnate in a new womb. This cycle of birth-death-reincarnation (*samsāra*) continues until the mind is pure enough to achieve enlightenment. The enlightened have no need to assume physical form again; as the Buddha said, "they have realized what has to be realized; they have done what has to be done."

□ *THE BUDDHA CONVERTS A MURDERER* (Figure B.19)
There are many stories of the Buddha's healing effect on those he met. Here he converts a particularly nasty character, a *dacoit* (murderer) called Angulīmālā. *Angulīmālā* means "necklace of fingers," and the man was so called because he was surrounded by a negative aura of 999 bloody fingers, representing the number of people he had killed. So keen was he to notch up his thousandth victim, that he was considering murdering his own mother. Luckily for all concerned, the Buddha intervened. On seeing the Master, Angulīmālā decided to get his thousandth finger from the Enlightened One himself, but his sword was unable to penetrate the Buddha's aura. He calmly bid the *dacoit*, "Be still, as I am still." So saying, he expounded the *dharma* to the

astonished murderer and that evening received him into his order.

Symbolically, Angulīmālā represents the negative ego, prepared to "kill" even the deeper self (the mother), which nourishes it in its blind and vicious ignorance. The calming power of meditation leads to a more universal sense of being.

□ *THE PLOT AGAINST THE BUDDHA* (Figure B.20)
One of the monks, the Buddha's cousin Devadatta, plotted to gain control of the order and enlisted the help of King Bimbisāra's son and heir, Prince Ajāshatru. Here the two conspirators plan to murder the Master, but the assassins they hired were won over by the power of the Enlightened One. Later both Devadatta and Ajāshatru repented and were forgiven.

□ *ĀNANDA ACCEPTS WATER FROM AN UNTOUCHABLE*
    (Figure B.21)
Buddhism did not acknowledge the caste system. Even today, many Buddhist converts come from the lower end of the Hindu social scale. There are four main castes: priests (*brāhmanas* or *brāhmins*), warriors (*kshatriyas*), merchants (*vaishyas*), and manual workers (*shūdras*). There is also a fifth group, the "untouchables" (*chandalas*)—now called "scheduled castes," who, until recently, were "outcastes," enjoying none of the privileges of the Hindu social order. A *kshatriya* himself, Buddha repudiated the caste system as being inhuman and admitted anyone who was sincere into his order.

One of the most famous converts to Buddhism was Dr. Ambedeka, who was born an "untouchable," became a lawyer, and eventually drafted the Indian Constitution, which made discrimination on the grounds of caste illegal.

When Ānanda asked an untouchable girl at a well for a drink of water, she replied that she was not fit to serve him. He told her that caste meant nothing to him, whereupon she was so delighted that she begged him to be allowed to serve the order. On hearing of this and other similar cases, the Buddha decided to admit women into the order under eight additional rules.

□ *THE DEATH OF THE BUDDHA* (Figure B.22)
After almost fifty years of Enlightenment, the Buddha spent the last rainy season retreat near Vaishālī, and then traveled with five hundred monks to the part of the country where he had grown up. He knew his death was imminent and prepared his disciples for the inevitable. They reached the town of Pāvā, where the Buddha ate a meal of truffles. Soon after he was attacked by dysentery but moved on to the nearby town of Kushinagara. Here he lay down under a *shāla* tree and asked

any of the assembled monks who had doubts about the teaching to voice them for the last time. None had any. The Master appointed no successor but said that the *dharma* itself was to be their guide. His last words were "Decay is inherent in all compounded things. Work toward your Enlightenment with dedication. Be a light unto yourselves, a refuge unto yourselves." When the Master's body was put on the funeral pyre, a flame burst out of his breast and consumed the corpse, for it is said that he who sets in motion the Wheel of Truth cannot be burned by normal fire.

☐

Leaving the temple, we can retrace the Buddha's footsteps. When he arrived here from Bodh Gayā after attaining Enlightenment, he came from the east, along the footpath that connected the ancient city of Banāras with the Deer Park. His first encounter was with the five ascetics, and this took place at the spot now marked by the Dharmekha Stūpa.

The path from the Mūla Gandhakutī Temple to the *stūpa* is lined by *ashoka* trees, whose leaves are considered lucky and are widely used for festivals and healing. You will see them strung over doorways of houses where there has recently been a marriage.

*Dharmekha Stūpa
(from the west).*

Gupta carving on the Dharmekha Stūpa.

Dharmekha Stūpa (Figure A.4)

This solid cylindrical tower rises to a height of over 130 feet (40 meters) and rests on a circular stone base. Halfway up this base are eight niches, each of which would originally have held images. The stones in each layer of the base were bonded together by means of iron clamps, in the traditional Indian way. The *stūpa* is an enlargement of an original brick edifice that was probably erected by Emperor Ashoka in the third century B.C., to commemorate one of the holiest places of Buddhism, for it was on this spot, after his meeting with the five ascetics, that the Enlightened One set in motion the Wheel of Truth. (The name Dharmekha is a corruption of *dharmachakra*, "Wheel of Truth.") Remains of this original *stūpa* were found by Sir Alexander Cunningham in 1836, when he was investigating the present *stūpa* for relics. There were no relics, but he did come across a stone slab, carved with the Buddhist creed in characters of the sixth century A.D. (the Gupta period). The present base of the *stūpa* dates from this time. It is remarkable for the exquisite carved ornamentation, in which geometrical and floral motifs are intertwined with human and animal figures. This magnificent example of Gupta decoration, some of which resembles Mayan art, was a stone copy of the sumptuously embroidered cloth (*devadūshya*), which was originally draped over the whole *stūpa*. The finest carving is to be found on the southwest side of the *stūpa* (A.5).

The Deer Park is also holy to the Jains, for it was here that the eleventh *tīrthankara*, Shreyāmshanātha, died. The modern temple to the southwest of the Dharmekha Stūpa is a Jain temple commemorating the event (A.6).

The Main Shrine
(Figure A.8)

After the first discourse, the Buddha left the dwelling of the five ascetics to settle down in the park. He walked westward and took up his abode in what is now known as the Main Shrine. Although little now remains, we can see from the thickness of the walls that they were originally intended to support a massive and lofty structure. From the style of building and decoration, we can date the temple from the sixth century. Presumably this temple marked the site of what was the Buddha's headquarters here in Sārnāth, though he spent much of his life traveling in northern India, mainly in what is now Bihār. It was certainly his preferred place of meditation (*mūlaghandhakutī*) and was known as the Mūlaghandhakutī Shrine. Both the concrete pavement around the shrine and the brick walls inside were added at a later date to reinforce the original. Nearby is the courtyard where the Buddha would take his daily walk (A.7). Inside the shrine can be seen the remains of a railing, cut from a single block of Chunār sandstone (A.9). It dates from about 200 B.C., and would probably have surmounted the Dharmarājikā Stūpa to the south.

☐

At the western end of the Main Shrine stands the stump of an Ashokan column (A.10), the famous capital of which you will see in the Archeological Museum. It was originally almost fifty feet (over fifteen meters) high and was one of the many pillars that the emperor had erected in his kingdom to proclaim the teachings and the glory of the *dharma*.

View over the ruins of the Main Shrine courtyard, showing the Dharmekha Stūpa (left) and the main temple (right).

The shaft of the pillar tapers slightly and bears three inscriptions. The earliest and most important of these dates from the second century B.C. and warns that anyone who created schisms in the order would be expelled. "His sacred Majesty further urges that his order should be made known to lay-members. The guardians of the *dharma* should familiarize themselves with the edict, and make its message known in their own circles and elsewhere." Even at this early stage of its history, Buddhism was evidently beginning to suffer the distortion and sectarianism that inevitably dilutes the teaching of an enlightened leader.

North of the Main Shrine lie the remains of the monasteries (A.11) which were erected as the order grew in strength.

The most interesting part of these ruins lies in the northwest corner of the compound. Here you can still see an underground passage, covered by stone slabs. The walkway is about 165 feet (50 meters) long and leads to a small medieval shrine. Cells for meditation were also here, and the structure may have belonged to an order of Buddhist nuns (A.12).

The path from this spot to the museum in the south of the precinct gives the best view back over the ruins, stretching up to and beyond the tall mass of the Dharmekha Stūpa, which dominates the park. We can get an idea of the considerable extent of the community here, which remained a thriving center of Buddhism from the time of its founding to the invasion of the Muslims in the twelfth century.

Dharmarājikā Stūpa (Figure A.13)

This *stūpa* was built by Ashoka to enshrine the bodily relics of the Buddha when the emperor was redistributing them to the eight most important *stūpas* in India. It was demolished by Jagat Singh, prime minister to the Mahārāja of Banāras, in 1794, a piece of historical irony, as the ruler of Banāras is the villain in many of the *jātaka* tales. But at least this tragic piece of vandalism alerted the world to the existence of Sārnāth. While demolishing the *stūpa*, Jagat Singh's workmen found a stone box containing a green marble casket. Within the casket were relics of the Buddha, which were thrown into the Ganges on Jagat Singh's orders. But Mr. Duncan, the British resident of Banāras at that time, published an account of the discovery, and Sārnāth was placed firmly on the archeological map. The casket was rediscovered by Cunningham's excavations in the 1830s, but it has since disappeared. The British excavations showed six distinct layers to the *stūpa* providing valuable evidence of how an original *stūpa* would be increased layer by layer by succeeding patrons of the Buddhist faith. As in Hinduism, improvement of an existing religious structure assured the benefactor great merit, and kings were always eager to commemorate themselves in this way.

The Archeological Museum
(Figure A.15)

The Archeological Museum was planned as a site museum to display the antiquities unearthed at Sárnáth. Built in 1910, it is modeled on a Buddhist monastery. Sculptures are arranged in the main hall, four galleries, and the outside verandahs.

The Main Hall

□ *THE LION CAPITAL*
As you enter the Main Hall, you come face to face with the celebrated Lion Capital, which originally topped the Ashokan column in the western end of the Main Shrine. One of the most famous pieces of Indian art, and the symbol adopted as the country's emblem, the Lion Capital originally comprised four pieces.

The Bell-shaped Base   This was in the form of an inverted lotus, the familiar symbol of enlightenment and creativity.

Round Abacus   This is carved with four sacred animals—an elephant, a bull, a horse, and a lion, each separated by a Wheel of Truth (*dharmachakra*). As well as being the most common symbols of the Buddha's teaching, these wheels represent the intermediate regions of space, whereas the animals represent the four quarters. As such, they hark back to the very beginnings of Indian civilization. Here they are portrayed in a lively, realistic manner and remind us of Greek sculpture. There was considerable Greek influence at the time of the Mauryan dynasty (second century B.C.), when this was carved. Alexander the Great's abortive invasion of India a hundred years earlier had left a legacy of more than just blue-eyed Indians, for the Greeks brought with them styles of stone carving that the native craftsmen adapted into their own rich vocabulary.

The Four Lions   These form the body of the capital and display the other major influence on Indian stone sculpture—ancient Irán. The symbol of the lion as a solar divinity can be found in the art of Irán, Mesopotamia, and Egypt, long before the time of Ashoka. This emblem of regal majesty and divine power was transposed to the Buddhist cause and perhaps even carved by sculptors who had produced the same image further west, before they came to India. Even the details of these magnificent creatures remind us of their prototypes: Their masklike heads, triangular eyes (whose sockets originally held sparkling gems), and muzzles etched with whiskered lines are all Iranian conventions. Indeed the very idea of erecting memorial columns is a feature of ancient Mesopotamian civilization, and carving edicts on stone to insure their "immortality" can be traced back to early Irān. So you can see that at this early date, India was open to a variety of influences from the West, whereas, for the next thousand years, until the coming of Islām, she was to remain comparatively isolated.

Nevertheless, Ashoka added new life to the conventions he inherited. Part of this vitality is due to the extraordinary quality of the stone. When the Chinese pilgrim Hiuen-tsang visited Sārnāth in the seventh century, he reported on the pillar's beauty: "The stone is altogether as bright as jade. It is glistening and sparkles like light." The sheen has not diminished. Made of local Chunār sandstone (as were all the Mauryan monuments), the capital has a brilliance, never captured in photographs, that makes it resemble marble and adds to its imperial authority.

The Wheel of Truth   The capital was originally crowned by a Wheel of Truth, of which only a few broken spokes survive. They are also in the museum.

□ THE BODHISATTVA
To the left of the Lion Capital stands a red sandstone *bodhisattva*. This dates from the first century A.D. and is a fine example of the Mathurā school of sculpture.

□ THE CHHATTRA
Behind the *bodhisattva* stands an octagonal shaft, which was originally crowned by a lotiform umbrella top (*chhattra*) now resting against the north wall of the hall. This massive parasol—a stylized version of the sacred tree/royal umbrella/thousand-petaled lotus image—is profusely carved with auspicious signs: animals, lotuses, sheaves of corn, fishes, and *svastikas*—emblems of good luck in Hindu, Buddhist, and Jain art. They have been found on the bricks of Mohenjodaro (ca. 2500 B.C.).

□ THE SEATED BUDDHA
The Main Hall also enshrines one of the greatest pieces of sculptural art in the world. This is the seated Buddha, shown "Setting in Motion the Wheel of Truth." It sits against the south wall, beside the doorway to the next gallery. A master-

piece of Gupta art (fifth century), the Buddha deserves close scrutiny. As with the best of Gupta art, the seated Buddha exudes a blissful serenity that is an extraordinary combination of the sensual and the spiritual. The face is a soft oval; the gently closed eyes and full, heavy lips smile with an inner certainty. The body is almost bursting with contained energy. This pregnant vitality is *prāna*—the life energy that sustains creation and positively radiates from those who have realized their own divinity. The vibrant glow of *prāna* suffuses the whole figure, even down to its well-formed toes, and its warm sensuousness is enhanced by the creamy peach color of the sandstone. Yet the whole tone of the figure is one of utter restraint. The energy is self-contained, its richness is modulated by the simplicity of the unadorned body surface, the supple gesture of the hands, which have the pliant twist of a growing plant, and the plain inner circle of the halo (*prabhāmandala*) framing the face. The whole effect of the Buddha is breathtaking, inducing in us the same indrawn calm it radiates.

Beautiful though this Buddha is, its primary purpose is to point beyond itself. We have seen time and again that the purpose of an image in Indian art is to serve as a springboard whereby the mind can ascend from the concrete world to the abstract realm of spirit. The viewer is led from an esthetic appreciation to higher insight, whereby the formal composition of the sculpture expresses certain truths which are

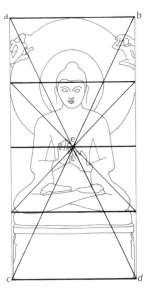

Figure C. Sārnāth Buddha (centered energy).

themselves beyond the world of form. In this Platonic conception of the purpose of art, an image is technically known as a support (*pratyaya*), and both Hindu and Buddhist texts refer to the image as a specific means (*upāya*) by which the perceiving consciousness is expanded. Let us examine the Sārnāth Buddha a little more closely in this light.

Centered Energy (Figure C)   The sculpture is basically a rectangle *a-b-c-d*, composed of four equal rectangles. The central point of the figure is the point *e* (the *anāhata chakra* of the Buddha), at which all the diagonals intersect. Appropriately enough, this central point is the place where the Buddha's fingers touch to form the *mudrā* of "Setting in Motion the Wheel of Truth." Thus the essential part of the figure's message—the birth of Buddhism—is also its physical center (*madhya bindu*).

Potential Energy (Figure D)   This unity of form and meaning is emphasized by the fact that point *e* is also the point at which the two triangles *a-b-e* and *c-d-e* touch. If you isolate these two triangles, you get a figure that is one of the archetypes of esoteric symbolism the world over. Here the top triangle, pointing downward, represents the male spiritual force, often likened to the sky, and the lower triangle represents the female material, earthy force. When these two triangles just touch each other, they are a symbol of potential

Figure D. Sārnāth Buddha (potential energy).

waiting to be realized: the moment before creation, which is pure possibility. The point where they touch is called, in cosmological terms, *bindu* ("seed"), and this point contains all creation in latent form. In Hindu iconography this state of potential is symbolized by the drum of Shiva, Lord of Time, which is shaped like an hourglass, itself a common Western symbol of time. On its side, this figure becomes a stylized representation of the mathematical sign for infinity.

Manifesting Energy (Figure E)   When the two triangles move and interpenetrate, then the male is joined with the female force, and creation has begun. All the potential of the *bindu* point begins to be manifested, just as an oak emerges out of the potential contained within an acorn. The most common representation of this creative union of male and female is the *satkona* ("six-pointed star"), whose Western counterpart is the Star of David (see page 320). The tantric *satkona* is elaborated into the *shrī yantra*—the universe arisen from the *bindu*.

Here in the Sārnāth Buddha, the *bindu* point is just where the Master is making the Wheel of Truth *mudrā*, by joining his left (female) and right (male) hands. Again this is entirely appropriate, because to the Buddhist this historical occasion of the first discourse was the moment when the Buddhist "creation" began—in other words, the doctrine was released to the world. The Buddhist calendar dates from this event,

Figure E. Sārnāth Buddha (manifesting energy).

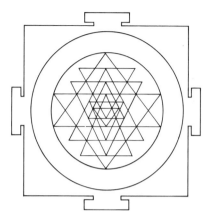

Figure F. Shrī yantra (manifested energy).

which, as the historical "grounding" of the Great Enlightenment, marks the beginning of time made sacred by the
Master's teaching.

The second half of the movement is also contained in the
sculpture. As the male triangle moves downward, it becomes
f-g-h, with its base as the heavenly attendants of the Buddha,
and its inverted apex "grounded" in the Wheel of Truth. This

*Figure G. Sārnāth Buddha
(impersonal energy).*

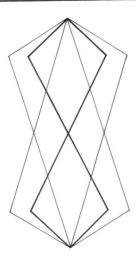

Figure H. Sārnāth Buddha (pure energy).

male triangle unites those parts of the sculpture that are accessory to the main figure, whereas the ascending female triangle *j-k-l* comprises the actual body of the Buddha.

Impersonal Energy (Figure G)   Within this configuration there is a further tension in the way the panel is composed that serves to reinforce its didactic message. Initially, your gaze is led up to the Buddha's face. Its tranquil and composed beauty serves as a natural focus within the ascending triangle *j-k-l*, but on reaching the face, your attention is held within the frame of the halo, a circle whose center is the Buddha's third eye (*o*). The floriate decoration of the nimbus catches your attention. Then the frame of the triangle *m-n-e*, emphasizing the shape of the Master's face and the downcast direction of his gaze, leads you back down from the head to the hands. You move from the personal teacher to the impersonal teaching, from the historical to the eternal, from the Buddha to the *dharma*. And this is just what the Master would have wanted.

Pure Energy (Figure H)   The final development of the Sārnāth Buddha is to expand into pure energy. What began as a piece of figurative sculpture of the highest quality has dissolved into the pure form of the diamond thunderbolt (*vajra*), a comprehensive symbol of the *dharma* much loved by Mahāyānist iconographers. Within the very body of this Gupta Buddha shines the indestructible brilliance of the Truth he taught.

18

BODH GAYĀ

THE TREE OF LIFE

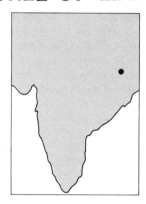

It was at Bodh Gayā, seven miles (eleven kilometers) south of present-day Gayā in Bihār, that the Buddha attained Enlightenment. The exact date of his *nirvāna* is not known, but most authorities agree it was sometime around 590 B.C. The Buddha was reluctant to describe the nature of *nirvāna* for fear that his description would degenerate into yet another intellectual or emotional barrier to people discovering the Truth for themselves. Nor did he write any of his teaching down; all we have by way of record is the scriptures assembled by his early followers and filtered down through the great Buddhist Councils of 486 B.C. and 386 B.C., when the doctrine became increasingly formalized. But what the Buddha did say about *nirvāna* alludes to a state that is beyond the restrictions of the individual ego and the self-centered desire (*tanhā*, literally "thirst") that binds us all to the wheel of suffering. The enlightened mind sees through the veil of conditioning and habitual response (*pratitya samutpāda*) that obscures Truth; it sees Reality face to face. This insight naturally engenders compassion (*karunā*) for the suffering of others and the desire to awaken them to freedom; the Buddha once said it was as natural for him to teach as for a flower to give out its scent. *Nirvāna* is to be experienced in this life, not in some imaginary realm after death, and the Master referred to the state as "a glorious city, stainless and undefiled, pure and white, unaging, deathless, secure, calm and happy." Buddhism has in essence remained true to the purity of its founder's message, for even to the restless modern mind its teachings are like an inexhaustible lake of wisdom, pellucid and without shadow.

The Mahābodhi Temple (Figure A.2)

The Enlightenment took place under the *bodhi* tree (*bodhi:* "enlightened mind"), a descendent of which is the spiritual axis of the Bodh Gayā site. But what first catches the visitor's attention is not the tree but the Mahābodhi Temple, which was built next to it. Rising clear above the jumble of the temple compound, the present structure dates from the second century A.D. It was erected on the site of one built by Emperor Ashoka when he visited Bodh Gayā about 250 B.C. It was due to Ashoka's conversion to Buddhism that the religion really gained a strong foothold; in fact he was to Buddhism what Constantine was to Christianity, both patron and popularizer. Ashoka came to power in 269 B.C., and for several years he continued the work of his predecessors in extending the limits of the mighty Mauryan empire. He laid siege to Orissā, and after a prolonged and brutal war, finally conquered its capital, Kalinga, in 264 B.C. But it was a pyrrhic victory: over 100,000 killed, 150,000 taken prisoner, and countless numbers made homeless and destitute. This, one of his inscriptions tells us, the great emperor found "very pitiful and grievous." So pitiful, in fact, that not long after the battle of Kalinga, Ashoka converted to Buddhism.

His conversion was sincere and lasting. He seems to have genuinely adopted the teaching of nonviolence (*ahimsā*) and instituted a number of humanitarian and altruistic reforms throughout his vast empire. He established a cadre of "Officers of Righteousness" to patrol his kingdom, and saw his role as becoming what he called "the moral leader of the civilized world." All his considerable energy was now directed toward establishing and propagating the teachings of the Master, not only throughout India but throughout the whole civilized world. Ashoka had sandstone columns, the famous Ashokan pillars, set up in different parts of the country. These were carved with inscriptions containing the message of the *dharma* and extolling the early monastic communities faithfully to observe the teachings of the Enlightened One. Ashoka also renovated the relic shrines that housed the remains of the Buddha, had hundreds of *stūpas* erected, and visited all the major centers of pilgrimage many times. It is due to his energy and patronage that Buddhist architecture emerged as a distinct and often glorious style.

Because of the custom of kings and visitors adding to the existing structure, it is hard to fix an exact chronology for the

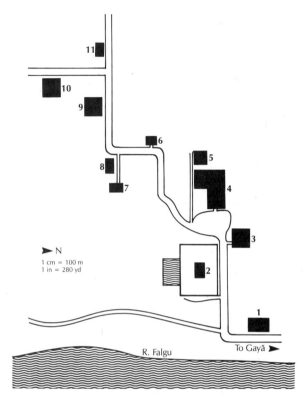

1 *Burmese temple.* 2 *Mahābodhi Temple.* 3 *Temple office.*
4 *Tibetan temple.* 5 *Bīrla temple.* 6 *Chinese temple.* 7 *Ashok
Travellers Lodge (ITDC).* 8 *Museum.* 9 *Thai temple.*
10 *Japanese temple.* 11 *Tourist bungalow.*

Figure A. Bodh Gayā Village.

temple. We know that the original was repaired in A.D. 450
by King Sado. And we can get some idea of its former glory
from the diaries of the Chinese monk and traveler Hiuen-
tsang, who visited Bodh Gayā in A.D. 637. He tells us that
"over every part of the ground surrounded by the wall there
were sacred monuments of all kinds, *stūpas* and monasteries. Kings, ministers and noble personages from all parts of
the world who had received the gift of the *dharma* had
constructed them to preserve the memory of the Master."
And of the temple itself, he says:

> To the East of the *bodhi* tree there is a *vihāra* between a
> hundred and sixty and a hundred and seventy feet high,
> with a base of about fifty feet. It is carved with several niches,
> each of which contains a gilded statue of the Buddha. On

all four sides the walls are covered with beautiful sculptures, festoons of pearls and figures of sages. On its summit there is a gilt copper *āmalaka* fruit. The architraves and pillars, the doors and the windows are all ornamented with gold and silver casings, amongst which pearls and precious stones are inserted. To the right and left of the outer door are two large niches, containing statues of Avalokiteshvara and the *buddha* Maitreya. Both statues are of solid silver, and about ten feet high.

But already at this time the precinct was badly damaged by flooding of the nearby River Falgu, and the courtyard was silted to a depth of almost three feet (one meter). We know that the temple was repaired by the Burmese in 1079 and again by a king of Siwālik in 1157. But from the time of the Muslim invasions in the twelfth century until the beginning

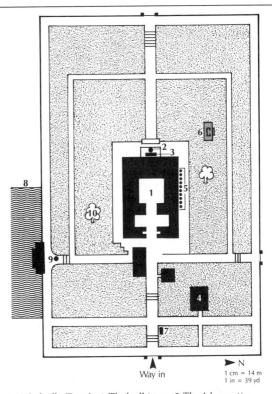

Way in

► N
1 cm = 14 m
1 in = 39 yd

1 *Mahābodhi Temple.* **2** *The* bodhi *tree.* **3** *The Adamantine Diamond Throne.* **4** *The Unblinking Shrine.* **5** *The Bejewelled Walk.* **6** *The Rainbow Shrine.* **7** *The Goatherd's Tree.* **8** *Muchalinda Lake.* **9** *Ashokan column.* **10** *The* rajata *tree.*

Figure B. Mahābodhi Temple site plan.

of the nineteenth century, we have very scanty information about the site.

The modern history of the temple begins with the renewed interest of the Burmese. In 1811 the King of Burma came here to investigate for himself the site of the Master's Enlightenment, and his successor, King Mindon, began restoration work of the temple some years later. This was continued by the British, under General Cunningham. At that time the temple was half buried. The entire courtyard area was underground, and the actual entrance was on a level with what is now the first (U.S. second) floor and main gate. The renovation work was completed in 1884.

The temple (see Figure B.1) is basically a truncated pyramid, crowned by a finial reminiscent of a miniature Burmese *stūpa*. This is shaped like an *āmalaka* fruit, a symbol of enlightenment. The four corner replicas of the central spire (*shikhara*) are generally thought to be later additions and conform to the Hindu *pancharatha* design. The niches that cover the facade were originally filled with Buddha figures— probably placed with reference to the four directions—and date from the Pāla period (eighth through twelfth centuries). They are at present occupied by a fairly haphazard collection of sculptures that were recovered during the course of restoration. The style of the square engaged columns between each niche in the podium, and the lion-head frieze above, as well as the way the main finial is repeated in miniature on the corners of each story of the *shikhara*, are motifs that we shall see continuing in Hindu temples up through the Middle Ages. And the Hindu technique of power through repetition is also employed here, both in the images set into the main temple and the accumulation of votive and commemorative *stūpas* in its grounds.

□ THE BUDDHA AND THE LINGA
Inside the sanctuary there is a huge image of the Buddha, in the earth-touching pose, facing east. There is also a Shiva *linga*, installed in about A.D. 860 by a local Hindu monarch, Rāja Dharmapala, so the place is sacred to both Hindus and Buddhists. Bodh Gayā is thus a living testimony to the renowned religious tolerance of the Indians. Here at the holiest Buddhist shrine in the world a Hindu ritual is performed by a brahmin priest every morning and evening.

□ UPSTAIRS
Visit the first (U.S. second) floor of the building. There is a meditation room with a small library, and some fine eighth-century steatite figures on the stairs and in the corner shrines of the balcony. This verandah also gives a spectacular view over the Bodhi Tree and the throne below.

The Mahābodhi Temple.

The Buddha stayed in Bodh Gayā for seven weeks after the great Enlightenment, enjoying the bliss of *nirvāna* and deciding whether to teach the Truth to the suffering and unregenerate world. Each of these weeks was spent in a different part of the temple complex.

□ *THE BODHI TREE* (Figure B.2)
The Buddha spent the first week under the *bodhi* tree. The legend is that the original *bodhi* tree sprang up on the day of Gautama's birth, and lived for several centuries as a shrine for his devotees. After the death of the Buddha, cuttings were taken from the tree to various parts of the country and shrines were established around them as a memorial to the Master. Mahendra, the nephew of Ashoka, took a cutting to Anurādhapura, the ancient capital of Srī Lankā. It is a cutting of that tree, brought here by General Cunningham in 1881, which we see today. The *bodhi* tree is a *pīpal* (*Ficus religiosa*), which, like the sacred *banyan* (*Ficus indica*) of the Hindus, is a type of fig tree.

□ *THE ADAMANTINE DIAMOND THRONE* (Figure B.3)
Situated between the tree and the back of the temple, the *vajrāsana* was the Buddha's seat of meditation. To the Buddhist this is the holiest spot on earth, the navel of the world. It was here that the Buddha sat facing east and medi-

The bodhi *tree,
showing entrance to
the Adamantine
Diamond Throne (left).*

tating, and it is said that no other celestial being can fly over
this spot, so powerful is its aura.

Pilgrims show their devotion by offering incense, flowers,
little lamps, and colored scarves tied onto the branches of the
tree. It was originally the custom to lustrate the tree; the
pious Emperor Ashoka was reputed to have poured 1,008
vases of holy water over the roots. In course of time, paved
walkways were put around the trees to make circumambulation possible over the muddy ground, and railings were added
to protect them. Ashoka himself donated the first railings
around the *bodhi* tree. The inner compound around the tree
can be opened for meditation; just ask the monk in charge at
the temple. It is closed so as to keep it as a place of worship,
not just a common thoroughfare.

□ *THE UNBLINKING SHRINE* (Figure B.4)
The second week of Enlightenment was spent at this spot.
The Master was so absorbed in bliss that he stood for a week
gazing at the *bodhi* tree, transfixed and unblinking. Built of
bricks, some of which are carved, this whitewashed shrine
contains a statue of the Buddha.

□ *THE BEJEWELLED WALK* (Figure B.5)
The Master spent the third week walking up and down this
north side of the temple in ecstatic contemplation. The plat-

form commemorates the place he walked, and the row of carved stone lotuses show where the Enlightened One's feet rested. This tradition harks back to legends of the Buddha's birth, when lotuses sprang up at the places he took his first seven steps. One Buddhist meditation technique involves a process of focusing the awareness on walking.

The platform was originally covered by a pillared roof—the remnants of the pillars can be seen alongside the row of lotuses.

□ THE RAINBOW SHRINE (Figure B.6)

Once he was accustomed to the ecstasy of his new state of awareness, the Buddha spent a week here in deep meditation. During this time he again became familiar with all the different levels of consciousness. While transcending the mind again and again, the Master emitted dazzling light from his body, which crystallized into rays of white, yellow, blue, red, and orange. These are the colors of the Buddhist flags tied to the *bodhi* tree.

Within this roofless shrine is a statue of the Buddha in meditation pose. The gilded figures in the garden are mostly Burmese, as is the beautiful carved bell, symbol of the *dharma*.

□ THE GOATHERD'S TREE (Figure B.7)

On the dawn of the day of Enlightenment, the daughter of a nearby farmer, Sujātā, approached this tree with an offering of milk rice in a golden dish that she was intending to offer to the presiding tree spirit in thanks for her newly born son. When she saw the noble figure of Gautama, however, she immediately offered him the dish instead. He broke his fast and accepted.

Most authorities give this site, now marked by a white plaque with a Burmese inscription, as the place where the tree under which he ate originally stood.

After his meal Gautama bathed in the River Nairanjanā (now called the Falgu) and tossed his begging bowl into the water, declaring that if the bowl floated upstream, he would attain Buddhahood. The bowl duly went against the current. After this he rested on the river bank, and as evening came, he made his way to the *bodhi* tree. As he arrived there a grasscutter named Sothiya, impressed by the young man, offered him eight handfuls of *kusha* grass as a seat. Gautama spread these out on a stone slab under the tree and took his seat, vowing not to move until he had achieved the great Awakening.

Some versions of the story say Gautama meditated for forty-nine days under the *bodhi* tree before *nirvāna* dawned, but all agree that he spent the fifth week of Enlightenment under the goatherd's tree again, absorbed in infinite peace.

□ *MUCHALINDA LAKE* (Figure B.8)

The site of the sixth week of Enlightenment is marked by the broken Ashokan column (B.9) probably reset by Cunningham. It stands next to a *pīpal* tree, by the entrance to the tank. The Master was meditating under an ancestor of this tree when a severe storm broke out as Māra, Lord of Chaos, tried to disturb his bliss. The serpent-king Muchalinda, who dwelt at the bottom of the lake, rose out of the depths and, encircling the Buddha with his coils, spread his seven hoods as a protective canopy over the Master's head. Thus the Buddha continued his meditation unperturbed. The story is one of many which illustrate the sovereignty of the enlightened man over the realms of nature, and his reintegration with the powers of the unconscious—universally symbolized by the snake or dragon.

□ *THE RAJATA TREE* (Figure B.10)

The seventh week of *nirvāna* was spent on the site of this tree. At that time there was a *rajata* tree growing here. The species is now extinct in India, but this one was brought from Burma and planted here about ten years ago. It was during this last week that the Buddha decided to spread his teaching to alleviate the sufferings of humanity.

The Garden

In all religions the garden is paradise. But the garden here at Bodh Gayā is not like Eden, watched over by a stern father god, nor does it have the contrived and intellectual order of the Islamic heaven. The garden here is unmistakably Indian: higgledy-piggledy, sprouting life in untamed and fertile abandon. It is a veritable jungle of creepers and bushes, gnarled stumps and twisted roots. The ground is littered with little clay votive lamps, burnt twists of wick, *pīpal* leaves, stubs of incense. Everywhere stand stone *stūpas* and brick shrines and monuments erected by kings, patrons, and believers from all over the Buddhist world. Clustered around the main spire, they are mute witnesses to the universality of the Master's message. Like the different forms of Buddhism, each has its own place, size, and height; each caters to the different needs and temperaments of man. Here, as so often in India, it is the juxtaposition of stone and vegetation that fills one with surprise and delight.

Just after the monsoon the place is a riot of color. The garden is splashed with vivid red and yellow canna lilies, speckled with delicate pink lantana. Flame-orange marigolds vie with pale ivory *mogra*, deep cream gardenias and scarlet zinnias are entwined by skeins of pure white jasmine. Trees abound. Stately *pīpals*, relatives of the *bodhi* tree, the

Commemorative stūpa *in the garden.*

feathery and feminine *nīm*, which is sometimes actually married to the *pīpal* and whose leaves have a healing effect; great palms and upright *ashoka* trees, which are dedicated to Kāma, the god of love, and are said to break into orange flower when touched by a beautiful virgin. And the trees are treated in a typically Indian way too; beneath a *pīpal* to the north of the garden, beyond the Bejewelled Walk, sit a group of five Hindu deities, on which the faithful have put flowers and the red *sindūr*. In and out of this leafy tangle float the monks robed as strikingly as exotic butterflies—Tibetans in deep burgundy, Srī Lankāns in saffron, Burmese in burnished amber, Japanese in jet black. The garden spawns a variety that encompasses all of Asia, yet somehow the place flows in an organic and unhurried unity, and man moves in harmony with the rhythm and power of nature. This little temple complex is an oasis in the unrelieved flat heat of surrounding Bihār.

The unmoving hub of all this movement is the *bodhi* tree. It really is extraordinarily protective. Here under its widespread branches, which seem to embrace all humanity, there is a constant and quiet devotion, very different from the noisy activity of so many Hindu temples. In its shaded tranquility the mind does begin to settle down, and becomes still enough to notice things normally overlooked, sights and sounds usually blotted out by the constant chatter of thought that prevents us from living in the present moment.

It is fitting that the Buddha attained Enlightenment at the roots of a tree. His teaching is radical. It undercuts the whole edifice on which Banāras is built: the priest, the rituals, the gods. The Buddha's message is to get to the root of your own mind, because all action is based on thought, and the quality of thought is based on the quality of the mind. The tool for this exploration is meditation. Any other approach to the problems of life is only cosmetic, like the gardener who sees a plant is wilting and tries to polish its leaves. The answer is to water the root. If you attend to the basis of the problem, its solution comes automatically. Meditation is like the sap that impartially nourishes all parts of the tree of life.

And somehow the *pīpal* tree is fitting, too. Look at its leaf (see Figure C), so finely shaped and delicate. It is like a thought, with its long tail, swimming up from the depths of the mind. The whole movement of meditation is to chase the tail of thought and go beyond it to an inner silence. This is the basic method of Buddhism, calming the mind so that you can see clearly, unclouded by fear, hope, or preconceptions. This dispassionate insight into the self and the world is one pillar on which the *dharma* rests. The other is compassion. Knowledge of reality must be balanced by loving kindness toward suffering mankind; the mind must be balanced by the heart. See how the *pīpal* leaf is heart-shaped, reminding us of the importance of love, lest we abandon our humanity in the search for divinity.

Figure C. Leaf of the pīpal tree.

There is no doubt that countries where Buddhism has taken root do have a gentleness about them. The people are friendly and welcoming and above all cheerful. It has a profoundly civilizing influence, and a simplicity that is perhaps most aptly summed up in the often repeated Buddhist refrain: "May all beings be happy! May all manner of beings be happy!"

19

BHUBA-NESHWAR

A CITY OF DEVOTION

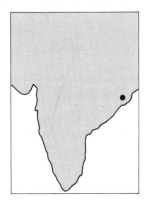

Once a place has become holy for a tribe or a group, it is holy for all. Time and again we see temples erected on the sites of ancient cult worship. What inspired a tree, a river, or a cave could also inspire a temple. And if a site was holy to Lord Shiva, it could just as well be holy to Lord Vishnu; if it was sacred to the Hindus, it could be sacred to the Buddhists or the Jains also. Clusters of temples sprang up, organically. They sprouted, like mushrooms after the rain, because the soil there had proved fertile for the spirit to grow and spread.

When Hinduism was at its height, from the seventh to the twelfth centuries, northern India was dotted with such temple cities, veritable conglomerations of the holy. They acted as the nodes of an arterial system that spread the length and breadth of ancient India, carrying the spiritual life blood through the country. They were the centers of pilgrimage, learning, and civilization, like the monastic complexes of medieval Europe.

Few of these temple cities now remain. Time, climate, and invaders have combined to destroy what must, in their prime, have been breathtaking displays of the Indian artistic genius. Luckily one site remains where literally hundreds of temples of all sizes still stand in a comparatively small area. This is Bhubaneshwar, in the northeastern state of Orissā.

Bhubaneshwar is an archeologist's dream (Figure A). The whole area is littered with remains of fortified towns that date back to the second and third centuries B.C. Though the exact nature of these settlements is in doubt, there is a definite connection here with one of the most important Indian monarchs, the Emperor Ashoka (269–230 B.C.). At Dhauli, five miles (eight kilometers) south of Bhubaneshwar, stands a set of his famous rock-cut edicts. It is significant that the thirteenth edict, which describes his bloody victory over the kingdom of Kalinga (modern Orissā) is omitted. It is replaced by two edicts, one of which contains the famous saying "All men are my children." Though such paternal sentiments must have rung somewhat hollow to the decimated survivors of Kalinga, they were not entirely out of place. For it was after the terrible carnage of the Kalinga campaign that Ashoka renounced the military life and was converted to Buddhism. His change of heart ushered in one of the most stable and civilized periods in India's history.

Dhauli had been an important center of the Jain religion. The hills of Udāyagiri and Khandagiri around Bhubaneshwar are still honeycombed with the caves of ascetics. But with the coming of Ashoka, it became one of the hubs of the

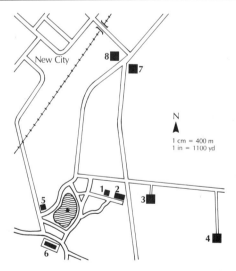

1 *Parashurāmeshvara Temple.* 2 *Mukteshvara Temple.*
3 *Rājārānī Temple.* 4 *Brahmeshvara Temple.* 5 *Vaitāl Deul Temple.* 6 *Lingarāja Temple.* 7 *Museum.* 8 *Hotel Kalinga Ashok (ITDC).*

Figure A. Bhubaneshwar.

new Buddhist empire. This continued until the fifth century, when a new religious force appeared on the scene. This was the Pāshupata sect of tantric Shaivism, founded by the great Shaiva *guru* and miracle worker Lakulīsha. The new faith soon had the land under its magical spell, and the rise of Bhubaneshwar as its capital was consolidated by the seventh century. From then until the thirteenth century, when Vaishnava cults were to assume supremacy, the building here developed in an independent and idiosyncratic way. It comprises a separate subdivision of the northern Indian *nagara* style, which is known as the Orissan (or Kalinga) Order.

Originally, there were no less than seven thousand temples in Bhubaneshwar. They were built around the sacred Lake Bindusagar, which was believed to be unequaled in its magic and healing powers. Now about five hundred temples remain. Although many of them are in a poor state of repair, they still provide a fascinating catalogue of styles and development. It is a measure of the Kalinga dynasty's priorities that, despite this incredible expenditure of effort in building the holy city, as far as we can tell, no attention whatever was paid to the town planning of Bhubaneshwar itself. As so often in India, the priority was the sacred rather than the secular. We can imagine Bhubaneshwar as a medieval Hindu Mecca, which, like the Islamic city today, hosted a vast pilgrim population that stayed in impermanent, perhaps tented, accommodation.

Orissan temple architecture is unusually well documented. Not only are there temples remaining in good repair, but we also have architectural texts (*Shilpa shāstras*) that lay down the names, proportions, and forms of the temples in minutest detail. This is unusual in India, where early historical records, written on leaf or bark, have generally not survived the monsoon climate. Added to which, all the ancient brotherhoods, whether priests, musicians, or architects, belonged to an esoteric tradition that was essentially oral. Knowledge was passed on in secret from *guru* to disciple, father to son. Orissā is also unusual in that some of these families of initiated architects (*sthāpatis*) still survive.

The very earliest temples were single, towered buildings erected on the site of an earlier shrine. Here in Bhubaneshwar there are remains of these early single-building temples dotted around the fields. Many of them seem to have reverted to the nature from which they came.

Orissan Temple Architecture   The typical Orissan temple proper is composed of two structures: the *deul* and the *jagamohana* (see Figure B). The *deul* is the sanctum, containing the principal image of the temple and surmounted by a curvilinear spire.

The *jagamohana* ("world-delighter") is a porch for the congregation. It has a pyramidal roof composed of receding steps. In conformity with the Hindu pattern, the interior of the sanctum is generally smaller and darker than that of the porch. All the energies of the holy are concentrated in this introverted little chamber. It is used for a glimpse (*darshana*) of the sacred image, or ritual, or individual worship under the watchful eye of the priest. The porch is more public, and used for group celebration, dancing, meditation, or reading.

The internal plan of both *deul* and *jagamohana* is square. The outer walls, however, are broken by various projections into sections known as *rathas*. In the earliest temples there was only one projection, and the temple is thus *triratha* ("three-sectioned"). This projection, whether on its own in the simplest temples or as the central one of several in the later ones, is called the *rāhā*. As time goes by, these projections increase in both number and ornateness. Thus the later buildings are *pancharatha* ("five-sectioned"), *saptaratha* ("seven-sectioned"), and so on. These outer projections are also carried over to the spire of the *deul* and are called *pagas*.

As the abode of the gods, the Hindu temple is the body of the Cosmic Man (Prajāpati) who, by self-sacrifice, created the world. It is also an idealized representation of the human figure, for the human nervous system contains the universe. Thus the temple unites macrocosm to microcosm. This function is particularly clear in the names of the principal parts of the Orissan temple. Both the *deul* and the *jagamohana* are composed of four main sections: plinth (*pishta*), base (*bāda*), "trunk" (*gandi*), and "head" (*mastaka*). The plinth is optional and is missing in many temples, including some of the most important. The *bāda* consists of the "foot" (*pābhāga*), "lower and upper shin" (*tala-* and *uparajāngha*), and the *varanda*, which separates the *bāda* from the *gandi*. The base of the *deul* is similar to that of the *jagamohana*, but with the "trunk" the buildings take their distinctive form. The "trunk" of the *deul* is a spire (*shikhara*) that rises steeply upward, until it flattens out near its summit. This creates the "shoulder" style of *shikhara*, which is unique to Orissā. The "trunk" itself is divided into horizontal tiers (*bhūmis*), each marked off by fluted disks. These disks are miniature versions of the ribbed cushion (*amlā*), which crowns the spire.

The *jagamohana* "trunk," on the other hand, is composed of a number of layers (*pidhās*) of diminishing size. They ascend to form a pyramid; the top *pidhā* being about half the size of the lowest one.

In both buildings the "head" is separated from the "trunk" by a "neck" (*beki*), a recessed cylindrical portion. In the fully developed *jagamohana*, this is followed by a huge bell-shaped

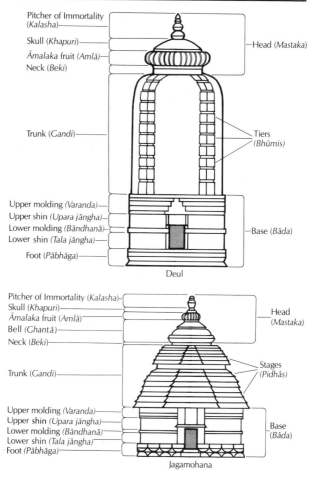

Pitcher of Immortality (Kalasha)
Skull (Khapuri)
Āmalaka fruit (Amlā)
Neck (Beki)
Head (Mastaka)

Trunk (Gandi)
Tiers (Bhūmis)

Upper molding (Varanda)
Upper shin (Upara jāngha)
Lower molding (Bāndhanā)
Lower shin (Tala jāngha)
Foot (Pābhāga)
Base (Bāda)

Deul

Pitcher of Immortality (Kalasha)
Skull (Khapuri)
Āmalaka fruit (Amlā)
Bell (Ghantā)
Neck (Beki)
Head (Mastaka)

Trunk (Gandi)
Stages (Pidhās)

Upper molding (Varanda)
Upper shin (Upara jāngha)
Lower molding (Bāndhanā)
Lower shin (Tala jāngha)
Foot (Pābhāga)
Base (Bāda)

Jagamohana

Figure B. Typical Orissan temple.

portion (*ghantā*). This supports the *amlā* which is named after the *āmalaka* fruit (emblic myrobalan). The resemblance is not merely visual. The fruit is believed to have great purifying properties, and is widely used in Ayurvedic medicine and yogic diet. The *amlā* also represents the thousand-petaled lotus that opens above the head in the enlightened being.

Next comes the "skull" (*khapuri*), which is crowned by the "vessel of immortality" (*kalasha*). In the macrocosm, this pitcher stands at the summit of Mount Meru. It is from here that the goddess Gangā begins her descent to earth. In the microcosm the pitcher contains the *soma* juice, that flows down inside the yogi's head, purifying the subtle with bliss. In accordance with a universal symbolism, the base and "trunk" are square, representing the grounding stability of the earth, whereas the "head" is circular, as befits the creative movement of the heavens.

The whole temple is crowned by the "divine weapon" (*āyudha*) of the resident deity. In the case of Shaiva temples, this is Lord Shiva's mystic trident (*trishūla*).

The inside of the *deul* also has several distinctive features. As with all truly Hindu building, the basic technique of structure is that of corbeling. Heavy slabs are laid on top of one another so that they gradually close off the inner space at the top. But there is an inherent weakness in this design, which can be seen by the numbers of spires that have collapsed inward over the centuries. To counteract such a possibility, the Orissan architects devised a system of "false ceilings" to span the inner space of the sanctum. Opposite walls were joined by massive slabs that formed ceilings (*mudas*). In all the temples, there is one of these ceilings directly above the cella, known as the *garbha-muda*. Moreover, in the larger temples, the hollow chamber created by the *garbha-muda* was in turn roofed off by a second ceiling (*ratna-muda*). The taller the temple, the more such hollow chambers were needed. They not only insured structural stability within the corbeling system but also provided hidden chambers in which the most esoteric rites of the temple were performed. As so often in sacred architecture, the form is perfectly suited to its purpose. Because these recondite chambers were above the image and thus "nearer" to the transcendent deity, they were the ideal place for the "higher" initiations to take place. Access to these secret chambers was often through an opening above the lintel of the sanctum doorway.

It is also noticeable that the interiors of the temples are almost invariably plain and austere in comparison with their highly ornamented exteriors. This is to encourage "one-pointedness" (*ekāgrata*) in the mind of the devotee. Free from the distractions of carving and embellishment, he is better able to concentrate on the image of the god within the womblike darkness of the holy of holies.

The temples are nearly all built of sandstone, around an inner core of laterite, which is also the material generally used for compound walls. The sandstone was quarried in the nearby Khandagiri and Udāyagiri Hills. On the evidence of contemporary sculpted panels, it seems likely that the stones were brought to the building up wooden ramps, which were supported on wooden posts to form an adjustable type of scaffolding. The stones were carried slung in ropes from poles. They were then laid with great precision into place on top of one another and kept in position by their weight and the use of iron dowels and clamps. No mortar was used. One unusual feature of the external decorative carving is that, to judge from unfinished temples, it was done *in situ*, after the stone blocks were placed in position.

As at other sites, such as Konārak and Khajurāho, the carving on the Bhubaneshwar temples may be broadly divided into four categories.

1. Hieratic deities, with characteristic iconographic features.
2. Human beings in a variety of domestic scenes. Prominent among these are the "relaxed damsels" (*alasa kanyās*)—the nymphs that radiate on the human level the sensuous enjoyment of the divine realms.
3. Composite and mythological figures, including *nāgas* and *vyālas*.
4. Geometric and floral decorative motifs.

We have seen at Khajurāho how Indian temples can blur the distinction between sculpture and architecture, as whole wall surfaces writhe with figures. But here at Bhubaneshwar, the skill is even more refined, as the carving becomes minuscule, pitting the stone with relentless ornamentation.

The Temples

Parashurāmeshvara, Eighth Century A.D.

At Bhubaneshwar, it is possible to trace the development of the Orissan temple step by step. The temples fall into three

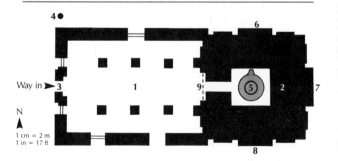

1 Jagamohana. 2 Deul. 3 *Main entrance*. 4 Sahasrā linga.
5 Yoni-linga. 6 *North* rāhā *niche and* kūdus. 7 *Kārttikeya*.
8 *Ganesha*. 9 *Eight-planet lintel*.

Figure C. Parashurāmeshvara Temple ground plan.

groups: early, middle, and late. The best preserved of the early group is the Parashurāmeshvara. It sits in a sunken courtyard protected by a wall. Its highly carved facade is lit by sunlight filtering through the leaves of an ancient *banyan* tree that leans protectively over the southern wall of the compound. The two component parts of the temple are easily distinguishable and combine to form a very pleasing whole. The porch illustrates a very early type of *jagamohana* (Figure C.1), being rectangular rather than cube shaped. Moreover, its roof is not pyramidal but terraced—sloping in two stages. The piercing of the roof allowed light and air into the chamber, as did the latticed windows. The porch has been extensively, but not always expertly, restored. In fact, it was a slightly later addition to the *deul*, as can be seen from the patched-up join between the two buildings. This covers up part of the intricately carved front face of the *deul*, which, as in the earliest shrine temples, originally stood alone.

□ *THE DEUL* (Figure C.2)
The *deul* itself is quite squat and thickset, a conical beehive of stone. Nevertheless, it already demonstrates the soaring-upward curve that is to distinguish Orissan *shikharas*. This movement is stabilized, rather than diminished, by the horizontal emphasis of the layered *bhūmis* with their detailed

Detail of Parashurā-meshvara Temple, showing bhūmis *of the* deul *terminating in miniature* amlās.

carvings. There is, throughout, a fine balance between the horizontal lines of the porch and the horizontally tiered upward thrust of the *deul*. As time went by, the vertical emphasis was to predominate, and the *bhūmis* became less and less of an architectural or decorative feature in their own right.

The Parashurāmeshvara *deul* is *triratha* in plan, each face of the building having one full projection. The line of these projections is reminiscent of the bamboo poles that were lashed together at the top to provide the roof of the earliest shrines (see Figure D). Despite this archaic echo, there is a hint of the future development on the temple form, as we can already see the beginnings of pilasters emerging on either side of this *rāhā* projection. These in time developed and became much more rounded, culminating in the fully blown lateral transepts that distinguish, for example, the mature Khaju-rāho temples. Another early feature is the treatment of the *varanda*. Here it is a highly ornate decorative frieze, separating the base from the "trunk." In later temples it ceased to be as ornate and became a mere separation between the two parts of the building.

Figure D. Bamboo-pole prototype shikhara.

A distinctive feature of all Orissan temples is the intricate rusticated carving that adorns the surfaces. The figures here convey a homely, domestic feeling. Their main purpose is to tell stories of the gods, or to depict scenes of everyday life. Even when hieratic deities are depicted, they have a charm that prevents them from becoming overstylized. There is everywhere a freshness and life, as if the sculptor had just perfected an art that had not yet grown stale.

☐ *THE JAGAMOHANA* (Figure C.1)
This liveliness is evident in the very varied collection of deities that is carved around the lowest panel of the exterior of the *jagamohana*. The all-embracing catholicity of Hinduism is well illustrated: Although this is a Pāshupata Shaiva temple, these figures include Sūrya, the sun god; Yama, god of death; and the Seven Mother Goddesses (*Sapta Mātrikās*), primeval fertility deities.

The lintel of the main (western) entrance (C.3) of the *jagamohana* is carved with Gaja-Lakshmī, the goddess of wealth being bathed by two elephants. The panel to the left shows wild elephants being captured by tame ones; and to the right there is a scene depicting the worship of the *linga*. The windows to either side of the entrance are exceptionally fine, being pierced by comely figures of musicians and dancers.

☐ *THE THOUSAND-LINGA LINGA* (Figure C.4)
In the northwest corner of the compound is a four-foot-high stone *linga*, with the serpent of immortality coiled around it. This is what is known as a *sahasrā linga*, "the Thousand-Linga Linga." One circumambulation of this is believed to be worth a thousand circumambulations of an ordinary *linga*, much as a journey to the Kailāsanātha Temple at Ellorā is the equivalent of a pilgrimage to the fabled mountain itself.

☐ *THE IMAGES*
The principal images, aside from the *yoni-linga* in the holy of holies (Figure C.5), are contained in the central projections of the three sides of the *deul*. It is customary in Hindu architecture to fill the niches on the outside of the temple with forms (or consorts) of the deity to whom the temple is dedicated. These accessory gods are known as *pārshva-devatās*. A Shaiva temple normally has as its *pārshva-devatās* Shiva's consort, Pārvatī, and his two sons Ganesha and Kārttikeya. A Vaishnava temple will have three of the ten incarnations of the god Vishnu. Here, Pārvatī was originally placed in the northern niche (C.6), but has since been stolen. It was the custom of the Bhubaneshwar architects to have freestanding *mūrtis* in such niches, but as time went by and many were stolen, the habit of carving them from blocks of stone that were actually part of the wall arose. Later still, the images were again freestanding. Unfortunately, temple looting is still rife in India today, often involving Indian officials and "respectable" Western collectors. There is a fine hunting scene over the empty niche.

One recurring motif in Orissan temple decoration is the miniature *chaitya* window design known as the *kūdu*. Adapted from the entrances of the earliest Buddhist caves, these horseshoe arches contain animals, heads, or figures. There are two conspicuous examples here above the empty Pārvatī niche. The lower one shows the familiar scene of Shiva resisting Rāvana's attempt to dislodge him from Mount Kailāsa; the upper, a figure of Shiva as Natarāja, Lord of the Dance.

The eastern niche contains the war god Kārttikeya ("Son of the Pleiades," C.7). He is especially popular in southern India, where he is called Subrahmanya, "Beloved of the brahmins." He has two arms, carries a spear in his left hand and a *mātulunga* fruit in his right—symbols of his twin powers of creation and destruction. His spear, which never misses its mark, returns to his hand after killing his enemies. His strength is immense, and he is the general of the army of the gods. He rides on the peacock called Year, which devours the serpent of Time.

One of Kārttikeya's names is Skanda, "The Spurt of Semen," and in this form he represents the power of chastity in yoga. For this reason women are forbidden to worship him.

Thus Kārttikeya's peacock devours the most subtle of instincts that bind the spirit of man in his body. Kārttikeya changes poison into ambrosia.

The lintel above the niche shows the marriage of Shiva and Pārvatī. They are attended by their other son Ganesha, the fire god Agni, and the creator Brahmā, who kneels and ladles *ghī* from a vase as an offering. Next to Brahmā is the sun god Sūrya.

High up on this eastern facade sits a *kūdu* cameo of the founder of the Pāshupata sect, Lakulīsha. He is surrounded by his four chief disciples. The figure could almost be Buddhist in its meditation posture, lack of adornment, long earlobes, and tightly curled hair. Pāshupata Shaivism took over from Buddhism in this area, and such images were no doubt modeled to attract converts, or at least make the point that the new sect was teaching essentially the same truths as its predecessor.

The persistence of the Lakulīsha figure on this temple gives us a clue as to its name. Parashurāmeshvara refers of course to Parashu-Rāma, the seventh incarnation of Lord

Lakulīsha, eastern facade, Parashurāmeshvara deul.

Vishnu. However, as this is a Shaiva temple, this must be a misnomer. It is probably a corrupt form of Parāshareshvara, which refers to Parāshara, one of the most famous of the Pāshupata *gurus*.

The *pārshva-devatā* of the southern face is Ganesha (C.8). He is seated on a throne with legs carved in the shape of lions (*singhāsana*), a traditional seat for kings or *gurus*. His trunk is happily tucked into a bowl of *laddus*, his favorite sweet. An interesting feature is that he is not accompanied by his usual vehicle, the mouse. This was a comparatively late iconographical convention that had not been widely adopted by the eighth century.

The story of how the mouse came to be Ganesha's constant companion is related in one of the later *Purānas*. Ganesha quarreled with his brother Kārttikeya over which of them was the greater. Shiva set them the test that whoever could go around the world faster would be the greater. Kārttikeya immediately set off on his peacock to fly round the globe. Ganesha was more cunning. Riding on a mouse, he went around Shiva himself saying: "As you are the Lord of the Universe, to go around you is to travel around the universe itself." Since then the mouse and Ganesha have been inseparable.

Above Ganesha the *kūdu* scene shows Shiva begging food from his consort Annapūrnā, "the food-filled one," who lives on the mountain of the same name. All these figures are carved in very low relief; they are almost flat. Nevertheless, the soft lines convey a feeling of gentle softness and plasticity, and their faces have that detached serenity that imbues the best of Indian sculpture.

As in all the earlier *jagamohanas*, the porch here has supporting pillars inside. Later this gave way to a cantilever construction technique. The lintel over the door to the holy of holies (C.9) is carved with representations of the planets. This is another indication of the date of this temple. Usually there are nine figures, but here, as in all early buildings, there are only eight.

Mukteshvara Temple, Tenth Century A.D. (Figure E)

Two hundred yards (one hundred eighty meters) down the road from the Parashurāmeshvara stands what has been called the gem of Orissan architecture, the Mukteshvara. It provides a good example of the transition between the earliest and the middle phases of the Kalinga school. Like most of the temples here its smallness immediately strikes the visitor. In fact the Mukteshvara is the smallest Bhubaneshwar temple; the *deul* is only thirty-five feet (ten meters) high and the *jagamohana* only twenty-five feet (eight meters).

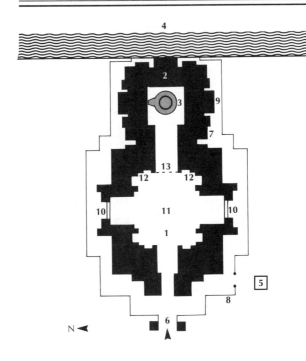

1 Jagamohana. 2 Deul. 3 Yoni-linga. 4 *Tank.* 5 *Sacred well.*
6 Torana *gateway.* 7 *Gangā and Yamunā.* 8 *Ascetic.* 9 Bho
motif. 10 *Latticed windows.* 11 *Ceiling lotus.* 12 *Lion-
dragons.* 13 *Nine-planet lintel.*

Figure E. Mukteshvara Temple ground plan.

The temple sits in a sunken, walled compound, which
connects to a sacred tank on the eastern side (E.4). In the
southwest corner of the compound is a well (E.5), the water
of which is believed to cure barren women. The lintel of its
doorframe is well carved, depicting the great *guru* Lakulīsha
surrounded by disciples and ascetics, all reading scriptures.

Several miniature shrines are dotted around the temple.
Many of them contain a *linga*, and they give a good idea of
the variety of this cult object. Some are carved, some plain,
some are sunken, some have double *yonis* and so on. These
were added after the main temple was built, as an offering or
in thanksgiving, just as a miniature *stūpa* would be added in
the Buddhist tradition.

The actual temple buildings are enclosed by a second, low
wall, which provides a tightly circumscribed path for *pradakshinā*. This path is entered from the west, through a corbeled
torana gateway (E.6), supported on massive pillars. This
gateway is one of the unique features of the temple. Its heavy

lines are relieved by delicate carvings: Female figures and little heads peep out from *kūdus*, radiating a sunny bliss.

☐ *THE JAGAMOHANA* (Figure E.1)
There is a radical development noticeable in the line of the *jagamohana*, which has become a building in its own right rather than just an appendage to the *deul*. It has now begun to assume the terraced pyramid of the mature Orissan porch, but it is still comparatively unadorned and devoid of the crowning elements, such as lions, that are found on later examples. Moreover, the internal plan is not yet fully square. Change is also noticeable in the iconography: Kārttikeya is shown with his customary attendant, the peacock, and Ganesha is accompanied by his vehicle, the mouse.

Generally speaking, all the figures here are more elongated—less flattened than their predecessors on the Parashurāmeshvara. This change is seen in the maturing of all Indian figurative art, whether Hindu or Buddhist. The folk motifs, typified by dwarfish fertility gods with exaggerated features, gradually give way to a more sophisticated representation in which esthetic considerations play as important a part as the direct transmission of feeling.

☐ *THE DEUL* (Figure E.2)
The *deul* also shows development. The plan is now a full *pancharatha*, and the lowest register (*pābhāga*) shows five distinct moldings. Above this the subsidiary pilasters are well defined. The figures that adorn the facade herald themes that were to be developed later, particularly the *nāgas* and *alasa kanyā* maidens.

Mukteshvara Temple.

The temple is more indented, vertically as well as horizontally. Both buildings stand on a small platform, and the divisions between their various parts ("foot," "shin," "trunk," and so on) are much more accentuated. Altogether a different temple is taking shape. Nevertheless, there is still an archaic look about the whole. The *amlā* finial is not yet supported by squatting figures or heraldic lions as in the later *deuls*, and the contours of the spire have been softened, each corner being smoothly rounded. The overall atmosphere of the building is one of homeliness, which is what has endeared it, no doubt, to both visitors and experts over the years.

□ *THE CARVINGS*

Some details of the carving are worth a mention. The *rāhā* niches are empty but flanked by the river goddesses Gangā and Yamunā (Figure E.7), common attendant deities in Hindu iconography, who hark back to earlier fertility cults. A most prominent theme around the temple is that of the naked ascetic. He is shown meditating or, more often, instructing a pupil. The detail with which these skeletal figures have been rendered is astonishing. There is little doubt that the temple was a center for tantric initiation. This is clear not only from the name (Mukteshvara: "the Lord who bestows freedom through yoga"), but from the prevalence of these figures. Part

Detail of outer wall of Mukteshvara Temple, showing ascetic surmounted by smiling face in kūdu.

of the tantric discipline involves meditation on the transience of all life and is often done in cemeteries and on burning *ghāts*. Thus the skeletal ascetic combines in his appearance the two major themes of austerity and impermanence that lie at the heart of the tantric doctrine. He is a walking example of his own teaching and simultaneously alludes to a favorite tantric deity, Shiva in extreme emaciation (Bhairava atiriktānga). Some particularly fine ascetics are found on the outer face of the small wall that encloses the temple. Here the figures are surmounted by lotus motifs that allude to the *chakras* of the subtle body, another crucial part of tantric doctrine. A good example is on the south face (E.8).

The southern *rāhā* displays an important motif (E.9). This is the *chaitya* window crowned by the head of a mythical lion, its jaws open. The head represents the all-devouring power of time and is often placed over temple doorways. It is especially common in the tantric temples of the Himālayas. The *chaitya* window is here flanked by two dwarfish attendants, and the whole tableau resembles a family crest. In effect, this is what it is, as the motif (known as the *bho*) appears only on Kalinga temples. The *bho* persists until very late, but nowhere else is such a fine example so visible.

There is also fine carving on the *jagamohana*. On the outside, the latticed windows (E.10) are particularly remark-

Bho *motif, southern* rāhā, *Mukteshvara Temple.*

Vaital Deul, showing vesara-*style roof modeled on Buddhist* chaitya *hall.*

able. Their outer frames depict humorous scenes of monkeys: picking lice from each other's fur, fighting crocodiles and crabs, and so on. The doorway is embellished with scrollwork. The interior is unusually ornate. The ceiling (E.11) is cusped and contains a central pendant of an eight-petaled lotus with *devatās* in the petals—another tantric motif. Each of the *chakras* is said to have gods and *mantras* resting on its petals. There is some good carving in the ornate cornice, and the corners of the chamber have mythical lion-dragons (E.12), which are very similar to the animals found in Nepalese and Tibetan tantric temples. The lintel over the doorway to the holy of holies (E.13), which contains a fine *yoni-linga*, is also a stylistic advance on the Parashurāmeshvara. Ketu has been added to the other eight, to make up the full complement of nine planets.

Vaitāl Deul Temple, Ninth Century A.D. (Figure A.5)

Chronologically placed between the Parashurāmeshvara and the Mukteshvara, the Vaitāl Deul demonstrates a different direction of Kalinga architecture. What we see clearly here is the emergence from imitation of existing Buddhist styles. The *deul* is rectangular and positioned on a transverse axis to the *jagamohana* hall. Its roof is clearly reminiscent of the *chaitya* hall vault; in end elevation it presents a large horse-shoe arch. The architect chose to leave the outer surface of the vault unadorned but crowned its top with three *kalasha* finials of Hindu design. The familiar Hindu *shikhara* is transposed, in miniature, to the four corners of the *jagamohana*. This, with its flat, two-tiered roof and latticed windows, is similar to what we have already seen at the Parashurā-meshvara. The lower portions of the *deul* are divided into deep *bhūmis*. Instead of *ratha* projections, there are shallow pilasters, all on the same plane. These pilasters are most elegantly carved, the intricacy of design being heightened by the severely plain recesses that separate them. The Vaitāl Deul belongs to the *khākharā* order of temples, a subdivision of the Kalinga style, which seems to have been reserved for temples dedicated to tantric *shakti* goddesses. The name *khākharā* comes perhaps from its resemblance to a local type of pumpkin gourd (*kakhāru*); elsewhere in India this shape is called the *vesara* order.

The carving on the facade is of a high standard, though it has the characteristics of early work. On the eastern face of the *deul*, overlooking the *jagamohana* roof, are two fine *kūdus*. The lower one contains a figure of Sūrya, the sun god, flanked by the twin sisters of the Dawn, with Aruna, messenger of the Dawn, driving a chariot of seven horses beneath. (This motif was to be developed in the Sun Temple of Konārak.) Above Sūrya is a graceful ten-armed Shiva Natarāja. The southern face has figures of Pārvatī, Shiva, and the *guru* Lakulīsha. Of particular interest here are some lion-elephant panels, another image that is to be developed at Konārak into a major decorative theme. The western face has the figure of Ardhanārīshvara, the androgynous god who is half-Shiva, half-Pārvatī. The northern face has a fearsome panel of Durgā, the consort of Shiva in his dreadful form of Bhairava. Durgā is goddess of war; she thrives on blood sacrifice. She is shown killing the demon buffalo, a victory that is reenacted when buffaloes are slaughtered to her today. She carries a snake, a bow, a shield, a trident (which stresses her affinity with Shiva), an arrow, and the *vajra* thunderbolt, symbol of esoteric knowledge.

Outside the entrance to the sanctum stands an unusual "four-faced" *linga* carved with weird figures. Next to that is a sacrificial post (*yūpa*), probably a stone replica of a wooden original, to which the sacrificial animals were tied. The *jagamohana* hall has no pillars. The wooden beams that cross the ceiling were a later addition, but the heavy wooden door to the hall is original. There are some good sculptures against the northern wall, which date from the eleventh century.

□ *CHĀMUNDĀ*
The focus of the sanctuary is the terrible goddess who sits behind the grille, barely visible in the darkness. She is

Chāmundā, a tantric goddess who is worshipped as a form of Durgā. Chāmundā is the most terrifying of the Seven Mother Goddesses of tantric rites, fertility deities that were incorporated into later Hinduism. Although they were brought into the fold of orthodoxy, they were never shorn of their awful powers, and to this day they receive blood sacrifice. Chāmundā is "the destroyer of demons," for she was created to rid the goddess Kālī of demons who were bothering her, and as such, she is protrayed as fearful beyond belief. She is black, draped with an orange cloak, and wears a garland of skulls around her neck. She is seated on a corpse, and flanked by the two animals of the night: an owl and a jackal. Her body is withered and emaciated; her eyes glittering and sunken. Her mouth hangs open in expectation of sacrifice. Chāmundā is surrounded by the Mother Goddesses and her attendants. One of the most striking of these, on the northern wall of the sanctum, holds a skullcup that he has just filled with the blood from a freshly severed head at his feet.

Altogether the darkness, the horrifying figures, and the legacy of many centuries' blood-sacrifice combine to give this shrine a peculiarly disquieting atmosphere. We are faced here with very primitive rites, and they have charged the temple with a strange power. The Vaitāl Deul is not for the squeamish.

Rājārāni Temple, Eleventh Century A.D. (Figure F)

Very different in atmosphere from the Vaitāl Deul is the Rājārānī. It is set in open fields and approached by a long path. The temple is surrounded by a walkway that is ringed by slabs of volcanic rock. This picturesque little temple is almost like an English village church, surrounded by the gravestones of its previous congregation. There is no darkness here.

Part of the temple's impact lies in the contrast between its two parts. The *jagamohana* (F.1) is very plain. Although *pancharatha* in plan, the building is virtually free of adornment, except for the decoration around its doors and windows. The entrance has rounded pilasters entwined with *nāgas*, the guardians of the deep, and is surmounted by an architrave of the nine planets. This projection is continued onto the roof, in the form of a solid gable on top of which sits a lion. These figures were to become an important part of the later temples. So successful was the combination of red and golden sandstone considered, that the stone was called *rājārānī*, after the temple.

The *deul* (F.2), on the other hand, has become quite ornate. What immediately strikes the visitor are the clusters of miniature *rekha* spires around the main *shikhara*. These give the effect of a gradual ascent to the finial and are the proto-

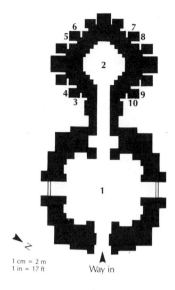

1 Jagamohana. 2 Deul. 3 *Indra.* 4 *Agni.* 5 *Yama.* 6 *Nirriti.*
7 *Varuna.* 8 *Vāyu.* 9 *Kubera.* 10 *Īshāna.*

Figure F. Rājārānī Temple ground plan.

types of what was to be fully developed by the architects of
Khajurāho. Here in Bhubaneshwar, the experiment was not
apparently found successful enough to continue on a larger
scale. The towering ascent of the *shikhara* is somewhat offset
by the size and volume of these *rekhas*, and they give the
deul an almost circular appearance.

The image in the *garbha-griha* is missing, but from the
carvings of *linga* worship, Shiva and Pārvatī and the *guru*
Lakulīsha, we can safely assume that the Rājārānī was dedicated to Shiva, perhaps in conjunction with his consort
(*Rājārānī:* "the King and his Queen").

The carving includes several figures that are to become
increasingly important in temple decoration. As well as the
lions just mentioned, we see here *alasa kanyās* carved in
high relief. These elegant and slender nymphs are shown in
a variety of familiar postures and domestic scenes, such as
washing, attending to their toilet, and enjoying amorous play.
Heraldic beasts are widely featured: the recesses between the
rathas of the *deul* have the rampant lions (*vyālas*) so beloved
by Orissan architects. There are also many erotic figures and
mithunas, another feature of medieval temples.

The most significant aspect of the Rājārānī iconography,
however, lies in the "Guardians of the Eight Directions"
(*ashtadikpālas*). These are deities who watch over the eight

cardinal points, and thus preserve the orientation and balance of the universe (see Figure G). Aligned to the image in the sanctum, they radiate its influence outward to all directions. They act as solid stained-glass windows, carved in stone yet transmitting the inner light. Circumambulating the temple, we come across them in the following order, all on the first register:

☐ *INDRA—LORD OF THE EAST* (Figure F.3)
He signifies power and courage. He is king of heaven, and protector of heroes. He carries a thunderbolt and an elephant goad. His elephant is below him, and there are two beautiful attendants above. Indra wears the *rudrāksha* bead amulets around his arms and wrists—the symbol of the power of yoga.

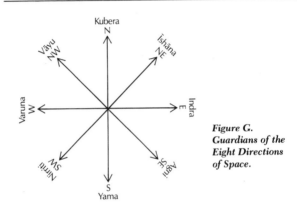

*Figure G.
Guardians of the
Eight Directions
of Space.*

☐ *AGNI—LORD OF THE SOUTHEAST* (Figure F.4)
Agni, as god of fire, presides over ritual sacrifice. Bearded and potbellied (those who sacrifice are rewarded with material well-being), he rides on the ram. The smooth protuberance of his portly figure contrasts with the tight scrollwork of the surrounding border.

Above Agni, on the second register, stands a king and his queen. The king has on his head the lotus crown of enlightenment. He carries an inverted parasol, another image of the thousand-petaled lotus.

☐ *YAMA—LORD OF THE SOUTH* (Figure F.5)
Yama is the god of death. His name means "controller." He dispenses cosmic justice and is Keeper of the Law. As such he carried the staff of power (*danda*). But there is a creative purpose to his apparent destruction, for set into the staff is a

skull. The true end of Yama's discipline is death of the self, and spiritual rebirth. This is the esoteric meaning of the skulls used in tantric ritual. He also carries the noose to catch his victims; Yama is inescapable.

His vehicle is the buffalo. In Himālayan Tantra, Yama is often buffalo-headed. The buffalo symbolizes our animal nature, which must be tamed. In Taoist and Zen art, the spiritual masters are often portrayed riding buffalo (for example, Lao Tse).

□ *NIRRITI—LORD OF THE SOUTHWEST* (Figure F.6)
The god of misery, Nirriti holds a sword and a severed head above a prostrate figure. His face has an expression of relish; his chest is thrown out as if in pride. But the figure below him has a look of great peace. It conveys the release that comes in meditation, sleep, or death. The blows of suffering can lead us to wisdom. And when the mind is left behind (the severed head), one is no longer touched by suffering. Similar teachings are conveyed by similar images in Western occult traditions—for example, the Tarot cards.

□ *VARUNA—LORD OF THE WEST* (Figure F.7)
The "Lord of the Waters," guardian of rites, and Lord of Destiny. Varuna, in the human sphere, rules over knowledge. One of the most beautiful of the figures, Varuna exudes beneficence. His smile tells us that all will be well in the end. He holds the noose of destiny in his left hand, and his right is extended in the *mudrā* of giving (*dānamudrā*). The whole tableau is beautifully composed, with the lord balanced between his vehicle (the *makara*) and a female attendant at the bottom and two celestial attendants watching over him from above.

□ *VĀYU—LORD OF THE NORTHWEST* (Figure F.8)
Vāyu is the wind god. He holds a fluttering banner. By a fitting irony, this figure has been worn almost smooth by the wind, its features fanned into ribbed lines, like sand blown by the breeze. It is a masterpiece of the art of decay.

□ *KUBERA—LORD OF THE NORTH* (Figure F.9)
The god of riches; king of men and genies. In the human realm he governs wealth. Below him stand the seven jars of plenty overflowing with gems (*nidhi*) like fabulous cornucopias. He holds flowers, to signify fruitfulness, and his grin and potbelly attest to the comforting power of prosperity.

□ *ĪSHĀNA—LORD OF THE NORTHEAST* (Figure F.10)
Lord of Purity, Īshāna is a remarkable figure. A form of Shiva, he has an erect phallus (*ūrdhvalinga*) and is attended by an

emaciated familiar, whose club mimics his master's *linga*. To the tantric initiate, true potency is the result of purity. Here again we have the esoteric tantric images—death, skulls, eroticism—which serve as codes to the initiated.

□

The Rājārānī Temple is important architecturally and iconographically. It provides a charming example of the development of Orissan style and is also a rarity in that it contains so many *mūrtis* of major deities in such good condition.

Brahmeshvara Temple, ca. A.D. 1050 (Figure A.4)

The next member of the later group of temples that should be visited is the Brahmeshvara, which despite its name, was originally built to house a *linga* symbol of Shiva. Thus the temple is typical of many Orissan shrines in that it is dedicated to Shiva but at the same time displays a propensity for religious synthesis that is a marked characteristic of the area.

The temple is *pancharatha* on plan, with four subsidiary shrines at the corners, mimicking the central *shikhara*. With its two enclosing walls separated by a tank on the southern side, the complex is attractively laid out.

Both the *deul* and *jagamohana* are in the mature Orissan style and are chiefly remarkable for the profuse detail of their carving. The door of the *jagamohana* is beautifully carved with floral and creeper motifs, interspersed with flying *gandharvas*. Notice, too, the fine pair of Shaiva doorkeepers stationed at the jambs, above double *vyālas* who also protect the threshold. The center of the lintel is a Gaja Lakshmī; in the architrave above, the nine planets are represented, flanked by an auspicious couple. As in the Mukteshvara, the interior of the *jagamohana* is also carved. An inverted lotus squared by *nāgas* dominates the ceiling, while the courses are carved with a variety of scenes that include the worship of the *linga* and a *guru* holding audience.

The *deul* has figures of the Guardians of the Eight Directions prominent in niches, and many different forms of Shiva— as Naṭarāja, Ardhanārīshvara, and the skeletal Bhairava—can be seen. The *bho* motif we saw on the Mukteshvara is here very common, sometimes being crowned by a rampant lion on a *kīrti mukha*, a design that is an unusual feature of this temple. But perhaps the most persistent motif noticeable here is the introduction of musicians and dancers among the female figures on all the exterior walls. Several of these *kanyās* are shown holding a lute or the *vīnā*, which is an innovation and is particularly significant when they appear on the balusters filling the windows of the latticed window projections on the north and south side of the *jagamohana*. Dancers and musicians placed here were to become a regular feature of later Orissan temples. There are also numerous female deities shown in dance poses (including the terrible Chāmundā), and on one of the four corner shrines there is a dancing Ganesha, which is unusual for the temples in this area. All these figures point to the tastes of the builders of the temple, the Somavamshī dynasty. Religiously eclectic, they introduced many tantric and erotic motifs into their architecture, and even referred to their king as Kāmadeva: "The God of Love." More important, the commemorative inscription of the Brahmeshvara tells us that the Somavamshī queen Kolāvatī presented "many beautiful women" to the temple. Thus it seems likely that she was responsible for introducing the cult of dancers dedicated to the temple (*devadāsīs:* "slaves of God") into Orissā, a cult originally popular in southern and central India that became an important part of Orissan religious life. It was to house the performances of the *devadāsīs* that an extra building (the *nātamandira:* "hall of dance") was added to the *deul* and *jagamohana* in all Orissan temples built after this time.

Lingarāja Temple, Eleventh Century A.D. (Figure A.6)

The Lingarāja is one of the most accomplished achievements of Indian architecture. Every inch of this huge temple—the *deul* stands over one hundred eighty feet (fifty-five meters) high—is covered with intricate carving, but the balance between line and ornamentation never falters, and the mighty

Lingarāja Temple, seen from north wall, showing mature deul *(right) and* jagamohana *(left).*

mass of the whole structure creates an unforgettable impression. The *deul* is *pancharatha* in plan, and the recesses between the *rathas* are filled with the eight *dikpālas, vyālas,* elegant *kanyās,* and a variety of major deities—Ganesha, Kārttikeya, Sūrya, Shiva, Pārvatī, and Brahmā—that attests to the catholic temperament of the Somavamshī builders. Moreover, the main image is not, as one might expect, a Shiva *linga* but a form of Shiva who is half-Vishnu, called Hari-Hara. The charm of the *kanyās,* some of whom are shown at their toilet, or writing a letter, caressing a pet bird, and so on, much in the style of Khajurāho, provides a welcome balance to the awesome atmosphere of the place, which is created partly by the dark laterite stone. The soaring ascent of the curvilinear *shikhara* is emphasized by deeply incised lines that run vertically to the *amlā* crown—an altogether considerable advance on the Rājārānī, which was built only a few years earlier. *Chaitya* window and ornamental *bho* motifs are prominent; so are the finely etched strata of numerous horizontal *bhūmis,* which provide a shimmering balance to the vertical energy of the *rekhās.* Most striking are the magnificent heraldic lions, which adorn the *shikhara* and sit underneath the massive *amlā* crown. We have seen these creatures already at the Brahmeshvara, but here they have a new confidence and are generally in better proportion to the building. The *deul* is topped by an elegant *kalasha* finial.

The *jagamohana* is also a self-confident building. The outer walls and steep pyramidal roof are both divided into two registers by horizontal moldings; its ascending tiers are deeply cut and adorned with the heraldic lion above a *bho* motif. The vertical sides of the *pidhā* tiers are carved with militaristic friezes of elephants, infantry, cavalry, and so on.

Two new buildings have been added to the standard *deul* and *jagamohana* on the same axis. These are the *nātamandira* ("Hall of Dance") and the *bhogamandapa* ("Hall of Celebration"). As their names imply, the *nātamandira* was for the ceremonial dancing of the *devadāsī* girls, and the *bhogamandapa* for communal celebration, feasting, and music in honor of the deity. This last structure has been altered since it was built, probably in the latter part of the thirteenth century. Scholars believe that the *bhogamandapa* was originally an open pillared hall, topped by a pyramidal roof similar to that of the *jagamohana,* in which lectures and sermons were delivered by learned *pandits* to the general public. This hall was joined to the *jagamohana* by a raised open platform which was used as a foundation for temporary structures for various seasonal festivals. The weight of the massive roof proved too great for the pillared hall, however, and its walls were filled and the roof reduced to turn it into the closed chamber it is today. As the importance of the temple grew, so the distinct chambers for dancing and celebration emerged as necessary. Certainly in its original form, the sweep up to the *shikhara* of the *deul* from the hall, across the low platform, would have been even more impressive than what we see today. As these new halls were added, the *jagamohana* became correspondingly more intimate in its function, so that the gradual progression from outer to inner, profane to sacred, was maintained.

The Lingarāja is surrounded by a hundred and eight subsidiary shrines, clustered around it like foothills around a mighty peak. All are protected by a forbidding walled enclosure. Above all, the place radiates power, the single most important attribute of the divine in Hindu eyes. Unfortunately, entrance is strictly forbidden to non-Hindus. It is, however, possible to view the imposing complex from a platform on the north wall of the compound. The scale and assured grandeur of this masterpiece of Orissan architecture are awe-inspiring. It is a fitting introduction to the most accessible of the Orissan cathedrals, the Sun Temple at nearby Konārak.

20

KONĀRAK

THE TEMPLE
OF THE SUN

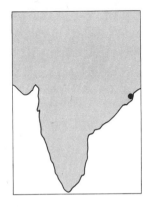

The Sun Temple of Konārak stands on a deserted stretch of coast in Orissā, overlooking the Bay of Bengāl. For centuries this once lofty building was used by sailors navigating the shore. They called it the "Black Pagoda," to distinguish it from the "White Pagoda"—the famous Jagannātha Temple twenty miles (thirty-two kilometers) up the coast in Purī.

There is something elemental about the place. Battered by storms and sea winds, nibbled by salt and sand, the temple seems to be gradually returning to its source, like some majestic galleon that is slowly but surely slipping under the waves. Now the Sun Temple stands nearly two miles (three kilometers) from the sea, but originally the Bay of Bengāl came to within a few yards of the walled enclosure. In times of storm during the monsoons, flood tides still advance menacingly toward it.

No one really knows why a temple was erected here, but there are many legends to account for its appearance. The most popular concerns Sāmba, the son of Lord Krishna. Sāmba was inordinately proud of his beauty. So proud that he once made the mistake of ridiculing a celebrated sage, Nārada, who was not renowned for his looks. Nārada was not amused. Always mischievous, he decided to have his revenge on the arrogant boy. He managed to lure the unsuspecting Sāmba to the pool where his stepmothers, the luscious consorts of Krishna, were bathing in joyful abandon. When Krishna heard that his son had become a peeping tom, he was furious and cursed him with leprosy. Realizing later that the innocent boy had been tricked by Nārada's cunning, Krishna was mortified. But he could not revoke his curse; all he could do was advise his son to worship the sun god Sūrya, healer of all diseases, and hope for a cure. After twelve years of penance and worship, Sāmba was at last instructed by Sūrya to go and bathe in the sea at Konārak. He did so and was cured of his awful affliction. Sāmba was so delighted that he decided there and then to erect a Sūrya temple on the spot. It was called Konārka, "Place of the Sun," from which the modern name comes.

Historical fact has always been interwoven with myth in India, and there may be an interesting connection here. We know that the temple was actually built by a king of the medieval Ganga dynasty, Narasingha Deva (1238–1264). The king was popularly known as *lānguliā*, "the one with a tail." It is possible that he built the temple as a supplication to Sūrya to remove a spinal protuberance of some sort. In the eyes of his subjects, such an act would imply that Narasingha was a descendant of, or even a reincarnation of, Krishna's very own son. It was not unheard of for kings to align themselves in this way with the great heroes of antiquity or even with gods. To discover the roots of one's family tree securely planted in heaven could be a distinct advantage!

A less romantic explanation is that Narasingha built the temple to commemorate his victories over the Muslims, who

The Sun Temple, from the south.

were pushing into Orissā from the west. We know that during his reign he won at least three resounding victories over the invaders.

In fact, Orissā has had a history of independence and military honor second only to that of the Rājputs. Since earliest times the main annual festivals of the Hindu calendar in this part of the country have been military, rather than religious, affairs. Until recently the autumn festival of Dussera, celebrated all over India as a worship of Durgā, consort of Shiva, was an aboriginal hunting festival in Orissā. Reserved forests were thrown open to the general public for hunting; the ancestral weapons were brought out and worshipped in each village, and the warlike past of the community was relived in ancient myth and songs. Leadership, bravery, and strength have always been the valued qualities here. Under the Ganga dynasty Orissā had a peasant militia of three hundred thousand men, with fifty thousand foot and ten thousand horse, and an elephant regiment twenty-five thousand strong. She was relied upon by the central power in times of crisis, her troops constituting what was, in effect, a national army. Even the Muslims grudgingly admitted that a Ganga king could, at a moment's notice, take the field with eighteen thousand men. And it was in Orissā that the first armed rebellions against the British took place in the early nineteenth century. This concern with martial arts invaded even the religious sphere. The priests at the Jagannātha Temple in Purī were renowned for their physical prowess and exercised daily in the famous religious gymnasia (*jagadhara*). The *pandits* were accomplished and respected wrestlers.

Many of the common Orissan surnames, such as Dalai ("group commander") and Senapati ("general"), originated in Ganga times. Interestingly, the higher posts in the army were held by the priestly brahmin caste; thus Bahīnapati ("commander-in-chief") is a common brahmin name. This unusual custom may explain the fact that in Orissā even the orthodox brahmins eat meat (though not beef), whereas elsewhere in India they are vegetarians. The country's great warriors—Sikhs, Rājputs, Marāthās—have always eaten meat. The British followed the national policy of selecting as troops those whose diet was most conducive to aggression. Thus until 1947 at least, soldiers were, if possible, always recruited from the meat-and-wheat eaters of, for example, the Punjāb, rather than the rice-and-lentil eaters of the Gangetic plain.

Narasingha himself was more renowned for his valor than his piety. This, combined with Orissā's impressive military history, supports the theory that Konārak was a colossal tower of victory, erected to the sun god in thanks for his earthly representative's victory over the dreaded Muslim. The profusion of carvings, on and around the temple, depicting military subjects, seems to confirm it.

At the end of the sixteenth century, Konārak was famous far beyond the borders of Orissā. By then, it had become a great center of pilgrimage and attracted the praise of even such a discriminating critic as Abul Fazl, the court biographer of Emperor Akbar the Great. He tells us:

> Near Jagannāth (Purī) is a temple dedicated to the sun. Its cost was defrayed by twelve years' revenue of the province. Even those whose judgment is critical stand astonished at the sight. . . . Twenty-eight temples stand in its vicinity; six before the entrance and twenty-two within the enclosure, each of which has its separate legend.

Those days are gone. All that now remains is half the main temple, and even that is damaged. Nevertheless, this mere fragment of Konārak's former glory constitutes what is often considered to be the most impressive temple in northern India.

History of the Temple

When you arrive, do not go immediately to the main entrance, but to the vantage point (Figure A.1). This is situated on the south wall of the complex, behind the two rearing figures of the Royal Horses (A.14). From here you can get the best view of the site as a whole and imagine how it must have looked in its heyday (see Figure B). The temple originally consisted of three parts: sanctuary (*deul*, A.3) surmounted by a colossal spire tower; porch (*jagamohana*, A.4); and the detached Hall of Dance (*Nātamandira*, A.5). The whole complex was surrounded by a wall.

The temple was conceived as a massive chariot lying on an east-west axis, in which the sun god, Sūrya, was pulled across the sky. Each day his journey brought life and light back to earth and his procession was a continual rejoicing. The chariot had twenty-four wheels, and was pulled by seven horses, representing the seven days of the week and the seven sages (*rishis*) who govern the constellations. Sun worship is central to India. The standard daily prayer of the brahmins is the *gāyatrī*, addressed to the sun, and, on an esoteric level, the sun symbolizes the divine Self within. The idea of procession is also an integral part of temple worship. Deities are shown to the public on feast days and festivals and are pulled around the town in brightly decorated chariots. The most famous of these processions takes place every July, in nearby Purī. This is the festival of the Jagannātha Temple. A form of Vishnu, Shrī Jagannātha, "Lord of the World," is paraded in an enormous chariot, from which comes the English word *juggernaut*.

To the west of the Sun Temple stand the remains of two

earlier structures: the Vaishnava Temple (A.6) and the Māyādevī Temple (A.7). Thus looking from left to right across the site (that is, west to east), you can trace a progression beginning with the earliest structure, the Vaishnava Temple, and ending with the latest, the Hall of Dance (A.5).

The *shikhara* must have been extremely impressive, since it dominated the rest of the complex. Various theories have been put forward to explain its collapse: earthquake, subsidence, lightning. In fact, both man and nature had a hand in it. We know from historical records that the *shikhara* was originally crowned by a finial in traditional Hindu style: a water pot (*kalasha*) on top of a heavy spheroid base (*amlā*). (See the illustration of a typical Orissan temple, Chapter 19, Figure B.) The *kalasha* was made of copper, most probably gilded, and the *amlā* of stone. We also know that the *kalasha* was removed at the beginning of the seventeenth century by the Muslims, who thought it was gold and wanted to melt it down. The *amlā* underneath it was made of several massive blocks of stone, clamped together by iron dowels. The very weight of the stone served to keep the corbeled walls of the spire in position by counteracting their tendency to fall inward. But when the *kalasha* was removed, the plaster covering the dowels was damaged and exposed and, over

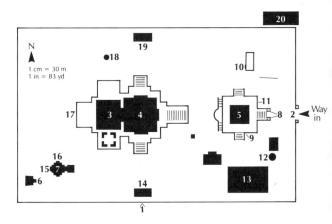

1 *Vantage point.* 2 *Main entrance.* 3 *Deul.* 4 Jagamohana.
5 *Hall of Dance*—Nātamandira. 6 *Vaishnava Temple.*
7 *Māyādevī Temple.* 8 *Guardian figures.* 9 *Gargoyle.*
10 *Ceiling lotus.* 11 *Ascetics.* 12 *Well.* 13 *Kitchens.* 14 *Royal horses.* 15 *Shiva.* 16 *Chlorite gargoyles.* 17 *Decayed figures.*
18 *Remains of statues (roof figures).* 19 *Royal elephants.*
20 *The nine planets.*

Figure A. Konārak.

Figure B. Reconstruction of how the Sun Temple originally looked. (After Percy Brown.)

time, washed away. The iron underneath now began to erode, disintegrate, and finally fell apart. As a result, the stone slabs fell down, damaging the rest of the building and exposing further capping stones to the ravages of the elements. Worse still, the essential tensile balance of the spire was destroyed. There was nothing to prevent its crumbling. Remnants of the *amlā* coping stone now lie to the north of the porch.

Added to this, any incentive to preserve the temple had been dealt another blow. Several years before the removal of the copper *kalasha*, the local *mahārāja* had removed the cult image of Sūrya from the sanctuary. It was taken to Purī, for safety from the approaching Muslim armies. Once the presiding deity had gone, the temple was shorn of its spiritual power, and local interest in it would have declined. (Time and again we see this in India: A building that the West would automatically wish to preserve for its architectural worth, is totally ignored because the main image—the spiritual "life" and *raison d'être* of any temple—is missing.) Added to which, the sanctity of the temple would have been further violated by the entry of the Muslims when they came to steal the *kalasha*. Though we have no record of any iconoclastic destruction, their very presence inside the hallowed ground of the temple would have violated its sanctity. All in all, there was little reason for the local people to prevent the place falling into total neglect, which is just what happened.

The decay was gradual. Even in 1848 a corner of the tower still stood to a considerable height. In 1820 this was about 120 feet (35 meters) according to the Scots traveler, A. Stirling, who saw it then. The English architect Markham Kittoe, writing in 1838, estimated it had diminished to "80 or 100 feet, and has at a distance the appearance of a crooked column." But this brave remnant was not to last long. Ten years later, in 1848, it was blown down in a ferocious gale. When the Indian writer Rajendralāla Mitra visited the site after another twenty years, even the sanctuary over which the proud *shikhara* had towered was reduced to "an enormous mass of stones, studded with a few *pīpal* trees here and there."

The porch—that part of the temple still standing—suffered more from the greedy hands of man than from the elements. The chief villain of the piece was a *rāja* of Kurda, who took a particular liking to the chlorite slabs that decorated the facade of the building. Again, on-the-spot evidence comes from Kittoe:

> The Kurda Rāja has demolished all three entrances and is removing the stones to Purī; the masons pick out the figures and throw them down to take their chances of being broken— which most of them are. These they leave on the spot; those that escape uninjured are taken away.

Nor were the local people averse to helping themselves to the iron clamps, for the sake of the metal. Fortunately, this vandalism was stopped by order of the government in 1838.

The story of the conservation and repair of the temple has become an inextricable part of its myth. Sadly, the early part of the story is a classic tale of bureaucratic bungling. The first suggestion to repair the ruin came from the unlikely direction of the Marine Board. In 1806 they submitted a proposal to have the temple repaired so that it could once more be a useful navigational landmark for the ships in the Bay of Bengāl! But the government considered the expense

Wheel, south face.

involved to be too great. This was again the reason given by the deputy governor of Bengāl in 1838, when he refused to do anything to preserve the temple. In 1882–83, some jungle clearance was undertaken and a few statues mounted on platforms around the site, but in the wrong places. In 1892 Lieutenant Governor Sir Charles Elliot refused to grant any money for restoration, though some individual pieces of sculpture were shifted to the Calcutta Museum a couple of years later. Elliot did suggest that some debris be cleared from the rear of the porch, but this was not done, because the superintendent engineer thought that such action would weaken what remained of the building.

Thus a hundred years were wasted before any constructive action was taken to improve the site. In 1900 Sir John Woodburn, the new lieutenant governor, visited Konārak and immediately issued an order that repair and restoration should begin without further delay. The problems faced were enormous. The porch was tottering, the stone crumbling and overgrown. The entire site was silted with sand, so that the platform of the porch was completely submerged. This, along with the Hall of Celebration, was gradually uncovered, and it was only after several years' work that the magnificent wheels, now famous all over the world, were fully exposed to view.

To prevent its collapse, the porch's interior was permanently filled in. After the ceiling was repaired, a lining of dry masonry about sixteen feet (almost five meters) thick was erected along the inside walls. The space left in the center was filled with sand. This filling initially took place through the north door, the only one left open. Then that was closed off and the filling continued through the hole in the roof caused by the falling stones of the *shikhara* tower years earlier. Finally this opening was also sealed, and the last of the sand poured through a hole twenty-five feet (seven and a half meters) long and only five inches (thirteen centimeters) in diameter. Extensive restoration work was then done on the exterior of the building.

These major repairs were buttressed by general renovation from 1915 to 1953. Gaps and crevices in the walls were pointed, loose stones reset, moss and lichen chemically removed, and damaging salt particles soaked off by paper pulp treatment. Trees were planted regularly to the south of the precinct, between the temple and the sea, to act as buffers to the corrosive salt- and sand-laden winds and to prevent the beach itself drifting into the site. There have been several government surveys whose recommendations have been carried out. The latest survey was by an international team from UNESCO who, in 1980, produced the extraordinary suggestion that the entire temple should be covered in a coat of fiberglass to protect it from the march of time.

To appreciate the temple fully, it is best to make two full circumambulations: the first at ground level, the second around the upper floor. To begin the first round, go through the main entrance (A.2).

The Temple Complex

The Guardian Figures (Figure A.8)

The first thing you see on coming through the main entrance is a pair of guardian figures composed of a lion, elephant, and man. These masterpieces of Orissan art are full of life; their vitality emphasized by the way the natural lines of the striated stone follow the flowing rhythms of the massive bodies, giving the whole figure a swirling yet contained energy. These, as the other colossi we shall see here, represent the military might of the Ganga kings. (*Narasingha* means "man-lion.") They are dynastic emblems, like the heraldic dragons of the Chandella rulers of Khajurāho. The rearing lions show traditional attributes of a deity expecting sacrifice: open mouth, bulging eyes, flared nostrils. The elephants are altogether more gentle; indeed, they seem to be grinning and their little eyes twinkle with merriment. These huge figures were originally guarding the steps of the eastern door of the porch, mounted on blocks and standing over sixteen feet (five meters) high. They were at that time covered in chocolate and pink plaster, like the Kailāsanātha temple at Ellorā. You can still see remnants of this paint, especially on the left elephant.

The Hall of Dance—Nātamandira (Figure A.5)

This pavilion was the scene of ritual celebrations held in honor of the sun god. Such halls are a distinctive feature of Orissan temple architecture. Here there would have been drama, music, dancing, and banquets, as well as daily rituals performed in honor of the lord of all life. One of the unique features of the Hindu temple was the degree to which it penetrated into the daily life of the people. The cathedrals of medieval Europe overlooked marketplaces where goods were sold and mystery plays enacted; the temples of ancient Greece served as stages for certain arts that were considered divine; but it was the Hindu temple that sought above all to glorify human life by turning it into a sacrificial celebration. Only the holy of holies was restricted to the priest; the outer parts of the temple were open to the public. Even today at a place like Madurai, in southern India, you can see the social role of

The Hall of Dance, from the east, with main temple behind.

the temple in full swing. Sacred happily mingles with profane. There are arcades of shops where you can do everything from buying cooking utensils to having your palm read by a professional fortune teller. You can meet your friends, sit and gossip, and conduct business deals—all under the gaze of the deities. The money changers are welcome; business is very much as usual.

□ *THE WALLS*
The walls of the platform of the Hall of Dance are covered by hundreds of figures, carved in living detail. The majority of these are heavenly nymphs (*alasa kanyās*) of the sort that are to be seen at Khajurāho. They twist and turn like sinuous corkscrews. Most are playing musical instruments—drums, flutes, cymbals—or dancing with their hands above their heads and their hips swinging in joyful movement. The whole wall pulsates with rhythm.

□ *THE SCULPTURES AROUND THE BASE*
Orissā had a particularly vital tradition of dance, and it was there that the *Nātamandira* became a separate structure, independent of the main temple. The sculptures around the base of the hall portray the principal poses as enumerated in the classic text on Orissan dance, the *Sangina darpana*. Other women are shown in a variety of poses, which illustrate their relaxed and sensuous enjoyment of everyday living. Some are at their toilet, bathing, or wringing out their wet hair; others caress a child or adjust a scarf. Everywhere there is a languorous dwelling on the physical charm of these damsels, the divine attendants of the sun god's court. As at Khajurāho,

life in all its pleasurable variety is seen as essentially feminine—delicate, creative, and beautiful.

□ *THE GARGOYLE* (Figure A.9)
As well as the *kanyās*, some deities are depicted, including
Ganesha and the Guardians of the Eight Directions of space,
a common motif on temple walls. Also there are instances
of a robust humor. One of these is in the gargoyle surmounting a pilaster. The gargoyle is in the form of a man, with the
water pipe coming out between his legs. To appreciate this
fully, you have to go right into the corner of the wall and look
back up at the gargoyle. Then you see that behind the man
crouches a woman, grinning as widely as her playmate.

□

The standing figures on the walls of the pavilion are arrayed
in three tiers. Each figure is set in a protruding panel framed
by running borders of vine leaves, tendrils, tiny elephants,
ducks, and animals. These tiers are punctuated further by
vignettes of erotic couples locked in close embrace, soldiers
on the march, and animals in various positions. The background to all this intricate carving is a wall surface that is
not continuous but regularly pitted with small holes, so that
it resembles a honeycomb. It seems barely substantial enough
to support the carvings that emerge so boisterously from its
checkered shadows. The whole effect is one of fragility
combined with softness. This impression is accentuated by
the way the scroll motifs tend to be concentrated at the corners
of the building, and thus serve to soften any angularity it
might have. Each register of frieze is deeply indented, and
this adds to the play of light and shade that reduces the wall
surface to one rippling arabesque that is at once lively and
contained. We are left with a feeling of profusion and unashamed vitality.

It is worth remembering that Hindu temple art is squarely
based on the indigenous craft traditions. This heritage has
several important implications. On the technical side it insures
the continuing skill of the stone carver, who inherits the trade
from his father. This skill is highly prized, for the carver who
fashions unworked stone into life acts as a microcosm of the
mysterious power that fashions the undifferentiated primordial matter into the world of name and form. Thus the stone-
mason bridges the gulf between God and man. He passively
receives the divine forms and actively transmits them to his
material. (The scribe does the same with different materials
and instruments.) In the Indian tradition both primordial
matter (*prakriti*) and pure spirit (*purusha*) are eternal and
divine; they represent the first duality to emerge from the
One.

The craft tradition dictated content as well as form. The crafts were rooted in a world view that was cosmological rather than theological. Their art is not morally didactic in the sense of teaching what ought to be done to become "holy"; temples such as Konārak and Khajurāho are non-moral. They communicate a vision of a world that is *already* holy by virtue of its beauty, richness, and exuberance. In this it is spiritually akin to early Christian art (for example, in the catacombs), in which craft traditions, originally from Egypt, still predominate. Both genres share insignia and motifs that are universal: solar circles, crosses, serpents, tendrils, volutes. Such art is "pre-historical" in that it employs a vocabulary of cyclical and cosmic motifs rather than focusing on the historical personages of the founder of the religion, its saints, and so on. Generally speaking, the farther an art moves from this craft base, the more morally didactic it becomes.

□ *DEVADĀSĪS*

The subjects of the carving are not merely decorative. They are records of what went on here. One important institution in the Hindu temple was the *devadāsīs*—the temple dancing girls. These girls entertained the public as well as performing dances to the temple god. They represented an incarnation of heavenly nymphs and portrayed myths and stories from the scriptures. The *devadāsīs* would have danced here in this hall.

But however pure its beginnings, the *devadāsī* institution went into a spectacular decline. By the eighteenth century there was an entire colony of the girls living in Purī, an old center of brahminical piety. Under royal guard, the girls were

The Hall of Dance, detail of south wall.

not allowed to marry, as they were officially "married" to Sūrya, the sun god they served. However, not only the deity enjoyed their charms. The colony was popularly known as "the place where bodies may enjoy relaxation," and out of the six categories of *devadāsīs* residing in this stately pleasure dome, one was called "those who are meant for the king only," and another "those who are meant for the inner apartments only." Perhaps the other four were generally available—at least to the upper echelons of society. We know from letters discovered in the possession of a former *devadāsī* at the beginning of this century that at one stage even the king had to write to the girls and reprimand them for the scandals they were causing. Their reputation sank so low that they came to be called *maharīs* ("scavengers") by the orthodox Orissan society, a reference not only to the lowest caste, but to the girls' indiscriminate acceptance of all comers. The secluded, clandestine life of the colony, redolent with illicit pleasure and courtly intrigue, must have been an endless source of righteous indignation for the local gossips.

The *devadāsī* system was kept alive by the random recruitment of young girls, often from poor families who were probably only too pleased to see their daughters assured of a good living and themselves freed from having to find a dowry they could ill afford. Nevertheless, it would be wrong to see the system as nothing but a front for wholesale prostitution. Even in its last hours, the custom retained some of its former glory,

A pair of lovers (maithuna), *detail from* jagamohana.

and some of the *devadāsīs* fulfilled their original duty. The Orissan historian, Dr. K. Mansingha, recalls seeing a brilliant performance of the dancing art in the Hall of Celebration of Orissā's holiest temple, the Jagannātha at Purī. This was in the early years of the present century. Sumptuously clad in heavy gold jewelry from the temple coffers, a young *deva-dāsī* danced silently in front of the image for almost an hour. She was accompanied only by her *guru*, an old man, who played the *pachawāj* drum. When she had finished, many of her spellbound audience—men and women of all ages—spontaneously rolled over the very ground on which she had danced, so great was their appreciation.

☐

In the classic Orissan temple, such as the Lingarāja at Bhubaneshwar, there was a hall of celebration (*bhoga-mandapa*) in addition to the Hall of Dance, in which the *devadāsīs* performed. Here at Konārak the two structures seem to have been amalgamated. The inner arrangement of the hall, divided into bays by thick pillars, falls into nine compartments, thus forming a ground plan known as the *graha-abja-mandapa*, used in ancient India for the construction of stages. This fact, together with the profuse carving of musicians, and so forth, would argue that this pavilion was a *nātamandira*. But it may well be that Narasingha intended to build another structure between this and the *jagamohana*, much as happened at the Lingarāja, and it is a fact that the building farthest from the *deul* is generally a *bhogamandapa* in Orissan temples. Whether this was his intention or not, this hall would also have been used for banquets. Food was ceremonially offered to the sun god, and a portion of the offering returned as blessed and given to the devotees as consecrated food (*prasāda*). This custom takes place in every living Hindu temple. There is also the important ritual of feeding the brahmins in order to gain spiritual merit, another custom still practiced, though times are hard and priestly potbellies less common than they were. The southern door of the hall led directly to the kitchens (Figure A.13).

From the inside you can see that the hall was aligned to the eastern door of the main temple. This was to allow the rising sun to fall on the image in the holy of holies each morning. There may well have been a ritual opening of doors to allow the light to shine through the hall, for there are large holes in the floor that were probably sockets for wooden doorjambs.

☐ *THE CEILING LOTUS* (Figure A.10)
The building would have had a pyramidal roof, similar in shape to the roof of the porch of the temple. There is a finely

carved piece from the ceiling now lying to the north of the hall. This is a fully opened lotus, with Sūrya on the pericarp surrounded by an inner ring of eight petals, and an outer one of sixteen. On each of the sixteen petals there is a dancer.

☐

One of the beautiful features of all the buildings here is the stone. A type of gneiss, it is garnetiferous, and time has exposed its glistening veins of different colors. Here in the hall, there is a predominance of muted heathery colors—purple, brown, and yellow. The tonal effect is one of mellow softness, emphasized by the rounded larval texture of the stone, weathered smooth by the years.

☐ *THE ASCETICS* (Figure A.11)
The hall contains more explicit references to the destructive power of time. On the northeast side of the building are a couple of remarkable sculptures. The right-hand one carries a pot, the left-hand one wears ascetic's beads and holds what looks like the remains of a musical instrument in his hand. Placed next to a cameo of a beautiful maiden preening herself, this skeletal pair are like a couple of grotesques from some Shakespearean graveyard, full of obscure but grim hints that all is vanity before the Lord of Time.

☐

Despite its undoubted charm, there are definite indications that the Hall of Dance was built later than the main temple, and its style is slightly decadent in comparison. The individual figures are not as fine as those we shall see in a few minutes: the proportions, particularly of head to body, seem often misjudged, and the uncarved base of the plinth in relation to the decorated wall it supports is really too squashed to be fully satisfying as a coherent structure. It is perhaps best to view the building as an appetizer for the feast that is yet to come.

From the Hall of Dance you can pass, via the well (A.12), to the kitchens (A.13). Here you can see stone slabs that were tabletops, their drainage channels and the depressions in which spices were pounded still visible. From here proceed to the southern edge of the compound.

The Royal Horses (Figure A.14)

These are another example of the genius of Ganga monolithic sculpture. The western one is the best perserved. Fully caparisoned, with a quiver full of arrows and a scabbard for a sword hanging from his back, he is crushing some hapless enemy, his tail lifted in arrogant ease. The dismounted rider, unfortunately headless, still conveys a powerful feeling of energy, compressed in his rounded shoulders and bulging thighs.

The defeated enemies under each horse are probably the contemporary sultans of Bengāl, Tughar Khān, and Iktiyar Yazbak, whom Narasingha Deva defeated a few years before Konārak was built. It was a resounding victory for the Orissan, and a contemporary copperplate inscription tells us gleefully that "the whitish stream of the Ganges became black with the collyrium (mascara) washed from the weeping eyes of the Muslim women of Bengāl." There has been rivalry between Orissā and Bengāl for centuries, so this victory was doubly welcome and fit to be commemorated by the Sun Temple.

The Main Temple (Figure C)

Begin the circumambulation of the main body of the temple, comprising the *jagamohana* and the *deul* (C.1, 2) starting with the seven horses.

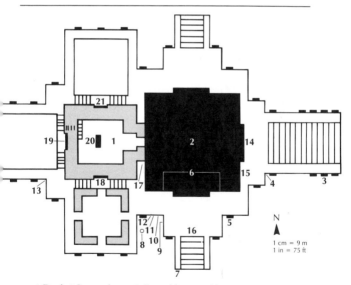

1 Deul. 2 Jagamohana. 3 *Second horse.* 4 Nāga *corner.*
5 *Wheel.* 6 *Brahmā and figures.* 7 *Elephant frieze.* 8 *Circles.*
9 *Man offering the* linga. 10 *The blissful couple.* 11 *The king meets the giraffe.* 12 *The happy monk.* 13 *The departure.*
14 *Eastern doorway.* 15 *Large* maithuna. 16 *Southern steps.*
17 *Southern recess.* 18 *The southern Sūrya.* 19 *The western Sūrya.* 20 The garbha-griha. 21 *The northern Sūrya.*

Figure C. Sun Temple ground plan.

□ SOUTHERN FACE

Since the days of the great Vedic horse sacrifices, the horse has been intimately associated with royalty. The second horse on the southern side (C.3) is the best preserved, his flanks beautifully marbled. His testicles are shiny from the touch of devotees, perhaps women wanting children, who worship him as a god of fertility, able to impart the mysterious life force to those who beseech him. Underneath the horses a frieze of elephants begins. It runs the entire way around the temple, and contains over seventeen hundred of these well-loved beasts. Elephants were prized equally for their military role and their practical work as beasts of burden in ancient India, and they are commemorated on most temples.

□ THE NĀGA CORNER (Figure C.4)

As you walk around, you notice three dominant themes in the carving: heavenly nymphs (*alasa kanyās*), divine serpent kings (*nāgarājas*) and queens (*nāgarānīs*), and fabulous beasts (*vyālas*). All these subjects are well represented in this corner.

The Kanyā Beginning from the east, you have the nymph: languorous, sensuous, inviting. The word *alasa* means "completely relaxed," and, as at Khajurāho, there is no erotic tension or compulsion in these figures' undoubted allure. They are innocent and natural, with the uninhibited grace and sensuality of a tribal girl who instinctively realizes she is the sweet-scented embodiment of the Great Mother goddess who creates and sustains all life.

The Nāgarāja Next to the *kanyā* is a *nāgarāja*, hands raised in the *namaste* gesture of greeting (*namaste* means: "I greet the light within you") still used today, and technically known as the *anjalimudrā*. *Nāgas* are the guardians of the underworld, and they watch over the treasures of the subconscious mind. In this role they are the equivalent to dragons in the Western mythical traditions, with the important difference that to the Eastern psyche the serpent was a creative and beneficial power, not something that was evil and had to be destroyed by a gallant Saint George or a noble Parsifal. The hoods that crown the *nāgas'* heads are a protective symbol of majesty, like the royal umbrella or the sacred tree. On an esoteric level, they allude to the thousand-petaled lotus that opens over the head of the enlightened who have discovered the treasure buried deep within.

The Vyāla Next to the *nāga* stands a fine leogryph (*vyāla*). As well as being heraldic devices of royalty, like the lion you saw

*Damsel (*alasa kanyā*) flanked by* nāga *king and queen.*

at the entrance to the Hall of Dance or the Chandella lions at Khajurāho, these fabulous creatures also belong to the inexhaustible richness of the subconscious that the temple embodies and toward which it leads us. Mythical beasts such as these were intended to awaken their archetypes in our own psyches.

The Nāga Couple   Lastly, you come to an astonishingly tender *nāga* couple in loving embrace. The male has three large hoods, the female three small ones. These hoods catch the light and emphasize the contrast between sun and shade in a highly dramatic manner. The couple positively glow with golden light as the sun strikes the honey-colored veins that run through the speckled texture of the stone. The female reclines, luxuriously content in the safety of her lover's arms. Her face is suffused with a dreamy joy, while his features radiate a tender and loving concern. It is remarkable how the sculptor has managed to convey feeling here through the way he has carved the hands of the pair. The female's left hand is spread, her index finger raised, as she tingles to her very fingertips with pleasure. Her other hand lightly supports the small of her partner's back. His right hand delicately cradles her breast, while his left one gently supports her hooded head. Altogether this couple is a marvelously observed tableau of loving joy.

The Boxed Frieze A similar warmth of feeling is found in the cameos that form the boxed frieze above these standing figures. Several of these are erotic couples. Particularly pleasing is a humorous panel, directly above the figures we have just seen, which shows a woman being attacked by monkeys who are trying to steal the pot of food she is carrying on her head. Such attacks are still a hazard today.

☐ *THE WHEEL* (Figure C.5)
This is the best preserved of the twenty-four chariot wheels. The wheel is one of those composite symbols that has many levels of meaning to the Indian psyche. It represents time—the passage of the sun and the passing of the seasons. It is an ancient symbol of royalty. It is also the round of *karma*, the cycle of cause and effect that keeps us acting from moment to moment and also carries the subtle body from life to life, reincarnation to reincarnation. The *Upanishads* talk about the gods "spinning the wheel of fate." Esoterically, the wheel is the lotus of enlightenment, and the *chakra*, or subtle energy center, through which the life force enters and vitalizes the physical body. In modern times the power of this symbol has also been recognized. Mahatma Gandhi knew what he was doing when he adopted the spinning wheel as the sign of the independence movement, and it is the wheel that sits in the center of the Indian flag today.

The detail here is noticeable, especially the carving in the hub, which depicts a king riding an elephant while his subjects stand in a worshipful ring around him. There is also some hapless enemy, or perhaps criminal, whom the elephant is nonchalantly crushing beneath his feet, much to the approval of the onlookers and no doubt his gracious majesty himself. The eight principal spokes are also well carved with erotic couples, *maithunas,* and maidens in various poses.

☐

As you move westward across the southern door, you see a lightning conductor that runs up over the new brickwork of the southern doorway and leads to the top of the temple. Let your eyes follow this conductor up until you come to the balcony with large standing figures arrayed around it. Some of these are very beautiful; the ones on this southern face are the four-headed Brahmā, god of creation, while some of the others are celestial musicians and dancing girls (C.6). Nowadays it is unfortunately too dangerous to climb that far up the temple to get a closer look at these figures, but even from down here on the ground you can get an idea of their radiant expressions of happiness. There are also fine friezes of people and elephants at ground level (C.7), hauling rocks to build the temple.

To the worshipper, the higher up the temple and the nearer to the heavens you are, the more the rapture increases. Thus the base friezes are of elephants, people, the workaday life of battles, building, and celebration, with figures of dancing and music on a human level interspersed with the *nāgas* of the underworld. By the time you get to the top of the building, you are in the world of the Titans, heavenly giants. According to the texts, each realm of creation enjoys one hundred times the bliss of the realm below it, a progression that culminates in the unspeakable bliss of the Absolute. In the temple this ultimate level is symbolized by the finial, the *kalasha* pot, which is filled with *soma*, the nectar of immortality.

☐ *THE PAVEMENT IN THE SOUTHWEST RECESS*
  (Figure C.8)
The pavement here is marked by various circles etched in the stone, some of them interlocking. No one knows for sure what they were used for. Although they are similar to *mandalas* that were drawn as part of the architectural plans of many temples, it is most likely they were for astrological calculations, some of them being sundials for daytime observations.

☐ *MAN OFFERING THE* LINGA (Figure C.9)
On the top register, third figure along, stands a man with his *linga* in his hand. On the ground between his legs is a fire. We have here an archaic fertility symbol, in which the life force of the sun god, the element fire, and human sexuality are all linked. Fire plays a crucial part in Hindu ritual. It is the receptacle of sacrifice in the Vedic rites. The unmarried student is given sacred fire when he receives the sacred thread and commanded to worship it all his life. When he marries, the fire is brought into the household and is the center of family rituals. As an adult, the Hindu makes offerings to the ancestors into fire, and when he dies, his body is consumed by fire. Fire is one of the principal manifestations of Sūrya; it is the mouth of the gods, consuming all. It is deified as Agni.

☐ *THE BLISSFUL COUPLE* (Figure C.10)
The register continues with an erotic couple, then, in the corner, a woman having some trouble with a demon. Then, on the south-facing wall of the recess, is one of Konārak's highlights. It is a couple, perhaps a king and his queen, standing under a tree. Although the piece is badly damaged, and only the top half remains, the couple convey an intense feeling. They are in paradise; their faces irradiated with a sunny, childhood happiness that reminds us of an Eden we all once inhabited. Here we have in a nutshell the difference between the Sun Temple and Khajurāho, with which it is often compared. At Khajurāho the figures, however charm-

The blissful couple (mithuna).

ing, inhabit a rarified world we cannot enter but only look upon from outside, like children with their noses pressed against a shop window. Their expressions are stylized, removed. But here at Konārak the feeling is intensely human; we can relate to it. As a result Konārak is psychologically accessible to us, which not all Hindu temples are. This couple represent the high noon of human life. Full of optimism and possibility, they bask in the warmth of the sun god's bounty, cheerfully unaware of the inevitable march of time.

□ *THE KING MEETS THE GIRAFFE* (Figure C.11)
To the left of the blissful couple there is a strange scene in which a group of men is paying homage to the king seated on an elephant. They are presenting him with a giraffe. We have here an interesting historical tidbit. Giraffes, of course, are found only in Africa, not in India, so this is probably a record of a trading ship that landed at Konārak, which was a flourishing port at the time the temple was built, and brought its strange cargo for the king to see. It is hard to tell who looks more surprised by the encounter—the people or the animals!

□ *THE HAPPY MONK* (Figure C.12)
At the end of this wall is an example of Konārak's impish satire. Here is a monk, rotund and worldly in the best Chaucerian tradition, deriving very unspiritual solace from three nubile ladies, who, from the look of it, are doing all they can to please him. His face is like an exuberant melon, split open with a toothy and triumphant laugh, as he holds a purse

above his head, keeping back his money until he is fully satisfied. Wherever they could, the masons here surreptitiously poked fun at the priesthood of their day.

☐

Even when they were first carved, scenes like these won the admiration of all who saw them, and the fame of Konārak spread far and wide. Narasingha Deva was delighted with the achievement of his craftsmen, as the following story shows.

One day, the king decided to see how the building of the Sun Temple was progressing. He disguised himself and wandered about the site, incognito, looking here and there to see that the work was to his satisfaction. In one corner of the vast camp he came across a famous craftsman, absorbed in carving out a block of stone. This artist had an attendant, a young apprentice whose sole job was to squat behind the master and supply him with refreshment whenever he needed it. This refreshment was in the form of *pān*—betel leaf wrapped around a bitter and heady mixture of chopped areca nut, chewing tobacco, and lime. (*Pān* is especially popular as a stimulant in the northeast of the country, staining both mouths and pavements a vivid blood-red.) The king motioned to the attendant to move, and silently took his place. So absorbed was the master, that he did not notice anything had happened behind him. After a while, he stretched back his hand for more *pān*. The king, who had been gazing entranced at the beautiful work being done, quickly got out his own *pān* box of finest silver, took out a bundled leaf, and put it in the outstretched hand. The craftsman popped the *pān* in his mouth and went on working. For a few moments nothing happened, but then he suddenly realized that the *pān* he was chewing was of a far higher quality than normal. Turning around to find out what was going on, he recognized the face of his king. Spluttering profuse apologies, the sculptor prostrated himself before the squatting monarch. But Narasingha Deva would have none of it. Rising to his feet, he lifted up the artisan and then bowed down low before him, saying: "*Mahārāj!* You are so talented, you are indeed worthy to have the king as your attendant!"

☐ *THE DEPARTURE* (Figure C.13)
The sun god presides over decay and death just as much as growth and life. This poignant panel shows an aged woman taking leave of her family who cluster around her, begging her not to go. Her destination is probably Banāras, where all pious Hindus hope to end their days on the banks of the Ganges.

Vaishnava Temple (Figure A.6)

This is the oldest temple on the site, dedicated to Vishnu, showing us the simplest form of the temple: a small sanctuary that originally contained an image preceded by a porch. At the entrance to this there is a primitive door guardian who bears the stave of power to ward off the evil eye. This temple was uncovered in 1956 and was made from brick, plastered with lime and sand. Vishnu was from earliest times a solar deity, as his discus and lotus attributes remind us.

Māyādevī Temple (Figure A.7)

This was originally dedicated to Sūrya, the sun god, and was excavated in the first decade of the century. It used to contain an image of a form of Sūrya called Rāmachandi, who allegedly crept away in the middle of the night when he overheard two priests discussing the approach of the Muslims. He is now residing in a temple eight miles (thirteen kilometers) from here.

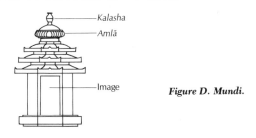

Figure D. Mundi.

There is some good carving on the outside walls, especially *nāga* figures and little faces set in *chaitya* window frames (*kūdus*). Guardians of the Eight Directions are also prominent, set in miniature temples called *mundis* (see Figure D). These *mundis* are a common feature of Orissan architecture and are also found at Khajurāho. Notice also a fine dancing Shiva waving a serpent above his head on the western wall (A.15). On the northern wall are two fine chlorite gargoyles in the form of crocodiles (A.16). One supports a couple in its mouth, the other a fish. These were drains to carry the ritual ablutions of water, clarified butter, and milk out of the temple to where they could be touched by devotees.

The Main Temple—Western Face

At first glance, this wall seems too badly damaged to be worth looking at. But if you do look, it gradually becomes apparent that the ravages of time have created a weathered effect that is haunting in its beauty. We have here an art of decay, a sculpture of dissolution that in its own way is as poignant and arresting as anything on the site. In some cases the erosion has revealed the striations of the rock, rippling and sparkling in undulating rhythms. Then the figures seem to be composed just of vibrating waves of energy, exposed by the ceaseless caress of winds and rain, and their forms seem to swim out of the swirling waters of the surrounding chaos. *Nāgas*, dancing girls, loving couples—all are reduced to mere ripples of movement in the ever-changing web of life that is constantly creating and dissolving forms. Take a moment or two to study this graceful dance of death captured, for example, by the group in the center of the western facade (Figure A.17). In their inevitable decay, these lovely figures pay an ironical yet supremely fitting tribute to the sun god, Sūrya, Lord of Time.

The Main Temple—Northern Face

Well preserved but deprived of sunlight, this face is difficult to approach, due to restoration work being done after falls of rock during recent monsoons. Much of the best work is high up on the wall, and its position, together with lack of direct light, makes it difficult even to photograph. Nevertheless, there is much good carving, dealing with subjects we have already come across.

Particularly remarkable in this northern side of the complex are the remains of the colossal figures that originally crowned the roof of the main temple (Figure A.18) and the pair of royal elephants that are situated near the northern wall of the compound (A.19).

The Nine Planets (Figure A.20)

In the wooded clearing outside the northeast corner of the compound stands a hut that enshrines a good carving of the nine planets. These are, from left to right: Sun, Moon, Mars, Mercury, potbellied Jupiter, Venus, Saturn, and two others. All are seated cross-legged on a lotus and carry a water pot in the left hand and a rosary in the right. The last two deities are Rāhu (ascending node) and Ketu (descending node). The fierce-looking Rāhu carries a crescent in each hand, whereas Ketu has a bowl of flames in the left hand and a staff in the right. These were originally part of an architrave of the eastern door but were moved to safety when the temple was excavated.

Astrology is vital to the Hindus. Planetary deities must be worshipped and appeased to secure success in life; the astrologer, along with the priest and the money lender, is a figure of enduring importance in village life. No marriage takes place unless the horoscopes are well matched (a reason given by Indians for the negligible divorce rate in India). No important occasion goes ahead unless the astrological signs are favorable to it, and eminent scientists, businessmen, and politicians pay careful heed to what their astrologers tell them is in store.

Each Saturday there is a fair here in the little clearing, and Saturn, the deity of Saturday, is worshipped to insure a favorable week ahead. Priests come and conduct *pūjā* for the pilgrims, decorating the images with flowers, vermilion, and sandal paste and offering coconuts, rice, and money. Ancient fire sacrifices (*homa*) are also performed in specially dug pits outside the hut. These take place at sunrise and date back four thousand years, to Vedic times.

The Main Temple—First (U.S. Second) Floor
(Figure C.14)

The frame of this door is the best preserved; except for a small missing piece near the base it is virtually complete. Made of chlorite, all the doorframes here are alike in composition and technique. They are composed of seven intricately carved bands, containing little figures, scrollwork, serpents, *mithuna*, and so on. Each band is "supported" by a figure at its base, and the lintel is surmounted by protective figures also.

These doorways echo their wooden prototypes, which can still be seen, brightly painted and decorated, in the Himālayan temples, especially in Bhūtan and Ladākh. Indeed, Himālayan art was much influenced by the Pāla-Sena school, which thrived in Bengāl and northern Orissā in the ninth century and went up to the Himālayas with the Buddhists who fled the Muslim armies.

☐ *LARGE MAITHUNA* (Figure C.15)
A fine example of a couple in close embrace. This level has some very large *mithuna* figures, which would have been out of proportion had they occurred lower down the wall but blend perfectly with the less adorned upper reaches.

☐ *SOUTHERN STEPS* (Figure C.16)
As you walk around the temple, you cross the top of the southern steps. Covered in larval rock that has been weathered away by erosion, they resemble nothing so much as seaweed. It is as if the whole temple is slipping slowly back into the deep, its molten steps already half submerged. The higher you climb, the nearer the gods you get, and the wilder

the journey becomes. Walking here is like clambering over childhood rocks. After the rain the stone is slippery, and glistens with little pools trapped in its pitted depressions. In the warm sun, it seems just right for the bare feet that pad across its well-worn softness with a dry, slapping sound.

Decay works its own magic. The ravages of time can spark off associations and nuances of feeling that would have remained unprompted by a more perfectly preserved work of art. Here crumbling rocks, mossy lichen, and sudden green glimpses of sprouting plant life act as triggers to memory and fantasy. Sea monsters and strange beasts peep out from hidden corners in the walls, luring you on into unexplored depths, as the spirit of the temple slowly but surely takes hold of you. Konârak's bones are turning to coral, its eyes are becoming pearls, and the whole temple is suffering "a sea-change, into something rich and strange."

□ SOUTHERN RECESS (Figure C.17)
Just before the short flight of steps leading up to the Sūrya image, on the right, is a superb recess. This recess typifies the site, since it maintains a balance between mass and detail that is everywhere here and contains stone that varies tremendously in color, texture, and workmanship. Here monolithic figures overlook pillars carved in the tiniest detail. On the west side rears up a man mounted on a lion, which is on top of an elephant crushing an enemy soldier. There is a tremendous dynamism in this proud tableau, which must be six feet (two meters) high and is still in pretty good condition. War is balanced by love; on the opposite wall stand a glorious *maithuna* couple, again very large, which catches the honeyed evening light from the west. We can get an idea of how impressive the main *shikhara* must have been as it soared up into the sky, adorned by carvings such as these.

Due to damage, many of these sculptures are now visibly part of the mammoth rock. They seem to be reverting to the undifferentiated stuff from which they were once fashioned. Sucked back into a wall of solid quicksand, they are frozen in time. The carvings that adorn every inch of the pillars here urge the same metamorphosis on us. Their tracery swirls and twists to produce curling introverted patterns—stone seaweed caught and turned by the pull of the tide. Like the Celtic motifs they so resemble, like all art shaped by the restless sea, the Konârak scrolls ebb and flow in a cadence of ceaseless flux. Meandering like the illuminations of a medieval manuscript, they echo the patterns with which the Lindisfarne monks embellished their Gospel and their brethren in Ireland decorated the Book of Kells. Such patterns act as gentle mazes, ensnaring the heart with the promise of hidden secrets.

☐ *THE SOUTHERN SŪRYA* (Figure C.18)

Sūrya is one of the three chief deities of the Vedas. As the source of light, of warmth, of life, and of knowledge, he is the source of all.

One of the wonders of Konārak are the three forms of Sūrya, which are set in the southern, western, and northern walls. Made of chlorite, these accessory deities (*pārshva-devatās*) were originally framed, but the frames have long since disappeared. The walls and roof around them are thus all modern.

Sūrya towers majestically over the south side of the compound. His gaze is unflinching yet compassionate, and the full, almost flat quality of the face with its almond-shaped eyes and flattish nose look more Southeast Asian, perhaps Burmese or Thai, than Indian. Konārak had extensive maritime connections with Southeast Asia, so it is quite possible that the model for these features came from there. Yet the face is not heavy; the smooth polished stone is shadowed by the gently smiling lips, as the cheeks swell out from the nose and catch the light. It has an assured, self-absorbed tranquillity that reminds us of the height of Gupta art, nearly eight hundred years earlier.

Sūrya's body radiates an adamantine strength. Broad-shouldered, narrow-waisted, and long-limbed, it is hung with the signs of royalty: earrings, sacred thread, necklaces, an exquisitely worked *dhotī* closed with a magnificent belt and clasp, with a long pendule hanging down at the front. Sūrya is the only Indian god who wears boots—a legacy from Iranian iconography, as is the work on the *dhotī*. Again, the body has the same fullness of contained energy that vitalizes the sculpted figures of the Gupta period.

At first sight the sun god may appear rather too stylized by comparison with the other, more naturalistic carving that adorns the walls of Konārak. It is true that hieratic deities are always carved according to canonical convention. But there are several little details that prevent it becoming too formal a figure. The taut body is etched with fineness at the armpits, waist, and ankles; there is no heaviness at all. The subsidiary figures add a touch of relief to the main one. By Sūrya's right foot kneels the king, his sword laid down in submission; by his left, the priest. Church and state, the two worlds of man, bow down before the omnipotent source of life. Their faces have the sweetness of mature Pāla-Sena art.

Speaking of the universal spirit that the sun most perfectly symbolizes, the *Brihadāranyaka Upanishad* asks:

> Who really knows the One,
> To whom the priests and the warriors are but food,
> And death is but a sauce?

*Sūrya, the sun god
(southern face of
deul).*

Behind these two stand a charming couple of figures: the bearded Dandi and the bearded and potbellied Pingala, the two attendants of Sūrya. Beyond them, in a *mundi* niche, are two warriors, while at the very ends are Ushā and Pratyushā, the twin divinities of light who in Vedic mythology dispel the darkness with their rosy-tipped arrows. Below is the charioteer Aruna ("the Dawn"), who drives the god's one-wheeled golden chariot, controls the seven horses, and shields the world from the sun's fury. The chariot bears dancers and musicians.

The four standing figures flanking the image are Sūrya's wives, two on each side. Above these are deities: On the left is Vishnu with his mace and lotus; on the right Brahmā, bearded and potbellied, with three of his four heads visible and with matted hair. This portly god is carrying his water pot, stave, sacrificial ladle, and rosary. He is in his role of priest-ascetic. Sūrya's halo is fringed with tongues of flame and surrounded by various attendants, who frame the ineffable beauty of the main face.

This wealth of subsidiary detail, carved with feeling and vitality, presents a variety that rescues the enormous central figure from appearing too massive or conventional. Altogether, it is a triumph of the Ganga sculptor's art.

☐ *THE WESTERN SŪRYA* (Figure C.19)

The best time to see this image is in the afternoon, when the otherwise dull chlorite is enlivened by the sun. Wearing the traditional crown of kings and gods, this Sūrya is very similar to the one you just saw. The stone is so finely carved it looks as if the statue had been cast in metal.

Again, some of the attendant figures here are superb. The sun god's halo is composed of smiling musicians whose faces glow with happiness like the blissful couple on the southern wall. They remind one of an ancient creation myth, which tells us:

> When the sun appeared, there was a great cry from which all beings and all their pleasures were born. Hence at his rising and setting, cries and songs are heard; all beings and desires rise towards it. Those who worship the sun as the Absolute ever hear beautiful sounds and are always filled with joy.   *Chandogya Upanishad*

On the top left of Sūrya stands Brahmā, the creator; on the right, Vishnu, the preserver, for the sun both quickens and sustains all life. Here the flanking deities are flexed, so as to give the whole figure a serpentine motion and a touch of lightness. And again the lower part of the piece is blackened with the patina from the touch of hundreds of thousands of pious hands.

☐ *THE GARBHA-GRIHA* (Figure C.20)

This was the holy of holies, originally approached from the east. Now it is empty except for a carved chlorite platform, on which the image of the deity was originally set. The platform is divided into three horizontal divisions. In the recessed middle division is the moustached King Narasingha Deva, kneeling with folded hands in the company of priests. His sword, the emblem of kingship, is held in his armpit. One of the priests is garlanding the monarch, while another carries a royal charter pertaining to the founding of the temple. To the left of the king kneels his queen, surrounded by six of her female attendants. The dress of all these figures shows considerable variety, and all their little faces are lit with that sunny contentment that is a hallmark of Konārak sculpture.

☐ *THE NORTHERN SŪRYA* (Figure C.21)

Here the sun god is shown sitting on a spirited charger, while the king and priest stand as attending servants. Sūrya himself is wearing a high crown, and the *tilak* mark on his forehead. Although the body is badly damaged, the god's face is again a masterful achievement.

Sūrya is shown riding a horse to indicate that he is facing north, that part of the sky where the sun is principally absent. The presence of the horse also alludes to a *Mahābhārata* myth in which Sūrya's brightness was so great that Knowledge left, unable to bear it, leaving Shadow alone by his side. She retired into the forest to devote herself to a life of contemplation. To hide, she took the form of a mare. The Sun, however, discovered her, and, taking the form of a horse, approached her. She bore him two sons, the Ashwins, who are the twin gods of agriculture.

It is perhaps fitting that we should end our Indian journey with the Konārak sun temple. The sun is the beginning of all life, and yet, as the measure of time, it relentlessly takes back what it has given. The desire to transcend time lies at the very heart of Indian culture. It is the basis of her religions, her art, her social system. So to the Indian psyche, the sun symbolizes not only time but that which lies beyond time, the Eternal. These faces of the sun are not incompatible opposites. On the contrary, they are the two complementary aspects of the One Life.

The didactic purpose of the best of Indian art is to bring the timeless into the transitory. It seeks to make us realize that deep within the ever-changing world lies the unchanging spirit, the Self of all creation. Places like Konārak attempt to bring us to the threshold of this unifying vision, so we discover our true nature. Perhaps eight centuries before Christ the poet of the *Īsha Upanishad* hymned the sun as the image of his own potential divinity:

> O Lord of Light, the knowing one,
> The golden guardian, giver of life to all,
> Spread apart thy rays, gather up thy brilliance,
> That I may perceive thy finest and most splendrous nature,
> That cosmic spirit which lies at thy heart,
> For I myself am That!

SOME
USEFUL DATES

B.C.

ca. 3000–ca. 500	Indus Valley civilization (Harappā and Mohenjodaro).
ca. 1800–ca. 800	Vedic Āryans settle across northern India.
ca. 800	*Upanishads* composed; Hinduism begins to take form.
ca. 599–527	Mahāvīra, founder of Jainism.
ca. 566–483	Gautama the Buddha.
327–325	Alexander invades northern India.
324	Chandragupta defeats the Greeks and founds Mauryan dynasty.
269–232	Reign of Ashoka, who spreads Buddhism throughout the Mauryan Empire, which extends as far south as Mysore.

A.D.

ca. 100	Mahāyāna Buddhism founded.
320	Chandra Gupta founds Gupta dynasty in northern India; Golden Age of Indian art begins.
ca. 454	Huns invade India for the first time.
ca. 600	Gupta dynasty ends.
712	Arabs occupy Sind.
ca. 788–820	Shankara, the great Hindu teacher.
816–1192	Rājput kingdoms in Rājasthān.
1001–1026	Mahmūd of Ghaznī invades.
1193	Qutbuddīn Aibak takes Delhi.
1193–1526	Various Muslim dynasties (the Delhi Sultanate) rule from Delhi. Islamic influence permeates into Indian architecture.
1336–1565	Hindu Vijayanagar empire rules in Deccan.
1398	Tīmūr the Lame invades India.
1469–1538	Guru Nānak, founder of Sikhism.
1498	Vasco da Gama lands in Calicut.

1510	Portuguese capture Goa.
1526–1530	Reign of Bābur, founder of the Mughal dynasty.
1530–1556	Reign of Humāyūn, who brings Persian influence into Indian art and architecture.
1556–1605	Reign of Akbar, the greatest Mughal, builder of fort cities at Āgra and Fatehpur Sīkrī.
1600	Elizabeth I of England grants charter to East India Company.
1605–1627	Reign of Jahāngīr. Mughal Empire covers all of India except the Deccan and the extreme south, and Mughal art reaches new heights, especially in miniature painting.
1611	East India Company builds factories at Surat.
1627–1658	Reign of Shāh Jahān, builder of Tāj Mahal and the fort city of Shāhjahānābād (Old Delhi).
1658–1707	Reign of Aurangzeb, able administrator and religious zealot, the last of the great Mughals.
1744–1748	First Anglo-French War in India.
1757	British supremacy established at Battle of Plassey.
1792	Ranjīt Singh, Sikh leader, signs peace treaty with British.
1853	Introduction of telegraph system and railways.
1857	The Indian Mutiny.
1858	India comes under direct control of British government.
1869–1948	Mahatma Gandhi, father of the nation.
1885	Indian National Congress founded.
1906	Muslim League founded.
1920–1922	Noncooperation Movement.
1930–1935	Civil disobedience campaigns.
1945–1946	General elections; communal riots in Calcutta and Punjāb.
1947	Partition: India and Pakistān gain independence.
1950	India becomes a republic within the British Commonwealth.
1952	Jawaharlal Nehru becomes India's first prime minister.
1971	Bangladesh becomes independent.

SOME
USEFUL READING

HISTORY

Allen, C., ed. *Plain Tales from the Raj*. London: Futura, 1977.

Basham, A. L. *The Wonder That Was India*. London: Fontana, 1971.

Collins, L., and D. Lapierre. *Freedom at Midnight*. New York: Avon, 1976; St. Albans: Granada, 1982.

Gascoigne, B. *The Great Mughals*. London: Cape, 1976.

Watson, F. *A History of India*. New York and London: Thames & Hudson, 1979.

ART AND ARCHITECTURE

Boner, A. *Principles of Composition in Hindu Sculpture*. Leiden: Brill, 1962.

Burckhardt, T. *Sacred Art East and West*. Bedfont, Middlesex: Perennnial, 1976.

————. *The Art of Islam*. London: World of Islam Festival Publishing Co., 1976.

Coomaraswamy, A. *The Transformation of Nature in Art*. New York: Dover, 1937; New Delhi: Munshiram Manoharlal, 1974.

Craven, R. *A Concise History of Indian Art*. New York: Oxford University Press, 1976; London: Thames & Hudson, 1976.

James, D. *Islamic Art*. New York and London: Hamlyn, 1974.

Kramrisch, S. *The Hindu Temple*. Columbia, Mo.: South Asia Books 1980; New Delhi: Motilal Banarsidass, 1977.

Lannoy, R. *The Eye of Love*. New York: Grove Press, 1976; London: Hutchinson, 1976.

Michell, G. *The Hindu Temple*. New York: Harper & Row, 1978; London; Elek, 1977.

Rowland, B. *The Art and Architecture of India*. New York and London: Pelican, 1977.

Zimmer, H. *Myths and Symbols in Indian Art*. Princeton, N.J.: Princeton University Press, 1971.

RELIGION AND PHILOSOPHY

Conze, E., trans. *Buddhist Scriptures*. New York and London: Penguin, 1959.

Dawood, N., trans. *The Koran*. New York and London: Penguin, 1964.

Maharishi, Mahesh Yogi. *The Bhagavad Gita*. New York and London: Penguin, 1969.

Mascaro, J., trans. *The Dhammapada*. New York and London: Penguin, 1973.

Mookerjee, A., and M. Khanna. *The Tantric Way*. London: Thames & Hudson, 1977.

O'Flaherty, W. *Hindu Myths*. London: Penguin, 1976.

Radhakrishnan, S. *The Hindu View of Life*. New York and London: Allen & Unwin, 1980.

———, trans. *The Bhagavad Gita*. New York: Harper & Row; 1949 London: Allen & Unwin, 1949.

Rahula, W. *What the Buddha Taught*. New York: Grove Press, 1974; Bedford, England: Gordon Fraser, 1959.

Rajagopalachari, C. *The Mahabharata*. Pomona, Cal.: Auromere, 1979; Bombay: Bharatiya Vidya Bhavan, 1976.

———. *The Ramayana*. Pomona, Cal.: Auromere, 1979; Bombay: Bharatiya Vidya Bhavan, 1975.

Ross, N. W. *Buddhism: A Way of Life and Thought*. New York: Alfred A. Knopf, 1980; London: William Collins, 1981.

Sen, R. *Hinduism*. London: Penguin, 1981.

Shah, I. *The Sufis*. New York: Anchor, 1971; London: Cape, 1969.

Shearer, A., and P. Russell, trans. *The Upanishads*. New York: Harper & Row, 1978; London: Wildwood House, 1978.

Shearer, A. *Effortless Being*. London: Wildwood House, 1982.

Smart, N. *The Religious Experience of Mankind*. New York: Charles Scribner's Sons, 1976; London: Fontana, 1971.

Suzuki, D. *Outlines of Mahayana Buddhism*. New York: Schocken, 1963.

Zimmer, H. *Philosophies of India*. Princeton, N.J.: Princeton University Press, 1969.

FICTION

Forster, E. M. *A Passage to India*. New York: Harcourt Brace, 1949; London: Penguin, 1970.

Hesse, H. *Siddhartha*. New York: New Directions, 1951; London: Picador, 1973.

Jhabvala, R. P. *Heat and Dust*. New York: Harper & Row, 1977; London: Futura, 1975.

Kaye, M. M. *The Far Pavilions*. New York: Bantam, 1979; London: Penguin, 1979.

Kipling, R. *Kim*. New York: Dell, 1976; London: Pan, 1976.

———. *Plain Tales from the Hills*. London: Macmillan, 1924.

Masters, J. *The Nightrunners of Bengal*. London: Sphere, 1978.

Narayan, R. K. *The Financial Expert*. Chicago, Ill.: University of Chicago Press; London: Heinemann, 1981.

Rao, R. *Kanthapura*. New York: New Directions, 1967.

Rushdie, S. *Midnight's Children*. New York: Alfred A. Knopf; London: Picador, 1981.

Scott, P. *The Raj Quartet*. London: Granada, 1982.

AUTOBIOGRAPHY

Bharati, A. *The Ochre Robe*. Santa Barbara, Cal.: Ross Erikson, 1980.

Chaudhuri, N. *Autobiography of an Unknown Indian*. Berkeley: University of California Press, 1968.

Gandhi, M. K. *An Autobiography: The Story of My Experiments with Truth*. Boston: Beacon Press, 1972; London: Penguin, 1982.

Masters, J. *Bugles and a Tiger*. London: Michael Joseph, 1956.

Nehru, J. *Autobiography*. London: Bodley Head, 1949; New Delhi: Allied, 1962.

Yogananda, P. *Autobiography of a Yogi*. Los Angeles, Cal.: Self Realization Fellowship, 1971.

GENERAL

Basham, A. L. *A Cultural History of India*. Oxford: Clarendon Press, 1975.

Brough J., trans. *Poems from the Sanskrit*. London: Penguin, 1969.

Chaudhuri, N. *The Continent of Circe*. Bombay: Jaico, 1978.

Eck, D. L. *Banāras: City of Light*. New York: Alfred A. Knopf, 1982; London: Routledge, 1983.

Godden, J., and R. *Shiva's Pigeons*. New York: Viking, 1972; London: Chatto & Windus, 1972.

Keay, J. *Into India*. London: John Murray, 1973.

Lannoy, R. *The Speaking Tree*. New York and Oxford: Oxford University Press, 1971.

Moorhouse, G. *Calcutta*. London: Penguin, 1983.

Moraes, F., and E. Howe, eds. *India*. London: André Deutsch, 1974.

Newby, E. *Slowly Down the Ganges*. London: Hodder & Stoughton, 1966.

GLOSSARY

Abhaya mudrā Gesture of "Fear not!" The right hand is held up, palm facing outward.

Aghorī Member of a sect of tantric ascetics.

Agni Fire; the Vedic fire god.

Āgyā chakra The sixth *chakra*, situated in the middle of the forehead, popularly known as "the third eye."

Alasa kanyā "Languid maiden" that adorns temple walls.

Amlā Spheroid base of finial on northern Indian temple.

Amrita Nectar of immortality, also known as *soma*.

Anāhata The fourth *chakra*, situated in the center of the chest.

Anda "Egg"; the hemispherical dome of a Buddhist *stūpa*.

Andhakāsura A demon defeated by Shiva.

Annapūrnā "The giver of food and plenty"; a form of the great goddess Shakti.

Apsaras (pl. apsarases) Celestial dancer; a nymph belonging to Indra's heaven, often shown flying in the air.

Āratī Worship of the image of the deity, especially that involving the waving of lights.

Ardhanārīshvara A form of Shiva that is half-male and half-female.

Āsana Seat, throne; a posture in *hatha yoga* and in iconography.

Āshram Place of retreat where a *guru* instructs disciples.

Asura Demon.

Ātman The Self, pure consciousness beyond the mind.

Avalokiteshvara Mahāyāna *bodhisattva* of compassion.

Avatāra An incarnation of God, usually of Vishnu.

Bāgh A garden. The term is Islamic and implies formal arrangement.

Bhagavad Gītā Eighteenth chapter of the *Mahābhārata* and the most popular scripture of the Hindus.

Bhairava A fearsome form of Shiva worshipped especially by tantric sects.

Bhakti Devotion.

Bhogamandapa Hall used for offerings in Orissan temple.

Bhūdevī Mother Earth as one of Vishnu's consorts.

Bhūmi Horizontal course of a temple *shikhara*.

Bhūmisparsha mudrā Gesture of touching the earth, made with the right hand, palm facing inward.

Bhūta Ghost; evil spirit.

Bodhisattva Celestial being in Mahāyāna Buddhism; a future *buddha*.

Brahmā God as creator, member of the Hindu trinity with Vishnu and Shiva.

Brahmachārin Student; celibate.

Brahmachārya Period of studentship; celibacy.

Brahman Ultimate Reality, the one Supreme Consciousness that manifests as the world.

Brahmin Priest; member of the highest of the four ancient *varnas*.

Chahār bāgh A formal Mughal garden laid out with straight walkways radiating out from a central pond or platform.

Chaitya Buddhist temple in the form of a basilica.

Chakra "Circle"; energy-center in the subtle body.

Chhatrī Domed pavilion or cupola, especially in Indo-Islamic architecture.

Chhattra Royal umbrella; stone parasol erected on top of a *stūpa* as a finial.

Damaru Hourglass-shaped drum carried by Shiva, symbolizing time.

Dāna mudrā Gesture of giving or generosity, with right hand held down, palm outward.

Darbār Muslim word for royal court or assembly; a special audience chamber.

Darshana Sight of a saint, deity, or holy place.

Deul Sanctuary that houses the image in an Orissan temple.

Deva Deity

Devatā Minor deity.

Devī Benevolent consort of Shiva; general name for a goddess.

Dharma Truth; the teaching of the Buddha.

Dharmachakra The Wheel of Truth, symbol of Buddhist teaching.

Dharmachakra mudrā Gesture of preaching, with hands held in front of the chest, fingers touching.

Dhyāna mudrā Gesture of meditation, with both hands resting in the lap, palms upward, right hand on top of left.

Dhyāni buddha One of the five celestial *buddhas* of the Mahāyāna.

Dikpāla One of the Guardians of the Eight Directions.

Dīwān A court; also the name of a chief minister in Muslim India.

Durgā Terrible consort of Shiva.

Dvārapāla Door guardian in a temple.

Gana Fertility or nature spirit, attendant of Shiva, often a dwarf.

Gandharva Celestial musician in Indra's court.

Ganesha Elephant-headed deity, son of Shiva and Pārvatī.

Gangā The River Ganges as goddess.

Garbha-griha "Womb-house," holy of holies in a Hindu temple.

Garuda Fabulous creature, half-man, half-vulture, Vishnu's mount.

Gavāksha Miniature *chaitya* window motif in temple decoration, also known as *kūdu*.

Ghāt "Sloping place," used to describe steps going down to a river, or the sides of a range of hills (for example, Western Ghāts).

Grihastin Householder.

Guru Spiritual teacher.

Gyāna Spiritual knowledge.

Hammām Hot or "Turkish" baths; ultimately derived from the Romans and popular all over the Muslim world.

Hanumān The monkey god, attendant of Lord Rāma.

Haram "Forbidden by religious law," thence the women of a Muslim household and the part of the building reserved for them.

Harmikā Pavilion; railed balcony surmounting dome of *stūpa*.

Hasta Hand pose in Hindu art (also called *mudrā*).

Hatha yoga Type of yoga that concentrates on physical postures.

Hauz Ablution tank in a mosque.

Hijra The flight of the Prophet Muhammad from Mecca to Medina in A.D. 622. This marks the start of the Muslim lunar calendar, which loses about one year in every thirty-three years of the Roman calendar. The Muslim year is often marked A.H. (i.e., After *Hijra*).

Hīnayāna "The Small Vehicle," name given to original Buddhists by the Mahāyāna school.

Hujra Domed chamber in Islamic architecture.

Idā One of the three main *nādīs* (nerves) in the subtle body.

Imām Leader of the prayers in the congregational mosque (any adult male Muslim is entitled to act as *imām*, providing he is sane).

Indra Principal Vedic god, ruler of the heavens.

Ishtadevatā Personally chosen god.

Jagamohana Enclosed porch, preceding the sanctuary in Orissan temples, used as an assembly and dancing hall.

Jainism Sect founded in fifth century B.C. by Mahāvīra, a contemporary of the Buddha.

Jālī Perforated stone screen.

Jatā Matted hair as worn by ascetics, and Shiva.

Jātakas Tales of previous incarnations of the Buddha, when he was a *bodhisattva*.

Jati Subcaste.

Kaʻba The shrine at Mecca, center of the Muslim universe, said to be built by Abraham on the site of his intended sacrifice of Ishmael.

Kailāsa Shiva's mountain home in the Himālayas.

Kalasha Pot-shaped finial on Hindu temples, containing the nectar of immortality.

Kālī Fearsome aspect of the great goddess Shakti, one of Shiva's consorts.

Kanyā Maiden, often used in temple decoration.

Karma Action; the law—"As you sow, so shall you reap."

Kārttikeya One of Shiva's sons, also known as Skanda, Kumāra, or Subrahmanya.

Katahra Low wooden or stone railing that encloses an area. Very common at Fatehpur Sīkrī.

Khās "Private," used, as in *dīwān-i-khās*, for chambers of private audience.

Khass tattīs Screens made from dry, aromatic grasses, which were sprinkled with water to cool rooms.

Krishna Eighth incarnation of Vishnu, hero of the *Mahābhārata*.

Kshatriya Warrior; member of the second of the ancient *varnas*..

Kūdu Miniature *chaitya* window motif in temple decorations, also known as *gavāksha*.

Kundalinī Creative life energy latent in the nervous system.

Lakshana One of the thirty-two bodily marks that distinguish a *buddha*.

Lakshmī Goddess of fortune, consort of Vishnu.

Līlā Play, sport; the universe as the play of God.

Linga Phallic emblem of Shiva.

Liwān Prayer hall of a mosque.

Loka "Realm" (there are fourteen *lokas* in the universe: six above the earth, the earth itself, and seven below the earth).

Madhya bindu Central point in a sculptural composition.

Madhya sūtra Central axis in a sculptural composition.

Mahal House or palace.

Mahāyāna "Great Vehicle," the later, theistic form of Buddhism.

Mahāyogi Shiva in his form as the great yogi.

Maheshvara "The Great Lord"; a general name for Shiva.

Maithuna Sexual intercourse; also used to describe a sculpture portraying the same, or lovers in close embrace.

Makara Mythical aquatic animal, sea dragon.

Mālā Rosary.

Mandala Circular diagram of cosmos, used as meditational aid.

Mandapa Hall of a temple, usually pillared.

Mantra Sound used for meditation.

Maqbara Underground chamber containing the real grave (*qabr*) in an Islamic mausoleum.

Masjid "Place of prostration"; a mosque

Māyā "Magical play"; the illusory and impermanent nature of the world.

Mihrāb Arched alcove in a mosque that indicates the direction of Mecca.

Mīnār Tower, often attached to mosque (as in "minaret").

Minbar Pulpit in a mosque.

Mithuna "The state of being a couple," used to describe the auspicious couples that are represented on Hindu, Buddhist, and Jain shrines.

Moksha Freedom; Hindu term for enlightenment.

Mudrā Symbolic hand gesture, especially in Buddhist iconography.

Mūlādhāra Lowest *chakra*, situated at the perineum.

Mūrti General term for image.

Nādī Nerve of the subtle body, through which vital force flows.

Nāga Mythical serpent god, symbol of water, guardian of the underworld.

Nagara Northern Indian (or Indo-Āryan) style of temple.

Nandin Sacred bull, mount of Shiva.

Narasingha "Man-lion," fourth incarnation of Vishnu.

Naskh Script in which the *Qur'ān* is usually written. Modern Arabic print is also generally called *naskh*.

Natarāja Shiva as Lord of the Dance.

Nātyashāstra The main classical text on dance and drama.

Nirvāna Buddhist term for enlightenment.

Padmāsana The "lotus posture."

Pancharatha Type of temple with four subsidiary shrines grouped around a central one.

Parinirvāna Death of the Buddha.

Pārvatī Benign wife of Shiva.

Pingalā One of the three principal *nādīs* (nerves) in the subtle body.

Pīpal Sacred fig tree; the *bodhi* tree of the Buddhists, the *ashwattha* of the Hindus.

Pradakshinā Circumambulation of a sacred site, image, or person.

Pragya Insight, wisdom.

Prāna Life breath; the vital force in living beings.

Pratibimba Reconstruction of the cosmos in architectural structure.

Pūjā Ritual worship.

Pūjāris Specialists in ritual, nearly always brahmins.

Purāna Ancient historical myth (there are eighteen principal ones).

Pūrnaghata Vase-and-foliage motif, often used in pillar capitals, signifying well-being and material prosperity.

Qabr Real grave in an Islamic mausoleum; often in an underground chamber.

Qibla Direction of the Kā'ba at Mecca.

Rāma Hero of the *Rāmāyana.*

Rasa Mood, feeling; theory of esthetics.

Rishi Sage, seer of Vedic hymns.

Riwāqs Cloisters in Islamic buildings.

Rūpakāya Visible form of a divinity or *buddha.*

Sādhu Wandering holy man.

Sahasrāra Highest *chakra,* the "thousand-petaled lotus," situated at the crown of the head.

Sahn Mosque courtyard.

Samsāra The continual bondage of life, death, and rebirth experienced by the unenlightened.

Sangha Buddhist monastic community.

Sannyāsin One who has taken the vow of renunciation.

Sarasvatī Goddess of speech and learning, consort of Brahmā.

Satkona Six-pointed star, a tantric design.

Shaiva Worshipper of Shiva.

Shakti The Goddess; primal energy; power; general name for a god's consort.

Shāstra Sacred text.

Shikhara Spire in northern Indian temple.

Shilpashāstras Texts on architecture.

Shilpin Craftsman.

Shiva God as destruction and re-creation; third member of Hindu trinity.

Shringāra Erotic sculpture.

Shrīvasta Emblem in the center of Jain *tīrthankara*'s chest.

Shūdra Laborer; member of the lowest of the ancient *varnas.*

Siddhi Supernormal power.

Soma Nectar of immortality.

Stūpa Buddhist relic mound.

Sūfīs The esoteric brotherhoods of Islām.

Sushumnā Principal *nādī* (nerve) of the subtle body.

Svadisthāna Second *chakra,* situated between *mūlādhāra* and navel.

Svastika Emblem of good luck.

Tantra Religious philosophy centered on *shakti* worship.

Tathāgata Name for Buddha, especially in the Mahāyāna pantheon.

Theravāda "Doctrine of the Elders," the school of Buddhism more popularly known as Hīnayāna.

Tīrtha "Ford" or "place of crossing," used to describe a pilgrimage center, or specially sacred place of the Hindus.

Tīrthankara One of the twenty-four Jain sages.

Torana Gate of the enclosure of a Buddhist *stūpa.*

Tribhanga Favorite sculptural pose, bending at the neck, shoulders, and waist.

Trishūla Shiva's trident.

Tulasī The plant basil, sacred to Vaishnavas.

Ulamā Collective name for experts in Muslim canon law.

Urnā Curled hair on brow of Buddha; third-eye protuberance on brow.

Urushringa Small turrets clustered on a *shikhara,* duplicating its shape.

Ushnīsha Protuberance on head of Buddha signifying Enlightenment.

Vāhana Vehicle or mount of a deity.

Vaishnava Worshipper of Vishnu.

Vaishya Merchant, member of the third of the *varnas.*

Vajra "Thunderbolt" or "diamond," signifying indestructibility of a deity.

Varadā mudrā Gesture bestowing boons, with hand down, palm open.

Varna Ancient division of Indian society, nowadays synonymous with caste.

Vedas Sacred scriptures of the Hindus.

Vedikā Railing or fence of a sacred enclosure, such as *stūpa.*

Vihāra Buddhist monastery.

Vīnā Indian lute.

Vināyaka Another name for Ganesha, "Lord of Obstacles."

Vishnu God as preserver, second member of the Hindu trinity.

Vishuddha Fifth *chakra,* situated at the throat.

Yaksha (m.); ***Yakshī*** (f.) Nature spirits, symbols of fertility.

Yantra Geometric diagram similar to *mandala* but square.

Yoga Any method of union with the divine.

Yogi Practitioner of *yoga.*

Yoni Womb; vagina.

Yoni-linga Image combining male *(linga)* and female *(yoni)* emblems, as representations of Shiva and Shakti.

Zanāna "Female"; the word commonly used in India for those parts of a building reserved for women, and the women themselves as a group.

Zarīth Cenotaph in Islamic architecture.

TRAVELING TIPS

The majority of people using this book will probably be traveling by package tour. Much of what follows will not apply to them. But for the independent traveler, India is one of the few countries left in the world where traveling is still an adventure: unpredictable, exciting, and colorful. Even en route to the sites in this book, all of which are comparatively well known, anything can happen! The tips below are gleaned from the many years I have been traveling in this fascinating and mysterious land. My one overall piece of advice would be: Don't be in too much of a hurry! India has proceeded at her stately pace for over five thousand years; one or two impatient Westerners aren't going to change her way of doing things. If we can just relax and enter into the rhythm of the country, she has much to teach us.

INFORMATION

The main organ for information on tourism in India is the *Government of India Department of Tourism* and its offshoot *The Indian Tourism Development Corporation.* The *Government of India Tourist Offices* will answer all your queries and provide in addition a wealth of pamphlets, maps, road routes, and so on, covering every aspect of your stay in India. This service is free of charge. If you are planning a trip to India, the first thing to do is to get in touch with your nearest *Government of India Tourist Office;* the main international addresses are in the following list:

AUSTRALIA
Sydney
Carlton Centre
55 Elizabeth Street
Sydney NSW 2000
Tel: 02-232-1600

AUSTRIA
Vienna
Opernring 1
1010 Vienna
Tel: 57 14 62

BELGIUM
Brussels
Revenstein 60-Boite 15
B-1000 Brussels
Tel: 02/511 1796

CANADA
Toronto
Suite 1016
Royal Trust Tower
PO Box 342
Toronto Dominion Centre
Toronto M5K 1K7 Ontario
Tel: 416-362-3188

FRANCE
Paris
8 Boulevard de la Madeleine
75009 Paris
Tel: 073-00-84

ITALY
Milan
Via Albricci 9
20122 Milan
Tel: 804952

JAPAN
Tokyo
Pearl Building
9-18 Ginza
7 Chome
Chuo-ku
Tokyo
Tel: 571-5062

KUWAIT
Kuwait
Saadoun Al-Jassim Bldg
Fahad Al-Salem Street
Post Box 4769
Safat
Tel: 426088

SINGAPORE
Singapore
Podium Block
4th Floor
Ming Court Hotel
Tanglin Road
Singapore 10
Tel: 235 5737

SWEDEN
Stockholm
Sveavagen 9-11
Box 40016
103-41 Stockholm 40
Tel: 08 215081

SWITZERLAND
Geneva
1-3 Rue de Chantepoulet
1201 Geneva
Tel: 321813

UNITED KINGDOM
London
21 New Bond Street
London W1Y 0DY
Tel: 01-493-0769

UNITED STATES
New York
30 Rockefeller Plaza
North Mezzanine
New York, NY 10020
Tel: 212-586-4901

Chicago
201 North Michigan Avenue
Chicago, IL 60601
Tel: 312-236-6899

Los Angeles
3550 Wilshire Blvd
Suite 204
Los Angeles, CA 90010
Tel: 213-380-8855

WEST GERMANY
Frankfurt
Kaiser Strasse 77-111
6 Frankfurt Main
Tel: 232380

When in India, it is worth remembering that each state also has its own *Tourist Information Office.* These may have to be consulted if you are planning a journey off the beaten track, using, for example, state-run rather than national transport. Addresses of state tourist information offices can be obtained either at the local *Government of India Tourist Office* or at your hotel.

TRAVEL

AGENTS

If you are not traveling with a group, the easiest way to make all your arrangements in India is to use the services of travel agents. They will advise on itineraries, book and buy tickets, reserve rooms in hotels, and provide you with all the necessary information you require. Such things as buying tickets can be a lengthy and tiring process in India, especially if you are not familiar with all the procedures involved (it is not always just a case of going to the counter and paying your money!). It really saves a great deal of time and effort to let someone who knows the job do it for you, and is well worth the fee they charge. Added to which, quotas for tickets are sometimes limited, and a local agent who speaks the language and has the right contacts stands a much better chance of getting what he wants than the uninformed tourist.

There are several good travel agents who have connections all over the country. I use **Trade Wings Ltd.**, whom I have always found to be friendly, helpful, and efficient. Their main offices are:

Bombay
30 K. Dubash Marg
Fort, Bombay 400021
Tel: 244334

Delhi
60 Janpath
New Delhi 110001
Tel: 321322

If you contact the relevant office, they will advise you on your itinerary, make whatever arrangements you wish, and give you the addresses of their local branches or subagents in the areas you plan to visit.

Other good travel agents are:

Thomas Cook India Ltd.
Bombay
Thomas Cook Buildings
Dr. D. Naoroji Road,
Bombay 400001
Tel: 258556

Delhi
Hotel Imperial
Janpath
New Delhi 110001
Tel: 312402

Travel Corporation of India (TCI)
Bombay
Chander Mukhi
Nariman Point
Bombay 400021
Tel: 231881

Delhi
Hotel Metro
N-49 Connaught Circus
New Delhi 110001
Tel: 45181

Cox & Kings
Bombay
270-272 Dr. D. Naoroji Road
Bombay, 400001
Tel: 263065

Delhi
Indra Palace
Connaught Circus
New Delhi 110001
Tel: 321428

TRAINS

If you wish to travel in India by train and want to fix up your itinerary before you arrive in the country, there is a firm that will advise and book train itineraries in advance:

The Romance of India by Rail
(International Railtours)
60 Cable Road
Whitehead, Co. Antrim
Northern Ireland BT 38 9 P2
Tel: (09603) 72446 *or* (0232) 29483

As your journeys will often be lengthy, it is always advisable to reserve a seat and, if the trip includes even part of a night, a bunk or sleeper. This should be done *at least* three days before you travel. Every train has a "tourist quota" of reserved seats, so if you are told that a particular train is fully booked, search out the **Tourist Quota Office** in the station to make sure you get your reservation.

PLANES

The national airline is **Air India**, whose main offices are:

Bombay
Air India Building
Nariman Point
Fort, Bombay
Tel: 233747

Delhi
1 Scindia House
Janpath, New Delhi
Tel: 344225

The domestic airline is *Indian Airlines,* whose main offices are:

Bombay	**Delhi**
Air India Building	Kanchanjunga Building
Nariman Point	18 Barakhamba Road
Fort, Bombay	New Delhi
Tel: 233031	Tel: 40084/40071

Outside India, the *Air India* offices will give you information about *Indian Airlines* schedules, prices, and booking.

HOTELS

There is a very wide range of hotels in India, and, as everywhere else, you get what you pay for. In general, though, you can find a very comfortable hotel for prices that are reasonable, or even cheap, by Western standards. Service in hotels is generally friendly, courteous, and very willing—usually much pleasanter than its Western counterpart—but it is as well to allow longer than you would in a comparable Western hotel for meals, room service, and so on, to arrive. For the purposes of this brief guide, hotels are divided into three categories; price ranges, of course, are provisional at press time.

LUXURY

Upward from Rs. 350 ($45) per night. The luxury hotels in India are among the best in the world. Many, like the converted palaces of the *mahārājas,* are unique, and preserve a style that has long since disappeared in the West. Some of these top-class hotels are owned by American companies and managed by Indians (for example, Wellcome/Sheraton Group); the result is not exactly Indian but certainly comfortable.

MEDIUM

Ranging from Rs. 120 ($15) to Rs. 350 ($45) a night. In this range there is a very reasonable nationwide chain run by the Ashok Group, a branch of the Indian Tourist Development Corporation (ITDC). In the smaller towns, ITDC hotels can be as little as Rs. 60 ($7) a night, though in the big cities they can come into the luxury class.

BUDGET

Under Rs. 120 ($15) a night. It is quite possible to find a good hotel in this range in India; often a refreshing change from the standardized international-type hotel chains with obligatory disco, and so forth. As well as private hotels in this category, there are rest houses run by the state government known as *dak bungalows.* These are usually clean and simple and can cost as little as Rs. 20 ($2.50) a night, but they are more common in the smaller towns. Your travel agent will advise you of their availability. If you are traveling by train and arrive late or have a very early connection to make, it is possible to stay in the station "retiring rooms" on the larger railway stations. Ask to see the station master on your arrival. Bedding can sometimes be rented for the night.

I have personal experience of all the hotels listed in the site notes that follow, with the exception of two or three, which I include on reliable recommendation. The rating of the hotel is shown after its name: (L) = luxury; (M) = medium, and (B) = budget.

DOCUMENTS

As a general rule, keep a copy of every single official letter you write to inquire about something, reserve a room, and so on, and keep every single reply or confirmation you receive. You should also keep every single receipt you are given, including those you get from changing your money. These bits of paper can prove invaluable; nothing speeds up the elephantine slowness of Indian bureaucracy more than the ability to produce the relevant documents. You should also make a note of the date of booking if you did it by phone and the name of the person you dealt with on each particular occasion. Indian bureaucrats are not renowned for their ability to improvise or take what may appear to be the quickest course of action; what is important to them is doing the thing in the prescribed way. If you have all the relevant details from your side you will make life easier for all concerned. If you don't, you may well find yourself wasting precious time sitting around various offices while the details of your case are painstakingly sorted out.

HOURS

It is also worthwhile to check carefully on opening hours for all banks, offices, and so on. These can vary considerably from day to day and place to place, and are subject to religious holidays, and so on.

RECONFIRMATION

Always remember, or get your travel agent to remember, to *reconfirm* a hotel booking or a plane or train seat. This should be done shortly before the intended journey or stay. Some places will not take a booking seriously unless it is reconfirmed in this way, and both Air India and Indian Airlines are prone to double-booking.

LANGUAGE

Unless you are going off the beaten track, all the Indians you come across for official reasons will speak good English. The Indians are excellent linguists. Nevertheless, it is worth remembering that the person you deal with will probably speak English as his third or fourth language (being naturally more at home with Punjābī, Hindī, or Bengālī), and it is well to make allowances for this. Just because the Indians speak English so well, it is sometimes easy to forget that misunderstandings can occur.

LOCAL CUSTOMS

The Indians are a friendly, tolerant, and patient people. That they remain so toward tourists is all the more astonishing when you consider that, being a religious society, they live by a strict set of rules that the average Westerner often unwittingly breaks or willfully disregards. Some ignorance on our part is inevitable; but as tourists we are guests of the Indian people, and have a responsibility to respect their way of life.

Many forms of behavior that are accepted or encouraged in the West are considered gross in India. Generally speaking, women should dress modestly at all times, especially when visiting temples or shrines, and cover their arms and heads when visiting a mosque. Men should not wear shorts to visit a mosque or temple. Shoes should always be removed before entering a holy place that is under worship (carry a pair of "temple socks" with you). No leather articles should be taken into a Hindu, Jain, or Sikh temple that is in use; you may be asked to remove all leather articles such as belts, and so on, and deposit them outside.

It is worth remembering that Indians find demonstrations of affection between couples in public offensive, even to the extent of holding hands.

Generally speaking, you should bargain in all tourist shops that are not government or state enterprises. The first price asked in shops that are not "fixed price" is often absurdly high, and the shopkeeper will take anything up to 50 percent less in the end.

PHOTOGRAPHY

Film is very expensive in India (often twice the U.S. or European price), so it is best to take all you need with you. It is safest to have it developed at home.

Photography is usually permitted in holy places, but there may be local restrictions. Check first. If you are photographing inside a temple, remember it is primarily a place of worship, not just a subject for your photo collection back home. Just imagine what would happen if a noisy party of Indians barged into a New England church on a Sunday morning and elbowed the congregation out of the way to get shots of the altar! A similar violation takes place every day when tourists visit the Hindu or Buddhist shrines.

BAKSHEESH

India has been bedeviled by the "Oxfam Image," which paints her as a country of starvation, poverty, and misery. This is just not true. Although, like any Third World country, she has her share of problems, India displays a remarkable strength and cheerfulness when dealing with her economic and climatic difficulties. Travelers in India are often amazed at how little of what they see agrees with the Western media image of the country, largely created by reporters who can only think in sensational or controversial terms.

Nevertheless, you may well encounter beggars, particularly at the major pilgrimage sites (giving to the needy is a religious duty and merit for the Hindu and Muslim). Visitors are often most sympathetic to the beggars who have least need of their concern: the children. If you wish to give to the elderly or the infirm, that's your business, but ignore those children who ask for *baksheesh* ("gift" in Arabic). The wise traveler gives them nothing. No rupees, no foreign money, no stamps, no sweets, *nothing!* The child who can scratch a living by skipping school and pestering every tourist he sees will have no incentive to do anything else for the rest of his days. Compared with

Orientals, we are terribly sentimental about children, and the reason that these children appear with their "no mama, no papa" routine is solely because unthinking visitors have shelled out a wide variety of useless goodies in the past. (You never find children begging off the tourist routes.) Incalculable damage has been done by previous generations of tourists who, if you'll pardon the pun, had more dollars than sense. These little beggars, however appealing, are just playing their version of the international game called "soak the tourist," and the minute your back is turned, their practiced expressions of distress will vanish along with their limps, as they skip off laughingly to find the next sucker. Handouts don't help anyone; they merely insure that every succeeding visitor will be pestered unnecessarily.

ELEPHANTA: BOMBAY
Photoflash, Flashlight

The cave-temple is situated on Elephanta Island, about six miles (ten kilometers) off the tip of the elongated island that is Bombay. Boats leave regularly from the **Gateway of India** on **Apollo Bunder**; the journey takes about an hour each way. The area around **Apollo Bunder** is known as **Fort** and is the center of Bombay's cosmopolitan life.

WHERE TO SHOP

Good all around **Fort**, especially along **Churchgate Street**. The sidewalks are lined with stalls selling silks, leather, jewelry (a specialty of Bombay), etc. Bargaining compulsory. Visit **Jhaveri Bazaar** (for jewerly) and **Chor Bazaar**–"Thieves Market"–(for anything).

Two shops are especially recommended for handmade goods:

> **Khadi Village Industries Emporium**
> 286 Dadabhai Naoroji Road
> Fort, Bombay
> Set up on Gandhian lines.

> **Central Cottage Industries Emporium**
> 34 Chhatrapati Shivaji Marg
> Fort, Bombay
> Next to Gateway of India.

> PHOTOGRAPHIC
> **Dave Bros.**
> Shop No. 9
> Indian Mercantile Mansion
> Bombay 1
> Opposite Regal Cinema.

MUSEUMS

The Prince of Wales Museum, one of India's best, contains an especially fine collection of paintings, particularly Mughal and Rājput miniatures; some European works (Gainsborough, Poussin, Titian); sculpture, including important Buddhist pieces from Amarāvati and Gandhāra; and a natural history section. There is also a good collection of Oriental arms, jade, china, and silver. The museum is closed on Mondays.

The Victoria and Albert Museum has a collection of prints, maps, photographs, etc., illustrating the history of Bombay. Also over thirty acres (twelve hectares) of gardens.

ART GALLERIES

The Jahāngīr Art Gallery, adjacent to the Prince of Wales Museum, this is India's leading gallery for contemporary art. The café here is a useful place to meet people, and there is also a good souvenir shop.

ARCHITECTURE

Bombay is full of glorious Victorian Gothic. See for example the **University** buildings, or one of the main stations, **Victoria Terminus** (V.T.). There is a Railway Information Bureau here, and the General Post Office is close by.

WHAT TO SEE

A journey to **Malabar Hill** about three miles (five kilometers) from **Fort**, is well worthwhile. In the center of the hill are the **Hanging Gardens** and **Kamala Nehru Park**, which give a fine view of the harbor and city. Also the **Towers of Silence** (where the Parsees dispose of their dead) and the surrounding gardens. There are many beaches in and near Bombay; **Juhu** tends to be crowded, but **Versova, Madh,** and **Manori** are quieter. **Chowpatty Beach** is fun in the evening, when Bombay relaxes after a day's work.

WHERE TO STAY

> **The Tāj Mahal Hotel** (L)
> Apollo Bunder
> Bombay, I
> Close to the Gateway of India, one of the great hotels of the world.

> **Hotel Moti International** (M)
> 10 Ormiston Road
> Colaba, Bombay

> **YMCA International Guest House** (B)
> Madama Cama Road
> Fort, Bombay

> **Red Shield Hostel** (B)
> Mereweather Road
> Fort, Bombay

Bombay Airport (Santa Cruz) is about ten miles (sixteen kilometers) from the center of the city. If for any reason you have to spend a night there, hotels are:

> **Centaur Hotel (ITDC)** (L)
> Santa Cruz Airport
> Bombay

> **Hotel Transit** (M)
> Off Nehru Road
> Vile Parle (East)
> Bombay

ELLORĀ AND AJANTĀ
Photoflash, Flashlight

Both these sites are best reached by day excursion from Aurangābād, where there is an airport. Ellorā is 26 miles (42 kilometers) from Aurangābād, Ajantā 66 miles (106 kilometers).

WHERE TO STAY

> **Ajantā Ambassador Hotel** (L)
> Jalna Road
> Aurangabād
>
> **Aurangabād Ashoka Hotel** (ITDC) (M)
> Dr. Rajendra Prasad Marg
> Aurangabād

ITDC buses leave regularly for both Ellorā and Ajantā from the *Aurangabād Ashoka Hotel.*

If you have time, however, it is possible to stay overnight at each site, which is worth considering, as the sites are at their best in the early morning and evening.

> **Ellorā**
> **Kailās Hotel** (B)
> Ellorā Dist.
> Aurangabād
>
> **Ajantā**
> **Ajantā Rest House** (B)
> Ajantā Caves
> Near Aurangabād

MOUNT ĀBŪ

Mount Ābū is best reached from Udaipur, itself one of the most popular tourist places in northern India. Udaipur is not discussed in this book, since it has no sacred sites to speak of, but it is a beautiful and romantic town where you can see the *mahārāja*'s palaces and well laid out flower gardens; stay in the famous **Lake Palace Hotel** (L), a converted palace set in the middle of Picchola Lake; and wander through genuine and colorful bazaars. There is also a good ITDC hotel, the **Lakshmī Vilas** (M).

Ābū is about four hours by road from Udaipur, but very well worth the journey.

WHERE TO STAY

> **Hotel Hilltone** (M)
> Mount Ābū
> The attached **Madhuban** restaurant is good.
>
> **Jaipur House Hotel** (M)
> Mount Ābū
>
> **Tourist Bungalow** (B)
> Mount Ābū

JAIPUR

The capital of Rājasthān, Jaipur is well worth several days' visit. It is a famous center for culture and the arts, best known for gemstones (especially emeralds); brass, gold, silver, and enamel ware; miniature painting, and cloth. You can see the craftsmen at work in their traditional studios.

WHERE TO SHOP

Johri Bazaar for gemstones.

Chandpole Bazaar for marble.

Nehru Bazaar for cloth.

Gangauri Bazaar (Saturday afternoons) is the weekly market. It's a photographer's paradise.

Rājasthān State Handicraft Emporium
Mirza Ismail Marg
Jaipur

PAINTING

India's greatest living miniaturist lives in Jaipur in a traditional Rājasthānī house (*haveli*), running an atelier as his forebears have done for the last ten generations. He is Ved Pal Sharma, better known as Banu. Banu restores miniatures for museums all over the world (including the *mahārāja*'s private collection of twenty thousand), has four thousand students throughout the world, and does original work, too. He can be contacted through Rām Gopāl Sharma, who works at the **Albert Hall Museum** (Tel: 67796) and is himself one of Jaipur's most knowledgeable and fascinating characters.

A more commercial studio, but of high quality, can be seen at the atelier of Sangram Singh of Nawalgarh, Sarsen Chand Road, Jaipur.

MUSEUM

The **Albert Hall Museum,** set in the middle of the **Public Gardens,** has a very good collection, especially of folk art and costumes; musical instruments; miniatures and painted panels; and old photographs of the city. It also has the oldest and most beautiful Persian Garden Carpet in the world, made in 1630, probably for Mahārāja Jai Singh I.

WHAT TO SEE

Apart from the **City Palace** and **Jantar Mantar,** see the **Palace of the Winds** (*Hawā Mahal*), the fort-palace of **Amber**—six miles (ten kilometers) from Jaipur—where you can ride up to the palace on an elephant, and the **Jagat Shiromānī Temple** nearby, dedicated to Krishna. The royal cenotaphs at **Gethore**, just outside the city, and the **Pundriki-ki-Haveli**, a traditionally decorated house in **Brahmāpurī**, the old brahmin quarter of Jaipur, should also be visited.

To get a good overall view of the layout of Jaipur, visit the **Tiger Fort** or **Sūrya Temple** overlooking the city; the view is magnificent. For modern magnificence, visit the **Rāj Mandir Cinema**, built by a local family of jewelers. It is one of the most opulent cinemas in Asia.

Sanganer, about eight miles (thirteen kilometers) south of Jaipur, is a center for hand-woven and printed fabrics. You can see the process of dying and printing carried out in the traditional way and buy lengths of material if you wish. There is also a center for hand-made paper here, and Jain temples.

WHERE TO STAY

Rambagh Palace (L)
Bhawani Singh Marg
Jaipur
One of the *mahārāja*'s palaces turned into a hotel with extensive gardens, rambling corridors, and some sumptuous *art deco* rooms.

Jaipur Ashok (ITDC) (M)
Jai Singh Circle
Bani Park
Jaipur

Narain Niwas (M)
Kandir Bagh
Jaipur
An old family house, a veritable museum of Rājput memorabilia, run as a small hotel.

Gangaur Tourist Bungalow (M)
Off Mirza Ismail Road
Jaipur

Youth Hostel (B)
Bhawani Singh Marg
Jaipur

DELHI

As the capital city of India, Delhi has all the expected attractions of good shops, restaurants, entertainment, and so on, and some unexpected ones as well. A good guide to these is:

Delhi—A Legend that Lives, published by the Delhi Tourism Development Corporation.

Delhi Welcomes You, a free magazine that comes out each month with a calendar of the month's cultural activities.

WHERE TO SHOP

Baba Karak Singh Marg
Off Connaught Place
New Delhi
Emporia from all the Indian states, a variety of hand-made articles.

The Central Cottage Industries Emporium
Janpath
New Delhi
A wide range of goods of quality, with an excellent selection of materials, especially silk.

ANTIQUES
The Chatta Chowk Bazaar
Red Fort
Old Delhi

PHOTOGRAPHIC
India Photographic Co.
22-A Janpath
New Delhi

CAMERA REPAIRS
Mahatta & Co.
59 M Block
Connaught Place
New Delhi

BOOKS
Oxford Book Shop
Scindia House (near Regal Cinema)
Connaught Circus
New Delhi

The Bookworm
Block B
Connaught Place
New Delhi

MAPS
Survey of India Sales Office
Above Central Cottage Industries Emporium
Janpath
New Delhi

MUSEUMS

The National Museum, Janpath, has a renowned collection that includes some pieces from the Indus Valley civilization; sculpture; many fine bronzes; paintings, and textiles.

Tibet House, Institutional Area, Lodi Road, New Delhi, has a small but good collection of Tibetan art, some of it from the Dalai Lama's personal collection. There is also a shop.

The Craft Museum, Thapar House, 124 Janpath, deserves a visit.

WHAT TO SEE

In addition to the sites covered in this book, there are many places of interest in Delhi, including **Humāyūn's Tomb, Purana Qila** (the Old Fort), **Jantar Mantar Observatory**, the bazaars of **Old Delhi**, the **Government Secretariat Complex** on Raisina Hill, **Tughluq's Tomb** and ruined fort, and the **Birla Temple**, New Delhi.

WHERE TO STAY

Tāj Mahal Hotel (L)
1 Man Singh Road
New Delhi

Oberoi Intercontinental (L)
Dr. Zakir Hussain Marg
New Delhi

Ashoka (ITDC) (L)
50B Chanakyapuri
New Delhi

Hotel Janpath (ITDC) (M)
Janpath
New Delhi

Lodhi Hotel (ITDC) (M)
Lala Lajpat Rai Marg
New Delhi
An excellent southern Indian vegetarian restaurant here.

Imperial Hotel (M)
Janpath
New Delhi
Good Chinese food here.

Nirula's Hotel (B)
L-Block
Connaught Circus
New Delhi

YMCA International Guest House (B)
Parliament St.
New Delhi

Vishva Yuvak Kendra (Youth Hostel) (B)
Off Teen Murti Marg
Chanakyapuri, New Delhi

AMRITSAR
Photoflash

Amritsar can be reached by train or plane from Delhi. When visiting the **Golden Temple**, take care to observe all the rules that are clearly posted outside the main entrance (for example, *all* visitors must cover their heads).

WHERE TO SHOP
The bazaars around the Golden Temple are interesting; Amritsar is famous for its textiles (especially *pashmīna*), embroidered shawls, and rugs.

WHERE TO STAY

Hotel Amritsar International (M)
City Center
Amritsar

Hotel Ritz (M)
The Mall
Amritsar

Hotel Airlines (M)
Cooper Road
Amritsar

It is also possible to stay in accommodations provided by the temple authorities. Inquire at the **Temple Administration Office**, next to the main entrance.

ĀGRA AND FATEHPUR SĪKRĪ
Photoflash, Flashlight

WHAT TO SEE
The **Fort,** where Shāh Jahān spent his last days gazing out over the river Yamunā at his beloved Tāj Mahal, should definitely be visited. At **Bhāratpur**, an old walled city with a ruined fort about 25 miles (40 kilometers) due west of Āgra, is the **Ghana Bird Sanctuary**, one of the best in India. There is a good, new motel.

WHERE TO STAY

Hotel Mughal Sheraton (L)
Tāj Ganj
Āgra

Clark's Shiraz Hotel (L)
Tāj Road
Āgra

Mumtaz Ashok Hotel (ITDC) (M)
Fatehabād Road
Āgra

Jaiwal Hotel (M)
3 Tāj Road
Sadar Bazaar
Āgra

Fatehpur Sīkrī is best reached by day excursion from Āgra.

SĀNCHĪ

WHAT TO SEE

There is a good *museum* on the left of the road going up to the site.

WHERE TO STAY

Ashok Travellers Lodge (ITDC) (B)
Sānchī

Railway Retiring Rooms (B)
Sānchī

KHAJURĀHO

Photoflash, Flashlight

WHAT TO SEE

As well as the western group described in the text, the eastern group of temples are also of considerable interest, the best being the **Javari Temple** (ca. 1080). These are best reached by cycle-rickshaw from the center of the town. About five hundred yards (meters) southeast of the eastern group are the Jain temples, and a mile south of the eastern group lies the southern group, the best example of which is the small **Chaturbhuja Temple** (ca. 1100), dedicated to Shiva in his form as the Great Teacher (Dakshināmūrti).

The *Museum* is small and well laid out and is worth a visit. It has a particularly fine dancing Ganesha.

Flash needed for inside temples and museum.

WHERE TO STAY

Hotel Chandella (L)
Khajurāho

Khajurāho Ashoka Hotel (ITDC) (M)
Khajurāho

Tourist Bungalow (B)
Khajurāho

BANĀRAS

WHAT TO SEE

The most spectacular sight in Banāras is the *ghāts*; best seen in the early morning or evening. The most impressive temples are the **Durgā** (or **Monkey**) **Temple**, near Asi Ghat; the **Golden Temple**, between Mīr Ghāt and Jalasaī Ghāt; and the **Annapūrnā Temple**, just along the street from the Golden Temple. Local guides will be found to take you around these temples; a small fee may have to be paid since sometimes Westerners are not encouraged to enter. For a completely different style of architecture, the **Nepalese Temple**, near Mīr Ghāt, should be visited. Rāja Jai Singh, the founder of Jaipur, built an *observatory* here at Banāras; it overlooks the Man Mandir Ghāt.

WHERE TO SHOP

Banāras is famous for brass, silks, embroideries, and brocades. There are many fascinating shops and stalls in the *galis* leading down to the *ghāts*. You can see silk being woven, and buy the finished product, at:

Oriental Arts
Sunder Villa
S. 10/252 Maqbool Alam Road
Chowkaghāt, Banāras.

WHERE TO STAY

Clark's Hotel (L)
The Mall
Banāras
The oldest hotel, full of the slightly crazy bustle that typifies the city. Usually heavily booked.

Hotel Tāj Ganges (L)
Built in 1981.

Hotel de Paris (M)
The Mall
Banāras

Hotel Vārānasī Ashok (ITDC) (M)
The Mall
Banāras
This has an excellent bookshop.

SĀRNĀTH
Photoflash

The **Deer Park** is four miles (six and a half kilometers) north of Banāras and is usually visited on a day excursion from the city.

WHAT TO SEE

As mentioned in the text, the **museum** is an integral part of the site and should not be missed.

Half a mile (one kilometer) to the south of the site is a modern **Tibetan temple** that is interesting.

BODH GAYĀ
Photoflash

The nearest town is Gayā (seven miles, or eleven kilometers), an unimpressive town, with taxis and buses to Bodh Gayā.

WHAT TO SEE

One fascinating thing about the site is that here you can see temples of various forms of Buddhism—Tibetan, Thai, Japanese, Chinese, Burmese—side by side, and get an idea of how the religion changed its forms as it spread. The **Tibetan temple** is particularly lively. Near the Travellers Lodge is a small museum.

WHERE TO STAY

Ashok Travellers Lodge (ITDC) (B)
Bodh Gayā

BHUBANESHWAR
Photoflash, Flashlight

As there is an airport here, Bhubaneshwar is the jumping-off point for the rest of Orissā.

WHAT TO SEE

Five miles (eight kilometers) southeast of Bhubaneshwar is the famous **Dhauli Rock**, where the best-preserved stone-cut edicts of the Buddhist Emperor Ashoka are found. There is also a modern *stūpa* here. In **Gautam Nagar** there is a *museum* with tribal artifacts.

WHERE TO SHOP

There is an **Orissan State Handicrafts Emporium** in the New Town.

WHERE TO STAY

> **Hotel Kaliaga Ashok** (ITDC) (M)
> Gautam Nagar
> Bhubaneshwar
>
> **Hotel Pratchi** (M)
> Main Street
> Bhubaneshwar

KONĀRAK

Can be reached by road from Bhubaneshwar.

WHERE TO STAY

> **Ashok Travellers Lodge** (ITDC) (B)
> Konārak
>
> The museum is close by.

As well as the listed sites in Orissā, **Purī** should definitely be visited. It is one of the seven holiest cities in India, and the site of the **Jagannātha Temple**, sacred to the followers of Vishnu. Every June there is a huge festival here, when the deities are paraded in the Jagannātha temple-chariot. Unfortunately, the temple is not open to non-Hindus, but the outside can be viewed from a balcony of the nearby **Raghunandan Library**, which has a good collection of palm-leaf manuscripts and is a center of research into Orissan history. Purī can be reached by road or rail from Bhubaneshwar.

The large **market place** in front of the temple is full of stalls, and the surrounding bazaars are interesting and very photogenic. Orissā has a lively tradition of folk art. Particularly attractive are the *pata* paintings on palm leaf, cotton, or silk, which illustrate scenes from Indian mythology. These can be found in Purī and Bhubaneshwar.

WHERE TO STAY

> **The South Eastern Railway Hotel** (M)
> Purī
> This is on the beach, and is a marvel of Edwardian India. Not to be missed.
>
> **Tourist Bungalow** (B)
> Purī

INDEX

A Note About the Author

Alistair Shearer read English Literature at Cambridge and later took a postgraduate degree in Comparative Religious Studies. He has translated some of the most important yoga texts from Sanskrit. An inveterate traveler—having visited more than forty countries—he is a specialist in the art and architecture of the Indian subcontinent and South East Asia, where he spends each winter leading tours.

A Note on the Type

This book was film set in a face called Primer, designed by Rudolph Ruzicka (1883–1978). Mr. Ruzicka was earlier responsible for the design of Fairfield and Fairfield Medium, faces whose virtues have for some time been accorded wide recognition.

The complete range of sizes of Primer was first made available in 1954, although the pilot size of 12-point was ready as early as 1951. The design of the face makes general reference to Century—long a serviceable type, totally lacking in manner or frills of any kind—but brilliantly corrects its characterless quality.

Composed by Centennial Graphics, Inc., Ephrata, Pennsylvania. Printed and bound by R. R. Donnelly & Sons, Crawfordsville, Indiana. Designed by Christine Aulicino.